DEVELOPMENT AND UNDERDEVELOPMENT

DEVELOPMENT AND UNDERDEVELOPMENT

The Political Economy of Global Inequality

EDITED BY

Mitchell A. Seligson and John T Passé-Smith

LYNNE
RIENNER
PUBLISHERS

BOULDER
LONDON

Published in the United States of America in 2003 by
Lynne Rienner Publishers, Inc.
1800 30th Street, Boulder, Colorado 80301
www.rienner.com

and in the United Kingdom by
Lynne Rienner Publishers, Inc.
3 Henrietta Street, Covent Garden, London WC2E 8LU

Library of Congress Cataloging-in-Publication Data
Development and underdevelopment : the political economy of global inequality / Mitchell
  A. Seligson and John T Passé-Smith, editors.—3rd ed.
      p. cm.
    Includes bibliographical references and index.
    ISBN 1-58826-206-5 (alk. paper)
      1. Developing countries—Economic conditions.   2. Economic development.
    3. Income distribution.   4. Capitalism.   5. Economic history—1945–   6. Social history—
    1945–   I. Seligson, Mitchell A.   II. Passé-Smith, John T
    HC59.7.D4453   2003
    338.9—dc21

                                                                            2003043239

British Cataloguing in Publication Data
A Cataloguing in Publication record for this book
is available from the British Library.

Printed and bound in the United States of America

⊗   The paper used in this publication meets the requirements
      of the American National Standard for Permanence of
      Paper for Printed Library Materials Z39.48-1992.

    5   4   3   2

CONTENTS

PREFACE

The end of the Cold War was seen by some as "the end of history," and with that, the end of international conflict. Sadly, our experiences in the post–Cold War period have not met that expectation. Indeed, it seems as if the world is more unstable and conflict-prone than ever. Many conflicts revolve around issues of ethnic or religious difference, but a constant theme in armed conflicts worldwide is the struggle over resources and the wealth that goes with them. The yawning gaps in wealth that so sharply demarcate rich nations from poor and rich people from poor people seem to be relentless promoters of conflict.

This book is about the international gap in wealth between rich and poor nations and the domestic gap in wealth between rich and poor people. It is a substantially revised version of its three predecessors, *The Gap Between Rich and Poor* (1984) and the first two editions (1993 and 1998) of the present book.

We have updated the book with recent contributions to the literature, but also retained many of the classics included in the earlier editions. (Of the thirty-three contributions to this edition, twenty appeared in one or more of the prior editions, and thirteen are new.) We also reorganized the volume to make it more logical and easier for students to use.

Beginning with a new selection, Part 1 offers strong evidence that the gap between rich and poor countries has been growing over the long term. Angus Maddison provides data that goes back 1,000 years, showing us that the gap was much narrower a millennium ago than it is today. The remaining contributions in this section examine more recent data and show the same pattern.

Part 2, which focuses on the domestic gap between rich and poor, now includes further recent evidence of the link between inequality and violence. Part 3 expands our analysis of the convergence thesis. It begins with W. W. Rostow's classic work on the stages of economic growth, which implies that eventually all countries will become rich. This view is supported by the work of Moses Abramovitz. William J. Baumol found a more limited form of convergence, but J. Bradford De Long disputed Baumol's findings by showing that selection bias affected Baumol's results. A large, contemporary, cross-national study by Roberto Patricio Korzeniewicz and Timothy Patrick Moran reinforces the argument against convergence, but Glenn Firebaugh shows that there has been neither convergence nor divergence in recent years, if one looks at income distribution weighted by the population size of countries. Here the "China effect" plays a major role.

Part 4, on the impact of culture on development, includes the classic contributions of David C. McClelland, Herman Kahn, and Oscar Lewis, along with Jim Granato, Ronald Inglehart, and David Leblang's recent empirical evidence.

Dependency theory is covered in Part 5. Along with Theotonio dos Santos's classic contribution, this section includes studies of Ireland and Canada, critiques of dependency theory, and a very recent piece examining the impact of dependency on the domestic distribution of income.

Part 6 opens with Mancur Olson's fascinating "Big Bills Left on the Sidewalk," which makes a strong case that poor countries are poor because they have bad policies. Olson's argument is strengthened by a study of Mauritius, as well as by a more global look at weak states. This section also includes Michael Lipton's classic work on urban bias and a newer piece by Adam Przeworski and Fernando Limongi on the impact of democracy on growth. The section ends with Nancy Birdsall and Richard Sabot's comparison of Latin America and Asia and Paul Krugman's critique of the Asian model.

As the book is organized, any one part could be assigned to students as a self-contained unit. The order in which the parts are presented here, however, does create a logical path that students can easily follow. Parts 1 and 2 provide the basic facts of the gap. Part 3 deals with the dynamics question: Is the gap widening or narrowing? Part 4 presents culture-based explanations for the gap. Part 5 covers dependency and world-system theories, with much empirical evidence and case-study data supporting both sides of the debate. Part 6 covers the role of the state in stimulating or inhibiting growth and inequality. And in Part 7, we offer some conclusions and directions for future research.

*   *   *

We are indebted to numerous people for helping us to prepare the manuscript for this new edition. In particular, we thank Leia Isanhart for her assistance with many of the administrative chores associated with the volume. Also, Mary Sue Passé-Smith worked relentlessly and offered invaluable advice; the book would not have been completed without her help. At the University of Pittsburgh, Professor Seligson's graduate and undergraduate assistants, José René Argueta and Katherine Good, ably assisted in the process. Finally, we thank the many authors and publishers who so kindly granted permission for their works to appear here.

—*Mitchell A. Seligson,*
John T Passé-Smith

CHAPTER 1

The Dual Gaps: An Overview of Theory and Research

MITCHELL A. SELIGSON

C LASSICAL ECONOMIC THEORY TELLS US THAT IN THE END WE WILL ALL BE rich, but this volume contains a great deal of evidence that contradicts that theory. According to W. W. Rostow's thesis (see Chapter 10), underdevelopment is only a stage that nations pass through on their way to becoming developed. But the data we have at hand tell a different story. The income gap between rich and poor countries has grown dramatically since World War II. In 1950 the average per capita income (in 1980 U.S. dollars) of low-income countries was $164, whereas the per capita income of the industrialized countries averaged $3,841, yielding an absolute income gap of $3,677. By 1980, incomes in the poor countries had risen to an average of only $245, whereas those in the industrialized countries had soared to $9,648; the absolute gap in 1980 stood at $9,403 (World Bank 1980: 34). For this period, then, there is clear evidence to support the old adage that "the rich get richer." It is not true, however, that the poor get poorer—not literally, anyway—but that would be a perverse way of looking at these data. A more realistic view of the increases in "wealth" in the poor countries would show that in this thirty-year period their citizens increased their incomes by an average of only $2.70 a year, about what a North American might spend for lunch at a neighborhood fast-food stand. And in terms of relative wealth, the poor countries certainly did get poorer; the total income (gross national product, or GNP) of the high-income countries declined from 4.3 percent of the income earned by the industrialized countries in 1950 to a mere 2.5 percent by 1980.

The growth in the gap has continued into the new century. By 2001 the gap was wider than ever, according to the World Bank. In that year the low-income countries averaged only $430 (in 2001 U.S. dollars) in gross national income (GNI, the revised term for gross national product) while the high-income countries averaged $26,710, resulting in a gap of $26,280! The relative gap by 2001 had become even greater than it was in 1980, with the income of the low-income countries equal to only 1.8 percent of that of the industrialized countries. In other terms, since 1950 the relative gap between rich and poor countries had widened by 60 percent (World Bank 2003: 234–235).

One might suspect that these data do not reflect the general pattern of growth found throughout the world but may be excessively influenced by the disappointing performance of a few "basket case" nations. That suspicion is unfounded. The low-income countries comprise two-fifths of the world's population; 2.5 billion of the world's 6.1 billion people live in countries with per capita incomes that average $430 a year. It is also incorrect to speculate that because the growth rates of some poor countries have recently outperformed those of the industrialized countries that the gap will soon be narrowed. In Chapter 3, John Passé-Smith tells us that it could take Pakistan's 142 million people 579 years to close the gap. Even in the "miracle countries" such as South Korea and Taiwan, where growth rates have been twice as high as in the industrialized countries, the gap has doubled.

There is another gap separating rich from poor: many developing nations have long experienced a growing gap between their own rich and poor citizens, as the chapters in Part 2 of this volume demonstrate. Many poor people who live in poor countries are falling further behind not only the world's rich but also their more affluent countrymen. Moreover, precisely the opposite phenomenon has taken place within many of the richer countries, where the gap between rich and poor is far narrower today than it was a century ago. (Although in some industrialized countries, such as the United States, income inequality seems to have been increasing in recent decades.) The world's poor, therefore, find themselves in double jeopardy.

The consequences of these yawning gaps can be witnessed every day. In the international arena, tensions between the "haves" and "have-nots" dominate debate in the United Nations and other international forums. The poor countries demand a "new international economic order" (NIEO), which they hope will result in the transfer of wealth away from the rich countries, or at least stem the hemorrhage of their own wealth. The industrialized countries have responded with foreign aid programs that, by all accounts, have at best only made a small dent in the problem. Indeed, some argue that foreign aid actually exacerbates the gap (Bornschier, Chase-Dunn, and Rubinson 1978). Within the developing countries, domestic stability may be tenuous at best, as victims of the gap between rich and poor (along with their sympathizers) seek redress through violent means. The guerrilla fighting that spotted the globe during the Cold War may have been fueled by international conflict, but, as Edward N. Muller and Mitchell A. Seligson show in Chapter 8, its root cause invariably can be traced to domestic inequality and deprivation, whether relative or absolute. This remains true in the post–Cold War era.

Thinking and research on the international and domestic gaps between rich and poor have been going through a protracted period of debate that can be traced back to the end of World War II. The war elevated the United States to the position of world leader, and in that position the nation found itself confronted with a Western Europe in ruins. The motivations behind the Marshall Plan for rebuilding Europe are debated to this day, but two things remain evident: unprecedented amounts of aid were given and the expected results were rapidly achieved. War-torn industries were rebuilt, new ones were begun, and economic growth quickly resumed. Similarly, Japan, devastated by conventional and nuclear attack, was able to rebuild its economy and become a world leader in high-technology industrial production.

The successful rebuilding of Europe and Japan encouraged many to believe that similar success would meet efforts to stimulate growth in the developing world. More often than not, however, such efforts have failed or fallen far below expectations. Even when programs have been effective and nations have seemed well on the way toward rapid growth, many of them nonetheless continued to fall further and further behind the wealthy countries. Moreover, growth inevitably seemed to be accompanied by a widening income gap within the developing countries. Only in Asia have we seen some reversal of this worldwide trend; there, poor nations have grown rapidly while income inequality has not worsened, and in some cases it has even improved. The lessons of Asia therefore are important ones.

Over the years, an impressive volume of research on explaining the gap question has been generated, and we have attempted to include some of the very best of it in this collection. The authors represented here offer a wide-ranging treatment of the thinking that is evolving on the subject of the international and domestic gaps between rich and poor. Their studies are not confined to a single academic discipline or geographic area. Rather, their work reflects a variety of fields, including anthropology, economics, political science, psychology, and sociology, and they have examined the problems from the perspective of a single country or region as well as with a microanalytic approach.

The volume is organized to first present to the reader a broad picture defining the international and domestic gaps between the rich and the poor. This picture is contained in Parts 1 and 2. Part 3 challenges the conventional wisdom on the existence of the international gap. Parts 4 through 6 attempt to explain the existence of the gaps.

In Part 1 we present a broad overview of the facts of the international gap. The chapters here show that the international gap existed 1,000 years ago and has been increasing ever since. In Chapter 3, John Passé-Smith demonstrates that even though some countries manage to narrow the gap, most do not. These findings are robust even when purchasing power parity is used to calculate per capita incomes. Part 2 examines domestic inequality. Simon Kuznets (Chapter 6) sees widening domestic income inequality as an almost inevitable by-product of development. Kuznets traces a path that industrialized nations seem to have followed quite closely. It begins with relative domestic equality in the distribution of income. The onset of industrialization produces a significant shift in the direction of inequality and creates a widening gap. Once the industrialization process matures, however, the gap is again reduced. Those who regard the Marshall Plan as the model for the resolution of world poverty still hold this view. Part 2 also shows that inequality is linked to violence in the form of domestic insurgency (Chapter 8); therefore, there are real societal costs to pay beyond the ethical ones.

Whereas Parts 1 and 2 present the basic argument on the extent and duration of the international and domestic gap, Part 3 examines the evidence for the so-called convergence thesis. This thesis argues that even though Kuznets may have been right, in the long run rich and poor countries all will follow the same stages of growth (Chapter 10) and will eventually converge (Chapter 11). Several authors in Part 3 show, however, that convergence between rich and poor is in fact an ever-receding dream.

Explanations for the gaps have often focused on different aspects of national culture. We have all heard the claim that the Germans or Japanese are wealthy because they are so industrious. Part 4 of this volume presents evidence for and against the role of culture in development. Specifically, the cultural values associated with industrialization are seen as foreign to many developing nations, which are deeply attached to more traditional values. According to the cultural thesis, punctuality, hard work, achievement, and other "industrial" values are the keys to unlocking the economic potential of poor countries.

Most adherents of this perspective believe that such values can be inculcated through deliberate effort (Chapter 16). Others argue that the values will emerge naturally as the result of a worldwide process of diffusion of values functional for development. This perspective has been incorporated into a more general school of thought focusing on the process called "modernization." Development occurs and the international gap is narrowed when a broad set of modern values and institutions is present. The success of the Asian economies in recent years has led some to speculate that there are cultural values found there that foster growth. This view, a variant on Max Weber's old notion of the value of the "Protestant ethic," is termed the "Confucian ethic," as is shown in Chapter 17.

In marked contrast to these two perspectives, which suggest that the phenomena of rich and poor disparity are transitory, a third school of thought comes to rather different conclusions. The scholars supporting this approach—known as *dependentistas*—observe that the economies of the developing nations have been shaped in response to forces and conditions established by the industrialized nations and that their development has been both delayed and dependent as a result. The *dependentistas* conclude that the failure of poor countries is a product of the distorted development brought on by dependency relations. In Part 5 the dependency and world-system perspectives are presented by the major writers in the field, and refuted by others using careful studies of large data sets. The case studies of Canada (Chapter 21) and Ireland (Chapter 22) suggest that dependency is not only a problem for the developing world but for some parts of the industrialized world as well.

Part 6 presents the most recent explanation of the gaps, one that focuses on the role of states within the third world. As socialist economies worldwide proved incapable of keeping up with the capitalist industrialized countries, international development agencies shifted their attention to the need for policy reforms within the third world. This emphasis brought with it a host of neoliberal policy prescriptions, including privatization, trade liberalization, and the end of import substitution industrialization (ISI) policies. The collapse of the Soviet Union and the socialist states of Eastern Europe, along with a move toward capitalist economics in China, has reinforced this tendency.

According to the perspective that focuses on the state, errors of state policy are largely responsible for the gaps. One way these policies get distorted is from "urban bias" (Chapter 29). Proponents of this view see numerous policies in the third world that favor the cities over the countryside, with the result that growth is slowed and the gap between rich and poor nations widens.

Because of the dramatic increase in the number of democratic governments in recent years, the focus on states has raised concerns over the connection between democracy on the one hand and growth and inequality on the other. Some have argued that democratic political systems are less capable than their authoritarian counterparts of setting a clear economic agenda, whereas others have argued that democracies not only are good for growth but also are inherently egalitarian in nature and hence help reduce the domestic gap between rich and poor. Chapter 30, by Adam Przeworski and Fernando Limongi, presents the evidence in this debate.

Finally, the dramatic successes in both growth and equality in the so-called miracle economies of Asia, the "gang of four" and the "little tigers," have led to a careful examination of state policy in those countries. These economies have shown consistent growth that far exceeds that of the third world and that of the industrialized countries. Moreover, this growth has been achieved in countries such as Taiwan, South Korea, and Japan at the same time as income inequality has been *reduced*. Some observers, such as Herman Kahn (Chapter 17), believe that the success can be largely explained by cultural factors, especially the "Confucian ethic." But others believe that it is state policies that have driven these successes. The evidence is ably summarized by Nancy Birdsall and Richard Sabot (Chapter 31), who show how the failure to invest in human capital in Latin America is responsible for slowed growth and high inequality, as compared to Asia.

The readers of this volume will come away from it with a clear sense of the causes of the gaps between the rich and poor. It is to be hoped that some of those readers might someday help in implementing the "cure."

References

Bornschier, Volker, Christopher Chase-Dunn, and Richard Rubinson. 1978. "Cross-National Evidence of the Effects of Foreign Investment and Aid on Economic Growth and Inequality: A Survey of the Findings." *American Sociological Review* 84: 651–683.

World Bank. 1980. *World Development Report 1980*. New York: Oxford University Press.

———. 2003. *World Development Report 2003*. New York: Oxford University Press.

PART I

Is There a Gap Between Rich and Poor Countries?

CHAPTER 2

The World Economy: A Millennial Perspective

Angus Maddison

Angus Maddison has long been one of the most prominent economic historians, providing development scholars with some of the most reliable historical data with which to judge long-term economic growth patters. In this chapter, Maddison discusses world economic growth since 1000 C.E. Maddison provides evidence that after reaching a low point around 1000, western Europe began to grow such that it surpassed the production per capita of the rest of the world by the year 1500. After this point the gap between western Europe and the rest of the world widens. By 1820 western Europe produces about twice that produced by the rest of the world and from that point on the gap grows very rapidly. In Part 3 of this book, we turn to convergence theory, which proposes that over the long run, per capita incomes will converge. Maddison's conclusions suggest that the long-term pattern is one marked by divergence rather than convergence.

GDP Per Capita

LONG-TERM ESTIMATES OF WORLD GDP ARE VERY RECENT. RESEARCH ON REAL income growth by quantitative economic historians has been heavily concentrated on Europe, and generally confined to the past two centuries. Until recently what was known about earlier centuries was in large degree conjectural.

Maddison (1995) contained detailed estimates for different parts of the world economy for 1820 onwards, with a very crude provisional assessment for 1500 to 1820. Here I have made a much more careful scrutiny of the evidence for centuries before 1820 and incorporated the results of Maddison (1998) on Chinese economic performance over two millennia.

The level and movement of per capita GDP is the primary general purpose indicator of changes in well-being and production potential, but one should keep in mind that per capita consumption has increased less over the long run because of the increased share of product allocated to investment and government. Labour productivity does not always move parallel to per capita income. The advances achieved in Sung China (960–1279) and in Japan in the seventeenth and eighteenth centuries required substantial increases in per capita labour effort. In the twentieth century we find the opposite phenomenon. Labour input per person fell substantially in Western Europe and Western Offshoots.

Table 2.1 summarises my findings for the past millennium. It shows clearly the exceptionalism of Western Europe's very lengthy ascension, and origins of the great divergence between the West (Group A) and the rest of the world (Group B).

The major conclusions I draw from the long term quantitative evidence are as follows:

(a) West European income was at a nadir around the year 1000. Its level was significantly lower than it had been in the first century. It was below that in China, India and other parts of East and West Asia;

(b) There was a turning point in the eleventh century when the economic ascension of Western Europe began. It proceeded at a slow pace, but by 1820 real income had tripled. The locus and characteristics of economic leadership changed. The North Italian city states and, in particular, Venice initiated the growth process and reopened Mediterranean trade. Portugal and Spain opened trade routes to the Americas and Asia, but were less dynamic than the Netherlands which became the economic leader around 1600, followed by the United Kingdom in the nineteenth century;

(c) Western Europe overtook China (the leading Asian economy) in per capita performance in the fourteenth century. Thereafter China and most of the rest of Asia were more or less stagnant in per capita terms until the second half of the twentieth century. The stagnation was initially due to indigenous institutions and policy, reinforced by colonial exploitation which derived from Western hegemony and was most marked from the eighteenth century onwards;

(d) West European appropriation of the natural resources of North America, introduction of European settlers, technology and organisation

Table 2.1   Growth of Per Capita GDP by Major Region, 1000–1998
(annual average compound growth rate)

	1000–1500	1500–1600	1600–1700	1700–1820	1820–1998
Western Europe	0.13	0.14	0.15	0.15	1.51
Western Offshoots	0.00	0.00	0.17	0.78	1.75
Japan	0.03	0.03	0.09	0.13	1.93
Average Group A	0.11	0.13	0.12	0.18	1.67
Latin America	0.01	0.09	0.19	0.19	1.22
Eastern Europe & Former USSR	0.04	0.10	0.10	0.10	1.06
Asia (excluding Japan)	0.05	0.01	–0.01	0.01	0.92
Africa	–0.01	0.00	0.00	0.04	0.67
Average Group B	0.04	0.02	0.00	0.03	0.95

Table 2.1b   Level of Per Capita GDP, Groups A and B, 1000–1998 (1990 international dollars)

	1000	1500	1600	1700	1820	1998
Average Group A	405	704	805	907	1,130	21,470
Average Group B	440	535	548	551	573	3,102

Table 2.1c   Popualation of Groups A and B, 1000–1998 (millions)

	1000	1500	1600	1700	1820	1998
Total Group A	35	76	95	110	175	838
Total Group B	233	362	461	493	866	5,069

Table 2.1d   GDP of Groups A and B, 1000–1998 (billions of 1990 international dollars)

	1000	1500	1600	1700	1820	1998
Total Group A	14.1	53.2	76.1	100.0	198.0	17,998
Total Group B	102.7	194.0	252.9	271.8	496.5	15,727

Source: Appendix B [of original text; not included here].

added a substantial new dimension to Western economic ascension from the eighteenth century onwards. Towards the end of the nineteenth century, the United States became the world economic leader;

(e) Japan was an exception to the Asian norm. In the course of the seventeenth, eighteenth and the first half of the nineteenth century, it caught up with and overtook China in per capita income. The Meiji takeover in 1868 involved massive institutional change aimed at catching up with the West. This was achieved in income terms in the 1980s, but not yet in productivity;

(f) The colonial takeover in Latin America had some analogy to that in North America, but Iberian institutions were less propitious to capitalist development than those in North America. Latin America included a much larger indigenous population which was treated as an underclass without access to land or education. The social order was not greatly changed after independence. Over the long run the rise in per capita income was much smaller than in North America, but faster than in Asia or Africa;

(g) African per capita income was lower in 1820 than in the first century. Since then there has been slower advance than in all other regions. The income level in 1998 was little better than that of Western Europe in 1820. Population growth is now faster than in any other region—eight times as fast as in Western Europe;

(h) The most dynamic growth performance has been concentrated on the past two centuries. Since 1820 per capita income has risen 19-fold in Group A, and more than 5-fold in the rest of the world—dwarfing any earlier advance and compressing it into a very short time span.

One may ask what is new in these findings. In the first place there is the quantification which clarifies issues that qualitative analysis leaves fuzzy. It helps to separate stylised facts from the stylised fantasies which are sometimes perceived to be reality. It is more readily contestable and likely to be contested. It sharpens scholarly discussion, and contributes to the dynamics of the research process. It is also useful to have a world picture because it helps to identify what is normal and what is exceptional.

My findings differ in some respects from earlier interpretations of the length and pace of Western Europe's economic ascension. There has been a general tendency to date it from 1500 when Europeans encountered America and first made a direct entry into the trading world of Asia. Max Weber attributed Europe's advance to the rise of Protestantism, and this thesis attracted attention because it was congruent with the conventional wisdom about the beginning of the European ascension. I no longer believe that there was a sharp break in the pace of advance of per capita income around 1500.

Kuznets (1966, Chapter 1) suggested that "modern economic growth" is a distinctive economic epoch preceded by merchant capitalism in Western Europe "from the end of the fifteenth to the second half of the eighteenth century," and an "antecedent epoch of feudal organisation." In Kuznets (1973, pp. 139–41), he advanced what seemed to be a reasonable view about the rate of per capita GDP growth in Western Europe in the merchant capitalist period. In Maddison (1995), I accepted Kuznets' hypothesis for his merchant capitalist period, but I now believe that growth was slower then than Kuznets suggested, and that the pace of advance between the eleventh and the fifteenth centuries was not much different. For this reason, it does not seem valid to distinguish between epochs of "feudal organisation" and "merchant capitalism." Instead I would characterise the whole period 1000–1820 as "proto-capitalist."

I also differ from Kuznets on the timing of the transition to what he called "modern economic growth" (which I call "capitalist development"). The evidence now available suggests that the transition took place around 1820 rather than in 1760. The revisionist work of Crafts (1983 and 1992) and others has helped to break the old notion of a sudden take-off in the second half of the eighteenth century in England. Recent research on the Netherlands shows income to have been higher there than in the United Kingdom at the end of the eighteenth century. Work in the past twenty years on the quantitative history of other West European countries provides further reason for postdating the transition and modifying the old emphasis on British exceptionalism.

My analysis of US economic performance shows a rapid advance in the eighteenth century in contrast to the findings of Gallman (1972) and Mancall and Weiss (1999). The essential reason for the difference is that I include rough estimates of the indigenous population and its GDP as well as the activity of European settlers (I also did this for Australia, Canada and New Zealand).

My assessment of Japanese development differs from the conventional wisdom. I have quantified its economic performance in the Tokugawa period and compared it with China. Most analysts concentrate on comparisons between Japan and Western Europe in the Meiji period, and ignore the Asian context.

Gerschenkron (1965) and Rostow (1960 and 1963) both emphasised the idea that "take-offs" were staggered throughout the nineteenth century in West European countries. Kuznets (1979, p. 131) endorsed this view. In fact growth acceleration was more synchronous in Western Europe than they believed.

There are two schools of thought about the relative performance of Europe and Asia. The mainstream view was clearly expressed by Adam Smith in 1776. He was not a practitioner of political arithmetic but on the basis of the "price of labour" and other evidence, his ordinal ranking from the top downwards was as follows for the 1770s: Netherlands, England, France, British North American colonies, Scotland, Spain, Spanish colonies in America, China, Bengal (depressed by the East India Company's plundering).

This mainstream view is reflected in Landes (1969, pp. 13–14) whose overall assessment, like that of Smith, was similar to mine. "Western Europe was already rich before the Industrial Revolution— rich by comparison with other parts of the world of that day. This wealth was the product of centuries of slow accumulation, based in turn on investment, the appropriation of extra-European resources and labour, and substantial technological progress, not only in the production of material goods, but in the organisation and financing of their exchange and distribution . . . it seems clear that over the near-millennium from the year 1000 to the eighteenth century, income per head rose appreciably—perhaps tripled."

In Maddison (1983), I contrasted the Landes view with Bairoch's (1981) assessment of relative income per head. He suggested that China was well ahead of Western Europe in 1800, Japan and the rest of Asia only 5 per cent lower than Europe, Latin America well ahead of North America, and Africa about two thirds of the West European level. This highly improbable scenario was never documented in the case of Asia, Latin America or Africa. His figures for these areas were essentially guesstimates. Bairoch consistently took the position that the third world had been impoverished by the rich countries (see Bairoch, 1967), and he was, in fact, fabricating ammunition for this hypothesis (see the critique of Chesnais, 1987).

In spite of its shaky foundations, Bairoch's assessment has been influential. Braudel (1985, vol. 3 pp. 533–4) acknowledged "the great service Paul Bairoch has rendered to historians" and believed "it is virtually beyond question that Europe was less rich than the worlds it was exploiting, even after the fall of Napoleon." Andre Gunder Frank (1998, pp. 171 and 284) cites Bairoch and suggests that "around 1800 Europe and the United States, after long lagging behind, suddenly caught up and then overtook Asia economically and politically. Pomeranz (2000) cites Bairoch more cautiously (p. 16) but his sinophilia drives him to the same conclusion. He suggests (p. 111), there is "little reason to think that West Europeans were more productive than their contemporaries in various other densely populated regions of the Old World prior to 1750 or even 1800."

Maddison (1983) contrasted the assessments of Landes and Bairoch and commented: "These remarkably different quantitative conclusions have very different analytical implications. If Bairoch is right, then much of the backwardness of the third world presumably has to be explained by colonial exploitation, and much less of Europe's advantage can be due to scientific precocity, centuries of slow accumulation, and organisational and financial prosperity."

In view of the laborious efforts I have since made to accumulate quantitative evidence on this topic, I now conclude that Bairoch and his epigoni are quite wrong. To reject them is not to deny the role of colonial exploitation, but this can be better understood by taking a more realistic view of Western strength and Asian weakness around 1800.

The major problem in growth analysis is to explain why such a large divergence developed between the advanced capitalist group and the rest of the world. There are, of course, some examples of past convergence, e.g. Europe's rise from its nadir to overtake China, the Japanese catch-up with China in Tokugawa times, and subsequently with the advanced capitalist group. Western Europe achieved a very substantial degree of catch-up on the United States in the golden age after the second world war; resurgent Asia (China, India, the so-called tigers and others) have narrowed their degree of backwardness substantially over the past quarter century.

In attempting to understand the causes of divergence and the possibilities for catch-up in different parts of the world economy, there is no universal schema which covers the whole millennium. The operative forces have varied between place and period.

References

Bairoch, P. 1967. *Diagnostic de l'évolution économique du tiers-monde 1900–1966,* Gauthiers-Villars, Paris.

Bairoch, P. 1981. "The Main Trends in National Economic Disparities since the Industrial Revolution." Pp. 3–17 in *Disparities in Economic Development since the Industrial Revolution,* edited by P. Bairoch and M. Levy-Leboyer. London: Macmillan.

Braudel. F. 1985. *Civilisation and Capitalism, 15th–18th Century,* 3 vols., Fontana, London.

Chesnais, J.-C. 1987. *La Revanche du Tiers-Monde,* Laffont, Paris.

Crafts, N.F.R. 1983. "British Economic Growth, 1700–1831: A Review of the Evidence," *Economic History Review,* May, pp. 177–199.

Crafts, N.F.R., and C. K. Harley. 1992. "Output Growth and the British Industrial Revolution: A Restatement of the Crafts-Harley View," *Economic History Review,* November, pp. 703–730.

Frank. A.G. 1998. *Reorient: Global Economy in the Asian Age,* University of California Press, Berkeley.

Gallman, R.E. 1972. "The Pace and Pattern of American Economic Growth," in Davis and Associates.

Gerschenkron, A. 1965. *Economic Backwardness in Historical Perspective*, Praeger, New York.

Kuznets, S. 1979, *Growth, Population and Income Distribution*, Norton, New York.

Kuznets, S. 1973. *Population, Capital and Growth: Selected Essays*, Norton, New York.

Kuznets, S. 1966. *Modern Economic Growth*, Yale.

Landes, D.S. 1969. *The Unbound Prometheus*, Cambridge University Press, Cambridge.

Maddison, A. 1998. *Chinese Economic Performance in the Long Run*, OECD Development Centre, Paris.

Maddison, A. 1995. *Monitoring the World Economy 1820–1992*, OECD Development Centre, Paris.

Maddison, A. 1983. "A Comparison of Levels of GDP Per Capita in Developed and Developing Countries, 1700–1980," *Journal of Economic History*, March, pp. 27–41.

Mancall, Peter C., and Thomas Weiss. 1999. "Was Economic Growth Likely in Colonial British North America?" *Journal of Economic History*, Vol. 59, Issue 1, pp. 17–40.

Pomeranz, K. 2000. *The Great Divergence*, Princeton University Press, Princeton.

Rostow, W.W. 1963. *The Economics of Takeoff into Sustained Growth*, MacMillan, London.

Rostow, W.W. 1960. *The Stages of Economic Growth*, Cambridge University Press, Cambridge.

CHAPTER 3

The Persistence of the Gap Between Rich and Poor Countries, 1960–1998

JOHN T PASSÉ-SMITH

O NE OF THE PRIMARY GOALS OF THIS BOOK IS TO TRACE THE DEBATE OVER the causes of the gap between rich and poor countries, referred to as the external gap. Before its causes can be fruitfully discussed, however, the student of development should have an understanding of the extent of the gap and the characteristics of worldwide economic growth. In Chapter 2 Angus Maddison provided a valuable picture of historical patterns of growth. This chapter focuses on the more recent period, 1960 to 1998. In examining trends in and characteristics of economic growth, I have divided the chapter into four sections: rates of growth, the absolute gap, the relative gap, and country mobility.

Rates of Economic Growth

Following Western Europe's fast recovery after World War II, the governments of the industrialized countries turned their attention to aiding the third world nations in their development efforts. In the 1950s and early 1960s, economic growth became the centerpiece of economists' development plans. To that end the United Nations declared the 1960s the "development decade" and set a goal of 6 percent annual growth as necessary to raise the poverty-stricken to a decent standard of living (Dube 1988: 2–3). About two decades later David Morawetz (1977) was commissioned by the World Bank to take stock of what had been accomplished in the area of development. Morawetz evaluated the world's growth between 1950 and 1975, concluding that although the whole world had experienced relatively rapid growth, the gap between the high-income and poor countries in terms of per capita gross national product (GNP/pc) was growing wider.

For the period under investigation in this chapter, 1960 to 1998, data were obtained from the *World Development Indicators, 2000* (World Bank 2000) and the International Monetary Fund's *International Financial Statistics: Supplement on Output Statistics,* no. 8 (IMF 1984). Figures on GNP/pc are presented in constant 1995 U.S. dollars, and growth rates were computed from the constant per capita GNPs using the regression method described by the World Bank in the *World Development Report* (1988: 288–289).[1] The income groupings and regional designations were borrowed from the World Bank's *World Development Indicators, 2000* (see the Tables, Quick Reference section where the technical notes offer the "Classification of economies by income and region").[2] The cutoffs for the income groups were defined as follows: those countries with a GNP/pc of $9,361 or greater are considered high-income; middle-income countries have a GNP/pc of $761 to $9,360; and the poor countries are those with a GNP/pc of less than $761. GNP/pc is expressed in 1995 U.S. dollars.

Over the thirty-nine-year period 1960–1998, the annual average rate of GNP/pc growth for the world has been about 1.7 percent (see Table 3.1). To put this achievement in perspective, we must realize that modern growth among those countries considered developed today began in the middle of the nineteenth century. During the hundred years prior to 1950, according to Simon Kuznets (1972: 19), those countries experienced a century of unprecedented rates of growth (1.6 percent annual). Since 1960 the entire world—not just the fastest-growing countries—has surpassed the 1.6 percent mark. In fact, in the 1960s the world grew at almost 2.9 percent per annum. A more sobering observation is that every decade since the 1960s has witnessed a decelerating growth rate until the 1990s, when the world's economies recovered from less than 1 percent growth in the 1980s, rising to 1.22 percent in

Table 3.1   Growth Rates by Income Grouping

	1960–1998	1960–1969	1970–1979	1980–1989	1990–1998
World	1.71	2.86	2.63	0.72	1.22
Rich	2.10	4.13	2.24	1.83	2.75
Middle	2.21	3.81	3.07	0.39	1.20
Poor	0.78	1.34	1.30	0.27	0.34
Less than 1 million	2.32	3.39	4.14	0.76	0.88

Source: World Bank, *World Development Indicators, 2000* (Washington, D.C.: World Bank, 2000).

the 1990s. The largest drop came between the 1970s (2.6 percent) and the 1980s (0.7 percent).

For the period as a whole, the middle-income countries had the highest growth rates. The mean growth rate of the middle-income countries between 1960 and 1998 was 2.21 percent, while the high-income countries grew at an average annual rate of 1.71 percent and the poor countries grew the slowest at 0.78 percent. Although the poorest countries are left behind, these facts at least partially support the expectations of convergence theorists who assert that the gap between rich and poor will disappear over the long run. They argue that the poorer countries have the highest growth potential (see convergence theorists' possible explanation for these growth rates in Chapter 11 by Moses Abramovitz and Chapter 12 by William Baumol) and that as this potential is realized the gap will dissolve. The partial support of convergence is probably due to the fact that the World Bank's income categories placed Canada, Italy, and Japan in the middle-income group in 1960. If these three countries are removed the middle-income countries achieve a growth rate that is equal to but does not exceed that of the high-income countries (2.1 percent for both). It should be noted, however, that in the 1970s the economic growth rate of middle-income countries significantly surpassed that of the high-income countries.

If convergence in its purest form were occurring today, the growth rates of the poorest countries would be the highest, followed by the middle-income countries, and the high-income countries would have the lowest growth rates. In his 1982 study of world growth between 1960 and 1978, Robert Jackman found that while middle-income countries were growing faster than the high-income countries, the poor suffered the lowest growth rates. Jackman labeled this the "modified Matthew effect" (1982: 175). In the Bible, the Book of Matthew contains a reference to the continued accumulation of wealth by the rich and the further impoverishment of the poor; by the modified Matthew effect, Jackman meant that both the high-income and middle-income countries were growing richer. In fact, he discovered that the middle-income countries were growing faster than the high-income (converging). Alas, the poor fell further behind.

Looking back to Table 3.1, the annual average rates of growth for the high-income, middle-income, and poor countries are broken down by decades. The modified Matthew effect is found only in the 1970s. During this decade the middle-income countries grew at an impressive annual average rate of 3.07 percent, while the high-income achieved a rate of 2.24 percent. Although the poor grew the slowest, at 1.3 percent, only the 1960s were more prosperous. The forces that modified the

Matthew effect during the 1970s weakened during the following decades, and any hope for closing the gap was extinguished. It could be that the oil shocks of the 1970s—quadrupling the cost of imported oil—hurt the energy-hungry, high-income economies more than the middle-income and low-income countries, at least initially. In the 1970s the growth rate of the high-income economies fell to 2.24 percent from the 1960s average of 4.13 percent. Awash in petrodollars reinvested in the high-income countries by the oil-exporting nations, bankers in the first world hoped to avoid inflation by making more money available to developing countries.

During the 1970s the middle-income countries grew at a healthy 3.07 percent and the poor at 1.3 percent. While the 1970s was a time of relatively easy money and economic growth for the middle-income and poor countries, the debt came due; the 1980s is now referred to as "the lost decade." Development plans contrived during the 1970s period of easy money gave way to the debt crisis in the 1980s. The middle-income countries saw their economic growth fall to 0.39 percent in the 1980s and the poor could only muster 0.27 percent. Fortunately, the economy bottomed out in the 1990s and all three income groups improved. Between 1990 and 1998, the high-income countries grew at an annual average rate of 2.75 percent, while the middle-income and poor grew at 1.2 percent and 0.34 percent respectively.

The economic growth rates of the World Bank's geographic regions are presented in Table 3.2. High-income countries and those with populations under 1 million are extracted from their geographic regions by the World Bank and displayed as separate groups. Table 3.2 shows that east Asia, containing the so-called Asian newly industrializing countries

Table 3.2   Growth Rates by Region

	1960–1998	1960–1969	1970–1979	1980–1989	1990–1998
High income	2.57	4.51	2.56	2.14	2.75
Americas	0.97	2.30	2.50	−0.93	1.66
Middle East/north Africa	2.66	3.40	4.48	0.92	0.48
Eastern Europe/central Asia	1.88	5.34	4.50	2.12	−3.14
South Asia	1.89	1.33	1.09	2.73	3.09
East Asia/Pacific	4.03	3.36	4.11	3.72	4.46
West Africa	−0.03	1.04	0.87	−0.59	−0.40
East/south Africa	1.05	1.65	2.35	0.57	−0.72
Less than 1 million	2.32	3.39	4.14	0.76	0.88

Source: Computed from World Bank, *World Development Indicators, 2000* (Washington, D.C.: World Bank, 2000).

(NICs), is the fastest growing region with an annual growth rate of 4.03 between 1960 and 1998. East Asia/Pacific maintained the most stable and strong growth rate throughout the entire period, even though it was not necessarily the fastest growing region each decade. During the 1960s eastern Europe/central Asia achieved the highest rate of growth (5.34 percent) and maintained a relatively high 4.5 percent rate through the 1970s, but the 1980s witnessed a halving of their growth rate and the 1990s brought economic contraction at an alarming pace (–3.14 percent). The slowest decade of economic growth was the 1980s with global economic expansion reaching 2.14 percent. During this decade both the Americas (–0.93) and west Africa (–0.59) experienced negative growth rates. While the economies of the Americas recovered in the 1990s returning to a positive rate of growth (1.66), eastern Europe/central Asia (–3.14), west Africa (–0.40), and east/south Africa (–0.72) all contracted.

Analysis of income groups and regions makes it difficult to judge the performance of individual states. Table 3.3 remedies this by highlighting the ten fastest- and slowest-growing countries. The fastest growing countries in the world between 1960 and 1998 grew at an annual average rate of from 4.8 percent (Swaziland) to 7.7 percent (Botswana). One of the more striking features of Table 3.3 is that six of the ten fastest-growing countries in the world between 1960 and 1998— Botswana, China, Oman, Dominica, Thailand, and Swaziland—started the period with GNP/pcs of less than $761 (in the poor income group). As may be expected, the region containing the Asian NICs, east Asia/Pacific, is well represented on the list with five countries (the Republic of Korea, Singapore, China, Hong Kong, and Thailand). East/south Africa is represented by Botswana and Swaziland. The Middle East/north African region is represented by Oman and Malta, and Dominica is the sole country from the Americas on the top-ten list. Although they represent less than one-half of 1 percent of the world's population, five countries with populations of less than 1 million are among the fastest-growing countries in the world (Botswana, Malta, Oman, Dominica, and Swaziland). No high-income country made the list of the ten fastest- or ten slowest-growing countries.

Unfortunately, one region of the world dominates the list of the slowest-growing countries. Of the ten slowest-growing countries in the world between 1960 and 1998, seven are from sub-Saharan Africa (east/south Africa and west Africa): the Democratic Republic of Congo, Niger, Madagascar, Zambia, Sierra Leone, the Central African Republic, and Chad. Of the remaining countries, two belong to the Middle East/north African region (Qatar and Kuwait), and one is from

Table 3.3   The Fastest- and Slowest-Growing Countries, 1960–1998

The Ten Fastest-Growing Countries

Rank	Country	Economic Growth Rate, 1960–1998	Income Group, 1960
1	Botswana	7.7	LT 1 million/poor
2	Korea, Republic of	6.5	Middle income
3	Singapore	6.5	Middle income
4	China	6.4	Poor
5	Malta	6.3	LT 1 million/middle income
6	Hong Kong	5.7	Middle income
7	Oman	5.6	LT 1 million/poor
8	Dominica	5.5	LT 1 million/poor
9	Thailand	5.0	Poor
10	Swaziland	4.8	LT 1 million/poor

The Ten Slowest-Growing Countries

Rank	Country	Economic Growth Rate, 1960–1998	Income Group, 1960
1	Qatar	−5.2	LT 1 million/rich
2	Congo, Democratic Republic of	−3.1	Poor
3	Nicaragua	−2.3	Poor
4	Niger	−2.3	Poor
5	Kuwait	−2.0	LT 1 million/rich
6	Madagascar	−1.6	Poor
7	Zambia	−1.6	Poor
8	Sierra Leone	−1.1	Poor
9	Central African Republic	−1.0	Poor
10	Chad	−0.8	Poor

Source: World Bank, *World Development Indicators, 2000* (Washington, D.C.: World Bank, 2000).

Note: LT 1 million refers to countries with populations less than 1 million.

the Americas (Nicaragua). The slowest-growing countries in the world all experienced negative growth of from –0.8 percent (Chad) to –5.2 percent (Qatar).

The Absolute Gap

In 1965 Simon Kuznets reported that the mean GNP/pc of the high-income countries was $1,900, whereas that of the poor was $120.[3] One of the major trends over the previous 100 to 125 years, Kuznets argued, was that the absolute gap widened very slowly up until World War II and then began to accelerate. "A reasonable conjecture is that, in comparison with the quintupling of the per capita product of developed countries over the last century, the per capita product of the 'poor' LDCs [less-developed countries] rose two-thirds at most" (1972: 19).

The absolute gap, as defined by David Morawetz (1977), is the difference between the mean GNP/pc of a set of high-income countries and that of poorer countries or groups of countries. Morawetz found that the absolute gap between members of the Organization for Economic Cooperation and Development (OECD) and developing countries between 1950 and 1975 had more than doubled (from $2,191 to $4,839 in 1975 U.S. dollars). Neither the developing countries as a group nor any of the geographic regions reported by Morawetz were able to achieve a narrowing of the absolute gap.

Comparable results obtain for the 1960 to 1998 period. The data presented in Table 3.4 show that the dollar amount (as measured by GNP/pc) separating the high-income and middle-income countries has grown from $9,623 to $22,317 (1995 U.S. dollars) and from $12,081 to $25,016 between the high-income and poor countries for the 1960–1998 period. The far-right-hand column of Table 3.4 lists the annual average

Table 3.4   The Absolute Gap, 1960–1998 (1995 U.S. dollars)

	1960	1980	1998	Annual Average Increase in the Gap
Income Group				
Middle income	9,623	15,333	22,317	325
Poor	12,081	17,739	25,016	332
Region				
Americas	10,730	15,306	22,268	296
Middle East/north Africa	11,371	15,279	22,708	291
Eastern Europe/central Asia	11,380	15,348	22,627	288
South Asia	12,262	17,855	24,933	325
East Asia/Pacific	11,845	16,724	22,336	269
West Africa	12,030	17,463	24,810	328
East/south Africa	11,931	17,259	24,280	317
Less than 1 million	3,689	6,028	12,614	229
Countries That Have Closed the Absolute Gap				
Japan	4,267		–17,291	
Singapore	9,329		–7,208	
Hong Kong	9,453		3,668	
Ireland	7,352		5,925	
French Polynesia	7,487		6,366	

Source: World Bank, *World Development Indicators, 2000* (Washington, D.C.: World Bank, 2000).

increase in the absolute gap. It shows that on average the gap between the high-income and middle-income countries increases $325 per year while the gap between the average GNP/pc of the high-income and poor widens $332 per year. In fact, only 5 of 114 countries have been able to close the absolute gap: Japan, Singapore, Hong Kong, Ireland, and French Polynesia.

If, over the thirty-nine years covered in this chapter, the percentage of people who lived in poor countries had dropped to a relatively small number, or even if the number of people was moderate but they lived in only a few countries, then interest in the gap would probably wane. But poverty has remained a persistent problem for more than half the world's population. Table 3.5 provides information on the percentage of the world's population living in high-income, middle-income, and poor countries. The data indicate that in 1998 59.7 percent of the world's population lived in countries with per capita GNPs of less than $760 (1995 U.S. dollars). This is a grim statistic. Table 3.5 also shows, however, that a larger percentage of people lived in middle-income countries in 1998 than in 1960, while both the high-income and the poor groups shrank in size. Unfortunately, the population distribution means that the gap between high-income, middle-income, and poor countries is not just affecting a small percentage of the world's population.

The data set out thus far demonstrate that the gap between the high-income and the other two groups is growing. But does this prove the adage that "the rich get richer while the poor get poorer"? In previous editions of this volume the data showed that while the gap was opening, the middle-income and poor countries were gradually increasing the average size of their economies. Figure 3.1 shows that for the period under examination, the middle-income countries do increase their average GNP/pc from $2,850 in 1960 to $3,077 in 1998; however, the middle-income countries' GNP/pc actually contracts seventeen of the thirty-

Table 3.5 World Population Living in Rich, Middle-Income, and Poor Countries (percentage)

Income Group	1960	1980	1998
Rich	14.1	18.8	16.7
Middle	21.2	17.7	23.5
Poor	64.2	63.3	59.7
Less than 1 million	0.4	0.2	0.1

Source: World Bank, *World Development Indicators, 2000* (Washington, D.C.: World Bank, 2000).

**Figure 3.1   GNP/pc of High-Income, Middle-Income,
and Poor Countries (U.S. dollars)**

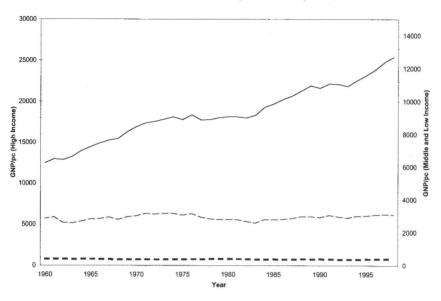

Source: World Bank, *World Bank Indicators, 2000* (Washington, DC: World Bank, 2000).

nine years. The poor do become poorer. In 1960 the GNP/pc of the poor
countries was $392 but by 1998 it had dropped to $378. Perhaps even
more disheartening is the fact that the average GNP/pc for the poor
dropped to $351 in 1987 but never once climbed above $400.

   In order to eventually catch up with the high-income countries'
GNP/pc, low-income countries must simply grow faster than the rich.
But catching up could take hundreds if not thousands of years if the
countries are relatively poor and their growth rates are only slightly
faster than those of the high-income. Indeed, in such a case the absolute
gap will widen for years before it begins to shrink. This is due to what
Morawetz called the "simple algebra of the gap." The gap between
high-income and poor countries will not close until the ratio of their
GNP/pcs is equal to the inverse ratio of their growth rates. A relatively
simple way to determine if a poor or middle-income country can close
the absolute gap is to divide the growth rate of the high-income countries by the ratio of the poor or middle-income country's GNP/pc to the
high-income countries' GNP/pc. This equation yields the growth rate
the country must exceed in order to begin closing the absolute gap. If,
for example, the high-income countries have a mean GNP/pc of $8,000

and a growth rate of 2 percent, a country with a GNP/pc of $1,000 must exceed a growth rate of 16 percent in order to begin closing the absolute gap that year. Very few are able to achieve or maintain such a rate of economic expansion for very long.

Can any country close the absolute gap? Replicating the projections of David Morawetz, I have attempted to find out if there exists any country capable of catching up to the high-income group. The results presented in Table 3.6 assume that countries will maintain the same growth rate as they achieved between 1960 and 1998. Given this assumption, only twenty-two countries can ever hope to catch up to the high-income countries. Only six countries—Botswana, Oman, Dominica, Thailand, China, and Malaysia—have the opportunity to catch up to the high-income within the twenty-first century. Five more countries would catch up in the twenty-second century.

Table 3.6   Closing the Absolute Gap

Country	GNP/pc (1995 U.S. dollars)	Annual Average Growth Rate, 1960–1998 (percent)	Number of Years Until the Gap Is Closed
Rich[a]	25,394	2.1	
Botswana	3,460	7.7	38
Oman	4,893	5.6	49
Dominica	3,099	5.5	65
Thailand	2,579	5.0	82
China	711	6.4	87
Malaysia	4,107	4.0	99
Swaziland	1,534	4.8	108
Seychelles	6,810	3.1	136
Indonesia	896	4.3	157
Mauritius	3,999	3.3	159
Trinidad and Tobago	4,468	3.0	198
Lesotho	696	3.7	232
Hungary	4,726	2.8	247
Belize	2,607	3.0	260
Egypt, Arab Republic of	1,162	3.3	264
Tunisia	2,185	2.9	315
Sri Lanka	792	2.9	445
Brazil	4,453	2.5	446
Pakistan	489	2.8	579
Turkey	3,269	2.4	699
Paraguay	1,789	2.4	905
Dominican Republic	1,697	2.4	923

Source: World Bank, *World Development Indicators, 2000* (Washington, D.C.: World Bank, 2000).
Note: a. Those countries with a GNP/pc of more than $9,361 in 1998.

The Relative Gap

The relative gap measures the GNP/pc of the poor or middle-income groups as a percentage of that of the developed countries. Morawetz (1977) reported that the developing countries had narrowed the relative gap by about one-half of a percentage point between 1950 and 1975. He added that it might be easier for them to narrow the relative gap than the absolute gap, thereby making it a more accessible development goal.

However, my results, as shown in Table 3.7 indicate that the middle-income countries' GNP/pc expressed as a percentage of the GNP/pc of the high-income has grown smaller over time. The middle-income countries' percentage of the high-income declined such that by 1998 the GNP/pc of the middle-income countries as a percentage of the high-income had dropped below the 1960 level. In 1960 the relative gap between the high-income and middle-income countries was 22.9 percent. By 1998 the middle-income countries had a relative gap score of only 12.1 percent. The same was true for poor countries. Their relative gap score fell from 3.1 percent to 1.5 percent over the thirty-nine-year period. In other words, the relative gap between high-income and middle-income countries and high-income and poor countries widened between 1960 and 1998.

Mobility

Can countries move from one income group to another or substantially improve their ranking within a grouping? In terms of upward mobility

Table 3.7   The Relative Gap, 1960–1998

Income Group	1960	1980	1998
Middle Income	22.9	15.4	12.1
Poor	3.1	2.1	1.5
Region			
Americas	14.0	15.6[a]	12.3
Middle East/north Africa	8.8	15.7[a]	10.6
Eastern Europe/central Asia	8.8	15.3[a]	10.9
South Asia	1.7	1.5	1.8[a]
East Asia/Pacific	5.0	7.7[a]	12.0[a]
West Africa	3.5	3.7[a]	2.3
East/south Africa	4.3	4.8[a]	4.4
Less than 1 million	70.4	66.7	50.3

Source: World Bank, *World Development Indicators, 2000* (Washington, D.C.: World Bank, 2000).

Note: a. Denotes an improvement in the relative gap over the previous period reported.

across income groups, the record has been unimpressive. Table 3.8 summarizes the movement of countries from one income group to another between 1960 and 1998. Of the 114 countries, 87 remained in the same category in 1998 that they occupied in 1960. Even though the number of upwardly mobile countries was relatively small, not one country moved down from one income group to the next. Ten countries were able to move up from the middle-income group to the high-income. Eighteen that started out in the poor group in 1960 became middle-income countries by 1998.

Although 76 percent of the countries in this sample remained within the same income group, Table 3.9 shows that there was quite a bit of movement within the ranks. Table 3.9 lists the ten countries that moved the most between 1960 and 1998, up or down, in terms of GNP/pc rank. Botswana (+41) and Swaziland (+34) made the most impressive jumps. Among the top ten movers, China ranked the lowest in 1960 at 114 but was able to move up thirty-three places. Qatar experienced the most severe drop in the rankings, falling thirty places. Six of the countries

Table 3.8   Mobility Across Income Groups, 1960 and 1998

Rich
Rich in 1960 and 1998 (N=22): Austria, Australia, Bahamas,[a] Belgium, Bermuda,[a] Denmark, Finland, France, Iceland,[a] Kuwait, Luxembourg,[a] Netherlands, New Zealand, Norway, Portugal, Qatar,[a] Singapore, Spain, Sweden, Switzerland, United States, United Kingdom.

Joined rich from the middle-income category (N=10): Canada, French Polynesia,[a] Greece, Hong Kong, Ireland, Israel, Italy, Japan, Korea (Republic of), Malta.[a]

Middle-Income
Middle-income in 1960 and 1998 (N=30): Algeria, Argentina, Barbados,[a] Belize,[a] Brazil, Chile, Colombia, Costa Rica, Ecuador, El Salvador, Fiji,[a] Gabon, Guatemala, Hungary, Jamaica, Latvia, Malaysia, Mauritius, Mexico, Panama, Paraguay, Peru, Puerto Rico, Saudi Arabia, Seychelles,[a] South Africa, Trinidad and Tobago, Turkey, Uruguay, Venezuela.

Joined middle-income from the poor category (N=18): Botswana, Côte d'Ivoire, Dominica,[a] Dominican Republic, Egypt (Arab Republic of), Guyana,[a] Indonesia, Morocco, Oman, Papua New Guinea, Philippines, Sri Lanka, Suriname,[a] Swaziland,[a] Syrian Arab Republic, Thailand, Tunisia.

Poor
Poor in 1960 and 1998 (N=35): Bangladesh, Benin, Burkina Faso, Burundi, Cameroon, Central African Republic, Chad, China, Congo (Democratic Republic of), Congo (Republic of), Gambia, Georgia, Ghana, Guinea-Bissau, Haiti, Honduras, India, Kenya, Lesotho, Madagascar, Malawi, Mali, Mauritania, Nepal, Nicaragua, Niger, Nigeria, Pakistan, Rwanda, Senegal, Sierra Leone, Sudan, Togo, Zambia, Zimbabwe.

Source: World Bank, World Development Indicators, 2000 (Washington, D.C.: World Bank, 2000).
Note: a. Less than 1 million population throughout the entire period.

Table 3.9   Mobility in Rankings of GNP/pc (Differences in Rankings, 1960–1998)

| | The Upwardly Mobile | | | | The Downwardly Mobile | | |
| | GNP/pc Rank | | | | GNP/pc Rank | | |
Country	1960	1998	Difference	Country	1960	1998	Difference
Botswana	91	50	+41	Qatar	1	31	−30
Swaziland	100	66	+34	Congo, Democratic Republic of	87	114	−27
China	114	81	+33	Niger	86	109	−23
Oman	67	39	+28	Algeria	48	69	−21
Thailand	83	56	+27	Zambia	74	95	−21
Singapore	33	8	+25	Venezuela	29	49	−20
Lesotho	108	83	+25	Senegal	68	87	−19
Indonesia	99	76	+23	Haiti	75	94	−19
Pakistan	110	88	+22	Central African Republic	80	98	−18
Malta	53	32	+21	Georgia	63	80	−17

Source: World Bank, *World Development Indicators, 2000* (Washington, D.C.: World Bank, 2000).

that dropped the most in rankings were from Africa and two were from the Americas.

Conclusion

If scholars such as Simon Kuznets (1972) and Michael Lipton (1977) are correct, the worldwide economic growth experienced since World War II is unprecedented. Between 1850 and 1950 the countries considered high-income in 1950 experienced economic expansion averaging 1.6 percent. Between 1960 and 1998 the entire world grew at an annual average rate of 1.71 percent, and between 1960 and 1969 the growth rate hovered at 2.86 percent. Post–World War II generations have grown accustomed to rapid economic growth, leading many people to believe that it will continue. However, the research of Kuznets and others suggests that, over time, countries have likely experienced long periods of stagnation, or periods of economic expansion followed by periods of contraction.

Second, the data above indicate that not everyone has shared in the growth. The absolute gap between high-income and middle-income and between high-income and poor countries has grown steadily since 1960. For the middle-income countries the absolute gap grew from $9,623 to

$22,317, and the poor fell from a deficit of $12,081 to $25,016. On average, the absolute gap widened $325 for the middle-income countries and $332 for the poor countries every year. In addition, neither the middle-income nor the poor group improved the relative gap. Four of the six regions, however, were able to increase their GNP/pc as a percentage of that of the high-income countries. The Americas and West Africa experienced a worsening of their relative gap score. East Asia/Pacific made the greatest relative gap gain with a 7 percent increase, from 5 percent of the high-income countries in 1960 to 12 percent in 1998.

Third, this analysis of income groups would have proven irrelevant if the percentage of the world's population in the lowest-income group had fallen significantly. Unfortunately, such was not the case. In 1998 the percentage of the world's population living in countries with a GNP/pc of less than $760 was 59.7 percent, or approximately 3 billion people, up from about 1.4 billion in 1960. If there is positive news to be had, it is that the percentage of people living in poor countries dropped from about 64 percent in 1960 to about 60 percent in 1998.

Fourth, the number of high-income countries increased from thirteen (plus five high-income countries with populations less than 1 million) in 1960 to twenty-five (plus six high-income countries with populations less than 1 million) in 1998. Ten countries joined the high-income during the thirty-nine-year period and eighteen moved up into the middle-income category. In all, twenty-eight countries became mobile and crossed from one income category to another; not one country dropped to a lower income level.

It appears that only six countries can close the gap with the high-income within the next century: Botswana, Oman, Dominica, Thailand, China, and Malaysia. If growth rates remain similar to those of the entire thirty-nine-year period, Botswana will be the first African country to join the high-income countries.

Notes

1. The growth rates are calculated by the regression method described in the *World Development Report, 1988*. The least squares method finds the growth rate by fitting a least-squares trend line to the log of the gross national product per capita. This takes the equation form of $X_t = a + bt + e_t$, where X equals the log of the GNP/pc, a is the intercept, b is the parameter to be estimated, t is time, and e is the error term. The growth rate, r, is the [antilog (b)]–1. GNP/pcs for the following countries and years were estimated using the growth rate of the five years before or after the missing data. The least squares regression

method used to estimate the missing data is described above: Bermuda, 1998; French Polynesia, 1998; Gambia, 1960–1965; Georgia, 1960–1964; Guinea-Bissau, 1960–1969; India, 1960–1969; Kuwait, 1960–1961, 1996–1998; Latvia, 1960–1964; mali, 1960–1966; Malta, 1996–1998; Oman, 1996–1998; Puerto Rico, 1998; Qatar, 1960–1969, 1996–1998; Saudi Arabia, 1970; Senegal, 1960–1967; Sierra Leone, 1960–1963; Syrian Arab Republic, 1960–1964; Tunisia, 1960; Venezuela, 1960–1966; Zimbabwe, 1960–1964. For further information, see World Bank (1988: 288–289). For a discussion of different methods of computing growth rates see Jackman (1982: 604–610).

2. The regional categories were drawn from World Bank (2000).

3. Kuznets defined the high-income countries as those with a GNP/pc greater than $1,000 (1965 U.S. dollars). A "narrow" definition of the poor countries set the GNP/pc cutoff point at $120 or less. For his more broadly defined poor category, Kuznets raised the cutoff point to $300. The middle-income group varied according to Kuznets's choice of the narrowly or broadly defined poor group in any particular example. Kuwait and Qatar were excluded because their growth had been dependent on a single commodity and did not reflect diversified growth. Puerto Rico was excluded because its GNP/pc was so tightly connected to the United States. Japan was included in the high-income group even though its GNP/pc was below the cutoff point because it had managed tremendous growth with very few natural resources. Thus, its growth was achieved through diversified development of the economy. For further information on how Kuznets defined his income groups, see Ranis (1972).

References

Dube, S. C. 1988. *Modernization and Development: The Search for Alternative Paradigms.* London and New Jersey: Zed Books Ltd.

Durning, A. B. 1990. "Ending Poverty." In L. Starke, ed., *State of the World, 1990.* New York and London: W. W. Norton.

IMF (International Monetary Fund). 1984. *International Financial Statistics: Supplement on Output Statistics,* no. 8. Washington, D.C.: IMF.

Jackman, R. W. 1980. "A Note on the Measurement of Growth Rates in Cross-National Research." *American Journal of Sociology* 86: 604–610.

———. 1982. "Dependence on Foreign Investment and Economic Growth in the Third World." *World Politics* 34: 175–197.

Kahn, H. 1979. *World Economic Development: 1979 and Beyond.* Boulder, Colo.: Westview.

Kuznets, S. 1972. "The Gap: Concept, Measurement, Trends." In G. Ranis, ed., *The Gap Between Rich and Poor Nations.* London: Macmillan.

———. 1979. *Growth, Population, and Income Distribution.* New York: W. W. Norton.

———. 1984. "Economic Growth and Income Inequality." In M. A. Seligson, ed., *The Gap Between Rich and Poor.* Boulder, Colo.: Westview.

Lipton, M. 1977. *Why the Poor People Stay Poor: A Study of Urban Bias in World Development.* London: Temple Smith.

———. 1989. *New Seeds and Poor People.* London: Unwin Hyman.

Morawetz, D. 1977. *Twenty-Five Years of Economic Development: 1950–1975.* Washington, D.C.: World Bank.

Ranis, Gustav. 1972. *The Gap Between Rich and Poor Nations: Proceedings of a Conference Held by the International Economic Association at Bled, Yugoslavia.* New York: St. Martin's Press.

World Bank. 1988. *World Development Report, 1988.* Oxford: Oxford University Press.

———. 1990. *World Development Report, 1990.* Oxford: Oxford University Press.

———. 1992. *The World Tables, 1992.* Washington D.C.: World Bank.

———. 2000. *World Development Indicators, 2000.* CD-rom. Washington, D.C.: International Bank for Reconstruction and Development/World Bank Group.

CHAPTER 4

The Rising Inequality of World Income Distribution

ROBERT HUNTER WADE

One of the important debates surrounding the gap between rich and poor countries is what, if anything, a government should do. Robert Hunter Wade argues that conflicting conclusions about the gap have arisen in part due to the measure of inequality used, whether and how the measure is weighted, and the method of converting to a common currency. The varying recipes produce eight different measures of income inequality. Wade concludes that seven of the eight measures of inequality clearly show that the gap is worsening and the last suggests that the gap is stable. His warnings about the consequences of ignoring a worsening gap are amplified in Chapter 8 by Edward N. Muller and Mitchell A. Seligson, who tie income inequality to domestic political violence.

D OES IT MATTER WHAT IS HAPPENING TO WORLD INCOME DISTRIBUTION (among all 6.2 billion people, regardless of where they live)? Amartya Sen, the recent Nobel laureate in economics, warns that arguing about the trend deflects attention from the central issue, which is the sheer magnitude of inequality and poverty on a world scale. Regardless of the trend, the magnitude is unacceptable (Sen, 2001). He is right, up to a point. The concentration of world income in the wealthiest quintile (fifth) of the world's population is indeed shocking and cannot meet any plausible test of legitimacy. The chart [Figure 4.1] shows the distribution of world income by population quintiles. Ironically, it resembles a

Reprinted with permission from *Finance and Development,* vol. 38, no. 4 (December 2001). Copyright © 2001 by the International Monetary Fund.

Figure 4.1   Distribution of World GDP, 1989
(percent of total with quantities of population ranked by income)

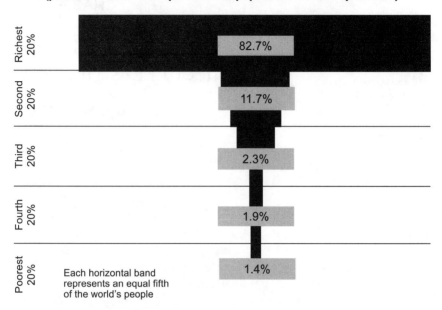

Source: United Nations Development Programme, *Human Development Report 1992* (New York: Oxford University Press for the UNDP, 1992).

champagne glass, with a wide, shallow bowl at the top and the slenderest of stems below.

But still, the trend does matter. Many champions of free trade and free capital movements say that world income distribution is becoming more equal as globalization proceeds, and on these grounds they resist the idea that reducing world income inequality should be an objective of international public policy. Moreover, many theories of growth and development generate predictions about *changes* in world income distribution; testing them requires information about trends. Indeed, the neoliberal paradigm—which has supplied the prescriptions known as the Washington Consensus that have dominated international public policy about development over the past twenty years—generates a strong expectation that as national economies become more densely interconnected through trade and investment, world income distribution tends to become more equal. And it is a fair bet that if presented with the statement, "World income distribution has become more equal over the past twenty years" and asked to agree, agree with qualifications, or disagree, a majority of Western economists would say, "agree" or "agree with qualifications."

If they are right, this would be powerful evidence in favor of the "law of *even* development," which says that all national economies gain from more integration into international markets (relative to less integration), and lower-cost, capital-scarce economies (developing countries) are likely to gain *more* from fuller integration than higher-cost, capital-abundant economies (developed countries). Developing countries wishing to catch up with standards of living in the West should therefore integrate fully into international markets (by lowering tariffs, removing trade restrictions, granting privileges to *foreign* direct investment, welcoming foreign banks, enforcing intellectual property rights, and so on) and let the decisions of private economic agents operating in free markets determine the composition and volume of economic activities carried out within the national territory. This "integrationist" strategy will maximize their rate of development; put the other way around, their development strategy should amount to an integrationist strategy—the two things are really one and the same.

Fortunately, the self-interest of the wealthy Western democracies coincides with this integrationist strategy for developing countries, because as developing countries grow richer, their demand for Western products expands and their capacity to absorb their population growth at home also expands, reducing the pressure on the West created by surging immigration. The World Bank, the IMF [International Monetary Fund], the World Trade Organization (WTO), and the other global supervisory organizations are therefore well justified in seeking to enforce maximum integration on developing countries for the good of all.

What Does the Evidence Show?

Therefore, a lot is at stake in the question of whether world income distribution has become more, or less, equal over the past twenty years or so. It turns out that there is no single correct answer, because the answer depends on which combination of measures one adopts. It depends on (1) the measure of inequality (a coefficient like the Gini, or quintile or decile [tenth] ratios), (2) the unit of inequality (countries weighted equally, or individuals weighted equally and countries weighted by population), and (3) the method of converting incomes in different countries to a common numeraire (current market exchange rates or purchasing power parity exchange rates). Treating these as either/or choices yields eight possible measures, each with some plausibility for certain purposes. Then there is the further question of what kind of data is used—the national income accounts or household income and expenditure surveys.

My reading of the evidence suggests that none of the eight alternative measures clearly shows that world income distribution has become more equal over the past twenty years. Seven of the eight show varying degrees of *increasing inequality.* The eighth—the one that uses the Gini coefficient, countries weighted by population, and purchasing power parity—shows no significant change in world income distribution. This is because the Gini coefficient gives excessive weight to changes around the middle of the distribution and insufficient weight to changes at the extremes and therefore, in this case, gives more weight (than a decile ratio) to fast-growing China; the use of countries weighted by population has the same effect; and the use of purchasing power parity tends to raise low incomes more than high incomes, compared with market exchange rates. Hence this combination generates the least rise in inequality. But a recent paper by Dowrick and Akmal (2001) suggests that the Penn World Tables, on which most calculations of purchasing power parity are based (see Heston and Summers, 1991), contain a bias that makes incomes of developing countries appear higher than they are. The tables consequently *understate* the degree and trend of inequality. When the bias is corrected, even the most favorable combination of measures shows rising inequality of world income distribution over the past twenty years, although the trend is less strong than the trend based on any of the other possible combinations.

It is often said that purchasing power parity measures should always be preferred to market exchange rates and that countries should always be weighted by population rather than treated as equal units of observation. Certainly, purchasing power parity measures are better for measuring relative purchasing power, or relative material welfare, though the available data are not good enough for them to be more than rough-and-ready approximations, especially for China and, before the early 1990s, the countries of the former Soviet Union. But data problems aside, we may also be interested in income for other purposes. Indeed, for most of the issues that concern the world at large—such as migration flows; the capacity of developing countries to repay foreign debts and import capital goods; the extent of marginalization of developing countries in the world polity; and, more broadly, the economic and geopolitical impact of a country (or region) on the rest of the world—then we should use market exchange rates to convert incomes in different countries into a common numeraire. After all, the reason why many poor countries are hardly represented in international negotiations whose outcomes profoundly affect them is that the cost of hotels, offices, and salaries in places like New York, Washington, and Geneva must be paid in U.S. dollars, not in purchasing power parity–adjusted dollars. Using market exchange rates, the conclusion is clear: all four combinations of measures using market exchange rates show that world income distribution has become *much more unequal*.

Causes of Increasing Inequality

What are the causes of the rise in world income inequality? The theory is not exactly what one might call watertight; the causality is very difficult to establish. Differential population growth between poorer and richer countries is one cause. The fall in non-oil commodity prices—by more than half in real terms between 1980 and the early 1990s—is another, affecting especially the poorest countries. The debt trap is a third. Fast-growing middle-income developing countries, seeking to invest and consume more than can be covered by domestic incomes, tend to borrow abroad; and they borrow on terms that are more favorable when their capacity to repay is high and less favorable when—as in a financial crisis—their capacity to repay is low. We saw repeatedly during the 1980s and 1990s that countries that liberalized and opened their financial systems and then borrowed heavily—even if to raise investment rather than consumption—ran a significant risk of costly financial crisis. A crisis pulls them back down the world income hierarchy. Hence the debt trap might be thought of as a force in the world economy that is somewhat analogous to gravity.

Another basic cause is technological change. Technological change of the kind we have seen in the past two decades tends to reinforce the tendency for high-value-added activities (including innovation) to cluster in the (high-cost) Western economies rather than disperse to lower-cost developing countries. Silicon Valley is the paradigm: the firms that are pioneering the collapse of distance themselves congregate tightly in one small space. Part of the reason is the continuing economic value of tacit knowledge and "handshake" relationships in high-value-added activities. Technological change might be thought of as distantly analogous to electromagnetic levitation—a force in the world economy that keeps the 20 percent of the world's population living in the member countries of the Organization for Economic Cooperation and Development (OECD) comfortably floating above the rest of the world in the world income hierarchy. If we have world economy analogues of gravity and electromagnetism, can the world economy analogue of relativity theory be far behind?

Consequences

Income divergence helps to explain another kind of polarization taking place in the world system, between a zone of peace and a zone of turmoil. On the one hand, the regions of the wealthy pole show a strengthening republican order of economic growth and liberal tolerance (except toward immigrants), with technological innovation able to substitute for depleting natural capital. On the other hand, the regions of the lower- and middle-income poles contain many states whose capacity to govern is stagnant or eroding, mainly in Africa, the Middle East, Central Asia, the former Soviet Union, and parts of East Asia. Here, a rising proportion of the people find their access to basic necessities restricted at the same time as they see others driving Mercedes.

The result is a large mass of unemployed and angry young people, mostly males, to whom the new information technologies have given the means to threaten the stability of the societies they live in and even threaten social stability in countries of the wealthy zone. Economic growth in these countries often depletes natural capital and therefore future growth potential. More and more people see migration to the wealthy zone as their only salvation, and a few are driven to redemptive terrorism directed at the symbolic centers of the powerful.

Reorienting International Organizations

The World Bank and the IMF have paid remarkably little attention to global inequality. The Bank's *World Development Report 2000: Attacking Poverty* says explicitly that rising income inequality "should not be seen as negative," provided the incomes at the bottom do not fall and the number of people in poverty falls or does not rise. But incomes in the lower deciles of world income distribution have probably fallen absolutely since the 1980s; and one should not accept the Bank's claim that the number of people living on less than $1 a day remained constant at 1.2 billion between 1987 and 1998, because the method used to compute the figure for 1998 contains a downward bias relative to that used to compute the figure for 1987. Suppose, though, that the incomes of the lower deciles had risen absolutely and the number of people in absolute poverty had fallen, while inequality increased. The Bank's view that the rise in inequality should not be seen as a negative ignores the associated political instabilities and flows of migrants that—all notions of justice and fairness and common humanity aside—can harm the lives of the citizens of the rich world and the democratic character of their states.

The global supervisory organizations like the Bank, the IMF, the WTO, and the United Nations system should be giving the issue of global income inequality much more attention. If we can act on global warming—whose effects are similarly diffuse and long term—can we not act on global inequality? We should start by rejecting the neoliberal assumption of the Bretton Woods institutions over the past two decades, now powerfully reinforced by the emergent WTO, that development strategy boils down to a strategy for maximum integration of each economy into the world economy, complemented by domestic reforms to make full integration viable. The evidence on world income distribution throws this assumption into question—as does a lot of evidence of other kinds. International public policy to reduce world income inequality must include a basic change in the policy orientation of the World Bank, the IMF, and the WTO so as to allow them to sanction government efforts to impart directional thrust and nourish homegrown institutional innovations.

References

Dowrick, Steve, and Muhammad Akmal. 2001. "Explaining Contradictory Trends in Global Income Inequality: A Tale of Two Biases," *Faculty of Economic and Commerce*. Australian National University.

Heston, Alan, and Robert Summers. 1991. "The Penn World Tables (Mark 5): An Expanded Set of International Comparisons, 1950–1988," *Quarterly Journal of Economics* (May), pp. 327–68.

Rodrik, Dani, 2001. "The Global Governance of Trade as If Development Really Mattered" (unpublished).

Sen, Amartya. 2001. "If It's Fair, It's Good: 10 Truths About Globalization," *International Herald Tribune,* July 14–15.

Wade, Robert Hunter. 1990. *Governing the Market: Economic Theory and the Role of Government in East Asia's Industrialization*. Princeton: Princeton University Press.

———. 2001a. "Winners and Losers," *Economist,* April 28.

———. 2001b. "Globalization and World Income Distribution: Trends, Causes, Consequences, and Public Policy" (unpublished, July).

CHAPTER 5

Could It Be That the Whole World Is Already Rich? A Comparison of RGDP/pc and GNP/pc Measures

JOHN T PASSÉ-SMITH

MEASURING GROWTH IS NOT AN EASY TASK. WHILE POVERTY AND WEALTH are easily discernable to anyone traveling across the frontiers of high-income and low-income countries, they are not easy to quantify. Visitors to foreign lands are confronted with the "traveler's dilemma": after conversion from U.S. coin into foreign currency, 1 dollar does not necessarily yield the same buying power in India as does 1 dollar in the United States, or Botswana, or France. The amount of cash it took to buy a feast in one country might purchase only a partial loaf of bread in the next. This dilemma alerted scholars to the need to replace exchange rates with a conversion factor that would better reflect comparable currency purchasing power.

Few people argue over the existence of a gap between high-income and low-income countries, but the extent of the gap is often disputed, in part because of a lack of confidence in the accuracy of exchange rate conversions. Comparing the general conditions in Burkina Faso to those in Switzerland, one may be satisfied that the gross national product per capita (GNP/pc) accurately reflects the differing standards of living; however, some have argued that this is not the case. Many scholars have suggested that conversions of GNP to a common currency utilizing official exchange rates overstates the poverty of low-income countries (Heston 1973; Kuznets 1972; Kravis, Kenessey, Heston, and Summers 1975; Morris 1979; Summers and Heston 1984; Ward 1985).

Exchange rate conversions are said to distort the actual purchasing power of currencies because they fluctuate away from a hypothesized equilibrium value. The fluctuations may occur rapidly—caused by inflation, changes in production techniques, import and export barriers (or perhaps the quick removal of present barriers), price shocks originating domestically or internationally, and so forth—but the restoration of equilibrium occurs much more slowly. Thus, exchange rate fluctuations represent malalignments of currency prices that will ultimately move back toward a relative unity value (Katseli-Papaefstratiou 1979: 4). M. D. Morris (1979: 10) pointed out that it is not uncommon for exchange rates to oscillate rather wildly in a relatively short time. For example, Brazil's official exchange rate during the first quarter of 1981 was 70.8 cruzeiros per U.S. dollar; the midyear rate climbed to 91.8, and by the end of the year the official rate stood at 118.[1] This represents a 60 percent shift in the exchange rate.

Some contend that the exchange rate/purchasing power parity (PPP) difference involves more than a lag time for correction of an equilibrium-tending exchange rate. Simon Kuznets, for example, asserts that because many low-income countries retain sizeable elements of precapitalistic production and noncash trade that go unreported in national accounts statistics, their GNP is understated (1972: 8). As countries become richer, Kuznets explains, these traditional sectors gradually give way, lessening the degree of distortion in GNP measurement. Therefore, the new conversion factor, the PPP, should cause little change in the GNP of high-income countries, but the poorer the country the more the PPP should increase their GNP over the official exchange rate conversion value.[2]

The United Nations commissioned a series of related projects, beginning in 1968 and continuing today, dubbed the International Comparison Project (ICP).[3] The purpose of the ICP study is to produce PPP conversion factors so that more accurate crossnational comparisons of national account statistics can be made. In 1984 Robert Summers and Alan Heston reported that the project had "develop[ed] a structural relationship between purchasing power parities and exchange rates . . . [that took] account of the variability of exchange rates" (1984: 207–208). Using extensive research in thirty-four "benchmark" countries, this relationship between PPP and exchange rates was to be extrapolated to the remaining "nonbenchmark" countries of similar size, economic structure, and so forth. In 1988, the sample of countries and the years of coverage were expanded to 130 countries covering the period 1950 to 1985. This sample has been regularly updated, and the current data set, the Penn World Tables 6, offers information for 168 countries between 1950 and 1998 (see http://pwt.econ.upenn.edu).

The following sections offer some simple comparisons of national accounts converted with exchange rates and purchasing power parity factors. Only those countries present in both data sets and covering every year are used.[4] The merged samples include ninety-seven countries for the years 1960 to 1998. At least two questions are raised: how different are the data for individual countries, and how has the change in data changed the extent of the gap between high-income and low-income as illustrated in Chapter 3?

GNP/pc and Real GDP/pc Compared

The gross national product of a country is equal to the gross domestic product (GDP) less factor payments abroad, so in comparing the two one should expect a difference even if the GDPs were not "real" GDPs (RGDPs) produced with a purchasing power parity index. Although factor payments often represent a negative flow, they are sometimes positive, so it cannot be readily assumed that the GNP will be slightly smaller than the GDP. A quick glance at the International Monetary Fund's *International Financial Statistics: Yearbook 1980* (IMF 1980) seems to show that the industrialized high-income countries of Europe and the United States are more likely to experience an inflow of factor payments than developing countries, but this is impressionistic not systematic evidence.

On the left-hand side of Table 5.1 is the RGDP/pc (the ICP data) for 1960 and 1998, the rankings for both years, and the annual average growth rate.[5] The right-hand side of the table includes comparable GNP/pc data (World Bank data set). The countries are also broken down by geographic regions as defined by the World Bank's *World Development Indicators, 2000*. The World Bank classifications include two nongeographically defined groups, the "high-income countries" and countries with less than 1 million in population; the non-high-income countries were divided into geographic regions: sub-Saharan Africa, Middle East/north Africa, Europe (non–high income Europe), and the Americas.

PPP proponents argue that exchange rate conversions make the rich look richer and the poor poorer than they actually are. Examining Table 5.1 this would mean that one should expect, when converted by PPP factors, the high-income countries to have mean per capita scores slightly lower than the exchange rate–converted scores. This does not mean, however, that the rankings will necessarily be altered. It could mean that there is simply a compression of values toward the mean. In examining the RGDP/pc and GNP/pc rankings for 1998 among the high-income countries, the mean change in rankings was zero. There were six countries that differed by more than five places, and nine of the twenty-three high-income countries have a higher PPP-converted GDP/pc ranking than GNP/pc ranking.

Table 5.1 Comparison of RGDP/pc and GNP/pc: Levels, Rank, and Growth Rates by Region

	Real Gross Domestic Product per Capita					Difference Between RGDP/pc and GNP/pc Rank, 1998	Difference Between RGDP/pc and GNP/pc, 1998	Gross National Product per Capita				
	1960	1998	Rank 1960	Rank 1998	Annual Growth 1960–1998			1960	1998	Rank 1960	Rank 1998	Annual Growth 1960–1998
High Income												
Singapore	$2,577	$31,302	45	2	6.55	-4	-$1,300	$3,145	$32,602	26	6	6.50
United States	$12,953	$31,048	2	3	2.18	-5	$1,732	$14,173	$29,316	4	8	1.70
Norway	$8,181	$27,133	11	4	3.22	-1	-$9,444	$11,143	$36,577	7	5	3.10
Switzerland	$15,162	$25,155	1	5	1.25	3	-$22,075	$26,677	$47,230	1	2	1.40
Hong Kong	$3,072	$24,785	38	6	6.02	-9	$3,059	$3,021	$21,726	27	15	5.70
Canada	$10,382	$24,480	6	7	2.20	-11	$4,683	$8,927	$19,797	16	18	2.00
Denmark	$10,088	$24,101	7	8	2.25	4	-$12,791	$14,884	$36,892	3	4	2.10
Australia	$10,398	$23,435	5	9	2.00	-7	$2,202	$9,433	$21,233	15	16	1.90
Japan	$4,512	$23,347	25	10	4.18	7	-$19,338	$8,207	$42,685	17	3	4.20
Netherlands	$9,111	$23,032	10	11	2.25	0	-$5,312	$11,563	$28,344	6	11	2.20
Sweden	$9,853	$22,890	8	13	1.92	-1	-$3,723	$12,976	$26,613	5	14	1.70
Belgium	$8,166	$22,838	12	14	2.60	5	-$6,446	$10,539	$29,284	9	9	2.60
Finland	$7,352	$22,444	17	15	2.75	2	-$5,363	$9,574	$27,807	13	13	2.60
Ireland	$4,839	$22,001	23	17	3.50	-2	$2,532	$5,122	$19,469	21	19	3.00
Austria	$7,473	$21,968	16	18	2.86	11	-$8,873	$10,501	$30,841	10	7	2.80
France	$8,042	$21,716	14	19	2.48	7	-$6,312	$10,653	$28,028	8	12	2.40
United Kingdom	$9,608	$21,076	9	20	2.02	3	$862	$9,561	$20,214	14	17	1.90
Italy	$6,880	$20,801	18	21	2.85	1	$1,438	$6,646	$19,363	18	20	2.80
Portugal	$3,172	$17,768	34	22	4.00	-3	$6,195	$2,673	$11,573	30	25	3.60
Spain	$4,391	$16,842	26	23	2.96	1	$1,437	$4,424	$15,405	22	22	2.80
Israel	$5,444	$16,619	21	24	2.74	3	$1,048	$5,150	$15,571	20	21	2.70
New Zealand	$11,132	$15,955	4	25	0.97	2	$661	$10,465	$15,294	11	23	0.90
Greece	$3,730	$13,819	31	26	3.12	2	$1,708	$3,397	$12,111	25	24	3.00
Mean	$7,675	$22,372	17	14	2.90	0	-$3,192	$9,255	$25,564	14	14	2.77

LT 1 million												
Luxembourg	$11,696	$39,129	3	1	3.12	0	–$11,722	$15,190	$50,851	2	1	3.60
Iceland	$8,127	$22,970	13	12	2.85	2	–$6,113	$9,977	$29,083	12	10	2.80
Barbados	$5,341	$22,161	22	16	3.07	–12	$15,068	$2,768	$7,093	28	28	2.10
Seychelles	$3,065	$11,682	39	30	3.70	1	$4,872	$2,563	$6,810	31	29	3.10
Fiji	$2,644	$7,981	42	36	2.16	–11	$5,671	$1,331	$2,310	41	47	1.70
Dominican Republic	$1,657	$4,984	62	49	2.35	–2	$3,287	$671	$1,697	56	51	2.40
Guyana	$2,424	$3,342	49	61	0.41	–3	$2,581	$607	$761	58	64	–0.50
Mean	$4,993	$16,036	33	29	2.52	–4	$1,949	$4,730	$14,086	33	33	2.22
Sub-Saharan Africa												
Mauritius	3,761	12,888	30	28	3.47	–9	8,889	1,137	3,999	46	37	3.3
South Africa	4,725	7,481	24	37	1.04	–1	3,652	2,701	3,829	29	38	0.6
Gabon	2,926	7,181	40	39	1.91	4	3,066	1,866	4,115	35	35	1.4
Botswana	1,022	6,531	81	41	5.56	1	3,071	321	3,460	76	40	7.7
Zimbabwe	1,943	3,023	57	65	1.42	–4	2,366	419	657	70	69	0.9
Lesotho	835	2,354	89	68	2.85	1	1,658	177	696	91	67	3.7
Cameroon	1,730	2,016	59	72	0.83	2	1,405	482	611	65	70	1.3
Côte d'Ivoire	1,710	1,995	60	73	–0.17	10	1,233	589	762	59	63	–0.1
Senegal	1,986	1,631	56	75	–0.56	4	1,056	679	575	55	71	–0.7
Congo, Republic of	917	1,582	85	76	2.11	10	884	462	698	67	66	1.6
Mauritania	1,221	1,444	74	78	0.1	5	984	288	460	77	73	0.5
Ghana	1,560	1,432	66	79	–0.53	3	1,033	459	399	68	76	–0.8
Kenya	883	1,300	87	80	1.1	–3	970	194	330	90	83	1.6
Benin	1,154	1,249	76	81	–0.13	4	860	350	389	74	77	0.1
Gambia	1,384	1,188	71	82	–0.34	1	841	270	347	80	81	0.7
Central African Republic	2,335	1,068	51	83	–2.24	1	733	462	335	66	82	–1
Burkina Faso	786	1,062	92	84	1.15	–2	804	176	258	92	86	0.9
Nigeria	1,045	1,025	79	85	–0.17	–3	795	213	230	89	88	0.1
Togo	983	1,023	82	86	–0.13	2	696	230	327	87	84	0.2
Rwanda	923	1,013	84	87	0.8	–4	798	268	215	81	91	0
Chad	1,316	1,010	73	88	–0.75	–1	783	286	227	78	89	–0.8
Sierra Leone	633	972	95	89	–0.49	–6	826	256	146	82	95	–1.1
Mali	1,032	921	80	90	0.06	5	658	234	263	86	85	0.2

(continues)

Table 5.1 continued

	Real Gross Domestic Product per Capita							Gross National Product per Capita				
	1960	1998	Rank 1960	Rank 1998	Annual Growth 1960–1998	Difference Between RGDP/pc and GNP/pc Rank, 1998	Difference Between RGDP/pc and GNP/pc, 1998	1960	1998	Rank 1960	Rank 1998	Annual Growth 1960–1998
Niger	1,604	902	65	91	-1.98	-1	690	405	212	71	92	-2.3
Madagascar	1,481	858	69	92	-1.73	5	625	367	233	73	87	-1.6
Zambia	1,652	843	63	93	-2.35	14	477	578	366	60	79	-1.6
Malawi	551	778	97	94	0.57	1	602	111	176	96	93	1
Guinea-Bissau	660	711	94	95	0.23	1	550	253	161	83	94	-0.6
Burundi	567	692	96	96	0.92	0	547	127	145	95	96	1.2
Congo, Democratic Republic of	923	191	83	97	-3.15	0	76	393	115	72	97	-3.1
Mean	$1,475	$2,212	72	78	0.31	1	$1,388	$492	$825	73	76	0.44
Middle East/north Africa												
Tunisia	$1,898	$6,375	58	43	3.13	-5	$4,190	$756	$2,185	52	48	2.90
Algeria	$3,108	$4,489	37	52	2.05	-3	$3,014	$1,335	$1,475	40	55	1.20
Morocco	$1,329	$4,129	72	54	2.52	-2	$2,790	$731	$1,339	53	56	1.80
Syrian Arab Republic	$1,408	$4,124	70	55	2.62	-4	$3,112	$530	$1,012	63	59	2.20
Egypt, Arab Republic of	$1,605	$4,013	64	56	2.40	-1	$2,851	$343	$1,162	75	57	3.30
Mean	$1,870	$4,626	60	52	2.54	-3	$3,191	$739	$1,435	57	55	2.28
Europe (other than high-income Europe)												
Turkey	$2,741	$7,334	41	38	2.47	-3	$4,065	$1,186	$3,269	45	41	2.40
Asia												
Korea, Republic of	$1,543	$13,251	67	27	6.58	1	$2,279	$1,321	$10,972	42	26	6.50
Malaysia	$2,146	$7,986	53	35	4.03	-1	$3,879	$959	$4,107	48	36	4.00
Thailand	$1,177	$5,852	75	45	4.88	1	$3,273	$451	$2,579	69	44	5.00

(continues)

Sri Lanka	1,532	68	57	2.62	−5	3,097	278	792	79	62	2.9
Indonesia	$820	91	60	5.00	−1	$2,627	$250	$896	84	61	4.30
Philippines	$2,090	55	62	1.16	4	$2,171	$701	$1,145	54	58	1.10
Papua New Guinea	$2,642	43	63	0.00	3	$2,310	$613	$996	57	60	0.90
China	$692	93	64	4.32	−1	$2,491	$96	$711	97	65	6.40
India	$894	86	67	2.44	−7	2,023	235	441	85	74	1.7
Pakistan	883	88	71	2.34	−1	1,564	175	489	93	72	2.8
Bangladesh	1,075	78	74	1.06	−6	1,304	214	361	88	80	1.1
Nepal	823	90	77	1.58	−13	1,235	150	222	94	90	1
Mean	$1,360	74	59	3.00	−2	$2,354	$454	$1,976	76	61	3.14
Americas											
Argentina	$7,520	15	29	0.60	2	$3,477	$5,319	$8,322	19	27	0.70
Uruguay	$5,989	19	31	1.29	1	$4,370	$3,757	$5,963	23	30	1.10
Chile	$3,994	28	32	1.83	1	$5,052	$1,971	$4,829	33	31	−0.80
Trinidad and Tobago	$4,068	27	33	2.19	1	$4,761	$1,432	$4,468	39	32	3.00
Mexico	$3,932	29	34	1.85	0	$3,748	$2,018	$4,312	32	34	1.80
Brazil	$2,472	48	40	2.86	7	$2,677	$1,849	$4,453	36	33	2.50
Venezuela	$5,677	20	42	0.17	3	$3,007	$3,531	$3,461	24	39	−0.40
Panama	$2,411	50	44	2.15	2	$3,355	$1,561	$2,995	37	42	1.10
Colombia	$2,511	47	46	2.24	0	$3,399	$1,075	$2,344	47	46	2.10
Costa Rica	$3,629	32	47	1.02	4	$2,830	$1,555	$2,714	38	43	1.60
Paraguay	$2,178	52	48	2.73	−1	$3,610	$882	$1,789	50	49	2.40
El Salvador	$3,437	33	50	0.20	0	$2,977	$1,302	$1,704	43	50	−0.10
Peru	$3,155	36	51	0.21	6	$2,176	$1,917	$2,482	34	45	0.00
Guatemala	$2,565	46	53	1.11	−1	$2,646	$918	$1,519	49	54	1.10
Ecuador	$2,124	54	58	1.85	5	$2,264	$763	$1,524	51	53	2.10
Jamaica	$2,619	44	59	0.78	7	$2,213	$1,288	$1,571	44	52	0.00
Haiti	$1,091	77	66	1.07	−12	$2,275	$545	$369	61	78	−0.70
Nicaragua	$3,162	35	69	−1.71	−6	$1,885	$534	$401	62	75	−2.30
Honduras	$1,702	61	70	0.78	2	$1,583	$513	$693	64	68	0.80
Mean	$3,381	40	48	1.22	1	$3,069	$1,723	$2,943	41	46	0.84

Sources: World Bank, *World Development Indicators, 2000* (Washington, D.C.: World Bank, 2000); and the Penn World Tables 6.0, see online at http://pwt.econ.upenn.edu/icp.html.

Contrary to what might be expected, twelve of the twenty-three high-income countries actually appear to be wealthier when the PPP conversion factors are used (United States, Canada, Denmark, Australia, Ireland, United Kingdom, Italy, Portugal, Spain, Israel, New Zealand, and Greece). The relatively high level of agricultural production in some of these high-income countries may explain why their RGDP/pc is larger than their GNP/pc. The mean RGDP/pc score, as PPP proponents would predict, is about $3,000 smaller than the GNP/pc. If the PPP-converted RGDP/pc is more accurate, then the wealth of the high-income countries is exaggerated.

Proponents of PPPs have argued that, even more than overstating the wealth of the rich, exchange rate conversions overstate the poverty of low-income countries. So, as might be expected, only two non-high-income countries, Luxembourg and Iceland, have an exchange rate–converted GNP/pc larger than their RGDP/pc. If either of these two countries had populations greater than 1 million, they would be classified as high-income countries. Not one country that would be considered middle- or low-income had an RGDP/pc lower than their exchange rate–converted GNP/pc. If these figures are accurate, then the ICP project demonstrates that not only is the poverty of the developing countries exaggerated, but the wealth of the high-income is at least partially an illusion as well. One discomforting fact, however, is that if GNP/pc levels used by the *World Development Indicators, 2000* to define income groupings were used to create RGDP/pc income groups, the poorest country in the Western Hemisphere, Haiti, with an RGDP/pc of over $1,000 in 1960, would be considered a middle-income country. Given the standard of living in Haiti, one would have to question what was poor if Haiti is considered middle-income.

As for the regional groupings, the Middle East/north African countries—Tunisia, Algeria, Morocco, Syria, and Egypt—experienced the largest apparent increase from the GNP/pc to RGDP/pc. The mean GNP/pc for this region was $1,435 in 1998—ranging from $1,012 for Syria to $2,185 for Tunisia—increasing to an RGDP/pc of $4,626. Here the GNP/pc is only 31 percent of the RGDP/pc. For every country in this group the change was very large. Indeed, Tunisia had a GNP/pc of $2,185 in 1998 but was reported to have the purchasing power equivalence of $6,375. This is either indicative of the type of overestimation of poverty that PPP proponents were speaking of or an overstatement of the wealth of Tunisia. With these changes, the Middle East/north African countries ranked on average three places higher than their GNP/pc ranking.

For the Americas the changes were only slightly less dramatic. For instance, the GNP/pc there was about 49 percent of their RGDP/pc. The average real GDP/pc was $3,069 higher than the GNP/pc. After the high-income countries, the other regions, ranked by their 1998 RGDP/pc and, in parentheses, the difference between RGDP/pc and GNP/pc were: Americas $6,012 ($3,069), Middle East/north Africa $4,626 ($3,191), Europe $7,334 ($3,191), sub-Saharan Africa $2,212 ($1,388). Every group other than the high-income countries had a significantly higher mean RGDP/pc than GNP/pc.

If PPP conversions correct for an overestimation of the gap between high-income and low-income countries, they must either increase the apparent wealth of the low-income, decrease the apparent wealth of the high-income, or both. The ICP project has observed both shifts. On average, the high-income countries' RGDP/pc is $3,192 less than their exchange rate–converted GNP/pc, while the nondeveloped countries' RGDP/pc is approximately $2,445 higher.

Table 5.2 isolates countries that have the largest disparity between the RGDP/pc and GNP/pc. The table also includes the income level designated by the World Bank in the *World Development Indicators, 2000*. As PPP proponents would predict, only two non-low-income countries are included on the list. The table shows that Sri Lanka and Guyana move from GNP/pcs of $792 and $761 to $3,889 and $3,342 respectively. Haiti experiences the most severe change among low-income countries, rising from a 1998 GNP/pc of $369 to an RGDP/pc of $2,644. Referring back to Table 5.1, this would mean that the purchasing power of Haitians in 1998 roughly equaled that of citizens of Greece in 1960. This statistic is somewhat less than convincing. At the very least it suggests the possible need for further refinement of the PPP conversion factors.

The Income Gap Between Countries

If the income groups employed in Chapter 3 were used here to analyze RGDP/pcs, the results would be in many ways quite different. Because the low-income countries' RGDP/pc increases significantly over the exchange rate conversion, there would only be three countries considered low-income in 1998. Although the champions of the PPP conversion factor argue that GNP/pc overstates poverty, they do not argue that there are only five impoverished countries in the world. For this reason, the categories used to discuss income groupings below utilized the *World Development Indicators, 2000* income groups, except the cutoff for the low-income group was set to $2,000 (up from $760). Of the ninety-seven countries, forty-two register as low-income in 1960 (see

Table 5.2   The Most Severe Changes in the Conversion from GNP/pc to RGDP/pc

Country	World Development Indicators, 2000 Income Grouping	Real GDP/pc 1998	GNP/pc 1998	Difference (RGDP/pc– GNP/pc)	GNP/pc as a percentage of RGDP/pc	HDI
Sri Lanka	Lower middle	$3,889	$792	$3,097	20.38	0.733
Guyana	Lower middle	$3,342	$761	$2,581	22.76	0.709
Haiti	Low income	$2,644	$369	$2,275	13.95	0.440
China	Low income	$3,202	$711	$2,491	22.21	0.706
Zimbabwe	Low income	$3,023	$657	$2,366	21.73	0.555
India	Low income	$2,464	$441	$2,023	17.88	0.563
Nicaragua	Low income	$2,286	$401	$1,885	17.54	0.631
Pakistan	Low income	$2,053	$489	$1,564	23.80	0.522
Bangladesh	Low income	$1,665	$361	$1,304	21.70	0.461
Nepal	Low income	$1,457	$222	$1,235	15.23	0.474
Burkina Faso	Low income	$1,062	$258	$804	24.25	0.303
Nigeria	Low income	$1,025	$230	$795	22.46	0.439
Rwanda	Low income	$1,013	$215	$798	21.25	0.382
Chad	Low income	$1,010	$227	$783	22.45	0.367
Sierra Leone	Low income	$972	$146	$826	15.04	0.252
Niger	Low income	$902	$212	$690	23.49	0.293
Malawi	Low income	$778	$176	$602	22.58	0.385
Guinea-Bissau	Low income	$711	$161	$550	22.70	0.331
Burundi	Low income	$692	$145	$547	20.96	0.321

Sources: World Bank, *World Development Indicators, 2000* (Washington, D.C.: World Bank, 2000); World Bank, *The Human Development Report, 2000* (Washington, D.C.: World Bank, 2000); and the Penn World Tables 6.0, see online at http://pwt.econ.upenn.edu/icp.html.
Note: HDI = Human Development Index.

Table 5.3   Income Groups' Percentage of World Population

	World Population[a] (billions)	High Income Percent	High Income Number of Countries	Middle Income Percent	Middle Income Number of Countries	Low Income Percent	Low Income Number of Countries
Year							
1960	2.405	11.7	9	23.9	46	64.4	42
1965	2.643	14.1	13	22.7	45	63.2	39
1970	2.952	19.1	18	19.8	46	61.0	33
1975	3.279	20.1	22	18.3	45	61.6	30
1980	3.588	19.7	27	18.9	43	61.5	27
1985	3.914	16.4	20	25.8	50	57.8	27
1990	4.271	15.5	20	25.9	49	58.5	28
1995	4.610	16.0	23	73.5	47	10.6[b]	27
1998	4.814	15.8	25	73.8	47	10.5	25

Source: World Bank, *World Development Indicators, 2000* (Washington, D.C.: World Bank, 2000).
Notes: a. The world total reflects population data for the 98 countries for which there is also GNP/pc data.
b. India and China moved from low income to middle income in 1995.

Table 5.3). This figure declines to thirty countries in 1975 and to twenty-five by 1998. The most striking fact presented in Table 5.3 is that the low-income countries comprise 64.4 percent of the world's population in 1960 (available data) and 10.5 percent in 1998. The percentage drops from 58.5 percent in 1990 to 10.6 percent in 1995 because both India and China move from the low-income group to the middle-income group. No matter how the income groups are defined, the compression of income in the early periods, in combination with the growth rates, makes for very unusual results. If one were to raise the high-income group cutoff over the *World Development Indicators, 2000* cutoff, then there would have been no high-income countries in 1960. If the cutoff is dropped at all, then the majority of countries in the world are rich by 1998.

Although the RGDP/pc appears to be indicating that exchange rate–converted GNP/pcs overstate poverty to some degree, it is doubtful that only twenty-five countries and 10.5 percent of the world's population remained impoverished in 1998. Given the way the RGDP/pc compresses and changes the apparent wealth of countries over time, either income groups are no longer useful ways to analyze levels of development or there are problems with the PPP conversion factor. Part of the problem, of course, is associated with arbitrarily dividing countries into groups, but it is doubtful that that explains everything. Admittedly, this brief presentation does not mathematically analyze the ICP project, but if the claim of the ICP is that the PPP conversion factor is demonstrating people's actual purchasing power across time, then an income group that identifies wealth and poverty in 1960 should mark wealth and poverty in 1998. It would be very difficult to show that in 1960, 64 percent of the world's population lived in impoverished conditions that were only experienced by 10.5 percent of the world in 1998. This is the reality that Table 5.3 is suggesting.

In examining the gap between rich and poor countries, it is possible to determine if the gap is widening or narrowing without defining income groups. A simple method of detecting such a trend is to examine annual standard deviations. If the gap is closing then the standard deviations should grow smaller, meaning that countries are moving closer to the world average RGDP/pc. Figure 5.1 shows the standard deviations of the RGDP/pc and the GNP/pc for the world (N=97). The figure illustrates that both the RGDP/pc and the GNP/pc are growing larger over time. The gap between richest and poorest countries is opening wider. The RGDP/pc (the white bar) shows that the RGDP/pc is larger than the GNP/pc, reflecting the "discovery" of wealth in poorer countries. Also, the standard deviation of the RGDP/pc is smaller than the GNP/pc,

Figure 5.1   Standard Deviations and
Means of World RGDP/pc and GNP/pc

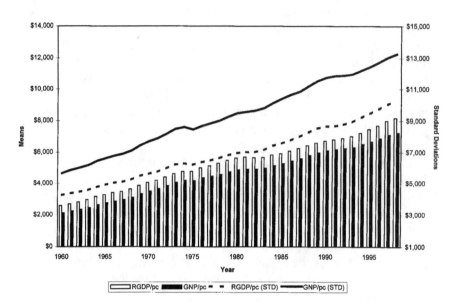

Source: World Bank, *World Bank Indicators, 2000* (Washington, D.C.: World Bank, 2000).

which means that the gap between rich and poor appears smaller when considering the RGDP/pc rather than the GNP/pc. It is interesting that the means and standard deviations of the two move in such concert. In 1974 it appears that both measures point to a very slight closing of the gap—or at least slowing its expansion. The heavy, dotted line in Figure 5.1 shows the world mean RGDP/pc while the solid line represents the average GNP/pc. As might be expected, the gap as expressed by the standard deviation of the RGDP/pc is consistently smaller than the GNP/pc, yet it is still of considerable size.

The gap as illustrated in Figure 5.1, however, may present a misleading picture. It would not be surprising that as the world grows richer, the increase in the standard deviation away from the mean would also grow larger as a reflection of that increase. The coefficient of variation standardizes the deviation score for changing means so that one can be relatively sure that an increase in the coefficient of variation is not a relic of an increasing mean value.[6] Figure 5.2 displays the coefficient of variation for the RGDP/pc and the GNP/pc and presents a slightly different picture of the world.

The coefficient of variation (the standard deviation divided by the

Figure 5.2   Coefficient of Variation, 1960–1998

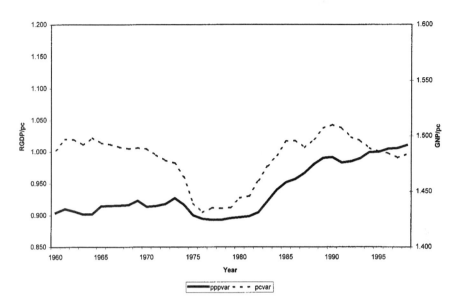

Source: World Bank, *World Bank Indicators, 2000* (Washington, D.C.: World Bank, 2000).

mean) grows larger as the gap grows wider and shrinks as the gap closes. The coefficient of variation for the RGDP/pc worsens between 1960 (0.904) and 1998 (1.01), while the coefficient of variation for the exchange rate–converted GNP/pc actually shows a very slight improvement, moving from 1.49 in 1960 to 1.48 in 1998. Both coefficients move together, indicating a slight worsening of the gap between 1960 and about 1965, and then suggest that the gap between rich and poor was narrowing (slightly) between about 1965 and 1976. In about 1980 both the coefficients of variation show that the gap between rich and poor opened until about 1990 and then leveled off. It is remarkable that with all of the differences between the two measures, they show a remarkably similar trend in both the coefficients of variations and the world means. The main difference between the two is that the PPP conversions produce a slightly smaller gap. It would also appear that the difference between the two is slightly smaller in 1998 than in 1960.

Growth Rates

The world economy grew at an average annual rate of 1.74 percent for the RGDP/pc and 1.65 percent for the GNP/pc for the ninety-seven

Table 5.4   Annual Average Growth Rates by Geographic Region (percentage)

	RGDP/pc					GNP/pc				
	1960–1998	1960–1969	1970–1979	1980–1989	1990–1998	1960–1998	1960–1969	1970–1979	1980–1989	1990–1998
World	1.74	2.81	2.48	0.63	1.43	1.65	2.57	2.42	0.77	1.39
High Income	2.91	4.52	2.87	2.42	2.29	2.77	4.81	2.71	2.33	2.13
LT 1 million	2.52	2.47	3.75	0.62	4.08	2.17	2.13	3.27	0.53	2.86
Sub-Saharan Africa	0.31	1.84	1.41	–0.59	–1.34	0.44	1.37	1.45	–0.26	–0.68
Asia	3.00	2.58	2.70	2.88	3.56	3.14	2.51	2.86	3.31	3.88
Middle-East/ north Africa	2.54	2.94	4.67	0.25	1.42	2.28	1.32	4.46	0.82	1.20
Europe (non–high income)	2.47	3.43	3.59	2.23	2.50	2.40	3.80	2.60	2.80	2.90
Americas	1.22	2.50	2.44	–1.02	2.38	0.84	2.22	2.47	–1.15	1.58

Source: World Bank, *World Development Indicators, 2000* (Washington, D.C.: World Bank, 2000).

countries in the sample (see Table 5.4). As explained in Chapter 3, this is quite impressive, yet the data from both methods of conversion showed that the decade of the 1960s was the fastest growing. Both the RGDP/pc and the GNP/pc growth rates for the world slowed to less than 1 percent during the 1980s. Thus, both measures show very similar growth patterns for the entire period and the subperiods.

Except in a few instances the RGDP/pc growth rates are very similar to the exchange rate–converted GNP/pcs. The regions, however, change order when ranked by rate of growth. For the entire period, the regions are ranked the same for the two conversion methods except for Europe (non–high income), which swaps positions with the Middle East/north Africa: Asia, Middle East/north Africa, Europe (non–high income), the Americas, and Africa. During the 1960s non–high income Europe has the highest growth, but the rankings of the other regions are scrambled. Similar changes in the rankings of growth rates can be found across the table. Another difference between the two is that the growth rates for the RGDP/pcs tend to be slightly higher than those of the exchange rate–converted GNP/pcs.

Conclusion

This chapter has two goals: (1) to outline the motivations for the purchasing power parity; (2) to compare the results of the ICP project

(RGDP/pcs) and World Bank/IMF exchange rate GNP/pcs. Fundamentally, the argument for PPP conversion factors, based on supporting evidence, is that exchange rate conversions of national account statistics may introduce distortions, especially in low-income countries.

Although Tables 5.1 and 5.2 highlight some extreme changes for individual countries, these changes do not have a visible impact on *trends* in the gap between high-income and low-income countries or in annual average growth rates. The growth rates calculated from RGDP/pcs tend to be slightly smaller than those calculated from the GNP/pcs, but they appear to be very highly correlated.

Second, the RGDP/pcs raise the level of growth of the regional groups, as PPP proponents might have suggested, and they *lower* the apparent level of growth of the high-income group from $25,564 (GNP/pc 1998) to $22,372 (RGDP/pc 1998). Thus, the gap between the richest and poorest countries is automatically compressed. This and the rapid growth of countries across the time period render the analysis of economic groups problematic. Unless the "low-income" category offered by the *World Development Indicators, 2000* is altered, only three countries register as low-income in 1998. Also, the RGDP/pc of Haiti in 1998 appears to put it on par with Greece in 1960, which raises some questions about the levels of growth as indicated by the RGDP/pc.

Third, analysis of standard deviations indicates that both PPP conversion factors and exchange rates lead to the conclusion that the gap between high-income and low-income countries is growing wider. However, the coefficient of deviation points to contrasting conclusions with reference to the gap. The PPP conversion factor shows a slight worsening of the gap and the exchange rate conversion factor shows a slight narrowing of the gap. On closer scrutiny, the coefficient of variation demonstrates that the gap widened slightly between 1960 and 1965, narrowed between 1965 and 1976, then began to widen again.

Fourth, overall the growth rates are very similar for both the ICP and World Bank data. Both point to the 1960s as the period of fastest growth, while the 1980s was the slowest growth period. It is also interesting to note that growth rates produced from the RGDP/pc tend to be slightly higher than the growth rates calculated from the exchange rate conversions.

More research needs to be done to define a poverty level with respect to the ICP data. The traveler's dilemma demonstrates that exchange rates do not reflect the purchasing power of the people across countries. However, there is a problem when an analysis that finds 64 percent of the world's people in poverty in 1960 suggests that only 10.5 percent of the world's population remained poor in 1998. Not even the

most optimistic analyst would suggest that this is an accurate description of the world. More needs to be done to better understand the data
that the ICP is producing. What does it mean to have a real gross
domestic product per capita of $2,000 in terms of the living standards of
people?

Notes

1. The example follows the logic of Morris (1979: 10–11).
2. Kuznets (1972) also noted that if the currency of a rich country is used
as the numeraire currency, the PPP conversion for richer countries is not affected by the conversion and the poorer the country the more the PPP conversion
inflates the resulting figure. This means the PPP-converted GNP/pcs make the
gap between high-income and poor countries look smaller. However, when the
numeraire currency is that of a poor country, the opposite is true. Poor countries
are not affected by the conversion and the richer the country the more the PPP
conversion inflates the resulting GNP/pc. In other words the gap looks wider.
3. Other institutions making significant contributions to this work have
been the University of Pennsylvania, the Ford Foundation, and the World Bank.
For a more complete history of this project, see Kravis et al. (1975).
4. GNP/pcs for the following countries and years were estimated using the
growth rate of the five years before or after the missing data. The least squares
regression method used to estimate the missing data is described in note 5:
Sierra Leone, 1960, 1997, 1998; Tunisia, 1960; Angola, 1997, 1998; Barbados,
1997, 1998; Cyprus, 1997, 1998; Fiji, 1997, 1998; Equitorial Guinea, 1997,
1998; New Zealand, 1998; Portugal, 1998; Zaire, 1998.
5. The growth rates for both the RGDP/pcs and GNP/pcs are calculated by
the regression method described in the *World Development Report, 1988*
(World Bank 1988: 288–289). The least squares method finds the growth rate
by fitting a least squares trend line to the log of the gross national product per
capita. This takes the equation form of $X_t=a+bt+e_t$. Where X equals the log of
the GNP/pc, t is time, and b is the parameter to be estimated. The growth rate, r,
is the [antilog (b)]–1. For a discussion of different methods of computing
growth rates, see Jackman (1980).
6. The coefficient of variation is the standard deviation divided by the
mean.

References

Bairoch, P. 1981. "The Main Trends in National Economic Disparities Since
the Industrial Revolution." In P. Bairoch and M. Lévy-Leboyer, eds.,
Disparities in Economic Development Since the Industrial Revolution.
London: Macmillan.
Beckerman, W. 1966. *International Comparisons of Real Income.* Paris: OECD
Development Center.
Gilbert, M., and I. Kravis. 1954. *An International Comparison of National*

Products and the Purchasing Power of Currencies. Paris: Organization for European Economic Cooperation.

————. 1958. *An International Comparison of Comparative National Products and Price Levels: A Study of Western Europe and the United States.* Paris: Organization for European Economic Cooperation.

Heston, A. 1973. "A Comparison of Some Short-Cut Methods of Estimating Real Product per Capita." *Review of Income and Wealth* (March): 79–104.

IMF (International Money Fund). 1980. *International Financial Statistics: Yearbook 1980.* Washington, D.C.: IMF.

————. 1984. *International Financial Statistics: Supplement on Output Statistics,* no. 8. Washington, D.C.: IMF.

Jackman, R. W. 1980. "A Note on the Measurement of Growth Rates in Cross-National Research." *American Journal of Sociology* 86: 604–610.

Katseli-Papaefstratiou, Louka T. 1979. *The Reemergence of the Purchasing Power Parity Doctrine in the 1970s.* Princeton, N.J.: International Finance Section, Department of Economics, Princeton University.

Kravis, I. B., Z. Kenessey, A. Heston, and R. Summers. 1975. *A System of International Comparisons of Gross Product and Purchasing Power.* Baltimore: Johns Hopkins University Press.

Kuznets, S. 1972. "The Gap: Concept, Measurement, Trends." In G. Ranis, ed., *The Gap Between Rich and Poor Nations.* London: Macmillan.

Morris, M. D. 1979. *Measuring the Condition of the World's Poor: The Physical Quality of Life Index.* New York: Pergamon Press.

Summers, R., and A. Heston. 1984. "Improved International Comparisons of Real Product and Its Composition: 1950–1980." *Review of Income and Wealth* (September): 207–259.

————. 1988. "A New Set of International Comparisons of Real Product and Prices: Estimates for 130 Countries, 1950–1985." *Review of Income and Wealth* (March): 1–25.

Ward, M. 1985. *Purchasing Power Parities and Real Expenditures in the OECD.* Paris: OECD Press.

World Bank. 1988. *World Development Report.* Oxford: Oxford University Press.

————. 1992. *The World Tables of Economic and Social Indicators, 1960–1986.* Washington, D.C.: World Bank.

————. 2000. *World Development Indicators, 2000.* Washington, D.C.: World Bank.

PART 2

The Other Gap:
Domestic Income Inequality

CHAPTER 6

Economic Growth
and Income Inequality

SIMON KUZNETS

Most debate on the internal gap between rich and poor people in developing nations begins with this seminal presidential address delivered by Simon Kuznets to the American Economic Association in 1954. The address, portions of which are reprinted here, uses limited data from Germany, the United Kingdom, and the United States to show that since the 1920s, and perhaps even earlier, there has been a trend toward equalization in the distribution of income. Kuznets discusses in some detail the possible causes for this trend, examining those factors in the process of industrialization that tend to counteract the concentration of savings in the hands of the wealthy. That particular discussion is not included here, but the interested reader can consult the original piece. Our interest lies in Kuznets's conclusion that the central factor in equalizing income must have been the rising incomes of the poorer sectors outside of the traditional agricultural economy. Kuznets introduces the critically important notion of the "Inverted U-curve" (although he does not label it as such in the address), arguing that there seems to be increasing inequality in the early phases of industrialization, followed by declines in the later phases only. Finally, Kuznets opens the debate over the relevance of these findings for the developing nations by examining data from India, Ceylon (Sri Lanka), and Puerto Rico. The findings that income inequality in the developing countries is greater than that in the advanced countries and that such inequality may be growing form the basis of virtually all subsequent research and debate on this subject.

Reprinted with permission from the *American Economic Review,* vol. 45 (March 1955): 1, 3–6, 17–26.

T HE CENTRAL THEME OF THIS CHAPTER IS THE CHARACTER AND CAUSES OF long-term changes in the personal distribution of income. Does inequality in the distribution of income increase or decrease in the course of a country's economic growth? What factors determine the secular level and trends of income inequalities?

These are broad questions in a field of study that has been plagued by looseness in definitions, unusual scarcity of data, and pressures of strongly held opinions. . . .

Trends in Income Inequality

Forewarned of the difficulties, we turn now to the available data. These data, even when relating to complete populations, invariably classify units by income for a given year. From our standpoint, this is their major limitation. Because the data often do not permit many size group-ings, and because the difference between annual income incidence and longer-term income status has less effect if the number of classes is small and the limits of each class are wide, we use a few wide classes. This does not resolve the difficulty; and there are others due to the scantiness of data for long periods, inadequacy of the unit used—which is, at best, a family and very often a reporting unit—errors in the data, and so on through a long list. Consequently, the trends in the income structure can be discerned but dimly, and the results considered as pre-liminary informed guesses.

The data are for the United States, England, and Germany—a scant sample, but at least a starting point for some inferences concerning long-term changes in the presently developed countries. The general conclusion suggested is that the relative distribution of income, as measured by annual income incidence in rather broad classes, has been moving toward equality—with these trends particularly noticeable since the 1920s but beginning perhaps in the period before the first world war.

Let me cite some figures, all for income before direct taxes, in sup-port of this impression. In the United States, in the distribution of income among families (excluding single individuals), the shares of the two lowest quintiles rise from 13.5 percent in 1929 to 18 percent in the years after the second world war (average of 1944, 1946, 1947, and 1950); whereas the share of the top quintile declines from 55 to 44 per-cent, and that of the top 5 percent from 31 to 20 percent. In the United Kingdom, the share of the top 5 percent of units declines from 46 per-cent in 1880 to 43 percent in 1910 or 1913, to 33 percent in 1929, to 31 percent in 1938, and to 24 percent in 1947; the share of the lower 85 percent remains fairly constant between 1880 and 1913, between 41 and 43 percent, but then rises to 46 percent in 1929 and 55 percent in 1947. In Prussia, income inequality increases slightly between 1875 and 1913—the shares of the top quintile rising from 48 to 50 percent, of the top 5 percent from 26 to 30 percent; the share of the lower 60 percent, however, remains about the same. In Saxony, the change between 1880 and 1913 is minor: the share of the two lowest quintiles declines from 15 to 14.5 percent; that of the third quintile rises from 12 to 13 percent, of the fourth quintile from 16.5 to about 18 percent; that of the top quintile declines from 56.5 to 54.5 percent, and of the top 5 percent from 34 to 33 percent. In Germany as a whole, relative income inequality drops fairly sharply from 1913 to the 1920s, apparently due to decimation of large fortunes and property incomes during the war and inflation, but then begins to return to prewar levels during the depression of the 1930s.[1]

Even for what they are assumed to represent, let alone as approximations to shares in distribution by secular income levels, the data are such that differences of two or three percentage points cannot be assigned significance. One must judge by the general weight and consensus of the evidence—which unfortunately is limited to a few countries. It justifies a tentative impression of constancy in the relative distribution of income before taxes, followed by some narrowing of relative income inequality after the first world war—or earlier.

Three aspects of this finding should be stressed. First, the data are for income before direct taxes and exclude contributions by government (e.g., relief and free assistance). It is fair to argue that both the proportion and progressivity of direct taxes and the proportion of total income of individuals accounted for by government assistance to the less privileged economic groups have grown during recent decades. This is certainly true of the United States and the United Kingdom, but in the case of Germany is subject to further examination. It follows that the distribution of income after direct taxes and including free contributions by government would show an even greater narrowing of inequality in developed countries with size distributions of pretax, ex-government-benefits income similar to those for the United States and the United Kingdom.

Second, such stability or reduction in the inequality of the percentage shares was accompanied by significant rises in real income per capita. The countries now classified as developed have enjoyed rising per capita incomes except during catastrophic periods such as years of active world conflict. Hence, if the shares of groups classified by their annual income position can be viewed as approximations to shares of groups classified by their secular income levels, a constant percentage share of a given group means that its per capita real income is rising at the same rate as the average for all units in the country; and a reduction in inequality of the shares means that the per capita income of the lower-income groups is rising at a more rapid rate than the per capita income of the upper-income groups.

The third point can be put in the form of a question. Do the distributions by annual incomes properly reflect trends in distribution by secular incomes? As technology and economic performance rise to higher levels, incomes are less subject to transient disturbances, not necessarily of the cyclical order that can be recognized and allowed for by reference to business cycle chronology, but of a more irregular type. If in the earlier years the economic fortunes of units were subject to greater vicissitudes—poor crops for some farmers, natural calamity losses for some nonfarm business units—if the over-all proportion of individual entrepreneurs whose incomes were subject to such calamities, more yesterday but some even today, was larger in earlier decades, these earlier distributions of income would be more affected by transient disturbances. In these earlier distributions the temporarily unfortunate might crowd the lower quintiles and depress their shares unduly, and the temporarily fortunate might dominate the top quintile and raise its share unduly—proportionately more than in the distributions for later years. If so, distributions by longer-term average incomes might show less reduction in inequality than do the distributions by annual incomes; they might even show an opposite trend.

One may doubt whether this qualification would upset a narrowing of inequality as marked as that for the United States, and in as short a period as twenty-five years. Nor is it likely to affect the persistent downward drift in the spread of the distributions in the United Kingdom. But I must admit a strong element of judgment in deciding how far this qualification modifies the finding of long-term stability followed by reduction in income inequality in the few developed countries for which it is observed or is likely to be revealed by existing data. The important point is that the qualification is relevant; it suggests need for further study if we are to learn much from the available data concerning the secular income structure; and such study is likely to yield results of interest in themselves in their bearing upon the problem of trends in temporal instability of income flows to individual units or to economically significant groups of units in different sectors of the national economy. . . .

Hence we may conclude that the major offset to the widening of income inequality associated with the shift from agriculture and the countryside to industry and the city must have been a rise in the income share of the lower groups within the nonagricultural sector of the population. This provides a lead for exploration in what seems to me a most promising direction: consideration of the pace and character of the economic growth of the urban population, with particular reference to the relative position of lower-income groups. Much is to be said for the notion that once the early turbulent phases of industrialization and urbanization had passed, a variety of forces converged to bolster the economic position of the lower-income groups within the urban population. The very fact that, after a while, an increasing proportion of the urban population was "native," i.e., born in cities rather than in the rural areas, and hence more able to take advantage of the possibilities of city life in preparation for the economic struggle, meant a better chance for organization and adaptation, a better basis for securing greater income shares than was possible for the newly "immigrant" population coming from the countryside or from abroad. The increasing efficiency of the older, established urban population should also be taken into account. Furthermore, in democratic societies the growing political power of the urban lower-income groups led to a variety of protective and supporting legislation, much of it aimed to counteract the worst effects of rapid industrialization and urbanization and to support the claims of the broad masses for more adequate shares of the growing income of the country. Space does not permit the discussion of demographic, political, and social considerations that could be brought to bear to explain the offsets to any declines in the shares of the lower groups, declines otherwise deducible from the trends suggested in the numerical illustration.

Other Trends Related to Those in Income Inequality

One aspect of the conjectural conclusion just reached deserves emphasis because of its possible interrelation with other important elements in the process and theory of economic growth. The scanty empirical evidence suggests that the narrowing of income inequality in the developed countries is relatively recent and probably did not characterize the earlier stages of their growth. Likewise, the various factors that have been suggested above would explain stability and narrowing in income inequality in the later rather than in the earlier phases of industrialization and urbanization. Indeed, they would suggest widening inequality in these early phases of economic growth, especially in the older countries where the emergence of the new industrial system had shattering effects on long-established pre-industrial economic and social institutions. This timing characteristic is particularly applicable to factors bearing upon the lower-income groups: the dislocating effects of the agricultural and industrial revolutions, combined with the "swarming" of population incident upon a rapid decline in death rates and the maintenance or even rise of birth rates, would be unfavorable to the relative economic position of lower-income groups. Furthermore, there may also have been a preponderance in the earlier periods of factors favoring maintenance or increase in the shares of top-income groups: in so far as their position was bolstered by gains arising out of new industries, by an unusually rapid rate of creation of new fortunes, we would expect these forces to be relatively stronger in the early phases of industrialization than in the later when the pace of industrial growth slackens.

One might thus assume a long swing in the inequality characterizing the secular income structure: widening in the early phases of economic growth when the transition from the pre-industrial to the industrial civilization was most rapid; becoming stabilized for a while; and then narrowing in the later phases. This long secular swing would be most pronounced for older countries where the dislocation effects of the earlier phases of modern economic growth were most conspicuous; but it might be found also in the "younger" countries like the United States if the period preceding marked industrialization could be compared with the early phases of industrialization, and if the latter could be compared with the subsequent phases of greater maturity.

If there is some evidence for assuming this long swing in relative inequality in the distribution of income before direct taxes and excluding free benefits from government, there is surely a stronger case for assuming a long swing in inequality of income net of direct taxes and including government benefits. Progressivity of income taxes and, indeed, their very importance characterize only the more recent phases of development of the presently developed countries; in narrowing income inequality they must have accentuated the downward phase of the long swing, contributing to the reversal of trend in the secular widening and narrowing of income inequality.

No adequate empirical evidence is available for checking this conjecture of a long secular swing in income inequality;[2] nor can the phases be dated precisely. However, to make it more specific, I would place the early phase in which income inequality might have been widening from about 1780 to 1850 in England; from about 1840 to 1890, and particularly from 1870 on in the United States; and from the 1840s to the 1890s in Germany. I would put the phase of narrowing income inequality somewhat later in the United States and Germany than in England—perhaps beginning with the first world war in the former and the last quarter of the nineteenth century in the latter.

Is there a possible relation between this secular swing in income inequality and the long swing in other important components of the growth process? For the older countries a long swing is observed in the rate of growth of population—the upward phase represented by acceleration in the rate of growth reflecting the early reduction in the death rate which was not offset by a decline in the birth rate (and in some cases was accompanied by a rise in the birth rate); and the downward phase represented by a shrinking in the rate of growth reflecting the more pronounced downward trend in the birth rate. Again, in the older countries, and also perhaps in the younger, there may have been a secular swing in the rate of urbanization, in the sense that the proportional additions to urban population and the measures of internal migration that produced this shift of population probably increased for a while—from the earlier much lower levels; but then tended to diminish as urban population came to dominate the country and as the rural reservoirs of migration became proportionally much smaller. For old, and perhaps for young countries also, there must have been a secular swing in the proportions of savings or capital formation to total economic product. Per capita product in pre-industrial times was not large enough to permit as high a nationwide rate of saving or capital formation as was attained in the course of industrial development: this is suggested by present comparisons between net capital formation rates of 3 to 5 percent of national product in underdeveloped countries and rates of 10 to 15 percent in developed countries. If then, at least in the older countries, and perhaps even in the younger ones—prior to initiation of the process of modern development—we begin with low secular levels in the savings proportions, there would be a rise in the early phases to appreciably higher levels. We also know that during recent periods the net capital formation proportion, and even the gross, failed to rise and perhaps even declined.

Other trends might be suggested that would possibly trace long swings similar to those for inequality in income structure, rate of growth of population, rate of urbanization and internal migration, and the proportion of savings or capital formation to national product. For example, such swings might be found in the ratio of foreign trade to domestic activities; in the aspects, if we could only measure them properly, of government activity that bear upon market forces (there must have been a phase of increasing freedom of market forces, giving way to greater intervention by government). But the suggestions already made suffice to indicate that the long swing in income inequality must be viewed as part of a wider process of economic growth, and interrelated with similar movements in other elements. The long alternation in the rate of growth of population can be seen partly as a cause, partly as an effect of the long swing in income inequality which was associated with a secular rise in real per capital income levels. The long swing in income inequality is also probably closely associated with the swing in capital formation proportions—in so far as wider inequality makes for higher, and narrower inequality for lower, countrywide savings proportions.

Comparison of Developed and Underdeveloped Countries

What is the bearing of the experience of the developed countries upon the economic growth of underdeveloped countries? Let us examine briefly the data on income distribution in the latter, and speculate upon some of the implications.

As might have been expected, such data for underdeveloped countries are scanty. For the present purpose, distributions of family income for India in 1949–50, for Ceylon in 1950, and for Puerto Rico in 1948 were used. While the coverage is narrow and the margin of error wide, the data show that income distribution in these underdeveloped countries is somewhat *more* unequal than in the developed countries during the period after the second world war. Thus the shares of the lower 3 quintiles are 28 percent in India, 30 percent in Ceylon, and 24 percent in Puerto Rico—compared with 34 percent in the United States and 36 percent in the United Kingdom. The shares of the top quintile are 55 percent in India, 50 percent in Ceylon, and 56 percent in Puerto Rico, compared with 44 percent in the United States and 45 percent in the United Kingdom.[3]

This comparison is for income before direct taxes and excluding free benefits from governments. Since the burden and progressivity of direct taxes are much greater in developed countries, and since it is in the latter that substantial volumes of free economic assistance are extended to the lower-income groups, a comparison in terms of income net of direct taxes and including government benefits would only accentuate the wider inequality of income distributions in the underdeveloped countries. Is this difference a reliable reflection of wider inequality also in the distribution of *secular* income levels in underdeveloped countries? Even disregarding the margins of error in the data, the possibility raised earlier in this chapter that transient disturbances in income levels may be more conspicuous under conditions of primitive material and economic technology would affect the comparison just made. Since the distributions cited reflect the annual income levels, a greater allowance should perhaps be made for transient disturbances in the distributions for the underdeveloped than in those for the developed countries. Whether such a correction would obliterate the difference is a matter on which I have no relevant evidence.

Another consideration might tend to support this qualification. Underdeveloped countries are characterized by low average levels of income per capita, low enough to raise the question of how the populations manage to survive. Let us assume that these countries represent fairly unified population groups, and exclude, for the moment, areas that combine large native populations with small enclaves of nonnative, privileged minorities, e.g., Kenya and Rhodesia, where income inequality, because of the excessively high income shares of the privileged minority, is appreciably wider than even in the underdeveloped countries cited above.[4] On this assumption, one may infer that in countries with low average income, the secular level of income in the lower brackets could not be below a fairly sizable proportion of average income—otherwise, the groups could not survive. This means, to use a purely hypothetical figure, that the secular level of the share of the lowest decile could not fall far short of 6 or 7 percent, i.e., the lowest decile could not have a per capita income less than six- or seven-tenths of the countrywide average. In more advanced countries, with higher average per capita incomes, even the *secular* share of the lowest bracket could easily be a smaller fraction of the countrywide average, say as small as 2 or 3 percent for the lowest decile, i.e., from a fifth to a third of the countrywide average—without implying a materially impossible economic position for that group. To be sure, there is in all countries continuous pressure to raise the relative position of the bottom-income groups; but the fact remains that the lower limit of the proportional share in the secular income structure is higher when the real countrywide per capita income is low than when it is high.

If the long-term share of the lower-income groups is larger in the underdeveloped than in the average countries, income inequality in the former should be narrower, not wider as we have found. However, if the lower brackets receive larger shares, and at the same time the very top brackets also receive larger shares—which would mean that the intermediate income classes would not show as great a progression from the bottom—the net effect may well be wider inequality. To illustrate, let us compare the distributions for India and the United States. The first quintile in India receives 8 percent of total income, more than the 6 percent share of the first quintile in the United States. But the second quintile in India receives only 9 percent, the third 11, and the fourth 16; whereas in the United States, the shares of these quintiles are 12, 16, and 22 respectively. This is a rough statistical reflection of a fairly common observation relating to income distributions in underdeveloped compared with developed countries. The former have no "middle" classes: there is a sharp contrast between the preponderant proportion of population whose average income is well below the generally low countrywide average, and a small top group with a very large relative income excess. The developed countries, on the other hand, are characterized by a much more gradual rise from low to high shares, with substantial groups receiving more than the high countrywide income average, and the top groups securing smaller shares than the comparable ordinal groups in underdeveloped countries.

It is, therefore, possible that even the distributions of secular income levels would be more unequal in underdeveloped than in developed countries—not in the sense that the shares of the lower brackets would be lower in the former than in the latter, but in the sense that the shares of the very top groups would be higher and that those of the groups below the top would all be significantly lower than a low countrywide income average. This is even more likely to be true of the distribution of income net of direct taxes and inclusive of free government benefits. But whether a high probability weight can be attached to this conjecture is a matter for further study.

In the absence of evidence to the contrary, I assume that it is true: that the secular income structure is somewhat more unequal in underdeveloped countries than in the more advanced—particularly in those of Western and Northern Europe and their economically developed descendants in the New World (the United States, Canada, Australia, and New Zealand). This conclusion has a variety of important implications and leads to some pregnant questions, of which only a few can be stated here.

In the first place, the wider inequality in the secular income structure of underdeveloped countries is associated with a much lower level of average income per capita. Two corollaries follow—and they would follow even if the income inequalities were of the same relative range in the two groups of countries. First, the impact is far sharper in the underdeveloped countries, where the failure to reach an already low countrywide average spells much greater material and psychological misery than similar proportional deviations from the average in the richer, more advanced countries. Second, positive savings are obviously possible only at much higher relative income levels in the underdeveloped countries: if in the more advanced countries some savings are possible in the fourth quintile, in the underdeveloped countries savings could be realized only at the very peak of the income pyramid, say by the top 5 or 3 percent. If so, the concentration of savings and of assets is even more pronounced than in the developed countries; and the effects of such concentration in the past may serve to explain the peculiar characteristics of the secular income structure in underdeveloped countries today.

The second implication is that this unequal income structure presumably coexisted with a low rate of growth of income per capita. The underdeveloped countries today have not always lagged behind the presently developed areas in level of economic performance; indeed, some of the former may have been the economic leaders of the world in the centuries preceding the last two. The countries of Latin America, Africa, and particularly those of Asia, are underdeveloped today because in the last two centuries, and even in recent decades, their rate of economic growth has been far lower than that in the Western World—and low indeed, if any growth there was, on a per capita basis. The underlying shifts in industrial structure, the opportunities for internal mobility and for economic improvement, were far more limited than in the more rapidly growing countries now in the developed category. There was no hope, within the lifetime of a generation, of a significantly perceptible rise in the level of real income, or even that the next generation might fare much better. It was this hope that served as an important and realistic compensation for the wide inequality in income distribution that characterized the presently developed countries during the earlier phases of their growth.

The third implication follows from the preceding two. It is quite possible that income inequality has not narrowed in the underdeveloped countries within recent decades. There is no empirical evidence to check this conjectural implication, but it is suggested by the absence, in these areas, of the dynamic forces associated with rapid growth that in the developed countries checked the upward trend of the upper-income shares that was due to the cumulative effect of continuous concentration of past savings; and it is also indicated by the failure of the political and social systems of underdeveloped countries to initiate the governmental or political practices that effectively bolster the weak positions of the lower-income classes. Indeed, there is a possibility that inequality in the secular income structure of underdeveloped countries may have widened in recent decades—the only qualification being that where there has been a recent shift from colonial to independent status, a privileged, *nonnative* minority may have been eliminated. But the implication, in terms of the income distribution among the *native* population proper, still remains plausible.

The somber picture just presented may be an oversimplified one. But I believe that it is sufficiently realistic to lend weight to the questions it poses—questions as to the bearing of the recent levels and trends in income inequality, and the factors that determine them, upon the future prospect of underdeveloped countries within the orbit of the free world.

The questions are difficult, but they must be faced unless we are willing completely to disregard past experience or to extrapolate mechanically oversimplified impressions of past development. The first question is: Is the pattern of the older developed countries likely to be repeated in the sense that in the early phases of industrialization in the underdeveloped countries income inequalities will tend to widen before the leveling forces become strong enough first to stabilize and then reduce income inequalities? While the future cannot be an exact repetition of the past, there are already certain elements in the present conditions of underdeveloped societies, e.g., "swarming" of population due to sharp cuts in death rates unaccompanied by declines in birth rates, that threaten to widen inequality by depressing the relative position of lower-income groups even further. Furthermore, if and when industrialization begins, the dislocating effects on these societies, in which there is often an old hardened crust of economic and social institutions, are likely to be quite sharp—so sharp as to destroy the positions of some of the lower groups more rapidly than opportunities elsewhere in the economy may be created for them.

The next question follows from an affirmative answer to the first. Can the political framework of the underdeveloped societies withstand the strain which further widening of income inequality is likely to generate? This query is pertinent if it is realized that the real per capita income level of many underdeveloped societies today is lower than the per capita income level of the presently developed societies before *their* initial phases of industrialization. And yet the stresses of the dislocations incident to early phases of industrialization in the developed countries were sufficiently acute to strain the political and social fabric of society, force major political reforms, and sometimes result in civil war.

The answer to the second question may be negative, even granted that industrialization may be accompanied by a rise in real per capita product. If, for many groups in society, the rise is even partly offset by a decline in their proportional share in total product; if, consequently, it is accompanied by widening of income inequality, the resulting pressures and conflicts may necessitate drastic changes in social and political organization. This gives rise to the next and crucial question: How can either the institutional and political framework of the underdeveloped societies or the processes of economic growth and industrialization be modified to favor a sustained rise to higher levels of economic performance and yet avoid the fatally simple remedy of an authoritarian regime that would use the population as cannon-fodder in the fight for economic achievement? How to minimize the cost of transition and avoid paying the heavy price—in internal tensions, in long-run inefficiency in providing means for satisfying wants of human beings as individuals—which the inflation of political power represented by authoritarian regimes requires?

Facing these acute problems, one is cognizant of the dangers of taking an extreme position. One extreme—particularly tempting to us—is to favor repetition of past patterns of the now developed countries, patterns that, under the markedly different conditions of the presently underdeveloped countries, are almost bound to put a strain on the existing social and economic institutions and eventuate in revolutionary explosions and authoritarian regimes. There is danger in simple analogies; in arguing that because an unequal income distribution in Western Europe in the past led to accumulation of savings and financing of basic capital formation, the preservation or accentuation of present income inequalities in the underdeveloped countries is necessary to secure the same result. Even disregarding the implications for the lower-income groups, we may find that in at least some of these countries today the consumption propensities of upper-income groups are far higher and savings propensities far lower than were those of the more puritanical upper-income groups of the presently developed countries. Because they may have proved favorable in the past, it is dangerous to argue that completely free markets, lack of penalties implicit in progressive taxation, and the like are indispensable for the economic growth of the now underdeveloped countries. Under present conditions the results may be quite the opposite—withdrawal of accumulated assets to relatively "safe" channels, either by flight abroad or into real estate; and the inability of governments to serve as basic agents in the kind of capital formation that is indispensable to economic growth. It is dangerous to argue that, because in the past foreign investment provided capital resources to spark satisfactory economic growth in some of the smaller European countries or in Europe's descendants across the seas, similar effects can be expected today if only the underdeveloped countries can be convinced of the need of a "favorable climate." Yet, it is equally dangerous to take the opposite position and claim that the present problems are entirely new and that we must devise solutions that are the product of imagination unrestrained by knowledge of the past, and therefore full of romantic violence. What we need, and I am afraid it is but a truism, is a clear perception of past trends and of conditions under which they occurred, as well as knowledge of the conditions that characterize the underdeveloped countries today. With this as a beginning, we can then attempt to translate the elements of a properly understood past into the conditions of an adequately understood present.

Notes

1. The following sources were used in calculating the figures cited: *United States.* For recent years we used *Income Distribution by Size, 1944–1950* (Washington, 1953) and Selma Goldsmith and others, "Size Distribution of Income Since the Mid-Thirties," *Rev. Econ. Stat.,* Feb. 1954, XXXVI, 1–32; for 1929, the Brookings Institution data as adjusted in Simon Kuznets, *Shares of Upper Groups in Income and Savings* (New York, 1953), p. 220.

United Kingdom. For 1938 and 1947, Dudley Seers, *The Levelling of Income Since 1938* (Oxford, 1951), p. 39; for 1929, Colin Clark, *National Income and Outlay* (London, 1937) Table 47, p. 109; for 1880, 1910, and 1913, A. Bowley, *The Change in the Distribution of the National Income, 1880–1913* (Oxford, 1920).

Germany. For the constituent areas (Prussia, Saxony and others) for years before the first world war, based on S. Prokopovich, *National Income of Western European Countries* (published in Moscow in the 1920s). Some summary results are given in Prokopovich, "The Distribution of National Income," *Econ. Jour.,* March 1926, XXXVI, 69–82. See also, "Das Deutsche Volkseinkommen vor und nach dem Kriege," *Einzelschrift zur Stat. des Deutschen Reichs,* no. 24 (Berlin, 1932), and W. S. and E. S. Woytinsky, *World Population and Production* (New York, 1953) Table 192, p. 709.

2. Prokopovich's data on Prussia, from the source cited in footnote 1, indicate a substantial widening in income inequality in the early period. The share of the lower 90 percent of the population declines from 73 percent in 1854 to 65 percent in 1875; the share of the top 5 percent rises from 21 to 25 percent. But I do not know enough about the data for the early years to evaluate the reliability of the finding.

3. For sources of these data see "Regional Economic Trends and Levels of Living," submitted at the Norman Waite Harris Foundation Institute of the University of Chicago in November 1954 (in press in the volume of proceedings). This paper, and an earlier one, "Underdeveloped Countries and the Preindustrial Phases in the Advanced Countries: An Attempt at Comparison," prepared for the World Population Meetings in Rome held in September 1954 (in press) discuss issues raised in this section.

4. In one year since the second world war, the non-African group in

Southern Rhodesia, which accounted for only 5 percent of total population, received 57 percent of total income; in Kenya, the minority of only 2.9 percent of total population, received 51 percent of total income; in Northern Rhodesia, the minority of only 1.4 percent of total population, received 45 percent of total income. See United Nations, *National Income and Its Distribution in Underdeveloped Countries,* Statistical Paper, Ser. E, no. 3, 1951, Table 12, p. 19.

CHAPTER 7

Should Equity Be a Goal of Economic Policy?

IMF Fiscal Affairs Department

In Chapter 4, Robert Hunter Wade discusses the expanding external gap and warns against policymakers ignoring it. In this chapter, International Monetary Fund staff working in the IMF Fiscal Affairs Department pose the question: Should governments be concerned with issues of equity? After concluding that widespread economic expansion has not been met with declining inequalities, the authors attempt to determine the impact of globalization on the distribution of income. They conclude by suggesting that one of the more promising strategies for economic growth with equity involves investing in human capital. The reader should also consult Chapter 31 for an argument based on human capital.

OVER THE PAST DECADE, GLOBAL OUTPUT HAS GROWN BY MORE THAN 3 percent a year and inflation has slowed in most regions. The fruits of this growth have not been shared equally, however, and income disparities have grown in many countries, developed as well as developing. One of the most pressing issues facing policymakers today is how to respond to these trends. To what extent are growth and equity complementary, and to what extent is there a trade-off between the two?

Why Is Equity Important?

The answers to these questions depend on how equity is defined. Different societies have different perceptions of what is equitable, and these social and cultural norms shape the policies they will adopt to promote equity. Although there is a consensus that extreme inequality of income, wealth, or opportunity is unfair and that efforts should be made to raise the incomes of the poorest members of society, there is little agreement on the desirability of greater income equality for its own sake or on what constitutes a fair distribution of income. Equity issues are especially knotty because they are inextricably intertwined with social values. Nonetheless, economic policymakers are devoting greater attention to them for a number of reasons:

• Some societies view equity as a worthy goal in and of itself because of its moral implications and its intimate link with fairness and social justice.

• Policies that promote equity can help, directly and indirectly, to reduce poverty. When incomes are more evenly distributed, fewer individuals fall below the poverty line. Equity-enhancing policies, particularly such investment in human capital as education, can, in the long run, boost economic growth, which, in turn, has been shown to alleviate poverty.

• Heightened awareness of the discrimination suffered by certain groups because of their gender, race, or ethnic origin has focused attention on the need to ensure that these groups have adequate access to government services and receive fair treatment in the labor market.

• Many of today's policies will affect the welfare of future generations, which raises the issue of intergenerational equity. For instance, the provision of very generous pension benefits to today's retirees could be at the expense of tomorrow's retirees—an important issue in many transition and industrial countries.

• Policies that promote equity can boost social cohesion and reduce political conflict. To be effective, most policies require broad political support, which is more likely to be forthcoming when the distribution of income is seen as fair. However, macroeconomic adjustment that entails growth-enhancing structural reforms such as privatization may increase unemployment and worsen inequality in the short run. In such circumstances, well-targeted social safety nets to shelter the consumption levels of the poor are critically important.

Growing Inequality

Income inequality varies greatly from region to region. It is greatest in Latin America and sub-Saharan Africa, and lowest in Eastern Europe;

other regions fall between these two extremes. In Latin America, the average "Gini coefficient"—the most commonly used measure of inequality, with 0 representing perfect equality and 1 representing total inequality—is nearly 0.5. The average Gini coefficient in sub-Saharan Africa is slightly lower, but there is considerable variation among countries. Income inequality has a regional dimension in both Africa and Latin America—average incomes are significantly higher in urban areas than in rural areas.

In recent years, income inequality has been increasing in a large number of countries. This increase has been most striking in the economies in transition to market-oriented systems, where the average Gini coefficient had been about 0.25 until the late 1980s; by the mid-1990s, it had risen to more than 0.30. Although this may not appear to be a large increase, it is quite significant for such a short period of time, since Gini coefficients tend to be relatively stable in countries over long periods. In the past decade, income inequality has also increased in several Group of Seven countries (for example, Germany, Japan, the United Kingdom, and the United States) and is beginning to rise in some East Asian countries (China and Thailand).

Much of the debate about income distribution has centered on wage earnings. But wages tell only part of the story. The distribution of wealth (and, by implication, capital income) is more concentrated than labor income. In Africa and Latin America, unequal ownership of land has been identified as an important factor in the overall distribution of income. Furthermore, in recent years, there has been a shift from labor to capital income (including from self-employment) in many countries. In transition economies, this shift has been due primarily to the privatization of state-owned assets. The analysis of trends in nonlabor income in countries with well-developed capital markets and pension funds is more complicated. Pension funds and other financial institutions receive a sizable portion of capital income, and the share of capital income in total household income typically changes over the life cycle of the individuals in the household.

Is Globalization to Blame?

Globalization has linked the labor, product, and capital markets of economies around the world. Increased trade, capital and labor movements, and technological progress have led to greater specialization in production and the dispersion of specialized production processes to geographically distant locations. Developing countries, with their abundant supply of unskilled labor, have a comparative advantage relative to developed countries in the production of unskilled-labor-intensive goods and services. As a result, production of these goods in developed countries has come under increased competitive pressure. Economic theory tells us this should apply downward pressure on the relative compensation of unskilled workers in developed countries and upward pressure on the compensation of their counterparts in developing countries.

On the basis of this theory, some have claimed that globalization is to blame for growing income inequality in developed countries. Others argue that the widening gap between the wages of skilled workers and unskilled workers in the industrial countries is due to the development and dispersion of skill-intensive technologies rather than to increased trade. Several empirical studies have tried to gauge the relative importance of trade versus technological progress for the decline in wages of unskilled workers in developed countries. Estimates of the contribution of increased trade to the total increase of the wage differential between unskilled and skilled workers range from negligible to 50 percent. This large variation reflects the structure of production in developed countries and the share of the labor market that is in direct competition with low-skilled workers in developing countries.

The debate regarding the effect of globalization on income distribution in developing countries mirrors the debate on developed countries. Although, all other things being equal, increased openness would be expected to boost the relative wage of unskilled workers in developing countries, experience has been mixed. Evidence suggests that the relative wages of unskilled workers rose in East Asian countries in the 1960s and 1970s but fell in Latin America in the 1980s and early 1990s. There are two possible explanations for why wages fell in Latin America: first, the opening up of developing Asian countries—Bangladesh, India, China, Indonesia, and Pakistan—where unskilled labor is even more abundant; second, the availability of new production technologies that are biased toward skilled labor.

Globalization's effect on income distribution appears to be determined to some extent by a country's level of development and the technologies available to it. Similarly, exposure to international competition may change institutions (for example, trade unions), and thereby affect income distribution. Some observers contend that, because of the mobility of capital, globalization limits the ability of union workers to achieve a "union wage premium," decreasing the bargaining power of workers vis-à-vis capital. In addition, globalization may lead to sharp short-run changes in the distribution of income, as barriers to trade are reduced and the distribution of production is reallocated among sectors.

Many argue that globalization makes it more difficult for governments to carry out equitable policies. Increasingly mobile capital and labor have limited the ability of governments to levy taxes and transfer them to those affected by globalization. To the extent that capital is more mobile than labor, the incidence of taxes to finance safety nets for those affected by globalization is shifted to labor. . . .

Summary

Despite widespread economic expansion, income gaps have widened during the past decade in many parts of the world, including in the industrial countries. This trend has heightened concerns about the treatment of equity in the formulation of economic policy. Equity and growth can be complementary: some policies that promote equity—particularly investment in human capital—can boost growth in the long run and thus alleviate extreme poverty, increase social cohesion, and reduce the scope for political conflict. Policy choices are not always so easy, however: when growth and equity do not go hand in hand, when and how should governments intervene?

The strategies that countries have adopted vary widely. The most effective tool for redistributing income is fiscal policy. And of the two sides of the budget—taxation and spending—the expenditure side, especially spending on health and education, has offered the better opportunities for reducing income inequality over the long term. But governments have also pursued income redistribution through labor market measures, monetary policy, and the overall stance of macroeconomic policy.

An important question is whether governments should focus on outcomes (such as decreasing broad measures of income inequality) or on ensuring that all members of society have equal opportunities (for example, through policies that facilitate mobility among income classes and by setting up a well-functioning judicial system and reducing the scope for corruption). In all these efforts, governments face difficult obstacles: lack of financial resources, difficult-to-reach target groups, weak administrative capacity, and legal and political constraints. A consensus is forming nevertheless that governments should sometimes intervene to ensure not only that the size of the pie increases, but that everybody gets a fair share.

CHAPTER 8

Inequality and Insurgency

EDWARD N. MULLER AND MITCHELL A. SELIGSON

What are the consequences of the widespread domestic income inequality that have been noted in Part 2 of this volume? In this chapter Edward Muller and Mitchell Seligson conduct a cross-national test using a large database. They find that when income inequality is high, the probability of domestic political violence increases substantially. This finding suggests that income inequality can lead to uprisings, guerrilla movements, and civil wars, as have occurred in Vietnam, Central America, and elsewhere. Since the violence invariably causes considerable destruction of property, not to speak of the lives lost, economic growth is adversely affected. Thus, in addition to creating normative problems, income inequality also seems to be responsible for violence and, in turn, slowed economic growth. The inescapable conclusion is that income inequality matters a great deal, for when it is high, a vicious circle of violence and slowed growth is the result.

MANY STUDENTS OF DOMESTIC POLITICAL CONFLICT CONSIDER INEQUALITY in the distribution of land and/or lack of land ownership (landlessness) to be among the more fundamental economic preconditions of insurgency and revolution (e.g., Huntington 1968; Midlarsky 1981, 1982; Midlarsky and Roberts 1985; Paige 1975; Prosterman 1976; Prosterman and Riedinger 1982; Russett 1964; Tanter and Midlarsky 1967). Huntington (1968, 375), whose writing on the subject has been particularly influential, advanced a strong version of the land maldistri-

---

Reprinted with permission of the American Political Science Association from *American Political Science Review,* vol. 81, no. 2 (1987): 425–450.

bution hypothesis as follows: "Where the conditions of land-ownership are equitable and provide a viable living for the peasant, revolution is unlikely. Where they are inequitable and where the peasant lives in poverty and suffering, revolution is likely, if not inevitable, unless the government takes prompt measures to remedy these conditions." However, because mass revolutions are rare events, it is more plausible to relax the postulate that revolution is an inevitable consequence of land maldistribution and to restate the hypothesis: the greater the maldistribution of land, the greater the probability of mass-based political insurgency and, consequently, the greater the *vulnerability* of a country to revolution from below. This weaker, necessary-but-not-sufficient version of the land-maldistribution-leads-to-revolution hypothesis directs attention to the relationship between land distribution and mass political violence.

The land maldistribution hypothesis is based on the assumption that discontent resulting from a highly concentrated distribution of land and/or lack of land ownership (landlessness) in agrarian societies is an important direct cause of mass political violence. Advocates of what has come to be called the "resource mobilization" approach to the explanation of collective protest and violence (e.g., Gamson 1975; Oberschall 1973; Tilly 1978) reject such discontent hypotheses for the reason that inequality and discontent are more or less always present in virtually all societies and that consequently the most direct and influential explanatory factor must not be discontent per se but rather the *organization* of discontent. Thus Skocpol (1979, 112–57), who is skeptical of discontent theories of revolution, argues that the peasant revolts that were a crucial insurrectionary ingredient in the French, Russian, and Chinese revolutions occurred not because of the maldistribution of landholdings but rather because communities of French, Russian, and Chinese peasants had sufficient autonomy from local landlords to enable them to mobilize collectively. By contrast, Midlarsky (1982, 15–20), a proponent of discontent theory, explains the peasant revolts in each of these cases by the fact that rapid population growth severely exacerbated land inequality until a level of deprivation was reached that no longer could be tolerated.

Two contemporary cases cited by Midlarsky and Roberts (1985) in support of the land maldistribution hypothesis are El Salvador and Nicaragua.[1] Compared with other middle-income developing countries, population growth in El Salvador and Nicaragua was above average during the 1960s and 1970s (see World Bank 1981, tbl. 17). Maldistribution of land also was a serious problem, as the Gini coefficient of land concentration was .80 for Nicaragua and .81 for El

Salvador (values well above the global mean of .60) and agricultural households without land (i.e., tenants, sharecroppers, and agricultural laborers) amounted to 40% of the total labor force in El Salvador circa 1970, which was the highest level of landlessness in the world at that time (data are not available for Nicaragua).[2] Each country subsequently experienced a relatively high rate of mass political violence, which in the Nicaraguan case culminated in revolution.

But the seemingly obvious conclusion that land maldistribution must have been a primary cause of political violence in El Salvador and Nicaragua ignores the fact that, during the same period of time, two other Central American states, Costa Rica and Panama, remained quite peaceful despite the presence of exactly the same preconditions supposed to have caused the insurgency in El Salvador and Nicaragua. Costa Rica and Panama experienced above-average population growth (in fact, Costa Rica's 3.4% annual population-growth rate during 1960–70 not only exceeded the 2.9% rate registered by El Salvador and Nicaragua but was also among the highest in the entire world); land was concentrated in the hands of the few to about the same degree in Costa Rica (the Gini coefficient was .82) and Panama (Gini coefficient of .78) as in El Salvador and Nicaragua; and the amount of landlessness in Costa Rica (24%) and in Panama (36.2%) ranked ninth and third highest in the world, respectively. Nevertheless, during 1970–77 Panama registered only a single death from political violence, and there were no instances of deadly political violence in Costa Rica (see Taylor and Jodice 1983, vol. 2, tbl. 2.7).

Comparison of Costa Rica and Panama with El Salvador and Nicaragua thus raises the issue of the general validity of the land maldistribution hypothesis: Are Costa Rica and Panama merely exceptions to the rule, or is maldistribution of land in reality a minor or even irrelevant factor in the process that generates insurgency and revolution? That question is significant not only because inequality is frequently assumed in academic writing to be an important determinant of political instability; it also has profound policy implications because land reform has traditionally been a cornerstone of U.S. efforts to promote political stability in developing countries.

Inequality, Resource Mobilization, and the Structure of the State

We argue that theories emphasizing land maldistribution as a fundamental precondition of insurgency and revolution are misspecified. They attribute direct causal significance to an inequality variable that plays only a relatively small, indirect part in the generation of mass political violence. We hypothesize that the more important direct cause of variation in rates of political violence cross-nationally is inequality in the distribution of income rather than maldistribution of land. This hypothesis is predicated on the following assumptions:

1. Inequality in the contemporary world generates discontent;
2. Although inequality is present to some degree in all societies, some societies are significantly more inegalitarian than others;
3. Inequality in the distribution of land and inequality in the distribution of income are not necessarily tightly connected; in particular, they are sufficiently independent of each other that an effect of one on a response variable such as the rate of political violence does not necessarily imply that the other will have a similar effect;
4. Given the existence of inequality-based discontent, it is more difficult to mobilize peasant communities than urban populations for political protest; peasants normally become the foot soldiers of insurgent movements only if they are effectively organized by a "vanguard" of urban professional revolutionaries.

From these assumptions we derive the following postulates:

1. A high level of income inequality nationwide significantly raises the probability that at least some dissident groups will be able to organize for aggressive collective action. This is because, first, the pool of discontented persons from which members can be drawn will include the more easily mobilized urban areas; and, second, it may be possible for urban revolutionaries to establish cross-cutting alliances with groups in the countryside.
2. A high level of agrarian inequality does not necessarily raise the probability that dissident groups will be able to organize for aggressive collective action; this is because the pool of discontented persons from which members can be drawn may be restricted to the countryside, which is difficult to mobilize; consequently, we predict that if income inequality is relatively low, the rate of political violence will tend to be relatively low, even if agrarian inequality is relatively high; whereas if income inequality is relatively high, the rate of political violence will tend to be relatively high, even if agrarian inequality is relatively low.

Our inequality hypothesis, which is based on an integration of dis-content (or relative deprivation) arguments (e.g., Gurr 1970) with the resource mobilization approach, can be illustrated by the cases of Costa Rica and Venezuela, where egalitarian redistribution of income occurred despite persisting high agrarian inequality; and the case of Iran, where income inequality worsened, especially in urban areas, despite an egalitarian land reform.

Costa Rica circa 1960 had a relatively inegalitarian distribution of land (the 1963 Gini coefficient was .78) and an extremely inegalitarian distribution of income (the richest 20% of families received 61% of total personal income in 1961). During the decade of the 1960s the dis-tribution of land in Costa Rica became slightly more concentrated (the 1973 Gini coefficient was .82). The distribution of income, however, was substantially altered in an egalitarian direction by democratically elected reformist administrations who pursued welfare-state policies similar to those of European social democratic governments. By 1970 the share of national income accruing to the richest quintile of Costa Rican households had been reduced to 50%.[3] As mentioned above, vio-lent conflict was absent from Costa Rican politics during the 1970s.

Venezuela was a similarly inegalitarian society circa 1960, when a democratic regime was inaugurated. The 1956 Gini index of land con-centration was .91—the second highest in the world next to Peru—and the richest quintile of Venezuelan households received 59% of total per-sonal income in 1962. During the 1960s the distribution of land in Venezuela remained highly concentrated (the 1971 Gini coefficient was .91), but the distribution of income became more egalitarian—although not as dramatically so as in Costa Rica—due to a combination of reformist administrations and an expanding petroleum-based economic pie (by 1970 the income share of the richest quintile of households had been reduced to 54%). Deaths from political violence in Venezuela reg-istered a sharp decline over this period (according to Taylor and Jodice 1983, vol. 2, tbl. 2.7, they amounted to 1,392 during the years 1958–62; 155 during 1963–67; 53 during 1968–72; and 9 during 1973–77). . . .

Of course, income inequality is not the only cause of mass political violence. In Panama, for example, income was distributed very unequally circa 1970, as the richest 20% of households earned 62% of total national income. But by the early 1970s, General Omar Torrijos Herrera, who had led a successful coup d'etat by officers of the national guard in 1968, had crushed all opposition, established firm censorship of the media, and taken control of the judiciary. Ratings of political rights and civil liberties in Panama during the mid-1970s on a scale of one to seven (most free to least free) averaged 6.5.[4] During this period

(1973–77) the Torrijos regime in Panama was the most repressive in the Western Hemisphere next to Cuba, where the rating of political rights and civil liberties averaged 6.9. Inequality-induced discontent presumably existed in Panama, and it probably was relatively widespread, but there was little or no opportunity to organize it.

By contrast, Panama's next-door neighbor to the northwest, Costa Rica, enjoyed the distinction in the mid-1970s of being the oldest democracy in Latin America. Since 1949 Costa Rica had held regularly scheduled free and fair elections, the media were uncensored, unions were free to organize, the judiciary was independent of the executive and legislative branches of government, and citizens were not subject to arbitrary arrest. Costa Rica's political and civil rights ratings averaged a maximum score of 1.0 during 1973–77.

The "open" and "closed" political systems of Costa Rica and Panama exemplify polar extremes of regime repressiveness. Differences in regime structure are relevant to the explanation of cross-national variation in mass political violence because they can be assumed to affect three important variables emphasized in some versions of resource mobilization theory (e.g., McAdam 1982): (1) the extent to which dissident groups are able to develop strong organizations, (2) their belief in the likelihood of success of collective action, and (3) the range of political opportunities available to them for achieving their goals.

In the context of an extremely repressive regime, dissident groups are severely restricted in their ability to organize; their belief in the likelihood of success of collective action will probably be low; and opportunities to engage in collective action of any kind will be quite limited. Consequently, under the condition of a high level of regime repressiveness, rational actors most likely will attach a relatively low utility to violent collective action, and the rate of mass political violence therefore should be relatively low.

In the context of a nonrepressive or "democratic" regime, dissident groups will not face significant restrictions on their ability to organize for collective action, and their belief in the likelihood of achieving at least some success from collective action will probably be relatively high. Moreover, a democratic regime structure will afford a variety of opportunities for dissident groups to participate legally and peacefully in the political process. Because the costs of peaceful collective action will be lower than those of violent collective action and because the likelihood of success of peaceful collective action will be reasonably high, rational actors under the condition of a nonrepressive regime structure presumably will usually attach a much higher utility to peaceful as opposed to violent collective action, and, therefore, the rate of mass political violence here too should be relatively low.

In the context of a semirepressive regime, it is possible for dissident groups to develop relatively strong organizations. However, opportunities to engage in nonviolent forms of collective action that effectively exert influence on the political process are limited. Semirepressive regimes allow only for, in Green's (1984, 154) apt terminology, "pseudoparticipation . . . an elaborate charade of the participatory process." Polities with pseudoparticipation typically have elections that are not free and fair, legislatures that are little more than debating societies, and a judiciary that is not independent of the will of the executive; the media are subject to censorship at the whim of the executive; and citizens are subject to arbitrary arrest and detention by security forces, which are under the exclusive control of the executive. In short, semirepressive regimes erect a facade of participatory institutions but do not permit popular input to significantly influence governmental output. Because opportunities for genuine participation are restricted, many politically activated citizens may come to perceive civil disobedience and violence as being more efficacious than legal means of pseudoparticipation; and since the expected costs of insurgency may not be perceived to be prohibitive, rational actors may well attach a relatively high utility to aggressive political behavior. Therefore, it is plausible to expect that the rate of mass political violence cross-nationally will be highest under semirepressive authoritarian regimes.

The analysis of the causes of the Iranian revolution by Green (1982, 1984) documents in detail how the Shah vacillated between fully restricting mass participation and allowing pseudoparticipation and concludes that "the effects of such tactics served to increase popular hostility among those socially mobilized Iranians eager to have a measure of influence over the manner in which their society was ruled" (Green, 1984, 155). Green's case study description is corroborated by global comparative measures of regime repressiveness, which show that Iran in the late 1950s was classified as having a "semi-competitive" regime (Coleman 1960); was scored for 1960 and 1965 as intermediate (34.9 and 45.0, respectively) on a 0–100 scale of extent of political democracy (Bollen 1980); was ranked circa 1969 at an intermediate level on a scale of opportunity for political opposition (Dahl 1971); received a mean rating of 5.7 on political and civil rights for 1973–77; and had shifted in 1978 to a mean rating of 5.0 on political and civil rights. Thus, while pursuing a strategy of economic development that had the short-term consequence of increasing inequality in the distribution of income, the Pahlavi government would appear to have added fuel to the fire by following a semirepressive political development strategy that allowed opposition groups to organize but did not enable them to participate effectively.

If one takes income inequality and the repressiveness of the regime into account simultaneously, it might be argued that each variable could have an independent causal impact on the likelihood of mass political violence. An equally plausible specification of the joint relationship is that discontent resulting from income inequality will affect political violence only (or most strongly) in countries with semirepressive regime structures; whereas in countries with nonrepressive regime structures, inequality-induced discontent will tend to be channeled into peaceful participation; and in countries with repressive regime structures, it will be borne apathetically or else perhaps lead to various kinds of nonpolitical deviant behavior. . . .

A Cross-National Test of the Causal Model

There have been no studies reported to date that compare the causal importance of land maldistribution versus income inequality as determinants of mass political violence cross-nationally.[5] Until the 1970s, reasonably reliable information on the distribution of land and income was available for only a limited number of countries. Thus in Hibbs's (1973) comprehensive cross-national study of determinants of mass political violence during the 1948–67 period, inequality variables had to be excluded because of insufficient data. We now have been able to compile a relatively comprehensive data set on inequality circa 1970 [appendix in original—Eds.]. Information on land inequality is available for approximately three-quarters of the population of independent political units in 1970, while information on landlessness and income inequality is available for approximately one-half of the population. Regionally, these data are quite comprehensive for Europe and the Americas. In regard to landlessness and, especially, income distribution, coverage is poor for states in the Middle East and North Africa, and it is somewhat limited for the states of sub-Saharan Africa. Since it is unlikely that much new data on inequality circa 1970 will emerge in the future, results using the current data set can probably be regarded as being about as definitive as possible for this time period.

Measurement of the Dependent Variable

Political violence is measured by the natural logarithm of the death rate from domestic conflict per one million population.[6] Annual death counts are from Table 2.7 of Taylor and Jodice (1983, vol. 2). Current political violence is the logged sum of annual deaths from domestic political conflict during 1973–77 divided by midinterval population; lagged political violence is the logged sum of annual deaths from domestic political conflict during 1968–72 divided by midinterval population. Countries where domestic political conflict overlaps with major interstate wars are excluded: Kampuchea, Laos, and South Vietnam for the 1968–77 period; and Pakistan for the 1968–72 period (where an extremely high death rate reflects the conflict between India and Pakistan in 1971 over the secession of Bangladesh). Ireland also is excluded for the 1973–77 period because the relatively high death rate there reflects a spillover from the Northern Ireland conflict.

In the vast majority of countries, the death rate from political violence per one million population is less than 50. A few countries register very extreme scores, however; for example, Zimbabwe's 1973–77 death rate from political violence was 544 per million and Argentina's death rate was 177 per million. Even after logging, countries with political violence death rates of 50 or more almost always show up as outliers in regression equations (i.e., they usually have extremely high standardized residuals). Consequently, in order to reduce the problem of extreme scores on the dependent variable, it is desirable to set a ceiling on the death rate. The upper limit that we have selected is 50 deaths per million. The adjusted death rate variables thus range from a minimum value of 0 to a maximum value of 50 or more; and the range of the logged death rate variables is from 0 to 3.93.

Measurement of the Independent Variables

The data on land inequality circa 1970 encompass 85 states in which agriculture was not collectivized. Land inequality is measured by the Gini coefficient of land concentration. A weighted index of land inequality is the geometric mean of the Gini coefficient (expressed as a percentage) and the percentage of the labor force employed in agriculture in 1970 (see Taylor and Jodice 1983, vol. 1). Apart from measurement of the extent to which land is concentrated in the hands of the few, we also take into account a second aspect of land maldistribution, landlessness, as measured by agricultural households without land as a proportion of the total labor force. These data are derived from estimates by Prosterman and Riedinger (1982) of the proportion in 64 countries of agricultural households without land.

Income inequality is measured by the size of the share of personal income accruing to the richest quintile of recipients, based on information about the nationwide distribution of income in 63 countries compiled principally from publications of the World Bank. Although some previous studies have used Gini coefficients of income concentration, this measure tends to be unduly sensitive to inequality in the middle of the distribution, whereas inequality in reference to the top of the distribution probably is more relevant to political violence. In any event, income shares also have a more direct meaning than Gini coefficients and are currently more frequently used in research on income inequality.

Regime repressiveness is measured by a country's 1973–77 average annual combined rating on 7-point rank-order scales of political rights and civil liberties that have been reported by Raymond D. Gastil since 1973 (the data are from Taylor and Jodice 1983). A semirepressive regime structure is defined operationally as a mean political rights and civil liberties rank in the range of 2.6–5.5. These cutpoints are identical to those used by Gastil for classifying political systems as "free" (1.0–2.5), "partly free" (2.6–5.5), and "not free" (5.6–7.0).

The indicator of governmental acts of coercion is the negative sanctions variable (imposition of sanctions) from Taylor and Jodice 1983 (vol. 2, tbl. 3.1). Current negative sanctions is the frequency of negative sanctions summed over the years 1973–77 and divided by midinterval total population in millions; lagged negative sanctions are the 1968–72 frequency per one million midinterval population. The negative sanctions variables are expressed as natural logarithms (after adding an increment of one).

The indicator of intensity of separatism is an ordinal scale developed by Ted and Erika Gurr. The data for circa 1975 are from Taylor and Jodice 1983, 55–57 and tbl. 2.5. We express intensity of separatism as a dummy variable, scored 1 (i.e., high intensity) if groups or regions actively advocating greater autonomy were forcibly incorporated into the state (codes 3 and 4) and 0 (i.e., low intensity) otherwise (codes 0, 1, and 2).[7]

Level of economic development is measured by energy consumption per capita in 1970 (from Taylor and Jodice 1983, vol. 1). Values of this variable are expressed as natural logarithms.

Land Maldistribution, Income Inequality, and Political Violence

According to what is generally considered to be the most appropriate specification of the land inequality hypothesis (e.g., Huntington 1968; Nagel 1976; Prosterman 1976), the strongest effect on political violence should be observed when inequality in the distribution of land is weighted by the proportion of the labor force employed in the agricultural sector of the economy. This specification implies a multiplicative interaction between land inequality and the size of the agricultural labor force, which we call *agrarian inequality*, defined operationally as the geometric mean of Gini land concentration and the percentage of the labor force employed in agriculture (i.e., the square root of the product of these variables). . . .

Results

The results of testing the inequality hypotheses in the context of a multivariate model of determinants of political violence are summarized in Figure 8.1. All of the evidence that we have considered points to the presence of a robust, positive monotonic (positively accelerated) relationship between income inequality and political violence that is independent of the other variables in the model. The effect of income inequality on political violence may be enhanced by the presence of a semirepressive regime, but the evidence is not conclusive in that regard, so we represent the possibility of an interaction between income inequality and semirepressiveness by dashed arrows. The other solid arrows linking explanatory variables to political violence also denote relationships that hold for change as well as level of violence and seem to be robust. We have tested the regime-repressiveness hypothesis with a dummy variable in this study (in order to take into account the possibility of an interaction with income inequality). It should be noted, however, that the same kind of effect appears if regime repressiveness

Figure 8.1   Observed Causal Paths in the Multivariate Causal Model

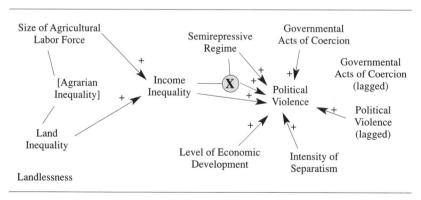

is expressed as a continuous quantitative variable—that is, if the semi-repressive-regime dummy variable is replaced by regime repressiveness and its square, a statistically significant nonmonotonic-inverted-U-curve relationship between regime repressiveness and political violence is consistently observed in multivariate equations that include income inequality and the other explanatory variables. We have not tested for the possibility of an instantaneous reciprocal relationship between political violence and governmental acts of coercion (see Hibbs 1973) because that is a complex topic requiring a separate paper. From preliminary work, however, we are confident that it is valid to infer the presence of a positive effect of current governmental acts of coercion on current political violence. . . .

The only completely irrelevant variable in the model is landlessness, a finding that runs counter to the strong claim of causal importance for this variable made by Prosterman (1976). Moreover, at least as a general determinant of mass political violence, the condition of high agrarian inequality also fails to warrant the strong causal claims made for it by many scholars. The components of agrarian inequality, land inequality and size of the agricultural labor force, affect income inequality and, therefore, are indirectly relevant to political violence, but neither the weighted index of agrarian inequality nor land inequality per se has any direct effect on political violence.

Discussion

The finding that agrarian inequality is relevant only to the extent that it is associated with inequality in the nationwide distribution of income has important policy implications. Land reform in third world countries all too often is considered to be a panacea for problems of inequality. However, as Huntington (1968, 385) points out, redistribution of land is the most difficult of reforms for modernizing governments because it almost always entails some degree of outright confiscation. And our study indicates that land redistribution is also not necessarily the most meaningful of reforms. If land redistribution is carried through to the point of actually effecting an egalitarian redistribution of income, as seems to have been the case in countries as diverse as Taiwan and Egypt, and/or if other economic development policies do not exacerbate income inequality, then land reform can make a contribution to the promotion of political stability. However, there are cases such as Bolivia and Mexico in which land reform has not been associated with egalitarian income redistribution. Land reform without income redistribution is probably at best merely a temporary palliative; and at worst, as the case of Iran demonstrates, it can be quite counterproductive by alienating powerful conservative groups such as the nobility and the clergy. Indeed, by simultaneously encouraging both land reform and a policy of rapid economic growth that ignored inegalitarian distributional consequences, U.S. advisors to the Shah would appear unwittingly to have exacerbated the economic preconditions of revolution in Iran.

If the effect of income inequality on change in political violence and its level, observed for 60 and 62 cases, is reliable and more or less generalizable across time in the contemporary world (at least for nontraditional societies where modern values like equality can be assumed to have become salient), it follows that redistribution of income must be ranked as one of the more meaningful reforms that a modernizing government can undertake in the interest of achieving political stability. Unfortunately, redistribution of income may conflict not only with the class interests of many third world governments but also with their predilection for rapid industrialization. The Shah's great dream of surpassing Sweden by the year 2000 was dashed in part by his single-minded concern with economic growth and the raising of per capita income. As Green (1982, 70–71) points out, "the premise of the Pahlavi development ethos rested on the assumption that economic development was more important than political rights or justice." Iran in the years immediately preceding the revolution indeed registered an extraordinary growth of per capita gross national product, which averaged an increase of 13.3% annually during 1970–78, the highest rate of growth of GNP per capita in the world (see Taylor and Jodice 1983, vol. 1, tbl. 3.6); but at the same time that per capita income was increasing phenomenally, the distribution of that income was apparently becoming more concentrated at the top, presumably heightening perceptions of economic injustice. It is important to emphasize, however, that there is no necessary trade-off between rapid economic growth and income inequality. Taiwan's average annual growth of GNP per capita during 1960–78 was 6.6% (see World Bank 1980, tbl. 1), a rate that, although surpassed by Iran (the world leader excluding Romania), was nevertheless almost twice as high as the average rate (3.7%) for all middle-income countries. At the same time (1964–78), the income share of the richest 20% of households in Taiwan declined from 41.1% to 37.2% (see Tsiang 1984, tbl. 9). Thus, by following a different set of economic policies than the Shah, the government of Taiwan achieved growth with equity. And the death rate from political violence in Taiwan during 1973–77 was .06, as compared with Iran's rate of .91. . . .

Notes

A version of this paper was presented at the 1985 Midwest Political Science Association meeting in Chicago, April 18–21. Support for this research was provided by National Science Foundation Grant SES83-2021.

1. Midlarsky and Roberts distinguish between these cases in regard to the dynamics of coalition formation leading to different kinds of revolutionary movements. Although both countries had inegalitarian distributions of land, creating a potential for insurgency in each case, the revolutionary movement in El Salvador was more narrowly class-based than in Nicaragua, due to differences in population density that produced greater land scarcity in El Salvador than in Nicaragua. This difference is thought to have enhanced the likelihood of a successful revolution in Nicaragua.

2. Unless otherwise noted, data on land and income distribution referred to in the text are either from Table A-1 [see original work] or, for years other than those in Table A-1, from the sources cited therein.

3. Based on a study reported by Céspedes (1979). Trejos (1983) reports the income share of the richest 20% of households in Costa Rica as 51.1% in 1971, 52.1% in 1974, and 53% in 1977.

4. These and all subsequent data on civil and political liberties referred to in the text are calculated from the data file of the *World Handbook of Political and Social Indicators*. For a description of the ratings, see Taylor and Jodice 1983 (1:58–65).

5. The only previous research on this topic is reported in Midlarsky 1981, where income distribution is measured by an index of intersectoral inequality. As Sigelman and Simpson (1977, 111) have pointed out, however, this index "is at best a second-rate measurement proxy for personal income, lacking theoretical interest of its own."

6. Deaths from political violence are an attribute of political-protest events like riots, armed attacks, and assassinations. Deaths are thus a summary measure of the intensity of political-protest events. Deaths are used in preference to a composite index for the following reasons: (1) a single-variable indicator is more easily interpretable than a composite measure; (2) deaths will necessarily correlate very strongly with a composite measure such as that constructed by Hibbs (1973), which includes deaths, armed attacks, and assassinations; and (3) there is probably less reporting bias for deaths than for indicators such as armed attacks (see Weede 1981). Death *rate* is preferred over raw counts because the former is an indicator of the extent to which the regime is threatened by insurgency, which depends not on the absolute frequency of political violence but rather on its frequency relative to size of population (for further discussion of this issue see Linehan 1976; Muller 1985; and Weede 1981). The logarithmic transformation is theoretically appropriate because death rate from political violence is expected to vary as a positively accelerated function of inequality; it is also necessary because of the presence of extreme values—although the problem of extreme values still exists after logging. An increment of one is added to each death score before logging because the log of zero is undefined.

7. In testing the multivariate model across 62 cases, the following countries are missing data on intensity of separatism: Barbados, Gabon, Honduras,

Ivory Coast, Malawi, Nepal, Sierra Leone, and Trinidad and Tobago. Based on country descriptions from Banks 1976, these countries were scored zero on intensity of separatism.

References

Ahluwalia, Montak S. 1976. Inequality, Poverty, and Development. *Journal of Development Economics* 3:307–42.

Bandura, Albert. 1973. *Aggression: A Social Learning Analysis.* Englewood Cliffs, NJ: Prentice-Hall.

Banks, Arthur S., ed. 1976. *Political Handbook of the World: 1976.* New York: McGraw-Hill.

Bharier, Julian. 1971. *Economic Development in Iran 1900–1970.* New York: Oxford University Press.

Bollen, Kenneth A. 1980. Issues in the Comparative Measurement of Political Democracy. *American Sociological Review* 45:370–90.

Bornschier Volker, and Peter Heintz, eds. 1979. *Compendium of Data for World System Analysis.* Zurich: Soziologisches Institut der Universität.

Buss, Arnold H. 1961. *A Psychology of Aggression.* New York: Wiley.

Céspedes, Victor H. 1979. *Evolución de la distribución del ingreso en Costa Rica.* Serie divulgación económica, No. 18. Costa Rica: Ciudad Universitaria Rodrigo Facio.

Coleman, James S. 1960. Conclusion: The Political Systems of the Developing Areas. In *The Politics of the Developing Areas,* ed. Gabriel A. Almond and James S. Coleman. Princeton: Princeton University Press.

Dahl, Robert A. 1971. *Polyarchy.* New Haven: Yale University Press.

Fei, John C. H., Gustav Ranis, and Shirley W. Y. Kuo. 1979. *Growth with Equity: The Taiwan Case.* New York: Oxford University Press.

Food and Agriculture Organization of the United States. 1981. *Nineteen Seventy World Census of Agriculture: Analysis and International Comparison of the Results.* Rome: author.

Gamson, William A. 1975. *The Strategy of Social Protest.* Homewood, IL: Dorsey.

Green, Jerrold D. 1982. *Revolution in Iran.* New York: Praeger.

Green, Jerrold D. 1984. Countermobilization as a Revolutionary Form. *Comparative Politics* 16:153–69.

Gurr, Ted Robert. 1970. *Why Men Rebel.* Princeton: Princeton University Press.

Hardy, Melissa A. 1979. Economic Growth, Distributional Inequality, and Political Conflict in Industrial Societies. *Journal of Political and Military Sociology* 5:209–27.

Hibbs, Douglas A. 1973. *Mass Political Violence.* New York: Wiley.

Huntington, Samuel P. 1968. *Political Order in Changing Societies.* New Haven: Yale University Press.

Jabbari, Ahmad. 1981. Economic Factors in Iran's Revolution: Poverty, Inequality, and Inflation. In *Iran: Essays on a Revolution in the Making,* ed. Ahmad Jabbari and Robert Olson. Lexington, KY: Mazda.

Jain, Shail. 1975. *Size Distribution of Income.* Washington, DC: World Bank.

Keddie, Nikki R. 1968. The Iranian Village before and after Land Reform. *Journal of Contemporary History* 3:69–91.

Leal, Maria Angela. 1983. Heritage of Hunger: Population, Land, and Survival. In *Revolution in Central America*, ed. Stanford Central America Action Network. Boulder, CO: Westview.

Linehan, William J. 1976. Models for the Measurement of Political Instability. *Political Methodology* 3:441–86.

McAdam, Doug. 1982. *Political Process and the Development of Black Insurgency*. Chicago: University of Chicago Press.

Midlarsky, Manus I. 1981. The Revolutionary Transformation of Foreign Policy: Agrarianism and Its International Impact. In *The Political Economy of Foreign Policy Behavior*, ed. Charles W. Kegley and Patrick J. McGowan. Beverly Hills, CA: Sage.

Midlarsky, Manus I. 1982. Scarcity and Inequality. *Journal of Conflict Resolution* 26:3–38.

Midlarsky, Manus I., and Kenneth Roberts. 1985. Class, State, and Revolution in Central America: Nicaragua and El Salvador Compared. *Journal of Conflict Resolution* 29:163–93.

Muller, Edward N. 1985. Income Inequality, Regime Repressiveness, and Political Violence. *American Sociological Review* 50:47–61.

Muller, Edward N. 1986. Income Inequality and Political Violence: The Effect of Influential Cases. *American Sociological Review* 51:441–45.

Nagel, Jack. 1976. Erratum. *World Politics* 28:315.

Norusis, Marija J. 1986. *SPSS/PC+*. Chicago: SPSS.

Oberschall, Anthony. 1973. *Social Conflict and Social Movements*. Englewood Cliffs, NJ: Prentice-Hall.

Paige, Jeffery M. 1975. *Agrarian Revolution*. New York: Free Press.

Paukert, Felix. 1973. Income Distribution at Different Levels of Development: A Survey of Evidence. *International Labour Review* 108:97–125.

Prosterman, Roy L. 1976. IRI: A Simplified Predictive Index of Rural Instability. *Comparative Politics* 8:339–54.

Prosterman, Roy L., and Jeffrey M. Riedinger. 1982. Toward an Index of Democratic Development. In *Freedom in the World: Political Rights and Civil Liberties 1982*, ed. Raymond D. Gastil. Westport, CT: Greenwood Press.

Roberti, Paolo. 1974. Income Distribution: A Time-Series and a Cross-Section Survey. *Economic Journal* 84:629–38.

Russett, Bruce M. 1964. Inequality and Instability: The Relation of Land Tenure to Politics. *World Politics* 16:442–54.

Sawyer, Malcolm. 1976. Income Distribution in OECD Countries. *OECD Economic Outlook*, Occasional Studies, July, 3–36.

Seligson, Mitchell A., Richard Hough, John Kelley, Stephen Miller, Russell Derossier, and Fred L. Mann. 1983. *Land and Labor in Guatemala: An Assessment*. Washington, DC: Agency for International Development and Development Associates.

Sigelman, Lee, and Miles Simpson. 1977. A Cross-National Test of the Linkage between Economic Inequality and Political Violence. *Journal of Conflict Resolution* 21:105–28.

Skocpol, Theda. 1979. *States and Social Revolutions*. New York: Cambridge University Press.

Tanter, Raymond, and Manus I. Midlarsky. 1967. A Theory of Revolution. *Journal of Conflict Resolution* 11:264–80.

Taylor, Charles L., and Michael C. Hudson. 1972. *World Handbook of Political and Social Indicators.* 2d ed. New Haven: Yale University Press.

Taylor, Charles L., and David A. Jodice. 1983. *World Handbook of Political and Social Indicators.* 3d ed. Vols. 1 and 2. New Haven: Yale University Press.

Tilly, Charles. 1969. Collective Violence in European Perspective. In *Violence in America: Historical and Comparative Perspectives,* ed. Hugh Davis Graham and Ted Robert Gurr. New York: Signet Books.

Tilly, Charles. 1978. *From Mobilization to Revolution.* Reading, MA: Addison-Wesley.

Trejos, Juan Diego. 1983. *La distribución del ingreso de las familias Costarricenses: Algunas caracteristicas en 1977.* San Jose: Instituto investigaciones en ciencias económicas, Universidad de Costa Rica, No. 50.

Tsiang, S. C. 1984. Taiwan's Economic Miracle: Lessons in Economic Development. In *World Economic Growth,* ed. Arnold C. Harberger. San Francisco: Institute for Contemporary Studies.

United States Agency for International Development. 1983. *Country Development Strategy Statement: Jamaica, FY 1985.* Washington, DC: Government Printing Office.

Webb, Richard C. 1976. The Distribution of Income in Peru. In *Income Distribution in Latin America,* ed. Alejandro Foxley. New York: Cambridge University Press.

Weede, Erich. 1981. Income Inequality, Average Income, and Domestic Violence. *Journal of Conflict Resolution* 25:639–53.

Weede, Erich. 1986. Income Inequality and Political Violence Reconsidered. *American Sociological Review* 51:438–41.

World Bank. 1979, 1980, 1981, 1982, 1983, 1984, 1985. *World Development Report.* New York: Oxford University Press.

CHAPTER 9

Some New Evidence on Correlates of Political Violence: Income Inequality, Regime Repressiveness, and Economic Development

ERICH WEEDE

In the previous chapter, Edward Muller and Mitchell Seligson concluded that a high level of income inequality increases the likelihood of political violence, thereby producing slowed economic growth. The astute policymaker would conclude that policies to alleviate income inequality would have the dual impact of lowering the likelihood of political violence and clearing an impediment to economic growth. Although he was directly addressing an earlier article by Edward Muller, here, Erich Weede contends that the proposed tie between income inequality, levels of economic development, and violence was wrong. Utilizing an updated dataset, Weede examines cross-national evidence and concludes that neither inequality nor levels of economic development contribute to political violence.

Introduction

KARL MARX SUGGESTED THAT CAPITALISM CANNOT AVOID IMPOSING HARDSHIP upon the working class, which therefore has no choice but to rebel and to overthrow capitalism. Some may dispute whether Marx had absolute or relative deprivation in mind, but he certainly belongs to a sociological tradition which explains political violence by deprivation. Influenced by psychological work on frustration and aggression (Dollard *et al.*, 1939), more recent writers (Davies, 1962; Feierabend and Feierabend, 1966; Gurr, 1968, 1970; Huntington, 1968), focus on

Reprinted with permission of Oxford University Press from *European Sociological Review*, vol. 3, no. 2. Copyright © 1987 by Oxford University Press.

discontent, frustration or *relative* deprivation in order to explain political protest and violence. From a macrosociological, sociological and comparative perspective, one would like to know whether there are objective and measurable background characteristics linked to relative deprivation and ultimately to violence. If so, we could arrive at general statements linking broad societal characteristics on the one hand and protest, violence, or even revolution on the other hand—as Marx sought to do in the nineteenth century.

Contemporary *macro*sociological research on political conflict and deprivation falls into two categories. It is possible to argue that imbalances in socio-economic development lead to relative deprivation which, in turn, leads to protest and violence (Deutsch, 1961; Feierabend and Feierabend, 1966, Gurr, 1968; Gurr and Duvall, 1973; Huntington, 1968). Excessive social mobilisation, creating wants which cannot be satisfied because of rather slow economic development, provides an example of such imbalances. Then the task is to construct indices of relative deprivation or social frustration from a variety of background variables and to relate these indices to protest or violence. In my view, these efforts have not proved to be cumulative (for more or less critical appraisals see Eckstein, 1980; Snyder, 1978; Weede, 1975, 1986a; Zimmermann, 1980, 1983). Moreover, there seems to be less interest in this enterprise in the 1980s than there was in the late 1960s or early 1970s.

Alternatively, one may argue that inequality is the most obvious background condition of relative deprivation and political violence. Disregarding studies which focus on some particular aspect of inequality such as land distribution (Russett, 1964; Nagel, 1974, 1976) or which rely on sectoral inequality data (Parvin, 1973), there are only five cross-national studies which investigate the relationship between (personal or household) income inequality and political violence (Sigelman and Simpson, 1977; Hardy, 1979; Weede, 1981; Powell, 1982; Muller, 1985 challenged by Weede, 1986b, and defended by Muller, 1986). In their pioneering study Sigelman and Simpson (1977: 124) conclude "that the overall level of societal well-being is a more critical determinant of political violence than is income inequality, a measure of relative well-being." While Sigelman and Simpson still admitted some marginal contribution of income inequality to political violence. Hardy (1979) and Weede (1981) even denied the existence of a relationship between inequality and violence once economic development is controlled. Analysing the relationships between *per capita* income, income inequality and deaths from political violence across democracies only,

Powell (1982: 51) arrived at the very same conclusion. Despite some major disagreements about research design and the proper way of analysing the data, results from Sigelman and Simpson (1977), Hardy (1979), Weede (1981) and Powell (1982) were cumulative in casting ever-growing doubts upon the plausible proposition that income inequality strongly affects political violence.

Recently, the emerging consensus has been challenged. Muller (1985) claims that income inequality does indeed contribute to political violence. While the contradictory findings of Muller (1985) on the one hand and earlier researchers, on the other, necessitate a renewed effort at analysing the inequality-violence linkage, it is important also to note Muller's (1985: 58) strongest finding: that the death rate from political violence is a non-monotonic function of regime repressiveness, where deaths are maximised at intermediate levels of regime repressiveness. This latter result easily fits with a rational action, resource mobilisation or political process explanation of political violence (Coleman, 1978; Oberschall, 1973; Tilly, 1975, 1978; Tullock, 1974; Weede, 1985, 1986a): If there is a lot of consistently applied repression, then resource mobilisation by dissidents is more or less impossible, and violent as well as non-violent opposition is deterred. If there is almost no repression, then dissidents may organise themselves, but low cost and non-violent means of exerting influence are available and preferred. At intermediate levels of repressiveness, however, peaceful opposition seems ineffective, while violent opposition is not effectively deterred. Muller's (1985) findings on the inequality-violence linkage, however, seem to favour a discontent or relative deprivation approach (e.g. Davies, 1962; Feierabend and Feierabend, 1966; Gurr, 1968, 1970). Some may find Muller's even-handedness in his evaluation of contending theoretical approaches and his note of caution, concerning the rather weak correspondence between micro-explanations of why men rebel and macro-relationships between inequality and violence, reassuring. Others may deplore the fact that we make so little progress in choosing rationally between contending paradigms or research programs.

Of course, it is possible to argue that relative deprivation matters in producing political violence without claiming that income inequality matters. Relative deprivation may result from different characteristics of nations or even be a purely psychic state largely independent of objective or measurable macro-characteristic of nations. Or, the impact of the size distribution of income on violence may depend on the presence or absence of some widely accepted ideological justification of inequality. Moreover, from *micro*sociological research (Muller, 1979,

1980), we know that utilitarian and normative justifications of violence itself matter. Unfortunately, there are no measures for these variables at the cross-national level of analysis. It is also possible to reconcile an inequality-violence linkage with a resource mobilisation, political process, or rational action approach.

A robust and strong linkage between inequality and political violence *in an additive model* implies that more inequality *always* contributes to more political violence. This is a relative deprivation view. From a rational action perspective, action by the underpriviledged *depends* on their chances of success which are, to say the least, not improved by being underprivileged. From a resource mobilisation perspective, the linkage between being underprivileged and political violence should *depend* on the connectedness of underprivileged people, on their organisation for collective action—none of which is a necessary corollary of lacking privileges or suffering from exploitation. If the inequality-violence linkage is conditional on other variables, then *unconditional* effects of inequality on violence *in additive models* should be fairly weak or absent.

In this paper I shall not investigate those conditional effects of inequality on violence which are compatible with a rational action, resource mobilisation and political process perspective. I shall restrict myself, rather, to an investigation of the additive and general effects of inequality on violence which are to be expected according to a straightforward application of the relative deprivation approach. I limit my research agenda, because it is almost impossible to find cross-nationally valid measures for many variables which play a central role in rational action, resource mobilisation, or political process explanations of violence. Moreover, it makes methodological sense to investigate the simpler additive models first, before moving to a more complicated explanatory approach which includes some interaction effects (Allison, 1977).

While there are no final verdicts in empirical research, while there always remain anomalies (Kuhn, 1962; Lakatos, 1968/69), it is conceivable to strengthen the case against relative deprivation and to promote resource mobilisation, political process, and rational action approaches to political violence. This can be done by calling into question Muller's (1985) finding on the relationship between inequality and violence and by thus reaffirming the earlier consensus (Sigelman and Simpson, 1977; Hardy, 1979; Weede, 1981) that inequality makes little, if any, difference, and by preserving Muller's valuable and welcome[1] finding on the nonmonotonic relationship between regime regressiveness and political violence. This is the agenda of the present paper.

Differences between Previous Studies

There is little need to discuss the differences between the Sigelman and Simpson (1977), Hardy (1979), and Weede (1981) studies in detail. While Hardy (1979) accused Sigelman and Simpson (1977) of a defective research design, in particular of not consistently avoiding ratio variables, Weede (1981) could demonstrate that it does not really matter whether one applies Sigelman and Simpson's or Hardy's procedure. Moreover, substantial conclusions in all three studies are fairly similar to each other. Therefore, my attempt to uncover the reasons for Muller's deviant results will contrast his work on the one hand and the three pieces of previous work on the other hand.[2]

While Sigelman and Simpson, Hardy and, to a lesser degree, Weede relied on Paukert's (1973) inequality data, Muller thinks that we can and should do better. That is why he collected upper-quintile income shares *ca.* 1960 and *ca.* 1970 from a number of previous compilations. Previously, Weede (1986b) accepted the idea that Muller's (1985) data are somewhat better than those used by other researchers but still questioned his conclusions. The purpose of this paper is to move beyond Muller's data-base and to find out whether other inequality data-sets support Muller or not.

Muller's work, however, differs from *all* previous studies in other respects as well. His dependent variable is the natural logarithm of deaths from political violence per million inhabitants (plus one).[3] In choosing deaths from political violence as the only indicator of political violence, Muller (1985: 51) accepted Weede's (1981) previous warnings of reporting bias in armed attacks which might be transferred to a composite index. In insisting on the standardisation of deaths by population *before* the regression, he rejects Weede's (1981) and Sigelman and Simpson's (1977) or, for that matter, Hibbs'[4] (1973) procedure of implicitly standardising violence *within the regression* by entering population as another independent variable. Muller's procedure implies that we regard a nation that is twice as populous as another one as equally violent as the smaller one only if we observe exactly twice as many deaths from political violence. Standardising violence within the regression avoids *a priori* commitments of this kind. Since it is difficult to argue persuasively in favour of either strategy, we should find out whether the difference in standardisation for population-size effects really matters. As previously noted (Weede, 1986b), it does not. Therefore, I can safety accept Muller's procedure.[5]

In so far as the time-spread of available inequality measures permitted, the previous work by Sigelman and Simpson, Hardy, and Weede was cross-sectional. By contrast, Muller argues that inequality today affects violence about five years later. That is why he specifies the death rate to be a time-lagged function of income inequality. While the difference between Muller's and previous practice is easy to grasp, I find it difficult to accept either the idea that time-lagging is a substantial improvement or that it should affect results. Neither Muller nor any previous researcher made a theoretical defense of lagging or not lagging. In general, income inequality is fairly stable over short periods of time, such as a mere five years.[6] If we had access to time-series data, we could rarely attribute observable short-run changes in income shares to true change rather than to measurement error.[7] Moreover, Muller is as incapable of sticking to five year lags as earlier researchers were of using truly simultaneous measurements. Since income inequality data refer to *different years* between either 1958–62 or 1968–72. Muller's lags differ from nation to nation.

Where inequality data refer to 1958 (or 1968), lags are longer than where they refer to 1962 (or 1972). In itself, the time spread of inequality measures makes it impossible to take a strong position on the lagging issue—whether in favor of lags or against lags.[8] That is why I feel that we—not only participants in the published debate but the social science community at large—are in trouble if lagging or not lagging matters. As earlier demonstrated (Weede, 1986b) we are indeed in trouble: without lagging, Muller's relationship between *ca.* 1970 income inequality and violence is reduced to insignificance.

In my view, the simple fact that inequality *ca.* 1970 seems related to violence in the mid-seventies, but *un*related to violence *ca.* 1970 should be sufficient reason for doubts and concern. Nevertheless, I shall accept Muller's five-year-lag and thereby bias my study in favor of reproducing his results. If I do not replicate them, then there are very strong reasons to doubt his positive link between inequality and violence.

In multiple regression analysis the relationship between inequality and political violence is affected by control variables. Again, Muller applies a different and somewhat longer list of control variables than previous researchers. In one respect, Muller's list is obviously superior to the earlier ones. He alone included regime repressiveness in his equations. This variable turned out to have a stronger impact on political violence than any other one. Therefore, one might reject earlier research and accept Muller's results as the best available.

In my view, this would be a premature response. Muller (1985: 58) also applies ethnolinguistic fractionalisation and government sanctions per million as control variables. Since the former control variable does not even come close to significance, we should omit it, as Muller himself recognised for the mid-1970s. It is plausible to stipulate that government sanctions affect political violence. But does it make sense to standardise sanctions—for example: press censorship, curfew, or martial law—by population? Does a government ruling twice as populous a nation as another one require twice as many such sanctions in order to be considered equally coercive? In my view, the imposition of press censorship or martial law (if it ever happened) would be as coercive in Canada as in the US rather than about ten times as coercive because of the different population size. Moreover, it is hard to understand not only why Muller standardises sanctions by population, but also why he keeps this insignificant predictor in his equation. Admittedly, it is unlikely that the elimination of insignificant and poorly operationalised independent variables makes much difference. It is also easy to find out by focusing on the major and less dubious control variables only.

Since Muller's inclusion of the regime repressiveness variable looks more important than his inclusion of the dubious sanctions per million variable, one may still be inclined to accept his rather than earlier results. But there is another specification difference. None of the earlier researchers included a lagged violence term in his equations. Muller did. Since the lagged violence term is highly significant and contributes more to the explanation of later violence than inequality or most other independent variables do, this issue matters. Weede (1986b) demonstrated that the effects of inequality on later violence become insignificant once the lagged violence term has been eliminated. Is inclusion or exclusion of the lagged violence variable preferable? On the one hand, it is plausible to argue that violence begets violence. Therefore, the lagged term should be included. On the other hand, it is almost impossible to make theoretical sense out of the contradictory findings resulting from exclusion or inclusion of previous violence. The regression equation including a lagged violence term may be so rearranged that the left side of it contains the difference between current violence and (weighted) previous violence. Income inequality affects this difference between current and previous violence.[9] But it does not significantly increase current violence in an equation without previous violence. Why does inequality seem to affect the persistence of violence differently from new violence? In analysing a new and different data set, we might be lucky and get similar results whether we include or exclude a lagged violence term. (Or, we might be stuck with the problem.)

Weede's (1986b) criticism of Muller's (1985) paper claimed that Muller's positive link between inequality *ca.* 1970 and violence is more tenuous and less robust than Muller admits. First, it depends on relating inequality to later rather than simultaneous violence. Second, it depends on regressing *later* violence on inequality *and earlier violence* (and some other control variables like regime repressiveness). Third, it depends very much on Zimbabwe (formerly Rhodesia), which is the worst outlier on violence in Muller's sample. Muller's (1986) response to Weede very much focused on the outlier problem and argues that Panama is an even more influential case than Zimbabwe, and that one should not delete Zimbabwe only, but either Panama only or Panama and Zimbabwe or Panama, Zimbabwe, and Argentina in exploring the robustness of the inequality-violence linkage. I shall give special attention to these cases below.

Data and Analyses

Muller's (1995: 50) major source of upper quintile income shares *ca.* 1970 is the World Bank (1979, 1982). Muller also took some data from Ahluwalia (1976) and Jain (1975) who have previously been affiliated with the World Bank and published their data and analyses under World Bank auspices. Presumably, the World Bank team compiling income inequality data for the World Development Reports knew about Ahluwalia's (1976) and Jain's (1975) in-house efforts and probably about other available inequality data, but decided not to use all of them any more. In my view, non-publication of inequality data within the World Development Reports does not reflect a preference for missing values but a hesitation to include data of dubious quality.

Certainly, Muller was more critical about inequality data than previous authors including myself (Weede, 1981). But the World Bank (1977–1985) seems to be even more cautious and critical. In looking through all these World Development Reports, I could find top 20 per cent income shares in the 1968–72 period for only 25 nations. By contrast, Muller found 51 estimates from a wider variety of sources. These 25 nations constitute my *small* sample. Such a small number of cases is unfortunate. Therefore, I decided to run different risks in different analyses. It is dangerous to accept too wide a time spread of inequality data which are analysed later, *as if* they referred to a single year (Menard, 1986). But it is also dangerous to restrict one's sample size too much. In the small sample I tried to minimise the former danger, in the *large* sample I try to minimise the latter danger by accepting any inequality data in-between 1965 and 1977 published by the World Bank (1979–1985). Of course, where there is a choice the value closest to

1970 is taken. Still this yields top 20 per cent income shares for only 47 nations in the "large" sample.

The basic idea of the research design is to run cross-sectional regressions of violence on income inequality, the level of economic development, regime repressiveness, and earlier violence in both data-sets. The dependent variable is deaths from political violence 1973–77, taken from Taylor and Jodice (1983, 2nd vol.: 48–51). Following Muller's example, deaths are standardised by population *before* the regression and logarithmically transformed. Operationally, violence is ln (deaths per million +1). Of course, the lagged endogenous variable derives from the same source and is defined the same way.[10]

Again following Muller's example, energy consumption *per capita* in 1970 is the indicator of the level of economic development. The data source is Taylor and Jodice (1993, Vol. 1 and the corresponding tape).[11] Regime repressiveness refers to the average score of a nation on civil liberties and political liberties indices ranging from one to seven in the 1973–1977 period. Although originally collected by Gastil and Freedom House, the data are easily available in Taylor and Jodice (1983, Vol. 1 and the corresponding tape). According to Muller, the relationship between regime repressiveness and violence is curvilinear and non-monotonic. That is why we have to add a squared term of repressive-ness, too. Since the two standardised coefficients in a polynomial regression (one for the simple and one for the squared repressiveness term) do not permit a meaningful interpretation, we should use the *un*standardised coefficients from a first regression run as weights for the simple and squared terms respectively, and enter the weighted sum of simple and squared repressiveness instead of both terms in a second regression run. While the sign of the single standardised regression coefficient in the second run is necessarily positive and not meaningful, its absolute magnitude may be compared with other standardised coeffi-cients in the usual manner (see Jagodzinski and Weede, 1981, for tech-nical details).

Table 9.1 refers to the small sample. It defines violence in Muller's way. It accepts his insistence on relating *ca.* 1970 inequality to violence about five years later. It includes the independent variables which had the strongest effects in Muller's analysis or in other previous research. While lagged violence is excluded in the first (and third) column, it is included in the second (and fourth) column, as Muller insists on doing. But to no avail. Income inequality is not significantly related to vio-lence. Worse still, even the sign of the relationship contradicts Muller's expectations. In the small sample at least, more inequality seems (weakly and insignificantly) related to less violence. It is difficult to imagine results which more strongly contradict Muller's previous findings than the ones in Table 9.1.

Previously, I argued (Weede, 1986b) that there are three ways to call Muller's findings into question. One can relate inequality to simultaneous violence instead of later violence: this has not been done in Table 9.1, and could not have been done because there are no regime repressiveness data available for the 1968–72 period. Or, one can elimi-

Table 9.1   Regressions of ln (deaths from political violence per million+1) on Income Inequality, Economic Development, and Regime Repressiveness (small sample)[a]

	(b)	(c)	(b)	(c)
Top 20% income share	−0.024	−0.014	−0.0051	0.024
	0.59	0.74	0.91	0.55
	−.12	−0.07	−0.03	0.13
ln energy consumption	0.26	0.54	0.19	0.61
per capita 1970	0.34	0.06	0.48	0.03
	0.26	0.55	0.24	0.75
Death rate, 68–72		0.46		0.58
	—	0.04	—	0.01
		0.46		0.68
Regime repressiveness	2.81	2.41	1.82	1.00
1973–77	0.00	0.01	0.07	0.23
Regime repressiveness	−0.34	−0.28	−0.20	−0.078
squared	0.01	0.02	0.13	0.49
Beta of				
b1 regime	0.81	0.76	0.73	0.72
repressiveness				
+b2 regime				
repressiveness				
squared				
Constant	−3.57	−6.15	−2.90	−7.05
N	25	25	23	23
Adjusted R^2	0.26	0.38	0.16	0.44

Notes: (a) In the first five panels. First cell entries are unstandardised regression coefficients, second cell entries are significance levels in two-tailed tests, and third cell entries are standardised regression coefficients. For computation and interpretation of the standardised regression coefficient in the sixth panel, which summarises the curvilinear effect of repressiveness, see Jagodzinski and Weede (1981). The significance of the curvilinear effect should be judged according to the performance of simple and squared terms in the first regression run (panels 4 and 5).

(b) Lagged violence excluded.

(c) Lagged violence included.

nate the lagged violence term: in Table 9.1 this does not make much difference. Or one can eliminate the case of Zimbabwe. This has been
done in Table 9.1, for the World Bank did not publish the estimate
which Muller took from Jain (1975)—i.e., from an earlier World Bank
publication than later World Development Reports. The Bank seems to
have had some second thoughts. So, there might be two good reasons to
eliminate Zimbabwe from the calculations: its outlier status *and* the
dubious validity of its income inequality data.

In other respects, Table 9.1 reaffirms Muller's previous findings.
There is a curvilinear relationship between regime repressiveness and
violence. While either the absence of repression or the ruthless pursuit
of repression minimises violence, intermediate levels of repression look
dangerous, and there might be a positive relationship between a higher
level of economic development (and higher average incomes) on the
one hand and more violence on the other hand. While the strength and
significance of this relationship very much depends on the inclusion of
a lagged violence variable, the positive sign of the relationship fits well
with Muller's findings and contradicts strongly those of Sigelman and
Simpson (1977), Hardy (1979), or Weede (1981).

Muller (1986) suggested that if Zimbabwe is deleted, we should
better delete Panama and, maybe, Argentina. too. In the third and fourth
column of Table 9.1 both of these nations are deleted. Eliminating
Panama only affects results to a lesser degree. The elimination of these
two nations does *not* lead to the significant and positive relationship
between income inequality and violence which Muller (1985) supported
in his study. In particular if the elimination of Argentina and Panama is
combined with the inclusion of a lagged violence term as in the fourth
column of Table 9.1, then the *positive* relationship between the level of
economic development and violence becomes very strong indeed, while
the curvilinear relationship between regime repressiveness and violence
loses significance. Certainly, some results in Table 9.1 constitute problems. The relationships between energy consumption *per capita* and
regime repressiveness on the one hand and violence on the other are
rather strongly affected by the inclusion or exclusion of two influential
cases. But there is a single unambiguous result in Table 9.1: top 20 per
cent income shares and violence are *un*related to each other.

The difference between Tables 9.1 and 9.2 derives from sample
size. Moreover, the lag between inequality and violence, although
close to five years in many cases, varies quite a bit from nation to
nation in Table 9.2 because inequality data refer to different years in
the 1965–77 period. The larger sample has been achieved at a price in
other respects. Fortunately, results in Tables 9.1 and 9.2 are fairly simi-

Table 9.2   Regressions of ln (deaths from political violence per million+1) on Income Inequality, Economic Development, and Regime Repressiveness (large sample)[a]

	(b)	(c)	(b)	(c)
Top 20% income share	F-level insufficient	0.016 0.55 0.06	0.0088 0.74 0.06	0.034 0.21 0.23
ln energy consumption per capita 1970	0.069 0.68 0.09	0.30 0.11 0.36	F-level insufficient	0.31 0.09 0.41
Death rate, 68–72	—	0.46 0.00 0.45	—	0.49 0.00 0.54
Regime repressiveness 1973–77	1.72 0.00	1.62 0.01	1.12 0.06	0.88 0.12
Regime repressiveness squared	−0.22 0.01	−0.20 0.01	−0.14 0.09	−0.095 0.23
Beta of b1 regime repressiveness +b2 regime repressiveness squared	0.51	0.50	0.38	0.42
Constant	−1.75	−4.58	−0.95	−4.71
N	47	46	45	44
Adjusted R^2	0.16	0.29	0.11	0.30

Notes: (a) For explanation of table see note (a) to Table 9.1.
(b) Lagged violence excluded.
(c) Lagged violence included.

lar to each other. Income inequality is still not significantly related to more violence. And this result is robust over the inclusion or exclusion of influential cases and over the inclusion or exclusion of a lagged violence term. Replacing Muller's data by those in which the World Bank puts some confidence unambiguously destroys the inequality-violence link, even if Muller's (1985, 1986) prescriptions on lagging the inequality-violence relationship, on inclusion of a lagged violence term, and on the influential cases of Argentina and Panama are accepted.

Unfortunately, those results in Table 9.2 which concern the linkages between the level of economic development or repressiveness and violence seem less clear. Exclusion of the two influential cases and inclusion of a lagged violence term weakens the curvilinear relationship between regime repressiveness and violence, while strengthening the relationship between energy consumption *per capita* and violence. But note that the larger sample in Table 9.2 does not produce so strong a positive link between the level of economic development and violence as the smaller sample did in Table 9.1 above.

In analysing the relationship between inequality and violence, we have no choice but to restrict our analysis to a sample where information on inequality is available. Once it has been established that inequality does not affect violence, as has been done above, there is no reason to investigate the linkages between energy consumption *per capita* or regime repressiveness and violence in so small a sample. Using the same data sources as above, we may easily expand the larger sample by a factor of three. Such an expansion should reduce the weight of influential cases. If we are lucky, even inclusion or exclusion of a lagged violence variable no longer affects the very existence of a significant relationship between the level of economic development or repressiveness and violence.

The sample in Table 9.3 refers to all nations for which the World Handbook (Taylor and Jodice, 1983) provides data. Thus, some small, underdeveloped societies with authoritarian governments had to be neglected. But there are no major omissions in the data-set. Whereas the effects of lagged energy consumption *per capita* and regime repressiveness in Table 9.2 above very much depended on the inclusion or exclusion of influential cases, i.e., of Argentina and Panama, and on the inclusion or exclusion of a lagged violence term, Table 9.3 permits a simple and straightforward evaluation of the effects of the level of economic development and regime repressiveness. The level of economic development does not significantly affect (logged) deaths from political violence (per million). There is a weak to moderate curvilinear relationship between regime repressiveness and violence, i.e., intermediate repressiveness evokes more violence than either more or less repression. But smaller samples restricted by data availability on income inequality (Tables 9.1 and 9.2 above; Muller, 1985) seem to exaggerate the strength of the relationship somewhat. Fortunately, previously influential cases (Argentina and Panama) are no longer influential. And the inclusion or exclusion of a lagged death rate affects only the percentage of variance explained, as was to be expected.

Table 9.3   Regressions of ln (deaths from political violence per million+1) on Income Inequality, Economic Development, and Regime Repressiveness (very large sample)[a]

	(b)	(c)	(b)	(c)
Top 20% income share	-0.81	0.094	-0.095	0.082
	0.50	0.40	0.43	0.46
	-0.07	0.08	-0.08	0.07
Death rate, 68–72		0.40		0.40
	—	0.00	—	0.00
		0.47		0.48
Regime repressiveness	1.35	1.11	1.23	1.00
1973–77	0.01	0.01	0.01	0.02
Regime repressiveness	-1.17	-0.14	-0.15	-0.12
squared	0.01	0.01	0.01	0.02
Beta of				
b1 regime	0.26	0.22	0.24	0.20
repressiveness				
+b2 regime				
repressiveness				
squared				
Constant	-1.14	-1.55	0.079	-1.34
N	126	126	124	124
Adjusted R^2	0.06	0.26	0.06	0.26

Notes: (a) For explanation of table see note (a) to Table 9.1.
(b) Lagged violence excluded.
(c) Lagged violence included.

Conclusion

For good reasons Muller (1985: 52) underlined that macro-hypotheses about the relationship between income inequality and violence do not *necessarily* correspond to any particular micro-theory about individual behavior. This caveat notwithstanding, it seems most straightforward to link macro-relationships between the level of economic development or inequality and violence with a deprivation perspective and to link a macro-relationship between regime repressiveness and violence with a rational action, resource mobilisation or political power approach.

Except for Muller's contribution, most previous researchers seemed to discover a negative relationship between the level of economic development and violence and a negligible, although occasionally significant relationship between inequality and violence. According to

Muller, the relationship between the level of economic development and violence might be positive rather than negative and there is a moderately strong relationship between inequality and violence. As Weede (1986b) has outlined in his criticism of Muller's (1985) paper, Muller's results depend heavily on relating inequality or development in t to violence in t+5, on explaining later violence by earlier violence among other causes, and on influential cases like Zimbabwe. Muller's (1986) response largely focused on the influential cases issue, on whether Argentina and Panama or Zimbabwe or all of them should be deleted in order to reduce the weight of outliers. Whether they prefer Muller's or Weede's arguments and conclusions, most readers of the debate are likely to be rather unhappy with the weight of technical considerations.

That is why this paper has attempted a new approach by moving beyond Muller's inequality data set and analysing World Bank data on income inequality only. Muller's divergent results should be replicable with other data, too. Moreover, I hoped that the effects of inequality on violence would not depend as much on the inclusion or exclusion of a lagged violence term and on influential cases in the new data set as in Muller's. Fortunately, this hope has been largely fulfilled. So, we get rather unambiguous results from the new analyses.

First, income inequality does *not* increase violence in the data set compiled from World Development Reports. This finding rests on analyses which accepted Muller's five year lag between inequality and violence. It still holds if one accepts Muller's suggestion to include earlier violence as a determinant of later violence. It holds whether you include or exclude Argentina or Panama. If *all* the technical problems disputed between Muller (1986) and Weede (1986b) are resolved in Muller's favour, but another compilation of data is analysed, then we reproduce the close-to-zero relationship between inequality and violence reported by earlier researchers (Sigelman and Simpson, 1977; Hardy, 1979; Weede, 1981; Powell, 1982) and not Muller's (1985, 1986) moderately strong link between inequality and violence. As Weede (1986b) has demonstrated before, acceptance of Muller's data in itself is insufficient to produce his results. You have to accept all of his technical recommendations on lags, earlier violence and outliers, too.[12] Summarising earlier research and controversy, I cannot see convincing and easily replicable evidence in favour of a theoretically or statistically significant relationship between inequality and violence.

Second, the effects of the level of economic development, as operationalised by logged energy consumption per capita, and regime repressiveness on violence seem affected by influential cases like Argentina and Panama and by the inclusion or exclusion of earlier violence as a determinant of later violence, but only if analyses are based on a sample restricted by data availability on income inequality. But since income inequality does not robustly and significantly affect violence, there is no reason to accept a major limitation of the sample size where the purpose is to evaluate the effects of development and/or regime repressiveness on violence.

Third, in large global samples there is no significant relationship between the level of economic development and violence. All contrary reports from much smaller samples (Sigelman and Simpson, 1977; Hardy, 1979; Weede, 1981; Muller, 1985) should be viewed with equal suspicion, whether they report a negative link or come close to suggesting that it might be positive.

Fourth, in large global samples there still is a significant curvilinear relationship between regime repressiveness and violence where intermediate repressiveness maximises violence and either extreme reduces it. While the relationship is not as strong as Muller's (1985) much smaller sample suggested, it at least survives.

Taken together the macro-relationships give little comfort to deprivation theorists. Neither the level of development which is, of course, closely related to average incomes and standards of living, nor income inequality seems to affect violence. Neither average nor relative deprivation seems to matter. But regime repressiveness influences the incidence of violence, as it should if people behave rationally, consider the likely consequences of their actions, and take the realities of power into account. While the relationship between regime repressiveness and violence is rather weak in a large sample, it is the only robust and significant cross-national result and it is compatible with a rational action, resource mobilisation or political power view of social conflict.

Notes

1. "Welcome," that is, from a rational action, resource mobilisation or political process approach to political violence.

2. Since Powell's (1982) analysis refers to democracies only, while all other studies concern all political regimes where data are available, I shall not investigate the reasons why Powell (1982) and Muller (1985) arrive at different conclusions on the inequality-violence relationship. By restricting his analysis to democracies Powell (1982) implicitly controlled for regime repressiveness, i.e., for the dominant explanatory variable in Muller's (1985) study. By definition, regime repressiveness in democracies is low.

3. Since some nations score zero deaths from political violence and since the log of zero is not defined, the increment has to be added before logging.

4. Sigelman and Simpson (1977) and Weede (1981) borrowed the procedure from Hibbs (1973).

5. I also did it the other way, following the example of Hibbs (1973), Sigelman and Simpson (1977), or Weede (1981) and obtained more or less the same results.

6. The correlation between Muller's inequality data *ca.* 1960 and *ca.* 1970 is 0.85. For a five year difference it should be still higher. But see Menard (1986) for a dissenting view on the stability of income inequality.

7. The reliability of difference scores approaches zero if the average reliability of cross-sectional measures is of the same order of magnitude as is stability over time. See Guilford (1954: 394) for the relevant formula.

8. Of course, the aggregation of deaths from political violence over five years also adds to the problem of lags differing from nation to nation. Most of the violence might occur in the first year of the aggregation period and thereby effectively shorten the lag. Or, most of the violence might occur in the last year of the period and thereby lengthen the lag.

9. The difference between current violence and previous violence is almost certainly much less reliable than raw violence are. The reliability of difference scores depends on the reliability of both sets of raw scores and on their stability over time (see Guilford 1954: 394). The correlation of violence 1968–72 with violence 1973–77 is 0.51 in Muller's sample. If the reliability of raw scores were 0.9. the reliability of difference scores would be only 0.8. If the reliability of raw scores were 0.8, the reliability of difference scores would be only 0.59.

10. Since earlier violence data are missing for Bangladesh, this case has to be deleted wherever there is a lagged violence term.

11. Since Taylor and Jodice (1993) do not report energy consumption *per capita* for Bangladesh in 1970, I took the 1973 estimate from Ballmer-Cao and Scheidegger (1979: 185).

12. In particular (if you want to reproduce Muller's findings), you must not eliminate only Zimbabwe from the analysis, as I did. But the World Bank did not reprint information about Zimbabwe's income distribution from an earlier World Bank source on which Muller relied. This fact in itself makes the Zimbabwe data suspect. Moreover, the meaning of Zimbabwe's income inequality (whatever it was *ca.* 1970 when the country still was named Rhodesia) is different from elsewhere. Except for South Africa there are few nations where race and income are as closely correlated as they probably were in Rhodesia. The racial stigmata of the poor in southern Africa affect mobility opportunities and thereby an obvious alternative to collective action.

References

Ahluwalia M S. (1976): "Inequality, Poverty, and Development." *Journal of Development Economics*. 3: 307–342.

Allison P D. (1977): "Testing for Interaction in Multiple Regression." *American Journal of Sociology*. 83: 144–153.

Ballmer-Cao T-H and Scheidegger J. (1979): *Compendium of Data for World System Analysis*. Zurich: Soziologisches Institut der Universität.

Coleman J S. (1978): "A Theory of Revolt Within an Authority Structure." *Peace Science Society International Papers*. 28: 15–28.

Davies J C. (1962): "Toward a Theory of Revolution." *American Sociological Review*. 27: 5–19.

Deutsch K W. (1961): "Social Mobilization and Political Development." *American Political Science Review*. 55: 493–514.

Dollard J *et al.* (1939): *Frustration and Aggression*. New Haven. Conn.: Yale University Press.

Eckstein H. (1980): "Theoretical Approaches to Explaining Collective Political Violence." Pp. 135–166 in Gurr T R. (ed): *Handbook of Political Conflict*. New York: Free Press.

Feierabend I K and R L. (1966): "Aggressive Behaviors within Polities 1948–1962: A Cross-National Study." *Journal of Conflict Resolution*. 10: 249–271.

Guilford J P. (1954): *Psychometric Methods*. New York: McGraw-Hill.

Gurr T R. (1968): "A Causal Model of Civil Strife." *American Political Science Review*. 62: 1104–1124:

——— (1970): *Why Men Rebel*. Princeton: University Press.

Gurr T R and Duvall R. (1973): "Civil Conflict in the 1960s." *Comparative Political Studies*. 6: 135–169.

Hardy M A. (1979): "Economic Growth, Distributional Inequality, and Political Conflict in Industrial Societies." *Journal of Political and Military Sociology*. 5: 209–227

Hibbs D A. (1973): *Mass Political Violence*. New York: Wiley.

Huntington S P. (1968): *Political Order in Changing Societies*. New Haven. Conn.: Yale University Press.

Jagodzinski W and Weede E. (1981): "Testing Curvilinear Propositions by Polynomial Regression with Particular Reference to the Interpretation of Standardized Solutions." *Quality and Quantity*. 15: 447–463.

Jain S. (1975): *The Size Distribution of Income. A Compilation of Data*, Washington. D.C.: World Bank.

Kuhn T. (1962): *The Structure of Scientific Revolutions*. Chicago: University Press.

Lakatos I. (1968/69): "Criticism and the Methodology of Scientific Research Programs." *Proceedings of the Aristotelean Society*. LXIX: 149–186.

Menard S. (1986): "A Research Note on International Comparisons of Inequality of Income," *Social Forces*. 64: 778–793.

Muller E N. (1979): *Aggressive Political Participation*. Princeton University Press.

——— (1980): "The Psychology of Political Protest and Violence." Pp. 69–99 in Gurr T R. (ed): *Handbook of Political Conflict*. New York: Free Press.

——— (1985): "Income Inequality, Regime Repressiveness, and Political Violence." *American Sociological Review*. 50: 47–61.

——— (1986): "Income Inequality and Political Violence. The Effect of Influential Cases." *American Sociological Review*. 51: 441–445.

Nagel J. (1974): "Inequality and Discontent." *World Politics* 26: 453–472.

——— (1976): "Erratum." *World Politics*. 28: 315.

Oberschall A. (1973): *Social Conflict and Social Movements*. Englewood Cliffs, New Jersey: Prentice-Hall.

Parvin M. (1973): "Economic Determinants of Political Unrest." *Journal of Conflict Resolution*. 17: 271–296.

Paukert F. (1973): "Income Distribution at Different Levels of Development." *International Labour Review*. 108: 97–125.

Powell G B. (1982): *Contemporary Democracies. Participation, Stability, and Violence*, Cambridge, Mass.: Harvard University Press.

Russett B M. (1964): "Inequality and Instability. The Relation of Land Tenure to Politics." *World Politics*. 16: 442–454.

Sigelman L and Simpson M. (1977): "A Cross-National Test of the Linkage between Economic Inequality and Political Violence." *Journal of Conflict Resolution*. 21: 105–128.

Snyder D. (1978): "Collective Violence." *Journal of Conflict Resolution*. 22: 499–534.

Taylor C L and Judice D A. (1983): *World Handbook of Political and Social Indicators*. 3rd ed. 2 vols, New Haven, Conn.: Yale University Press.

Tilly C. (1975): "Revolutions and Collective Violence." Pp. 483–555 in Greenstein F I and Polsby N W. (eds): *Handbook of* Political Science. vol. III, Reading, Mass: Addison-Wesley.

———— (1978): *From Mobilization to Revolution*. Reading, Mass.: Addison-Wesley.

Tullock G. (1974): *The Social Dilemma: The Economics of War and Revolution*. Blacksburg, Virginia: University Publications.

Weede E. (1975): "Unzufriedenheit. Protest und Gewalt." *Politische Vierteljahresschrift*. 16: 409–428.

———— (1977): *Hypothesen, Gleichungen und Daten*, Kronsberg/Taunus: Athenaeum.

———— (1981): "Income Inequality, Average Income, and Domestic Violence." *Journal of Conflict Resolution*. 25: 639–653.

———— (1985): "Dilemmas of Social Order: Collective and Positional Goods, Leadership and Political Conflict." *Sociological Theory*. 3(2): 46–57.

———— (1986a): *Konfliktforschung, Opladen: Westdeutsher Verlag*.

———— (1986b): "Income Inequality and Political Violence Reconsidered. Comment on Muller." *American Sociological Review*. 51: 438–441.

World Bank (1979 to 1985): *World Development Report(s)*. yearly. New York: Oxford University Press.

Zimmermann E. (1980): "Macro-Quantitative Research on Political Protest." Pp. 167–237 in Gurr T R. (ed): *Handbook of Political Conflict*. New York: Free Press.

———— (1983): *Political Violence. Crises and Revolutions*. Cambridge. Mass.: Schenkman.

PART 3

The Classic Thesis:
Convergence or Divergence?

CHAPTER 10

The Five Stages of Growth

W. W. ROSTOW

Early research on economic underdevelopment suggested that the problem was only short-term and that in the end all countries would become rich. In this excerpt from W. W. Rostow's classic work, *The Stages of Economic Growth,* Rostow outlines this optimistic scenario by positing five stages of economic development all societies eventually experience as they mature into industrialized developed countries: tradition, the preconditions for takeoff, the takeoff, the drive to maturity, and the age of high mass consumption. Although this tremendously influential publication did not focus specifically on the causes of the gaps, the author suggests the reason they arise and their potential resolution. As a country moves out of the traditional stage and prepares for economic takeoff, its economy begins to grow much faster than the economies of countries that remain in the first stage. The gap between rich and poor would then be explained by the fact that not all countries enter the development process at the same time. Thus the gap between rich and poor countries would be expected to disappear as the countries progress into the later stages of growth. As a country progresses through the stages of development, those who adopt the new economic rules and succeed accumulate the profits of their success and internal inequality arises. As more people join the monied economy and play by the new rules, the extent of the inequality should diminish.

Reprinted with permission of Cambridge University Press from *The Stages of Economic Growth* by W. W. Rostow, pp. 4–12. New York: Cambridge University Press, 1990.

I T IS POSSIBLE TO IDENTIFY ALL SOCIETIES, IN THEIR ECONOMIC DIMENSIONS, as lying within one of five categories: the traditional society, the preconditions for take-off, the take-off, the drive to maturity, and the age of high mass-consumption.

The Traditional Society

First, the traditional society. A traditional society is one whose structure is developed within limited production functions, based on pre-Newtonian science and technology, and on pre-Newtonian attitudes towards the physical world. Newton is here used as a symbol for that watershed in history when men came widely to believe that the external world was subject to a few knowable laws, and was systematically capable of productive manipulation.

The conception of the traditional society is, however, in no sense static; and it would not exclude increases in output. Acreage could be expanded; some *ad hoc* technical innovations, often highly productive innovations, could be introduced in trade, industry and agriculture; productivity could rise with, for example, the improvement of irrigation works or the discovery and diffusion of a new crop. But the central fact about the traditional society was that a ceiling existed on the level of attainable output per head. This ceiling resulted from the fact that the potentialities which flow from modern science and technology were either not available or not regularly and systematically applied.

Both in the longer past and in recent times the story of traditional societies was thus a story of endless change. The area and volume of trade within them and between them fluctuated, for example, with the degree of political and social turbulence, the efficiency of central rule, the upkeep of the roads. Population—and, within limits, the level of life—rose and fell not only with the sequence of the harvests, but with the incidence of war and of plague. Varying degrees of manufacture developed; but, as in agriculture, the level of productivity was limited by the inaccessibility of modern science, its applications, and its frame of mind.

Generally speaking, these societies, because of the limitation on productivity, had to devote a very high proportion of their resources to agriculture; and flowing from the agricultural system there was an hierarchical social structure, with relatively narrow scope—but some scope—for vertical mobility. Family and clan connexions played a large role in social organization. The value system of these societies was generally geared to what might be called a long-run fatalism; that is, the assumption that the range of possibilities open to one's grandchildren would be just about what it had been for one's grandparents. But this long-run fatalism by no means excluded the short-run option that, within a considerable range, it was possible and legitimate for the individual to strive to improve his lot, within his lifetime. In Chinese villages, for example, there was an endless struggle to acquire or to avoid losing land, yielding a situation where land rarely remained within the same family for a century.

Although central political rule—in one form or another—often existed in traditional societies, transcending the relatively self-sufficient regions, the centre of gravity of political power generally lay in the regions, in the hands of those who owned or controlled the land. The landowner maintained fluctuating but usually profound influence over such central political power as existed, backed by its entourage of civil servants and soldiers, imbued with attitudes and controlled by interests transcending the regions.

In terms of history then, with the phrase "traditional society" we are grouping the whole pre-Newtonian world: the dynasties in China; the civilization of the Middle East and the Mediterranean; the world of medieval Europe. And to them we add the post-Newtonian societies which, for a time, remained untouched or unmoved by man's new capability for regularly manipulating his environment to his economic advantage.

To place these infinitely various, changing societies in a single category, on the ground that they all shared a ceiling on the productivity of their economic techniques, is to say very little indeed. But we are, after all, merely clearing the way in order to get at the subject of this book; that is, the post-traditional societies, in which each of the major characteristics of the traditional society was altered in such ways as to permit regular growth: its politics, social structure, and (to a degree) its values, as well as its economy.

The Preconditions for Take-off

The second stage of growth embraces societies in the process of transition; that is, the period when the preconditions for take-off are developed; for it takes time to transform a traditional society in the ways necessary for it to exploit the fruits of modern science, to fend off diminishing returns, and thus to enjoy the blessings and choices opened up by the march of compound interest.

The preconditions for take-off were initially developed, in a clearly marked way, in Western Europe of the late seventeenth and early eighteenth centuries as the insights of modern science began to be translated into new production functions in both agriculture and industry, in a setting given dynamism by the lateral expansion of world markets and the international competition for them. But all that lies behind the break-up of the Middle Ages is relevant to the creation of the preconditions for take-off in Western Europe. Among the Western European states, Britain, favoured by geography, natural resources, trading possibilities, social and political structure, was the first to develop fully the preconditions for take-off.

The more general case in modern history, however, saw the stage of preconditions arise not endogenously but from some external intrusion by more advanced societies. These invasions—literal or figurative— shocked the traditional society and began or hastened its undoing; but they also set in motion ideas and sentiments which initiated the process by which a modern alternative to the traditional society was constructed out of the old culture.

The idea spreads not merely that economic progress is possible, but that economic progress is a necessary condition for some other purpose, judged to be good: be it national dignity, private profit, the general welfare, or a better life for the children. Education, for some at least, broadens and changes to suit the needs of modern economic activity. New types of enterprising men come forward—in the private economy, in government, or both—willing to mobilize savings and to take risks in pursuit of profit or modernization. Banks and other institutions for mobilizing capital appear. Investment increases, notably in transport, communications, and in raw materials in which other nations may have an economic interest. The scope of commerce, internal and external, widens. And, here and there, modern manufacturing enterprise appears, using the new methods. But all this activity proceeds at a limited pace within an economy and a society still mainly characterized by traditional low-productivity methods, by the old social structure and values, and by the regionally based political institutions that developed in conjunction with them.

In many recent cases, for example, the traditional society persisted side by side with modern economic activities, conducted for limited economic purposes by a colonial or quasi-colonial power.

Although the period of transition—between the traditional society and the take-off—saw major changes in both the economy itself and in the balance of social values, a decisive feature was often political. Politically, the building of an effective centralized national state—on the basis of coalitions touched with a new nationalism, in opposition to the traditional landed regional interests, the colonial power, or both, was a decisive aspect of the preconditions period; and it was, almost universally, a necessary condition for take-off. . . .

The Take-off

We come now to the great watershed in the life of modern societies: the third stage in this sequence, the take-off. The take-off is the interval when the old blocks and resistances to steady growth are finally overcome. The forces making for economic progress, which yielded limited bursts and enclaves of modern activity, expand and come to dominate the society. Growth becomes its normal condition. Compound interest becomes built, as it were, into its habits and institutional structure.

In Britain and the well-endowed parts of the world populated substantially from Britain (the United States, Canada, etc.) the proximate stimulus for take-off was mainly (but not wholly) technological. In the more general case, the take-off awaited not only the build-up of social overhead capital and a surge of technological development in industry and agriculture, but also the emergence to political power of a group prepared to regard the modernization of the economy as serious, high-order political business.

During the take-off, the rate of effective investment and savings may rise from say, 5 percent of the national income to 10 percent or more; although where heavy social overhead capital investment was required to create the technical preconditions for take-off the investment rate in the preconditions period could be higher than 5 percent, as, for example, in Canada before the 1890s and Argentina before 1914. In such cases capital imports usually formed a high proportion of total investment in the preconditions period and sometimes even during the take-off itself, as in Russia and Canada during their pre-1914 railway booms.

During the take-off new industries expand rapidly, yielding profits a large proportion of which are reinvested in new plants; and these new industries, in turn, stimulate, through their rapidly expanding requirement for factory workers, the services to support them, and for other manufactured goods, a further expansion in urban areas and in other modern industrial plants. The whole process of expansion in the modern sector yields an increase of income in the hands of those who not only save at high rates but place their savings at the disposal of those engaged in modern sector activities. The new class of entrepreneurs expands; and it directs the enlarging flows of investment in the private sector. The economy exploits hitherto unused natural resources and methods of production.

New techniques spread in agriculture as well as industry, as agriculture is commercialized, and increasing numbers of farmers are prepared to accept the new methods and the deep changes they bring to ways of life. The revolutionary changes in agricultural productivity are an essential condition for successful take-off; for modernization of a society increases radically its bill for agricultural products. In a decade or two both the basic structure of the economy and the social and political structure of the society are transformed in such a way that a steady rate of growth can be, thereafter, regularly sustained.

. . . One can approximately allocate the take-off of Britain to the two decades after 1783; France and the United States to the several decades preceding 1860; Germany, the third quarter of the nineteenth century; Japan, the fourth quarter of the nineteenth century; Russia and China the quarter-century or so preceding 1914; while during the 1950s India and China have, in quite different ways, launched their respective take-offs.

The Drive to Maturity

After take-off there follows a long interval of sustained if fluctuating progress, as the now regularly growing economy drives to extend modern technology over the whole front of its economic activity. Some 10–20 percent of the national income is steadily invested, permitting output regularly to outstrip the increase in population. The make-up of the economy changes unceasingly as technique improves, new industries accelerate, older industries level off. The economy finds its place in the international economy: goods formerly imported are produced at home; new import requirements develop, and new export commodities to match them. The society makes such terms as it will with the requirements of modern efficient production, balancing off the new against the older values and institutions, or revising the latter in such ways as to support rather than to retard the growth process.

Some sixty years after take-off begins (say, forty years after the end of take-off) what may be called maturity is generally attained. The economy, focused during the take-off around a relatively narrow complex of industry and technology, has extended its range into more refined and technologically often more complex processes; for example, there may be a shift in focus from the coal, iron, and heavy engineering industries of the railway phase to machine-tools, chemicals, and electrical equipment. This, for example, was the transition through which Germany, Britain, France, and the United States had passed by the end of the nineteenth century or shortly thereafter. But there are other sectoral patterns which have been followed in the sequence from take-off to maturity. . . .

Formally, we can define maturity as the stage in which an economy demonstrates the capacity to move beyond the original industries which powered its take-off and to absorb and to apply efficiently over a very wide range of its resources—if not the whole range—the most advanced fruits of (then) modern technology. This is the stage in which an economy demonstrates that it has the technological and entrepreneurial skills to produce not everything, but anything that it chooses to produce. It may lack (like contemporary Sweden and Switzerland, for example) the raw materials or other supply conditions required to produce a given type of output economically; but its dependence is a matter of economic choice or political priority rather than a technological or institutional necessity.

Historically, it would appear that something like sixty years was required to move a society from the beginning of take-off to maturity. Analytically the explanation for some such interval may lie in the powerful arithmetic of compound interest applied to the capital stock, combined with the broader consequences for a society's ability to absorb modern technology of three successive generations living under a regime where growth is the normal condition. But, clearly, no dogmatism is justified about the exact length of the interval from take-off to maturity.

The Age of High Mass-Consumption

We come now to the age of high mass-consumption, where, in time, the leading sectors shift towards durable consumers' goods and services: a phase from which Americans are beginning to emerge; whose not unequivocal joys Western Europe and Japan are beginning energetically to probe; and with which Soviet society is engaged in an uneasy flirtation.

As societies achieved maturity in the twentieth century two things happened: real income per head rose to a point where a large number of persons gained a command over consumption which transcended basic food, shelter, and clothing; and the structure of the working force changed in ways which increased not only the proportion of urban to total population, but also the proportion of the population working in offices or in skilled factory jobs—aware of and anxious to acquire the consumption fruits of a mature economy.

In addition to these economic changes, the society ceased to accept the further extension of modern technology as an overriding objective. It is in this post-maturity stage, for example, that, through the political process, Western societies have chosen to allocate increased resources to social welfare and security. The emergence of the welfare state is one manifestation of a society's moving beyond technical maturity; but it is also at this stage that resources tend increasingly to be directed to the production of consumers' durables and to the diffusion of services on a mass basis, if consumers' sovereignty reigns. The sewing-machine, the bicycle, and then the various electric-powered household gadgets were gradually diffused. Historically, however, the decisive element has been the cheap mass automobile with its quite revolutionary effects—social as well as economic—on the life and expectations of society.

For the United States, the turning point was, perhaps, Henry Ford's moving assembly line of 1913–14; but it was in the 1920s, and again in the post-war decade, 1946–56, that this stage of growth was pressed to, virtually, its logical conclusion. In the 1950s Western Europe and Japan appeared to have fully entered this phase, accounting substantially for a momentum in their economies quite unexpected in the immediate post-war years. The Soviet Union is technically ready for this stage, and, by every sign, its citizens hunger for it; but Communist leaders face difficult political and social problems of adjustment if this stage is launched.

Beyond Consumption

Beyond, it is impossible to predict, except perhaps to observe that Americans, at least, have behaved in the past decade as if diminishing relative marginal utility sets in, after a point, for durable consumers' goods; and they have chosen, at the margin, larger families—behavior in the pattern of Buddenbrooks dynamics.[1] Americans have behaved as if, having been born into a system that provided economic security and high mass-consumption, they placed a lower valuation on acquiring additional increments of real income in the conventional form as opposed to the advantages and values of an enlarged family. But even in this adventure in generalization it is a shade too soon to create—on the basis of one case—a new stage-of-growth, based on babies, in succession to the age of consumers' durables: as economists might say, the income-elasticity of demand for babies may well vary from society to society. But it is true that the implications of the baby boom along with the not wholly unrelated deficit in social overhead capital are likely to dominate the American economy over the next decade rather than the further diffusion of consumers' durables.

Here then, in an impressionistic rather than an analytic way, are the stages-of-growth which can be distinguished once a traditional society begins its modernization: the transitional period when the preconditions for take-off are created generally in response to the forces making for modernization; the take-off itself; the sweep into maturity generally taking up the life of about two further generations; and then, finally, if the rise of income has matched the spread of technological virtuosity (which, as we shall see, it need not immediately do) the diversion of the fully mature economy to the provision of durable consumers' goods and services (as well as the welfare state) for its increasingly urban—and then suburban—populations. Beyond lies the question of whether or not secular spiritual stagnation will arise, and, if it does, how man might fend it off. . . .

Notes

1. In Thomas Mann's novel of three generations, the first sought money; the second, born to money, sought social and civic position; the third, born to comfort and family prestige, looked to the life of music. The phrase is designed to suggest, then, the changing aspirations of generations, as they place a low value on what they take for granted and seek new forms of satisfaction.

CHAPTER 11

Catching Up, Forging Ahead, and Falling Behind

MOSES ABRAMOVITZ

In this chapter, Moses Abramovitz explains convergence theory, the idea that there is an inverse relationship between the level and rate of productivity growth: labor productivity in poor countries is thought to have a higher potential for rapid growth than in rich countries. The expectation is that over time the GNP/pc growth rates of poor countries will be more rapid than those of the rich, and thus the gap between rich and poor countries will close. However, not all poor countries have higher labor productivity rates than rich countries, according to Abramovitz, because they lack the "social capacity" to utilize modern technology. Recently there has been considerable discussion of how developed countries can remain "competitive" with developing countries, where labor costs are often a fraction of those in the developed countries. Abramovitz suggests that this is as much a political as an economic question.

A MONG THE MANY EXPLANATIONS OF THE SURGE OF PRODUCTIVITY growth during the quarter century following World War II, the most prominent is the hypothesis that the countries of the industrialized "West" were able to bring into production a large backlog of unexploited technology. The principal part of this backlog is deemed to have consisted of methods of production and of industrial and commercial organization already in use in the United States at the end of the war, but not yet employed in the other countries of the West. In this hypothesis, the United States is viewed as the "leader," the other countries as "followers" who had the opportunity to "catch up." In conformity with this view, a waning of the opportunity for catching up is frequently advanced as an explanation of the retardation in productivity growth suffered by the same group of followers since 1973. Needless to say, the size of the initial backlog and its subsequent reduction are rarely offered as sole explanations of the speedup and slowdown, but they stand as important parts of the story.

These views about postwar following and catching up suggest a more general hypothesis that the productivity levels of countries tend to converge. And this in turn brings to mind old questions about the emergence of new leaders and the historical and theoretical puzzles that shifts in leadership and relative standing present—matters that in some respects fit only awkwardly with the convergence hypothesis. . . .

I. The Catch-up Hypothesis

The hypothesis asserts that being backward in level of productivity carries a *potential* for rapid advance. Stated more definitely the proposition is that in comparisons across countries the growth rates of productivity in any long period tend to be inversely related to the initial levels of productivity.

The central idea is simple enough. It has to do with the level of technology embodied in a country's capital stock. Imagine that the level of labor productivity were governed entirely by the level of technology embodied in capital stock. In a "leading country," to state things sharply, one may suppose that the technology embodied in each vintage of its stock was at the very frontier of technology at the time of investment. The *technological* age of the stock is, so to speak, the same as its *chronological* age. In an otherwise similar follower whose productivity level is lower, the technological age of the stock is high relative to its chronological age. The stock is obsolete even for its age. When a leader discards old stock and replaces it, the accompanying productivity increase is governed and limited by the advance of knowledge between the time when the old capital was installed and the time it is replaced. Those who are behind, however, have the potential to make a larger leap. New capital can embody the frontier of knowledge, but the capital it replaces was technologically superannuated. So—the larger the technological and, therefore, the productivity gap between leader and follower, the stronger the follower's potential for growth in productivity;

and, other things being equal, the faster one expects the follower's growth rate to be. Followers tend to catch up faster if they are initially more backward.

Viewed in the same simple way, the catch-up process would be self-limiting because as a follower catches up, the possibility of making large leaps by replacing superannuated with best-practice technology becomes smaller and smaller. A follower's potential for growth weakens as its productivity level converges towards that of the leader.

This is the simple central idea. It needs extension and qualification. There are at least four extensions:

(1) The same technological opportunity that permits rapid progress by modernization encourages rapid growth of the capital stock partly because of the returns to modernization itself, and partly because technological progress reduces the price of capital goods relative to the price of labor. So—besides a reduction of technological age towards chronological age, the rate of rise of the capital-labor ratio tends to be higher. Productivity growth benefits on both counts. And if circumstances make for an acceleration in the growth of the capital stock its chronological age also falls.[1]

(2) Growth of productivity also makes for increase in aggregate output. A broader horizon of scale-dependent technological progress then comes into view.

(3) Backwardness carries an opportunity for modernization in disembodied, as well as in embodied, technology.

(4) If countries at relatively low levels of industrialization contain large numbers of redundant workers in farming and petty trade, as is normally the case, there is also an opportunity for productivity growth by improving the allocation of labor.

Besides extension, the simple hypothesis also needs qualification.

First, technological backwardness is not usually a mere accident. Tenacious societal characteristics normally account for a portion, perhaps a substantial portion, of a country's past failure to achieve as high a level of productivity as economically more advanced countries. The same deficiencies, perhaps in attenuated form, normally remain to keep a backward country from making the full technological leap envisaged by the simple hypothesis. I have a name for these characteristics. Following Kazushi Ohkawa and Henry Rosovsky, I call them "social capability."[2] One can summarize the matter in this way. Having regard to technological backwardness alone leads to the simple hypothesis about catch-up and convergence already advanced. Having regard to social capability, however, we expect that the developments anticipated by that hypothesis will be clearly displayed in cross-country comparisons only if countries' social capabilities are about the same. One should say, therefore, that a country's potential for rapid growth is strong not when it is backward without qualification, but rather when it is technologically backward but socially advanced.

The trouble with absorbing social capability into the catch-up hypothesis is that no one knows just what it means or how to measure it. In past work I identified a country's social capability with technical competence, for which—at least among Western countries—years of education may be a rough proxy, and with its political, commercial, industrial, and financial institutions, which I characterized in more qualitative ways.[3] I had in mind mainly experience with the organization and management of large-scale enterprise and with financial institutions and markets capable of mobilizing capital for individual firms on a similarly large scale. On some occasions the situation for a selection of countries may be sufficiently clear. In explaining postwar growth in Europe and Japan, for example, one may be able to say with some confidence that these countries were competent to absorb and exploit then existing best-practice technology. More generally, however, judgments about social capability remain highly problematic. A few comments may serve to suggest some of the considerations involved as well as the speculative nature of the subject.

One concerns the familiar notion of a trade-off between specialization and adaptability. The content of education in a country and the character of its industrial, commercial, and financial organizations may be well designed to exploit fully the power of an existing technology; they may be less well fitted to adapt to the requirements of change. Presumably, some capacity to adapt is present everywhere, but countries may differ from one another in this respect, and their capacities to adapt may change over time.

Next, the notion of adaptability suggests that there is an interaction between social capability and technological opportunity. The state of education embodied in a nation's population and its existing institutional arrangements constrains it in its choice of technology. But technological opportunity presses for change. So countries learn to modify their institutional arrangements and then to improve them as they gain experience. The constraints imposed by social capability on the successful adoption of a more advanced technology gradually weaken and permit its fuller exploitation. . . .

Social capability, finally, depends on more than the content of education and the organization of firms. Other aspects of economic systems count as well—their openness to competition, to the establishment and operation of new firms, and to the sale and purchase of new goods and services. Viewed from the other side, it is a question of the obstacles to change raised by vested interests, established positions, and customary relations among firms and between employers and employees. The view from this side is what led Mancur Olson to identify defeat in war and accompanying political convulsion as a radical ground-clearing experience opening the way for new men, new organizations, and new modes of operation and trade better fitted to technological potential.[4]

These considerations have a bearing on the notion that a follower's potential for rapid growth weakens as its technological level converges on the leader's. This is not necessarily the case if social capability is itself endogenous, becoming stronger—or perhaps weaker—as technological gaps close. In the one case, the evolution of social capability connected with catching up itself raises the possibility that followers may forge ahead of even progressive leaders. In the other, a leader may fall back or a follower's pursuit may be slowed.

There is a somewhat technical point that has a similar bearing. This is the fact, noticed by Kravis and Denison, that as followers' levels of per capita income converge on the leader's, so do their structures of consumption and prices. R.C.O.[5] Matthews then observed that the convergence of consumption and production patterns should make it easier, rather than more difficult, for followers to borrow technology with advantage as productivity gaps close.[6] This, therefore, stands as still another qualification to the idea that the catch-up process is steadily self-limiting.

The combination of technological gap and social capability defines a country's *potentiality* for productivity advance by way of catch-up. This, however, should be regarded as a potentiality in the long run. The pace at which the potentiality is realized depends on still another set of causes that are largely independent of those governing the potentiality itself. There is a long story to tell about the factors controlling the rate of realization of potential.[7] Its general plot, however, can be suggested by noting three principal chapter headings:

(1) The facilities for the diffusion of knowledge—for example, channels of international technical communication, multinational corporations, the state of international trade and of direct capital investment.

(2) Conditions facilitating or hindering structural change in the composition of output, in the occupational and industrial distribution of the workforce, and in the geographical location of industry and popula-

tion. Among other factors, this is where conditions of labor supply, the existence of labor reserves in agriculture, and the factors controlling internal and international migration come in.

(3) Macroeconomic and monetary conditions encouraging and sustaining capital investment and the level and growth of effective demand.

Having considered the technological catch-up idea, with its several extensions and qualifications, I can summarize by proposing a restatement of the hypothesis as follows:

Countries that are technologically backward have a potentiality for generating growth more rapid than that of more advanced countries, provided their social capabilities are sufficiently developed to permit successful exploitation of technologies already employed by the technological leaders. The pace at which potential for catch-up is actually realized in a particular period depends on factors limiting the diffusion of knowledge, the rate of structural change, the accumulation of capital, and the expansion of demand. The process of catching up tends to be self-limiting, but the strength of the tendency may be weakened or overcome, at least for limited periods, by advantages connected with the convergence of production patterns as followers advance towards leaders or by an endogenous enlargement of social capabilities.

II. Historical Experience with Catching Up

I go on now to review some evidence bearing on the catch-up process. The survey I make is limited to the 16 countries covered by the new Maddison estimates of product per worker-hour for nine key years from 1870 to 1979.[8] The estimates are consistently derived as regards gross domestic product and worker hours and are adjusted as regards levels of product per worker hour by the Kravis estimates of purchasing power parities for postwar years. I have compressed the message of these data into three measures (see Tables 11.1 and 11.2):

(1) Averages of the productivity levels of the various countries relative to that of the United States, which was the leading country for most of the period. (For 1870 and 1890, I have also calculated averages of relatives based on the United Kingdom.) I calculate these averages for each of the nine key years and use them to indicate whether productivity levels of followers, *as a group,* were tending to converge on that of the leader.[9]

(2) Measures of relative variance around the mean levels of relative

Table 11.1   Comparative Levels of Productivity, 1870–1979: Means and Relative Variance of the Relatives of 15 Countries Compared with the United States (U.S. GDP per manhour = 100)[a]

	(1) Mean	(2) Coefficient of Variance[b]
1870	77 (66)	.51 (.51)
1890	68 (68)	.48 (.48)
1913	61	.33
1929	57	.29
1938	61	.22
1950	46	.36
1960	52	.29
1973	69	.14
1979	75	.15

a. 1870 and 1890. Figures in parentheses are based on relatives with the United Kingdom = 100.

b. Standard deviation divided by mean.

Source: Calculated from Angus Maddison, *Phases of Capitalist Development* (New York, 1982), Tables 5.2 and C.10.

Table 11.2   The Association (Rank Correlation) Between Initial Levels and Subsequent Growth Rates of Labor Productivity (GDP per manhour in 16 countries, 1870–1979)

Shorter Periods			Lengthening Periods Since 1870	
	(1)	(2)		(3)
1870–1913	−.59		1870–1890	−.32
1870–1890		−.32	−1913	−.59
1890–1913		−.56	−1929	−.72
			−1938	−.83
1913–1938	−.70		−1950	−.16
1913–29		−.35	−1960	−.66
1929–38		−.57	−1973	−.95
			−1979	−.97
1938–1950	+.48			
1950–1979	−.92			
1950–60		−.81		
1960–73		−.90		
1973–79		−.13		

Source of underlying data: Maddison, *Phases,* Tables 5.1, 5.2, and C.10.

productivity. These provide one sort of answer to the question of whether the countries that started at relatively low level of productivity tended to advance faster than those with initially higher levels.

(3) Rank correlations between initial levels of productivity and sub-

sequent growth rates. If the potential supposedly inherent in technological backwardness is being realized, there is likely to be some inverse correlation; and if it works with enough strength to dominate other forces the coefficients will be high.

The data I use and the measures I make have a number of drawbacks. The data, of course, have the weaknesses that are inherent in any set of estimates of GDP and manhours, however ably contrived, that stretch back far into the nineteenth century. Beyond that, however, simple calculations such as I have made fail, in a number of respects, to isolate the influence of the catch-up hypothesis proper.

To begin with, my measures do not allow for variation in the richness of countries' natural resources in relation to their populations. Labor productivity levels, therefore, are not pure reflections of levels of technology. In the same way, these levels will also reflect past accumulations of reproducible capital, both physical and human, and these may also be independent of technological levels in one degree or another. Further, the measured growth rates of labor of productivity will be influenced by the pace of capital accumulation. As already said, differences in rates of accumulation may reflect countries' opportunities to make advances in technology, but rates of capital formation may also be independent, to some degree, of countries' potentials for technological advance. Finally, my measures make no allowance for countries' variant abilities to employ current best-practice technology for reasons other than the differences in social capability already discussed. Their access to economies of scale is perhaps the most important matter. If advanced technology at any time is heavily scale-dependent and if obstacles to trade across national frontiers, political or otherwise, are important, large countries will have a stronger potential for growth than smaller ones.

There are many reasons, therefore, why one cannot suppose that the expectations implied by the catch-up hypothesis will display themselves clearly in the measures I present. It will be something if the data show some systematic evidence of development consistent with the hypothesis. And it will be useful if this provides a chance to speculate about the reasons why the connections between productivity levels and growth rates appear to have been strong in some periods and weak in others.

Other countries, on the average, made no net gain on the United States in a period longer than a century (Table 11.1, col. 1). The indication of very limited, or even zero, convergence is really stronger than the figures suggest. This is because the productivity measures reflect more than gaps in technology and in reproducible capital intensity, with respect to which catch-up is presumably possible. As already said, they also reflect differences in natural resource availabilities which, of course, are generally favorable to America and were far more important to America and to all the other countries in 1870 than they are today. In 1870, the agricultural share of United States employment was 50 percent; in 1979, 3.5 percent. For the other 15 countries, the corresponding figures are 48 and 8 percent on the average. The declines were large in all the countries.[10] So the American advantage in 1870 depended much more on our favorable land-man ratio than it did in 1979. Putting it the other way, other countries on the average must have fallen back over the century in respect to the productivity determinants in respect to which catch-up is possible.

In other respects, however, one can see the influence of the potential for catching up clearly. The variance among the productivity levels of the 15 "follower" countries declines drastically over the century—from a coefficient of variation of 0.5 in 1870 to 0.15 in 1979. Not only that: the decline in variance was continuous from one key year to the next, with only one reversal—in the period across World War II. In the same way, the inverse rank correlation between the initial productivity levels in 1870 and subsequent growth rates over increasingly long periods becomes stronger and stronger, until we reach the correlation coefficient of −.97 across the entire 109 years.[11] (Again there was the single reversal across World War II when the association was actually—and presumably accidentally—positive.)

I believe the steadily declining variance measures and the steadily rising correlation coefficients should be interpreted to mean that initial productivity gaps did indeed constitute a potentiality for fast growth that had its effect later if not sooner. The effect of the potentiality became visible in a very limited degree very early. But if a country was incapable of, or prevented from, exploiting that opportunity promptly, the technological growth potential became strong, and the country's later rate of advance was all the faster. Though it may have taken a century for obstacles or inhibitions to be fully overcome, the net outcome was that levels of productivity tended steadily to even out—at least within the group of presently advanced countries in my sample.

This last phrase is important. Mine is a biased sample in that its members consist of countries all of whom have successfully entered into the process of modern economic growth. This implies that they have acquired the educational and institutional characteristics needed to make use of modern technologies to some advanced degree. It is by no means assured—indeed, it is unlikely—that a more comprehensive sample of countries would show the same tendency for levels of productivity to even out over the same period of time.[12]

This is the big picture. How do things look if we consider shorter periods? There are two matters to keep in mind: the tendency to converge *within* the group of followers; and the convergence—or lack of it—of the group of followers vis-à-vis the United States. I take up the second matter in Section III. As to the convergence *within* the follower group, the figures suggest that the process varied in strength markedly from period to period. The main difference was that before World War II it operated weakly or at best with moderate strength. For almost a quarter-century following the war it apparently worked with very great strength. Why?

Before World War II, it is useful to consider two periods, roughly the decades before 1913, and those that followed. In the years of relative peace before 1913 I suggest that the process left a weak mark on the record for two reasons, both connected with the still early state of industrialization in many of the countries. First, the impress of the process was masked because farming was still so very important; measured levels of productivity, therefore, depended heavily on the amount and quality of farmland in relation to population. Productivity levels, in consequence, were erratic indicators of gaps between existing and best-practice technology. Secondly, social competence for exploiting the then most advanced methods was still limited, particularly in the earlier years and in the more recent latecomers. As the pre–World War I decades wore on, however, both these qualifying circumstances became less important. One might therefore have expected a much stronger tendency to convergence after 1913. But this was frustrated by the irregular effects of the Great War and of the years of disturbed political and financial conditions that followed, by the uneven impacts of the Great Depression itself and of the restrictions on international trade.

The unfulfilled potential of the years 1913–1938 was then enormously enlarged by the effects of World War II. The average productivity gap behind the United States increased by 39 percent between 1938 and 1950; the poorer countries were hit harder than the richer. These were years of dispersion, not convergence.

The post–World War II decades then proved to be the period when—exceptionally—the three elements required for rapid growth by catching up came together.[13] The elements are large technological gaps; enlarged social competence, reflecting higher levels of education and greater experience with large-scale production, distribution, and finance; and conditions favoring rapid realization of potential. This last element refers to several matters. There was *on this occasion* (it was otherwise after World War I) a strong reaction to the experience of defeat in war, and a chance for political reconstruction. The postwar political and economic reorganization and reform weakened the power of monopolistic groupings, brought new men to the fore, and focused the attention of governments on the tasks of recovery and growth, as Mancur Olson has argued.[14] The facilities for the diffusion of technology improved. International markets were opened. Large labor reserves in home agriculture and immigration from Southern and Eastern Europe provided a flexible and mobile labor supply. Government support, technological opportunity, and an environment of stable international money favored heavy and sustained capital investment. The outcome was the great speed and strength of the postwar catch-up process.[15]

Looking back now on the record of more than a century, we can see that catching up was a powerful continuing element in the growth experience of the presently advanced industrial countries. The strength of the process varied from period to period. For decades it operated only erratically and with weakened force. The trouble at first lay in deficient social capability, a sluggish adaptation of education and of industrial and financial organization to the requirements of modern large-scale technology. Later, the process was checked and made irregular by the effects of the two world wars and the ensuing political and financial troubles and by the impact of the Great Depression. It was at last released after World War II. The results were the rapid growth rates of the postwar period, the close cross-country association between initial productivity levels and growth rates, and a marked reduction of differences in productivity levels, among the follower countries, and between them and the United States.

Looking to the future, it seems likely that this very success will have weakened the potentiality for growth by catching up among the group of presently advanced countries. The great opportunities carried by that potential now pass to the less developed countries of Latin America and Asia.

III. Forging Ahead and Falling Behind

The catch-up hypothesis in its simple form does not anticipate changes in leadership nor, indeed, any changes in the ranks of countries in their relative levels of productivity. It contemplates only a reduction among countries in productivity differentials. Yet there have been many changes in ranks since 1870 and, of course, the notable shift of leadership from Britain to America towards the end of the last century.[16] This was followed by the continuing decline of Britain's standing in the productivity scale. Today there is a widely held opinion that America is about to fall behind a new candidate for leadership, Japan, and that both Europe and America must contemplate serious injury from the rise of both Japan and a group of still newer industrializing countries. . . .

The Congruity of Technology and Resources: United States as Leader

Why did the gap between the United States and the average of other countries resist reduction so long? Indeed, why did it even appear to become larger between 1870 and 1929—before the impact of World War II made it larger still? I offer three reasons:

(1) The path of technological change which in those years offered the greatest opportunities for advance was at once heavily scale-dependent and biased in a labor-saving but capital- and resource-using direction. In both respects America enjoyed great advantages compared with Europe or Japan. Large-scale production was favored by a large, rapidly growing, and increasingly prosperous population. It was supported also by a striking homogeneity of tastes. This reflected the country's comparative youth, its rapid settlement by migration from a common base on the Atlantic, and the weakness and fluidity of its class divisions. . . .

(2) By comparison with America and Britain, many, though not all, of the "followers" were also latecomers in respect to social capability. In the decades following 1870, they lacked experience with large-scale production and commerce, and in one degree or another they needed to advance in levels of general and technical education.

(3) World War I was a serious setback for many countries but a stimulus to growth in the United States. European recovery and growth in the following years were delayed and slowed by financial disturbances and by the impact of territorial and political change. Protection, not unification, was the response to the new political map. The rise of social democratic electoral strength in Europe favored the expansion of union power, but failed to curb the development and activities of industrial cartels. Britain's ability to support and enforce stable monetary conditions had been weakened, but the United States was not yet able or, indeed, willing to assume the role of leadership that Britain was losing. In all these ways, the response to the challenge of war losses and

defeat after the First World War stands in contrast to that after the Second.

Points (2) and (3) were anticipated in earlier argument, but Point (1) constitutes a qualification to the simple catch-up hypothesis. In that view, different countries, subject only to their social capability, are equally competent to exploit a leader's path of technological progress. That is not so, however, if that path is biased in resource intensity or if it is scale-dependent. Resource-rich countries will be favored in the first instance, large countries in the second. If the historical argument of this section is correct, the United States was favored on both counts for a long time; it may not be so favored in the future. Whether or not this interpretation of American experience is correct, the general proposition remains: countries have unequal abilities to pursue paths of progress that are resource-biased or scale-dependent.

Interaction Between Followers and Leaders

The catch-up hypothesis in its simple form is concerned with only one aspect of the economic relations among countries: technological borrowing by followers. In this view, a one-way stream of benefits flows from leaders to followers. A moment's reflection, however, exposes the inadequacy of that idea. The rise of British factory-made cotton textiles in the first industrial revolution ruined the Irish linen industry. The attractions of British and American jobs denuded the Irish population of its young men. The beginnings of modern growth in Ireland suffered a protracted delay. This is an example of the negative effects of leadership on the economies of those who are behind. Besides technological borrowing, there are interactions by way of trade and its rivalries, capital flows, and population movements. Moreover, the knowledge flows are not solely from leader to followers. A satisfactory account of the catch-up process must take account of these multiple forms of interaction. Again, there is space only for brief comment.

Trade and Its Rivalries. I have referred to the sometimes negative effects of leading-country exports on the economies of less developed countries. Countries in the course of catching up, however, exploit the possibilities of advanced scale-dependent technologies by import substitution and expansion of exports. When they are successful there are possible negative effects on the economies of leaders. This is an old historical theme. The successful competition of Germany, America, and other European countries is supposed to have retarded British growth from 1870 to 1913 and perhaps longer.[17] Analogous questions arise today. The expansion of exports from Japan and the newer industrializing countries has had a serious impact on the older industries of America and Europe, as well as some of the newer industries.

Is there a generalized effect on the productivity growth of the leaders? The effect is less than it may seem to be because some of the trade shifts are a reflection of overall productivity growth in the leader countries themselves. As the average level of productivity rises, so does the level of wages across industries generally. There are then relative increases in the product prices of those industries—usually older industries—in which productivity growth is lagging and relative declines in the product prices of those industries enjoying rapid productivity growth. The former must suffer a loss of comparative advantage, the latter a gain. One must keep an eye on both.

Other causes of trade shifts that are connected with the catch-up process itself may, however, carry real generalized productivity effects. There are changes that stem from the evolution of "product cycles," such as Raymond Vernon has made familiar. And perhaps most important, there is the achievement of higher levels of social capability. This permits followers to extend their borrowing and adaptation of more advanced methods, and enables them to compete in markets they could not contest earlier.

What difference does it make to the general prospects for the productivity growth of the leading industrial countries if they are losing markets to followers who are catching up?

There is an employment effect. Demand for the products of export- and import-competing industries is depressed. Failing a high degree of flexibility in exchange rates and wages and of occupational and geographical mobility, aggregate demand tends to be reduced. Unless macroeconomic policy is successful, there is general unemployment and underutilization of resources. Profits and the inducements to invest and innovate are reduced. And if this condition causes economies to succumb to protectionism, particularly to competitive protectionism, the difficulty is aggravated.

International trade theory assures us that these effects are transitory. Autonomous capital movements aside, trade must, in the end, balance. But the macroeconomic effects of the balancing process may be long drawn out, and while it is in progress, countries can suffer the repressive effects of restricted demand on investment and innovation.

There is also a Verdoorn effect. It is harder for an industry to push the technological frontier forward, or even to keep up with it, if its own rate of expansion slows down—and still harder if it is contracting. This is unavoidable but tolerable when the growth of old industries is restricted by the rise of newer, more progressive home industries. But when retardation of older home industries is due to the rise of competing industries abroad, a tendency to generalized slowdown may be present.

Interactions via Population Movements.   Nineteenth-century migration ran in good part from the farms of Western and Southern Europe to the farms and cities of the New World and Australia. In the early twentieth century, Eastern Europe joined in. These migrations responded in part to the impact on world markets of the cheap grains and animal products produced by the regions of recent settlement. Insofar they represent an additional but special effect of development in some members of the Atlantic community of industrializing countries on the economies of other members.

Productivity growth in the countries of destination was aided by migration in two respects. It helped them exploit scale economies; and by making labor supply more responsive to increase in demand, it helped sustain periods of rapid growth. Countries of origin were relieved of the presence of partly redundant and desperately poor people. On the other hand, the loss of population brought such scale disadvantages as accompany slower population growth, and it made labor supply less responsive to industrial demand.

Migration in the postwar growth boom presents a picture of largely similar design and significance. In this period the movement was from the poorer, more slowly growing countries of Southern Europe and North Africa to the richer and more rapidly growing countries of Western and Northern Europe.[18] There is, however, this difference: The movement in more recent decades was induced by actual and expected income differences that were largely independent of the market connections of countries of origin and destination. There is no evidence that the growth boom of the West itself contributed to the low incomes of the South.

Needless to say, migrations are influenced by considerations other than relative levels of income and changing comparative advantage. I stress these matters, however, because they help us understand the complexities of the process of catch-up and convergence within a group of connected countries.

Interaction via Capital Flows.   A familiar generalization is that capital tends to flow from countries of high income and slow growth to those with opposite characteristics or, roughly speaking, from leaders to followers. One remembers, however, that that description applies to gross new investments. There are also reverse flows that reflect the maturing of past investments. So in the early stages of a great wave of investment, followers' rates of investment and productivity growth are supported by capital movement while those of leaders are retarded. Later however, this effect may become smaller or be reversed, as we see today in relations between Western leaders and Latin American followers.

Once more, I add that the true picture is far more complicated than this idealized summary. It will hardly accommodate such extraordinary developments as the huge American capital import of recent years, to say nothing of the Arabian-European flows of the 1970s and their reversal now under way.

Interactions via Flows of Applied Knowledge. The flow of knowledge from leader to followers is, of course, the very essence of the catch-up hypothesis. As the technological gaps narrow, however, the direction changes. Countries that are still a distance behind the leader in average productivity may move into the lead in particular branches and become sources of new knowledge for older leaders. As they are surpassed in particular fields, old leaders can make gains by borrowing as well as by generating new knowledge. In this respect the growth potential of old leaders is enhanced as the pursuit draws closer. Moreover, competitive pressure can be a stimulus to research and innovation as well as an excuse for protection. It remains to be seen whether the newly rising economies will seek to guard a working knowledge of their operations more closely than American companies have done, and still more whether American and European firms will be as quick to discover, acquire, and adapt foreign methods as Japanese firms have been in the past.

Development as a Constraint on Change: Tangible Capital

The rise of followers in the course of catching up brings old leaders a mixed bag of injuries and potential benefits. Old leaders, however, or followers who have enjoyed a period of successful development, may come to suffer disabilities other than those caused by the burgeoning competitive power of new rivals. When Britain suffered her growth climacteric nearly a century ago, observers thought that her slowdown was itself due in part to her early lead. Thorstein Veblen was a pioneer proponent of this suggestion, and Charles Kindleberger and others have picked it up again.[19] One basis for this view is the idea that the capital stock of a country consists of an intricate web of interlocking elements. They are built to fit together, and it is difficult to replace one part of the complex with more modern and efficient elements without a costly rebuilding of other components. This may be handled efficiently if all the costs and benefits are internal to a firm. When they are divided among different firms and industries and between the private and public sectors, the adaptation of old capital structures to new technologies may be a difficult and halting process.

What this may have meant for Britain's climacteric is still unsettled. Whatever that may be, however, the problem needs study on a wider scale as it arises both historically and in a contemporaneous setting. After World War II, France undertook a great extension and modernization of its public transportation and power systems to provide a basis for later development of private industry and agriculture. Were the technological advances embodied in that investment program easier for France to carry out because its infrastructure was technically older, battered, and badly maintained? Or was it simply a heavy burden more in need of being borne? There is a widespread complaint today that the public capital structure of the United States stands in need of modernization and extension. Is this true, and, if it is, does it militate seriously against the installation of improved capital by private industry? One cannot now assume that such problems are the exclusive concern of a topmost productivity leader. All advanced industrial countries have large accumulations of capital, interdependent in use but divided in ownership among many firms and between private and public authorities. One may assume, however, that the problem so raised differs in its impact over time and among countries and, depending on its importance, might have some influence on the changes that occur in the productivity rankings of countries.

Development as a Constraint on Change: Intangible Capital and Political Institutions

Attention now returns to matters akin to social capability. In the simple catch-up hypothesis, that capability is viewed as either exogenously determined or else as adjusting steadily to the requirements of technological opportunity. The educational and institutional commitments induced by past development may, however, stand as an obstacle. That is a question that calls for study. The comments that follow are no more than brief indications of prominent possibilities.

The United States was the pioneer of mass production as embodied in the huge plant, the complex and rigid assembly line, the standardized product, and the long production run. It is also the pioneer and developer of the mammoth diversified conglomerate corporation. The vision of business carried on within such organizations, their highly indirect, statistical, and bureaucratic methods of consultation, planning and decision, the inevitable distractions of trading in assets rather than production of goods—these mental biases have sunk deep into the American business outlook and into the doctrine and training of young American managers. The necessary decentralization of operations into multiple profit centers directs the attention of managers and their superiors to the quarterly profit report and draws their energies away from the development of improved products and processes that require years of attention.[20] One may well ask how well this older vision of management and enterprise and the organizational scheme in which it is embodied will accommodate the problems and potentialities of the emerging computer and communications revolution. Or will that occur more easily in countries where educational systems, forms of corporate organization, and managerial outlook can better make a fresh start?

The long period of leadership and development enjoyed by the United States and the entire North Atlantic community meant, of course, a great increase of incomes. The rise of incomes, in turn, afforded a chance to satisfy latent desires for all sorts of non-market goods ranging from maintenance in old age to a safe-guarded natural environment. Satisfying these demands, largely by public action, has also afforded an ample opportunity for special interest groups to obtain privileges and protection in a process that Mancur Olson and others have generalized.

The outcome of this conjuncture of circumstances and forces is the Mixed Economy of the West, the complex system of transfers, taxes, regulations, and public activity, as well as organizations of union and business power, that had its roots long before the War, that expanded rapidly during the growth boom of the fifties and sixties, and that reached very high levels in the seventies. This trend is very broadly consistent with the suggestion that the elaboration of the mixed economy is a function of economic growth itself. To this one has to add the widely held idea advanced by Olson and many others that the system operates to reduce enterprise, work, saving, investment, and mobility and, therefore, to constrict the processes of innovation and change that productivity growth involves.

How much is there in all this? The answer turns only partly on a calculation of the direct effects of the system on economic incentives.

These have proved difficult to pin down, and attempts to measure them have generally not yielded large numbers, at least for the United States.[21] The answer requires an equally difficult evaluation of the positive roles of government activity. These include not only the government's support of education, research, and information, and its provision of physical overhead capital and of the host of local functions required for urban life. We must remember also that the occupational and geographical adjustments needed to absorb new technology impose heavy costs on individuals. The accompanying changes alter the positions, prospects, and power of established groups, and they transform the structure of families and their roles in caring for children, the sick, and the old. Technical advance, therefore, engenders conflict and resistance; and the Welfare State with its transfers and regulations constitutes a mode of conflict resolution and a means of mitigating the costs of change that would otherwise induce resistance to growth. The existing empirical studies that bear on the economic responses to government intervention are, therefore, far from meeting the problem fully.

If the growth-inhibiting forces embodied in the Welfare State and in private expressions of market power were straightforward, positive functions of income levels, uniform across countries, that would be another reason for supposing that the catch-up process was self-limiting. The productivity levels of followers would, on this account, converge towards but not exceed the leader's. But these forces are clearly not simple, uniform functions of income. The institutions of the Welfare State have reached a higher degree of elaboration in Europe than in the United States. The objects of expenditure, the structures of transfers and taxes, and people's responses to both differ from country to country. These institutional developments, therefore, besides having some influence on growth rates generally, may constitute a wide card in the deck of growth forces. They will tend to produce changes in the ranks of countries in the productivity scale and these may include the top rank itself.

A sense that forces of institutional change are now acting to limit the growth of Western countries pervades the writings of many economists—and, of course, other observers. Olson, Fellner, Scitovsky, Kindleberger, Lindbeck, and Giersch are only a partial list of those who see these economies as afflicted by institutional arthritis or sclerosis or other metaphorical malady associated with age and wealth.

These are the suggestions of serious scholars, and they need to be taken seriously. One may ask, however, whether these views take account of still other, rejuvenating forces which, though they act slowly, may yet work effectively to limit and counter those of decay—at least for the calculable future. In the United States, interregional competition, supported by free movement of goods, people, and capital, is such a force. It limits the power of unions and checks the expansion of taxation, transfers, and regulation.[22] International competition, so long as it is permitted to operate, works in a similar direction for the United States and other countries as well, and it is strengthened by the development in recent years of a more highly integrated world capital market and by more vigorous international movements of corporate enterprise. . . .

Finally, it is widely recognized that the process of institutional aging, whatever its significance, is not one without limits. Powerful forces continue to push that way, and they are surely strong in resisting reversal. Yet it is also apparent that there is a drift of public opinion that works for modification both in Europe and North America. There is a fine balance to be struck between productivity growth and the material incomes it brings and the other dimensions of social welfare. Countries are now in the course of readjusting that balance in favor of productivity growth. How far they can go and, indeed, how far they should go are both still in question. . . .

Notes

1. W.E.G. Salter, *Productivity and Technical Change* (Cambridge, 1960) provides a rigorous theoretical exposition of the factors determining rates of turnover and those governing the relation between productivity with capital embodying best-practice and average (economically efficient) technology.

2. *Japanese Economic Growth: Trend Acceleration in the Twentieth Century* (Stanford, 1973), especially chap. 9.

3. Moses Abramovitz, "Rapid Growth Potential and Its Realization: The Experience of Capitalist Economies in the Postwar Period," in Edmond Malinvaud, ed., *Economic Growth and Resources,* Proceedings of the Fifth World Congress of the International Economic Association, vol. 1 (London, 1979), pp. 1–30.

4. Mancur Olson, *The Rise and Fall of Nations: Economic Growth, Stagflation and Social Rigidities* (New Haven, 1982).

5. Kravis et al., *International Comparisons;* Edward F. Denison, assisted by Jean-Pierre Poullier, *Why Growth Rates Differ, Postwar Experience of Nine Western Countries* (Washington, D.C., 1967), pp. 239–45.

6. R.C.O. Matthews, Review of Denison (1967), *Economic Journal* (June 1969), pp. 261–68.

7. My paper cited earlier describes the operation of these factors in the 1950s and 1960s and tries to show how they worked to permit productivity growth to rise in so many countries rapidly, in concert and for such an extended period ("Rapid Growth Potential and Its Realization," pp. 18–30).

8. The countries are Australia, Austria, Belgium, Canada, Denmark, Finland, France, Germany, Italy, Japan, Netherlands, Norway, Sweden, Switzerland, United Kingdom, and United States.

9. In these calculations I have treated either the United States or the United Kingdom as the productivity leader from 1870 to 1913. Literal acceptance of Maddison's estimates, however, make Australia the leader from 1870–1913. Moreover, Belgium and the Netherlands stand slightly higher than the United States in 1870. Here are Maddison's relatives for those years (from *Phases,* Table 5.2):

	1870	1890	1913
Australia	186	153	102
Belgium	106	96	75
Netherlands	106	92	74
United Kingdom	114	100	81
United States	100	100	100

Since Australia's high standing in this period mainly reflected an outstandingly favorable situation of natural resources relative to population, it would be misleading to regard that country as the technological leader or to treat the productivity changes in other countries relative to Australia's as indicators of the catch-up process. Similarly, the small size and specialized character of the Belgian and Dutch economies make them inappropriate benchmarks.

10. Maddison, *Phases,* Table C5.

11. Since growth rates are calculated as rates of change between standings at the terminal dates of periods, errors in the estimates of such standings will generate errors in the derived growth rates. If errors at both terminal dates were random, and if those at the end-year were independent of those at the initial year, there would be a tendency on that account for growth rates to be inversely correlated with initial-year standings. The inverse correlation coefficients would be biased upwards. Note, however, that if errors at terminal years were random and independent and of equal magnitude, there would be no tendency *on that account* for the variance of standings about the mean to decline between initial and end-year dates. The error bias would run against the marked decline in variance that we observe. Errors in late-year data, however, are unlikely to be so large, so an error bias is present.

12. See also William J. Baumol, "Productivity Growth, Convergence and Welfare: What the Long-run Data Show." C. V. Starr Center for Applied Economics, New York University, Research Report No. 85–27, August 1985.

13. See Abramovitz, "Rapid Growth Potential and Its Realization."

14. Olson, *Rise and Fall.*

15. Some comments on the catch-up process after 1973 may be found in Abramovitz, "Catching Up and Falling Behind" (Stockholm, 1986), pp. 33–39.

16. If one follows Maddison's estimates (*Phases,* Table C.19), the long period from 1870 to 1979 saw Australia fall by 8 places in the ranking of his 16 countries, Italy by 2.5, Switzerland by 8, and the United Kingdom by 10. Meanwhile the United States rose by 4, Germany by 4.5, Norway by 5, Sweden by 7, and France by 8.

17. See also R.C.O. Matthews, Charles Feinstein, and John Odling-Smee, *British Economic Growth, 1856–1973* (Stanford, 1983), chaps, 14, 15, 17.

Their analysis does not find a large effect on British productivity growth from 1870 to 1913.

18. The migration from East to West Germany in the 1950s was a special case. It brought to West Germany educated and skilled countrymen strongly motivated to rebuild their lives and restore their fortunes.

19. Charles P. Kindleberger, "Obsolescence and Technical Change." *Oxford Institute of Statistics Bulletin* (Aug. 1961), pp. 281–97.

20. These and similar questions are raised by experienced observers of American business. They are well summarized by Edward Denison, *Trends in American Economic Growth, 1929–1982* (Washington, D.C., 1985), chap. 3.

21. Representative arguments supporting the idea that social capability has suffered, together with some quantitative evidence, may be found in Olson, *Rise and Fall;* William Fellner, "The Declining Growth of American Productivity: An Introductory Note," in W. Fellner, ed., *Contemporary Economic Problems, 1979* (Washington, D.C., 1979); and Assar Lindbeck, "Limits to the Welfare State," *Challenge* (Dec. 1985). For argument and evidence on the other side, see Sheldon Danzigar, Robert Haveman, and Robert Plotnick, "How Income Transfers Affect Work, Savings and Income Distribution," *Journal of Economic Literature* 19 (Sept. 1982), pp. 975–1028; and Edw. F. Denison, *Accounting for Slower Economic Growth* (Washington, D.C., 1979), pp. 127–38.

22. See R. D. Norton, "Regional Life Cycles and US Industrial Rejuvenation," in Herbert Giersch, ed., "Industrial Policy and American Renewal," *Journal of Economic Literature,* 24 (March 1986).

CHAPTER 12

Productivity Growth, Convergence, and Welfare: What the Long-Run Data Show

WILLIAM J. BAUMOL

William Baumol provides empirical analysis of convergence theory and finds that for a sample of sixteen countries between 1870 and 1979 labor productivity and its growth are inversely related. In Chapter 11, Moses Abramovitz explained that not all countries will experience convergence because they lack the social capacity to utilize technology to achieve rapid growth. Baumol turns to the post–World War II era (1950–1980) to see if this relationship can be found for all countries. Using RGDP/pcs and growth rates as proxies for labor productivity, Baumol finds that the poorest countries have the slowest RGDP/pc growth, thus failing to converge with the rich. The rest of the countries belong to what Baumol calls a "convergence club." Hence, if Baumol is correct, convergence will take place but the poorest countries will be excluded from the process, meaning that the gap will widen between them and the rest of the world.

> No matter how refined and how elaborate the analysis, if it rests solely on the short view it will still be . . . a structure built on shifting sands.
> —Jacob Viner (1958, pp. 112–131)

RECENT YEARS HAVE WITNESSED A REEMERGENCE OF INTEREST ON THE PART OF economists and the general public in issues relating to long-run economic growth. There has been a recurrence of doubts and fears for the

Reprinted with permission from the *American Economic Review,* vol. 76 (December 1986): 1072–1084.

future—aroused in this case by the protracted slowdown in productivity growth since the late 1960s, the seeming erosion of the competitiveness of U.S. industries in world markets, and the spectre of "deindustrialization" and massive structural unemployment. These anxieties have succeeded in redirecting attention to long-run supply-side phenomena that formerly were a central preoccupation of economists in the industrializing West, before being pushed aside in the crisis of the Great Depression and the ensuing triumph of Keynesian ideas.

Anxiety may compel attention, but it is not necessarily an aid to clear thinking. For all the interest now expressed in the subject of long-run economic growth and policies ostensibly directed to its stimulation, it does not seem to be widely recognized that adequate economic analysis of such issues calls for the careful study of economic history—if only because it is there that the pertinent evidence is to be found. Economic historians have provided the necessary materials, in the form of brilliant insights, powerful analysis as well as a surprising profusion of long-period data. Yet none of these has received the full measure of attention they deserve from members of the economics profession at large.

To dramatize the sort of reorientation long-term information can suggest, imagine a convincing prediction that over the next century, U.S. productivity growth will permit a trebling of per capita GNP while cutting nearly by half the number of hours in the average work year, and that this will be accompanied by a sevenfold increase in exports. One might well consider this a very rosy forecast. But none of these figures is fictitious. For these developments in fact lay before the United Kingdom in 1870, just as its economic leadership began to erode.

This chapter outlines some implications of the available long-period data on productivity and related variables—some tentative, some previously noted by economic historians, and some throwing a somewhat surprising light on developments among industrialized nations since World War II. Among the main observations that will emerge here is the remarkable convergence of output per labor hour among industrialized nations. Almost all of the leading free enterprise economies have moved closer to the leader, and there is a strong inverse correlation between a country's productivity standing in 1870 and its average rate of productivity growth since then. Postwar data suggest that the convergence phenomenon also extends to both "intermediate" and centrally planned economies. Only the poorer less developed countries show no such trend.

It will also emerge that over the century, the U.S. productivity growth rate has been surprisingly steady, and despite frequently expressed fears, there is no sign recently of any *long-term* slowdown in growth of either total factor productivity or labor productivity in the United States. And while, except in wartime, *for the better part of a century,* U.S. productivity growth rates have been low relative to those of Germany, Japan, and a number of other countries, this may be no more than a manifestation of the convergence phenomenon which requires countries that were previously behind to grow more rapidly. Thus, the chapter will seek to dispel these and a number of other misapprehensions apparently widespread among those who have not studied economic history.

Nonspecialists may well be surprised at the remarkably long periods spanned in time-series contributed by Beveridge, Deane, Kuznets, Gallman, Kendrick, Abramovitz, David, and others. The Phelps Brown-Hopkins indices of prices and real wages extend over seven centuries. Maddison, Feinstein (and his colleagues), and Kendrick cover productivity, investment, and a number of other crucial variables for more than 100 years. Obviously, the magnitudes of the earlier figures are more than a little questionable, as their compilers never cease to warn us. Yet the general qualitative character of the time paths is persuasive, given the broad consistency of the statistics, their apparent internal logic and the care exercised in collecting them. In this chapter, the period used will vary with topic and data availability. In most cases, something near a century will be examined, using primarily data provided by Angus Maddison (1982) and R.C.O. Matthews, C. H. Feinstein, and J. C. Odling-Smee (1982—henceforth, M-F-O).

Magnitude of the Accomplishment

The magnitude of the productivity achievement of the past 150 years resists intuitive grasp, and contrasts sharply with the preceding centuries. As the *Communist Manifesto* put the matter in 1848, with remarkable foresight, "The bourgeoisie, during its rule of scarce one hundred years, has created more massive and more colossal productive forces than have all preceding generations together." There obviously are no reliable measures of productivity in antiquity, but available descriptions of living standards in Ancient Rome suggest that they were in many respects higher than in eighteenth-century England (see Colin Clark, 1957, p. 677). This is probably true even for the lower classes— certainly for the free urban proletariat, and perhaps even with the inclusion of slaves. An upper-class household was served by sophisticated devices for heating and bathing not found in eighteenth-century homes of the rich. A wealthy Roman magically transported into an eighteenth-century English home would probably have been puzzled by the technology of only a few products—clocks, window panes, printed books and newspapers, and the musket over the fireplace.

It is true that even during the Middle Ages (see, for example, Carlo Cipolla, 1976), there was substantial technological change in the workplace and elsewhere. Ship design improved greatly. Lenses and, with them, the telescope and microscope appeared in the sixteenth century, and the eighteenth century brought the ship's chronometer which revolutionized water transport by permitting calculation of longitude. Yet, none of this led to rates of productivity growth anywhere near those of the nineteenth and twentieth centuries.

Nonhistorians do not usually recognize that initially the Industrial Revolution was a fairly minor affair for the economy as a whole. At first, much of the new equipment was confined to textile production (though some progress in fields such as iron making had also occurred). And, as David Landes (1969) indicates, an entrepreneur could undertake the new types of textile operations with little capital, perhaps only a few hundred pounds, which (using the Phelps Brown-Hopkins data) translates into some 100,000 1980 dollars. Jeffrey Williamson (1983) tells us that in England during the first half-century of the Industrial Revolution, real per capita income grew only about 0.3 percent per annum,[1] in contrast with the nearly 3 percent achieved in the Third World in the 1970s (despite the decade's economic crises).

Table 12.1 shows the remarkable contrast of developments since 1870 for Maddison's 16 countries. We see (col. 1) that growth in output per work-hour ranged for the next 110 years from approximately 400 percent for Australia all the way to 2500 percent (in the case of Japan). The 1100 percent increase of labor productivity in the United States placed it somewhat below the middle of the group, and even the United Kingdom managed a 600 percent rise. Thus, after not manifesting any substantial long-period increase for at least 15 centuries, in the course of 11 decades the median increase in productivity among the 16 industrialized leaders in Maddison's sample was about 1150 percent. The rise in productivity was sufficient to permit output per capita (col. 2) to increase more than 300 percent in the United Kingdom, 800 percent in West Germany, 1700 percent in Japan, and nearly 700 percent in France and the United States. Using Robert Summers and Alan Heston's sophisticated international comparison data (1984), this implies that in 1870, U.S. output per capita was comparable to 1980 output per capita in Honduras and the Philippines, and slightly below that of China, Bolivia, and Egypt!

Table 12.1   Total Growth from 1870 to 1979[a]: Productivity, GDP per Capita, and Exports, Sixteen Industrialized Countries[b]

	Real GDP per Work-Hour	Real GDP per Capita	Volume of Exports
Australia	398	221	—
United Kingdom	585	310	930
Switzerland	830	471	4,400
Belgium	887	439	6,250
Netherlands	910	429	8,040
Canada	1,050	766	9,860
United States	1,080	693	9,240
Denmark	1,098	684	6,750
Italy	1,225	503	6,210
Austria	1,270	643	4,740
Germany	1,510	824	3,730
Norway	1,560	873	7,740
France	1,590	694	4,140
Finland	1,710	1,016	6,240
Sweden	2,060	1,083	5,070
Japan	2,480	1,661	293,060

a. In 1970 U.S. dollars.
b. Shown in percent.
Source: Angus Maddison (1982, pp. 8, 212, 248–53).

The growth rates of other pertinent variables were also remarkable. One more example will suffice to show this. Table 12.1, which also shows the rise in volume of exports from 1870 to 1979 (col. 3), indicates that the median increase was over 6,000 percent.

The Convergence of National Productivity Levels

There is a long and reasonably illustrious tradition among economic historians centered on the phenomenon of convergence. While the literature devoted to the subject is complex and multifaceted, as revealed by the recent reconsideration of these ideas by Moses Abramovitz (1985), one central theme is that forces accelerating the growth of nations who were latecomers to industrialization and economic development give rise to a long-run tendency towards convergence of levels of per capita product or, alternatively, of per worker product. Such ideas found expression in the works of Alexander Gerschenkron (see, for example, 1952), who saw his own views on the advantages of "relative backwardness" as having been anticipated in important respects by Thorstein Veblen's writings on the penalties of being the industrial leader (1915). Although such propositions also have been challenged and qualified (for example, Edward Ames and Nathan Rosenberg, 1963), it is difficult to dismiss the idea of convergence on the basis of the historical experience of the industrialized world. (For more recent discussions, see also the paper by Robin Marris, with comments by Feinstein and Matthews in Matthews, 1982, pp. 12–13, 128–147, as well as Dennis Mueller, 1983.)

Using 1870–1973 data on gross domestic product (GDP) per work-year for 7 industrialized countries, M-F-O have shown graphically that those nations' productivity levels have tended to approach ever closer to one another. . . .[2]

The convergence toward the vanguard (led in the first decades by Australia—see Richard Caves and Laurence Krause, 1984—and the United Kingdom and, approximately since World War I, by the United States) is sharper than it may appear to the naked eye. In 1870, the ratio of output per work-hour in Australia, then the leader in Maddison's sample, was about eight times as great as Japan's (the laggard). By 1979, that ratio for the leader (the United States) to the laggard (still Japan) had fallen to about 2. The ratio of the standard deviation from the mean of GDP per work-hour for the 16 countries has also fallen quite steadily, except for a brief but sharp rise during World War II.

The convergence phenomenon and its pervasiveness are confirmed by Figure 12.1, on which my discussion will focus. The horizontal axis indicates each Maddison country's absolute level of GDP per work-hour in 1870. The vertical axis represents the growth rate of GDP per work-hour in the 110 years since 1870. The high inverse correlation between the two is evident. Indeed, we obtain an equation (subject to all sorts of statistical reservations)[3]

$$Growth\ Rate\ (1870-1979) = 5.25 - 0.75\ln\ (GDP\ per\ WorkHr,\ 1870),$$
$$R^2 = 0.88.$$

That is, with a very high correlation coefficient, the higher a country's productivity level in 1870 the more slowly that level grew in the following century.

Implications of the Inverse Correlation: Public Goods Property of Productivity Policy

The strong inverse correlation between the 1870 productivity levels of the 16 nations and their subsequent productivity growth record seems to

**Figure 12.1   Productivity Growth
Rate, 1870–1979 vs. 1870 Level (in percent)**

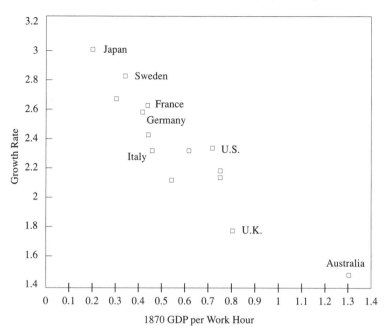

Source: Maddison (p. 212).

have a startling implication. Of course, hindsight always permits "fore-casts" of great accuracy—that itself is not surprising. Rather, what is striking is the apparent implication that *only one variable,* a country's 1870 GDP per work-hour, or its relation to that of the productivity leader matters to any substantial degree, and that other variables have only a peripheral influence. It seems not to have mattered much whether or not a particular country had free markets, a high propensity to invest, or used policy to stimulate growth. Whatever its behavior, that nation was apparently fated to land close to its predestined position in Figure 12.1.

However, a plausible alternative interpretation is that while national policies and behavior patterns do substantially affect productivity growth, the spillovers from leader economies to followers are large—at least among the group of industrial nations. If country A's extraordinary investment level and superior record of innovation enhance its own productivity, they will almost automatically do the same in the long run for industrialized country B, though perhaps to a somewhat more limited extent. In other words, for such nations a successful productivity-enhancing measure has the nature of a public good. And because the fruits of each industrialized country's productivity-enhancement efforts are ultimately shared by others, each country remains in what appears to be its predestined *relative* place along the growth curve of Figure 12.1. I will note later some considerations which might lead one to doubt that the less developed countries will benefit comparably from this sharing process.

This sharing of productivity growth benefits by industrialized countries involves both innovation and investment. The innovation-sharing process is straightforward. If industry in country A benefits from a significant innovation, those industries in other countries which produce competing products will find themselves under pressure to obtain access to the innovation, or to an imitation or to some other substitute. Industrialized countries, whose product lines overlap substantially and which sell a good deal in markets where foreign producers of similar items are also present, will find themselves constantly running in this Schumpeterian race, while those less developed countries which supply few products competing with those of the industrialized economies will not participate to the same degree.

There is reason to suspect that the pressures for rapidity in imitation of innovation in industrial countries have been growing. The explosion in exports reported in Table 12.1 has given them a considerably larger share of gross national product than they had in 1870. This suggests that more of each nation's output faces the direct competition of foreign rivals. Thus, the penalties for failure to keep abreast of innovations *in other countries* and to imitate them where appropriate have grown.

Second, the means required for successful imitations have improved and expanded enormously. World communications are now practically instantaneous, but required weeks and even months at the birth of the Industrial Revolution. While today meetings of scientists and technicians are widely encouraged, earlier mercantilist practices entailed measures by each country to prevent other nations from learning its industrial techniques, and the emigration of specialized workers was often forbidden. Though figures in this arena are difficult to interpret, much less substantiate, one estimate claims that employment in "information activities" in the United States has grown from less than 1 percent of the labor force in 1830 to some 45 percent today (James Beniger, forthcoming, p. 364, leaning heavily on Marc Porat, 1977). Presumably, growth of the information sector in other industrialized nations has been similar. This must surely facilitate and speed the innovative, counterinnovative, and imitative tasks of the entrepreneur. The combination of direct U.S. manufacturing investment in Europe, and the technology transfer activities of multinational corporations in the postwar era were also of great significance (see, for example, David Teece, 1976). All of this, incidentally, suggests that as the forces making for convergence were stronger in the postwar era than previously, the rate of convergence should have been higher. The evidence assembled by Abramovitz (1985) on the basis of Maddison's data indicates that this is in fact what has happened.

The process that has just been described, then, provides mutual benefits, but it inherently helps productivity laggards more than leaders. For the laggards have more to learn from the leaders, and that is why the process makes for convergence.

Like innovation, investment, generally considered the second main source of growth in labor productivity, may also exhibit international public good properties. Suppose two industrialized countries, A and B, each produce two traded products: say automobiles and shoes, with the former more capital intensive. If A's investment rate is greater than B's then, with time, A's output mix will shift toward the cars while B's will move toward shoes. The increased demand for auto workers in A will raise their real wages, while A's increased demand for imports of B's shoes will raise real wages in B, and will raise the *value* of gross domestic product per labor hour in that country. Thus, even investment in country A automatically tends to have a spillover effect on value productivity and real wages *in those other countries that produce and trade in a similar array of goods.*

While, strictly speaking, the factor-price equalization theorem is not applicable to my discussion because it assumes, among other things, that technology is identical in all the countries involved, it does suggest why (for the reasons just discussed) a high investment rate may fail to bring a relative wage advantage to the investing country. In practice, the conditions of the theorem are not satisfied precisely, so countries in which investment rates are relatively high do seem to obtain increased relative real wages. Yet the analysis suggests that the absolute benefits are contagious—that one country's successful investment policy will also raise productivity and living standards in other industrialized countries.[4]

Thus, effective growth policy does contribute to a nation's living standards, but it may also help other industrialized countries and to almost the same degree; meaning that relative deviations from the patterns indicated in Figure 12.1 will be fairly small, just as the diagram shows. (However, see Abramovitz, 1985, for a discussion of the counterhypothesis, that growth of a leader creates "backwash" effects inhibiting growth of the followers.)

All this raises an obvious policy issue. If productivity growth does indeed have such public good properties, what will induce each country to invest the socially optimal effort and other resources in productivity growth, when it can instead hope to be a free rider? In part, the answer is that in Western capitalistic economies, investment is decentralized and individual firms can gain little by free riding on the actions of investors in other economies, so that the problem does not appear to be a serious one at the national policy level.

Is Convergence Ubiquitous?

Does convergence of productivity levels extend beyond the free-market industrialized countries? Or is the convergence "club" a very exclusive organization? While century-long data are not available for any large number of countries, Summers and Heston provide pertinent figures for the 30-year period 1950–80 (data for more countries are available for briefer periods).[5] Instead of labor productivity figures, they give output per capita, whose trends can with considerable reservations be used as a rough proxy for those in productivity, as Maddison's figures confirm.

Figure 12.2 tells the story. Constructed just like Figure 12.1, it plots the 1950–80 real growth rate of GDP per capita for all 72 Summers-Heston countries against the initial (1950) level of this variable. The points form no tight relationship, and unlike those for the industrial countries, the dots show no negatively sloping pattern. Indeed, a regression yields a slightly positive slope. Thus, rather than sharing in convergence, some of the poorest countries have also been growing most slowly.

Figure 12.2 brings out the patterns more clearly by surrounding the set of points representing Maddison's 16 countries with a thin boundary and the centrally planned economy points[6] with a heavier boundary. We see that the Maddison country points lie near a sort of upper-right-hand boundary, meaning that most of them had the high incomes in 1950 (as was to be expected) and, for any given per capita income, the highest growth rates between 1950 and 1980. This region is very long, narrow, and negatively sloped, with the absolute slope declining toward the right. As in the Figure 12.1, productivity data for a 110-year period, this is exactly the shape one expects with convergence. Second, we see that the centrally planned economies are members of a convergence club of their own, forming a negatively sloping region lying below and to the left of the Maddison countries. The relationship is less tight, so convergence within the group is less pronounced, but it is clearly there.

Finally, there is the region of remaining points (aside from the

Figure 12.2   Growth Rate, 1950–80, GDP/pc vs. 1950 Level, 72 Countries

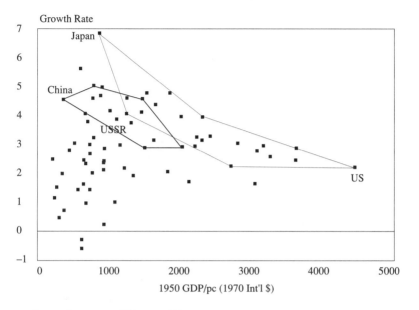

Source: Summers and Heston, 1984.

rightmost non-Maddison points in the graph) which lies close to the origin of the graph and occupies something like a distorted circle without any apparent slope. The points closest to the origin are less developed countries which were poor in 1950, and have grown relatively slowly since. They show no convergence among themselves, much less with other groups.

A few numbers suggest the difference in performance of various subgroups of the 72 countries. Using a four-set classification Summers, I. B. Kravis and Heston (1984, p. 254) provide Gini coefficients by decade from 1950 to 1980. For their set of industrialized countries, this coefficient falls precipitously from 0.302 in 1950 to 0.129 in 1980–a sharp drop in inequality. For the centrally planned economies the drop is much smaller—from 0.381 to 0.301. The middle-income group exhibits an even smaller decline, from 0.269 to 0.258. But the low-income countries underwent a small *rise* over the period, from 0.103 to 0.112, and the world as a whole experienced a tiny rise from 0.493 to 0.498.

There has also been little convergence among the groups. For the entire period, Summers et al. report (p. 245) an average annual growth rate in per capita real GDP of 3.1 percent for industrialized countries, 3.6 percent for centrally planned economies, 3.0 percent for middle-income market economies, and only 1.5 percent for the low-income group, with a world average group rate of 2.7 percent.

This suggests that there is more than one convergence club. Rather, there are perhaps three, with the centrally planned and the intermediate groups somewhat inferior in performance to that of the free-market industrialized countries. It is also clear that the poorer less developed countries are still largely barred from the homogenization processes. Since any search for "the causes" of a complex economic phenomenon of reality is likely to prove fruitless, no attempt will be made here to explain systematically why poorer less developed countries have benefited to a relatively small degree from the public good properties of the innovations and investments of other nations. But part of the explanation may well be related to product mix and education. A less developed country that produces no cars cannot benefit from the invention and adoption of a better car-producing robot in Japan (though it does benefit to a lesser degree from new textile and rice-growing technology), nor can it benefit from the factor-price equalization effect of the accompanying Japanese investments, since it cannot shift labor force out of its (nonexistent) auto industry as the theorem's logic requires. Lack of education and the associated skills prevent both the presence of high-tech industries and the effective imitation (adoption) of the Japanese innovation. Obviously, there is much more to any reasonably fuller explanation of the exclusion of many less developed countries from the convergence process, but that is not my purpose here. . . .

Notes

1. This observation does not quite seem to square with Charles Feinstein's estimates (1972, pp. 82–94) which indicate that while output per worker in the United Kingdom increased 0.2 percent per year between 1761 and 1800, between 1801 and 1830 the growth rate leaped up to 1.4 percent per annum. He estimates that total factor productivity behaved similarly. However, between 1801 and 1810, total annual investment fell to 10 percent of gross domestic product, in comparison with its 14 percent rate in the immediately preceding and succeeding periods.

2. Space prevents extensive consideration of Paul Romer's (1985) objection to the evidence offered for the convergence hypothesis provided here and elsewhere, i.e., that the sample of countries studied is an *ex post* selection of successful economies. Successes, by definition, are those which have done best relative to the leader. However, the Summers-Heston 1950–80 data for 72 countries represented in Figure 12.2 do permit an *ex ante* selection. Tests ranking countries both by 1950 and by 1960 GDP levels confirm that even an *ex ante* sample of the wealthiest countries yields a pattern of convergence which, while less pronounced than that calculated from an *ex post* group, is still unambiguous.

3. The high correlation should not be taken too seriously. Aside from the reasons why its explanation may be misunderstood that are presently discussed in the text, the tight fit of the data points is undoubtedly ascribable in good part to several biasing features of the underlying calculation. First, the 1870 figures were calculated by Maddison using backward extrapolation of growth rates, and hence their correlation is hardly surprising. Second, since growth rate, r, is calculated by solving $y_t = e^{rt}y_0$ for r, to obtain $r = (\ln y_t - \ln y_0)/t$, where $y_t = GDP$ per capita in period t, a regression equation $r = f(y_0)$ contains the same variable, y_0 on both sides of the equation, thus tending to produce a spurious appearance of close relationship. Indeed, if the convergence process were perfect, so that we would have $y_t = k$ with k the same for every country in the sample, every dot in the diagram would necessarily perfectly fit the curve $r = \ln k/t - \ln y_0/t$, and the r^2 would be unity, identically. The 72-country data depicted in Figure 12.2 hardly constitute a close fit (the R^2 is virtually zero), and do not even yield a negatively sloping regression line. Thus, a relationship such as that in Figure 12.1 is no tautology, nor even a foregone conclusion.

In addition, if the 1870 productivity levels are measured with considerable error, this must result in some significant downward bias in the regression coefficient on $\ln(GDP$ per $WorkHr$, 1870). This is a point distinct from the one concerning the size of the correlation coefficient, although the latter is affected by the fact that relatively large measurement errors in the 1870 productivity levels enter as inversely correlated measurement errors in the 1870–1979 growth rate. The argument that this bias is not sufficient to induce a negative correlation in the 72-country sample may not be wholly germane, as the relative seriousness of the measurement errors in the initial and terminal observations may be much the same for observations confined to the period 1950–80.

4. It must be conceded that the longer-run data do not seem to offer impressive support for the hypothesis that the forces of factor-price equalization have, albeit imperfectly, extended the benefits of exceptional rates of investment from those economies that carried out the successful investment programs to other industrialized economies. Since we have estimates of relative real wages, capital stock, and other pertinent variables for the United Kingdom and Germany, these have been compared below:

	Period	Ratio: German Increase to U.K. Increase[b]
Real Wages	1860–1980	4.25
GDP per Labor Hour	1870–1979	2.35
Capital Stock[a]	1870–1979	6.26
Capital Stock per Worker	1870–1979	3.8
Capital Stock per Capita	1870–1979	5.4

Sources: Real wages, same as in Note 6 [of original text; not included here]; all other data from Maddison.

a. Net nonresidential fixed tangible capital stock.

b. (German 1979 figure/German 1870 figure)/(U.K. 1979 figure/U.K. 1987 figure) with appropriate modification of the dates for the wage figures.

If the public goods attribute hypothesis about the effects of investment in one country were valid and if factor-price equalization were an effective force, we would expect the relative rise in German real wages and in productivity to be small (on some criterion) in comparison with the relative increase in its capital stock. However, the figures do not seem to exhibit such a pattern.

5. There are at least two sources of such data: the World Bank and the University of Pennsylvania group. Here I report only data drawn from the latter, since their international comparisons have been carried out with unique sophistication and insight. Instead of translating the different currencies into one another using inadequate exchange rate comparisons, they use carefully constructed indices of relative purchasing power. I have also replicated my calculations using World Bank data and obtained exactly the same qualitative results.

6. The centrally planned economies are Bulgaria, China, Czechoslovakia, East Germany, Hungary, Poland, Romania, USSR, and Yugoslavia. The 5 countries with relatively high 1950 incomes included neither in Maddison's sample nor in the planned group are, in descending order of GDP per capita, Luxembourg, New Zealand, Iceland, Venezuela, and Argentina. The countries with negative growth rates are Uganda and Nigeria.

References

Abramovitz, Moses. 1979. "Rapid Growth Potential and Its Realization: The Experience of the Capitalist Economies in the Postwar Period," in Edmond Malinvaud, ed., *Economic Growth and Resources, Proceedings of the Fifth World Congress of the International Economic Association,* Vol. 1, London: Macmillan.

———. 1985. "Catching Up and Falling Behind," delivered at the Economic History Association, September 20, 1985.

Ames, Edward and Rosenberg, Nathan. 1963. "Changing Technological Leadership and Industrial Growth," *Economic Journal* 73 (March): 13–31.

Beniger, James R. Forthcoming. *The Control Revolution: Technological and Economic Origins of the Information Society.* Cambridge: Harvard University Press.

Caves, Richard E. and Krause, Lawrence B. 1984. *The Australian Economy: A View from the North.* Washington: The Brookings Institution.

Cipolla, Carlo M. 1976. *Before the Industrial Revolution: European Society and Economy, 1000–1700.* New York: W. W. Norton.

Clark, Colin. 1957. *The Conditions of Economic Progress,* 3rd ed. London: Macmillan.

Darby, Michael. 1984. "The U.S. Productivity Slowdown: A Case of Statistical Myopia," *American Economic Review,* 74 (June): 301–322.

David, Paul A. 1977. "Invention and Accumulation in America's Economic Growth: A Nineteenth-Century Parable," in K. Brunner and A. H. Meltzer, eds., *International Organization, National Policies and Economic Development,* pp. 179–228. Amsterdam: North-Holland.

Deane, Phyllis and Cole, W. A. 1962. *British Economic Growth 1688–1959.* Cambridge: Cambridge University Press.

Feinstein, Charles. 1972. *National Income, Expenditure and Output of the United Kingdom, 1855–1965*. Cambridge: Cambridge University Press.

Gerschenkron, Alexander. 1952. "Economic Backwardness in Historical Perspective," in Bert F. Hoselitz, ed., *The Progress of Underdeveloped Areas*. Chicago: University of Chicago Press.

Landes, David S. 1969. *The Unbound Prometheus*. Cambridge: Cambridge University Press.

Lawrence, Robert Z. 1984. *Can America Compete?* Washington: The Brookings Institution.

McCloskey, D. N. 1981. *Enterprise and Trade in Victorian Britain*. London: Allen & Unwin.

Maddison, Angus. 1982. *Phases of Capitalist Development*. New York: Oxford University Press.

Marx, Karl and Engels, Friedrich. 1946. *Manifesto of the Communist Party* (1848). London: Lawrence and Wishart.

Matthews, R.C.O. 1982. *Slower Growth in the Western World*. London: Heinemann.

———, Feinstein, C. H. and Odling-Smee, J. C. 1982. *British Economic Growth, 1856–1973*. Stanford: Stanford University Press.

Mueller, Dennis C. 1983. *The Political Economy of Growth*. New Haven: Yale University Press.

Phelps Brown, E. H. and Hopkins, S. V. 1955. "Seven Centuries of Building Wages," *Economica*, 22 (August): 195–206.

———. 1956. "Seven Centuries of the Prices of Consumables," *Economica*, 23 (November): 296–314.

Porat, Marc Uri. 1977. "The Information Economy, Definitions and Measurement," Office of Telecommunications, Special Publication, 77-12(1), U.S. Department of Commerce, Washington.

Romer, Paul M. 1985. "Increasing Returns and Long Run Growth," Working Paper No. 27. University of Rochester, October.

Summers, Robert and Heston, Alan. 1984. "Improved International Comparisons of Real Product and Its Composition, 1950–1980," *Review of Income and Wealth*, 30 (June): 207–262.

Summers, Robert, Kravis, I. B., and Heston, Alan. 1986. "Changes in World Income Distribution," *Journal of Policy Modeling*, 6 (May): 237–269.

Teece, David J. 1976. *The Multinational Corporation and the Resources Cost of International Technology Transfer*. Cambridge: Ballinger.

U.S. Bureau of Census. 1973. *Long Term Economic Growth 1860–1970*. Washington, D.C., June.

Veblen, Thorstein. 1915. *Imperial Germany and the Industrial Revolution*. New York: Macmillan.

Viner, Jacob. 1958. *The Long View and the Short*. Glencoe: Free Press.

Williamson, Jeffrey G. 1983. "Why Was British Growth So Slow During the Industrial Revolution?" Unpublished, Harvard Institute of Economic Research.

CHAPTER 13

Productivity Growth, Convergence, and Welfare: Comment

J. BRADFORD DE LONG

In the previous chapter, William Baumol confirmed the expectations of convergence theory by finding that between 1870 and 1979 productivity rates of poorer countries grew more rapidly than those of richer countries. In this chapter, J. Bradford De Long argues that because only countries that converged by 1979 were included in the data set used by Baumol, convergence was assured. When De Long corrects for this sample-selection bias, convergence disappears. De Long then analyzes other variables to determine if the pattern of growth that he found can be explained. He does not find an association between democracy in 1870 and subsequent growth. De Long did find a significant relationship between religion and growth: Protestant cultures grew faster. But the author notes that the correlations will not hold for long given the growth rates of countries such as Japan and Italy. The optimistic view that there is a process of economic homogenization, a closing of the gap between rich and poor, is not sustained by the data. As the author concludes, "It pushes us away from the belief that even the nations of the now industrial West will have roughly equal standards of living in 2090 or 2190."

E CONOMISTS HAVE ALWAYS EXPECTED THE "CONVERGENCE" OF NATIONAL productivity levels. The theoretical logic behind this belief is powerful. The per capita income edge of the West is based on its application of the storehouse of industrial and administrative technology of the

---

Reprinted with permission from the *American Economic Review,* vol. 78, no. 5 (1986): 1038–1048.

Industrial Revolution. This storehouse is open: modern technology is a public good. The benefits of tapping this storehouse are great, and so nations will strain every nerve to assimilate modern technology and their incomes will converge to those of industrial nations.

William Baumol (1986) argues that convergence has shown itself strongly in the growth of industrial nations since 1870.[1] According to Baumol, those nations positioned to industrialize are much closer together in productivity now than a century ago. He bases this conclusion on a regression of growth since 1870 on 1870 productivity for sixteen countries covered by Angus Maddison (1982).[2]

Baumol's finding of convergence might—even though Baumol himself does not believe that it should—naturally be read to support two further conclusions. First, slow relative growth in the United States since World War II was inevitable: convergence implies that in the long run divergent national cultures, institutions, or policies cannot sustain significant productivity edges over the rest of the developed world. Second, one can be optimistic about future development. Maddison's sixteen all assimilated modern technology and converged; perhaps all developing nations will converge to Western living standards once they acquire a foundation of technological literacy.

But when properly interpreted Baumol's finding is less informative than one might think. For Baumol's regression uses an *ex post* sample of countries that are now rich and have successfully developed. By Maddison's choice, those nations that have not converged are excluded from his sample because of their resulting present relative poverty. Convergence is thus all but guaranteed in Baumol's regression, which tells us little about the strength of the forces making for convergence among nations that in 1870 belonged to what Baumol calls the "convergence club."

Only a regression run on an *ex ante* sample, a sample not of nations that have converged but of nations that seemed in 1870 likely to converge, can tell us whether growth since 1870 exhibits "convergence." The answer to this *ex ante* question—have those nations that a century ago appeared well placed to appropriate and utilize industrial technology converged?—is no. . . .

Maddison (1982) compiles long-run national income and aggregate productivity data for sixteen successful capitalist nations.[3] Because he focuses on nations which (a) have a rich data base for the construction of historical national accounts and (b) have successfully developed, the nations in Maddison's sixteen are among the richest nations in the world today. Baumol regresses the average rate of annual labor productivity growth over 1870–1979 on a constant and on the log of labor productivity in 1870 for this sample. He finds the inverse relationship of the first line of Table 13.1. The slope is large enough to erase by 1979 almost all initial income gaps, and the residual variance is small.

Regressing the log difference in per capita income between 1870 and 1979 on a constant and the log of per capita income in 1870 provides a slightly stronger case for convergence, as detailed in the second line of Table 13.1. The logarithmic income specification offers two advantages. The slope has the intuitive interpretation that a value of minus one means that 1979 and 1870 relative incomes are uncorrelated, and extension of the sample to include additional nations becomes easier.

Baumol's regression line tells us little about the strength of forces making for convergence since 1870 among industrial nations. The sample suffers from selection bias, and the independent variable is unavoidably measured with error. Both of these create the appearance of convergence whether or not it exists in reality. Sample selection bias arises because any nations relatively rich in 1870 that have not converged fail to make it into Maddison's sixteen. Maddison's sixteen thus include Norway but not Spain, Canada but not Argentina, and Italy but not Ireland. . . .

The unbiased sample used here meets three criteria. First, it is made up of nations that had high potential for economic growth as of 1870, in which modern economic growth had begun to take hold by the middle of the nineteenth century. Second, inclusion in the sample is not conditional on subsequent rapid growth. Third, the sample matches Baumol's as closely as possible, both because the best data exist for Maddison's sixteen and because analyzing an unbiased sample close to Baumol's shows that different conclusions arise not from different estimates but from removing sample selection and errors in variables' biases.

Table 13.1   Regressions Using Maddison's Sixteen

Independent Variable	Dependent Variable	Constant	Slope Coefficient	Standard Error of Estimate	R^2
Natural Log of 1870 Productivity	Annual Percent Productivity Growth	5.251	−0.749 .075	.14	.87
Natural Log of 1870 Income	Log Difference of 1979 and 1870 Income	8.457	−0.995 .094	.15	.88

Source: Data from Maddison (1982).

Per capita income in 1870 is an obvious measure of whether a nation was sufficiently technologically literate and integrated into world trade in 1870 to be counted among the potential convergers. . . .

. . . The choice of cutoff level itself requires balancing three goals: including only nations which really did in 1870 possess the social capability for rapid industrialization; including as many nations in Baumol's sample as possible; and building as large a sample as possible. . . .

If the convergence club membership cutoff is set low enough to include all Maddison's sixteen, then nations with 1870 incomes above 300 1975 dollars are included. This sample covers half the world. All Europe including Russia, all of South America, and perhaps others (Mexico and Cuba?) were richer than Japan in 1870. This sample does not provide a fair test of convergence. The Japanese miracle is a miracle largely because there was little sign in 1870 that Japan—or any nation as poor as Japan—was a candidate for rapid industrialization.

The second poorest of Maddison's sixteen in 1870 was Finland. Taking Finland's 1870 income as a cutoff leads to a sample in which Japan is removed, while Argentina, Chile, East Germany,[4] Ireland, New Zealand, Portugal, and Spain are added. . . .

All the additional nations have strong claims to belong to the 1870 convergence club. All were well integrated into the Europe-based international economy. All had bright development prospects as of 1870. . . . Argentina, Chile, and New Zealand were grouped in the nineteenth century with Australia and Canada as countries with temperate climates, richly endowed with natural resources, attracting large-scale immigration and investment, and exporting large quantities of raw and processed agricultural commodities. They were all seen as natural candidates for the next wave of industrialization.

Ireland's economy was closely integrated with the most industrialized economy in the world. Spain and Portugal had been the technological leaders of Europe during the initial centuries of overseas expansion—their per capita incomes were still above the European mean in the 1830s (Paul Bairoch, 1981)—and had retained close trading links with the heart of industrial Europe. Coke was used to smelt iron in Asturias in the 1850s, and by 1877 3,950 miles of railroad had been built in Spain. It is difficult to see how one could exclude Portugal and Spain from the convergence club without also excluding nations like Sweden and Finland.

Baumol's sample failed to include those nations that should have belonged to any hypothetical convergence club but that nevertheless did not converge. The enlarged sample might include nations not in the 1870 convergence club. Consider Kuwait today: Kuwait is rich, yet few would take its failure to maintain its relative standard of living over the next fifty years as evidence against convergence. For Kuwait's present wealth does not necessarily carry with it the institutional capability to turn oil wealth into next generation's industrial wealth. . . .

The volume of overseas investment poured into the additional nations by investors from London and Paris between 1870 and 1913 tells us that investors thought these nations' development prospects good. Herbert Feis' (1930) standard estimates of French and British overseas investment [the interested reader should refer to Table 2, p. 1,143 of the original article] show the six non-European nations among the top ten[5] recipients of investment per capita from France and Britain, and four of the five top recipients of investment belong to the once-rich twenty-two.[6] Every pound or franc invested is an explicit bet that the recipient country's rate of profit will remain high and an implicit bet that its rate of economic growth will be rapid. The coincidence of the nations added on a per capita income basis and the nations that would have been added on a foreign investment basis is powerful evidence that these nations do belong in the potential convergence club.

Errors in estimating 1870 income are unavoidable and produce equal and opposite errors in 1870–1979 growth. These errors therefore create the appearance of convergence where it does not exist in reality. . . .[7]

From one point of view, the relatively poor quality of much of the nineteenth century data is not a severe liability for this chapter. Only if there is less measurement error than allowed for will the results be biased against convergence. A more direct check on the importance of measurement error can be performed by examining convergence starting at some later date for which income estimates are based on a firmer foundation. A natural such date is 1913.[8] The relationship between initial income and subsequent growth is examined for the period 1913–1979 in Table 13.2.

The longer 1870–1979 sample of Table 13.3 . . . is slightly more hospitable to convergence than is the 1913–1979 sample, but for neither sample do the regression lines reveal a significant inverse relationship between initial income and subsequent growth. When it is assumed that there is no measurement error in 1870 income, there is a large negative slope to the regression line. But even in this case the residual disturbance term is large. When measurement error variance is assumed equal to half disturbance variance, the slope is slightly but not significantly negative.

For the central case of equal variances growth since 1870 is unrelated to income in 1870. There is no convergence. Those countries with

Table 13.2   Maximum Likelihood Estimation for the Once-Rich Twenty-Two, 1913–1979

p	Slope Coefficient B	Standard Error of Slope	Standard Error of Regression	Standard Error in 1870 PCI
0.0	−.333	.116	.171	.000
0.5	−.140	.136	.151	.107
1.0	0.021	.158	.133	.133
2.0	0.206	.191	.106	.150
Infinity	0.444	.238	.000	.167

Source: Data from Maddison (1982).

Table 13.3   Maximum Likelihood Estimation for the Once-Rich Twenty-Two, 1870–1979

p	Slope Coefficient B	Standard Error of Slope	Standard Error of Regression	Standard Error in 1870 PCI
0.0	−.566	.144	.207	.000
0.5	−.292	.192	.192	.136
1.0	0.110	.283	.170	.170
2.0	0.669	.463	.134	.190
Infinity	1.381	.760	.000	.196

Source: Data from Maddison (1982).

income edges have on average maintained them. If measurement error is assumed larger than the regression disturbance there is not convergence but divergence. Nations rich in 1870 or 1913 have subsequently widened relative income gaps. The evidence can be presented in other ways. The standard deviations of log income are given in Table 13.4. Maddison's sixteen do converge: the standard deviation of log income in 1979 is only 35 percent of its 1870 value. But the appearance of convergence is due to selection bias: the once-rich twenty-two have as wide a spread of relative incomes today as in 1870.

The failure of convergence to emerge for nations rich in 1870 is due to the nations—Chile, Argentina, Spain, and Portugal. In the early 1970s none of these was a democracy. Perhaps only industrial nations with democratic political systems converge. A dummy variable for democracy over 1950–80 is significant in the central ($p = 1$) case in the once-rich twenty-two regression in *a* at the 1 percent level, as detailed in Table 13.5.

But whether a nation is a democracy over 1950–80 is not exogenous but is partly determined by growth over the preceding century. As of 1870 it was not at all clear which nations would become stable democracies. Of the once-rich twenty-two, France, Austria (including Czechoslovakia), and Germany were empires; Britain had a restricted franchise; Spain and Portugal were semiconstitutional monarchies; the United States had just undergone a civil war; and Ireland was under foreign occupation. That all of these countries would be stable democracies by 1950 seems *ex ante* unlikely. Table 13.6 shows that shifting to an *ex ante* measure of democracy[9] removes the correlation. Whether a nation's politics are democratic in 1870 has little to do with growth since. The elective affinity of democracy and opulence is not one way with democracy as cause and opulence as effect.

There is one striking *ex ante* association between growth over 1870–1979 and a predetermined variable: a nation's dominant religious establishment. As Table 13.7 shows, a religious establishment variable that is one for Protestant, one-half for mixed, and zero for Catholic

Table 13.4   Standard Deviations of Log Output for Maddison's Sixteen and the Once-Rich Twenty-Two

Sample	1870	1913	1979
Maddison's 16	.411	.355	.145
Once-Rich 22	.315	.324	.329

Source: Data from Maddison (1982).

Table 13.5   Democracy over 1950–1980 and Long-Run Growth for the Once-Rich Twenty-Two, 1870–1979

p	Slope Coefficient *B*	Standard Error of Slope	Coefficient on Democracy Variable	Standard Error	Standard Error in 1870 PCI	Standard Error of Regression
0.0	−.817	.277	.495	.085	.155	.000
0.5	−.744	.203	.476	.084	.154	.109
1.0	−.599	.208	.437	.090	.150	.150
2.0	0.104	.227	.248	.071	.131	.185
Infinity	1.137	.019	.044	.003	.000	.198

Source: Data from Maddison (1982).

Table 13.6   Democracy in 1870 and Long-Run Growth for the Once-Rich Twenty-Two, 1870–1979

p	Slope Coefficient B	Standard Error of Slope	Coefficient on Democracy Variable	Standard Error	Standard Error in 1870 PCI	Standard Error of Regression
0.0	–.567	.342	.001	.091	.207	.000
0.5	–.272	.322	–.038	.094	.192	.136
1.0	0.164	.454	–.095	.115	.169	.169
2.0	0.742	.976	–.170	.180	.131	.155
Infinity	1.231	.167	–.195	.022	.000	.194

Source: Data from Maddison (1982).

Table 13.7   Dominant Religion in 1870 and Long-Run Growth for the Once-Rich Twenty-Two, 1870–1979

p	Slope Coefficient B	Standard Error of Slope	Coefficient on Democracy Variable	Standard Error	Standard Error in 1870 PCI	Standard Error of Regression
0.0	–.789	.252	.429	.088	.166	.000
0.5	–.688	.225	.403	.088	.164	.116
1.0	–.470	.248	.347	.098	.158	.158
2.0	0.375	.232	.132	.061	.132	.187
Infinity	1.199	.021	–.003	.004	.000	.197

Source: Data from Maddison (1982).

nations is significantly correlated with growth as long as measurement error variance is not too high.[10]

This regression is very difficult to interpret.[11] It does serve as an example of how culture may be associated with substantial divergence in growth performance. But "Protestantism" is correlated with many things—early specialization in manufacturing (for a given level of income), a high investment ratio, and a northern latitude, to name three. Almost any view—except a belief in convergence—of what determines long-run growth is consistent with this correlation between growth and religious establishment. Moreover, this correlation will not last: neither fast grower Japan nor fast grower Italy owes anything to the Protestant ethic. The main message of Table 13.7 is that, for the once-rich twenty-two, a country's religious establishment has been a surprisingly good proxy for the social capability to assimilate modern technology.

The long-run data do not show convergence on any but the most optimistic reading. They do not support the claim that those nations that should have been able to rapidly assimilate industrial technology have all converged. Nations rich among the once-rich twenty-two in 1870 have not grown more slowly than the average of the sample. And of the nations outside this sample, only Japan has joined the industrial leaders.

This is not to say that there are no forces pushing for convergence. Convergence does sometimes happen. Technology is a public good. Western Europe (except Iberia) and the British settlement colonies of Australia, Canada, and the United States are now all developed. Even Italy, which seemed outside the sphere of advanced capitalism two generations ago, is near the present income frontier reached by the richest nations. The convergence of Japan and Western Europe toward U.S. standards of productivity in the years after World War II is an amazing achievement, and this does suggest that those present at the creation of the post–World War II international order did a very good job. But others—Spain, Portugal, Ireland, Argentina, and Chile—that one would in 1870 have thought capable of equally sharing this prosperity have not done so.[12] The capability to assimilate industrial technology appears to be surprisingly hard to acquire, and it may be distressingly easy to lose.

The forces making for "convergence" even among industrial nations appear little stronger than the forces making for "divergence." The absence of convergence pushes us away from a belief that in the long run technology transfer both is inevitable and is the key factor in economic growth. It pushes us away from the belief that even the nations of the now industrial West will have roughly equal standards of living in 2090 or 2190. And the absence of convergence even among nations relatively rich in 1870 forces us to take seriously arguments like Romer's (1986) that the relative income gap between rich and poor may tend to widen.

Notes

1. Consider Baumol (1986): "Among the main observations . . . is the remarkable convergence. . . . [T]here is a strong inverse correlation between a country's productivity . . . in 1870 and its . . . productivity growth since then," and Baumol (1987): "Even more remarkable . . . is the convergence in . . . living standards of the leading industrial countries. . . . In 1870 . . . productivity in Australia, the leader, was 8 times . . . Japan's (the laggard). By 1979, the ratio . . . had fallen to about two."

2. Moses Abramovitz (1986) follows the behavior of these sixteen over time and notes that even among these nations "convergence" is almost entirely a post–World War II phenomenon. Abramovitz' remarks on how the absence of the "social capability" to grasp the benefits of the Industrial Revolution may

prevent even nations that could benefit greatly from industrializing are well worth reading. Also very good on the possible determinants of the social capability to assimilate technology are Irma Adelman and Cynthia Taft Morris (1980), Gregory Clark (1987), and Richard Easterlin (1981).

3. Maddison's focus on nations that have been economically successful is deliberate; his aim in (1964), (1982), and (1987) is to investigate the features of successful capitalist development. In works like Maddison (1970, 1983) he has analyzed the long-run growth and development of less successful nations.

4. Perhaps only nations that have remained capitalist should be included in the sample, for occupation by the Red Army and subsequent relative economic stagnation have no bearing on whether the forces making for convergence among industrial capitalist economies are strong. There is only one centrally planned economy in the unbiased sample, and its removal has negligible quantitative effects on the estimated degree of convergence.

5. The foreign investment figures do provide a powerful argument for adding other Latin American nations—Mexico, Brazil, and Cuba—to the sample of those that ought to have been in the convergence club. Inclusion of these nations would weigh heavily against convergence.

6. Japan would not merit inclusion in the 1870 convergence club on the basis of foreign investment before World War I, for Japanese industrialization was not financed by British capital. Foreign investors' taste for Japan was much less, investment being equal to about one pound sterling per head and far below investment in such nations as Venezuela, Russia, Turkey, and Egypt. Admittedly, Japan was far away and not well known, but who would have predicted that Japan would have five times the measured per capita GNP of Argentina by 1979?

7. By contrast, errors in measuring 1979 per capita income induce no systematic bias in the relationship between standard of living in 1870 and growth since, although they do diminish the precision of coefficient estimates.

8. The data for 1913 are much more plentiful and solid than for other years in the early years of the twentieth century because of the concentration of historians' efforts on obtaining a pre–World War I benchmark. Beginning the sample at 1913 does mean that changes in country's "social capability" for development as a result of World War I appear in the error term in the regression. If those nations that suffered most badly in World War I were nations relatively poor in World War I, there would be cause for alarm that the choice of 1913 had biased the sample against finding convergence when it was really present. But the major battlefields of World War I lay in and the largest proportional casualties were suffered by relatively rich nations at the core of industrial Europe.

9. Defined as inclusion of the electorate of more than half the adult male population.

10. The once-rich twenty-two are split into nations that had Protestant religious establishments in 1870 (Australia, Denmark, Finland, E. Germany, Netherlands, New Zealand, Norway, Sweden, U.K., and United States), intermediate nations—nations that either were split in established religion in 1870 or that had undergone violent and prolonged religious wars between Protestant and Catholics in the centuries after the Protestant Reformation—(Belgium, Canada, France, West Germany, and Switzerland), and nations that had solid

Catholic religious establishments in 1870 (Argentina, Austria, Chile, Ireland, Italy, Portugal, and Spain). This classification is judgmental and a matter of taste: are the Netherlands one of the heartlands of the Protestant Ethic or are they one of the few nations tolerant and pluralistic on matters of religion in the seventeenth century?

11. The easy explanation would begin with the medieval maxim *homo mercato vix aut numquam placere potest Deo:* the merchant's business can never please God. Medieval religious discipline was hostile to market capitalism, the Protestant Reformation broke this discipline down in some places, and capitalism flourished most and modern democratic growth took hold strongest where this breakdown of medieval discipline had been most complete.

But this easy explanation is at best incomplete. Initially the Reformation did not see a relaxation of religious control. Strong Protestantism—Calvin's Geneva or Cromwell's Republic of the Saints—saw theology and economy closely linked in a manner not unlike the Ayatollah's Iran. And religious fanaticism is not often thought of as a source of economic growth.

Nevertheless the disapproval of self-interested profit seeking by radical Protestantism went hand-in-hand with seventeenth century economic development. And by 1800 profit seeking and accumulation for accumulation's sake had become morally praiseworthy activities in many nations with Protestant religious establishments. How was the original Protestant disapproval for the market transformed? Accounting for the evolution of the economic ethic of the Protestant West from Jean Calvin to Cotton Mather to Benjamin Franklin to Andrew Carnegie is a deep puzzle in economic history. The best analysis may still be the psychological account given by Max Weber (1958). Originally published in 1905.

12. One can find good reasons—ranging from the Red Army to landlord political dominance to the legacy of imperialism—for the failure of each of the additional nations to have reached the world's achieved per capita income frontier in 1979. But the fact that there are good reasons for the relative economic failure of each of these seven nations casts substantial doubt on the claim that the future will see convergence, for "good reasons" for economic failure will always be widespread. It is a safe bet that in 2090 one will be able *ex post* to identify similar "good reasons" lying behind the relative economic decline of those nations that will have fallen out of the industrial core.

References

Abramovitz, M. 1986. "Catching Up, Forging Ahead, and Falling Behind," *Journal of Economic History,* June, 46: 385–406.

Adelman, I. and C. T. Morris. 1980. "Patterns of Industrialization in the Nineteenth and Early Twentieth Centuries," in Paul Uselding, ed., *Research in Economic History,* Vol. 5, Greenwich: JAI Press, 217–46.

Bairoch, P. 1981. "The Main Trends in National Economic Disparities Since the Industrial Revolution," in P. Bairoch and M. Lévy-Leboyer, eds., *Disparities in Economic Development Since the Industrial Revolution,* New York: St. Martin's Press.

Baumol, W. 1987. "America's Productivity 'Crisis'," *The New York Times,* February 15, 3:2.

———. 1986. "Productivity Growth, Convergence, and Welfare," *American Economic Review,* December, 76: 1072–85.

Clark, G. 1987. "Why Isn't the Whole World Developed? Lessons from the Cotton Mills," *Journal of Economic History,* March, 47: 141–74.

Easterlin, R. 1981. "Why Isn't the Whole World Developed?," *Journal of Economic History,* March, 41: 1–19.

Feis, H. 1930. *Europe, The World's Banker,* New Haven: Yale.

Maddison, A. 1987. "Growth and Slowdown in Advanced Capitalist Economies," *Journal of Economic Literature,* June, 25: 649–98.

———. 1983. "A Comparison of Levels of GDP per Capita in Developed and Developing Countries, 1700–1980," *Journal of Economic History,* March, 43: 27–41.

———. 1982. *Phases of Capitalist Development,* Oxford: Oxford University Press.

———. 1970. *Economic Progress and Policy in Developing Countries,* London: Allen & Unwin.

———. 1964. *Economic Growth in the West,* New York: The Twentieth Century Fund.

Romer, P. 1986. "Increasing Returns and Long Run Growth," *Journal of Political Economy,* October, 94: 1002–37.

Weber, M. 1958. *The Protestant Ethic and the Spirit of Capitalism,* New York: Scribner's. Originally published in 1905.

CHAPTER 14

World-Economic Trends in the Distribution of Income, 1965–1992

ROBERTO PATRICIO KORZENIEWICZ
AND TIMOTHY PATRICK MORAN

It is helpful to look at recent worldwide trends in income distribution to see which school, convergence or divergence, receives more support. In this chapter the authors examine the period 1965–1992 and look at income distribution trends both within-country and between-country. They find very strong evidence of a worldwide increase in income inequality that is mainly a function of gaps between countries. Moreover, they find that income inequality worldwide has increased sharply over the period that they study. To draw this conclusion they use data from 121 nations that account for over 93 percent of the world's population. One striking finding is that the income earned by the world's poorest population declined in the 1965–1992 period from 5.1 percent to 3.2 percent. However, the richest 20 percent increased their income share from 69.5 percent to 83.4 percent. They also find that in the period of the worldwide recession in the 1980s, the gaps grew even wider than in periods of growth, suggesting that dependency theory (see Part 5 of this book), which has argued that poor countries can grow quickly when the industrial core countries are in decline, is not support-ed. At the same time, this research seems to show that the worldwide spread of neoliberal capitalism has not been helpful in bridging the gap between nations. However, the authors do find that there has been some decline in within-country inequality, suggesting perhaps that neoliberal polices may have been of some benefit in attenuating domestic income inequality. The reader should compare these findings with the Firebaugh paper that follows in Chapter 15.

Reprinted with permission of the University of Chicago Press and the authors from the *American Journal of Sociology,* vol. 102, no. 4 (1997): 1000–1039.

W HILE CONTENDING THEORETICAL APPROACHES HAVE ADVANCED QUITE different speculations about trends in the global distribution of income, there are few systematic comparisons of these interpretations. To be sure, efforts to synthesize the relevant literature are complicated by the sheer number of pertinent debates and interpretations (as the topic is addressed either directly or indirectly by virtually all theories and empirical researchers dealing with world capitalist development). What is more important, empirical researchers have pursued separate paths of inquiry, following the boundaries enforced within different academic disciplines with few cross references between the various studies. The resulting literature is thus characterized by considerable heterogeneity in methods of inquiry, analytical assumptions, and theoretical concerns.

Despite these difficulties, there are rather clear trends within the literature. Overall, there is a general theoretical and empirical consensus that, until the 1950s, the development of capitalism was characterized by growing disparities in the distribution of income between poor and rich nations (although with some disagreements as to whether a significant gap existed before the 19th century; see Kuznets 1965; Bairoch 1962, 1981, 1993; Maddison 1983; Zimmerman 1962). This consensus broke down, however, when considering trends between the 1950s and 1970s, with contentious debates as to whether the world distribution of income subsequently moved toward convergence or growing inequality. Since the 1980s, finally, the literature has undergone a gradual but perceptible shift from analytical contention toward theoretical consensus.

The Argument for Convergence

A theoretical case for convergence has been made by authors across the social sciences. Some emphasize growing social similarities among all nations (Inkeles and Rossi 1956; Hoselitz 1960; Hoselitz and Moore 1963; Levy 1967; Inkeles 1969). Others, particularly within economics, argue that successful development itself generates institutional obstacles to continuing rapid growth among the wealthiest of nations, while "backward[ness] in level of productivity carries a *potential* for rapid advance" among poorer nations (Abramovitz 1986, p. 386, emphasis in the original; see also Veblen 1915; Rostow 1960; Kindleberger 1961; Gerschenkron 1962). For many proponents of this perspective, world markets serve to circulate new technologies and innovations, so "international product and factor markets unobstructed by either cartelization or governmental intervention will bring irrepressible and rapid growth to any poor country" (Olson 1982, p. 176; see also Rostow 1960; Baumol 1986). . . .

The Argument for Divergence

There is an extensive theoretical literature that challenges the hypothesis of convergence. A long-standing line of Marxist interpretation portrays inequality as a structural component of capitalist accumulation in a world-economy (Lenin 1939; Luxemburg 1951; Baran 1957; Magdoff 1969). On a different track, policymakers working for the Economic Commission for Latin America (ECLA) of the United Nations after World War II contended that a deterioration of terms of trade was leading to growing inequality between wealthy and poor nations (Prebisch 1950 and 1964; ECLA 1969; Furtado 1971). Parallel arguments were developed by Singer (1950) and Myrdal (1957). Later, and often evolving as a critique of the previous interpretations, dependency studies argued that the very existence of a capitalist international economy, as embodied in global trade or an international division of labor, entailed a continual transfer of surplus from poor (or satellite) to wealthy (or core) areas (e.g., Cardoso 1974, 1977; Cardoso and Faletto 1969; Dos Santos 1970; Frank 1966, 1967, and 1978). A similar emphasis on the persistence of world inequality also prevails within the original world-systems literature (e.g., Portes and Walton 1981; Wallerstein 1974, 1979, 1980). . . .

Providing empirical support for such interpretations, several quantitative studies indicate that the gap between poor and rich nations is extensive and growing. Kirman and Tomasini (1969) indicate that, regardless of the specific techniques used to evaluate this gap, the distance between the two groups grew during the 1950s and 1960s. While acknowledging that the relative gap narrowed slightly for a few regions experiencing high rates of economic growth (China, East Asia, the Middle East), Morawetz (1977) analyzes gross national product per capita (GNPPC) data to indicate that the absolute gap continued to widen during the 1950–75 period, and that even the relative gap continued to grow in many regions (Latin America, Africa, South Asia). Passé-Smith (1993a) performs a similar exercise, showing a widening gap over the 1975–90 period in absolute as well as relative terms (except for a few countries, such as Italy and Japan, and for the East Asia/Pacific region). These conclusions are compatible with Jackman (1982), who argues that the overall gap between poor and wealthy nations increased in the 1970s, although with some convergence between the wealthiest nations and the most developed peripheral countries. . . .

The differences in the empirical findings within the convergence/divergence debate are striking. To what extent can these differences be explained as an outcome of the data or methodological procedures selected by these studies? A careful analysis . . . finds no clear pattern in either data sources or methodological procedures that might explain these differences, as the structure of these studies (i.e., data sources, measures of inequality, sample size, or time period) does not go far in explaining the direction of their findings. In fact, studies with very different conclusions use the exact same data set to provide their evidence (e.g., Breedlove and Nolan [1988] and Peacock et al. [1984] use the data of Summers and Heston [1984, 1988] to find evidence for divergence, but the same source is used by Ram [1989] to claim growing convergence). Further inquiry into these differences, however, has been hampered by subsequent developments in the literature during the 1980s and 1990s.

Toward Theoretical Convergence?

Regardless of methodological disagreements, theoretical shifts since the 1980s have altered the terms of the convergence/divergence debate. Moving away from the convergence hypothesis, influential authors in the field of economics are acknowledging that growth in poor nations can continue to be hindered by persistent institutional constraints, while wealthy countries can experience unexpected pressures (e.g., domestic competition among regions or political transformations) that serve to overcome institutional constraints and to promote renewed growth (e.g., Abramovitz 1986; Adelman and Morris 1980; Barro and Sala-i-Martin 1992; Baumol 1986; Baumol and Wolff 1988; Clark 1987; De Long 1988; Easterlin 1981; Zind 1991; and some of the essays in Baumol, Nelson, and Wolff [1994]). . . .

Combined, the shifts reviewed in these pages have produced a noteworthy theoretical convergence. As studies have moved to focus on the impact of technological change and institutional innovation on global patterns of competition and economic growth, considerable overlap has emerged both between disciplines (e.g., sociology and economics) and between theoretical perspectives (e.g., world-systems theory and the new institutional economics). In this sense, a theoretical convergence in the 1990s has displaced to a considerable degree the contentious debates of the 1970s and 1980s on the future of world income inequalities.

With the advance of this theoretical convergence, however, empirical research on world income inequality has lagged behind. Replacing such inquiries, the social sciences in general have come to be guided in the *1990s* by a series of general assumptions drawn from apparent patterns of growth in the contemporary world-economy. For example, the economic success of East Asia is often presumed to entail a substantial redistribution of world income from wealthy to poor nations. To be sure, the paucity of research on these trends suggests that such assumptions have gained ground through a selective assimilation of partial observations rather than through systematic empirical verification. These untested assumptions are legitimated primarily by their common-sense appeal, yet they have come to prevail in establishing the boundaries of reasonable empirical inquiry in fields such as economic development.

The main concern of this study is to address the current lack of empirical research by evaluating recent trends in world income inequality. Such an effort is designed to begin addressing the lag between theoretical development and empirical inquiry discussed above. As always, such empirical inquiries often facilitate the task of evaluating which of the existing theoretical approaches (e.g., among those reviewed in this section) provides the best fit to observed trends. As indicated in the concluding section of this article, however, an evaluation of trends in world income inequality can also prove to be useful in explaining the very patterns of *theoretical* development addressed in this section. . . .

The World Distribution of Income, 1965–92

Data Sources

We rely on the GNPPC and population data available through the World Bank (1988 and various years). Since our study is no longer constrained by the spotty availability of data on within-country income distributions, the sample now includes the population of 121 countries for which observations were available in 1965 and the subsequent years presented in this article (a sample that accounts for 93.6% of the world population in 1990). . . .

Trends

Figure 14.1 shows the Lorenz curves for world income distribution in 1965 and 1990. As in the previous section, both curves indicate a preva-

Figure 14.1   World Distribution of Income, 1965 and 1990

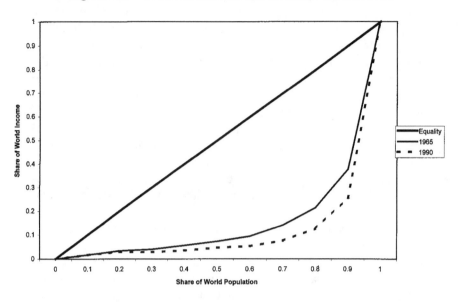

lence of profound inequality. Indeed, the summary measures show a constant increase throughout the period considered in this article, with the most pronounced increase taking place in the 1980s. As indicated in Table 14.1 and Figure 14.2 below, the Gini coefficient stood at .658 in 1965, and thereafter grew over every five-year period to reach .739 by 1990 (for an overall increase of 12.3%). Theil, with its greater sensitivity to transfers affecting low income earners, indicates an even larger increase, rising from .802 in 1965 to 1.107 by 1990 (for an overall increase of 38.0%).

There were significant differences in trends among each of the five-year intervals. Most important, income inequality changed relatively less over the 1965–70 and 1975–80 subperiods but became greatly accentuated between 1980 and 1990. For example, whereas the Gini coefficient increased by 3.5% in the 15 years between 1965 and 1980, the coefficient rose by 8.7% in the 10-year period between 1980 and 1990. Likewise, Theil increased by 8.5% between 1965 and 1980, but rose 27.2% in the subsequent decade. To make the same point in a different manner, the rise of inequality in the 1980s accounted for roughly three-quarters of the overall rise in global income inequality during the 1965–90 period (or 71.9% in the case of Gini; 77.7% in the case of Theil).

The character of these trends can be further specified by disaggre-

Table 14.1 World Income Distribution, 1965–90 (N = 121)

		1965	1970	1975	1980	1985	1990
Poorest 20%							
Quintile 5	GNPPC boundaries	30–90	60–110	90–170	120–140	110–290	80–350
	% of world GNPPC	2.25	2.17	2.11	1.65	1.82	1.38
	GNPPC	74	98	154	219	253	283
Quintile 4	GNPPC boundaries	90–100	110–130	170–180	240–300	290–320	350–370
	% of world GNPPC	2.87	2.77	2.45	2.21	2.26	1.78
	GNPPC	94	125	178	293	314	363
Quintile 3	GNPPC boundaries	100–270	130–280	180–500	300–1,030	320–810	370–730
	% of world GNPPC	4.15	3.81	3.68	3.52	3.25	2.11
	GNPPC	136	172	268	467	451	432
Quintile 2	GNPPC boundaries	270–1,110	280–1,790	500–1,550	1,030–4,443	810–4,123	760–4,060
	% of world GNPPC	21.23	21.29	16.42	18.28	15.39	11.29
	GNPPC	697	965	1,196	2,426	2,136	2,308
Richest 20%							
Quintile 1	GNPPC boundaries	1,110–3,650	1,790–4,980	1,550–9,070	4,443–17,800	4,123–16,770	4,060–32,790
	% of world GNPPC	69.50	69.97	75.35	75.38	77.27	83.44
	GNPPC	2,281	3,169	5,490	10,006	10,723	17,056
Richest 10%							
Decile 1	% of world GNPPC	47.26	46.86	48.73	46.27	52.19	56.09
Gini coefficient		.658	.662	.677	.682	.703	.740
		(.658)	(.655)	(.667)	(.664)	(.683)	(.712)
Theil coefficient		.802	.814	.862	.870	.945	1.108
		(.802)	(.791)	(.823)	(.813)	(.868)	(.990)

Figure 14.2   Summary of Measures of Inequality, 1964–1990

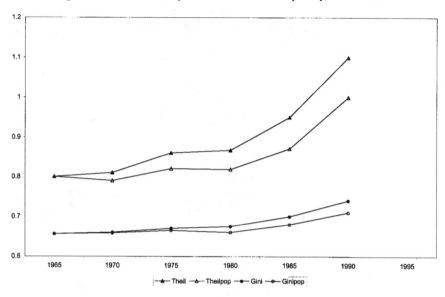

gating the between-country income data into population quintiles (see Table 14.1). The share of world income accruing to the poorest 40% of the world's population diminished over the 1965–90 period from 5.1% to 3.2%, for an overall decline of 37.3% (after increasing slightly between 1980 and 1985, the relative income of these two quintiles fell precipitously between 1985 and 1990). For the third quintile of the world's population, the share of world income diminished in every five-year period, for an overall decline of 49.2% between 1965 and 1990, with much of this decline taking place after 1985. Over the 1965–90 period as a whole, the three bottom quintiles of the world population experienced a noticeable convergence in their relative share of income (e.g., whereas the ratio of the average GNPPC of the third quintile to the poorest quintile was 1.8 in 1965, by 1990 it had declined slightly to 1.5).

The trends during the 1969–90 period as a whole were more unstable for the fourth population quintile. This quintile was characterized by considerable fluctuations, with its relative share of world income increasing during the 1965–70 and 1975–90 subperiods and declining over the other five-year periods (particularly during the 1980s). For the period as a whole, this quintile experienced a decline of 46.8% in its share of world income.

The richest 20% of the world's population was the only quintile to experience a sustained increase in its share of world income. Between 1965 and 1990, this quintile's relative share of world income increased from 69.5% to 83.4%, a change of 20.1%. The increase in its share of income rose more rapidly during the 1970–75 and 1980–90 subperiods. Given these trends, the overall distance between the poorest four quintiles and the richest quintile increased significantly over the 1965–90 period as a whole. Thus, whereas the ratio of the average GNPPC of the first quintile to the poorest quintile was 30.9 in 1965, by 1990 it had increased to 60.5. All quintiles lost relative ground to the wealthiest quintile between 1965 and 1990.

The trends that characterized the wealthiest quintile of the population, however, were not evenly distributed within the quintile. As suggested by the data in Table 14.1, while both top deciles increased their relative share of world income over the 1965–90 period, each of the two deciles was characterized by some fluctuations. For the period as a whole, the second decile experienced a relatively greater increase in income (23.0%) than the first decile (18.7%). By 1990, however, the top decile had reached its highest relative share of world income (56.1%) for the period as a whole, and all the increase in its relative income accrued during the 1980s (when its income rose by 21.2%). The second decile, on the other hand, experienced most of the growth in its relative share of world income prior to the 1980s (as its share rose 30.9% between 1969 and 1990), and then underwent an initial decline between 1980 and 1985 before slightly recovering by 1990.

These trends become even more stark if the disaggregation of income data by population shares is carried out with data that include both between- and within-country distributions of income. As can be observed in Table 14.2, between 1965 and 1992, the eight poorest world population deciles lost income shares relative to the top two population deciles. The decline was most pronounced for the poorest deciles: the world income share of the poorest 30% of the world population declined from 2.1% to 1.0%, for an overall decline of 51.6% during the 1965–92 period. For the four intermediate deciles (deciles 4–7 in Table 14.2), the world income share declined from 7.8% to 4.1%, for an overall decline of 46.9% during the same period. The decline was less pronounced in decile 8, but only the top 20% of the world population experienced an increase during the period under consideration, increasing their overall share of world income from 82.0% in 1965 to 88.9% by 1992. In either case, if these population deciles were represented as 10 runners in the midst of a race, with the lead runner already considerably

Table 14.2   World Income Distribution, 1965 and 1992 (N = 46)

Decile		1965	1992	% Change
Poorest 10%				
1	GNPPC boundaries	8–39	13–150	
	% world GNPPC	.51	0.24	–52.94
	Weighted average GNPPC	35.40	134.00	
2	GNPPC boundaries	39–59	150–239	
	% world GNPPC	.70	.33	–52.86
	Weighted average GNPPC	48.38	182.23	
3	GNPPC boundaries	59–72	239–259	
	% world GNPPC	.92	.46	–.50
	Weighted average GNPPC	63.61	254.29	
4	GNPPC boundaries	72–91	259–385	
	% world GNPPC	1.10	.58	–47.27
	Weighted average GNPPC	76.05	316.36	
5	GNPPC boundaries	91–100	385–373	
	% world GNPPC	1.43	.80	–44.06
	Weighted average GNPPC	99.02	437.39	
6	GNPPC boundaries	100–176	573–642	
	% world GNPPC	2.13	1.10	–48.36
	Weighted average GNPPC	147.64	605.13	
7	GNPPC boundaries	176–246	642–998	
	% world GNPPC	3.12	1.65	–47.12
	Weighted average GNPPC	216.21	903.87	
8	GNPPC boundaries	246–949	998–6,956	
	% world GNPPC	8.14	5.93	–27.15
	Weighted average GNPPC	564.79	3,248.61	
9	GNPPC boundaries	949–2,245	6,959–21,615	
	% world GNPPC	20.73	24.13	16.40
	Weighted average GNPPC	1,437.83	13,219.30	
Richest 10%				
10	GNPPC boundaries	2,245–7,501	21,615–54,093	
	% world GNPPC	61.23	64.77	5.78
	Weighted average GNPPC	4,246.10	35,481.06	

ahead of the slower nine in 1965, by 1992 runner 9 (decile 9) has broken away from the pack and is the only one to gain ground relative to the leader of the race. Meanwhile, the other eight runners (deciles 1–8) have dropped further and further behind.

Some may argue that this striking growth in income inequality could be primarily an outcome of differential rates of population growth in low and high-income nations. To evaluate this possibility, the study calculated T^*, which measures inequality in the case of unchanged population shares (Theil 1967, p. 110). Considering 1965 the fixed base year in which the population shares are $X_i, \ldots X_n$, new income shares can be calculated for each country in current year t as follows:

$$Y^*_{it} = \frac{X_i Z_{it}}{\sum\limits_{j=1}^{n} X_j Z_{jt}}, \; i = 1,...,n,$$

where Z equals the per capita income of country i and Y9, then, repre-sents the income share in any current year t if the population shares in t were held constant at 1965 levels and if the per capita incomes were actually observed in the current year. Hence,

$$T^* = \sum\limits_{i=1}^{n} Y^*_{it} \ln \frac{Y^*_{it}}{X_i},$$

is the level of inequality that exists when controlling for population.

As indicated by Table 14.1, even if population shares are held con-stant to their 1965 dimensions, world income inequality as measured by Gini would still have grown by 8.2% between 1965 and 1992 (as compared to the actual growth of 12.3% reported earlier in this sec-tion). Likewise, under the same assumption, Theil still shows an increase of 23.4% (as compared to the actual growth of 38.0% previ-ously reported). Furthermore, the overall direction of the trends in world income inequality for every five-year period are essentially sim-ilar (with 1965–70 and 1975–80 showing an attenuation of these inequalities, and the 1980s dramatically erasing all gains made in pre-vious years). In short, if population growth rates were identical among all areas of the world, income inequality would have increased slightly less, but the overall direction of the trends would not be significantly different.

We also evaluated whether the observed trends would be altered by the use of GDPPC [gross domestic product per capita] rather than GNPPC data, and no significant differences were found. Using avail-able World Bank (1995) data on GDPPC at market prices in current U.S. dollars for the 1965–90 period *(N = 112 countries, including China and India)*, the respective Gini coefficient rose from .671 in 1965, to .701 in 1980 and .738 by 1990. The Gini coefficient obtained for 1990 with the GDPPC data is virtually identical to the Gini coefficient report-ed for the GNPPC data (.739). The overall increase in inequality obtained through the GDPPC data (10.0%) was slightly less pronounced than observed in the GNPPC data (12.3%), but the direction of trends in each set of data coincided both for each five-year sub-period, and for the 1965–90 period as a whole.

Mobility

Given rising inequality, to what extent were the populations of particular nations able to challenge the general tendencies and increase their relative control, over income? As indicated earlier in the first section, such an evaluation is of considerable importance, as common sense in the field has come to represent the economic success of East Asia as involving a substantial redistribution of world income from wealthy to poor nations.

Focusing on the between-country data ($N = 121$), there was considerable stability over time in the distribution of world population among the income quintiles (see Table 14.3). A chi-square test was applied to the relationship between each country's quintile location in 1965 and in 1990, and this relationship was found to be statistically significant (overall, X_1 [16; $N = 124$] = 132.23, $P < .0001$; as indexed by Cramer's statistic, the strength of the relationship was 0.52). The population of 60.5% of the countries in our sample fell into the same quintile in both 1965 and 1990, and there were only 13 countries that were not classified in the same or adjacent quintiles in both years (upward mobility was most strongly featured in the cases of Botswana, Central African Republic, the Comoros, Indonesia, Lesotho, Oman, South Korea, and Taiwan; downward mobility was most evident for Niger, Nigeria, Madagascar, Mozambique, and Zaire). There were no cases of countries rising from the two poorest quintiles to the wealthiest quintile.

Similar results are suggested by the data that combine between- and within-country information on income distribution. The appendix table at the end of this article shows the 1965 and 1992 ranking and decile location of the country population quintiles in the sample. For descriptive purposes, "high upward mobility" involved those country quintiles that moved up either two or three deciles [the interested reader should refer to the appendix in the original text]. For the period under consideration, 6.4% of the world population was characterized by such mobility. Overall, this group of country quintiles increased its share of world GNP from 1.9% in 1965 to 6.5% by 1992.

If "very high upward mobility" involved a shift of four deciles or more between 1965 and 1992, 0.8% of the world population in 1965 (and 1.0% of the same population in 1992) underwent such mobility. These country quintiles were all related to six countries: Botswana (all four bottom quintiles), Lesotho (fourth quintile), Malaysia (poorest quintile), South Korea (two bottom quintiles), Thailand (second quintile), and Tunisia (second quintile). Overall, the group of country quintiles characterized by "very high upward mobility" increased its share of world GNP from 0.1% in 1965 to 0.4% by 1992.

Table 14.3 Position of Nations in World Income Distribution, 1965 and 1990

	1965				
	Quintile 5 (17)	Quintile 4 (5)	Quintile 3 (40)	Quintile 2 (31)	Quintile 1 (31)
1990					
Quintile 5 (18)	Afghanistan Bangladesh Burundi Chad Ethiopia Malawi Myanmar Nepal Rwanda Tanzania Upper Volta	Gambia India	Madagascar Mozambique Niger Nigeria Zaire		
Quintile 4 (3)	China	Haiti	India		
Quintile 3 (23)	Central Af. Rep. Comoros Indonesia Lesotho	Benin China	Angola Bolivia Ivory Coast Egypt Ghana Honduras Kenya Liberia Pakistan Senegal Sri Lanka Sudan Togo Zambia Zimbabwe	Nicaragua	
Quintile 2 (42)	Botswana		Algeria Cameroon Congo Dominica Philippines St. Lucia St. Vincent Swaziland	Belize Brazil Chile Colombia	Mauritainia Mexico Panama Peru

(continues)

Table 14.3 continued

	Dominican Rep.	Syria	Costa Rica	Romania	Luxembourg
	Morocco	Thailand	El Salvador	South Africa	Lybia
	Papua New Guinea	Tunisia	Gabon	Soviet Union	Netherlands
	Paraguay		Fiji	Suriname	New Zealand
			Guatemala	Turkey	Norway
			Jamaica	Uruguay	Soviet Union
			Malaysia	Australia	Spain
Quintile 1	Oman	Antigua and Barbuda	Portugal	Austria	Sweden
(38)	South Korea	Barbados	Saudi Arabia	Bahamas	Switzerland
	Taiwan	Greece	Seychelles	Belgium	USA
		Hong Kong	Singapore	Canada	West Germany
		Malta		Denmark	
				Finland	
				France	
				Great Britain	
				Iceland	
				Ireland	
				Israel	
				Italy	
				Japan	
				Kuwait	

Other country quintiles underwent opposite trends. Following equivalent criteria, "high downward mobility" involved country quintiles that moved down either two or three deciles. For the period under consideration, 1.0% of the world population in 1965 (and 1.3% of the same population in 1992) was characterized by such mobility. This mobility involved most clearly population quintiles from countries from Africa (e.g., the two wealthiest quintiles of Tanzania and the middle quintile of Zimbabwe) and Latin America (e.g., the three poorest quintiles of Guatemala, the poorest quintile of Peru and Panama, and the fourth quintile in Honduras), and to a lesser extent from Asia (e.g., the fourth quintile of Bangladesh). Overall, this group of country quintiles decreased its share of world GNP from 0.15% in 1965 to 0.06% by 1992.

In general terms, however, the main characteristic of the period was a striking stability in the relative standing of the population of poor and wealthy nations. "Stability" can be defined as involving country quintiles that remained in the same income decile or moved only to an adjacent income decile for the 1965–92 period as a whole. Hence defined, approximately 91.7% of the world population in 1965 (and 91.4% of the same population in 1992) experienced relative stability over the period as a whole. Overall, this share of the world population accounted for 93.1% of the 1992 world GNP in the sample under consideration (and 97.9% in 1965). Such stability further corroborates the few authors who have highlighted the growing inequalities of the 1980s (e.g., Arrighi 1991; Chase-Dunn 1989; Passé-Smith 1993a, 1993b), while challenging the hypothesis (e.g., as raised in Rain 1989) that world inequality in the distribution of income has been abating.

Discussion

The world distribution of income has become more unequal over the 1965–90 period, and while the gap between the populations of wealthy and poor nations has grown steadily since 1965, it intensified during the worldwide recession of the 1980s. These findings are robust even when controlling for population growth or using alternative sources of data. By decomposing world income inequality into between- and within-country components, we also found strong evidence that between-country inequalities are of significantly greater importance in shaping the trends in question. Overall, while between-country inequality has become more pronounced over the period under consideration, the opposite was the case of within-country inequality. However, the attenuation of income inequality within nations was not nearly sufficient to compensate for the accentuation of between-country inequality. Inequality in the distribution of income between-countries continues to be of essential importance to global social stratification.

The first section of this article notes that empirical studies on world income inequality are characterized by ambivalent findings. The trends in the distribution of world income found in this study, however, can be used to identify possible sources of these discrepant results. Most of these empirical studies were conducted with data from the 1960s and 1970s, a period in which trends of inequality were not as pronounced as they became in the 1980s. Given these conditions, minor differences in methodological procedures (e.g., in the percentage of the world population included in a sample, or in the indicator used to measure the distribution of income among nations) were likely to sway results in different directions. World income inequality grew at a more rapid pace during the 1980s, a decade when empirical research on this issue was lacking. Empirical studies that include this particular decade in their analysis, rather than restrict their investigation to the 1960s and 1970s, are likely to inevitably produce results that corroborate the main findings of this article.

The trends identified here also help understand the recent theoretical convergence discussed in the first section. On the one hand, indications of the persistence and deepening of world income inequality in the 1980s (slow growth in areas such as Latin America and Africa and high growth among core nations) are likely to have influenced scholars within the field of economics toward greater emphasis on the importance of institutional development and endogenous variables shaping growth. At the very least, such trends provided strong intuitive ammunition to analysts seeking to challenge the notion that exposure to markets alone would serve to reduce the income gap between wealthy and poor nations. On the other hand, such trends were accompanied by noteworthy exceptions. For the population of some poor and middle-income nations (such as those in East Asia), development strategies appeared to play an important role in generating sufficient economic growth to escape the polarization of income. These exceptions were particularly influential in shaping critical studies of the political economy of development within other disciplines in the social sciences.

While advancing our understanding of the current theoretical convergence that characterizes this field of inquiry, the findings reported in this article are insufficient to conclusively support one theoretical approach above all others in areas of continuing contention. Adherents of a world-systems perspective might claim that the persistence of inequality reflects the constraints inherent in the world-economy for the vast majority of the population. Other theoretical approaches might argue that such inequalities merely reflect the incomplete adoption of market-oriented strategies of growth in countries bounded by conflicts and negotiations involving rent-seeking interests, and that as countries abandon state-centered strategies of growth in favor of markets, a shift toward greater growth and social equality might be expected sometime in the future.

In this respect, however, the coming decade is likely to provide fundamental evidence as to whether a shift toward market-centered strategies of growth will deliver greater inequality or a more proportionate distribution of economic resources in the world-economy. This article joins others (e.g., Rubinson 1976; Breedlove and Nolan 1988; Peacock et al. 1988) to suggest easily implemented procedures that can be followed in the near future to continue tracing trends in world income inequality. By endorsing the use of easily available between-country data in such inquiries, the findings presented in this study will make it easier to closely track the future impact of market-centered strategies of growth on world income inequality and to further evaluate the relevance of alternative theoretical approaches.

Our findings indicate that efforts to account for patterns of development in the world-economy must include polarization as a crucial component of recent trends. Findings in this respect are rather clear. The world distribution of income became more unequal over the 1965–90 period, and inequality accelerated during the 1980s. Some populations (such as in East Asia) experienced upward mobility in a "world hierarchy of income," but such mobility is limited when compared to polarizing tendencies in the world distribution of income as a whole. These results highlight the continuing need for more detailed inquiries into the processes that generate growing inequality in the world distribution of income. In challenging current commonsense expectations regarding the economic opportunities easily available to the majority of the world population, such findings call at the very least for pause and critical reflection.

References

Abramovitz, Moses. 1986. "Catching Up, Forging Ahead, and Falling Behind." *Journal of Economic History* 46:385–406.

Adelman, Irma, and Amnon Levy. 1984. "Decomposing Theil's Index of Income Inequality into Between and Within Components." *Review of Income and Wealth* 30:119–21.

————. 1986. "Decomposing Theil's Index of Income Inequality: A Reply." *Review of Income and Wealth* 32:107–8.

Adelman, Irma, and Cynthia Taft Morris. 1967. *Society, Politics and Economic Development: A Quantitative Approach.* Baltimore: Johns Hopkins University Press.

————. 1980. "Patterns of Industrialization in the Nineteenth and Twentieth Centuries." 5:217–46 in *Research in Economic History,* edited by P. Uselding. Greenwich, Conn.: JAI Press.

Ahluwalia, Montek S. 1976. "Income Distribution and Development: Some Stylized Facts." *American Economic Review* 66:128–35.

————. 1993. "Income Inequality: Some Dimensions of the Problem." Pp. 31–9 in *Development and Underdevelopment: The Political Economy of Inequality,* edited by M. A. Seligson and J. T. Passé-Smith. Boulder, Colo.: Lynne Rienner.

Allison, P. D. 1978. "Measures of Inequality." *American Sociological Review* 43:865–80.

Altimir, Oscar. 1987. "Income Distribution Statistics in Latin America and Their Reliability." *Review of Income and Wealth* 33:111–55.

Ames, Edward, and Nathan Rosenberg. 1963. "Changing Technological Leadership and Industrial Growth." *Economic Journal* 73:13–31.

Amin, Samir. 1974. *Accumulation of a World Scale.* New York: Monthly Review Press.

Andic, S., and A. Peacock. 1961. "The International Distribution of Income." *Journal of the Royal Statistical Society,* ser. A, 124:206–18.

Arrighi, Giovanni. 1990. "The Developmentalist Illusion: A Reconceptualization of the Semiperiphery." Pp. 11–42 in *Semiperipheral States in the World-Economy,* edited by William G. Martin. New York: Greenwood Press.

————. 1991. "World Income Inequalities and the Future of Socialism." *New Left Review* 189:39–65.

————. 1994. *The Long Twentieth Century: Money, Power, and the Origins of Our Times.* London: Verso.

Arrighi, G., and Jessica Drangel. 1986. "The Stratification of the World-Economy: An Exploration of the Semiperipheral Zone." *Review* 10:9–74.

Arrighi, Giovanni, Roberto Patricio Korzeniewicz, and William Martin. 1986. "Three Crises, Three Zones: Core-Periphery Relations in the Long Twentieth Century." *Cahier du GIS Economie Mondiale, Tiers Monde, Developpement* 6:125–162.

Atkinson, Anthony. 1983. *The Economics of Inequality,* 2d ed. Oxford: Clarendon Press.

Bairoch, Paul. 1962. "Le mythe de la croissance iconomique rapide au XIX' siecle." *Revue de l'Institut de Sociologie* 2:307–31.

————. 1981. "The Main Trends in National Economic Disparities since the Industrial Revolution." Pp. 3–17 in *Disparities in Economic Development since the Industrial Revolution,* edited by P. Bairoch and M. Levy-Leboyer. London: Macmillan.

————. 1993. *Economic and World History: Myths and Paradoxes.* Chicago: University of Chicago Press.

Baran, Paul A. 1957. *The Political Economy of Growth.* New York: Monthly Review Press.

Barro, Robert J. 1990. "Government Spending in a Simple Model of Endogenous Growth." *Journal of Political Economy* 98:SI03–SI25.

———. 1991. "Economic Growth in a Cross Section of Countries." *Quarterly Journal of Economics* 106:407–43.

Barro, R. J., and Xavier Sala-i-Martin. 1992. "Convergence." *Journal of Political Economy* 100:223–51.

Baumol, William J. 1986. "Productivity Growth, Convergence, and Welfare: What the Long-Run Data Show." *American Economic Review* 76:1072–85.

Baumol, W. J., Richard R. Nelson, and Edward N. Wolff, eds. 1994. *Convergence of Productivity. Cross-National Studies and Historical Evidence.* New York: Oxford University Press.

Baumol, William J., and Edward N. Wolff. 1988. "Productivity Growth, Convergence and Welfare: Reply." *American Economic Review* 78:1155–59.

Beckerman, W., and R. Bacon. 1970. "The International Distribution of Income." Pp. 56–74 in *Unfashionable Economics,* edited by P. Streeten. London: Weidenfeld & Nicholson.

Benhabib, Jess, and Boyan Jovanovic. 1991. "Externalities and Growth Accounting." *American Economic Review* 81:82–113.

Berry, Albert. 1985. "On Trends in the Gap between Rich and Poor in Less Developed Countries: Why We Know So Little." *Review of Income and Wealth* 31:337–54.

———. 1987. "Evidence on Relationships among Alternative Measures of Concentration: A Tool for Analysis of LDC Inequality." *Review of Income and Wealth* 33:417–29.

Berry, Albert, François Bourguignon, and Christian Morrisson. 1983a. "Changes in the World Distribution of Income between 1950 and 1977." *Economic Journal* 93:331–50.

———. 1983b. "The Level of World Inequality. *Review of Income and Wealth* 29:217–41.

———. Bourguignon, François. 1979. "Decomposable Income Inequality Measures." *Econometrica* 47:901–20.

Breedlove, William L., and Patrick D. Nolan. 1988. "International Stratification and Inequality, 1960–1980." *International Journal of Contemporary Sociology* 25:105–23.

Cardoso, Fernando H. 1974. "Las contradicciones del desarrollo asociado." *Revista Paraguaya de Sociologia* 11:227–52.

———. 1977. "The Consumption of Dependency Theory in the United States." *Latin American Research Review* 12:7–21.

Cardoso, F. H., and Enzo Faletto. 1969. *Dependencia y desarrollo en Ambica Latina.* Mexico, D.F.: Siglo XXI.

Chase-Dunn, Christopher. 1989. *Global Formation: Structures of the World-Economy.* Cambridge: Blackwell.

Clark, Gregory. 1987. "Why Isn't the Whole World Developed? Lessons from the Cotton Mills." *Journal of Economic History* 47:141–74.

Coulter, Philip B. 1989. *Measuring Inequality: A Methodological Handbook.* Boulder, Colo.: Westview Press.

Cowell, Frank A. 1985. "Multilevel Decomposition of Theil's Index of Inequality." *Review of Income and Wealth* 31:201–5.

———. 1988. "Inequality Decomposition: Three Bad Measures." *Bulletin of Economic Research* 40:309–12.

Cumings, Bruce. 1984. "The Origins and Development of the Northeast Asian Political Economy." *International Organization* 38:1–40.

Das, T., and A. Parikh. 1982. "Decomposition of Inequality Measures and a Comparative Analysis." *Empirical Economics* 7:23–48.

De Long, J. Bradford. 1988. "Productivity Growth, Convergence, and Welfare: Comment." *American Economic Review* 78:1138–54.

Dos Santos, Theotonio. 1970. "The Structure of Dependence." *American Economic Review* 40:231–36.

Easterlin, Richard. 1981. "Why Isn't the Whole World Developed?" *Journal of Economic History* 41:1–19.

ECLA (Economic Commission for Latin America). 1969. *Development Problems in Latin America.* Austin: University of Texas Press.

Emmanuel, Arghiri. 1972. *Unequal Exchange: A Study of the Imperialism of Trade.* New York: Brian Pearce.

Evans, Peter. 1995. *Embedded Autonomy. States and Industrial Transformation.* Princeton, N.J.: Princeton University Press.

Firebaugh, Glenn. 1983. "Scale Economy or Scale Entropy? Country Size and Rate of Economic Growth, 1950–1977." *American Sociological Review* 48:257–69.

Fitzgerald, Frank T. 1981. "Sociologies of Development." *Journal of Contemporary Asia* 3:7–33.

Frank, Andre Gunder. 1966. "The Development of Underdevelopment." *Monthly Review* 18:17–31.

———. 1967. *Capitalism and Underdevelopment in Latin America.* New York: Monthly Review Press.

———. 1978. *Dependent Accumulation and Underdevelopment.* London: Macmillan.

Furtado, Celso. 1971. *Development and Underdevelopment: A Structural View.* Berkeley: University of California Press.

Gereffi, Gary. 1994. "The International Economy and Economic Development." Pp. 206–33 in *The Handbook of Economic Sociology,* edited by N. J. Smelser and R. Swedberg. Princeton, N.J.: Princeton University Press.

Gereffi, G., and Miguel E. Korzeniewicz, eds. 1994. *Commodity Chains and Global Capitalism.* Westport, Conn.: Greenwood Press.

Gereffi, Gary, and Donald Wyman, eds. 1990. *Manufacturing Miracles: Paths of Industrialization in Latin America and East Asia.* Princeton, N.J.: Princeton University Press.

Gerschenkron, Alexander. 1962. *Economic Backwardness in Historical Perspective.* Cambridge, Mass.: Harvard University.

Gini, Corrado. 1912. *Variabilita e mutabilita.* Bologna.

Griffin, Keith. 1978. *International Inequality and National Poverty.* New York: Holmes & Meier.

Grosh, Margaret E., and E. Wayne Nafziger. 1986. "The Computation of World Income Distribution." *Economic Development and Cultural Change* 34:347–59.

Haggard, Stephan. 1990. *Pathways from the Periphery. The Politics of Growth in Newly Industrializing Countries.* Ithaca, N.Y.: Cornell University Press.

Helpman, Elhanan. 1992. "Endogenous Macroeconomic Growth Theory." *European Economic Review* 36:237–67.

Hirschman, Albert. 1958. *The Strategy of Economic Development.* New Haven, Conn.: Yale University Press.

Horowitz, Irving L. 1966. *Three Worlds of Development.* New York: Oxford University Press.

Hoselitz, Bert F. 1960. *Sociological Aspects of Economic Growth.* Glencoe, Ill.: Free Press.

Hoselitz, B. F., and Wilbert E. Moore. 1963. *Industrialization and Society.* Paris: UNESCO.

Inkeles, Alex. 1969. "Making Men Modern: On the Causes and Consequences of Individual Change in Six Countries." *American Journal of Sociology* 75:208–25.

Inkeles, A., and P. H. Rossi. 1956. "National Comparisons of Occupational Prestige." *American Journal of Sociology* 61:329–39.

Jackman, R. W. 1982. "Dependence on Foreign Investment and Economic Growth in the Third World." *World Politics* 34:175–96.

Jazairy, Idriss, Mohiuddin Alamgir, and Theresa Panuccio. 1992. *The State of World Rural Poverty.* New York: New York University Press.

Jones, Charles I. 1995. "Time Series Tests of Endogenous Growth Models." *Quarterly Journal of Economics* 110:495–525.

Kindleberger, Charles P. 1961. "Obsolescense and Technical Change." *Oxford Institute of Statistics Bulletin,* March, pp. 281–97.

King, Robert G., and Sergio Rebelo. 1990. "Public Policy and Economic Growth: Developing Neoclassical Implications." *Journal of Political Economy* 98:S126–S150.

Kirman, Alan P., and Luigi M. Tomasini. 1969. "A New Look at International Income Inequalities." *Economia Internazionale* 22:437–61.

Korzeniewicz, Roberto P., and William Martin. 1994. "The Global Distribution of Commodity Chains." Pp. 67–91 in *Commodity Chains and Global Capitalism,* edited by G. Gereffi and M. Korzeniewicz. Westport, Conn.: Greenwood Press.

Kravis, Irving B., Alan W. Heston, and Robert Summers. 1978. "Real GNP per Capita for More Than One Hundred Countries." *Economic Journal* 88:215–42.

Kuznets, Simon. 1965. *Economic Growth and Structure.* New York: W. W. Norton.

———. 1971. *Economic Growth of Nations.* Cambridge, Mass.: Harvard University Press.

Lenin, V. I. 1939. *Imperialism, the Highest Stage of Capitalism.* New York: International Publishers.

Levy, Amnon, and Khorshed Chowdhury. 1994. "Intercountry Income Inequality: World Levels and Decomposition between and within Developmental Clusters and Regions." *Comparative Economic Studies* 26:33–50.

Levy, Marion J., Jr. 1967. "Social Patterns (Structures) and Problems of Modernization." Pp. 189–208 in *Readings on Social Change,* edited by W. Moore and R. M. Cook. Englewood Cliffs, N.J.: Prentice-Hall.

Lorenz, Max C. 1905. "Methods of Measuring the Concentration of Wealth." *Publications of the American Statistical Association* 9:209–19.

Lucas, Robert E., Jr. 1988. "On the Mechanics of Economic Development." *Journal of Monetary Economics* 22:3–42.

Luxemburg, Rosa. 1951. *The Accumulation of Capital* London: Routledge & Kegan Paul.

Maddison, Angus. 1983. "A Comparison of Levels of GDP Per Capita in Developed and Developing Countries, 1700–1980." *Journal of Economic History* 43:27–41.

Magdoff, Harry. 1969. *The Age of Imperialism*. New York: Monthly Review Press.

Morawetz, David. 1977. *Twenty-Five Years of Economic Development, 1950 to 1975*. Washington, D.C.: World Bank.

Myrdal, Gunnar. 1957. *Economic Theory and Under-Developed Regions*. London: Gerald Duckworth.

Nolan, Patrick D. 1983. "Status in the World System, Income Inequality, and Economic Growth." *American Journal of Sociology* 89:410–9.

North, Douglass C. 1981. *Structure and Change in Economic History*. New York: W. W. Norton.

———. 1989. "Institutions and Economic Growth: An Historical Interpretation." *World Development* 17:1319–32.

Olson, Mancur. 1982. *The Rise and Decline of Nations*. New Haven, Conn.: Yale University Press.

———. 1995. "The Devolution of the Nordic and Teutonic Economies." *American Economic Review* 85:22–27.

Oxaal, Ivaar, et al., eds. 1975. *Beyond the Sociology of Development. Economy and Society in Latin America and* Africa. London: Routledge & Kegan Paul.

Palma, Gabriel. 1978. "Dependency: A Formal Theory of Underdevelopment or a Methodology for the Analysis of Concrete Situations of Underdevelopment?" *World Development* 6:881–924.

Passé-Smith, John T. 1993a. "Could It Be That the Whole World Is Already Rich? A Comparison of RGDP/pc and GNP/pc Measures." Pp. 103–18 in *Development and Underdevelopment: The Political Economy of Inequality,* edited by M. A. Seligson and J. T Passé-Smith. Boulder, Colo.: Lynne Rienner.

———. 1993b. "The Persistence of the Gap: Taking Stock of Economic Growth in the Post–World War II Era. Pp. 15–30 in *Development and Underdevelopment. The Political Economy of Inequality,* edited by M. A. Seligson and J. T Passé Smith. Boulder, Colo.: Lynne Rienner.

Paukert, Felix. 1973. "Income Distribution at Different Levels of Development—A Survey of Evidence." *International Labor Review* 108:97–125.

Peacock, Walter, Greg Hoover, and Charles Killian. 1988. "Divergence and Convergence in International Development: A Decomposition Analysis of Inequality in the World System." *American Sociological Review* 53:838–52.

Portes, Alejandro. 1976. "On the Sociology of National Development: Theories and Issues." *American Journal of Sociology* 82:55–85.

Portes, Alejandro, and John Walton. 1981. *Labor, Class, and the International System.* New York: Academic Press.

Prebisch, Raúl. 1950. *The Economic Development of Latin America and Its Principal Problems.* New York: United Nations.

———. 1959. "Commercial Policy in the Underdeveloped Countries." *American Economic Review* 49:251–73.

———. 1964. *The Economic Development of Latin America.* New York. United Nations.

Pyatt, Graham. 1976. "On the Interpretation and Disaggregation of Gini Coefficients." *Economic Journal* 86:243–55.

Ram, Rati. 1989. "Level of Development and Income Inequality: An Extension of Kuznets-Hypothesis to the World-Economy." *Kyklos* 42:73–88.

Rau, William, and Dennis W. Roncek. 1987. "Industrialization and World Inequality: The Transformation of the Division of Labor in 59 Nations, 1960–1981." *American Sociological Review* 52:359–69.

Rock, Michael T. 1993. "'Twenty-Five Years of Economic Development' Revisited." *World Development* 21:1787–1801.

Romer, Paul M. 1986. "Increasing Returns and Long-Run Growth." *Journal of Political Economy* 94:1002–37.

———. 1990a. "Are Nonconvexities Important for Understanding Growth?" *American Economic Review* 80:97–103.

———. 1990b. "Endogenous Technological Change." *Journal of Political Economy* 98:S71–S102.

Rostow, W. W. 1960. *The Stages of Economic Growth: A Non-Communist Manifesto.* Cambridge: Cambridge University Press.

Roxborough, Ian. 1979. *Theories of Underdevelopment.* Atlantic Highlands, N.J.: Humanities Press.

Rubinson, Richard. 1976. "The World-Economy and the Distribution of Income within States: A Cross-National Study." *American Sociological Review* 41:638–59.

Sabel, Charles F. 1994. "Learning by Monitoring: The Institutions of Economic Development." Pp. 137–65 in *The Handbook of Economic Sociology,* edited by N. J. Smelser and R. Swedberg. Princeton, N.J.: Princeton University Press.

Schumpeter, Joseph A. 1934. *The Theory of Economic Development.* Cambridge, Mass.: Harvard University Press.

———. 1942. *Capitalism, Socialism and Democracy.* New York: Harper & Row.

Sen, Amartya. 1973. *On Economic Inequality.* New York: W. W. Norton.

Shafer, D. Michael. 1994. *Winners and Losers: How Sectors Shape the Developmental Prospects of States.* Ithaca, N.Y.: Cornell University Press.

Silber, Jacques. 1989. "Factor Components, Population Subgroups and the Computation of the Gini Index of Inequality." *Review of Economics and Statistics* 71:107–15.

Singer, Hans W. 1950. "The Distribution of Gains between Investing and Borrowing Countries." *American Economic Review* 40:472–99.

Singer, Hans W., and Javed A. Ansari. 1982. *Rich and Poor Countries.* London: George Allen & Unwin.

Singer, H. W., and Sumit Roy. 1993. *Economic Progress and Prospects in the Third World*. Cambridge: Edward Elgar.

Summers, Robert, and Alan Heston. 1984. "Improved International Comparisons of Real Product and Its Composition: 1950–1980." *Review of Income and Wealth* 30:207–62.

———. 1988. "A New Set of International Comparisons of Real Product and Prices: Estimates for 130 Countries, 1950–1985." *Review of Income and Wealth* 34:1–25.

Summers, Robert, Irving B. Kravis, and Alan Heston. 1980. "International Comparisons of Real Product and Its Composition: 1950–77." *Review of Income and Wealth* 26:19–66.

———. 1981. "Inequality among Nations: 1950 and 1975." Pp. 18–25 in *Disparities in Economic Development since the Industrial Revolution*, edited by P. Bairoch and M. Uvy-Leboyer. London: Macmillan.

Theil, Henri. 1967. *Economics and Information Theory*. Chicago: Rand McNally.

———. 1972. *Statistical Decomposition Analysis*. Amsterdam: North Holland.

Valenzuela, J. Samuel, and Arturo Valenzuela. 1978. "Modernization and Dependency: Alternative Perspectives in the Study of Latin American Underdevelopment." *Comparative Politics* 10:535–57.

Veblen, Thorstein. 1915. *Imperial Germany and the Industrial Revolution*. New York: Macmillan.

Wade, Robert. 1992. *Governing the Market. Economic Theory and the Role of Government in East Asian Industrialization*. Princeton, N.J.: Princeton University Press.

Wallerstein, Immanuel. 1974. *The Modern World-System 1: Capitalist Agriculture and the Origins of the European World-Economy in the Sixteenth Century*. New York: Academic Press.

———. 1979. *The Capitalist World-Economy*. Cambridge: Cambridge University Press.

———. 1980. *The Modern World-System II: Mercantilism and the Consolidation of the European World-Economy, 1600–1750*. New York: Academic Press.

———. 1983. *Historical Capitalism*. London: Verso.

Whalley, John. 1979. "The Worldwide Income Distribution: Some Speculative Calculations." *Review of Income and Wealth* 25:261–76.

World Bank. 1994. *World Development Report 1994*. New York: Oxford University Press.

———. 1993. *Social Indicators of Development 1993*. Baltimore: Johns Hopkins University Press.

———. 1990. *World Tables of Economic and Social Indicators, 1950–87, MRDF*. Washington, D.C.: World Bank, International Economics Department. Distributed by the Inter-University Consortium for Political and Social Research, Ann Arbor, Mich.

World Bank. Various years. *World Tables Update, MRDF*. Washington, D.C.: World Bank.

You, Jong-Il. 1994. "Macroeconomic Structure, Endogenous Technical Change and Growth." *Cambridge Journal of Economics* 18:213–33.

Zimmerman, L. J. 1962. "The Distribution of World Income." Pp. 28–47 in

Essays on Unbalanced Growth, edited by E. de Vries. The Hague: Institute of Social Studies.

Zind, Richard G. 1991. "Income Convergence and Divergence within and between LDC Groups." *World Development* 19:719–27.

CHAPTER 15

Empirics of World Income Inequality

GLENN FIREBAUGH

Glenn Firebaugh, whose important critical work on dependency theory is included in Part 5 of this book, reexamines the findings of Roberto Patricio Korzeniewicz and Timothy Patrick Moran in Chapter 14. Firebaugh disputes those findings, and those who have argued in favor of the divergence theory. His argument is that there are two ways of looking at world income distribution. The standard approach, used by Korzeniewicz and Moran, is to use the country as the unit of analysis, so that each country counts as one unit in the comparisons. The second way, the one that Firebaugh argues is more persuasive, is to treat each person as the unit of analysis. He accomplishes this by weighting the country data by population size. When this is done, large countries, especially China, play a great role. Since China's income grew at break-neck speed in recent years, and China's total population size has also grown enormously, the trends found in other studies are reversed. Firebaugh also uses PPP (i.e., purchasing power–based income) data rather than the exchange rate–based income data (see the discussion in Chapter 5). Firebaugh argues that this change in measuring income also helps to reverse the Korzeniewicz and Moran findings. Firebaugh concludes that there is no worldwide trend toward greater inequality and hence he does not find either convergence or divergence but stability in income distribution. The reader needs to determine which system of counting is the more persuasive. Should we calculate the gap between nations as a function of their total population size or limit ourselves to comparing each nation against all others irrespective of population

Reprinted with permission of the University of Chicago Press and the author from the *American Journal of Sociology,* vol. 104, no. 6 (1999): 1597–1630.

size? Good arguments can be made for each method, and Firebaugh is persuasive in arguing for the former. Yet, since we already know that income inequality is a major cause of insurgency (see Chapter 8), if two nations have widely different levels of income, it may not be too important what their respective population sizes are. Consider conflicts between Pakistan and India or tensions between China and North Korea. What seems to count in those cases is not the size of populations but many differences in culture, religion, income, and policy. In any event, even Firebaugh does not find evidence of convergence.

T HE INDUSTRIAL REVOLUTION PRODUCED A STUNNING INCREASE IN THE income disparity between nations. At the beginning of the 19th century, average incomes in the richest nations were perhaps four times greater than those in the poorest nations. At the end of the 20th century, average incomes in the richest nations are 30 times larger—annual incomes of about $18,000 versus $600 (Summers, Heston, Aten, and Nuxoll 1994).

Is the income disparity between nations still increasing? The answer to that question is critical. Because of the great disparity in average income from nation to nation, it is intercountry inequality—not inequality within nations—that is the major component of total income inequality in the world today. A recent sociological study estimates that inequality across countries accounts for over 90% of current world income inequality as measured by the Gini index. Other studies give lower estimates, but all agree with Berry, Bourguignon, and Morrisson (1983b, p. 217) that "it is clear that the level of world inequality is . . . primarily due to differences in average incomes across countries rather than to intra-country inequality."

Although I begin with the question of whether intercountry inequality is still rising, the analysis does not end there. My aim is to provide the foundation for a general sociological literature on intercountry income inequality by getting the facts right about its key dimensions: Whether increasing or declining, is the trend in intercountry inequality due to differential economic growth across nations or to differential population growth across nations? Which countries contribute most to change in intercountry inequality? Are results robust over different inequality measures and income series? Although sociological studies of these important issues are rare, there is no good reason for sociologists to continue to shy away from studying intercountry inequality. Careful income estimates are available for over 100 nations, which constitutes a near-universe of the world's population (Summers et al.

1994), and convenient methods have been developed for analyzing income inequality for aggregates (Firebaugh 1998). The time is ripe for systematic sociological research on intercountry inequality. . . .

Cross-National Evidence

Cross-national studies of convergence appear at first glance to present a mishmash of conflicting results. In this section I show that consistent findings do emerge when the studies are sorted carefully. I will also show that sociologists should not be too hasty to use the findings from economics to reach conclusions about trends in world income inequality because economists and sociologists are asking different questions.

It is useful first to place the convergence studies in historical perspective. At the outset of the Industrial Revolution average income in the richest nations was perhaps four times the average income in the poorest nations (Maddison 1995, chap. 2). Average income in the richest nations and poorest nations now differs by a factor of about 30. Over the long haul, then—from the late 18th century through much of the 20th—national incomes diverged. No one disputes that.

The more vexing question is what has happened since about 1960. Some studies conclude that there has been little or no change in intercountry inequality in recent decades (Berry et al. 1983a; Peacock et al. 1988; Schultz 1998) whereas other studies conclude that national incomes have continued to diverge (Jackman 1982; Sheehey 1996; Jones 1997; Korzeniewicz and Moran 1997).

There are three keys to making sense of these findings. The first key is weighting. Studies that do not weight generally find divergence, whereas studies that weight generally find very little change in intercountry inequality over recent decades. The second key is whether or not the national income data have been adjusted for "purchasing power parity" (PPP—elaborated in a subsequent section). The use of unadjusted data results in spurious divergence (Schultz 1998). The third key is China. Weighted studies that exclude China are suspect.

Studies of Unweighted Convergence

Table 15.1 summarizes key convergence studies from economics, sociology, and political science. In each of these studies the dependent variable is per capita income. Note that the income measure of choice is based on purchasing power parity; among recent studies only

Table 15.1 Summary of Major Studies of National Income Convergence*

Study	Data and Method	Conclusion
Unweighted by population:		
Jackman (1982; table 1, fig. 1)	Income Growth rate, † 1960 (N=98); regression of rate on initial level	Divergence with inverted-U pattern
Abramovitz (1986)	1870–1979 income; ‡ coefficient of variation; 16 industrial nations (from Maddison 1982)	Long-run convergence among rich nations
Baumol (1986).	Same historical data as Abramovitz (1986), but uses regression	Long-run convergence among rich nations
Barro and Sala-i-Martin (1992, table 3, fig. 4)	Income growth rate, ‡ 1960–85 (N=98); regression of rate on initial level	Divergence
Sheehey (1996, table 2)	Income growth rate, ‡ 1960–88 (N=107 non-OPEC nations)	Divergence with inverted-U pattern
Jones (1997, tables 2, 3)	1960 and 1990 income (N=74); ‡ SD of logged income	Divergence for world but rich converge
Weighted by population:		
Berry et al. (1983a)	1950–77 income (N=124); ‡ Gini, Theil, mean log deviation, Atkinson	No overall trend
Peacock, Hoover, and Killian (1988, figs. 1, 2)	1950–80 income (N=53); ‡Theil	No overall trend, with convergence within world system strata and divergence between strata
Ram (1989)		
Table 1	1960–80 income (N=115; excludes China); ‡ Theil§	divergence
Table 2	1960–80 inequality (N=21; regression of overall Theil on mean world income, 1960–80); excludes China in the Theil§	Inverted-U pattern
Korzeniewicz and Moran (1997)	1965–90 income (N=121); ‡ Gini, Theil	Divergence, especially in 1980s
Schulz (1998)	1960–89 income (N=120); ‖ Gini, variance of logged income, Theil	No trend for purchasing power parity income; divergence for foreign exchange (FX) rate income

Notes: *Because the object of this study is change in intercountry inequality, the table is restricted to studies of *unconditional* convergence, a term that refers to the absence of control variables. In regression analysis, unconditional convergence is examined by regressing growth rate of income per capita on intial level of income per capita. Conditional convergence is examined by adding control variables.

†Income estimates are based on foreign exchange rates.

‡Income estimates are based on purchasing power parity (PPP).

§The significance of excluding China in weighted analyses is addressed in the text. I do not note the unweighted analyses (top panel) that omit China because the omission of China hardly matters in those studies.

‖Income estimates are based both on foreign exchange rates and on purchasing power parity.

Korzeniewicz and Moran (1997) rely exclusively on income estimates that are based on the foreign exchange method.

The top panel of Table 15.1 summarizes studies that do not weight nations by size and the bottom panel summarizes studies that do. I begin with the studies in the top panel. One of the earliest reliable studies of cross-national convergence is Jackman's (1982) study of the relative income growth rates of 98 nations from 1960 to 1978. Jackman found an inverted-U pattern for the relationship between income growth rate and initial income—a pattern that was subsequently replicated in studies using different income measures and longer time periods (e.g., Summers and Heston 1991, table 4; Sheehey 1996). Despite this faster growth in the middle of the distribution, there is overall divergence because growth rates tend to be higher for the richest nations than for the poorest nations. Subsequent research has replicated the divergence finding as well (Barro and Sala-i-Martin 1992, table 3 and fig. 4; Sheehey 1996, table 2; Jones 1997, tables 2 and 3).

In short, when each national economy is given the same weight— the sort of convergence that interests economists because it bears on endogenous growth theory—there is an inverted-U pattern in which nations in the upper middle of the distribution tend to exhibit the fastest rates of income growth and those at the lower end of the distribution tend to exhibit the slowest rates of growth. The upshot is that national economies are diverging for the world as a whole even though there are convergence "clubs" (e.g., there is evidence of income convergence among Western European nations; see Abramovitz 1986; Baumol 1986; Jones 1997).

Studies of Weighted Convergence

Although it is weighted national convergence that bears most directly on sociologists' interest in world inequality, evidence on weighted national convergence is relatively scarce. In sharp contrast to the large and growing literature on unweighted convergence, the empirical literature on weighted convergence across nations consists of just a handful of studies.

The early study by Berry et al. (1983a) remains one of the best of these studies. Based on a large sample of nations containing most of the world's population, Berry et al. conclude, first, that economic growth in China was the most potent force equalizing world incomes from 1950 to 1977 and, second, that there was no clear-cut trend in intercountry income inequality from 1950 to 1977.

Remove China, then, and the data will show weighted divergence—precisely what Ram (1989) found for 1960–80 with China removed. Include China and the data will show no overall trend in intercountry income inequality in recent decades—precisely what Peacock et al. (1988) and Schultz (1998) found, replicating the main conclusion of Berry et al. (1983a). So the studies are quite consistent: Weighted by population, the data show no underlying trend in intercountry income inequality over recent decades; remove China, and the data show rising inequality.

Only one key finding remains to be explained: Korzeniewicz and Moran's (1997) anomalous finding of rising intercountry inequality despite their inclusion of China. Schultz (1998) provides the key to the puzzle. Schultz presents two sets of findings, one for income data based on purchasing power parity (PPP) and one for income data based on foreign exchange (FX) rates (the type of income data used by Korzeniewicz and Moran). Intercountry income inequality rises for the FX income series but not for the PPP income series.

The important lesson to be learned from Schultz's (1998) two sets of findings is that researchers should not rely on official exchange rates when studying trends in relative national incomes. Though early studies in economics used FX estimates because PPP estimates were unavailable, PPP-based income is now the industry standard (in addition to the studies listed in Table 15.1 above, see Barro 1991; Mankiw et al. 1992; Levine and Renelt 1992; Quah 1996). The rationale for the switch to PPP income measures will be elaborated later.

To summarize: When each national economy is given the same weight, the data indicate national divergence. Yet weighted studies find stability (the weighted studies that find divergence do so because they exclude China or use dubious income data). So the issue turns on weighting: Do we want to give nations or individuals equal weight?

Weighted versus Unweighted Convergence

Sociologists and economists are interested in intercountry convergence for different reasons. The stimulus for many economists is theoretical, to test theories of macroeconomic growth. Very often for economists, then, each nation represents one unit (one economy) and, in typical analyses, economic trends in Luxembourg count just as much as economic trends in China, even though China has nearly 3,000 times more people. By contrast, sociologists generally study intercountry income inequality because of what it can reveal about income inequality for the world as a whole (Korzeniewicz and Moran 1997), so sociologists are interested in whether there is intercountry convergence in the case where individuals, not nations, are given equal weight. Thus most sociologists are interested in weighted convergence. . . .

Weighting is likely to matter a lot in the case of intercountry inequality because nations vary so much in population size. Large nations such as China and India affect the weighted measure but have little effect on the unweighted measure, and the reverse is true for small, rich nations such as Luxembourg and Norway.

To verify the importance of weighting, Table 15.2 presents the weighted and unweighted trends in intercountry inequality from 1960 to 1989 (I use 1989 as the endpoint because the dissolution of the Soviet Union interrupts the income series at that point). I use variance of logged income (VarLog) because it is the inequality measure most often used in economic studies. Table 15.2 reports the results for five-year intervals.

The difference between the weighted and unweighted results is striking. The unweighted results confirm economists' findings of divergence. But when nations are weighted by size, intercountry inequality increases monotonically until 1975 and declines thereafter; as a result, there is little net change in inequality from 1960 to 1989. . . .

Table 15.2   The 1960–89 Trends in Intercountry Income Inequality: Weighted Versus Unweighted Results

Year	Average World Income*		Inequality (VarLog)	
	Weighted	Unweighted	Weighted	Unweighted (Varlog)
1960	2,277	2,294	.91	.74
1965	2,660	2,729	1.04	.84
1970	3,118	3,266	1.08	.90
1975	3,426	3,761	1.11	.96
1980	3,835	4,303	1.07	1.02
1985	4,059	4,421	.96	1.08
1989	4,367	4,826	.96	1.18
1960–89 change (%)	+92	+110	+5	+59

Source: Summers et al. (1994).

Note: Real gross domestic product per capita is given in constant U.S. dollars (variable RGDPPC in the Penn income series, ver. 5.6); N=120 nations containing 92%–93% of the world population.

*Average per capita income for the 120 nations, in constant U.S. dollars. "Weighted average" indicates that the national means are weighted by population size.

Trend in Intercountry Income Inequality

The Korzeniewicz-Moran (1997) study provides a convenient point of departure for studying the trend in intercountry income inequality. As noted earlier, Korzeniewicz and Moran conclude that intercountry income inequality is rising. Because that conclusion fits nicely with a large body of sociological literature on world polarization, the study is likely to attract a good deal of attention among sociologists. Moreover, the finding seems plausible, given the growth spurt in world income in recent decades (Easterlin 1998): careful estimates (Summers et al. 1994) indicate that the world's per capita income, stated in constant U.S. dollars, almost doubled from 1960 to 1989 (from $2,277 in 1960 to $4,367 in 1989), and an increase of this magnitude certainly has enormous potential for destabilizing the distribution of income across nations. Have Korzeniewicz and Moran uncovered an important trend that other weighted studies have missed?

The answer is no. The Korzeniewicz-Moran findings are based on the FX rate method, which is an unreliable method for comparing national incomes (e.g., Summers and Heston 1991; Horioka 1994). It is well documented that the use of official exchange rates exaggerates intercountry inequality (Ram 1979) and produces spurious divergence in intercountry inequality (Summers and Heston 1991, table 4; Schultz 1998). When industry-standard income data are substituted for the data used by Korzeniewicz and Moran, the rise in intercountry inequality disappears. What Korzeniewicz and Moran have demonstrated is not world polarization but the "dangers of using market exchange rates when making international comparisons" (Horioka 1994, p. 298).

To demonstrate these points, it is necessary first to summarize central issues regarding the comparison of income across nations.

Income Data. International comparisons of economic activity traditionally were obtained by using the FX rate to convert each country's national account data to a common currency, usually the U.S. dollar. But FX rates are highly flawed calibrators of currencies for two reasons. First, many goods and services are not traded on the international market, so exchange rates are based on a restricted bundle of goods and services (Grosh and Nafziger 1986, p. 351). Because this failure to capture economic activity is especially acute for non-monetized exchange in nonindustrial nations, FX measures of national income tend to miss significant economic activity in poorer nations. Second, FX markets are not totally "free" but are routinely distorted by government policy and speculative capital movement. As a result, exchange rates fail to reflect accurately the actual purchasing power parities (PPPs) of currencies.

To alleviate the deficiencies of FX-based income measures, several economists at the University of Pennsylvania spearheaded an ambitious effort to estimate national incomes using PPP to calibrate local currencies. Cross-nation parity for goods and services was determined through detailed studies of national price structures. As a result of those efforts, there is now an income series—the Penn series (Summers, Kravis, and Heston 1980; Kravis, Heston, and Summers 1982; Summers and Heston 1991; Summers et al. 1994)—that does not rely on FX rate. Even critics of the PPP measure concede that it represents a big improvement over the old FX measure (Dowrick and Quiggin 1997).

To appreciate the severity of the problem with using foreign exchange rates to compare national incomes, consider the FX income estimates for China and Japan. The remarkable economic growth of China since 1978 (Nee 1991, fig. 1; Chow 1994; Mastel 1997) is reflected in the PPP income series, where China's income ratio jumps roughly 40% between 1975 and 1989. Incredibly, though, the FX-based World Bank income series used by Korzeniewicz and Moran fails to capture that growth; instead it indicates that China's growth rate lagged so far behind the rest of the world that the FX income ratio for China declined by a whopping one-third from 1970 to 1989 (from .139 to .090).

The FX estimates for Japan are just as misleading. Though Japan experienced brisk economic growth through the 1970s and 1980s (Tachi 1993; Argy and Stein 1997), per capita income in Japan at the end of the 1980s still fell well short of incomes in the richest nations in the West (Horioka 1994). Yet FX-based income estimates place Japan's 1989 per capita income above per capita incomes in many rich Western nations (12% higher than Sweden and 16% higher than the United States; see World Bank 1993).

How do FX income estimates become so distorted? The Japanese case is illustrative. The use of foreign exchange rates to compare incomes leads one to conclude that Japanese per capita income as a percentage of U.S. per capita income rose from 67% in 1985 to 121% in 1988 (Horioka 1994, table 1). Obviously an increase of this magnitude in just three years would have been nothing short of miraculous. In fact this stupendous increase is "nothing more than a statistical illusion" (Horioka 1994, p. 297) caused by the too-rapid appreciation of the yen from 238 yen to the dollar in 1985 to 128 yen to the dollar in 1988. As Horioka (1994, table 1) demonstrates, more realistic measurement indicates that the Japan/U.S. income ratio rose only marginally over those three years, from 0.74 in 1985 to 0.76 in 1988.

In addition to the evidence that official exchange rates yield implausible income estimates for specific nations such as Japan and China, there are critical theoretical reasons for using PPP-based estimates when comparing incomes across nations (Summers and Heston 1980, 1991; Grosh and Nafziger 1986). Though Korzeniewicz and Moran (1997, p. 1011) state that the FX rate method "provides a better relational indicator of *command over income*" (emphasis in original), to the extent that exchange rates bear on command over income, they do so in the *world marketplace*—a largely hypothetical concept in the workaday world of the vast majority of the world's population. For the vast majority of the world's population, foreign-exchange-rate income is largely moot, since most of what is produced is not traded internationally. People face local prices, not international prices. This is not to deny that foreign-exchange-rate price can affect local price, but it is to say that an ox does not become half-an-ox when a nation decides to devalue its currency by half relative to the U.S. dollar.

Trends for FX versus PPP Income Estimates

Table 15.3 reports the 1965–89 trend in intercountry inequality based on both PPP and FX income. I try to replicate the Korzeniewicz and Moran (1997) study as closely as possible. First, I rely on the same

Table 15.3   Results for PPP-Based Versus FX-Based Income Estimates

			FX			
	PPP		Theil		Gini	
Year	Theil	Gini	Nominal	Adjusted	Nominal	Adjusted
1965	.552	.560	.816	.762	.661	.643
1970	.548	.558	.826	.771	.666	.647
1975	.540	.555	.847	.775	.674	.650
1980	.531	.550	.878	.782	.681	.650
1985	.512	.539	.963	.835	.706	.663
1989	.526	.543	1.079	.900	.733	.683
1965–89 Change (%)	−4.7	−3.0	+32.2	+18.1	+10.9	+6.2

Source: Summers et al. (1994) for the PPP income data and World Bank (1993) for the FX income data.

Note: There are 120 nations in the PPP data set and 112 nations in the FX data set. The data sets contain both capitalist and socialist nations and all populous nations and cover over 90% of the world's population. Theil and Gini results are reported to allow comparison with results offered by Korzeniewicz and Moran (1997). Results for V^2 and VarLog lead to the same conclusions. Under FX, "nominal" uses exchange-rate income estimates as given and "adjusted" uses more realistic estimates of income trends in China and Japan.

source for FX income estimates—the World Bank (1993)—and I use the same population data. Second, I use 1965 as the starting point. Third, I use the inequality indexes they used, the Theil and the Gini (results for V^2 and VarLog are similar). Finally, to ensure that results do not vary because of sampling differences, both "samples" here represent a near-universe of the world's people.

The results vividly demonstrate the difference in the two income series. According to the PPP-based income estimates, intercountry inequality declined modestly from 1965 to 1989. Yet according to the FX-based estimates, intercountry income inequality shot up 32.2% based on the Theil and 10.9% based on the Gini. Korzeniewicz and Moran (1997, table 3) report similar results (increases of 38.2% based on the Theil and 12.5% based on the Gini). These results reinforce the warning of, among others, Summers and Heston (1991, p. 355) that "it really makes a difference if exchange rates are used rather than PPPs" so "the practice of using exchange rates as quick, easily obtained estimates of PPPs is invalidated" (p. 335).

To see if the misleading FX income estimates for China and Japan matter much, I estimated a second, adjusted set of FX-based trends in intercountry income inequality [table not included here]. These results are based on the same FX income data as before, except that I use better income ratio estimates for China and Japan. Using more defensible income ratios (based on PPP) for just those two nations reduces the observed increase in the Theil and the Gini by over 40%.

In short, Korzeniewicz and Moran found divergence because they used a dubious income measure. Lest there be any doubt that the FX data yield a specious increase in intercountry inequality, it should be noted that a recent technical analysis of the PPP data used here (Dowrick and Quiggen 1997) concludes that the PPP data are, if anything, biased in favor of polarization. If so, then my failure to replicate the Korzeniewicz-Moran polarization result using PPP income cannot be dismissed on the ground that the use of PPP income as the yardstick stacks the deck against the polarization thesis.

If the FX income estimates tell the wrong story about recent trends in intercountry inequality, what is the right story? I now use PPP income estimates to answer that question. . . .

The Intercountry Income Inequality Plateau of 1960–89

It is well documented that, since about the mid-1970s, income inequality within the United States has risen after a long period of decline (Fischer et al. 1996; Nielsen and Alderson 1997). This phenomenon has been dubbed "the great U-turn" (Harrison and Bluestone 1988). Less appreciated is the pause in the long-run trend of rising intercountry inequality. This pause spans at least the 1960s, 1970s, and 1980s.

The discovery of a "great plateau" in the historical trend has important implications for our understanding of trends in world income inequality. One implication is that if income inequality across individuals has been increasing sharply for the world as a whole, as Korzeniewicz and Moran (1997) conclude, then the increase must be due to increases within nations. To cause the sort of increase in total world inequality that Korzeniewicz and Moran describe, the within-nation increase would need to be of colossal proportions because most of the total world income inequality is between, not within, nations.

A second implication of the plateau is that intercountry income inequality does not inevitably rise (or fall) with rising world income. Intercountry inequality was about the same in 1989 as it was 30 years earlier, and an important challenge for future studies is to determine why intercountry inequality remained so stable in a period when the world's average income shot up so rapidly. During a period of such great potential for destabilizing the distribution of income across nations, why did the variance neither increase nor decline? This study provides one part of the answer: offsetting trends in the most populous nations. The inequality-enhancing effects of rapid economic growth in Japan and sluggish economic growth in India were blunted by the inequality-reducing effects of rapid economic growth in China and slower-than-world-average population and economic growth in the United States over this period.

Finally, the discovery of the great plateau in weighted intercountry income inequality adds to the clamor for new sociological theories of national development (Gereffi 1989; Firebaugh 1992; Firebaugh and Beck 1994). Stable variance in the distribution of logged income across nations in a period of active core-periphery exchange calls into question fundamental assumptions sociologists have made about the impact of international exchange on national development. If the benefits of core-periphery movement of goods and capital in fact accrue primarily to rich nations and if this differential benefit is in fact the principal cause of intercountry income divergence (as dependency theory appears to claim), then it is hard to explain why the long-standing trend toward intercountry divergence was interrupted during an era of active core-periphery exchange.

References

Abramovitz, Moses. 1986. "Catching Up, Forging Ahead, and Falling Behind." *Journal of Economic History* 46:385–406.

Argy, Victor, and Leslie Stein. 1997. *The Japanese Economy*. New York: New York University Press.

Barro, Robert J. 1991. "Economic Growth in a Cross-Section of Countries." *Quarterly Journal of Economics* 106:407–43.

Barro, Robert J., and Xavier Sala-i-Martin. 1992. "Convergence." *Journal of Political Economy* 100:223–51.

Baumol, William J. 1986. "Productivity Growth, Convergence, and Welfare: What the Long-Run Data Show." *American Economic Review* 76:1072–85.

Berry, Albert, Francois Bourguignon, and Christian Morrisson. 1983a. "Changes in the World Distribution of Income between 1950 and 1977." *Economic Journal* 93:331–50.

———. 1983b. "The Level of World Inequality: How Much Can One Say?" *Review of Income and Wealth* 29:217–41.

Chow, Gregory C. 1994. *Understanding China's Economy*. Singapore: World Scientific.

Dowrick, Steve, and John Quiggin. 1997. "True Measures of GDP and Convergence." *American Economic Review* 87:41–64.

Easterlin, Richard A. 1998. *Growth Triumphant*. Ann Arbor: University of Michigan.

Firebaugh, Glenn. 1998. "Measuring Inequality: A Convenient Unifying Framework." Paper presented at the annual meeting of the Population Association of America, Chicago.

———. 1992. "Growth Effects of Foreign and Domestic Investment." *American Journal of Sociology* 98:105–30.

Firebaugh, Glenn, and Frank D. Beck. 1994. "Does Economic Growth Benefit the Masses? Growth, Dependence, and Welfare in the Third World." *American Sociological Review* 59:631–53.

Fischer, Claude S., Michael Hout, Martin Sanchez Jankowski, Samuel R. Lucas, Ann Swidler, and Kim Voss. 1996. *Inequality by Design*. Princeton, N.J.: Princeton University Press.

Gereffi, Gary. 1989. "Rethinking Development Theory: Insights from East Asia and Latin America." *Sociological Forum* 4:505–33.

Grosh, Margaret E., and E. Wayne Nafziger. 1986. "The Computation of World Income Distribution." *Economic Development and Cultural Change* 34:347–59.

Harrison, Bennett, and Barry Bluestone. 1988. *The Great U-Turn: Corporate Restructuring and the Polarizing of America*. New York: Basic Books.

Horioka, Charles Yuji. 1994. "Japan's Consumption and Saving in International Perspective." *Economic Development and Cultural Change* 42:293–316.

Jackman, Robert W. 1982. "Dependence on Foreign Investment and Economic Growth in the Third World." *World Politics* 34:175–96.

Jones, Charles I. 1997. "Convergence Revisited." *Journal of Economic Growth* 2:131–53.

Korzeniewicz, Roberto P., and Timothy P. Moran. 1997. "World-Economic

Trends in the Distribution of Income, 1965–1992." *American Journal of Sociology* 102:1000–39.

Kravis, Irving B., Alan Heston, and Robert Summers. 1982. *World Product and Income*. Baltimore: Johns Hopkins University Press.

Levine, Ross, and David Renelt. 1992. "A Sensitivity Analysis of Cross-Country Growth Regressions." *American Economic Review* 82:942–63.

Maddison, Angus. 1995. *Explaining the Economic Performance of Nations*. Brookfield, Vt.: Edward Elgar.

Mankiw, N. Gregory, David Romer, and David N. Weil. 1992. "A Contribution to the Empirics of Economic Growth." *Quarterly Journal of Economics* 107:407–37.

Mastel, Greg. 1997. *The Rise of the Chinese Economy*. London: M. E. Sharpe.

Nee, Victor. 1991. "Social Inequalities in Reforming State Socialism: Between Redistribution and Markets in China." *American Sociological Review* 56:267–82.

Nielsen, Francois, and Arthur S. Alderson. 1997. "The Kuznets Curve and the Great U-Turn: Income Inequality in U.S. Counties, 1970 to 1990." *American Sociological Review* 62:12–33.

Peacock, Walter Gillis, Greg A. Hoover, and Charles D. Killian. 1988. "Divergence and Convergence in International Development: A Decomposition Analysis of Inequality in the World System." *American Sociological Review* 53:838–52.

Quah, Danny T. 1996. "Convergence Empirics across Economies with (Some) Capital Mobility." *Journal of Economic Growth* 1:95–124.

Ram, Rati. 1979. "International Income Inequality: 1970 and 1978." *Economics Letters* 4:187–90.

Schultz, T. Paul. 1998. "Inequality in the Distribution of Personal Income in the World: How It Is Changing and Why." *Journal of Economics* 11:307–44.

Sheehey, Edmund J. 1996. "The Growing Gap between Rich and Poor Countries: A Proposed Explanation." *World Development* 24:1379–84.

Summers, Robert, and Alan Heston. 1991. "The Penn World Table (Mark 5): An Expanded Set of International Comparisons, 1950–1988." *Quarterly Journal of Economics* 106:327–68.

Summers, Robert, Alan Heston, Bettina Aten, and Daniel Nuxoll. 1994. *Penn World Table* (PWT) Mark 5.6a Data (MRDF). Center for International Comparisons, University of Pennsylvania.

Summers, Robert, Irving B. Kravis, and Alan Heston. 1980. "International Comparisons of Real Product and Its Composition, 1950–1977." *Review of Income and Wealth* 26:19–66.

Tachi, Ryuichiro. 1993. *The Contemporary Japanese Economy*, translated by Richard Walker. Tokyo: University of Tokyo Press.

World Bank. 1993. *World Tables of Economic and Social Indicators, 1950–1992* (MRDF). Washington, D.C.: World Bank, International Economics Department. Distributed by Inter-University Consortium for Political and Social Research, Ann Arbor. Michigan.

PART 4

Culture and Development

CHAPTER 16

The Achievement Motive in Economic Growth

DAVID C. MCCLELLAND

In this chapter, David C. McClelland, a psychologist, expands upon ideas developed by Max Weber, who examined the relationship between the Protestant ethic and the rise of capitalism. McClelland posits a more generalized psychological attribute he calls the "need for Achievement," or *n* Achievement. In this discussion, which is a summary of a book on the subject, McClelland presents some very interesting historical data he believes help explain the rise and decline of Athenian civilization. Turning to the present century, he produces data that show a close association between national levels of *n* Achievement and rates of economic growth. In seeking to determine what produces this psychological characteristic, McClelland finds that it is not hereditary but rather is instilled in people. It is therefore possible, he claims, to teach people how to increase their need to achieve and by so doing stimulate economic growth in developing countries. McClelland has been responsible for establishing training and management programs in developing countries in hopes that a change in the psychological orientation of public officials will help speed economic growth.

FROM THE BEGINNING OF RECORDED HISTORY, MEN HAVE BEEN FASCINATED by the fact that civilizations rise and fall. Culture growth, as A. L. Kroeber has demonstrated, is episodic, and sometimes occurs in quite different fields.[1] For example, the people living in the Italian peninsula at the time of ancient Rome produced a great civilization of law, politics, and military conquest; and at another time, during the Renaissance, the inhabitants of Italy produced a great civilization of art, music, letters, and science. What can account for such cultural flowerings? In our time we have theorists like Ellsworth Huntington, who stresses the importance of climate, or Arnold J. Toynbee, who also feels the right amount of challenge from the environment is crucial though he conceives of the environment as including its psychic effects. Others, like Kroeber, have difficulty imagining any general explanation; they perforce must accept the notion that a particular culture happens to hit on a particularly happy mode of self-expression, which it then pursues until it becomes overspecialized and sterile.

My concern is not with all culture growth, but with economic growth. Some wealth or leisure may be essential to development in other fields—the arts, politics, science, or war—but we need not insist on it. However, the question of why some countries develop rapidly in the economic sphere at certain times and not at others is in itself of great interest, whatever its relation to other types of culture growth. Usually, rapid economic growth has been explained in terms of "external" factors—favorable opportunities for trade, unusual natural resources, or conquests that have opened up new markets or produced internal political stability. But I am interested in the *internal* factors—in the values and motives men have that lead them to exploit opportunities, to take advantage of favorable trade conditions; in short, to shape their own destiny. . . .

Whatever else one thinks of Freud and the other psychoanalysts, they performed one extremely important service for psychology: once and for all, they persuaded us, rightly or wrongly, that what people said about their motives was not a reliable basis for determining what those motives really were. In his analyses of the psychopathology of everyday life and of dreams and neurotic symptoms, Freud demonstrated repeatedly that the "obvious" motives—the motives that the people themselves thought they had or that a reasonable observer would attribute to them—were not, in fact, the real motives for their often strange behavior. By the same token, Freud also showed the way to a better method of learning what people's motives were. He analyzed dreams and free associations: in short, fantasy or imaginative behavior. Stripped of its air of mystery and the occult, psychoanalysis has taught us that one can learn a great deal about people's motives through observing the things about which they are spontaneously concerned in their dreams and waking fantasies. About ten or twelve years ago, the research group in America with which I was connected decided to take this insight quite seriously and to see what we could learn about human motivation by coding objectively what people spontaneously thought about in their waking fantasies.[2] Our method was to collect such free fantasy, in the form of brief stories written about pictures, and to count the frequency with which certain themes appeared—rather as a medical technician counts the frequency with which red or white corpuscles appear in a blood sample. We were able to demonstrate that the frequency with which certain "inner concerns" appeared in these fantasies varied systematically as a function of specific experimental conditions by which we aroused or induced motivational states in the subjects. Eventually we were able to isolate several of these inner concerns, or motives, which, if present in great frequency in the fantasies of a particular person, enabled us to know something about how he would behave in many other areas of life.

Chief among these motives was what we termed "the need for Achievement" (*n* Achievement)—a desire to do well, not so much for the sake of social recognition or prestige, but to attain an inner feeling of personal accomplishment. This motive is my particular concern in this chapter. Our early laboratory studies showed that people "high" in *n* Achievement tend to work harder at certain tasks; to learn faster; to do their best work when it counts for the record, and not when special incentives, like money prizes, are introduced; to choose experts over friends as working partners; etc. Obviously, we cannot here review the many, many studies in this area. About five years ago, we became especially interested in the problem of what would happen in a society if a large number of people with a high need for achievement should happen to be present in it at a particular time. In other words, we became interested in a social-psychological question: What effect would a concentration of people with high *n* Achievement have on a society?

It might be relevant to describe how we began wondering about this. I had always been greatly impressed by the very perceptive analysis of the connection between Protestantism and the spirit of capitalism made by the great German sociologist, Max Weber.[3] He argues that the distinguishing characteristic of Protestant business entrepreneurs and of workers, particularly from the pietistic sects, was not that they had in any sense invented the institutions of capitalism or good craftsmanship, but that they went about their jobs with a new perfectionist spirit. The Calvinistic doctrine of predestination had forced them to rationalize every aspect of their lives and to strive hard for perfection in the positions in this world to which they had been assigned by God. As I read Weber's description of the behavior of these people, I concluded that they must certainly have had a high level of *n* Achievement. Perhaps the new spirit of capitalism Weber describes was none other than a high need for achievement—if so, then *n* Achievement has been responsible, in part, for the extraordinary economic development of the West. Another factor served to confirm this hypothesis. A careful study by M. R. Winterbottom had shown that boys with high n Achievement usually came from families in which the mothers stressed early self-reliance and mastery.[4] The boys whose mothers did not encourage their early self-reliance, or did not set such high standards of excellence, tended to develop lower need for achievement. Obviously, one of the key characteristics of the Protestant Reformation was its emphasis on self-reliance. Luther stressed the "priesthood of all believers" and translated the Bible so that every man could have direct access to God and religious thought. Calvin accentuated a rationalized perfection in this life for everyone. Certainly, the character of the Reformation seems to have set the stage, historically, for parents to encourage their children to attain earlier self-reliance and achievement. If the parents did in fact do so, they very possibly unintentionally produced the higher level of n Achievement in their children that was, in turn, responsible for the new spirit of capitalism.

This was the hypothesis that initiated our research. It was, of course, only a promising idea; much work was necessary to determine its validity. Very early in our studies, we decided that the events Weber discusses were probably only a special case of a much more general phenomenon—that it was n Achievement as such that was connected with economic development, and that the Protestant Reformation was connected only indirectly in the extent to which it had influenced the average n Achievement level of its adherents. If this assumption is correct, then a high average level of n Achievement should be equally associated with economic development in ancient Greece, in modern Japan, or in a preliterate tribe being studied by anthropologists in the South Pacific. In other words, in its most general form, the hypothesis attempts to isolate one of the key factors in the economic development, at least, of all civilizations. What evidence do we have that this extremely broad generalization will obtain? By now, a great deal has been collected—far more than I can summarize here; but I shall try to give a few key examples of the different types of evidence.

First, we have made historical studies. To do so, we had to find a way to obtain a measure of n Achievement level during time periods other than our own, whose individuals can no longer be tested. We have done this—instead of coding the brief stories written by an individual for a test, we code imaginative literary documents: poetry, drama, funeral orations, letters written by sea captains, epics, etc. Ancient Greece, which we studied first, supplies a good illustration. We are able to find literary documents written during three different historical periods and dealing with similar themes: the period of economic growth, 900 B.C.–475 B.C. (largely Homer and Hesiod); the period of climax, 475 B.C.–362 B.C.; and the period of decline, 362 B.C.–100 B.C. Thus, Hesiod wrote on farm and estate management in the early period; Xenophon, in the middle period; and Aristotle, in the late period. We have defined the period of "climax" in economic, rather than in cultural, terms, because it would be presumptuous to claim, for example, that Aristotle in any sense represented a "decline" from Plato or Thales. The measure of economic growth was computed from information supplied by F. Heichelheim in his *Wirtschaftsgeschichte des Altertums*.[5] Heichelheim records in detail the locations throughout Europe where the remains of Greek vases from different centuries have been found. Of course, these vases were the principal instrument of Greek foreign trade, since they were the containers for olive oil and wine, which were the most important Greek exports. Knowing where the vase fragments have been found, we could compute the trade area of Athenian Greece for different time periods. We purposely omitted any consideration of the later expansion of Hellenistic Greece, because this represents another civilization; our concern was Athenian Greece.

When all the documents had been coded, they demonstrated—as predicted—that the level of n Achievement was highest during the period of growth prior to the climax of economic development in Athenian Greece. (See Figure 16.1.) In other words, the maximum n Achievement level preceded the maximum economic level by at least a century. Furthermore, that high level had fallen off by the time of maximum prosperity, thus foreshadowing subsequent economic decline. A similar methodology was applied, with the same results, to the economic development of Spain in the sixteenth century[6] and to two waves of economic development in the history of England (one in the late sixteenth century and the other at the beginning of the industrial revolution, around 1800).[7] The n Achievement level in English history (as determined on the basis of dramas, sea captains' letters, and street ballads) rose, between 1400–1800, *twice,* a generation or two before waves of accelerated economic growth (incidentally, at times of Protestant revival). This point is significant because it shows that there is no "necessary" steady decline in a civilization's entrepreneurial energy from its earlier to its later periods. In the Spanish and English cases, as in the Greek, high levels of n Achievement preceded economic decline. Unfortunately, space limitations preclude more detailed discussion of these studies here.

We also tested the hypothesis by applying it to preliterate cultures of the sort that anthropologists investigate. At Yale University, an

**Figure 16.1   Average *n* Achievement Level
(plotted at midpoints of periods of growth, climax, and decline of
Athenian civilization as reflected in the extent of her trade area)**

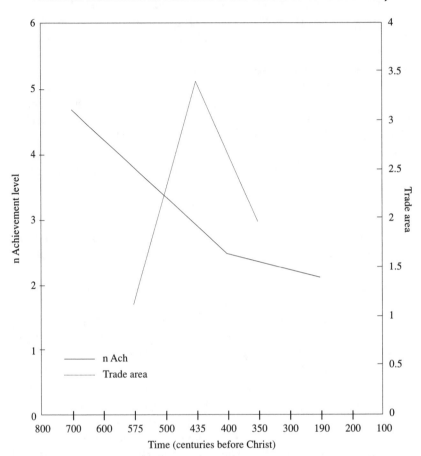

Note: Trade area measured for the sixth, fifth, and fourth centuries B.C. only.

organized effort has been made to collect everything that is known about all the primitive tribes that have been studied and to classify the information systematically for comparative purposes. We utilized this cross-cultural file to obtain the two measures that we needed to test our general hypothesis. For over fifty of these cultures, collections of folk tales existed that I. L. Child and others had coded,[8] just as we coded literary documents and individual imaginative stories, for *n* Achievement and other motives. These folk tales have the character of fantasy that we believe to be so essential for getting at "inner concerns." In the meantime, we were searching for a method of classifying the economic development of these cultures, so that we could determine whether those evincing high n Achievement in their folk tales had developed further than those showing lower n Achievement. The respective modes of gaining a livelihood were naturally very different in these cultures, since they came from every continent in the world and every type of physical habitat; yet we had to find a measure for comparing them. We finally thought of trying to estimate the number of full-time "business entrepreneurs" there were among the adults in each culture. We defined "entrepreneur" as "anyone who exercises control over the means of production and produces more than he can consume in order to sell it for individual or household income." Thus an entrepreneur was anyone who derived at least 75 percent of his income from such exchange or market practices. The entrepreneurs were mostly traders, independent artisans, or operators of small firms like stores, inns, etc. Nineteen cultures were classified as high in n Achievement on the basis of their folk tales; 74 percent of them contained some entrepreneurs. On the other hand, only 35 percent of the twenty cultures that were classified as low in n Achievement contained any entrepreneurs (as we defined it) at all. The difference is highly significant statistically (Chi square = 5.97, $p<.02$). Hence data about primitive tribes seem to confirm the hypothesis that high n Achievement leads to a more advanced type of economic activity.

But what about modern nations? Can we estimate their level of n Achievement and relate it to their economic development? The question is obviously one of the greatest importance, but the technical problems of getting measures of our two variables proved to be really formidable. What type of literary document could we use that would be equally representative of the motivational levels of people in India, Japan, Portugal, Germany, the United States, and Italy? We had discovered in our historical studies that certain types of literature usually contain much more achievement imagery than others. This is not too serious as long as we are dealing with time changes within a given culture; but it is very serious if we want to compare two cultures, each of which may express its achievement motivation in a different literary form. At last, we decided to use children's stories, for several reasons. They exist in standard form in every modern nation, since all modern nations are involved in teaching their children to read and use brief stories for this purpose. Furthermore, the stories are imaginative; and, if selected from those used in the earliest grades, they are not often influenced by temporary political events. (We were most impressed by this when reading the stories that every Russian child reads. In general, they cannot be distinguished, in style and content, from the stories read in all the countries of the West.)

We collected children's readers for the second, third, and fourth grades from every country where they could be found for two time periods, which were roughly centered around 1925 and around 1950. We got some thirteen hundred stories, which were all translated into English. In all, we had twenty-one stories from each of twenty-three countries about 1925, and the same number from each of thirty-nine countries about 1950. Code was used on proper names, so that our scorers would not know the national origins of the stories. The tales were then mixed together, and coded for n Achievement (and certain other motives and values that I shall mention only briefly).

The next task was to find a measure of economic development. Again, the problem was to ensure comparability. Some countries have much greater natural resources; some have developed industrially sooner than others; some concentrate in one area of production and some in another. Economists consider national income figures in per capita terms to be the best measure available; but they are difficult to obtain for all countries, and it is hard to translate them into equal purchasing power. Ultimately, we came to rely chiefly on the measure of electricity produced: the units of measurement are the same all over the world; the figures are available from the 1920s on; and electricity is the *form* of energy (regardless of how it is produced) that is essential to modern economic development. In fact, electricity produced per capita correlates with estimates of income per capita in the 1950s around .90 anyway. To equate for differences in natural re-sources, such as the amount of water power available, etc., we studied *gains* in kilowatt hours produced per capita between 1925 and 1950. The level of electrical production in 1925 is, as one would expect, highly correlated with the size of the gain between then and 1950. So it was necessary to resort to a regression analysis; that is, to calculate, from the average regression of gain on level for all countries, how much gain a particular country should have shown between 1925 and 1950. The actual gain could then be compared with the expected gain, and the country could be classified as gaining more or less rapidly than would have been expected on the basis of its 1925 performance. The procedure is directly comparable to what we do when we predict, on the basis of some measure of I.Q., what grades a child can be expected to get in school, and then classify him as an "under-" or "over-achiever."

The correlation between the n Achievement level in the children's readers in 1925 and the growth in electrical output between 1925 and 1950, as compared with expectation, is a quite substantial .53, which is highly significant statistically. It could hardly have arisen by chance. Furthermore, the correlation is also substantial with a measure of gain over the expected in per capita income, equated for purchasing power by Colin Clark. To check this result more definitively with the sample of forty countries for which we had reader estimates of n Achievement levels in 1950, we computed the equation for gains in electrical output in 1952–58 as a function of level in 1952. It turned out to be remarkably linear when translated into logarithmic units, as is so often the case with simple growth functions. Table 16.1 presents the performance of each of the countries, as compared with predictions from initial level in 1952, in standard score units and classified by high and low n Achievement in 1950. Once again we found that n Achievement levels predicted significantly ($r = .43$) the countries which would perform more or less rapidly than expected in terms of the average for all countries. The finding is more striking than the earlier one, because many Communist and underdeveloped countries are included in the sample. Apparently, n Achievement is a precursor of economic growth—and not only in the Western style of capitalism based on the small entrepreneur, but also in economies controlled and fostered largely by the state.

For those who believe in economic determinism, it is especially interesting that n Achievement level in 1950 is *not* correlated either with *previous* economic growth between 1925 and 1950, or with the level of prosperity in 1950. This strongly suggests that n Achievement is a *causative* factor—a change in the minds of men which produces economic growth rather than being produced by it. In a century dominated by economic determinism, in both Communist and Western thought, it is startling to find concrete evidence for psychological determinism, for psychological developments as preceding and presumably causing economic changes.

The many interesting results which our study of children's stories yielded have succeeded in convincing me that we chose the right material to analyze. Apparently, adults unconsciously flavor their stories for young children with the attitudes, the aspirations, the values, and the motives that they hold to be most important.

I want to mention briefly two other findings, one concerned with economic development, the other with totalitarianism. When the more and less rapidly developing economies are compared on all the other variables for which we scored the children's stories, one fact stands out. In stories from those countries which had developed more rapidly in both the earlier and later periods, there was a discernible tendency to emphasize, in 1925 and in 1950, what David Riesman has called "other-directedness"—namely, reliance on the opinion of particular others,

Table 16.1   Rate of Growth in Electrical Output (1952–1958) and National n Achievement Levels in 1950

Above Expectation Growth Rate			Below Expectation Growth Rate		
National n Achievement levels (1950)[a]	Country	Deviation from Expected Growth Rate[b]	National n Achievement Levels (1950)[a]	Country	Deviations from Expected Growth Rate[b]
High n Achievement Countries					
3.62	Turkey	+1.38			
2.71	India[c]	+1.12			
2.38	Australia	+0.42			
2.32	Israel	+1.18			
2.33	Spain	+0.01			
2.29	Pakistan[d]	+2.75			
2.29	Greece	+1.18	3.38	Argentina	−0.56
2.29	Canada	+0.08	2.71	Lebanon	−0.67
2.24	Bulgaria	+1.37	2.38	France	−0.24
2.24	U.S.A.	+0.47	2.33	South Africa	−0.06
2.14	West Germany	+0.53	2.29	Ireland	−0.41
2.10	U.S.S.R.	+1.61	2.14	Tunisia	−1.87
2.10	Portugal	+0.76	2.10	Syria	−0.25
Low n Achievement Countries					
1.95	Iraq	+0.29	2.05	New Zealand	−0.29
1.86	Austria	+0.38	1.86	Uruguay	−0.75
1.67	U.K.	+0.17	1.81	Hungary	−0.62
1.57	Mexico	+0.12	1.71	Norway	−0.77
0.86	Poland	+1.26	1.62	Sweden	−0.64
			1.52	Finland	−0.08
			1.48	Netherlands	−0.15
			1.33	Italy	−0.57
			1.29	Japan	−0.04
			1.20	Switzerland[e]	−1.92
			1.19	Chile	−1.81
			1.05	Denmark	−0.89
			0.57	Algeria	−0.83
			0.43	Belgium	−1.65

Note: Correlation of n Achievement level (1950) x deviations from expected growth rate = .43, $p < .01$.

a. Deviations in standard score units. The estimates are computed from the monthly average electrical production figures, in millions Kwh, for 1952 and 1958, from United Nations, *Monthly Bulletin of Statistics* (January, 1960), and *World Energy Supplies, 1951–1954* and 1955–1958 (Statistical Papers, Series 3). The correlation between log level 1952 and log gain 1952–1958 is .976. The regression equation based on these thirty-nine countries, plus four others from the same climatic zone on which data are available (China-Taiwan, Czechoslovakia, Rumania, Yugoslavia), is: log gain (1952–1958) = .9229 log level (1952) + .0480. Standard scores deviations from mean gain predicted by the regression formula (M = −.01831) divided by the standard deviation of the deviations from the mean predicted gain (SD = .159).

b. Based on twenty-one children's stories from second-, third-, and fourth-grade readers in each country.

c. Based on six Hindi, seven Telegu, and eight Tamil stories.

d. Based on twelve Urdu and eleven Bengali stories.

e. Based on twenty-one German Swiss stories, mean = .91; twenty-one French Swiss stories, mean = 1.71; overall mean obtained by weighting German mean double to give approximately proportionate representation of the two main ethnic populations.

rather than on tradition, for guidance in social behavior.[9] *Public opinion* had, in these countries, become a major source of guidance for the individual. Those countries which had developed the mass media further and faster—the press, the radio, the public-address system—were also the ones who were developing more rapidly economically. I think that "other-directedness" helped these countries to develop more rapidly because public opinion is basically more flexible than institutionalized moral or social traditions. Authorities can utilize it to inform people widely about the need for new ways of doing things. However, traditional institutionalized values may insist that people go on behaving in ways that are no longer adaptive to a changed social and economic order.

The other finding is not directly relevant to economic development, but it perhaps involves the means of achieving it. Quite unexpectedly, we discovered that every major dictatorial regime which came to power between the 1920s and 1950s (with the possible exception of Portugal's) was foreshadowed by a particular motive pattern in its stories for children: namely, a low need for affiliation (little interest in friendly relationships with people) and a high need for power (a great concern over controlling and influencing other people).

The German readers showed this pattern before Hitler; the Japanese readers, before Tojo; the Argentine readers, before Perón; the Spanish readers, before Franco; the South African readers, before the present authoritarian government in South Africa; etc. On the other hand, very few countries which did not have dictatorships manifested this particular motive combination. The difference was highly significant statistically, since there was only one exception in the first instance and very few in the second. Apparently, we stumbled on a psychological index of ruthlessness—i.e., the need to influence other people (n Power), unchecked by sufficient concern for their welfare (n Affiliation). It is interesting, and a little disturbing, to discover that the German readers of today still evince this particular combination of motives, just as they did in 1925. Let us hope that this is one case where a social science generalization will not be confirmed by the appearance of a totalitarian regime in Germany in the next ten years.

To return to our main theme—let us discuss the precise ways that higher n Achievement leads to more rapid economic development, and why it should lead to economic development rather than, for example, to military or artistic development. We must consider in more detail the mechanism by which the concentration of a particular type of human motive in a population leads to a complex social phenomenon like economic growth. The link between the two social phenomena is, obviously, the business entrepreneur. I am not using the term "entrepreneur" in the sense of "capitalist": in fact, I should like to divorce "entrepreneur" entirely from any connotations of ownership. An entrepreneur is someone who exercises control over production that is not just for his personal consumption. According to my definition, for example, an executive in a steel production unit in Russia is an entrepreneur.

It was Joseph Schumpeter who drew the attention of economists to the importance that the activity of these entrepreneurs had in creating industrialization in the West. Their vigorous endeavors put together firms and created productive units where there had been none before. In the beginning, at least, the entrepreneurs often collected material resources, organized a production unit to combine the resources into a new product, and sold the product, Until recently, nearly all economists—including not only Marx, but also Western classical economists—assumed that these men were moved primarily by the "profit motive." We are all familiar with the Marxian argument that they were so driven by their desire for profits that they exploited the workingman and ultimately forced him to revolt. Recently, economic historians have been studying the actual lives of such entrepreneurs and finding—certainly to the surprise of some of the investigators—that many of them seemingly were not interested in making money as such. In psychological terms, at least, Marx's picture is slightly out of focus. Had these entrepreneurs been above all interested in money, many more of them would have quit working as soon as they had made all the money that they could possibly use. They would not have continued to risk their money in further entrepreneurial ventures. Many of them, in fact, came from pietistic sects, like the Quakers in England, that prohibited the enjoyment of wealth in any of the ways cultivated so successfully by some members of the European nobility. However, the entrepreneurs often seemed consciously to be greatly concerned with expanding their businesses, with getting a greater share of the market, with "conquering brute nature," or even with altruistic schemes for bettering the lot of mankind or bringing about the kingdom of God on earth more rapidly. Such desires have frequently enough been labeled as hypocritical. However, if we assume that these men were really motivated by a desire for achievement rather than by a desire for money as such, the label no longer fits. This assumption also simplifies further matters considerably. It provides an explanation for the fact that these entrepreneurs were interested in money without wanting it for its own sake, namely, that money served as a ready quantitative index of how well they were doing—e.g., of how much they had achieved by their efforts over the past year. The need to achieve can never be satisfied by money; but estimates of profitability in money terms can supply direct knowledge of how well one is doing one's job.

The brief consideration of the lives of business entrepreneurs of the past suggested that their chief motive may well have been a high n Achievement. What evidence have we found in support of this? We made two approaches to the problem. First, we attempted to determine whether individuals with high n Achievement behave like entrepreneurs; and second, we investigated to learn whether actual entrepreneurs, particularly the more successful ones, in a number of countries, have higher n Achievement than do other people of roughly the same status. Of course, we had to establish what we meant by "behave like entrepreneurs"—what precisely distinguishes the way an entrepreneur behaves from the way other people behave?

The adequate answers to these questions would entail a long discussion of the sociology of occupations, involving the distinction originally made by Max Weber between capitalists and bureaucrats. Since this cannot be done here, a very brief report on our extensive investigations in this area will have to suffice. First, one of the defining characteristics of an entrepreneur is *taking risks* and/or innovating. A person who adds up a column of figures is not an entrepreneur—however carefully, efficiently, or correctly he adds them. He is simply following established rules. However, a man who decides to add a new line to his business is an entrepreneur, in that he cannot know in advance whether this decision will be correct. Nevertheless, he does not feel that he is in the position of a gambler who places some money on the turn of a card. Knowledge, judgment, and skill enter into his decision making; and, if his choice is justified by future developments, he can certainly feel a sense of personal achievement from having made a successful move.

Therefore, if people with high n Achievement are to behave in an entrepreneurial way, they must seek out and perform in situations in which there is some moderate risk of failure—a risk which can, presumably, be reduced by increased effort or skill. They should not work harder than other people at routine tasks, or perform functions which they are certain to do well simply by doing what everyone accepts as the correct traditional thing to do. On the other hand, they should avoid gambling situations, because, even if they win, they can receive no sense of personal achievement, since it was not skill but luck that produced the results. (And, of course, most of the time they would lose, which would be highly unpleasant to them.) The data on this point are very clear-cut. We have repeatedly found, for example, that boys with high *n* Achievement choose to play games of skill that incorporate a moderate risk of failure. . . .

Another quality that the entrepreneur seeks in his work is that his job be a kind that ordinarily provides him with accurate knowledge of the results of his decisions. As a rule, growth in sales, in output, or in profit margins tells him very precisely whether he has made the correct choice under uncertainty or not. Thus, the concern for profit enters in— profit is a measure of success. We have repeatedly found that boys with a high *n* Achievement work more efficiently when they know how well they are doing. Also, they will not work harder for money rewards; but if they are asked, they state that greater money rewards should be awarded for accomplishing more difficult things in games of skill. In the ring-toss game, subjects were asked how much money they thought should be awarded for successful throws from different distances. Subjects with high *n* Achievement and those with low *n* Achievement agreed substantially about the amounts for throws made close to the peg. However, as the distance from the peg increased, the amounts awarded for successful throws by the subjects with high *n* Achievement rose more rapidly than did the rewards by those with low *n* Achievement. Here, as elsewhere, individuals with high *n* Achievement behaved as they must if they are to be the successful entrepreneurs of society. They believed that greater achievement should be recognized by quantitatively larger reward.

What produces high *n* Achievement? Why do some societies produce a large number of people with this motive, while other societies produce so many fewer? We conducted long series of researches into this question. I can present only a few here.

One very important finding is essentially a negative one: *n* Achievement cannot be hereditary. Popular psychology has long maintained that some races are more energetic than others. Our data clearly contradict this in connection with *n* Achievement. The changes in *n* Achievement level within a given population are too rapid to be attributed to heredity. For example, the correlation between respective *n* Achievement levels in the 1925 and 1950 samples of readers is substantially zero. Many of the countries that were high in *n* Achievement at one or both times may be low or moderate in *n* Achievement now, and vice versa. Germany was low in 1925 and is high now; and certainly the hereditary makeup of the German nation has not changed in a generation.

However, there is substantiating evidence that *n* Achievement is a motive which a child can acquire quite early in life, say, by the age of eight or ten, as a result of the way his parents have brought him up. . . .

The principal results . . . indicate the differences between the parents of the "high n Achievement boys" and the parents of boys with low n Achievement. In general, the mothers and the fathers of the first group set higher levels of aspiration in a number of tasks for their sons. They were also much warmer, showing positive emotion in reacting to their sons' performances. In the area of authority or dominance, the data are quite interesting. The mothers of the "highs" were more domineering than the mothers of the "lows," but the *fathers* of the "highs" were significantly *less* domineering than the fathers of the "lows." In other words, the fathers of the "highs" set high standards and are warmly interested in their sons' performances, but they do not directly interfere. This gives the boys the chance to develop initiative and self-reliance.

What factors cause parents to behave in this way? Their behavior certainly is involved with their values and, possibly, ultimately with their religion or their general world view. At present, we cannot be sure that Protestant parents are more likely to behave this way than Catholic parents—there are too many subgroup variations within each religious portion of the community: the Lutheran father is probably as likely to be authoritarian as the Catholic father. However, there does seem to be one crucial variable discernible: the extent to which the religion of the family emphasizes individual, as contrasted with ritual, contact with God. The preliterate tribes that we studied in which the religion was the kind that stressed the individual contact had higher n Achievement; and in general, mystical sects in which this kind of religious self-reliance dominates have had higher n Achievement.

The extent to which the authoritarian father is away from the home while the boy is growing up may prove to be another crucial variable. If so, then one incidental consequence of prolonged wars may be an increase in n Achievement, because the fathers are away too much to interfere with their sons' development of it. And in Turkey, N. M. Bradburn found that those boys tended to have higher n Achievement who had left home early or whose fathers had died before they were eighteen.[10] Slavery was another factor which played an important role in the past. It probably lowered n Achievement—in the slaves, for whom obedience and responsibility, but not achievement, were obvious virtues; and in the slave-owners, because household slaves were often disposed to spoil the owner's children as a means for improving their own positions. This is both a plausible and a probable reason for the drop in n Achievement level in ancient Greece that occurred at about the time the middle-class entrepreneur was first able to afford, and obtain by conquest, as many as two slaves for each child. The idea also clarifies the slow economic development of the South in the United

States by attributing its dilatoriness to a lack of *n* Achievement in its elite; and it also indicates why lower-class American Negroes, who are closest to the slave tradition, possess very low *n* Achievement.[11]

I have outlined our research findings. Do they indicate ways of accelerating economic development? Increasing the level of *n* Achievement in a country suggests itself as an obvious first possibility. If *n* Achievement is so important, so specifically adapted to the business role, then it certainly should be raised in level, so that more young men have an "entrepreneurial drive." The difficulty in this excellent plan is that our studies of how *n* Achievement originates indicate that the family is the key formative influence; and it is very hard to change on a really large scale. To be sure, major historical events like wars have taken authoritarian fathers out of the home; and religious reform movements have sometimes converted the parents to a new achievement-oriented ideology. However, such matters are not ordinarily within the policymaking province of the agencies charged with speeding economic development.

Such agencies can, perhaps, effect the general acceptance of an achievement-oriented ideology as an absolute *sine qua non* of economic development. Furthermore, this ideology should be diffused not only in business and governmental circles, but throughout the nation, and in ways that will influence the thinking of all parents as they bring up their children. As B. C. Rosen and R. G. D'Andrade found, parents must, above all, set high standards for their children. The campaign to spread achievement-oriented ideology, if possible, could also incorporate an attack on the extreme authoritarianism in fathers that impedes or prevents the development of self-reliance in their sons. This is, however, a more delicate point, and attacking this, in many countries, would be to threaten values at the very center of social life. I believe that a more indirect approach would be more successful. One approach would be to take the boys out of the home and to camps. A more significant method would be to promote the rights of women, both legally and socially— one of the ways to undermine the absolute dominance of the male is to strengthen the rights of the female! Another reason for concentrating particularly on women is that they play the leading role in rearing the next generation. Yet, while men in underdeveloped countries come in contact with new achievement-oriented values and standards through their work, women may be left almost untouched by such influences. But if the sons are to have high *n* Achievement, the mothers must first be reached.

It may seem strange that a chapter on economic development should discuss the importance of feminism and the way children are reared; but this is precisely where a psychological analysis leads. If the motives of men are the agents that influence the speed with which the economic machine operates, then the speed can be increased only through affecting the factors that create the motives. Furthermore—to state this point less theoretically—I cannot think of evinced substantial, rapid long-term economic development where women have not been somewhat freed from their traditional setting of "Kinder, Küche und Kirche" and allowed to play a more powerful role in society, specifically as part of the working force. This generalization applies not only to the Western democracies like the United States, Sweden, or England, but also to the USSR, Japan, and now China.

In the present state of our knowledge, we can conceive of trying to raise n Achievement levels only in the next generation—although new research findings may soon indicate n Achievement in adults can be increased. Most economic planners, while accepting the long-range desirability of raising n Achievement in future generations, want to know what can be done during the next five to ten years. This immediacy inevitably focuses attention on the process or processes by which executives or entrepreneurs are selected. Foreigners with proved entrepreneurial drive can be hired, but at best this is a temporary and unsatisfactory solution. In most underdeveloped countries where government is playing a leading role in promoting economic development, it is clearly necessary for the government to adopt rigid achievement-oriented standards of performance like those in the USSR.[12] A government manager or, for that matter, a private entrepreneur, should have to produce "or else." Production targets must be set, as they are in most economic plans; and individuals must be held responsible for achieving them, even at the plant level. The philosophy should be one of "no excuses accepted." It is common for government officials or economic theorists in underdeveloped countries to be weighed down by all the difficulties which face the economy and render its rapid development difficult or impossible. They note that there is too rapid population growth, too little capital, too few technically competent people, etc. Such obstacles to growth are prevalent, and in many cases they are immensely hard to overcome; but talking about them can provide merely a comfortable rationalization for mediocre performance. It is difficult to fire an administrator, no matter how poor his performance, if so many objective reasons exist for his doing badly. Even worse, such rationalization permits, in the private sector, the continued employment of incompetent family members as executives. If these private firms were afraid of being penalized for poor performance, they might be impelled to find more able professional managers a little more quickly.

I am not an expert in the field, and the mechanisms I am suggesting may be far from appropriate. Still, they may serve to illustrate my main point: if a country short in entrepreneurial talent wants to advance rapidly, it must find ways and means of ensuring that only the most competent retain positions of responsibility. One of the obvious methods of doing so is to judge people in terms of their *performance*—and not according to their family or political connections, their skill in explaining why their unit failed to produce as expected, or their conscientiousness in following the rules. I would suggest the use of psychological tests as a means of selecting people with high *n* Achievement; but, to be perfectly frank, I think this approach is at present somewhat impractical on a large enough scale in most underdeveloped countries.

Finally, there is another approach which I think is promising for recruiting and developing more competent business leadership. It is the one called, in some circles, the "professionalization of management." Frederick Harbison and Charles A. Myers have recently completed a worldwide survey of the efforts made to develop professional schools of high-level management. They have concluded that, in most countries, progress in this direction is slow.[13] Professional management is important for three reasons: (1) It may endow a business career with higher prestige (as a kind of profession), so that business will attract more of the young men with high *n* Achievement from the elite groups in backward countries; (2) It stresses *performance* criteria of excellence in the management area—i.e., what a man can do and not what he is; (3) Advanced management schools can themselves be so achievement-oriented in their instruction that they are able to raise the *n* Achievement of those who attend them.

Applied toward explaining historical events, the results of our researches clearly shift attention away from external factors and to man— in particular, to his motives and values. That about which he thinks and dreams determines what will happen. The emphasis is quite different from the Darwinian or Marxist view of man as a creature who *adapts* to his environment. It is even different from the Freudian view of civilization as the sublimation of man's primitive urges. Civilization, at least in its economic aspects, is neither adaptation nor sublimation; it is a positive creation by a people made dynamic by a high level of *n* Achievement. Nor can we agree with Toynbee, who recognizes the importance of psychological factors as "the very forces which actually decide the issue when an encounter takes place," when he states that these factors "inherently are impossible to weigh and measure, and therefore to estimate scientifically in advance."[14] It is a measure of the pace at which the behavioral sciences are developing that even within

Toynbee's lifetime we can demonstrate that he was mistaken. The psychological factor responsible for a civilization's rising to a challenge is so far from being "inherently impossible to weigh and measure" that it has been weighed and measured and scientifically estimated in advance; and, so far as we can now tell, this factor is the achievement motive.

Notes

1. A. L. Kroeber, *Configurations of Culture Growth* (Berkeley, Calif., 1944).

2. J. W. Atkinson (Ed.), *Motives in Fantasy, Action, and Society* (Princeton, N.J., 1958).

3. Max Weber, *The Protestant Ethic and the Spirit of Capitalism,* trans. Talcott Parsons (New York, 1930).

4. M. R. Winterbottom, "The Relation of Need for Achievement to Learning and Experiences in Independence and Mastery," in Atkinson, *op. cit.,* pp. 453–478.

5. F. Heichelheim, *Wirtschaftsgeschichte des Altertums* (Leiden, 1938).

6. J. B. Cortés, "The Achievement Motive in the Spanish Economy Between the Thirteenth and the Eighteenth Centuries," *Economic Development and Cultural Change,* IX (1960), 144–163.

7. N. M. Bradburn and D. E. Berlew, "Need for Achievement and English Economic Growth," *Economic Development and Cultural Change,* 1961.

8. I. L. Child, T. Storm, and J. Veroff, "Achievement Themes in Folk Tales Related to Socialization Practices," in Atkinson, *op. cit.,* pp. 479–492.

9. David Riesman, with the assistance of Nathan Glazer and Reuel Denney, *The Lonely Crowd* (New Haven, Conn., 1950).

10. N. M. Bradburn, "The Managerial Role in Turkey" (unpublished Ph.D. dissertation, Harvard University, 1960).

11. B. C. Rosen, "Race, Ethnicity, and Achievement Syndrome," *American Sociological Review,* XXIV (1959), 47–60.

12. David Granick, *The Red Executive* (New York, 1960).

13. Frederick Harbison and Charles A. Myers, *Management in the Industrial World* (New York, 1959).

14. Arnold J. Toynbee, *A Study of History* (abridgment by D. C. Somervell; Vol. I; New York, 1947).

CHAPTER 17

The Confucian Ethic
and Economic Growth

HERMAN KAHN

The most recent theory on the cultural origins of economic growth derives from the observation that a group of countries that have made spectacular strides since World War II (e.g., Japan, South Korea, Taiwan) are Confucian societies. Until his recent death, Herman Kahn was director of the Hudson Institute think tank and was well known as a futurist. In this contribution, Kahn says that much of the success of these nations can be attributed directly to their cultures. It is interesting to compare the attributes of Confucianism that Kahn suggests are important for development with the attributes of *n* Achievement discussed in Chapter 16. It is also worth considering the implication of Kahn's argument for those nations in Latin America, Africa, and elsewhere that have dramatically different traditions. Has the absence of a "Confucian ethic" held back the development of these nations? If so, is it likely to make closing the gap between them and the developed nations an impossible dream?

M OST READERS OF THIS BOOK ARE FAMILIAR WITH THE ARGUMENT OF MAX Weber that the Protestant ethic was extremely useful in promoting the rise and spread of modernization.[1] Most readers, however, will be much less familiar with the notion that has gradually emerged in the last two decades that societies based upon the Confucian ethic may in many ways be superior to the West in the pursuit of industrialization,

Reprinted with permission from *World Economic Development: 1979 and Beyond,* by Herman Kahn (Indianapolis: Hudson Institute, 1979), pp. 121–122, 124–125.

affluence, and modernization. Let us see what some of the strengths of the Confucian ethic are in the modern world.

The Confucian Ethic

The Confucian ethic includes two quite different but connected sets of issues. First and perhaps foremost, Confucian societies uniformly promote in the individual and the family sobriety, a high value on education, a desire for accomplishment in various skills (particularly academic and cultural), and seriousness about tasks, job, family, and obligations. A properly trained member of a Confucian culture will be hard working, responsible, skillful, and (within the assigned or understood limits) ambitious and creative in helping the group (extended family, community, or company). There is much less emphasis on advancing individual (selfish) interests.

In some ways, the capacity for purposive and efficient communal and organizational activities and efforts is even more important in the modern world than the personal qualities, although both are important. Smoothly fitting, harmonious human relations in an organization are greatly encouraged in most neo-Confucian societies. This is partly because of a sense of hierarchy but even more because of a sense of complementarity of relations that is much stronger in Confucian than in Western societies.

The anthropologist Chie Nakane has pointed out that in Western societies there is a great tendency for "like to join like" in unions, student federations, women's groups, men's clubs, youth movements, economic classes, and so on.[2] This tends to set one group in society against another: students against teachers, employees against employers, youths against parents, and so on. In the Confucian hierarchic society, the emphasis is on cooperation among complementary elements, much as in the family (which is in fact the usual paradigm or model in a Confucian culture). The husband and wife work together and cooperate in raising the children; each has different assigned duties and responsibilities, as do the older and younger siblings and the grandparents. There is emphasis on fairness and equity, but it is fairness and equity in the institutional context, not for the individual as an individual. Synergism—complementarity and cooperation among parts of a whole—are emphasized, not equality and interchangeability. The major identification is with one's role in the organization or other institutional structure, whether it be the family, the business firm, or a bureau in the government.

Since the crucial issues in a modern society increasingly revolve around these equity issues and on making organizations work well, the neo-Confucian cultures have great advantages. As opposed to the earlier Protestant ethic, the modern Confucian ethic is superbly designed to create and foster loyalty, dedication, responsibility, and commitment and to intensify identification with the organization and one's role in the organization. All this makes the economy and society operate much more smoothly than one whose principles of identification and association tend to lead to egalitarianism, to disunity, to confrontation, and to excessive compensation or repression.

A society that emphasizes a like-to-like type of identification works out reasonably well as long as there is enough hierarchy, discipline, control, or motivation within the society to restrain excessive tendencies to egalitarianism, anarchy, self-indulgence, and so on. But as the society becomes more affluent and secular, there is less motivation, reduced commitment, more privatization, and increasingly impersonal and automatic welfare. Interest in group politics, group and individual selfishness, egoism, intergroup antagonisms, and perhaps even intergroup warfare all tend to increase. It becomes the old versus the young, insiders versus outsiders, men versus women, students versus teachers, and—most important of all—employees against employers. The tendencies toward anarchy, rivalry, and payoffs to the politically powerful or the organized militants become excessive and out of control.

For all these reasons we believe that both aspects of the Confucian ethic—the creation of dedicated, motivated, responsible, and educated individuals and the enhanced sense of commitment, organizational identity, and loyalty to various institutions—will result in all the neo-Confucian societies having at least potentially higher growth rates than other cultures. . . .

Whether or not one accepts our analysis of *why* neo-Confucian cultures are so competent in industrialization, the impressive data that support the final thesis are overwhelming. The performance of the People's Republic of China; of both North and South Korea; of Japan, Taiwan, Hong Kong, and Singapore; and of the various Chinese ethnic groups in Malaysia, Thailand, Indonesia, and the Philippines, discloses extraordinary talent (at least in the last twenty-five years) for economic development and for learning about and using modern technology. For example, the North Vietnamese operated one of the most complicated air defense networks in history more or less by themselves (once instructed by the Soviets), and the American army found that the South Vietnamese, if properly motivated, often went through training school in about half the time required by Americans. We do not gloss over the enormous differences among these neo-Confucian cultures. They vary almost as much

as do European cultures. But all of them seem amenable to modernization under current conditions.

Notes

1. Max Weber, *The Protestant Ethic and the Spirit of Capitalism,* translated by Talcott Parsons (New York: Charles Scribner's Sons, 1930).
2. Chie Nakane, *Japanese Society* (Berkeley, Calif.: University of
California Press, 1970).

CHAPTER 18

The Culture of Poverty

OSCAR LEWIS

The work of anthropologist Oscar Lewis has been distinctive in development literature. His studies tell fascinating stories of individual and family life in places like Cuba, Mexico, and Puerto Rico. So interesting have been Lewis's descriptions of the lives of families in the developing world struggling against the odds that filmmakers put *The Children of Sanchez* on the big screen. From these tales Oscar Lewis not only drew a picture of life among the poor but began to describe what he called the culture of poverty. The culture of poverty involves more than economic deprivation; it is a subculture with its own way of life, structure, and rules. According to Lewis, the culture of poverty is passed down from one generation to the next as a set of adaptive mechanisms to provide solutions to problems not resolved by the existing institutions of society. In this chapter, Lewis discusses the conditions that give rise to the culture of poverty and the impact it has on individuals and on the societies in which they live.

A LTHOUGH A GREAT DEAL HAS BEEN WRITTEN ABOUT POVERTY AND THE poor, . . . I first suggested [the concept of a culture of poverty] in 1959 in my book *Five Families: Mexican Case Studies in the Culture of Poverty. . . .*

Throughout recorded history, in literature, in proverbs, and in popular sayings, we find two opposite evaluations of the nature of the poor. Some characterize the poor as blessed, virtuous, upright, serene, independent, honest, kind, and happy. Others characterize them as evil, mean, violent, sordid, and criminal. These contradictory and confusing evaluations are also reflected in the in-fighting that is going on in the current war against poverty. Some stress the great potential of the poor for self-help, leadership, and community organization, while others point to the sometimes irreversible destructive effect of poverty upon individual character, and therefore emphasize the need for guidance and control to remain in the hands of the middle class, which presumably has better mental health.

These opposing views reflect a political power struggle between competing groups. However, some of the confusion results from the failure to distinguish between poverty *per se* and the culture of poverty, and from the tendency to focus upon the individual personality rather than upon the group—that is, the family and the slum community.

As an anthropologist I have tried to understand poverty and its associated traits as a culture or, more accurately, as a subculture[1] with its own structure and rationale, as a way of life which is passed down from generation to generation along family lines. This view directs attention to the fact that the culture of poverty in modern nations is not only a matter of economic deprivation, of disorganization, or of the absence of something. It is also something positive and provides some rewards without which the poor could hardly carry on.

Elsewhere I have suggested that the culture of poverty transcends regional, rural-urban, and national differences and shows remarkable similarities in family structure, interpersonal relations, time orientation, value systems, and spending patterns.[2] These cross-national similarities are examples of independent invention and convergence. They are common adaptations to common problems.

The culture of poverty can come into being in a variety of historical contexts. However, it tends to grow and flourish in societies with the following set of conditions: (1) a cash economy, wage labor, and production for profit; (2) a persistently high rate of unemployment and underemployment for unskilled labor; (3) low wages; (4) the failure to provide social, political, and economic organization, either on a voluntary basis or by government imposition, for the low-income population; (5) the existence of a bilateral kinship system rather than a unilateral one; and finally, (6) the existence of a set of values in the dominant class which stresses the accumulation of wealth and property, the possibility of upward mobility, and thrift, and explains low economic status as the result of personal inadequacy or inferiority.

The way of life which develops among some of the poor under these conditions is the culture of poverty. It can best be studied in urban or rural slums and can be described in terms of some seventy interrelated social, economic, and psychological traits. However, the number of traits and the relationships between them may vary from society to society and from family to family. For example, in a highly literate society, illiteracy may be more diagnostic of the culture of poverty than in a society where illiteracy is widespread and where even the well-to-do may be illiterate, as in some Mexican peasant villages before the Revolution.

The culture of poverty is both an adaptation and a reaction of the poor to their marginal position in a class-stratified, highly individuated, capitalistic society. It represents an effort to cope with feelings of hopelessness and despair which develop from the realization of the improbability of achieving success in terms of the values and goals of the larger society. Indeed, many of the traits of the culture of poverty can be viewed as attempts at local solutions for problems not met by existing institutions and agencies because the people are not eligible for them, cannot afford them, or are ignorant or suspicious of them. For example, unable to obtain credit from banks, they are thrown upon their own resources and organize informal credit devices without interest.

The culture of poverty, however, is not only an adaptation to a set objective conditions of the larger society. Once it comes into existence, it tends to perpetuate itself from generation to generation because of its effect on the children. By the time slum children are six or seven years old, they usually have absorbed the basic values and attitudes of their subculture and are not psychologically geared to take full advantage of changing conditions or increased opportunities which may occur in their lifetime.

Most frequently the culture of poverty develops when a stratified social and economic system is breaking down or is being replaced by another as in the case of the transition from feudalism to capitalism or during periods of rapid technological change. Often it results from imperial conquest in which the native social and economic structure is smashed and the natives are maintained in a servile colonial status, sometimes for many generations. It can also occur in the process of detribalization such as that now going on in Africa.

The most likely candidates for the culture of poverty are the people who come from the lower strata of a rapidly changing society and are already partially alienated from it. Thus, landless rural workers who migrate to the cities can be expected to develop a culture of poverty much more readily than migrants from stable peasant villages with a well-organized traditional culture. In this connection there is a striking contrast between Latin America, where the rural population long ago made the transition from a tribal to a peasant society, and Africa, which is still close to its tribal heritage. The more corporate nature of many of the African tribal societies, in contrast to Latin American rural communities, and the persistence of village ties tend to inhibit or delay the formation of a full-blown culture of poverty in many of the African towns and cities. The special conditions of apartheid in South Africa, where the migrants are segregated into separate "locations" and do not enjoy freedom of movement, create special problems. Here, the institutionalization of repression and discrimination tends to develop a greater sense of identity and group consciousness.

The culture of poverty is studied from various points of view: the relationship between the subculture and the larger society; the nature of the slum community; the nature of the family; and the attitudes, values, and character structure of the individual.

1. The lack of effective participation and integration of the poor in the major institutions of the larger society is one of the crucial characteristics of the culture of poverty. This is a complex matter and results from a variety of factors which may include lack of economic resources, segregation and discrimination, fear, suspicion, or apathy, and the development of local solutions for problems. However, participation in some of the institutions of the larger society—for example, in the jails, the army, and the public-relief system—does not *per se* eliminate the traits of the culture of poverty. In the case of a relief system which barely keeps people alive, both the basic poverty and the sense of hopelessness are perpetuated rather than eliminated.

Low wages, chronic unemployment, and underemployment lead to low income, lack of property ownership, absence of savings, absence of food reserves in the home, and a chronic shortage of cash. These conditions reduce the possibility of effective participation in the larger economic system. And as a response to these conditions, we find in the culture of poverty a high incidence of pawning of personal goods, borrowing from local money lenders at usurious rates of interest, spontaneous informal credit devices organized by neighbors, the use of second-hand clothing and furniture, and the pattern of frequent buying of small quantities of food many times a day as the need arises.

People with a culture of poverty produce very little wealth and receive little in return. They have a low level of literacy and education, do not belong to labor unions, are not members of political parties, generally do not participate in the national welfare agencies, and make very little use of banks, hospitals, department stores, museums, or art galleries. They have a critical attitude toward some of the basic institutions of the dominant classes, hatred of the police, mistrust of government and those in high position, and a cynicism which extends even to the church. This gives the culture of poverty a high potential for protest and for being used in political movements aimed against the existing social order.

People with a culture of poverty are aware of middle-class values, talk about them, and even claim some of them as their own; but on the whole, they do not live by them.[3] Thus it is important to distinguish between what they say and what they do. For example, many will tell you that marriage by law, by the church, or by both, is the ideal form of marriage; but few will marry. For men who have no steady jobs or other source of income, who do not own property and have no wealth to pass on to their children, who are present-time oriented and who want to avoid the expense and legal difficulties involved in formal marriage and divorce, free union or consensual marriage makes a lot of sense. Women will often turn down offers of marriage because they feel that marriage ties them down to men who are immature, punishing, and generally unreliable. Women feel that consensual union gives them a better break; it gives them some of the freedom and flexibility that men have. By not giving the fathers of their children legal status as husbands, the women have a stronger claim on their children if they decide to leave their men. It also gives women exclusive rights to a house or any other property they may own.

2. In describing the culture of poverty on the local community level, we find poor housing conditions, crowding, gregariousness, but above all, a minimum of organization beyond the level of the nuclear and extended family. Occasionally there are informal temporary groupings or voluntary associations within slums. The existence of neighborhood gangs which cut across slum settlements represents a considerable advance beyond the zero point of the continuum that I have in mind. Indeed, it is the low level of organization which gives the culture of poverty its marginal and anachronistic quality in our highly complex, specialized, organized society. Most primitive peoples have achieved a higher level of socio-cultural organization than our modern urban slum dwellers. . . .

3. On the family level the major traits of the culture of poverty are the absence of childhood as a specially prolonged and protected stage in the life cycle, early initiation into sex, free unions or consensual marriages, a relatively high incidence of the abandonment of wives and children, a trend toward female- or mother-centered families and consequently a much greater knowledge of maternal relatives, a strong predisposition to authoritarianism, lack of privacy, verbal emphasis upon

family solidarity, which is only rarely achieved because of sibling rivalry, and competition for limited goods and maternal affection.

4. On the level of the individual, the major characteristics are a strong feeling of marginality, of helplessness, of dependence, and of inferiority. I found this to be true of slum dwellers in Mexico City and San Juan among families that do not constitute a distinct ethnic or racial group and that do not suffer from racial discrimination. In the United States, of course, the culture of poverty of the Negroes has the additional disadvantage of racial discrimination; but as I have already suggested, this additional disadvantage contains a great potential for revolutionary protest and organization which seems to be absent in the slums of Mexico City or among the poor whites in the South.

Other traits include a high incidence of maternal deprivation, orality, weak ego structure, confusion of sexual identification, a lack of impulse control, a strong present-time orientation with relatively little ability to defer gratification and to plan for the future, a sense of resignation and fatalism, a widespread belief in male superiority, and a high tolerance for psychological pathology of all sorts.

People with a culture of poverty are provincial and locally oriented and have very little sense of history. They know only their own troubles, their own local conditions, their own neighborhood, their own way of life. Usually they do not have the knowledge, the vision, or the ideology to see the similarities between their problems and those of their counterparts elsewhere in the world. They are not class conscious although they are very sensitive indeed to status distinctions. . . .

I have not yet worked out a system of weighing each of the traits, but this could probably be done and a scale could be set up for many of the traits. Traits that reflect lack of participation in the institutions of the larger society or an outright rejection—in practice, if not in theory— would be the crucial traits; for example, illiteracy, provincialism, free unions, abandonment of women and children, lack of membership in voluntary associations beyond the extended family.

When the poor become class conscious or active members of trade-union organizations or when they adopt an internationalist outlook on the world, they are no longer part of the culture of poverty although they may still be desperately poor. Any movement, be it religious, pacifist, or revolutionary, which organizes and gives hope to the poor and which effectively promotes solidarity and a sense of identification with larger groups, destroys the psychological and social core of the culture of poverty. In this connection, I suspect that the civil-rights movement among the Negroes in the United States has done more to improve their self-image and self-respect than have their economic advances although, without a doubt, the two are mutually reinforcing.

The distinction between poverty and the culture of poverty is basic to the model described here. There are degrees of poverty and many kinds of poor people. The culture of poverty refers to one way of life shared by poor people in given historical and social contexts. The economic traits which I have listed for the culture of poverty are necessary but not sufficient to define the phenomena I have in mind. There are a number of historical examples of very poor segments of the population which do not have a way of life that I would describe as a subculture of poverty. Here I should like to give four examples:

a) Many of the primitive or preliterate peoples studied by anthropologists suffer from dire poverty which is the result of poor technology and/or poor natural resources or both, but they do not have the traits of the subculture of poverty. Indeed, they do not constitute a subculture because their societies are not highly stratified. In spite of their poverty, they have a relatively integrated, satisfying, and self-sufficient culture. Even the simplest food-gathering and hunting tribes have a considerable amount of organization—bands and band chiefs, tribal councils, and local self-government—elements which are not found in the culture of poverty.

b) In India the lower castes (the *Camars* or leatherworkers, and the *Bhangis* or sweepers) may be desperately poor both in the villages and in the cities, but most of them are integrated into the larger society and have their own *panchayat* organizations which cut across village lines and give them a considerable amount of power.[4] In addition to the caste system, which gives individuals a sense of identity and belonging, there is still another factor, the clan system. Wherever there are unilateral kinship systems or clans, one would not expect to find the culture of poverty because a clan system gives people a sense of belonging to a corporate body which has a history and a life of its own and therefore provides a sense of continuity, a sense of a past and of a future.

c) The Jews of Eastern Europe were very poor but they did not have many of the traits of the culture of poverty because of their tradition of literacy, the great value placed upon learning, the organization of the community around the rabbi, the proliferation of local voluntary associations, and their religion, which taught that they were the chosen people.

d) My fourth example is speculative and relates to socialism. On the basis of my limited experience in one socialist country— Cuba—and on the basis of my reading, I am inclined to believe that the culture of poverty does not exist in the socialist countries. I first went to Cuba in 1947 as a visiting professor for the State Department. At that time I began a study of a sugar plantation in Melena del Sur and of a slum in Havana. After the Castro Revolution I made my second trip to Cuba as a correspondent for a major magazine, and I revisited the same slum and some of the same families. The physical aspect of the slum had changed very little, except for a beautiful new nursery school. It was clear that the people were still desperately poor, but I found much less of the feelings of despair, apathy, and hopelessness which are so diagnostic of urban slums in the culture of poverty. They expressed great confidence in their leaders and hope for a better life in the future. The slum itself was now highly organized, with block committees, educational committees, party committees. The people had a new sense of power and importance. They were armed and were given a doctrine which glorified the lower class as the hope of humanity. (I was told by one Cuban official that they had practically eliminated delinquency by giving arms to the delinquents!)

It is my impression that the Castro regime, unlike Marx and Engels, did not write off the so-called lumpen proletariat as an inherently reactionary and anti-revolutionary force, but rather saw their revolutionary potential and tried to utilize it. In this connection, Frantz Fanon makes a similar evaluation of the role of the lumpen proletariat based upon his experience in the Algerian struggle for independence. In *The Wretched of the Earth* he writes:

> It is within this mass of humanity, this people of the shanty towns, at the core of the lumpen proletariat, that the rebellion will find its urban spearhead. For the lumpen-proletariat, that horde of starving men, uprooted from their tribe and from their clan, constitutes one of the most spontaneous and most radically revolutionary forces of a colonized people.[5]

My own studies of the urban poor in the slums of San Juan do not support the generalizations of Fanon. I have found little revolutionary spirit or radical ideology among low-income Puerto Ricans. On the contrary, most of the families I studied were quite conservative politically and about half of them were in favor of the Statehood Republican Party.

It seems to me that the revolutionary potential of people with a culture of poverty will vary considerably according to the national context and the particular historical circumstances. In a country like Algeria, which was fighting for its independence, the lumpen proletariat were drawn into the struggle and became a vital force. However, in countries like Puerto Rico, in which the movement for independence has very little mass support, and in countries like Mexico, which have achieved their independence a long time ago and are now in their post-Revolutionary period, the lumpen proletariat is not a leading source of rebellion or of revolutionary spirit.

In effect, we find that in primitive societies, and in caste societies, the culture of poverty does not develop. In socialist, fascist, and highly developed capitalist societies with a welfare state, the culture of poverty tends to decline. I suspect that the culture of poverty flourishes in, and is generic to, the early free enterprise stage of capitalism and that it is also endemic in colonialism. . . .

Notes

1. Although the term "subculture of poverty" is technically more accurate, I sometimes use "culture of poverty" as a shorter form.

2. Oscar Lewis, *Five Families: Mexican Case Studies in the Culture of Poverty* (New York: Basic Books, 1959).

3. In terms of Hyman Rodman's concept of "The Lower-Class Value Stretch" (*Social Forces,* vol. 42, No. 2 [December 1963], pp. 205–15), I would say that the culture of poverty exists where this value stretch is at a minimum, that is, where the belief in middle-class values is at a minimum.

4. It may be that in the slums of Calcutta and Bombay an incipient culture of poverty is developing. It would be highly desirable to do family studies there as a crucial test of the culture-of-poverty hypothesis.

5. New York: Grove, 1965, p. 103.

CHAPTER 19

The Effect of Cultural Values on Economic Development: Theory, Hypotheses, and Some Empirical Tests

JIM GRANATO, RONALD INGLEHART, AND DAVID LEBLANG

In this chapter, Jim Granato, Ronald Inglehart, and David Leblang examine the ties between cultural values and economic development. They utilize the "achievement motive" thesis developed by McClelland as a specific empirical point of reference. The authors test the theory using the World Values Survey, a database of interviews collected in many countries around the world. In this study, data are used for twenty-five countries, and strong evidence indicates that certain cultural values help to spur economic growth. In the same journal from which this chapter was drawn, however, the findings are disputed by other authors. The jury still seems to be out on this fascinating debate.

D O CULTURAL FACTORS INFLUENCE ECONOMIC DEVELOPMENT? IF SO, CAN they be measured and their effect compared with that of standard economic factors such as savings and investment? This article examines the explanatory power of the standard endogenous growth model and compares it with that of two types of cultural variables capturing motivational factors—achievement motivation and postmaterialist values. We believe that it is not an either/or proposition: cultural and economic factors play complementary roles. This belief is borne out empirically; we use recently developed econometric techniques to assess the relative merits of these alternative explanations.

Cultural factors alone do not explain all of the cross-national variation in economic growth rates. Every economy experiences significant

Reprinted with permission of Blackwell Publishing from *American Journal of Political Science,* vol. 40, no. 3 (August 1996): 607–631.

fluctuations in growth rates from year to year as a result of short-term factors such as technological shocks or unforeseen circumstances that affect output. These could not be attributed to cultural factors, which change gradually. A society's economic and political institutions also make a difference. For example, prior to 1945, North Korea and South Korea had a common culture, but South Korea's economic performance has been far superior.

On the other hand, the evidence suggests that cultural differences are an important part of the story. Over the past five decades, the Confucian-influenced economies of East Asia outperformed the rest of the world by a wide margin. This holds true despite the fact that they are shaped by a wide variety of economic and political institutions. Conversely, during the same period most African economies experienced low growth rates. Both societal-level and individual-level evidence suggests that a society's economic and political institutions are not the only factors determining economic development; cultural factors are also important.

Traditionally, the literature presents culture and economic determinants of growth as distinct. Political economists and political sociologists view their respective approaches as mutually exclusive. One reason lies in the level of analysis employed and with this the underlying assumptions about human behavior. Another reason is that we have had inadequate measures of cultural factors. Previous attempts to establish the role of culture either infer culture from economic performance or estimate cultural factors from impressionistic historical evidence. Both factors could be important, but until cultural factors are entered into a quantitative analysis, this possibility could not be tested.

By *culture*, we refer to a system of basic common values that help shape the behavior of the people in a given society. In most preindustrial societies, this value system takes the form of a religion and changes very slowly; but with industrialization and accompanying processes of modernization, these worldviews tend to become more secular, rational, and open to change.

For reasons discussed below, the cultures of virtually all preindustrial societies are hostile to social mobility and individual economic accumulation. Thus, both medieval Christianity and traditional Confucian culture stigmatized profit-making and entrepreneurship. But (as Weber argues), a Protestant version of Christianity played a key role in the rise of capitalism—and much later—a modernized version of Confucian society encourages economic growth, through its support of education and achievement.

The theory and evidence presented in this paper are organized as follows: section one discusses theories that deal with the effect of culture on economic development. This literature emphasizes the importance of motivational factors in the growth process. Section two introduces the data. This data, based on representative national surveys of basic values, enable us to construct two measures of cultures—achievement motivation and postmaterialist values. Section three discusses the baseline endogenous growth model. We draw upon a recent paper by Levine and Renelt (1992) to specify this model, and we augment it with cultural variables. Section four is the multivariate analysis. Economic and cultural variables each explain unique aspects of the cross-national variation in economic growth. Using the *encompassing* principles we find that an improved and parsimonious explanation for economic growth comes from a model that includes both economic and cultural variables. Section four also examines the robustness of this economic-cultural model and finds that the specification is robust to alterations in the conditioning set of information, the elimination of influential cases, and variations in estimation procedure. Section five concludes.

Culture, Motivational Factors, and Economic Growth

We first discuss the literature that views achievement motivation as an essential component in the process of economic development, and then we explore how cultural measures from the World Values Survey can be used to examine the effect of motivation on growth.

The motivational literature stresses the role of cultural emphasis on economic achievement. It grows out of Weber's (1904–1905) Protestant Ethic thesis. This school of thought gave rise to the historical research of Tawney (1926, 1955), case studies by Harrison (1992), and empirical work by McClelland et al. (1953) and McClelland (1961) on achievement motivation. Inglehart (1971, 1977, 1990) extends this work by examining the shift from materialist to postmaterialist value priorities. Although previous work mainly focuses on the political consequences of these values, their emergence represents a shift away from emphasis on economic accumulation and growth. These "new" values could be viewed as the erosion of Protestant Ethic among populations that experience high levels of economic security.

We suggest that Weber is correct in arguing that the rise of Protestantism is a crucial event in modernizing Europe. He emphasizes that the Calvinist version of Protestantism encourages norms favorable to economic achievement. But we view the rise of Protestantism as one case of a more general phenomenon. It is important, not only because of the specific content of early Protestant beliefs, but because this belief system undermines a set of religious norms that inhibit economic achievement and are common to most preindustrial societies.

Preindustrial economies are zero-sum systems: they are characterized by little or no economic growth which implies that upward social mobility only comes at the expense of someone else. A society's cultural system generally reflects this fact. Social status is hereditary rather than achieved, and social norms encourage one to accept one's social position in this life. Aspirations toward social mobility are sternly repressed. Such value systems help to maintain social solidarity but discourage economic accumulation.

Weber's emphasis on the role of Protestantism seems to capture an important part of reality. The Protestant Reformation combined with the emergence of scientific logic broke the grip of the medieval Christian Worldview on a significant part of Europe. Prior to the Reformation, Southern Europe was economically more advanced than Northern Europe. During the three centuries after the Reformation, capitalism emerged, mainly among the Protestant regions of Europe and the Protestant minorities in Catholic countries. Within this cultural context, individual economic accumulation was no longer rejected.

Protestant Europe manifested a subsequent economic dynamism that moved it far ahead of Catholic Europe. Shifting trade patterns, declining food production in Southern Europe and other factors also contributed to this shift, but the evidence suggests that cultural factors played a major role. Throughout the first 150 years of the Industrial Revolution, industrial development took place almost entirely within Protestant regions of Europe, and the Protestant portions of the New World. It was only during the second half of the twentieth century that an entrepreneurial outlook emerged in Catholic Europe and in the Far East. Both now show higher rates of economic growth than Protestant Europe. In short, the concept of the Protestant Ethic would be outdated if we take it to mean something that exists in historically Protestant countries. But Weber's more general concept, that certain cultural factors influence economic growth, is an important and valid insight.

McClelland et al. (1953) and McClelland's (1961) work on achievement motivation builds on the Weberian thesis but focuses on the values that were encouraged in children by their parents, schools, and other agencies of socialization. He hypothesizes that some societies emphasize economic achievement as a positive goal while others give it little emphasis. Since it was not feasible for him to measure directly the values emphasized in given societies through representative national surveys, McClelland attempts to measure them indirectly, through content analysis of the stories and school books used to educate children. He finds that some cultures emphasize achievement in their school books more heavily than others—and that the former showed considerably higher rates of economic growth than did the latter.

McClelland's work is criticized on various grounds. It is questioned whether his approach really measures the values taught to children, or simply those of textbook writers. Subsequently, writers of the dependency school argue that any attempt to trace differences in economic growth rates to factors within a given culture, rather than to global capitalist exploitation, is simply a means of justifying exploitation of the peripheral economies. Such criticism tends to discredit this type of research but is hardly an empirical refutation.

Survey research by Lenski (1963) and Alwin (1986) finds that Catholics and Protestants in the United States show significant differences in the values they emphasize as the most important things to teach children. These differences are more or less along the lines of the Protestant Ethic thesis. Alwin also demonstrates that these differences erode over time, with Protestants and Catholics gradually converging toward a common belief system.

The Data

The World Values Survey asks representative national samples of the publics in a number of societies, "Here is a list of qualities which children can be encouraged to learn at home. Which, if any, do you consider to be especially important?" This list includes qualities that reflect emphasis on autonomy and economic achievement, such as "thrift," "saving money and things," and "determination." Other items on the list reflect emphasis on conformity to traditional social norms, such as "obedience" and "religious faith."

We construct an index of achievement motivation that sums up the percentage in each country emphasizing the first two goals minus the percentage emphasizing the latter two goals. This method of index construction controls for the tendency of respondents in some societies to place relatively heavy emphasis on all of these goals, while respondents in other countries mention relatively few of them.

Figure 19.1 shows the simple bivariate relationship between this index and rates of per capita economic growth between 1960 and 1989. The zero-point on the achievement motivation index reflects the point where exactly as many people emphasize obedience and religion, as

Figure 19.1 Economic Growth Rate by Achievement Motivation Scores of Public

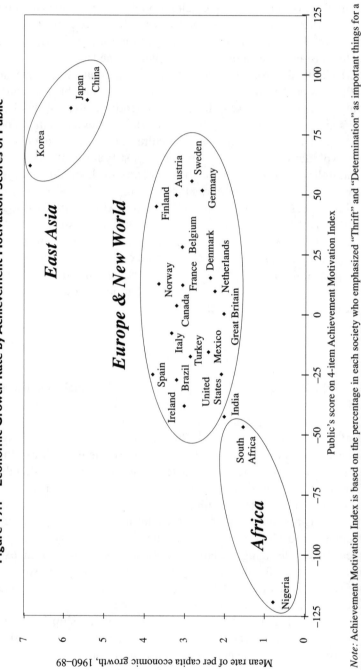

Note: Achievement Motivation Index is based on the percentage in each society who emphasized "Thrift" and "Determination" as important things for a child to learn *minus* the percentage emphasizing "Obedience" and "Religious Faith."

emphasize thrift and determination. As we move to the right, the latter values are given increasing emphasis. A given society's emphasis on thrift and determination *over* obedience and religious faith has a strong bivariate linkage with its rate of economic growth over the past three decades (r = .66; p = .001).

Though often stereotyped as having authoritarian cultures, Japan, China, and South Korea emerge near the pole that emphasizes thrift more heavily than obedience. The three East Asian societies rank highest on that dimension, while the two African societies included in this survey rank near the opposite end of the continuum, emphasizing obedience and religious faith.

The publics of India and the United States also fall toward the latter end of the scale. This is *not* an authoritarianism dimension. It reflects the balance between emphasis on two types of values. One set of values—thrift and determination—support economic achievement; while the other—obedience and religious faith—tend to discourage it, emphasizing conformity to traditional authority and group norms. These two types of values are not necessarily incompatible: some societies rank relatively high on both, while others rank relatively low on both. But, the relative *priority* given to them is strongly related to its growth rate.

Do cultural factors lead to economic growth, or does economic growth lead to cultural change? We believe that the causal flow can work in both directions. For example, there is strong evidence that post-materialist values emerge when a society attains relatively high levels of economic security. In this case, economic change reshapes culture. On the other hand, once these values become widespread, they are linked with relatively low subsequent rates of economic growth. Here, culture seems to be shaping economics—a parallel to the Weberian thesis, except that what is happening here is, in a sense, the rise of the Protestant Ethic in reverse.

Demonstrating causal connections is always difficult. In connection with our achievement motivation index, the obvious interpretation would be that emphasis on thrift and hard work, rather than on obedience and respect, is conducive to economic growth. The two most sensitive indicators of this dimension are thrift, on the one hand, and obedience on the other. For some time, economists have been aware that a nation's rate of gross domestic investment is a major influence on its long term growth rate. Investment, in turn, depends on savings. Thus, a society that emphasizes thrift produces savings, which leads to investment, and later to economic growth. We provide evidence below that this is probably the case. This does not rule out the possibility that economic growth might be conducive to thrift but this linkage is less obvious.

Emphasis on obedience is negatively linked with economic growth, for a converse reason. In preindustrial societies, obedience means conformity to traditional norms, which de-emphasize and even stigmatize economic accumulation. Obedience, respect for others, and religious faith all emphasize obligations to share with and support one's relatives, friends and neighbors. Such communal obligations are strongly felt in preindustrial societies. But from the perspective of a bureaucratized rational-legal society, these norms are antithetical to capital accumulation and conducive to nepotism. Furthermore, conformity to authority inhibits innovation and entrepreneurship.

The motivational component is also tapped by materialist/postmaterialist values, with postmaterialism having a negative relationship with economic growth. The achievement motivation variable is only modestly correlated with the materialist/postmaterialist dimension ($r = -.39$; p = .0581). Though both dimensions have significant linkages with economic growth, they affect it in different ways. The achievement motivation dimension seems to tap the transition from preindustrial to industrial values systems, linked with the modernization process.

The materialist/postmaterialist dimension reflects the transition to post-industrial society, linked with a shift away from emphasis on economic growth, toward increasing emphasis on protection of the environment and on the quality of life more generally. Previous research demonstrates that: (1) a gradual shift from materialist toward postmaterialist goals has been taking place throughout advanced industrial society; (2) that this shift is strongly related to the emergence of democracy ($r = .71$); but (3) that it has a tendency to be negatively linked with economic growth (Abramson and Inglehart 1995).

Multivariate Analysis

Our empirical approach is straightforward: we begin by estimating (via OLS) a baseline endogenous growth model that includes variables identified by Levine and Renelt (1992) as having robust partial correlations with economic growth. Using data for 25 countries[1] we first test the endogenous growth specification (Model 1 in Table 19.1). Following Equation [1], a nation's rate of per capita economic growth is regressed on its initial level of per capita income and human capital investment (education spending) as well as on its rate of physical capital accumulation. As expected, the results are quite compatible with the expectations of endogenous growth theory. The results of Model 1 are summarized as follows: (1) the significant negative coefficient on the initial level of per capita income indicates that there is evidence of "conditional convergence." That is, controlling for human and physical capital investment, poorer nations grow faster than richer nations; (2) investment in human capital (education spending) has a positive and statistically significant effect on subsequent economic growth; and (3) increasing the rate of physical capital accumulation increases a nation's rate of economic growth.

Overall this baseline economic model performs well: it accounts for 55% of the variation in cross-national growth rates and is consistent with prior cross-national tests of the conditional convergence hypothesis (e.g., Barro 1991; Mankiw, Romer, and Weil 1992). Model 1 also passes all diagnostic tests, indicating that the residuals are not serially correlated[2] (LM test), are normally distributed (Jarque-Bera test), and homoskedastic (White test).

Model 2 in Table 19.1 regresses the rate of per capita economic growth on a constant and the two cultural variables. As expected, both

Table 19.1 OLS Estimation of Economic Growth Models Dependent Variable: Mean Rate of per Capita Economic Growth (1960–1989)

Model Variable	Model 1	Model 2	Model 3	Model 4
Constant	−0.70	7.29*	3.16	2.40*
	(1.08)	(1.49)	(1.94)	(0.77)
Per Capita GDP in 1960	−0.63*		−0.42*	−0.43*
	(0.14)		(0.14)	(0.10)
Primary Education in 1960	2.69*		2.19*	2.09*
	(1.22)		(1.06)	(0.96)
Secondary Education	3.27*		1.21	
	(1.01)		(1.08)	
Investment	8.69*		3.09	
	(4.90)		(4.40)	
Achievement Motivation		2.07*	1.44*	1.88*
		(0.37)	(0.48)	(0.35)
Postmaterialism		−2.24*	−1.07	
		(0.77)	(1.03)	
R^2 Adjusted	.55	.59	.69	.70
SEE	.86	.83	.72	.71
LM ($x^2(1)$)	.42	.65	.68	.87
Jarque-Bera ($x^2(2)$)	.05	.30	.18	.57
White ($x^2(1)$)	.28	.24	.37	.18
SC	.119	−.117	−.095	−.352

Notes: Mean of dependent variable: 3.04; N is 25 for all models; standard errors in parentheses.

*t test: p < .05

achievement motivation and postmaterialism are significant predictors of economic growth and have the expected sign. Thus, the arguments of both Protestant Ethic and postmaterialist type theories cannot be rejected by this evidence. In addition, these variables, taken by themselves, do fairly well, accounting for 59% of the variance in growth rates. A glance at the diagnostics also indicates that the residuals are well behaved.

Comparing Competing Empirical Models: Encompassing Results

Both the economic and cultural models give similar goodness-of-fit performance. Each model's regressors are statistically significant. Yet, which model is superior? Or do both models possess explanatory factors that are missing in the other? . . .

In short, both models explain aspects of growth that the rival cannot. The implication is straightforward: growth rates are best understood as a consequence of both economic and cultural factors.

What happens when we combine the economic model with the cultural model? The results of this experiment are contained in Model 3. Beginning with the endogenous growth variables, adding the variables from Model 2 significantly alters the parameter estimates and standard errors on secondary education spending and physical capital investment. In fact, the coefficient on the physical capital investment variable changes dramatically. It decreases from 8.69 in Model 1 to 3.09 in Model 3. While this coefficient still has the expected sign, it is now far from significant.

Why is physical capital investment, a variable "robustly" correlated with economic growth in a number of other studies, now insignificant? Achievement motivation quite possibly is conducive to economic growth at least partly because it encourages relatively high rates of investment. Achievement motivation also has an important direct effect on economic growth rates, quite apart from its tendency to increase investment. Presumably the direct path from culture to economic growth reflects the effect of motivational factors on entrepreneurship and effort.

Returning to the analysis of Model 3 in Table 19.1, we now examine the direct effect of cultural values, particularly achievement motivation, on economic growth. As in Model 2, achievement motivation is positively and significantly related to economic growth. Combining Model 2 and Model 3 results in postmaterialism now being insignificant, however. This is probably due to the fact that countries with postmaterialist values are already fairly rich; the bivariate correlation between the initial level of wealth and postmaterialism is .75 and is significant at the .0000 level. Combining the regressors of these models (Model 3) we again have a model that does not violate any diagnostic test. In addition, the fit is more accurate (SEE).

Sensitivity Analysis

Table 19.1 contains an additional specification. In Model 4 we eliminate the three insignificant variables from Model 3—those for postmaterialism, investment, and secondary school enrollment—to check the stability of the remaining parameters. Model 4 is the most parsimonious and efficient model, explaining 70 percent of the variance in per capita growth rates with only three variables. . . .

Conclusion

The idea that economic growth is partly shaped by cultural factors has encountered considerable resistance. One reason for this resistance is because cultural values have been widely perceived as diffuse and permanent features of given societies: if cultural values determine economic growth, then the outlook for economic development seems hopeless, because culture cannot be changed. Another reason for opposition is that standard economic arguments supposedly suffice for international differences in savings and growth rates. For example, the standard life cycle model and not cultural arguments explains the difference in savings rates and growth rates between, say, Germany, Japan, and the United States.[3]

When we approach culture as something to be measured on a quantitative empirical basis, the illusion of diffuseness and permanence disappears. We no longer deal with gross stereotypes, such as the idea that "Germans have always been militaristic," or "Hispanic culture is unfavorable to development." We can move to the analysis of specific components of a given culture at a given time and place. Thus, we find that, from 1945 to 1975, West German political culture underwent a striking transformation from being relatively authoritarian to becoming increasingly democratic and participant (Baker, Dalton, and Hildebrandt 1981). And we find that, from 1970 to 1993, the United States and a number of West European societies experienced a gradual intergenerational shift from having predominantly materialist toward increasingly postmaterialist value priorities (Abramson and Inglehart 1995). Though these changes have been gradual, they demonstrate that central elements of culture can and do change.

Furthermore, empirical research can help identify specific components of culture that are relevant to economic development. One need not seek to change a society's entire way of life. The present findings suggest that one specific dimension—achievement motivation—is highly relevant to economic growth rates. In the short run, to change even a relatively narrow and well-defined cultural component such as this is not easy, but it should be far easier than attempting to change an entire culture. Furthermore, empirical research demonstrates that culture can and does change. Simply making parents, schools and other organizations aware of the potentially relevant factors may be a step in the right direction.

We find that economic theory already is augmented with "social norms" and "cultural" factors (Cole, Malaith, and Postlewaite 1992; Elster 1989; Fershtman and Weiss 1993). Where would cultural values fit theoretically in growth models? The economics literature is replete with models of savings behavior that focus on the "life cycle" and, more specifically, the bequest motive. Cultural variables matter here. Since savings and investment behavior holds an important place in growth models, a determination of how cultural and motivational factors can be used to augment these existing economic models, it seems to us, is the next step to uncovering a better understanding of economic growth.[4]

In the end, however, these arguments can only be resolved on the empirical battlefield. We use ordinary least squares regression to test economic and cultural models of growth on a cross section of 25 countries. We find that economic and cultural factors affect growth. . . .

The results in this article demonstrate that *both* cultural and economic arguments matter. Neither supplants the other. Future theoretical and empirical work is better served by treating these "separate" explanations as complementary.

Notes

1. The nations included in the multivariate analysis are: Austria, Belgium, Brazil, Canada, China, Denmark, Finland, France, Germany, Great Britain, India, Ireland, Italy, Japan, Korea, Mexico, Netherlands, Nigeria, Norway, South Africa, Spain, Sweden, Switzerland, Turkey, United States.

2. This is a check for spatial correlation between the errors of the cases.

3. In the post–World War II period, the life cycle model argues that since Japan and Germany had a substantial portion of their capital stock destroyed,

the "permanent income" of the population was going to be less than was expected at the onset of the war. The lower capital-labor ratio contributes to lower real wages and higher interest rates. In response the public raised its savings rate to "smooth" its postretirement income. The United States, on the other hand, saw a significant increase in its capital stock as a result of the war. This had the opposite effect since the higher capital-labor ratio depresses interest rates and raises real wages. The public's savings rate falls in this case since "permanent income" increases, while current consumption rises.

4. Institutional factors such as regime type and property rights have also been suggested as important determinants of economic growth (Helliwell 1994; Leblang 1996).

References

Abramson, Paul, and Ronald Inglehart. 1995. *Value Change in Global Perspective*. Ann Arbor: University of Michigan Press.

Achen, Christopher. 1982. *Interpreting and Using Regression*. Beverly Hills: Sage.

Alwin, Duane F. 1986. "Religion and Parental Child-Rearing Orientations: Evidence of a Catholic-Protestant Convergence." *American Journal of Sociology* 92:412–40.

Baker, Kendall L., Russell Dalton, and Kai Hildebrandt. 1981. *Germany Transformed* Cambridge: Harvard University Press.

Barro, Robert. 1991. "Economic Growth in a Cross Section of Countries." *Quarterly Journal of Economics* 106:407–44.

Bollen, Kenneth, and Robert Jackman. 1985. "Regression Diagnostics. An Expository Treatment of Outliers and Influential Cases." *Sociological Methods and Research* 13:510–42.

Chatterjee, S., and A. S. Hadi. 1988. *Sensitivity Analysis in Linear Regression*. New York: John Wiley.

Cole, Harold, George Malaith, and Andrew Postlewaite. 1992. "Social Norms, Savings Behavior, and Growth." *Journal of Political Economy* 100:1092–125.

Cook, R. D., and S. Weisberg. 1982. *Residuals* and *Influence in Regression*. London: Chapman and Hall.

Davidson, Ronald, and James MacKinnon. 1991. "Several Tests for Model Specification in the Presence of Alternative Hypotheses." *Econometrica* 49:781–93.

Elster, Jon. 1989. "Social Norms and Economic Theory." *Journal of Economic Perspectives* 3:99–117.

Fershtman, Chaim, and Yoram Weiss. 1993. "Social Status, Culture, and Economic Performance." *The Economic Journal* 103:946–59.

Fox, John. 1991. *Regression Diagnostics: An Introduction*. Sage University Paper on Quantitative Applications in the Social Sciences, 07-079. Newbury Park, CA: Sage.

Godfrey, Leslie. 1984. "On the Uses of Misspecification Checks and Tests of Non-nested Hypotheses in Empirical Econometrics." *Economic Journal* Supplement 96:69–81.

Granato, Jim, and Motoshi Suzuki. N.d. "The Use of the Encompassing Principle to Resolve Empirical Controversies in Voting Behavior: An Application to Voter Rationality in Congressional Elections." *Electoral Studies*. Forthcoming.

Hamilton, Lawrence. 1992. *Regression with Graphics: A Second Course in Applied Statistics*. Pacific Grove, CA: Brooks/Cole Publishing.

Harrison, Lawrence E. 1992. *Who Prospers? How Cultural Values Shape Economic and Political Success*. New York: Basic Books.

Helliwell, J. F. 1994. "Empirical Linkages Between Democracy and Growth." *British Journal of Political Science* 24:225–48.

Hendry, David, and Jean-Francois Richard. 1989. "Recent Developments in the Theory of Encompassing." In *Contributions to Operations Research and Econometrics: The XXth Anniversary of CORE*, ed. B. Comet and H. Tulkens. Boston: MIT Press.

Inglehart, Ronald. 1971. "The Silent Revolution in Europe." *American Political Science Review* 4:991–1017.

Inglehart, Ronald. 1977. *The Silent Revolution: Changing Values and Political Styles*. Princeton: Princeton University Press.

Inglehart, Ronald. 1990. *Culture Shift in Advanced Industrial Society*. Princeton: Princeton University Press.

Jackman, Robert. 1987. "The Politics of Economic Growth in Industrialized Democracies, 1974–1980." *Journal of Politics* 49:242–56.

Leamer, Edward. 1983. "Let's Take the 'Con' Out of Econometrics." *American Economic Review* 73:31–43.

Leblang, David. 1996. "Property Rights, Democracy, and Economic Growth." *Political Research Quarterly* 49:5–26.

Lenski, Gerhard. 1963. *The Religious Factor*. New York: Anchor-Doubleday.

Levine, Ross, and David Renelt. 1992. "A Sensitivity Analysis of Cross-Country Growth Regressions." *American Economic Review* 82:942–63.

Lucas, Robert. 1988. "On the Mechanics of Economic Development." *Journal of Monetary Economics* 1:3–32.

Mankiw, N. Gregory, David Romer, and David Weil. 1992. "A Contribution to the Empirics of Economic Growth." *Quarterly Journal of Economics* 152:407–37.

McClelland, David. 1961. *The Achieving Society*. Princeton: Van Nostrand.

McClelland, David, et al. 1953. *The Achievement Motive*. New York: Appleton-Century-Crofts.

Mizon, Grayham, and Jean-Francois Richard. 1986. "The Encompassing Principle and Its Application to Non-nested Hypothesis Tests." *Econometrica* 54:657–78.

Mooney, Christopher, and Robert Duval. 1993. *Bootstrapping: A Nonparametric Approach to Statistical Inference*. Sage University Paper Series on Quantitative Applications in the Social Sciences, 07-095. Newbury Park, CA: Sage.

Romer, Paul. 1990. "Endogenous Technological Change." *Journal of Political Economy* 98:71–102.

Solow, Robert. 1956. "A Contribution to the Theory of Economic Growth." *Quarterly Journal of Economics* 70:65–94.

Stine, Robert. 1990. "An Introduction to Bootstrap Methods." *Sociological Methods and Research* 18:243–91.

Swan, Trevor. 1956. "Economic Growth and Capital Accumulation." *Economic Record* 22:334–61.

Tawney, Richard. 1926. *Religion and the Rise of Capitalism: A History.* Gloucester, MA: P. Smith.

Tawney, Richard. [1922] 1955. *The Acquisitive Society.* Reprint. New York: Harcourt Brace.

Welsch, Roy. 1980. "Regression Sensitivity Analysis and Bounded-Influence Estimation." In *Evaluation of Econometric Models*, ed. Jan Kmenta and James Ramsey. New York: Academic Press.

Dependency Theory

CHAPTER 20

The Structure of Dependence

THEOTONIO DOS SANTOS

In Part 4 of this book we examined internal causes of slow growth among the poor countries. In Part 5, we examine external causes, starting with dependency. In this chapter, Theotonio dos Santos, a Brazilian economist, provides a classical definition of dependency. Dos Santos is a member of what has been called the "*dependentista* school" of development thinkers, the great majority of whom are Latin American intellectuals. Dependency theory comes in many varieties; indeed, some argue that there is no such thing as dependency "theory." Nonetheless, there is a body of thinking common to many of those in the *dependentista* school, and in this chapter dos Santos presents a concise statement of some of its fundamental tenets. He defines dependence and shows its linkages to Marxian theory, then goes on to elaborate three basic forms of dependence: (1) colonial, (2) financial-industrial, and (3) multinational. This latter form, arising out of the power of the large multinational corporations that maintain operations in developing countries, is of greatest concern to dos Santos because he sees it as limiting the developmental potential of newly industrializing nations. This new form of dependence restricts the size of the local market and thus contributes to income inequality in developing nations. Ultimately, according to dos Santos, dependent development must culminate in revolutionary movements of the left or right.

T HIS CHAPTER ATTEMPTS TO DEMONSTRATE THAT THE DEPENDENCE OF Latin American countries on other countries cannot be overcome

Reprinted with permission from *The American Economic Review,* vol. 60 (May 1970): 231–236.

without a qualitative change in their internal structures and external relations. We shall attempt to show that the relations of dependence to which these countries are subjected conform to a type of international and internal structure which leads them to underdevelopment or more precisely to a dependent structure that deepens and aggravates the fundamental problems of their peoples.

I. What Is Dependence?

By dependence we mean a situation in which the economy of certain countries is conditioned by the development and expansion of another economy to which the former is subjected. The relation of interdependence between two or more economies, and between these and world trade, assumes the form of dependence when some countries (the dominant ones) can expand and can be self-sustaining, while other countries (the dependent ones) can do this only as a reflection of that expansion, which can have either a positive or a negative effect on their immediate development [see reference no. 7, p. 6].

The concept of dependence permits us to see the internal situation of these countries as part of world economy. In the Marxian tradition, the theory of imperialism has been developed as a study of the process of expansion of the imperialist centers and of their world domination. In the epoch of the revolutionary movement of the Third World, we have to develop the theory of laws of internal development in those countries that are the object of such expansion and are governed by them. This theoretical step transcends the theory of development which seeks to explain the situation of the underdeveloped countries as a product of their slowness or failure to adopt the patterns of efficiency characteristic of developed countries (or to "modernize" or "develop" themselves). Although capitalist development theory admits the existence of an "external" dependence, it is unable to perceive underdevelopment in the way our present theory perceives it, as a consequence and part of the process of the world expansion of capitalism—a part that is necessary to and integrally linked with it.

In analyzing the process of constituting a world economy that integrates the so-called "national economies" in a world market of commodities, capital, and even of labor power, we see that the relations produced by this market are unequal and combined—unequal because development of parts of the system occurs at the expense of other parts. Trade relations are based on monopolistic control of the market, which leads to the transfer of surplus generated in the dependent countries to the dominant countries; financial relations are, from the viewpoint of the dominant powers, based on loans and the export of capital, which permit them to receive interest and profits, thus increasing their domestic surplus and strengthening their control over the economies of the other countries. For the dependent countries these relations represent an export of profits and interest which carries off part of the surplus generated domestically and leads to a loss of control over their productive resources. In order to permit these disadvantageous relations, the dependent countries must generate large surpluses, not in such a way as to create higher levels of technology but rather creating superexploited manpower. The result is to limit the development of their internal market and their technical and cultural capacity, as well as the moral and physical health of their people. We call this combined development because it is the combination of these inequalities and the transfer of resources from the most backward and dependent sectors to the most advanced and dominant ones which explains the inequality, deepens it, and transforms it into a necessary and structural element of the world economy.

II. Historic Forms of Dependence

Historic forms of dependence are conditioned by: (1) the basic forms of this world economy which has its own laws of development; (2) the type of economic relations dominant in the capitalist centers and the ways in which the latter expand outward; and (3) the types of economic relations existing inside the peripheral countries which are incorporated into the situation of dependence within the network of international economic relations generated by capitalist expansion. It is not within the purview of this chapter to study these forms in detail but only to distinguish broad characteristics of development.

Drawing on an earlier study, we may distinguish: (1) Colonial dependence, trade export in nature, in which commercial and financial capital in alliance with the colonialist state dominated the economic relations of the Europeans and the colonies by means of a trade monopoly, complemented by a colonial monopoly of land, mines, and manpower (self or slave) in the colonized countries. (2) Financial-industrial dependence, which consolidated itself at the end of the nineteenth century, characterized by the domination of big capital in the hegemonic centers, and its expansion abroad through investment in the production of raw materials and agricultural products for consumption in the hegemonic centers. A productive structure grew up in the dependent countries devoted to the export of these products (which I. V. Lenin labeled export economies [11]; other analysis in other regions [12] [13]), producing what the Economic Commission for Latin America (ECLA) has called "foreign-oriented development" (*desarrollo hacia afuera*) [4]. (3) In the postwar period a new type of dependence has been consolidated, based on multinational corporations which began to invest in industries geared to the internal market of underdeveloped countries. This form of dependence is basically technological-industrial dependence [6].

Each of these forms of dependence corresponds to a situation which conditioned not only the international relations of these countries but also their internal structures: the orientation of production, the forms of capital accumulation, the reproduction of the economy, and, simultaneously, their social and political structure.

III. The Export Economies

In forms (1) and (2) of dependence, production is geared to those products destined for export (gold, silver, and tropical products in the colonial epoch; raw materials and agricultural products in the epoch of industrial-financial dependence); i.e., production is determined by demand from the hegemonic centers. The internal productive structure is characterized by rigid specialization and monoculture in entire regions (the Caribbean, the Brazilian Northeast, etc.). Alongside these export sectors there grew up certain complementary economic activities (cattle-raising and some manufacturing, for example) which were dependent, in general, on the export sector to which they sell their products. There was a third, subsistence economy which provided manpower for the export sector under favorable conditions and toward which excess population shifted during periods unfavorable to international trade.

Under these conditions, the existing internal market was restricted by four factors: (1) Most of the national income was derived from export, which was used to purchase the inputs required by export production (slaves, for example) or luxury goods consumed by the hacienda- and mine-owners, and by the more prosperous employees. (2) The available manpower was subject to very arduous forms of superexploitation, which limited its consumption. (3) Part of the consumption of these workers was provided by the subsistence economy, which served as a complement to their income and as a refuge during periods of depression. (4) A fourth factor was to be found in those countries in which land and mines were in the hands of foreigners (cases of an enclave economy): a great part of the accumulated surplus was destined to be sent abroad in the form of profits, limiting not only internal consumption but also possibilities of reinvestment [1]. In the case of enclave economies the relations of the foreign companies with the hegemonic center were even more exploitative and were complemented by the fact that purchases by the enclave were made directly abroad.

IV. The New Dependence

The new form of dependence, (3) above, is in process of developing and is conditioned by the exigencies of the international commodity and capital markets. The possibility of generating new investments depends on the existence of financial resources in foreign currency for the purchase of machinery and processed raw materials not produced domestically. Such purchases are subject to two limitations: the limit of resources generated by the export sector (reflected in the balance of payments, which includes not only trade but also service relations); and the limitations of monopoly on patents which leads monopolistic firms to prefer to transfer their machines in the form of capital rather than as commodities for sale. It is necessary to analyze these relations of dependence if we are to understand the fundamental structural limits they place on the development of these economies.

1. Industrial development is dependent on an export sector for the foreign currency to buy the inputs utilized by the industrial sector. The first consequence of this dependence is the need to preserve the traditional export sector, which limits economically the development of the internal market by the conservation of backward relations of production and signifies, politically, the maintenance of power by traditional decadent oligarchies. In the countries where these sectors are controlled by foreign capital, it signifies the remittance abroad of high profits, and political dependence on those interests. Only in rare instances does foreign capital not control at least the marketing of these products. In response to these limitations, dependent countries in the 1930s and 1940s developed a policy of exchange restrictions and taxes on the national and foreign export sector; today they tend toward the gradual nationalization of production and toward the imposition of certain timid limitations on foreign control of the marketing of exported products. Furthermore, they seek, still somewhat timidly, to obtain better terms for the sale of their products. In recent decades, they have created mechanisms for international price agreements, and today the United

Nations Conference on Trade and Development (UNCTAD) and ECLA press to obtain more favorable tariff conditions for these products on the part of the hegemonic centers. It is important to point out that the industrial development of these countries is dependent on the situation of the export sector, the continued existence of which they are obliged to accept.

2. Industrial development is, then, strongly conditioned by fluctuations in the balance of payments. This leads toward deficit due to the relations of dependence themselves. The causes of the deficit are three:

a. Trade relations take place in a highly monopolized international market, which tends to lower the price of raw materials and to raise the prices of industrial products, particularly inputs. In the second place, there is a tendency in modern technology to replace various primary products with synthetic raw materials. Consequently, the balance of trade in these countries tends to be less favorable (even though they show a general surplus). The overall Latin American balance of trade from 1946 to 1968 shows a surplus for each of those years. The same thing happens in almost every underdeveloped country. However, the losses due to deterioration of the terms of trade (on the basis of data from ECLA and the International Monetary Fund), excluding Cuba, were $26,383 million for the 1951–66 period, taking 1950 prices as a base. If Cuba and Venezuela are excluded, the total is $15,925 million.

b. For the reasons already given, foreign capital retains control over the most dynamic sectors of the economy and repatriates a high volume of profit; consequently, capital accounts are highly unfavorable to dependent countries. The data show that the amount of capital leaving the country is much greater than the amount entering; this produces an enslaving deficit in capital accounts. To this must be added the deficit in certain services which are virtually under total foreign control—such as freight transport, royalty payments, technical aid, etc. Consequently, an important deficit is produced in the total balance of payments; thus limiting the possibility of importation of inputs for industrialization.

c. The result is that "foreign financing" becomes necessary, in two forms: to cover the existing deficit, and to "finance" development by means of loans for the stimulation of investments and to "supply" an internal economic surplus which was decapitalized to a large extent by the remittance of part of the surplus generated domestically and sent abroad as profits.

Foreign capital and foreign "aid" thus fill up the holes that they themselves created. The real value of this aid, however, is doubtful. If overcharges resulting from the restrictive terms of the aid are subtracted from the total amount of the grants, the average net flow, according to calculations of the Inter-American Economic and Social Council, is approximately 54 percent of the gross flow [5].

If we take account of certain further facts—that a high proportion of aid is paid in local currencies, that Latin American countries make contributions to international financial institutions, and that credits are often "tied"—we find a "real component of foreign aid" of 42.2 percent on a very favorable hypothesis and of 38.3 percent on a more realistic one [5, II, p. 33]. The gravity of the situation becomes even clearer if we consider that these credits are used in large part to finance North American investments, to subsidize foreign imports which compete with national products, to introduce technology not adapted to the needs of underdeveloped countries, and to invest in low-priority sectors of the national economies. The hard truth is that the underdeveloped countries have to pay for all of the "aid" they receive. This situation is generating an enormous protest movement by Latin American governments seeking at least partial relief from such negative relations.

3. Finally, industrial development is strongly conditioned by the technological monopoly exercised by imperialist centers. We have seen that the underdeveloped countries depend on the importation of machinery and raw materials for the development of their industries. However, these goods are not freely available in the international market; they are patented and usually belong to the big companies. The big companies do not sell machinery and processed raw materials as simple merchandise: they demand either the payment of royalties, etc., for their utilization or, in most cases, they convert these goods into capital and introduce them in the form of their own investments. This is how machinery which is replaced in the hegemonic centers by more advanced technology is sent to dependent countries as capital for the installation of affiliates. Let us pause and examine these relations in order to understand their oppressive and exploitative character.

The dependent countries do not have sufficient foreign currency, for the reasons given. Local businessmen have financing difficulties, and they must pay for the utilization of certain patented techniques. These factors oblige the national bourgeois governments to facilitate the entry of foreign capital in order to supply the restricted national market, which is strongly protected by high tariffs in order to promote industrialization. Thus, foreign capital enters with all the advantages: in many cases, it is given exemption from exchange controls for the importation of machinery; financing of sites for installation of industries is provided; government financing agencies facilitate industrialization; loans are available from foreign and domestic banks, which prefer such clients; foreign aid often subsidizes such investments and finances complementary public investments; after installation, high profits obtained in such favorable circumstances can be reinvested freely. Thus it is not surprising that the data of the U.S. Department of Commerce reveal that the percentage of capital brought in from abroad by these companies is but a part of the total amount of invested capital. These data show that in the period from 1946 to 1967 the new entries of capital into Latin America for direct investment amounted to $5,415 million, while the sum of reinvested profits was $4,424 million. On the other hand, the transfers of profits from Latin America to the United States amounted to $14,775 million. If we estimate total profits as approximately equal to transfers plus reinvestments we have the sum of $18,983 million. In spite of enormous transfers of profits to the United States, the book value of the United States' direct investment in Latin America went from $3,045 million in 1946 to $10,213 million in 1967. From these data it is clear that: (1) Of the new investments made by U.S. companies in Latin America for the period 1946–67, 55 percent corresponds to new entries of capital and 45 percent to reinvestment of profits; in recent years, the trend is more marked, with reinvestments between 1960 and 1966 representing more than 60 percent of new investments. (2) Remittances remained at about 10 percent of book value throughout the period. (3) The ratio of remitted capital to new flow is around 2.7 for the period 1946–67; that is, for each dollar that enters $2.70 leaves. In the 1960s this ratio roughly doubled, and in some years was considerably higher.

The *Survey of Current Business* data on sources and uses of funds for direct North American investment in Latin America in the period 1957–64 show that, of the total sources of direct investment in Latin America, only 11.8 percent came from the United States. The remainder is, in large part, the result of the activities of North American firms in Latin America (46.4 percent net income, 27.7 percent under the heading of depreciation), and from "sources located abroad" (14.1 percent). It is significant that the funds obtained abroad that are external to the companies are greater than the funds originating in the United States.

V. Effects on the Productive Structure

It is easy to grasp, even if only superficially, the effects that this dependent structure has on the productive system itself in these countries and the role of this structure in determining a specified type of development, characterized by its dependent nature.

The productive system in the underdeveloped countries is essentially determined by these international relations. In the first place, the need to conserve the agrarian or mining export structure generates a combination between more advanced economic centers that extract surplus value from the more backward sectors and internal "metropolitan" centers on the one hand, and internal interdependent "colonial" centers on the other [10]. The unequal and combined character of capitalist development at the international level is reproduced internally in an acute form. In the second place the industrial and technological structure responds more closely to the interests of the multinational corporations than to internal developmental needs (conceived of not only in terms of the overall interests of the population, but also from the point of view of the interests of a national capitalist development). In the third place, the same technological and economic-financial concentration of the hegemonic economies is transferred without substantial alteration to very different economies and societies, giving rise to a highly unequal productive structure, a high concentration of incomes, underutilization of installed capacity, intensive exploitation of existing markets concentrated in large cities, etc.

The accumulation of capital in such circumstances assumes its own characteristics. In the first place, it is characterized by profound differences among domestic wage-levels, in the context of a local cheap labor market, combined with a capital-intensive technology. The result, from the point of view of relative surplus value, is a high rate of exploitation of labor power. (On measurements of forms of exploitation, see [3].)

This exploitation is further aggravated by the high prices of industrial products enforced by protectionism, exemptions and subsidies given by the national governments, and "aid" from hegemonic centers. Furthermore, since dependent accumulation is necessarily tied into the international economy, it is profoundly conditioned by the unequal and combined character of international capitalist economic relations, by the technological and financial control of the imperialist centers by the realities of the balance of payments, by the economic policies of the state, etc. The role of the state in the growth of national and foreign capital merits a much fuller analysis than can be made here.

Using the analysis offered here as a point of departure, it is possible to understand the limits that this productive system imposes on the growth of the internal markets of these countries. The survival of traditional relations in the countryside is a serious limitation on the size of the market, since industrialization does not offer hopeful prospects. The productive structure created by dependent industrialization limits the growth of the internal market.

First, it subjects the labor force to highly exploitative relations which limit its purchasing power. Second, in adopting a technology of intensive capital use, it creates very few jobs in comparison with population growth, and limits the generation of new sources of income. These two limitations affect the growth of the consumer goods market. Third, the remittance abroad of profits carries away part of the economic surplus generated within the country. In all these ways limits are put on the possible creation of basic national industries which could provide a market for the capital goods this surplus would make possible if it were not remitted abroad.

From this cursory analysis we see that the alleged backwardness of these economies is not due to a lack of integration with capitalism but that, to the contrary, the most powerful obstacles to their full development come from the way in which they are joined to this international system and its laws of development.

VI. Some Conclusions: Dependent Reproduction

In order to understand the system of dependent reproduction and the socio-economic institutions created by it, we must see it as part of a system of world economic relations based on monopolistic control of large-scale capital, on control of certain economic and financial centers over others, on a monopoly of complex technology that leads to unequal and combined development at a national and international level. Attempts to analyze backwardness as a failure to assimilate more advanced models of production or to modernize are nothing more than ideology disguised as science. The same is true of the attempts to analyze this international economy in terms of relations among elements in free competition, such as the theory of comparative costs which seeks to justify the inequalities of the world economic system and to conceal the relations of exploitation on which it is based [14].

In reality we can understand what is happening in the underdeveloped countries only when we see that they develop within the framework of a process of dependent production and reproduction. This system is a dependent one because it reproduces a productive system whose development is limited by those world relations which necessarily lead to: the development of only certain economic sectors, to trade under unequal conditions [9], to domestic competition with international capital under unequal conditions, to the imposition of relations of superexploitation of the domestic labor force with a view to dividing the economic surplus thus generated between internal and external forces of domination. (On economic surplus and its utilization in the dependent countries, see [1].)

In reproducing such a productive system and such international relations, the development of dependent capitalism reproduces the factors that prevent it from reaching a nationally and internationally advantageous situation; and it thus reproduces backwardness, misery, and social marginalization within its borders. The development that it produces benefits very narrow sectors, encounters unyielding domestic obstacles to its continued economic growth (with respect to both internal and foreign markets), and leads to the progressive accumulation of balance-of-payments deficits, which in turn generate more dependence and more superexploitation.

The political measures proposed by the developmentalists of ECLA, UNCTAD, Inter-American Development Bank (BID), etc., do not appear to permit destruction of these terrible chains imposed by dependent development. We have examined the alternative forms of development presented for Latin America and the dependent countries under such conditions elsewhere [8]. Everything now indicates that what can be expected is a long process of sharp political and military confrontations and of profound social radicalization which will lead these countries to a dilemma: governments of force, which open the way to fascism, or popular revolutionary governments, which open the way to socialism. Intermediate solutions have proved to be, in such a contradictory reality, empty and utopian.

References

1. Paul Baran, *Political Economy of Growth* (Monthly Review Press, 1967).

2. Thomas Balogh, *Unequal Partners* (Basil Blackwell, 1963).

3. Pablo Gonzalez Casanova, *Sociología de la explotación, Siglo XXI* (México, 1969).

4. Cepal, *La CEPAL y el análisis del desarrollo Latinoamericano* (Santiago, Chile, 1968).

5. Consejo Interamericano Economico Social (CIES) O.A.S., Interamerican Economic and Social Council, External Financing for Development in L.A. *El Financiamiento externo para el desarrollo de América Latina* (Pan-American Union, Washington, 1969).

6. Theotonio dos Santos, *El nuevo carácter de la dependencia,* CESO (Santiago de Chile, 1968).

7. ———, *La crisis de la teoría del desarrollo y las relaciones de dependencia en América Latina,* Boletin del CESO, 3 (Santiago, Chile, 1968).

8. ———, *La dependencia económica y las alternotivas de cambio en*

América Latina, Ponencia al IX Congreso Latinoamericano de Sociología (México, Nov. 1969).

9. A. Emmanuel, *L'Echange Inégal* (Maspero, Paris, 1969).

10. Andre G. Frank, *Development and Underdevelopment in Latin America* (Monthly Review Press, 1968).

11. I. V. Levin, *The Export Economies* (Harvard Univ. Press, 1964).

12. Gunnar Myrdal, *Asian Drama* (Pantheon, 1968).

13. K. Nkrumah, *Neocolonialismo, última etapa del imperialismo* (Siglo XXI, México, 1966).

14. Cristian Palloix, *Problèmes de la Croissance en Economie Ouverte* (Maspero, Paris, 1969).

CHAPTER 21

American Penetration and Canadian Development: A Case Study of Mature Dependency

HEATHER-JO HAMMER AND JOHN W. GARTRELL

Dependency theorists have found that extensive foreign capital penetration dampens long-term economic growth, but, in a previous edition of this volume, Edward Muller asserted that up to that point, dependency theory had been unable to explain how Canada—a country highly penetrated by foreign investment—could be wealthy, fast growing, and experiencing relatively low levels of income inequality. In this chapter, Heather-Jo Hammer and John Gartrell argue that dependency theorists had failed to acknowledge that a country could be both a member of the core and a dependent country. After noting some similarities between mature dependency and Peter Evans's dependent development, the authors provide a model for Canada's mature dependence and offer evidence of a negative long-term effect of change in American direct investment on change in Canadian economic growth.

THE DEPENDENCY PERSPECTIVE ON THE SOCIOLOGY OF DEVELOPMENT HAS had difficulties in coming to terms with the Canadian situation. Canada seems to fall between types of social formations, displaying the social relations of advanced capitalism and the economic structure of dependency (Drache 1983, 36). Indeed, the Innisian tradition of Canadian political economy[1] stems from a perceived need for both original theory and distinctive methodology in the explanation of Canadian development (Drache 1983, 38). There is little doubt within the dependency perspective that Canada is "profoundly dependent" in the critical

Reprinted with permission of the American Sociological Association and the authors from *American Sociological Review,* vol. 51, no. 2 (April 1986): 201–213.

sense that it is extensively penetrated by American direct investment. Nevertheless, Canadian dependency is of a "different genre" than classic peripheral dependency (Portes 1976, 78). . . .

As a theory of development, dependency cannot adequately explain why core economies are not susceptible to the negative consequences of penetration as long as dependency is defined as a structural distortion that is evident exclusively in peripheral modes of development. We think that a demonstration of the negative structural effect of dependency is possible in the case of extensively penetrated core countries. The situation of "relative" core underdevelopment is described with the concept "mature dependency" (Hammer 1982, 1984a, 1984b). The differentiation of mature dependency from other forms of economic power dependency requires that the theory be liberated from its focus on the periphery and the semi-periphery, and the empirical studies be liberated from cross-national analysis. Our endeavour to specify a model of the structural effect of mature dependency on economic growth in Canada reflects Duvall's suggestion to merge dialectical analysis with time series methodology (Duvall 1978).

Mature Dependency and Canadian Development: Reformulating Dependency Theory

Dialectical analysis requires that each new situation of dependency be specified in a "search for differences and diversity" (Cardoso and Faletto 1979, xiii). Contrary to Caporaso and Zare (1981, 47) who state that "The questions of identification and measurement must be answered before theoretical ones can be raised," the dialectical method suggests that ". . . before measuring, previous elaboration of adequate theories and categories is required to give sense to the data" (Cardoso and Faletto 1979, xiii). In brief, Cardoso and Faletto's strategy is to establish the evidence on theoretical grounds and to interpret the data historically. Shifting to the language of empirical models, historical arguments must be interpreted in terms of the important context-defining variables that specify the form of dependency (Duvall 1978, 74).

The existing form of dependency that is most relevant to the Canadian case is Evans's (1979) statement of dependent development. There are some striking similarities between the Canadian and Brazilian developmental histories, particularly in relation to changes in the concentration of foreign capital. In both countries there is an historical shift from British portfolio to American direct investment, and from concentration in resources to concentration in industry. The key difference rests with the timing of the changes and the initial mode of incorpora-tion into the world economy. During the period of Canada's initial industrialization at the end of the nineteenth century, American direct investment in Canadian manufacturing accounted for about 34 percent of total manufacturing investment, compared to less than 4 percent in Brazil. The proportion of American to total direct investment in Canadian manufacturing was 55.6 percent by 1924 (Lewis 1938); in Brazil, by 1929, American direct investment accounted for only 24 per-cent of total manufacturing investment (Evans 1979, 78). It was not until the 1950s that American direct investment in Brazilian manufac-turing attained the concentration levels evident in Canada before the 1920s.

Most of the American MNEs that are currently dominant in Canada had already been established by the end of 1920 (Gonick 1970, 62). By 1897, Canada accounted for about 25 percent of total American direct investment abroad. By 1913, there were 450 American branch plants in Canada, including such giants as Singer, Bell, and Houston Electric (now General Electric) (Field 1914). When the American MNEs assert-ed their interests in Canadian manufacturing, Canada was the eighth largest manufacturing country in the world, not a peripheral country in transition (Maizels 1963). In 1870, manufacturing accounted for 19 per-cent of Canada's gross national product, with the production of iron and steel leading the composition.

"Production moves to the periphery only after the technology has become routinized" (Evans 1979, 28). Therefore, the comparative advantage of the periphery in the international market becomes the low cost of its labor (Evans 1979, 28). In addition to the economic disarticu-lation that results from the lack of integration between subsidiary firms,[2] there exists a disarticulation between technology and social structure. The problem is evident in the failure of imported technology to absorb the huge reserves of underemployed agricultural labor that have been excluded from urban industrialization (Evans 1979, 29). For the elite, disarticulation is an obstacle to self-sustained, autocentric accumulation (Evans 1979, 29). For the masses, economic exclusion is followed by political repression in order to prevent a rise in wages that would mean a loss in comparative advantage (Evans 1979, 48). Evans (1979, 29) describes both exclusion and disarticulation as the constant features of dependency, in the case of dependent development.[3]

Certainly, there is evidence of internal economic disarticulation in Canada. The establishment and protection of foreign technology and the control of the market by oligopolistic MNEs has resulted in a miniature replica effect. The Canadian goods market is fragmented due to an excess of buyers and sellers relative to size, and the concentration of MNEs in central Canada has resulted in regional disparity (Britton and Gilmour 1978, 93–96). However, the only way one can argue for the exclusion of the Canadian masses is in a relative sense, and only in comparison to the U.S. Historically, the wage levels of Canadian workers have been considerably higher than the wage levels of European workers. In fact, when American direct investment moved into Canadian industry at the end of the 1800s, Canada was at a comparative "disadvantage" because of its high wage levels. Where the wage differential does show up is in comparison to American industrial wages which were 60 percent higher than those in Canada during the period (Logan 1937, 90). Firestone's (1958) research suggests that real productivity in Canada outstripped real wages, but this relationship was reversed in the 1930s.

Canada had a reserve army of unskilled labor working in resources, construction and agriculture, whose wage rates were tied to the boom-bust cycle of export-led growth rather than to the import of technology (Drache 1983). This relation is accounted for by Canada's unique situation of being extensively penetrated by MNE investment simultaneously in resource extraction and manufacturing (Gherson 1980). In this sense the Canadian economy remains classically dependent, in that its export composition is predominated by primary resources.[4] In 1913, Canada was exporting an average of 31 percent less finished manufactures than the largest seven manufacturing countries (Maizels 1963). It was not the case that Canada lacked domestic savings for investment in the technology needed to further develop the manufacturing sector. Instead, Canadian funds were being directed into an elaborate banking and financial system to support the domestic transportation and utilities infrastructure needed for the export of wheat (Laxer 1984).

Technology was being imported at a much faster rate than manufactured goods were being exported. Consequently, foreign capital inflows were solicited to maintain the overall rate of economic growth (Ingram 1957). Gonick (1970, 70) argues that the import-substitution mentality implicit in the Canadian National Policy of 1897 was motivated by the commercial capitalists' concern with protecting their trade monopoly in staple exports. The policy of establishing a tariff barrier around Canadian manufacturing was intended to force the American MNEs to finance the Canadian industrial sector in order to penetrate the Canadian market. Apart from sidestepping the Canadian tariff, the opportunity to compete under the terms of British preference in export trade was a further attraction to American direct investment. In addition, the MNEs were able to take advantage of tax benefits and offers of free land that were a result of the regional competition within Canada to attract investment (Scheinberg 1973, 85).

The Canadian railway and financial capitalists were the same central Canadian capitalists who stood to gain from the protection of Canadian manufacturing and from government assistance to the Canadian Pacific Railway. Levitt (1970, 50–51) explains that Canadian private capital flowed freely from railway enterprises into the financial sector and manufacturing industries. In dependent development, the industrial bourgeoisie has no choice but to ally with the state and foreign capital (Evans 1979), whereas in mature dependency, the position and privileges of the commercial industrialists are not contingent upon the tripartite alliance. The alliance is formed by invitation, not necessity.

Innis (1956) argues that even though Canada had liberal democratic institutions, it lacked "strong" popular and democratic traditions. He suggests that this anomaly is linked to Canada's historical dependence and the way Canada was settled. The white settlers who colonized Canada were either fleeing revolution or were exiled when their revolution failed. "It was the presence of a deeply entrenched counter-revolutionary tradition which fundamentally altered not only the liberal democratic character and institutions of Canada but class relations as well" (Drache 1983, 44). Nevertheless, the history of democratic government in Canada can hardly be described as repressive, particularly in comparison to the history of Brazilian government. Thus, the two constant features of dependent development, exclusion of the masses and disarticulation, are evident in Canada, but to a relatively small degree. We suggest that the historical evidence does not support the argument that Canada has experienced dependent development. Rather, Canadian dependency is mature.

Mature dependency diverges from dependent development in the following respects:

1. The mature dependent's economy is functionally complete at the time when the tripartite alliance is formed. External capital inputs are invited, not essential.
2. The economic disarticulation associated with MNE investment is superimposed upon an intact economy that has demonstrated the capacity for self-sustained, autocentric accumulation. Mature dependency is a concrete historical alternative to classic autocentric development rather than an advanced phase of dependent development.
3. Mature dependency does not require economic exclusion of the

masses, nor does it result in the associated conditions of political repression.

4. Mature dependency is the condition that causes rich, industrialized core countries to exhibit relative underdevelopment vis-à-vis some of the other core countries on some criteria. The variability in relative status is determined, to a large extent, by the effectiveness of a state's development policy.

In contrast to its non-core counterparts, the mature dependent has abundant social, economic, and political resources that can be mobilized to regulate the negative effects of dependency (Duvall 1978, 69; Bornschier 1980a, 166–67). The contemporary features of mature dependency reflect a slow, historical process that has extended over a period of at least 120 years. Similar to dependent development, mature dependency emerged during the period of classic colonial dependence on staple-export growth. The continuity between Canada's early reliance on staple exports and contemporary mature dependency is a result of the continued interest of the Canadian state and the dominant capital interests in the encouragement of American MNE investment.

The difficulty in modeling mature dependency empirically is that we do not expect that the negative structural effects associated with MNE penetration will be evident in a rich, industrialized host until after the division of labor within the multinationals has come to dominate economic structure and growth. The actual effect, according to the decapitalization thesis, will appear only when inflows of fresh foreign capital slow down, or as we will demonstrate for the Canadian case, in combination with actual disinvestment. Although 80 percent of total direct investment in Canada has been American (Government of Canada 1981, 10), British portfolio investment was the primary source of foreign long-term investment capital until 1926.

Circa 1926, American portfolio investment split the market with the U.K., and by 1933, total American long-term investment came to exceed total British investment. Yet, at the onset of World War I, American direct investment accounted for only 13.5 percent of total foreign long-term investment in Canada. Fully 73.2 percent of all foreign long-term investment capital in Canada was in the form of British portfolio investment, imported by the sale of government-guaranteed railway bonds in order to subsidize Canadian investments.

American economic domination was not perceived as a threat to the Canadian state (Marshall et al. 1976, 15), because of its relatively small proportion and because it was complementary to British and Canadian investment (Behrman 1970). Moreover, for the period 1930–1946, portfolio investment (American and British) accounted for twice as much foreign long-term investment as did American direct investment. Flows of portfolio capital generally contribute to economic growth whereas the structural effects of foreign direct investment reduce growth (Behrman 1970, 19). Direct investments are those in which control lies with the foreign investor (Aitken 1961, 24). The organizational form of foreign direct investment is the multinational (Evans 1979, 38). In contrast, portfolio investments involve the acquisition of foreign securities by individuals or institutions with limited control over the companies concerned. In fact, there is considerable agreement that portfolio investment does not involve foreign control at all (Aitken 1961, 24; Hood and Young 1979, 9; Levitt 1970, 58; Gonick 1970, 50). As an economy expands, the foreign sector recedes (Gonick 1970, 50), whereas foreign direct investment may well expand faster than the general economy due to its concentration in the most dynamic and profitable sectors.

World War II changed the balance of foreign capital investments in Canada. Prior to the war, foreign portfolio investment accounted for an average of 71 percent of total foreign capital investment. After World War II, the average dropped to 34.8 percent. American direct investment, which had accounted for only 19.3 percent of the pre-war average, increased to 42.9 percent of foreign long-term investment for the period after 1946. Although American direct exceeded British portfolio investment as a proportion of total foreign long-term investment for the first time in 1946, it took about six more years for American direct investment to emerge as the primary source of foreign capital investment in Canada. While World War II facilitated an important increase in Canadian-owned manufacturing, it also brought closer economic ties with the U.S. Prior to 1950, American direct investment was linked closely to changes in the Canadian economy, accelerating during periods of high tariffs and decelerating during periods of recession (Marshall et al. 1976, 21). Pope (1971, 24) and Aitken (1961, 104) suggest that by 1950, American direct investment had become so large that it not only exploited opportunities, it created them by molding the Canadian economic structure.

The acceleration of American direct investment in Canada during the post-war boom period (1946–1960) is related to both the loss of Canadian access to British portfolio investment and markets and the ascent of the American economy to world economic hegemony. However, the crucial years, according to Grant (1970, 8), were the early 1940s when it was decided that Canada would become a branch plant economy. Both the organization of the war and the postwar construction were carried out under the assumption that government supported business interests in all national economic decisions. World War II brought the Ogdensburg agreements of 1940 to establish a joint defense board, the Hyde Park Declaration on the specialization of munitions production in 1941, a Joint War Production Committee, and Article VII of the Lend-Lease Law, which provided for a reduction in trade barriers. At this point, states Scheinberg (1973), Canadian leaders did perceive a threat to sovereignty, but were not prepared to change course in a period of accelerated wartime production.

Levitt (1970) describes how American direct investment continued to flow into the Canadian economy after the recession of 1957–1958, despite rising rates of unemployment and a slowing of Canadian output. The most important feature of the post-recession expansion was that only a very small proportion of foreign investment actually involved the importation of foreign savings (Gonick 1970, 64). American direct investment was financed largely from corporate capital raised in Canada through the sale of Canadian resources extracted and processed by Canadian labor, or from the sale of branch plant manufactures back to Canadian consumers at tariff-protected prices (Levitt 1970, 63).

Levitt (1970, 63–64) estimates that between 1957 and 1964, American direct investment in manufacturing, petroleum and natural gas, and mining and smelting secured 73 percent of investment funds from retained earnings and depreciation reserves. The strongest cross-national evidence (Bornschier 1980a, 161) of the negative impact of MNE penetration on specific economic sectors is evident in two of the three areas of American concentration in Canada, manufacturing and mining and smelting.

Although the proportion of American direct investment declined in the late 1970s, Canada's liabilities to the U.S. continued to rise through the reinvestment of retained earnings. Since 1975, almost 90 percent of the net increase in the book value of the stock of foreign direct investment in Canada has been accounted for by this process (Government of Canada 1981, 10).

Within the post-war period, both Grant and Levitt select 1960 as an important turning point in Canadian economic history. Grant (1970, 8) argues that since 1960, Canada has developed as a "northern extension" of the continental economy. Levitt (1970, 65) divides the post-war period into a boom period followed by a period of stabilization and disinvestment that she dates precisely to 1960. Levitt describes the latter phase of Canadian economic history as the period of "American Corporate Imperialism." In our analysis, the specification of this structural break is critical in the demonstration of the long-term negative effect of American direct investment on Canadian economic growth.

Bergesen (1982) emphasizes the importance of considering structural breaks in world economic development as parameters that delineate the time frame of analysis. World wars are structural breaks, and in the context of dependency analysis World War II takes on particular significance as the demarcation of the emergence of the MNEs as the basic organizational units of world production (Bergesen 1982, 33; Bornschier and Ballmer-Cao 1979, 488; Blake and Walters 1983, 87; Hood and Young 1979, 18), and the establishment of American direct investment as the dominant form of foreign investment capital in Canada. Our restriction of the time series analysis to the post–World War II period is consistent with the literature. . . .

Results

The results of the time series regression analysis support our hypothesis. Change in American direct investment for the post-war period has a negative effect on change in Canadian GNP after a lag of nine years. This effect is evident after 1960. The equation is reported in Table 21.1.

According to the full equation with all the variables included, IL9USDI has a negative effect on GNP of –1.88. As indicated by the value of the Durbin-Watson statistic (2.14), the model is free of autocorrelation. The coefficient for the long-term negative effect, specified

Table 21.1   Change in American Direct Investment and Change in Canadian Gross National Product: Ordinary Least Squares Time Series Estimates for the Period 1947–1978

Variable	Estimated Coefficient	Standard Error	T
DIFF	4709.16	882.282	5.33748
GFCF	.992951	.253596	3.91549
USDI	1.31187	.441842	2.96909
L9USDI	–.118747	.207940	–.571065
IUSDI	–.560369	.615555	–.910347
IL9USDI	–1.87526	.899004	–2.08593

Sum of the squared residuals = .321235E+08.
Standard error of the regression = –1111.54.
Mean of the dependent variable = –3066.78.
Standard deviation = 1893.11.
Log of the likelihood function = –266.516.
Number of observations = 32.
Sum of the residuals = 3486.96.
Durbin-Watson statistic = 2.1452.

as an interaction, is significant at the .025 level. The main effect of the lagged change in American direct investment (L9USDI) is small, negative and not significant for the entire post-war period. There is no evidence of a negative effect for the boom period (this run is not reported). The difference between the pre- and post-1960 series is significant at the .005 level. This difference . . . is equal to $4,709 million. Also significant at this level are the coefficients for the short-term (synchronous) effect of GFCF and USDI. As predicted by dependency theory, these effects are positive, and the immediate effect of change in American direct investment on change in Canadian economic growth is .42 larger than the GFCF coefficient. The main effect of the interaction term (IUSDI) is negative and not significant.

Although the Durbin-Watson statistic does not call for reestimation of the full equation, the variables are taken as first differences; therefore, the time-series procedure does not calculate in R^2. For this reason, the Cochrane-Orcutt iterative procedure (see Pindyck and Rubinfeld 1981, 157) has been performed on the equation as a check on the amount of variance explained. The R^2 and the R^2 adjusted both exceed .90. Various specifications of this full model have been estimated, eliminating the nonsignificant variables. What is most remarkable about the restricted equations is the stability of the coefficients and reported statistics across the different models. In the equation that includes only the difference between the periods, GFCF, USDI and IL9USDI, the estimated long-term negative effect for the post-1960 period is −1.92, compared to −1.88 in the full model. The other statistics are comparably close (results are not reported).

The argument could be made that the negative effect of change in USDI is simply a reflection of an underlying business cycle of the Juglar type (7–10 years). If this were the case, it is likely that a similarly lagged GFCF would show a negative effect on change in GNP. In the equation which estimates both main and interaction effects, the Durbin-Watson statistic indicates a problem of autocorrelation (D.W. = 1.54). The Cochrane-Orcutt estimation indicates that the period difference and the short-term effect of change in GFCF are both significant at the .005 level. The coefficient for GFCF is 1.77. These are the only significant effects in the equation. The other coefficients are estimated with enormous standard errors. The R^2 and adjusted R^2 are reduced to .83 and .81 respectively.

American direct investment in Canada is part of the composite measure of total American long-term investment. If the structural effect of mature dependency is related to the organization of the multinationals, we would expect to see a similar structure in total American long-term investment, to the extent that direct investment is proportionally dominant. The other two components of total long-term investment, portfolio and miscellaneous investments, should not exhibit the dependency effect on growth when they are disaggregated from the composite. Because American miscellaneous investment in Canada has accounted for only about 2.7 percent of total American long-term investment since 1926 (Government of Canada 1978), we will elaborate on the total of investment and on portfolio investment disaggregated.

Again, the analyses support our hypotheses about the nature of mature dependency. Comparing the lagged effects of American long-term and American direct investment, there is a similarity in the magnitudes and relative size of the coefficients, although the lagged effect is not significant. The portfolio estimates exhibit very little similarity to the direct investment estimates, and the short-term effect of portfolio investment is not significant. In fact, there is no significant effect for any of the portfolio variables when the American direct investment model is used to structure the equation. The evidence suggests that foreign direct investment is the only component of foreign long-term capital investments that has a long-term negative effect on the growth of the host economy. Granted, the empirical demonstration of a structural economic effect of dependency is a narrow delineation of the complexity of the alliance of social forces whose coincidence of interests causes the internalization of MNE investment. In fact, Portes (1976, 77) describes the internal impact of the multinationals as a remolding of the domestic social structure. Although our demonstration is limited to the transformation of the domestic economic structure, the specificities of our model are clearly defined by the contextual specificity of the larger social structure.

The importance of the findings is enhanced by their application to Canada, a dependent and yet non-peripheral economy. In this sense the findings and the historical evidence upon which they are based, suggest that dependency theory requires some modification. According to economic theories of the internal markets of MNES, it is possible for core countries to experience MNE-based dependency. The implications for the social structure of the dependent mature economy are not as devastating as they are in the periphery and the semi-periphery, but the structural effect on long-term economic growth is precisely the same.

Discussion and Conclusions

For the researcher interested in the demonstration of dependency effects in non-peripheral countries, model specification is the key directive in research design. Duvall (1978, 74) argues that the design of dependency research must incorporate the notion that context affects causal relations. "To effectuate this requirement, it is necessary to interpret verbal historicist arguments in terms of the important context-defining variables that are implied in the contextually-specific analysis" (Duvall 1978, 74). The context of mature dependency is provided by both history and theory. The historical legacy of the process of incorporation into the world economy has resulted in a hierarchical division of labor that requires both the measurement of variation between different structural positions and the measurement of variations within positions.

The restriction of current empirical studies of dependency to comparative non–time series designs has meant that events which are major sources of variation in independent variables have been largely ignored (Esteb 1977, 13). In the case of Canada's mature dependency, a time series design is required to capture the structural break that occurs in 1960. Moreover, the cross-national analysis of core countries as a block has obscured the structural distinctions that differentiate Canada from other developed countries.

Dependency theory suggests that extensive foreign capital penetration will have a long-term negative effect on the host's economic growth. The critical importance of theory in the design of dependency research is evident in variable selection, specification of the functional form of the relationship between variables, and the identification of the structure of lagged effects. Dependency theory has integrated organizational economics to explain how the dominance of multinational enterprises has changed the structure of the postwar world economy (see Evans 1979; dos Santos 1970; Cardoso and Faletto 1979). However, dependency theory has not seriously considered the implications of cross-penetration within the core for the structure of developed economies.

New theories addressing the organizational economics of multinational enterprises suggest that the structural effect associated with dependency need not be confined to the peripheral economies of the world system. The couching of dependency arguments in terms of peripheral modes of development does not accommodate "deviant" case analyses without some modification to the theory. Although Wallerstein himself waivers between essays, he classifies Canada, Australia and New Zealand as members of the semi-periphery in order to deal with the "doubtful" economic structures of these countries (see Wallerstein 1974; 1976). Evans (1979, 293) does the same. On this point, we must disagree with both theorists.

The theoretical definition of what constitutes the semi-periphery is admittedly imprecise; however, the term is used as a catch-all category for those countries which cannot simply be considered "peripheral" and yet are structurally distinguishable from center countries (Evans 1979, 291; Wallerstein 1976). Wallerstein (1974) suggests that the coherence of the category is derived from the fact that the semi-periphery is formed by the more advanced exemplars of dependent development. According to Evans's (1979) theory or dependent development, Canada does not fit the category.

The resolution of the issue of Canada's status requires both theoretical and methodological innovation. We suggest that a country can be both a member of the core and dependent. The situation has been described by the concept "mature dependency." The demonstration of a negative long-term effect of change in American direct investment on change in Canadian economic growth provides strong evidence for the existence of mature dependency as a variation in core development. We suggest that future empirical research be directed into case-by-case analyses of core country dependency. Portes (1976) suggests that Australia may be a good candidate for analysis. The Canadian case was a good place to start, particularly because of the significance of retained earnings in Canada, a characteristic which sets Canada apart from other American dependencies (see Hood and Young 1979, 39). In conclusion, we may have inadvertently bridged the rift between the dialectical method of analysis and empirical dependency research. As we have demonstrated in this paper, theoretically and historically informed time series analysis is the appropriate design for modeling the contextual specificity of variations in dependency.

Notes

1. The Innisian tradition began with the work of Harold Innis in the 1930s. He explained Canadian development in terms of its domination by staple-export-led growth. The tradition is a reformulation or Marxism tailored to Canada's mode of capitalist accumulation. It negates the liberal argument Canada's development has been principally autonomous, introverted and autocentric (Drache 1983, 27).

2. "Firms in dependent countries buy their equipment and other capital goods from outside. so that the 'multiplier effect' of new investments is transferred back to the center" (Evans 1979, 28).

3. Because the masses are effectively barred from economic participation, "to allow them political participation would be disruptive. Social and cultural exclusion follow from political and economic exclusion" (Evans 1979, 29).

4. See Richards and Pratt (1979) on "advanced resource capitalism."

References

Aitken, Hugh G.J. 1961. *American Capital and Canadian Resources.* Cambridge, MA: Harvard University Press.

Behrman, Jack N. 1970. *National Interests and the Multinational Enterprise: Tensions Among the North Atlantic Countries.* Englewood Cliffs, NJ: Prentice-Hall.

Bergesen, Albert. 1982. "The Emerging Science of the World-System." *International Social Science Journal* 34:23–25.

Blake, David H. and Robert S. Walters. 1983. *The Politics of Global Economic Relations.* Englewood Cliffs, NJ: Prentice-Hall.

Bornschier, Volker. 1980a. "Multinational Corporations, Economic Policy and National Development in the World System." *International Social Sciences Journal* 32:158–72.

Bornschier, Volker and Thanh-Huyen Ballmer-Cao. 1979. "Income Inequality: A Cross-national Study of the Relationship Between MNC-Penetration, Dimensions of the Power Structure and Income Distribution." *American Sociological Review* 44:487–506.

Britton, John H. and James A. Gilmour. 1978. *The Weakest Link—A Technological Perspective on Canadian Industrial Underdevelopment.* Ottawa: Science Council of Canada.

Caporaso, James A. and Behrouz Zare. 1981. "An Interpretation and Evaluation of Dependency Theory." 43–56 in *From Dependency to Development: Strategies to Overcome Underdevelopment and Inequality*, edited by Herald Manoz. Boulder, CO: Westview Press.

Cardoso, Fernando Henrique and Enzo Faletto. 1979. *Dependency and Development in Latin America.* Berkeley, CA: University of California Press.

dos Santos, Theotonio. 1970. "The Structure of Dependence." *American Economic Review* 60:231–36.

Drache, Daniel. 1983. "The Crisis of Canadian Political Economy Dependency Theory Versus the New Orthodoxy." *Canadian Journal of Political and Social Theory* 7:25–49.

Duvall, Raymond. 1978. "Dependency and Dependencia Theory: Notes Towards Precision of Concept and Argument." *International Organization* 32:51–78.

Duvall, Raymond and John Freeman. 1981. "The State and Dependent Capitalism." *International Studies Quarterly* 25:99–118.

Esteb, Nancy. 1977. "Methods for World System Analysis: A Critical Appraisal." Paper presented at the 72nd annual meetings of the American Sociological Association in Chicago, September 5–9.

Evans, Peter. 1979. *Dependent Development: The Alliance of Multinational, State, and Local Capital in Brazil.* Princeton, NJ: Princeton University Press.

Field, F. W. 1914. *Capital Investments in Canada.* Montreal: The Monetary Times of Canada.

Firestone, O. John. 1958. *Canada's Economic Development, 1867–1953.* London: Bowes and Bowes.

Gherson, Joan. 1980. "U.S. Investment in Canada." *Foreign Investment Review* 3:11–14.

Gonick, Cyril Wolfe. 1970. "Foreign Ownership and Political Decay." 44–73 in *Close the 49th Parallel etc.: The Americanization of Canada*, edited by Ian Lumsden. Toronto: University of Toronto Press.

Government of Canada. Statistics Canada. 1983. *National Income and Expenditure Accounts 1965–1982*. Ottawa: Minister of Supply and Services (catalogue no. 13-201) GNP CANSIM MATRIX 000531. GNP CANSIM MATRIX 000528.

———. 1978. Canada's International Investment Position 1978. Ottawa: Minister of Supply and Services (catalogue no. 67-202).

———. 1981. Canada's International Investment Position 1978. Ottawa: Minister of Supply and Services (catalogue no. 67-202).

Grant, George. 1970. *Lament for a Nation*. Toronto: McClelland and Stewart.

Hammer, Heather-Jo. 1982. "Multinational Corporations and National Development: American Direct Investment in Canada." Paper presented at the 10th annual congress meetings of the International Sociological Association in Mexico City, August 16–21.

———. 1984a. Comment on "Dependency Theory and Taiwan: Analysis of a Deviant Case." *American Journal of Sociology* 89:932–36.

———. 1984b. "Mature Dependency: The Effects of American Direct Investment on Canadian Economic Growth." Unpublished Ph.D. dissertation. Department of Sociology, University of Alberta, Edmonton, Canada.

Hood, Neil and Stephen Young. 1979. *The Economics of Multinational Enterprise*. London: Longman Group Limited.

Ingram, James C. 1957. "Growth in Capacity in Canada's Balance of Payments." *American Economic Review* 47:93–104.

Innis, Harold. 1956. *Essays in Canadian Economic History*. Toronto: Toronto University Press.

Laxer, Gordon. 1984. "Foreign Ownership and Myths About Canadian Development." *Review of Canadian Sociology and Anthropology* 22:311–45.

Levitt, Kari. 1970. *Silent Surrender: The Multinational Corporation in Canada*. Toronto: Macmillan.

Lewis. Cleona. 1938. *America's Stake in International Investments*. Washington, DC: Brookings Institute.

Logan, Harold. 1937. "Labour Costs and Labour Standards." 63–97 in *Labour in Canadian-American Relations*, edited by H. Innis. Toronto: University of Toronto Press.

Maizels, Alfred. 1963. *Industrial Growth and World Trade*. London: Cambridge University Press.

Marshall, Herbert, Frank A. Southard Jr. and Kenneth W. Taylor. 1976. *Canadian-American Industry: A Study in International Investment*. New Haven: Yale University Press.

Pindyck, Robert S. and Daniel Rubinfeld. 1981. *Econometric Methods and Economic Forecasting*. New York: McGraw-Hill.

Pope, William H. 1971. *The Elephant and the Mouse*. Toronto: McClelland and Stewart.

Portes, Alejandro. 1976. "On the Sociology of National Development: Theories and Issues." *American Journal of Sociology* 82:55–85.

Richards, John and Larry Pratt. 1979. *Prairie Capitalism: Power and Influence in the New West*. Toronto: McClelland and Stewart.

Scheinberg, Stephen. 1973. "Invitation to Empire: Tariffs and American Economic Expansion in Canada." 80–100 in *Enterprise and National Development: Essays on Canadian Business and Economic History*, edited by Glenn Porter and Robert D. Cuff. Toronto: Hakkert.

Stoneman, Colin. 1975. "Foreign Capital and Economic Growth." *World Development* 3:11–26.

Wallerstein, Immanuel. 1974. "Dependence in an Interdependent World: The Limited Possibilities of Transformation Within the Capitalist World Economy." *African Studies Review* 17:1–26.

———. 1976. "Semi-Peripheral Countries and the Contemporary World Crisis." *Theory and Society* 3:461–83.

CHAPTER 22

The Irish Case of Dependency: An Exception to the Exception?

DENIS O'HEARN

According to dependency/world systems theory, transnational corporation (TNC) penetration depresses growth and worsens income inequality. In the previous chapter, Heather-Jo Hammer and John Gartrell point to the relatively high degree of TNC penetration and income equality in Canada, questioning why TNC investment in developing countries has one outcome but in penetrated developed countries another. In this chapter, Denis O'Hearn addresses Irish dependency and its record of economic growth and income inequality, arguing that some countries have regimes that make them vulnerable to dependency relations while others do not. He reports that Ireland's growth was undermined by decapitalization. He also notes that radical free-trade policies in Ireland are also related to rising income inequality

F OR THE PAST 20 YEARS, THE APPROACH LOOSELY TERMED AS *DEPENDENCY* enjoyed popularity in development studies, particularly among radical scholars. Many studies concentrated on the connections between foreign penetration, economic growth, and income distribution. Baran (1957) and others emphasized the *tendencies* of foreign penetration to limit economic growth in the LDCs. Later works (Frank 1969) implied "laws" of development, relating proximity to the "metropole" with underdevelopment in the periphery. A series of analysts then attempted to "test" the hypotheses that foreign penetration caused (1) low growth rates and (2) inequality in LDCs (Chase-Dunn 1975; Bornschier 1980;

Reprinted with permission of the American Sociological Association and the authors from *American Sociological Review* (1989): 578–594.

Biersteker 1978; Bornschier and Ballmer-Cao 1979; Evans and Timberlake 1980).

Within the past few years some scholars have strongly challenged the dependency approach. A number of empirical analyses concentrated on "exceptions" to dependency, particularly from East Asia (for a review, see Chakravarty 1987). In place of dependency, these analysts propose a return to orthodox principles of neoclassical development economics and modernization theory. . . .

In place of dependency, a series of trade theorists give the following reasons for the "gang of four's" [Taiwan, South Korea, Singapore, and Hong Kong—eds.] success:

a. maintenance of an outward-looking orientation throughout the rapid growth phase of these countries;
b. maintenance of a very hospitable climate for foreign investment;
c. and finally, "keeping the prices right," by which they imply a relatively low real price of labour, a relatively high real rate of interest and "realistic" exchange rates (Chakravarty 1987).

Sociological and political accounts of the success in East Asia concentrate less on openness to foreign penetration than on political and class variables—the nature of the colonial and post-colonial relationship with Japan, the emphasis on labor-intensive enterprises, and the absence of an entrenched bourgeoisie. In fairness, many of these "non-economic" analyses have taken great pains to point out that South Korea and Taiwan are special or deviant cases and, therefore, do not in themselves constitute a threat to the dependency approach. Barrett and Whyte, for example, argue that Taiwan is a "deviant case" of dependency theory because foreign penetration was linked neither to stagnation nor inequality (Barrett and Whyte 1982; see also Cummings 1984).

In the present chapter, I will challenge the new modernizationism in development studies by presenting the case study of Ireland (i.e., the 26 southern counties). Ireland represents not only an "exception" to the "exceptions" in the so-called gang of four. It is in many ways a truer representation of the open, foreign-dominated, free-enterprise regime that the new modernizationists prescribe. In development terms, it is also an abject failure. This is especially significant because Ireland has for 30 years been in the heart of European economic integration. For 15 years, Ireland has "enjoyed" full membership in the European Economic Community, one of the dominant economic powers of the "modern industrial West." Indeed, this close relationship to the core, in classical "dependency" terms, directly contributed to Ireland's development problems.

Specificity of Irish Dependency

Ireland is an island about the size of the state of Maine, lying 30–60 miles from the British mainland. Its population is about four and a half million, well below its mid-19th century population of eight million. Its modern history is dominated by British occupation, four major waves of emigration, and several famines, including the famous mid-19th century "potato famine." In the 19th century, Irish peasants won limited ownership of farms and limited rights against British landlords. Ireland's traditional industrial area, around Belfast, was based on shipbuilding and linen-making for the British empire. Industry in the rest of the island was impeded by British laws, which removed Irish tariffs on industrial goods and outlawed certain lines of industry and exports.

Ireland was partitioned in 1921, at the end of a war of independence. Britain retained six of the nine counties of the province of Ulster, which included industrial Belfast and the largest adjoining area with a built-in settler majority. The southern state of today, therefore, comprises an area of about four-fifths of the island, with a population of about 3 million.

The new postcolonial state in 1932 embarked on an attempt to build native industry through a classical program of import-substituting industrialization (ISI), with high levels of tariff protection. Despite an economic war waged by Britain against Ireland, this program was quite successful: between 1931 and 1947 the number of manufacturing establishments employing more than 10 grew by 63 percent, and those employing over a hundred more than doubled. In the same period, industrial employment grew by about 80 percent, from 110,588 to 197,605 (O'Hearn 1988, pp. 82, 89). But in the mid-1950s, because of rising dollar trade deficits, external political pressures tied to Marshall Aid and European integration, and economic recession, the Irish regime changed the industrialization program from ISI to export-led industrialization (ELI). The new ELI regime had three distinguishing characteristics: (1) radical free trade, (2) radical free enterprises, and (3) foreign industrial domination.

Radical Free Trade

Unlike many developing countries, which followed a "stop-and-go" pattern of deprotection and reprotection, Ireland was forced to free its trade rapidly and totally. The removal of protection began after Ireland joined the Organisation for European Economic Cooperation (OEEC) in the 1950s—a prerequisite for receiving Marshall Aid—and ended when Ireland joined the EEC in 1972. Table 22.1 clearly shows the fall of tar-

Table 22.1　Revenues from Customs Tariffs, and as Percentage of Total Net Government Receipts (million Irish punts[a])

Year	(1) Tariff Revenue	(2) Total Revenue	(1) As Percentage of (2)	Year	(1) Tariff Revenue	(2) Total Revenue	(1) As Percentage of (2)
1954	37	83	44.6	1970	88	338	26.0
1955	37	85	43.5	1971	92	398	27.2
1956	39	89	43.8	1972	101	469	21.5
1957	45	94	47.9	1973	117	540	21.7
1958	47	97	48.5	1974	139	665	20.8
1959	48	98	49.0	1975	176	901	19.5
1960	45	103	43.7	1976	25	1222	2.0
1961	41	107	38.3	1977	29	1445	2.0
1962	45	119	37.8	1978	35	1709	2.0
1963	47	129	36.4	1979	39	1991	2.0
1964	50	145	34.5	1980	46	2584	1.8
1965	56	177	31.6	1981	58	3274	1.8
1966	58	194	29.9	1982	62	4014	1.5
1967	68	222	30.6	1983	77	4503	1.7
1968	70	248	28.2	1984	94	5115	1.8
1969	76	282	27.0				

a. The punt is the Irish currency. Its value was tied to the British pound until Ireland joined the European Money System in 1979.

Source: Irish Revenue Commissioners (various years).

iff receipts during ELI, beginning in 1959 when OEEC free trade pressures became severe. In 1972, tariff revenues as a percentage of total Irish government revenues fell by almost 6 percent. Four years later, as a result of Ireland's terms of accession to the EEC, tariff revenues fell to practically nil.[1]

As a result, the Irish market was penetrated by competing imports. Between 1960 and 1980, imports took over the Irish market in nearly every category of manufactured goods. In footwear and clothing, imports rose from 8 percent of domestic consumption in 1960, to 70–80 percent in 1980. In nonelectrical machinery, the share of imports during the same period rose from 55 to 98 percent.

The results for Irish-owned industry were disastrous (Table 22.2). Between 1973 and 1986, 85 to 90 percent of the jobs in pre-1955 clothing and textiles firms were lost. Three-fourths of the jobs in domestic miscellaneous manufacturing and over half of the jobs in domestic chemicals and metals were lost. In the pre-ELI Irish manufacturing sector as a whole, half of the jobs held in 1973 were lost by 1986 (60 percent in the nonfood sector). Of course, this demolition of protected nationalist industry *could* be viewed as "restructuring"—that is, clearing out inefficient and unprofitable sectors to make way for more prof-

Table 22.2   Changes of Employment and Number of Firms in Domestic "Old" and "Adapted" Industry from 1973 to 1986, Ireland

	Employment			Number of Firms		
Sector	1973	1986	Percent Change	1973	1986	Percent Change
Food	27601	17330	−37.2	598	448	−25.1
Drink	3804	3197	−16.0	77	56	−27.3
Textiles	8561	894	−89.6	120	43	−64.2
Clothing	8084	1231	−84.8	213	78	−63.4
Wood	5186	2769	−46.6	361	284	−21.3
Paper	8446	4453	−47.3	218	176	−19.3
Clay	9861	7519	−23.8	211	161	−23.7
Chemical	2245	1047	−53.4	64	28	−56.3
Metals	12148	5172	−57.4	354	239	−32.5
Other mfg.	3267	766	−76.6	132	71	−46.2
Nonfood	58825	23851	−59.5	1673	1080	−35.4
Total	90230	44378	−50.8	2348	1584	−32.5

Source: Author's calculations from IDA Employment Surveys.

itable "modern" sectors. To validate the dependency approach, therefore, we must show that the new industry which replaced domestic manufacturing was not conducive to economic growth.

Radical Free Enterprise

From its inception, the ISI regime was based strictly on principles of "private enterprise." Interventions by the state into the "business of business" were few, and state industry was limited (in 1945 there were three infrastructural and two industrial state companies). These principles were intensified under ELI. The state's role was to market Ireland as a profitable location for business—to provide incentives for industry to locate in Ireland and to find firms that would respond to the incentives. After that, new foreign firms could avoid any kind of scrutiny. The disposition of profits is left entirely in the hands of the firm. No profits taxes are paid on most manufactured exports, and profits may be freely repatriated. Means of production are freely imported, and output is freely exported. The regime does not pressure TNCs to use Irish inputs or to create other linkages. In the words of an Irish Minister for Industry and Commerce at the beginning of ELI, "we aim to convince [U.S. industrialists] that Ireland is the best possible location because of its attitude to private enterprise. . . . the more profits they make the better we will like it" (Dail Eireann 1958).

Foreign Domination

The Irish regime perceives foreign industry as a substitute for—not a complement to—domestic industry. An early and influential proponent of ELI captured the Irish attitude, saying, "By far the most hopeful means of getting good management, technical knowledge, and capital all at once is from subsidiaries of large foreign companies. . . . a plant which is paid for by foreign capital is a great deal better than one which has to be paid for from the scanty saving of the Republic" (Carter 1957). Since the inception of ELI, the regime relies *first and foremost* on the attraction of new foreign capital for industrial expansion. . . .

During the first half of the 1960s, TNCs created more than half of the new manufacturing jobs. After 1965, at least 70 to 80 percent of the new manufacturing jobs were in TNCs (O'Hearn 1987).

Ireland's adherence to free trade, free enterprise, and foreign industrial domination sets it apart from "exceptional" cases, such as South Korea and Taiwan. Regimes in these countries are characterized by strong state intervention in business, widespread use of selective protection and import-substitution, and a definite preference for domestic industry. The "free market" in Singapore, another high-growth East Asian economy, has been described as a "myth" (Lim 1983; see also Rodan 1985; Islam and Kirkpatrick 1986).[2]. . .

Results I: Slow Economic Growth

How do the specificities of the Irish case affect the relation of foreign penetration to economic growth and inequality? Are the relations of "dependency" at work in Ireland?. . .

Linkages

Even if the resources for investment and expansion are available, productive outlets for investment must be found. For many years, orthodox development theorists stressed the desirability of balanced growth among economic sectors, to avoid bottlenecks and realization problems (see Nurkse 1953; Lewis 1955). Albert Hirschman (1958) challenged this orthodoxy in his seminal work *The Strategy of Economic Development*. According to Hirschman, investment opportunities are created by the imbalanced development of the economy. Bottlenecks and gaps induce productive investment to correct or fill them.

Hirschman lists three kinds of linkages, or investment inducements. (1) If a firm buys inputs locally, it induces someone to produce them (*backward linkages*). (2) If a firm makes a product which may be processed further, it may induce a local firm to make a new product (*forward linkages*). (3) If a firm's activities contribute to the state's economic resources (through taxes and import duties), it creates *fiscal linkages*. Hirschman's analysis of linkages is behind more recent concepts such as *disarticulation* between "modern" and "traditional" economic sectors (Amin 1974) and *economic dualism* (Myint 1970; Singer 1970).

Fiscal linkages are probably negative in Ireland because (1) the typical TNC pays no taxes due to "free enterprise" tax provisions and pays no import duties due to free trade, and (2) large incentives and infrastructural costs are incurred by the state to attract foreign investment. Since TNCs in Ireland export nearly all of their product, forward linkages are few. The only possible significant linkages from TNC operations in Ireland are *backward* linkages.

Irish data on backward linkages are sparse. There were surveys of industrial firms in 1966, 1971, 1974, and 1983 (Survey Team 1967; O hUiginn 1972; McAleese 1977). Unfortunately, the coverage and classification of firms differ among the surveys, so longitudinal comparisons are awkward. But it is still possible to construct a fairly good picture of TNCs' backward linkages. Buckley (1974) found that TNCs in 1971 purchased only 31.5 percent of their material inputs from Irish sources, while Irish firms purchased 68.3 percent locally. McAleese and McDonald (1978) found that new (post–1955) nonfood TNCs purchased 11.2 percent of their inputs in Ireland, while new domestic firms purchased 22.2 percent locally. Thus, we can conclude that (*a*) the rate of TNC-related linkages is very low, (*b*) domestic firms have twice as many linkages as TNCs, and (*c*) the rate of linkages created by new domestic industry is also low. It is important to note that linkages were reduced in Ireland not only by the predominance of TNCs in new industry, but also because free trade encouraged (or forced) *domestic* firms to turn to foreign sources of supply. . . .

TNCs' backward linkages in Ireland are also extremely low relative to other dependent countries. Table 22.3 compares the proportions of material inputs that are locally purchased by manufacturing subsidiaries of U.S. TNCs in Ireland, Brazil, and Mexico. TNCs' local purchases are uniformly lower in Ireland, particularly in the "modern" sectors. In manufacturing as a whole, U.S. affiliates purchased 76.4 percent of their material inputs locally in Brazil and 68.5 percent in Mexico, but less than 20 percent in Ireland. While this confirms the extremely low level of TNC-induced linkages in Ireland by comparison with other semiperipheral countries, it also indicates the importance of specificities of Irish development. In particular, the most important causes of

Table 22.3   Locally Purchased Materials as Percentage of Total Material Inputs in U.S. Affiliates Operating in Brazil, Mexico, and Ireland

			Ireland	
Sector	Brazil	Mexico	U.S. TNCs	All TNCs
Food	89.5	96.8	73.0	70.7
Textiles	*	94.1	13.8	18.1
Paper	91.4	93.5	33.3	55.3
Chemicals	44.7	54.8	19.3	18.2
Rubber	92.7	88.5	3.1	1.5
Clay/cement	81.7	66.7	15.3	49.6
Metals	83.8	90.8	7.0	15.4
Nonelectric machinery	63.6	45.7	12.6	15.4
Electric machinery	60.0	61.6	10.9	11.2
Transport	97.1	60.7	8.9	18.6
Instruments	11.2	44.7	21.9	18.9
Other	74.0	97.6	19.2	19.2
Total	76.4	68.5	19.7	27.7

Note: Irish data are for 1983; Brazilian and Mexican data are for 1972.
Source: IDA Components of Sales Survey data, Connor (1977).

low linkages in Ireland—unlike Mexico and Brazil—are (1) the predominance of TNC production for export rather than for local markets, and (2) the degree of free enterprise (absence of local-content regulations).

In an economy such as Ireland's, where the regime emphasizes the attraction of new foreign capital, and where imports have swamped the domestic consumer market, *linkages* are an important source of investment opportunities. The scarcity of linkages between TNCs and the local Irish economy means that the contribution of new TNCs to growth is practically restricted to the activities of the TNCs themselves. Foreign investment creates few multipliers that lead to the growth of domestic investment.

Foreign Penetration and Growth

The logic of the Irish development regime is deceptively simple, as is the logic of modernizationist analysis in general: attract as much foreign investment as possible, the foreign investors will export a lot, exports will bring new resources into the country, and economic development will surely follow, along with jobs and prosperity.

Irish ELI was *spectacularly* successful at attracting foreign investment and increasing exports. Real foreign investment grew at an annual rate of 25 percent between 1955 and 1983. Real exports grew by 7.5 percent annually between 1955 and 1985 (8.3 percent after 1972), and manufactured exports by more than 10 percent (calculated from OECD 1987). If foreign investments and exports are the key to growth, the Irish economy should have expanded especially rapidly during the 1970s and 1980s.

The actual Irish growth experience was very different (Table 22.4). Throughout ELI, gross fixed capital formation (GFCF) grew annually by only 5 percent. Since 1972 (when Ireland joined the EEC) per capita GFCF grew by less than 2 percent. Annual rates of growth of per capita GNP were even slower. At its highest, per capita GNP grew at an annual rate of 3.4 percent (1965–1970). During ELI as a whole, the annual growth rate of per capita GNP was a mere 2.3 percent. Most significantly, the annual per capita economic growth rate fell to 0.4 percent during the post-EEC period, and was negative (–1.25 percent) in the 1980s.

These rates of growth are strikingly low compared to rates of growth in other countries. Ireland's annual rate of economic growth over the 30 years of ELI was the lowest in Europe, well below rates of growth in the European periphery (4–6 percent) and the average rates of growth for upper-income LDCs (about 5 percent), and far below the "exceptional" East Asian economies (6–8 percent). Even in its so-called

Table 22.4   Annual Percentage Rates of Growth of Gross Fixed Capital Formation (GFCF) and GNP during ELI, 1955–85 (constant 1958 Irish punts)

Years	GFCF	Per Capita GFCF	GFCF (mfg.)	GNP	Per Capita GNP	Net Output (mfg.)
1955–60	–3.91	–3.31	3.6	1.22	1.83	4.4
1960–65	11.88	11.59	14.64	3.41	3.14	7.75
1965–70	6.34	5.87	7.82	3.9	3.41	8.23
1970–75	3.48	1.98	6.51	3.33	1.81	5.61
1975–80	6.89	5.34	6.61	3.53	2.16	6.99
1980–85	–0.39	–1.02	–6.12	–0.45	–1.25	6.88
1955–72	6.73	6.53	11.3	3.4	3.19	7.44
1972–85	3.24	1.97	1.61	1.65	0.38	5.9
1955–85	5.83	5.02	7.74	3.15	2.34	6.92

Note: Five-year rates of growth for each variable x are calculated according to the following formula: $[\log x(t+5) - \log x(t)] / 5$. Rates of growth for longer periods are calculated by least-square regression of the log of the variable on time in years.

Source: Central Statistics Office (various years); OECD (1987).

"miracle years" of the 1960s, Ireland's annual growth rate of per capita GNP never reached 4 percent over any five-year period. Can this poor growth performance be associated with foreign penetration, free trade, and free enterprise?[3]

Growth of output and investment became slower as foreign penetration became higher, and growth rates became particularly low (and finally negative) after Ireland joined the EEC and was forced into full-fledged free trade. *Every industrial sector except chemicals and metals experienced significantly lower rates of growth of net output after Ireland's accession to the EEC than in the pre-EEC period of ELI* (O'Hearn 1988, chap. 14). Textiles and clothing experienced negative post-EEC growth rates. Food, drink, wood, paper, and clay were stagnant after 1972. Only metals, chemicals, and other manufacturing experienced annual growth rates of more than 5 percent after Ireland entered the EEC and embarked on full free trade. . . .

Results II: Income Distribution

The second major claim of dependency is that foreign penetration either increases inequality or prevents its decrease. Here again most of the existing evidence is from cross-sectional studies, which do not adequately explain how the effects of dependency may unfold over time (for a review of findings, see Bornschier 1980b). Dependency posits three major types of arguments about foreign penetration and inequality: (1) arguments about structural unemployment and poverty, (2) arguments about class inequality, and (3) arguments about wage inequality.

Structural Unemployment and Poverty

Foreign penetration may cause unemployment for several reasons, two of which are particularly relevant in the Irish case. (*a*) Radical free trade and discrimination in favor of foreign industry may cause widescale displacement of domestic industry. To this may be added the migration of farmers to the cities and towns, which may further swell the ranks of the unemployed. (*b*) If new foreign industry is more capital-intensive than domestic industry, or is concentrated in capital- (or materials-) intensive sectors, the employment created per unit of foreign investment may be too low to offset employment *losses* associated with foreign-penetration (Rubinson 1976; Bornschier and Ballmer-Cao 1979).

Although Irish income distribution data are scarce,[4] structural unemployment has certainly been a major cause of inequality since Ireland joined the EEC. In Table 22.5 I show the distribution of direct incomes in 1973 and 1980. Unemployment is the source of the major differences between the two distributions. In 1973, the lowest 10 percent of Irish households received less than 1 percent of direct incomes, while the next decile received 1.7 percent. By 1980, the lowest decile received no direct income, while the next decile received a mere 0.7 percent of total incomes. Today, with unemployment exceeding 20 percent, the lowest *two* deciles receive no direct income. To the extent the ELI regime caused unemployment in Ireland, it unquestionably *caused* higher inequality of direct incomes.

Apart from industrial closures, rising capital intensity is the major cause of unemployment. Assets per hour of labor expended in Irish industry grew during ELI (1955–82) at an annual rate of 5.3 percent (O'Hearn 1988). Not only did highly capital-intensive foreign operations penetrate Irish industry, but the regime's generous capital grants encouraged local firms to replace labor with machines. These factors added considerably to unemployment in the 1970s and 1980s.

An important difference between the Irish case and other situations of dependency, however, is the degree to which popular demands for social welfare have been met. Ireland's proximity to England, its claim to full European membership and "modernity," and its national aspirations to regain its northern territory all contributed to pressures on the regime to keep its social welfare benefits roughly in line with Britain's. At the same time, Britain's claim over the North of Ireland necessitated

Table 22.5   Distribution of Incomes and Tax Payments, by Decile, 1973 and 1980

Decile	Direct Income		Gross Income		Indirect Tax, 1980
	1973	1980	1973	1980	
1	—	Nil	2.9	2.6	10.0
2	1.7	0.7	4.4	4.2	
3	4.4	3.5	5.3	5.1	6.7
4	6.1	5.7	6.5	6.2	7.2
5	7.6	7.5	7.5	7.4	8.3
6	9.0	9.3	8.8	8.8	9.6
7	11.0	11.2	10.3	10.4	11.1
8	13.5	13.9	12.4	12.7	12.5
9	17.0	18.0	15.5	16.1	14.6
10	29.6	30.1	26.3	26.5	20.1
	99.9	99.9	99.9	100.0	100.1

Source: Roche (1984); Revenue Commissioners (1985).

the introduction of social welfare benefits there at the same level as existed in England. Thus, when postwar welfare reforms were introduced in Britain, Ireland followed with a similar, if slightly less "grandiose" scheme. As a result, the distribution of *gross* incomes in Ireland is more equitable than direct incomes (Table 22.5), although the share of the bottom 20 percent of families is still falling. Unfortunately, data more recent than 1980 are not available. Social welfare cutbacks have increased dramatically in the 1980s because of severe public and foreign debt crisis in Ireland. When the effects of these cutbacks on gross income distribution are accounted, it will surely be shown that inequality rose significantly.

Finally, the introduction of free trade in Ireland led to a massive loss of tariff revenues for the state. As a result, highly regressive value-added taxes were introduced in 1964, and the rates were rapidly increased during the 1970s and 1980s. Indirect (value-added and excise) taxes now account for more than half of government revenues. As shown in Table 22.5, the proportion of *indirect* taxes paid by low-income receivers is much greater than the proportion of income they receive. Since indirect taxes have risen considerably during ELI—they made up 19.8 percent of government revenues in 1955 and 50.5 percent of revenues in 1985—they have added considerably to inequality over time. Thus, free trade is responsible for yet another dimension of income inequality in terms of spending power.

Class Inequality

Explanations of inequality that concentrate on income differences among classes emphasize the aspects of foreign penetration that increase elite power and decrease working-class power. Some analysts concentrate on the tendency of local elites to use their alliances with foreign capital in order to resist popular demands for income redistribution (Rubinson 1976; Bornschier and Ballmer-Cao 1979). Others concentrate on the power of TNCs to resist labor demands and weaken labor organization. A structural argument emphasizes that the high proportion of unskilled workers in TNC subsidiaries increases the number of the lowest industrial wage earners, while the failure to locate skilled work in subsidiaries leaves a gap in the middle ranges of the income scale. At the same time, foreign penetration may encourage the expansion of low-paying service jobs (Evans and Timberlake 1980).

Certain specific characteristics of the Irish case tend to make some of these effects inoperable. The most obvious is the difference between the Irish political system—where overt authoritarianism is largely avoided—and regimes in other developing countries. A related difference is the degree to which the very rich elites in pre-independence Ireland were *absentee* elites, since England was so close. Very rich landlords and very rich capitalists in Ireland tended to remove their incomes to England, where they do not figure in Irish income distribution statistics. Therefore, 20th-century Ireland never developed the kind of measurable elite-mass inequality that is observed throughout the developing world.

These special Irish characteristics are reflected in the movement of upper income shares between 1973 and 1980 (Table 22.5). The increases of higher-income shares that are associated with falling low-income shares are spread throughout the top 50 percent of income earners. The share of the top 20 percent of income receivers grew only a little, from 46.6 percent to 48.1 percent of total incomes. No identifiable small elite in Ireland appeared to benefit greatly from the worsening position of the lowest-income receivers. This is because the lost income of the lowest 20 percent was due less to lower wages than to the complete loss of wages. Wage earners who remained employed may not be better off absolutely but still moved up to higher income deciles as the unemployed filled up lower deciles.

The lack of significant "bunching" of income shares in the higher deciles is also consistent with the structural argument that there are few new high-salaried professionals and managers in TNC subsidiaries. Evidence in support of this conclusion comes from studies of the skill structure of TNCs in Ireland. In the electronics industry, for example, Wickham (1986) finds a large concentration of employees in assembly operations, and a particular preponderance of women in these occupations.

The most significant change of class inequality to come out of dependent Irish industrialization is absent from Irish income distribution statistics. This change involves the large-scale movement of incomes from wages to profits, and within profits from domestic industry to the TNCs. The high levels of profit repatriations simply reflect the rapid rise of TNC profits, and the duality of profit rates between foreign and domestic industry. During TNC-penetration (1955–85), the surplus-share of incomes rose by 2 percent a year in manufacturing as a whole, and by 3.5 percent annually in electronics and 6.4 percent in pharmaceuticals (O'Hearn 1988, chap. 16).

The level of *international* inequality that is engendered by dependency is clearly shown in Table 22.6, where I report profit rates in 1981 by economic sector and nationality of ownership. The duality of profit rates is particularly large in the "modern" sectors—electronics, pharma-

Figure 22.6   Profit Rates by Sector and Country of Ownership, Irish Manufacturing, 1983

Sector	(a) Irish	(b) British	(c) Other Foreign	$\dfrac{c}{a}$
Food	2.26	3.01	5.23	2.31
Drink	9.29	18.60	26.95	2.90
Textiles	0.90	7.23	2.09	2.32
Clothing	−1.88	6.71	1.33	—
Wood	0.98	1.55	27.68	28.24
Paper	0.95	1.63	8.12	8.55
Clay	4.13	−8.90	27.32	6.62
Chemicals	−12.04	3.04	5.34	—
Pharmaceutical	10.15	22.02	48.66	4.79
Metals	1.09	5.52	10.25	9.40
Electric	−1.47	−196.00	22.65	—
Other	3.74	5.62	25.09	6.70
Total	1.82	7.03	22.09	12.14

Note: Profit rate refers to pretax profits as a percentage of total sales.
Source: Author's calculations form IDA Components of Sales Survey.

ceuticals, and other manufacturing—and a few "traditional" sectors such as drink, wood, and clay. Profits in certain foreign sectors—soft drinks, pharmaceuticals, healthcare, computers, instrument engineering, and others—were well in excess of 25 percent of sales and in some cases as high as *60 percent*. Overall, non-British TNCs' profit rates in Ireland averaged 22 percent, while domestic firms' profit rates averaged less than 2 percent. It is clearly possible, therefore, that the effects of dependency on inequality *among countries* are much greater than its effects on local inequality.

Finally, the relationship between elites, TNCs, and trade union power may differ significantly in Ireland from many other cases of dependency. The Irish working class developed in close proximity to the highly-unionized British working class. Trade unionists were involved in the struggle for national liberation, and their support for early nationalist governments was very important. By 1958, 92 percent of Irish industrial workers were unionized (Registrar of Friendly Societies 1959). At the same time, the uneasy alliance between governments and trade unions, which is an important factor that neutralizes working-class opposition to foreign penetration, led most unions to become nonmilitant. For many years, the IDA advised TNCs who located in Ireland to recognize trade unions. An incoming TNC commonly made a "sweetheart" agreement with an Irish trade union, giving it sole organizing rights in return for guarantees of labor peace. Recently, however, as the Irish regime became desperate for new TNC investments, they acceded to the wishes of the latest wave of entrants—the "yuppie" U.S. electronic firms—and dropped their pressure for unionization of TNC subsidiaries. The first major TNC to "go nonunion" was the computer firm Digital, which is now one of the largest employers in the country. The consequences on interclass income distribution of these successes of TNC power over Irish trade unions have yet to be worked out.

Wage Inequality

The effects of foreign penetration on wage differentials have probably been the most widely discussed aspect of dependency and inequality. Much has been written about *dualism*, where a thriving foreign-dominated "modern" sector exists alongside a stagnant "traditional" sector (Myint 1970; Singer 1970). According to this approach, wages in the "modern" sectors are expected to be higher than in the "traditional" sectors, and this encourages *wage* inequality.

On the other hand, the expectation that subsidiaries' employment structures are weighted toward unskilled jobs, with the more skilled and professional positions kept in the parent country, contradicts the *dualism* argument. If TNCs concentrate their employment in unskilled assembly trades, they *decrease* wage inequality, even if their unskilled workers are paid more than unskilled workers in domestic firms. Finally, in a labor-rich economy, with high unemployment—and particularly with a highly educated working class as in Ireland—there may be little reason to expect the TNCs to pay higher wages than local firms. This is particularly true where centralized wage-setting or wage-bargaining structures exist, as they do not only in Ireland, but also in some of the East Asian economies (e.g., Singapore).

There is little evidence that foreign penetration caused significant *wage* inequality in Ireland. Average wage rates within industrial sectors in 1983 were quite similar among Irish, British, and other foreign firms (Table 22.7). Neither are wage rates particularly high in the "modern" sectors. Wages in electronics, metals, and "other manufacturing" are at or below the average for industry. Among foreign sectors, only chemicals and pharmaceuticals have relatively high average wages. Clearly, the sectoral differentials in wage rates are tied to the structure of the labor force within those sectors. Electronics, healthcare products, textiles, and clothing have a high proportion of female assembly-type workers. The drink and chemicals industries are highly capital-intensive and have a higher proportion of technical and other skilled workers.

Table 22.7   Wages by Sector and Country of Ownership, Irish Manufacturing, 1983 (annual wage per capita in Irish punts)

Sector	Irish	British	Other Foreign
Food	9,445	10,822	9,600
Drink	12,694	15,840	12,652
Textiles	6,545	7,025	9,208
Clothing	5,619	5,567	4,838
Wood	7,114	10,383	4,039
Paper	12,787	9,276	9,781
Clay	12,424	13,821	15,561
Chemicals	15,455	10,191	12,925
Pharmaceutical	9,720	10,675	13,830
Metals	8,967	10,520	9,139
Electric	7,861	10,202	9,867
Other	7,664	9,251	8,837
Total	9,502	9,235	9,307

Source: Author's calculations form IDA Components of Sales Survey.

Specific local factors are more important than foreign penetration or "duality" in determining the Irish wage distribution. The Irish wage bargaining structure—where wages are negotiated in a series of central-ized "wage rounds" with tripartite participation of capital, trade unions, and the state—is the most important determinant of wage distribution. It is in the area of wage determination that the specificities of dependent cases, rather than any general "laws" of dependency, are likely to be most important.

Still, there are important dependency-related trends—economic decline, capital intensity, and unemployment—which have a strong influence in favor of *income* (as opposed to wage) inequality. These "pure dependency" effects of foreign penetration on income distribution differ significantly from other developing regimes, where localized political factors—often connected with authoritarian regimes—play a more important role in determining inequality.

Conclusions

The "dependency" approach to development studies has come under fire in recent years because of the seemingly "deviant" cases of East Asia. Proponents of modernization cite Taiwan and South Korea as instances where foreign penetration was *not* accompanied by either slow growth or rising inequality. They imply that other developing countries may also achieve rapid growth *with* equality by following a radical regime of free trade, free enterprise, and openness to foreign enterprise.

Unfortunately for the new modernizationists, neither South Korea nor Taiwan is really characterized by these traits. Both regimes intervene strongly in business, use selective protection and import-substitution, and have a definite preference for domestic industry. If South Korea, Taiwan, and even Singapore are "getting the prices right," it is because of their regimes' extensive intervention, not their reliance on "the market."

Ireland, on the other hand, has closely followed the prescriptions of the modernizationists. Since the 1950s, it has been highly penetrated by foreign industry, in preference to domestic industry; it removed its protective barriers and allows free movement of goods and profits in and out of the country; it disdained any form of control of business, including the use of indirect economic instruments such as credit and foreign exchange manipulations.

Ireland has also grown at a snail's pace and, recently, experienced negative economic growth. While the level of inequality has been reduced by social welfare policies—a remnant of the country's proximity to Europe—there is an underlying trend toward rising inequality, resulting from slow growth and tax policies that are forced by free trade and free enterprise. Since Ireland is among the top five debtor countries in the world (foreign debt as a percentage of GNP), the regime has already begun social welfare cutbacks that will drive it toward greater inequality. It is a classic case of "dependent" relations: slow growth and inequality caused by foreign penetration.[5]

There are other countries that are like Ireland in many respects, although the *specific* nature of dependent relations always differs significantly from country to country. The present analysis of Ireland does not resolve the problems of using dependency as a general approach to the study of development. Rather, it demonstrates how dependency-type mechanisms may thrive in a liberal, open atmosphere. Liberalness and openness, however, do not predominate in the periphery today—deviations from liberal regimes reinforce the need to rigorously examine the specificity of dependent situations. Thus, the Peruvian case of export-led "bonanza development"—where the state tries to maximize its share of TNC profits—is quite different from Irish ELI, where the state tries to maximize TNC investment and depend on trickle-down. The Brazilian case, where the state attempts to maximize linkages of TNCs with local capital, differs from the Irish regime, where linkages are simply hoped for.

Still, there are strong pressures afoot for liberalization, as proposed by the new modernizationists. These pressures are seen less in East Asia, however, than in places like Mexico and in the conditional lending of the IMF. The experience of foreign penetration, limited growth, and inequality—despite the exceptional cases of East Asia—is still much more common among developing countries than so-called "success." Students of development may have a lot to learn from the "exceptions"— particularly about ways to bring about economic development while avoiding the extreme authoritarianism of the East Asian cases. They have still more to learn from careful comparative historical analyses of specific cases of dependent development. The route of free trade, free enterprise, foreign penetration, and the new modernizationism is not the way to go.

Notes

1. Care should be taken not to confuse tariff revenues with categories such as "taxes on international trade and transactions" (e.g., in *World Development Report*). For Ireland, the latter is primarily excise taxes on alcohol and tobacco, a consumption tax which has partly replaced tariffs as a source of government revenues. Excise taxes are not a form of protection because locally produced alcoholic drinks and tobacco products are taxed at the same rate as imports. In addition, because excise taxes are placed on goods that are highly price inelastic, they have a limited effect on consumption of taxed items.

2. Apart from the level of state intervention in Singapore, its special characteristics as a city-state—like Hong Kong—reduce its usefulness as a "model of development" (Rodan 1985, pp. 9–10).

3. Critics of the present approach may suggest that Ireland's poor per capita growth performance is caused by its high rate of population growth. This is not the case. It is true that Ireland has the highest rate of natural increase in Western Europe, and that population grew more rapidly in the 1960s and 1970s than in previous periods (when it actually declined, because of emigration). Thus, population growth did exacerbate the slow growth of the 1970s. In the 1980s, however, Irish population is again declining—emigration is reaching its highest levels ever (see Irish Census of Population 1986). Most experts agree that emigration and population decline will continue at a rapid rate for some years to come, barring an unforeseen economic recovery. While there is some reciprocity Irish population growth rates (which change according to emigration rates) clearly respond to economic growth rates more than they "cause" them.

4. The Irish census contains no questions about income. There are a few tax-based surveys of income distribution, but these have gaps in coverage, because many people pay no income taxes. A few household budget surveys were conducted (in 1951/52, 1965/66, 1973, and 1981) and these seem to provide the best information on income distribution. For existing studies of Irish income distribution. see Stark (1977) and Roche (1984).

5. A similar analysis could be made regarding the North of Ireland. It has

also experienced severe economic decline and inequality during the postwar period. The reasons for stagnation and inequality in the North, however, are quite different from the South. Stagnation is mainly a result of the decline in importance to England of shipbuilding and natural fibers. The North has been allowed to decline as part of a British regional policy which favors Southern England at the expense of the so-called "Celtic fringe" and the old industrial regions of Northern England. In other words, Britain has largely withdrawn economically from its Northern Irish colony, although it refuses to withdraw militarily and politically. Inequality in the North of Ireland, unlike the South, is affected not only by class relations and economic decline, but also by sectarianism. The unemployment rate among the settler ("Protestant") population, for example, remains below the British average, at the expense of the native ("Catholic") population, which suffers unemployment averaging over 35 percent (above 80 percent in some Catholic areas).

References

Amin, S. 1974. *Accumulation on a World Scale*. New York: Monthly Review.

Baran, P. 1957. *The Political Economy of Growth*. New York: Monthly Review.

Barrett, R. E., and M. K. Whyte. 1982. "Dependency Theory and Taiwan: Analysis of a Deviant Case." *American Journal of Sociology* 87: 1064–89.

Biersteker, T. 1978. *Distortion or Development? Contending Perspectives on the Multinational Corporation*. Cambridge, MA: M.I.T. Press.

Bornschier, V. 1980a. "Multinational Corporations and Economic Growth: A Cross-National Test of the Decapitalization Thesis." *Journal of Development Economics* 7: 191–210.

———. 1980b. "Multinational Corporations, Economic Policy and National Development in the World System." *International Social Sciences* 32: 158–71.

Bornschier, V., and T.-H. Ballmer-Cao. 1978. "Income Inequality: A Cross-National Study of the Relationships between MNC-Penetration, Dimensions of the Power Structure and Income Distribution." *American Sociological Review* 44: 487–506.

Buckley, P. J. 1974. "Some Aspects of Foreign Private Investment in the Manufacturing Sector of the Economy of the Irish Republic." *Economic and Social Review* 5: 301–21.

Carter, C. 1957. "The Irish Economy Viewed from Without." *Studies* 46: 137–43.

Central Statistics Office. Various years. *National Income Accountants*. Dublin: Stationery Office.

Chakravarty, S. 1987. "Marxist Economics and Contemporary Developing Economies." *Cambridge Journal of Economics* 11: 3–22.

Chase-Dunn, C. 1975. "The Effects of International Economic Dependence on Development and Inequality." *American Sociological Review* 40: 720–38.

Connor, J. M. 1977. *The Market Power of Multinationals: A Quantitative Analysis of U.S. Corporations in Brazil and Mexico*. New York: Praeger.

Cummings, B. 1983. "The Origins and Development of the Northeast Asian

Political Economy: Industrial Sectors, Product Cycles, and Political Consequences." *International Organization* 38: 1–40.

Dail Eireann. 1958. Parliamentary Debates 165. Dublin: Stationery Office.

Evans, P., and M. Timberlake. 1980. "Dependence, Inequality, and Growth in Less Developed Countries." *American Sociological Review* 45: 531–52.

Frank, A. G. 1969. *Latin America: Underdevelopment or Revolution*. New York: Monthly Review.

Hirschman, A. O. 1958. *The Strategy of Economic Development*. New York: Norton.

Islam, I., and C. Kirkpatrick. 1986. "Export-Led Development, Labour-Market Conditions and the Distribution of Income: The Case of Singapore." *Cambridge Journal of Economics*. 10: 113–27.

Lewis, W. A. 1955. *Theory of Economic Growth*. Homewood, IL: Irwin.

Lim, L. 1983. "Singapore's Success: The Myth of the Free Market Economy." *Asian Survey* 23: 752–64.

McAleese, D. 1977. *A Profile of Grant-Aided Industry in Ireland*. Dublin: Institute of Public Administration.

McAleese, D., and D. McDonald. 1978. "Employment Growth and the Development of Linkages in Foreign-Owned and Domestic Manufacturing Enterprises." *Oxford Bulletin of Economics and Statistics* 40: 321–39.

Myint, H. 1970. "Dualism and the International Integration of the Underdeveloped Economies." *Banca Nazionale del Lavoro Quarterly Review* 93: 128–56.

Nurkse, R. 1953. *Problems of Capital Formation in Underdeveloped Countries*. Oxford: Oxford University Press.

O'Hearn, Denis. 1987. "Estimates of New Foreign Manufacturing Employment in Ireland (1956–1972)." *Economic and Social Review* 18: 173–88.

———. 1988. *Export-led Industrialization in Ireland: A Specific Case of Dependent Development*. Ph.D. diss., University of Michigan.

O hUiginn, P. 1972. *Regional Development and Industrial Location in Ireland. Volume 1, Locational Decisions and Experiences of New Industrial Establishments 1960–1970*. Dublin: An Foras Forbartha.

Organization for Economic Cooperation and Development (OECD). 1987. *National Accounts: Main Aggregates 1960–1985*. Paris: OECD.

Registrar of Friendly Societies (Ireland). 1959. *Annual Report*. Dublin: Stationery Office.

Revenue Commissioners (Ireland). Various years. *Annual Report*. Dublin: Stationery Office.

Roche, J. D. 1984. *Poverty and Income Maintenance Policies in Ireland*. Dublin: Institute of Public Administration.

Rodan, G. 1985. *Singapore's "Second Industrial Revolution": State Intervention and Foreign Investment*. Kuala Lumpur: ASEAN-Australian Joint Research Project.

Rubinson, R. 1976. "The World Economy and the Distribution of Income within States: A Cross-National Study." *American Sociological Review* 41: 638–50.

Singer, H. 1970. "Dualism Revisited: A New Approach to the Problems of the Dual Society in Developing Countries." *Journal of Development Studies* 7: 60–75.

Stark, T. 1977. *The Distribution of Income in Eight Countries*. London: HMSO.

Survey Team. 1967. *Survey of Grant-Aided Industry, 1967*. Dublin: Stationery Office.

U.S. Department of Commerce. 1980. "U.S. Direct Investment Abroad." *Survey of Current Business* 60: 16–38.

Wickham, J. 1986. *Trends in Employment and Skill in the Irish Electronics Industry*. Report to National Board for Science and Technology, Dublin.

World Bank. 1981. *World Development Report 1981*. Washington, DC: World Bank.

CHAPTER 23

Growth Effects of Foreign and Domestic Investment

GLENN FIREBAUGH

Dependency theorists have produced an extensive body of quantitative research that supports the thesis that dependency slows the economic growth of poor countries over the long run. It does so, in part, by replacing domestic investment with foreign investment. In this chapter, Glenn Firebaugh argues that the quantitative evidence has been seriously misinterpreted and that although domestic investment is better for growth than foreign investment, both spur growth in the short and long terms. This chapter, therefore, helps to undermine the dependency perspective.

A MONG THE MOST FUNDAMENTAL PRINCIPLES IN ECONOMICS IS THE principle that economic growth requires capital investment. Indeed, capital is generally thought to constitute one of the three basic categories of the factors of production (the other two categories being land and labor). A long and hallowed tradition in economics assumes positive effects for all three. Other endowments being equal, the more land, the more output; the more labor, the more output; and the more capital, the more output.

Recent work in sociology breaks sharply with this tradition by arguing that a particular type of capital—foreign investment stock—retards and distorts development in the Third World (Bornschier and Chase-Dunn 1983, 1985; Bornschier, Chase-Dunn, and Rubinson 1978; Boswell and Dixon 1990; London 1987, 1988; London and Robinson 1989; London and Smith 1988; London and Williams 1988, 1990;

Reprinted with permission of the University of Chicago Press and the author from *American Journal of Sociology,* vol. 98, no. 1 (1992): 105–130.

Wimberley 1990, 1991). The claim is that capital-poor Third World nations actually tend to be better-off in the long run if they eschew foreign capital. To quote Boswell and Dixon (1990, 554), "Previous research has documented the negative effects of economic dependency [foreign investment] on domestic growth." Such claims are legion in sociology.[1]

In this four-part article, I test the adverse-effects claim. . . .

The Source of Capital: Does It Matter?

In the antiseptic world of some economic theories, capital and labor are completely mobile, political leaders are all wise and altruistic, and class interests do not exist. In such a world capital is capital; its source is irrelevant. However, in the real world of structural barriers, ineffective and corrupt governments, and class interests, the source of capital could matter—plenty (e.g., Amin 1974, 1976; Barnet and Mueller 1974; Bornschier and Chase-Dunn 1985; Hymer 1979).

There are certainly compelling reasons for expecting Third World countries to benefit less from foreign investment than from the indigenous kind. Compared with domestic investment, foreign investment is (1) less likely to contribute to public revenues, as transnational corporations are often able to avoid taxes through mechanisms such as "transfer pricing" (e.g., Streeten 1973), (2) less likely to encourage the development of indigenous entrepreneurship, (3) more likely to use inappropriate capital-intensive technology (though this is controversial; see White 1978), (4) less likely to reinvest profits in the host country, and (5) more likely to be "linkage weak" (Hirschman 1977).

These last two reasons are especially important. Foreign investment may be "outward looking" in two respects. Not only does the profit flow outward, but the products often do as well. In such cases output "can slip out of a country without leaving much trace in the rest of the economy," as Hirschman (1958, 110) so aptly puts it. Domestic industries, in contrast, are more likely to form links with other industries in the domestic economy. According to Hirschman (1977, 80–81), such linkages are the stuff of economic development: "A linkage exists whenever an ongoing activity gives rise to economic or other pressures to lead to the taking up of a new activity," and "development is essentially the record of how one thing leads to another, and the linkages are that record." In a similar vein, Amin (1974, 1976) argues that poor nations tend to remain poor because their internal economic sectors are "disarticulated," and—like Hirschman—he believes that an outward-looking economy is more likely to be disarticulated. If these arguments are correct, then surely the growth effects of foreign investment fall well short of those of domestic investment.

Capital Dependency Research

It is one thing to claim that foreign investment is *not as good* as the homegrown variety. It is quite another matter to claim that foreign investment is bad. To actually retard growth, foreign investment must impede domestic enterprises. There are several possibilities. Transnational corporations could destroy nascent or even well-established local businesses (e.g., Amin 1976, chap. 4). Or they could co-opt local entrepreneurial talent. Or they could stimulate inappropriate consumption patterns, thereby lowering domestic savings rates. The result would be "investment decapitalization"—long-run decline in investment—if the shortfall due to lower savings exceeded the capital pumped into the economy from the outside.

Capital dependency or PEN research—so-called because it is based on the PEN (foreign capital penetration) measure of Bornschier and Chase-Dunn (1985)—*does* claim that foreign investment is pernicious for Third-World nations. Indeed, recent cross-national research in sociology appears to be preoccupied with demonstrating how foreign investment is a full-fledged menace in the Third World: how it reduces economic growth, increases inequality, impedes fertility reduction, promotes mortality, incites rebellion, fuels urban bias, and, in general, makes life miserable for residents. Lest there be any doubt as to whether PEN researchers really mean to say that foreign investment is bad (and not just "less good"), consider these conclusions culled from studies that use the PEN variable to measure investment dependence or "multinational corporation (MNC) penetration":

> [Foreign] capital formation (PEN) has clearly disadvantageous consequences for economic growth [in LDCS]. [Bornschier and Chase-Dunn 1985, 96]

> [PEN] clearly distorts development in ways that impede fertility decline. [London 1988, 615]

> This analysis shows that MNC penetration [PEN] promotes high mortality levels in the Third World. [Wimberley 1990, 87]

> Taken together, the findings above lead to the conclusion that it is

> multinational corporate penetration [PEN], not income inequality, that directly accounts for increased levels of collective political violence experienced by nations. [London and Robinson 1989, 307]

> Our overall conclusion is that dependency [PEN and military dependence] in the world economy and international state system gives rise to rebellion. [Boswell and Dixon 1990, 555]

> The results . . . reveal a significant positive relationship between penetration [PEN] and urban bias. [London and Smith 1988, 461]

> There is a significant negative relation between multinational corporate penetration [PEN] and basic needs provision. [London and Williams 1988, 761]

> This study adds strong empirical support to the world-system and dependency perspectives' claim that economic ties between the core and non-core harm the majority of noncore inhabitants. [Wimberley 1991, 427]

> Transnational corporate investment [TNC] dependence has an exceptionally strong harmful effect on [food] consumption.... [TNCs] promote immiseration in the non-core. [Wimberley and Bello, 1992]

Unless they are used vacuously, "harm," "immiserate," and similar words must mean that foreign investment actually is bad for the Third World—and not just that it is "less good" than domestic investment. Yet what precisely do PEN researchers mean when they say foreign capital "immiserates"? Dependency writers of the 1960s "stagnationist" school appear to claim that dependency precludes growth (see Gereffi 1983, chap. 1). The growth of many LDCs since then has deflated that claim, so the revised claim is that dependency tends to reduce—not preclude—economic growth. Hence by "immiseration" PEN researchers appear not to mean that capital penetration renders LDCs incapable of growth; rather, their claim is only that capital-penetrated LDCs are poorer than they would have been without the foreign investment.

There are, then, three viable positions regarding foreign investment's effect on economic growth. (1) Capital is capital. Foreign investment's effect is positive and the same size as that of domestic investment. (2) Foreign investment on balance tends to promote growth, albeit its effect is often not as large as that of domestic investment. This middle-of-the-road position is popular in development economics (see Gillis et al. 1983, chap. 14). (3) Foreign investment reduces growth. This is the conclusion of PEN research. Distinguishing between numbers 2 and 3—growth-promoting and growth-reducing investment—clearly is not hairsplitting. Naturally, LDCs try to encourage growth-promoting investment and avoid the other kind. So it is important to know which of these three positions characterizes foreign investment.

Data and Measures

The three positions can be tested using existing data. To avoid the accusation that the results are stacked against dependency theory, I use the PEN data set (from Ballmer-Cao and Scheidegger [1979], supplemented by data in Bornschier and Chase-Dunn [1985]). As in Bornschier and Chase-Dunn, the dependent variable is economic growth rate. In the PEN data set economic growth rate is measured by rate of growth of per capita GNP over the period 1965–77, expressed as an annual percentage.

Investment rate (I_τ) is the crucial independent variable. Here "rate" refers of course to change relative to initial level, so investment rate is change in capital relative to initial stock of capital. The PEN studies are based on foreign capital stock as of 1967 and 1973. To ensure that my results do not depend on the way I calculate investment rate, I do it three ways. The first is simply the percentage increase from 1967 to 1973:

$$\%I\gamma = [(1973K - 1967K)/1967K] \times 100, \tag{1}$$

where K is capital stock. The second is annual rate of change, expressed as a percentage:

$$\text{ann}I_\gamma = [\sqrt[6]{(1973K/1967K)} - 1] \times 100, \tag{2}$$

where $\sqrt[6]{(1973K/1967K)}$ denotes sixth root of $1973K/1967K$. The third measure is the continuous-time analogue to annual I_γ. To distinguish it from (2), I refer to the continuous-time annual rate as "annualized I_γ," ($\text{annz}I_\gamma$). It is calculated as follows:

$$\text{annz}I_\gamma = \{[\ln(1973K/1967K)]/6\} \times 100, \tag{3}$$

where ln is the natural logarithm.

From the PEN data, foreign and domestic investment rates can be calculated for 76 LDCs and 15 wealthy nations for a total of 91 nations (see App. A). To be consistent with earlier research, I include the conventional PEN control variables in my analysis, using the measures and data given in Bornschier and Chase-Dunn (1985). These measures are: (1) the logarithm of total energy consumption in 1967, to control for the effect of domestic market demand or "size"; (2) the average value of exports as a percentage of gross domestic product for the years 1965, 1970, and 1973, to control for the effect of export activity; (3) the logarithm of gross national product per capita (GNP/c) in 1965, to control for the effect of 1965 GNP/c on 1965–77 *growth rate* of GNP/c. Again, to be consistent with PEN research, I include this third variable as both log(GNP/c) and [log(GNP/c)]^2, so that I can model the presumed quadratic effect of initial GNP on subsequent GNP growth (Bornschier and Chase-Dunn 1985, 92). . . .

Results for Growth Rate

What do we find? There is strong support for the view that foreign is *not as good* as domestic investment (Table 23.1). Other things constant, annual economic growth is boosted by an estimated .23% for every 1% annual increase in domestic investment, but only by .08% for every 1% annual increase in foreign investment (see Table 23.1, col. 3). The difference between the slopes (domestic vs. foreign I_γ) is significant ($P <$ .05) in every instance (significance tests not shown). Regardless of measure—investment rate as percentage increase or annual rate or annualized rate—domestic investment is better.

Hence the results contradict the view that "capital is capital." But they also contradict the PEN view that foreign investment impedes growth. In every instance the slope for foreign investment is *positive* ($P < .01$). This holds whether investment is measured as percentage increase (Table 23.1, cols. 1 and 2), as annual rate (cols. 3 and 4), or as annualized rate (cols. 5 and 6); it holds when *per capita* investment rates are used (results not shown in Table 23.1), it holds when collinearity is reduced by dropping [log(GNP/c)]^2 (cols. 2, 4, 6); and it holds when the PEN controls are dropped altogether (results not shown in Table 23.1). The robustness of the foreign-investment effect is in sharp contrast to the usual instability of cross-national research. The positive investment effects reported in Table 23.1 are typical of what I found in estimating literally dozens of models.

In contrast to the investment slopes, the slopes for the PEN controls tend to be small and nonsignificant. Aside from market demand, the coefficients for the PEN control variables all fall well short of statistical significance. Using the PEN data set, I find that LDCs with greater rates of foreign investment tend to exhibit faster rates of economic growth, independent of the effects of domestic investment, export activity, and

Table 23.1   Estimated Economic Effects of Foreign and Domestic Investment: Growth Rate Models

Independent Variable	Investment Rate Measure[a]					
	$\%I_\tau$		AnnI_γ		AnnzI_γ	
	(1)	(2)	(3)	(4)	(5)	(6)
Foreign investment rate:						
Metric b	.005**	.005**	.077**	.076**	.084**	.083**
t-value	3.1	3.1	3.6	3.6	3.6	3.6
Standardized b	.29	.29	.33	.33	.33	.33
Domestic investment rate:						
Metric b	.029**	.029**	.233**	.233**	.253**	.254**
t-value	4.0	4.0	3.8	3.9	3.9	4.0
Standardized b	.39	.38	.36	.36	.36	.37
PEN control variables:						
Market demand:						
Metric b	.50	.50	.56*	.56*	.57*	.57*
t-value	1.9	2.0	2.2	2.2	2.2	2.3
Standardized b	.23	.23	.25	.25	.26	.26
Exports:						
Metric b	.004	.004	.004	.004	.004	.005
t-value	.3	.3	.3	.3	.3	.3
Standardized b	.02	.02	.03	.03	.03	.03
1965 GNP/c (log):[b]						
Metric b	−.35	.76	.87	.63	1.2	.61
t-value	−.1	1.3	.2	1.1	.2	1.1
Standardized b	−.07	.15	.17	.12	.22	.12
$[\text{Log}(1965) \text{ GNP/c})]^2$:						
Metric b	.21		−.05		−.10	
t-value	.2		−.04		−.1	
Standardized b	.22		−.05		−.11	
Adjusted R^2	.50	.51	.51	.52	.51	.42
Adjusted R^2 without control variables	.42		.42		.42	

Notes: In order to be consistent with PEN research, coefficients are reported for the model in which both log (1965 GNP/c) and its square are included (see cols. 1, 3, and 5). Because the two variables correlate +.997, results are also reported for the model without the squared term (see cols. 2, 4, and 6). Partial regression plots and diagnostic statistics indicate that results are not due to outliers. $N = 76$ LDCs.

a. See eqq. (1)–(3) in text for definitions of the three rates.
b. GNP/c denotes GNP per capita.
* $P < .05$ (two-tailed)
** $P < .01$ (two-tailed)

so on (Table 23.1). Nevertheless, PEN researchers conclude that LDCs tend to be richer if they eschew foreign investment. The argument is based on a sharp distinction between foreign investment's short-run and long-run effects (Bornschier and Chase-Dunn 1985, xi): "We find that, while flows of foreign investment have short-run positive effects on economic growth, accumulated stock of foreign capital (indicating a high degree of penetration and control by transnational corporations) has a long-run retardant effect on economic growth."

The claim then is that, other endowments equal, LDCs with higher accumulations of foreign capital are worse off in the long run than those with lower accumulations of foreign capital. Growth rate per se is not the concern here, since rates reflect short-run effects; rather, I want to determine the *cumulative* economic effect of foreign investment. Will LDCs eventually prosper more—enjoy higher levels of income per capita—with or without foreign investment? To answer that question I must determine foreign investment's total (direct + indirect) long-run effects on GNP/c.

Without wishing to belabor the obvious, it is important to stress that a long-run effect is a cumulation of short-run effects. So if PEN researchers are right about the positive short-run effects of foreign investment—and Table 23.1 certainly supports their view—then one wonders how positive short-run effects "add up" to a negative long-run effect.

The dependency answer lies in the notion of "decapitalization." Though decapitalization stories can be complex (Vernon 1971, chap. 5)—involving trade, balance of payments, and so forth—the PEN version is based on Bornschier's thesis that foreign capital harms LDCs by severely depressing their domestic investment. Lest there be any doubt, Bornschier (1980, fig. 1) formalizes his thesis by ordering the variables as follows: foreign capital → domestic capital → GNP growth. The critical test of decapitalization, then, is whether the path coefficient from cumulated foreign capital to cumulated domestic capital is negative (since all agree that domestic investment has a positive effect on GNP).[2]

Development economists most often tell a very different story. The famous Harrod-Domar capital theory, for example, assumes augmentation, not decapitalization (Gillis et al. 1983): "In a Harrod-Domar world . . . the role of foreign saving of all kinds is to *augment* domestic saving to increase investment and thus accelerate growth" (374; emphasis added). Thus Harrod-Domar theory claims that foreign investment boosts total investment: foreign investment → total investment → economic performance. . . . Contrary to what one might infer from PEN studies, the augmentation view is not bereft of empirical support. Indeed, Salvatore (1983) claims that "It has been conclusively confirmed empirically that foreign capital inflows . . . make a positive net contribution to the rate of foreign formation" (69–70; see Sprout and Weaver [1990] for recent evidence supporting augmentation).

Because it contains *cumulated* data on foreign and domestic investment, the PEN data set is especially well suited for testing the long-run effects of capital. Stock in 1967 refers to cumulated investment *as of* 1967. Domestic stock goes back 18 years; hence 1967 domestic stock reflects investment cumulated from 1950 to 1967 (see Ballmer-Cao and Scheidegger [1979, 73] for the depreciation formula used). The foreign stock measure goes back even further: it refers to the net book value of foreign holdings. So the PEN data on foreign stock are ideal for determining foreign investment's long-run effects, since, in principle, book value reflects investment from day 1. Moreover, "day 1" for foreign investment is well before 1950 for many LDCs, so there is a built-in lag for the foreign stock relative to the domestic stock. This is a critical point in view of the claim that foreign investment reduces domestic investment over the long run. If that claim is true, the reduction certainly should be evident in the PEN data.

Table 23.2 summarizes the PEN-data results for decapitalization and augmentation. In the 1967 models, accumulated capital as of 1967 (domestic capital in the case of decapitalization, total capital in the case of augmentation) is regressed on accumulated foreign capital as of 1967. To repeat, foreign capital is exogenous in PEN decapitalization models (Bornschier 1980), so it is exogenous here. Capital is in dollars per capita (logged to reduce skew; see Jackman 1980). Results are given for regressions with and without the PEN controls.[3] The 1973 models use accumulated capital as of 1973, rather than as of 1967. If, perchance, book value of foreign holdings from day 1 fails to capture all time-delay dependency effects, the PEN data permit an additional six-year lag by regressing 1973 domestic cumulation on 1967 foreign cumulation.

The results are unambiguous: augmentation, not decapitalization. The coefficient for cumulated foreign investment is always positive, and always statistically significant at $P < .0001$ or better (see Table 23.2).

What about the long-run *economic* effect of foreign investment? As just observed (Table 23.2), cumulated foreign investment boosts cumulated total investment. Of course, countries with more cumulated total investment tend to be richer than those with lower cumulations, so some of the long-run economic effect of foreign investment is indirect, through its positive effect on total investment. By contrast, the unmediated effect of foreign investment should be negative, reflecting the earlier finding that foreign investment is *not as good* as domestic investment.[4]

The dependent variable—logged GNP/*c*—is not cumulated output, but rather output for a single year. Unless vacuous, the claim that for-

Table 23.2   Estimated Effect of Accumulated Foreign Capital on Accumulated Domestic Capital and Accumulated Total Capital[a]

Model	Accumulated Domestic K (Decapitalization Test)	Accumulated Domestic K (Augmentation Test)
	Dependent Variable	
Accumulation as of 1967:		
No controls:		
Standardized b	.74	.78
t-value	9.5	10.9
PEN controls:		
Standardized b	.66	.71
t-value	10.0	11.5
Accumulation as of 1973:		
No controls:		
Standardized b	.76	.80
t-value	10.1	11.7
PEN controls:		
Standardized b	.65	.70
t-value	10.3	12.0
Accumulation as of 1973, with additional lag:		
No controls:		
Standardized b	.73	.77
t-value	9.1	10.3
PEN controls:		
Standardized b	.63	.67
t-value	9.5	10.7

Notes: Standardized coefficients are used because they are handier here for calculating indirect and total effects (see Table 23.3). Partial regression plots and diagnostic statistics indicate that results are not due to outliers.

a. Accumulated total capital = total foreign stock plus an 18-year accumulation of domestic stock.

b. Demand and exports, as in Table 23.1. GNP/c is not controlled for, because both decapitalization and augmentation assume that GNP is endogenous with respect to accumulated capital.

c. 1973 accumulation is regressed on 1967 accumulation, allowing an additional six years for foreign investment effects to appear.

eign investment has a long-run retardant economic effect must mean that at some point in time accumulated foreign capital demonstrably lowers output.

The estimates are given in Table 23.3. By boosting accumulated total capital, accumulated foreign capital boosts economic level in the long run. This indirect effect is large. The unmediated long-run effect of foreign capital—reflecting the earlier finding that foreign investment is less beneficial than domestic investment—is negative, but much smaller

Table 23.3   Estimated Long-Run Economic Effect on Foreign Investment[a]

Model	Even Through Total Investment[b]	Direct Investment[c]	Total Effect[d]
Accumulation as of 1967:			
No controls	.83**	−.16*	.67**
PEN controls	.67**	−.06	.61**
Accumulation as of 1973:			
No controls	.88**	−.21*	.67**
PEN controls	.68**	−.11	.57**
Accumulation as of 1973 with additional lag:			
No controls	.81**	−.17*	.64**
PEN controls	.62**	−.06	.56**

Notes: Partial regression plots and diagnostic statistics indicate that results are not due to outliers. $N = 76$ LDCs.

  a. Total accumulation of foreign stock; 18-year accumulation of domestic stock.

  b. Product of standardized regression coefficients for foreign accumulation→total accumulation→GNP.

  c. Expressed as a standardized regression coefficient. A negative coefficient is consistent with the view that foreign investment is *not as good* as domestic investment.

  d. Direct effect plus indirect effect through total investment.

  * $P < .05$ (two-tailed)

  ** $P < .01$ (two-tailed)

(and statistically insignificant when the PEN controls are added). As a result, the total effect of foreign investment is positive; the estimates range from +0.56 to +0.67. In short, *according to the PEN data,* foreign investment has a *positive* long-run economic effect in the Third World. This conclusion holds whether I use capital cumulation as of 1967 or as of 1973; it holds whether or not the PEN control variables are included; and it holds when I allow an additional six-year lag.

Accounting for the Contrary Conclusions of Earlier Research

If the PEN data in fact show that foreign investment has a beneficial long-run effect, why do PEN studies conclude otherwise? The problem lies not in wrong coefficients but in wrong interpretations of coefficients. The PEN researchers arrive at conclusions that are at odds with their results. To understand how this has happened, we must first understand the importance these studies attach to the distinction between capital stock and capital flow.

Capital Stock Versus Capital Flow

The long-standing economic distinction between capital flow and capital stock was popularized in sociology in an early dependency study by Bornschier et al. (1978). By distinguishing foreign capital stock—"total cumulated value of foreign-owned capital in a country"—from foreign capital flow—"current account inflows of foreign capital for some time period" (661)—Bornschier et al. try to account for an interesting pattern in cross-national studies of foreign capital and economic growth. Studies using capital flow to measure the effect of foreign capital (e.g., Papanek 1973) typically find beneficial investment effects, whereas those using capital stock with flow controlled for (e.g., Stoneman 1975) typically find the opposite. "What this pattern suggests is that the immediate effect of inflows of foreign capital . . . is to increase the rate of economic growth, while the long-run cumulative effects operate to reduce the rate of economic growth" (Bornschier et al. 1978, 667).

The Bornschier et al. thesis about stock and flow effects spawned the PEN research that still dominates cross-national work in sociology. From 1987 to 1990 in the *American Sociological Review* alone there were eight studies that used PEN or its log. Such interest is understandable: the capital dependency issue is timely, the theory controversial, the studies often painstaking. Unfortunately, though, this line of research is based on a faulty premise. A negative coefficient for stock, controlling for flow, does *not* mean that investment has a long-run adverse effect.

This point is easy to demonstrate by using the formula for investment rate as percentage increase (eq. [1]). The numerator is change in capital stock, 1967–73; PEN researchers call this *flow*. The denominator is capital accumulation as of 1967, that is, *stock*. So, in the stock and flow terminology, investment rate is simply flow divided by stock:

$$\%I_{\gamma} = (\text{flow/stock}) \times 100. \tag{4}$$

Observe that equation (4) still holds when flow and stock are each expressed as a percentage of GDP—that is, when total flow and total stock both are divided by GDP—as is typical in PEN research.

From equation (4) it is immediately apparent that, with stock constant, the faster the flow the *greater* the investment rate; and with flow constant, the larger the stock the *smaller* the investment rate. So when stock and flow are entered as separate variables in a regression equation it follows logically that

1. a positive flow coefficient and a negative stock coefficient indicate a beneficial investment effect;
2. a negative flow coefficient and a positive stock coefficient indicate an adverse investment effect.

These principles hold whether investment rate is measured as percentage increase (eq. [1]), as annual rate (eq. [2]), or as annualized rate (eq. [3]).

Now we see why PEN researchers get the results they do. When the flow coefficient (controlling for stock) is positive, and the stock coefficient (controlling for flow) is negative—precisely what PEN researchers find—investment has a beneficial effect. . . . Because domestic investment is *better* than foreign investment, the ratio of foreign to domestic stock . . . will have a negative slope. Because investment rate has a beneficial effect, stock per capita . . . will also have a negative slope. The latter factor dominates. . . . The overriding point, however, is that either way—whether PEN is capturing the denominator effect, or the effect of foreign investment relative to that of domestic investment—PEN researchers have misinterpreted their results.

PEN Research on the
Noneconomic Effects of Foreign Investment

The PEN studies of the noneconomic effects of foreign investment likewise routinely reach conclusions that are at odds with their findings.

A recent study well illustrates the point. In a painstaking analysis of the effect of foreign investment on Third World mortality, Wimberley (1990, 89) concludes that "in the long run, the greater the penetration of non-core areas by the capitalist world economy, the greater the privation of the majority in those areas." His findings indicate just the opposite, however. Using the three-components PEN model, he consistently finds a positive flow coefficient and a negative stock (PEN) coefficient for life expectancy.

Still other PEN studies of the noneconomic effects of foreign investment use *one*-component (PEN only) models. Because such one-component models have no defensible interpretation, conclusions from those studies remain suspect until they can be confirmed using sensible models of investment's effect.

Summing Up

Piqued by dependency and world-system theory, sociologists have begun to study a subject previously thought to be the stuff of development economics; that is, foreign investment's economic and welfare effects in the Third World.[5] The sociological studies draw on published estimates of cumulated capital as of 1967 and 1973—the "PEN data." Analyses of this data set are not altogether satisfactory, however, because the analysts' findings and conclusions are antipodal.

Dependency theory is too important to be ignored (as it is, by and large, in economics). Regrettably, its study in sociology has used illogic. A fresh start is needed. Reanalysis of the PEN data provides such a start. The reanalysis yields three major conclusions.

1. From the host country's perspective, all capital is not equal; the source *does* matter. Homegrown capital outperforms imported capital. This is true whether investment rate is measured as percentage increase, annual rate, or annualized rate.

2. If the PEN data are reliable, foreign investment benefits LDCs. The coefficients for foreign investment rate are always positive and statistically significant. Contrary to the earlier conclusions of sociologists, foreign investment apparently promotes growth over the long run as well as over the short run. This is not to deny that particular nations at particular times for particular reasons are hurt by foreign investment (see O'Hearn 1989; contrast Barrett and Whyte [1982], and Bradshaw [1988]). There is nonetheless no evidence in the PEN data of a general tendency for foreign investment to retard growth.

3. The capital dependency tradition that has recently dominated cross-national research in sociology is based on an error. Although the error has methodological implications, it is more aptly described as an error in logic. The PEN researchers employ growth rate or panel models, that is, models based on change in the dependent variable over the short run. In those models, salutary investment effects have paraded as negative stock coefficients. This is just as it should be since—flow constant—the greater the stock the *lower* the investment rate. Researchers have overlooked that mathematical fact, however, and have concluded that negative stock (PEN) slopes somehow reflect harmful "long-run" effects.

I close on a more upbeat note. Sociological models of Third World development can be improved by a quantum leap merely by adding appropriate measures of investment. Investment rate should be included routinely in panel and rate models. In this study I use data from capital dependency researchers—a conservative strategy, since such researchers would hardly want to choose data that exaggerate the benefits of investment—yet in that data investment is by far the *most important determinant* of economic growth in the Third World. In efforts to show how our perspectives add to those of "mere economics" then, we sociologists must not eschew all things economic. Foreign and domestic investment have important effects, albeit not necessarily of the sort described in recent sociological research.

Appendix A

Nations in Study[6]

Seventy-six less developed countries. Burundi, Cameroon, Central African Republic, Chad, Dahomey (Benin) Ethiopia, Ghana, Guinea, Ivory Coast, Kenya, Liberia, Madagascar, Malawi, Mali, Mauritania, Niger, Nigeria, Rwanda, Senegal, Sierra Leone, Somalia, South Africa, Zimbabwe, (South Rhodesia), Tanzania, Togo, Uganda, Upper Volta, Zaire, Zambia, Algeria, Egypt, Morocco, Sudan, Tunisia, Costa Rica, Dominican Republic, El Salvador, Guatemala, Honduras, Jamaica, Mexico, Nicaragua, Panama, Argentina, Bolivia, Brazil, Chile, Colombia, Ecuador, Paraguay, Peru, Uruguay, Venezuela, Iran, Iraq, Turkey, Afghanistan, Burma, Hong Kong, India, Indonesia, Japan, South Korea, Malaysia, Pakistan, Philippines, Sri Lanka, Thailand, Greece, Ireland, Italy, Portugal, Spain, Papua New Guinea, Taiwan, and Trinidad and Tobago.

Fifteen rich nations. Canada, United States, Austria, Belgium, Denmark, Finland, France, Germany (West), Netherlands, Norway, Sweden, Switzerland, United Kingdom, Australia, and New Zealand.

Notes

1. By "Previous research" Boswell and Dixon (1990) refer to research in sociology, not economics. Economists most often find that foreign investment augments domestic investment (see below), thus spurring growth.
2. Research in the PEN tradition keys on the Bornschier (1980) "depressed investment" model, so that is the decapitalization model I test here. The PEN data do not permit tests of trade- or remittance-based decapitalization stories.

3. I do not control for GNP/c because it is the criterion variable in both the decapitalization and augmentation models. Bornschier and Chase-Dunn fault Jackman (1982) for failing to control for the effect of "the level of economic development . . . [on] the degree of transnational penetration" (Bornschier and Chase-Dunn 1985, 86). Here, however, level of economic development is measured by GNP/c at time t, and transnational penetration is measured by *accumulated* foreign capital *as of t*. And GNP/c obviously does not work backward in time to determine earlier investment.

4. When total investment is constant, the more foreign investment there is, the higher the ratio of foreign investment to domestic investment. Hence if foreign investment is not as good as domestic investment, the coefficient for foreign investment, total investment controlled, should be negative.

5. A common misperception is that most foreign investment goes to LDCs. Multinational corporations are much more likely to invest in rich nations, especially in recent years. From 1985–89, new foreign investment in *all* LDCs totaled $78 billion; in the United States alone the total was $231 billion (Turner 1991, tables 12 and 13). The United States in fact is the leading recipient of foreign direct investment by far, accounting for over 40% of the world total since 1985. While foreign investment in the United States exploded during the 1980s, such investment in LDCs stagnated, giving rise to a new worry about the adverse global effect of "reconcentration of industrial capital in core areas" (Sassen 1988, 188).

6. The 76 LDCs and the 15 rich nations are defined as such in Bornschier and Chase-Dunn (1985).

References

Amin, Samir. 1974. *Accumulation on a World Scale: A Critique of the Theory of Underdevelopment*, 2 vols. New York: Monthly Review.

———. 1976. *Unequal Development: An Essay on the Social Formations of Peripheral Capitalism*. New York: Monthly Review.

Ballmer-Cao, Thanh-Huyen, and Juerg Scheidegger. 1979. *Compendium of Data for World-System Analysis: Bulletin of the Sociological Institute of the University of Zurich*. March.

Barnet, Richard, and Ronald Mueller. 1974. *Global Reach: The Power of Multinational Corporations*. New York: Simon & Schuster.

Barrett, Richard E., and Martin K. Whyte. 1982. "Dependency Theory and Taiwan: Analysis of a Deviant Case." *American Journal of Sociology* 82:1064–89.

Bornschier, Volker. 1980. "Multinational Corporations and Economic Growth: A Cross-national Test of the Decapitalization Thesis." *Journal of Development Economics* 7:191–210.

Bornschier, Volker, and Christopher Chase-Dunn. 1983. "Reply to Szymanski." *American Journal of Sociology* 89:694–99.

———. 1985. *Transnational Corporations and Underdevelopment*. New York: Praeger.

Bornschier, Volker, Christopher Chase-Dunn, and Richard Robinson. 1978. "Cross-national Evidence of the Effects of Foreign Investment and Aid on

Economic Growth and Inequality: A Survey of Findings and a Reanalysis." *American Journal of Sociology* 84:651–83.

Boswell, Terry, and William J. Dixon. 1990. "Dependency and Rebellion: A Cross-national Analysis." *American Sociological Review* 55:540–59.

Bradshaw, York W. 1988. "Reassessing Economic Dependency and Uneven Development: The Kenyan Experience." *American Sociological Review* 53:693–708.

Crenshaw, Edward. 1991. "Foreign Investment as a Dependent Variable: Determinants of Foreign Investment and Capital Penetration in Developing Nations, 1967–1978." *Social Forces* 69:1169–82.

Domar, Evsey. 1946. "Capital Expansion, Rate of Growth and Employment." *Econometrica* 14:137–47.

———. 1947. "Expansion and Employment." *American Economic Review* 37:34–55.

Firebaugh, Glenn, and Jack P. Gibbs. 1985. "User's Guide to Ratio Variables." *American Sociological Review* 50:713–22.

Gereffi, Gary. 1983. *The Pharmaceutical Industry and Dependency in the Third World*. Princeton, N.J.: Princeton University Press.

Gillis, Malcolm, Dwight H. Perkins, Michael Roemer, and Donald Snodgrass. 1983. *Economics of Development*. New York: Norton.

Harrod, Roy F. 1939. "An Essay in Dynamic Theory." *Economic Journal* 49:14–33.

Hirschman, Albert O. 1958. *The Strategy of Economic Development*. New Haven, Conn.: Yale University Press.

———. 1977. "A Generalized Linkage Approach to Development, with Special Reference to Staples." 67–98 in *Essays on Economic Development and Cultural Change in Honor of B. F. Hoselitz*, edited by Manning Nash. Chicago: University of Chicago Press.

Hymer, Stephen H. 1979. *The Multinational Corporation: A Radical Approach*. Cambridge: Cambridge University Press.

Jackman, Robert W. 1980. "A Note on the Measurement of Growth Rates in Cross-national Research." *American Journal of Sociology* 86:604–17.

———. 1982. "Dependence on Foreign Investment and Economic Growth in the Third World." *World Politics* 34:175–96.

London, Bruce. 1987. "Structural Determinants of Third World Urban Change: An Ecological and Political Economic Analysis." *American Sociological Review* 52:28–43.

———. 1988. "Dependence, Distorted Development, and Fertility Trends in Noncore Nations: A Structural Analysis of Cross-national Data." *American Sociological Review* 53:606–18.

London, Bruce, and Thomas D. Robinson. 1989. "The Effect of International Dependence on Income Inequality and Political Violence." *American Sociological Review* 54:305–8.

London, Bruce, and David A. Smith. 1988. "Urban Bias, Dependence, and Economic Stagnation in Noncore Nations." *American Sociological Review* 53:454–63.

London, Bruce, and Bruce A. Williams. 1988. "Multinational Corporate Penetration, Protest, and Basic Needs Provision in Non-core Nations: A Cross-national Analysis." *Social Forces* 66:747–73.

————. 1990. "National Politics, International Dependency, and Basic Needs Provision: A Cross-national Study." *Social Forces* 69:565–84.

O'Hearn, Denis. 1989. "The Irish Case of Dependency: An Exception to the Exceptions?" *American Sociological Review* 54:578–96.

Papanek, Gustav F. 1973. "Aid, Foreign Private Investment, Savings, and Growth in Less Developed Countries." *Journal of Political Economy* 81:120–30.

Salvatore, Dominick. 1983. "A Simultaneous Equations Model of Trade and Development with Dynamic Policy Simulations." *Kyklos* 36:66–90.

Sassen, Saskia. 1988. *The Mobility of Labor and Capital*. Cambridge: Cambridge University Press.

Sprout, Ronald V. A., and James H. Weaver. 1990. "Exports and Economic Growth: Neoclassical and Dependency Theory Contrasted." American University Department of Economics Working Paper no. 130. Washington, D.C.

Stoneman, Colin. 1975. "Foreign Capital and Economic Growth." *World Development* 3:11–26.

Streeten, Paul. 1973. "The Multinational Enterprise and the Theory of Development Policy." *World Development* 1:1–14.

Szymanski, Albert. 1983. "Comment on Bornschier, Chase-Dunn, and Rubinson." *American Journal of Sociology* 89:690–94.

Todaro, Michael P. 1981. *Economic Development in the Third World*, 2d ed. New York: Longman.

Turner, Philip. 1991. *Capital Flows in the 1980s: A Survey of Major Trends*. Economic Paper no. 30. Basel: Bank for International Settlements.

Vernon, Raymond W. 1971. *Sovereignty at Bay: The Multinational Spread of U.S. Enterprises*. New York: Basic.

White, Lawrence J. 1978. "The Evidence on Appropriate Factor Proportions for Manufacturing in Less Developed Countries: A Survey." *Economic Development and Cultural Change* 27:27–59.

Wimberley, Dale W. 1990. "Investment Dependence and Alternative Explanations of Third World Mortality: A Cross-national Study." *American Sociological Review* 55:75–91.

————. 1991. "Transnational Corporate Investment and Food Consumption in the Third World: A Cross-national Analysis." *Rural Sociology* 56:406–31.

Wimberley, Dale W., and Rosario Bello. 1992. "Effects of Foreign Investment, Exports, and Economic Growth on Third World Food Consumption." *Social Forces*. In press.

CHAPTER 24

The Long-Term Effects of Foreign Investment Dependence on Economic Growth, 1940–1990

JEFFREY KENTOR

In Chapter 23, Glenn Firebaugh makes a strong case that foreign investment, while not as beneficial as domestic investment, still makes a positive contribution to growth over the short and long term. Those findings
disputed dependency theory. In this chapter, Jeffrey Kentor disputes
Firebaugh, making the case that the limitation of his research was that it
was focused on too short a time span (1967–1973), whereas dependency theory looks at far longer periods of time to conclude that over the
long run, foreign investment slows growth. Kentor expands the time
period by covering 1938–1990 and finds that foreign capital penetration
does indeed appear to slow growth. The reader needs to consider this
argument carefully, but also wonder about the generalizability of the
findings since the long time frame yields many instances of missing
data and confines the analysis in a number of places to only about thir-
ty-six countries, many of which are advanced industrial countries from
the "core" rather than the "periphery." Of the remaining countries, five
are nonmarket economies.

D OES DEPENDENCE OF A NATIONAL ECONOMY ON FOREIGN INVESTMENT
promote economic growth or underdevelopment? The recent
exchanges between Glenn Firebaugh and William J. Dixon and Terry
Boswell suggest the contentious nature of this debate. This study analyzes models similar to those tested in previous research but with data
from earlier time points to examine the long-term effects of foreign cap-

---

Reprinted with permission of the University of Chicago Press and the author from
the *American Journal of Sociology,* vol. 103, no. 4 (1999): 1024–1046.

ital penetration. Accumulated stocks of foreign capital/GDP [gross domestic product] in 1938 have a short-term (five-year) positive effect on economic growth followed by a 20-year lagged negative effect on economic growth beginning in 1960 and lasting at least 30 years. Similar effects are found using a second indicator of foreign investment dependence, debits on investment income, for the 1950–90 period.

> The international migration of capital has facilitated development of the world's natural resources and has been instrumental in transmitting the direct effects of the industrial revolution from area to area. Thereby it has helped to increase the quantities and varieties of goods and services generally available and has raised living standards for some or most of the world's populations (Cleona Lewis, *Debtor and Creditor Countries, 1948*).
>
> Following an initial growth spurt this (foreign investment) will create an industrial structure in which monopoly is predominant, labor is insufficiently absorbed, and there is underutilization of the productive forces. Thus, the peripheral countries that adopt this path of uneven development based on income inequality and foreign capital imports will experience economic stagnation, under- and unemployment, and increasing marginalization of the population relative to countries that are less penetrated by transnational corporations and relative to the growth potential of the country (Volker Bornschier and Christopher Chase-Dunn, *Transnational Corporations and Underdevelopment, 1985*).

The above quotes summarize the debate that has continued for more than 20 years. Does dependence of a national economy on foreign investment promote economic growth or underdevelopment? The answer to this question has far-reaching implications. A country's level of economic development has an obvious impact on nearly all aspects of social life, so it is worthwhile to examine the mechanisms that have contributed to the historically large and growing economic inequalities existing across the core-periphery distribution of countries (Korzeniewicz and Moran 1997).

The classical modernization perspective, as reflected in Lewis's (1948) comments above, argued that the export of capital to undeveloped countries promoted economic growth by creating industries, transferring technology, and fostering a "modern" perspective in the local population. Dependency theory (Amin 1974; Frank 1979) challenged this pervasive belief. The dependency school argued that ownership of capital determined its effect on the underdeveloped economy. An economy controlled by foreign interests would not develop organically. It would grow in a disarticulated manner. The natural linkages that would evolve from locally controlled capital would not occur. Profits would be exported. The interests of the ruling elite would be allied with those of owners of the foreign capital. Income inequality would grow. The economy would stagnate.

The empirical work of Chase-Dunn (1975) and Bornschier and Chase-Dunn (1985) supported the above theoretical argument. They found that their measure of foreign capital penetration (PEN: a ratio of foreign investments to total capital stocks) in 1967 had a negative effect on GNP [gross national product] per capita growth, 1965–75. Bornschier and Chase-Dunn characterized these results within Wallerstein's (1974, 1979, 1980, 1989) world-systems perspective, arguing that foreign capital structured peripheral economies in the interests of core economies and in a manner that reproduced the core-periphery division of labor.

Subsequently, a diverse literature exploring the negative effects of foreign capital emerged along a spectrum of economic, social, and political dimensions including income inequality (Chase-Dunn 1975a; Bornschier 1980), unemployment (Bornschier and Ballmer-Cao 1979), overurbanization (Kentor 1981; Timberlake and Kentor 1983), fertility rates (London 1988), rebellions (Boswell and Dixon 1990), among many others. There appeared to be clear agreement that penetration of foreign capital promoted a host of negative effects on the penetrated economy.

The validity of Bornschier and Chase-Dunn's findings was questioned by Firebaugh (1992), who argued that these negative effects were spurious, a statistical artifact of the "denominator effect" of PEN. Firebaugh concluded from his reanalysis of Bornschier and Chase-Dunn's data that penetration of foreign capital has a positive effect on economic growth but one that is smaller than the positive effect that domestic capital investment has.

Dixon and Boswell (1996) addressed Firebaugh's concerns by constructing two new measures of foreign capital penetration: the ratios of (1) foreign stocks to total capital stocks and (2) foreign stocks to gross domestic product (GDP). Their reanalyses of the data with these new measures of foreign investment dependence supported Bornschier and Chase-Dunn's earlier findings of the negative effect of foreign investment dependence.

Dixon and Boswell (1996) pursued their critique of Firebaugh (1992) on a theoretical level. They argued that Firebaugh failed to distinguish between foreign capital investment and foreign investment dependence. It is not foreign capital per se that has a negative effect on economic growth but rather the control of foreign capital over the host economy that has a negative impact. Dixon and Boswell outlined the mechanisms by which penetration of foreign capital retards economic growth. They distinguished between the "differential productivity" associated with foreign investment—the disarticulated growth that occurs as the peripheral economy is reoriented toward the interests of the core—and the "negative externalities" of foreign capital penetration—the social and political consequences of this restructuring that goes beyond the economic "drag" of foreign investment, such as overurbanization and income inequality. Firebaugh (1996) responded to Dixon and Boswell's critique by asserting that they failed to account for the ratio problem, arguing that the substitution of GDP for total capital stocks in the denominator of their measure of foreign capital penetration was not meaningful since the correlation of GDP and total capital stocks is .99 for the countries studied.

A serious problem with both of these studies, however, is that they examine the effects of foreign capital penetration over a relatively short time period, 1967–73. The mechanisms by which these negative effects are hypothesized to occur would seem to suggest longer time frames. Bornschier and Chase-Dunn (1985) hypothesized that foreign investment dependence would have a short-term positive effect on the host economy as capital flows generated employment and purchases that represented the start-up costs of the new ventures. This would be followed by a longer term negative effect as the host economy is restructured for the benefit of the core. This distinction between short- and long-term effects anticipates Dixon and Boswell's theoretical understanding of the mechanisms by which foreign capital exerts negative effects on penetrated economies.

Fortunately, earlier data are available from two sources to examine these long-term effects: the Brookings Institution, which compiled cross-national data on accumulated foreign stocks in 1938, and the International Monetary Fund (IMF), which provides data on debits on investment income for 1938 and then annually beginning in 1946. 1 will use these two alternative measures to examine the long-term effects of foreign capital penetration on economic growth in peripheral countries. . . .

Results

Panel Regression Analyses

The results for the first series of panel regression examining the effects of LFANGS38GDP on economic growth are presented in Table 24.1

Table 24.1 OLS Regression of Effects of LFANGS38GDP on Economic Growth (GDP/pc), 1940–90

	1945			1950			1955			1960			1965		
	b	β	t-ratio	b	β	t-ratio	b	β	t-ratio	b	β	t-ratio	b	β	t-ratio
LGDPpc40	1.04	1.04	17.4**	1.1	1.06	29**	1.06	1.04	25.6**	1.01	.99	23.3**	.99	.96	17.92**
LFANGS38GDP	.1	.15	2.58**	.02	.03	76	-.02	-.03	-.69	-.07	-.1	-2.42**	-.11	-.15	-2.92**
EXP40GDP	1.3E-05	.08	1.6	1.9E-05	.12	3.7**	2.5E-05	.16	4.54**	3E-05	.2	5.12**	3.4E-05	.22	4.52**
LDGP1940	.05	.07	1.18	-.01	-.01	-.2	7.3E-05	1.1E-05	0	.01	.01	.24	.01	.02	.36
Constant	-1.64		1.18	-.86		-1.96	-.13		-.27	.89		1.78	1.51		2.35*
Adjusted R	.95			.98			.97			.97			.96		

	1970			1975			1980			1985			1990		
	b	β	t-ratio	b	β	t-ratio	b	β	t-ratio	b	β	t-ratio	b	β	t-ratio
LGDPpc40	.94	.91	14.5**	.89	.88	11.26**	88	.88	10.16**	.85	.82	8.84**	.93	.67	6.11**
LFANGS38GDP	-.15	-.211	-3.47**	-.18	-.26	-3.38**	-.18	-.27	-3.16**	-.22	-.31	-3.43***	-.22	-.23	-2.17*
EXP40GDP	3.8E-05	.24	4.33**	4.2E-05	.27	3.93**	4.2E-05	.28	3.6**	4.8E-05	.3	3.68***	4E-05	-.19	-1.98*
LDGP1940	.02	.03	.49	.02	.03	.32	-.01	-.01	-.09	.02	.03	.31	-.04	-.04	-.35
Constant	2.41		3.18**	3.19		3.46**	3.59		3.57**	4.09		3.67**	.89		1.78
Adjusted R	.94			.89			.88			.85			.97		

Note: –N=32.
*P < .05.
**P < .01.

and offer clear support for the earlier findings of the negative effects of foreign capital penetration on economic growth.

My measure of foreign capital penetration in 1938 (LFANGS38GDP) has an initial short-term positive effect on GDP per capita growth, 1940–45 (ß = .10). Between 1960 and 1990, however, the results indicate a continuing significant lagged negative effect of foreign capital penetration on economic growth. This negative effect becomes significant in the 1940–60 period (ß = –.05) and increases through the 1940–90 period (ß = –.18).

A second series of panel regressions, not shown here, were run on the above model excluding high GDP/pc countries, leaving 20 cases in the analysis. The results of these analyses were consistent with those above, although the effects were larger. The results of the next series of panel regressions, using LDEB49GDP, are given in Table 24.2. The findings are comparable to those using LFANGS38GDP, except that the initial positive effect of LDEB49pc on economic development is not significant. There is a 20-year lagged negative effect of LDEB49pc on economic growth beginning in 1970 and persisting through 1990 (ß = –.31).

A comparison of the effects of LFANGS38GDP and LDEB49GDP on economic growth by lag periods is given in Table 24.3. The standardized coefficients are nearly equivalent, the only difference being the absence of a significant five-year positive effect of LDEB49GDP on GDP/pc. The 20-year to 40-year lagged negative effects are remarkably similar between the two measures of foreign investment dependence.
. . .

Discussion

These results provide clear support for the prior findings of Bornschier and Chase-Dunn (1985) and Dixon and Boswell (1996). The short-term positive effect of foreign investment on economic growth, generated by capital inflows and increased employment, is replaced by a consistent long-term lagged negative effect beginning 20 years later and lasting at least 30 years. The strongest support is found in Table 24.2 of the analyses. Two different measures of foreign investment dependence, measured at different times and analyzed over different cases, provide nearly equivalent results.

The only anomaly between the LFANGS38GDP and LDEB49GDP analyses was the absence of an initial positive effect of LDEB49GDP on GDP/pc in 1955. The most likely reason for this is a reflection of the

Table 24.2 OLS Estimates of Effects of LDEB49GDP on Economic Growth (GDP/pc), 1950–90

	1955			1960			1965			1970		
	b	β	t-ratio	b	β	t-ratio	b	β	t-ratio	b	β	t-ratio
LGDPpc50	1.02	.98	49.14**	1.01	.97	33**	1.04	.95	22.46**	1.08	.93	19**
LDEB49GDP	-.002	-.004	-.2	-.02	-.04	-1.13	-.05	-.08	-1.8	-.09	-.14	-2.68**
EXP50GDP	-.0004	-.02	-.92	-.0003	-.01	-.482	-.0004	-.02	-.4	.0004	.02	.36
LDGP1950	.01	.01	.63	.03	.04	1.22	.02	.03	.58	.05	.06	1.19
Constant	.02		.17	.14		.65	.13		.41	-.07		-.17
Adjusted R	.99			.98			.95			.94		

	1955			1960			1965			1990		
	b	β	t-ratio	b	β	t-ratio	b	β	t-ratio	b	β	t-ratio
LGDPpc50	1.09	.91	16.19**	1.08	.9	14.71**	1.07	.87	12**	1.09	.83	10.49**
LDEB49GDP	-.1	-.16	-2.6**	-.12	-.18	-2.77	-.16	-.23	-2.93**	-.2	-.28	-3.21
EXP50GDP	-.0004	-.001	-.03	.0005	.02	.35	.001	.06	.72	.002	.08	.98
LDGP1950	.03	.05	.77	.04	.06	.88	.07	.09	1.16	.1	.12	1.39
Constant	.06	.14	.89	.21		.4	.19		.31	-4.97		-6.91**
Adjusted R	.92			.9			.87			.84		

Note: –N=35.
*P < .05.
**P < .01.

Table 24.3 Comparison of the Effects of LFANGS38GDP and LDEB49GDP on Economic Growth, 1940–90, Standardized Regression Coefficients

	5-Year Lag	10-Year Lag	15-Year Lag	20-Year Lag	25-Year Lag	30-Year Lag	35-Year Lag	40-Year Lag	45-Year Lag	50-Year Lag
LFANGS38GDP	.15**	.03	-.03	-.1*	-.15**	-.21**	-.26**	-.27**	-.31**	-.23**
LDEB49GDP	0	-.03	-.08	-.14**	-.16**	-.18**	-.23**	-.28**		

*P < .05.
**P < .01.

characteristics of this measure. New enterprises do not usually generate profits immediately. Rather, there is a lag time of anywhere from one to four years before new ventures become profitable. LDEB49GDP is an average of profits from 1947 to 1949. As such, it may actually reflect accumulated stocks as early as 1942. When GDP/pc 1940 is used as the lagged dependent variable with GDP/pc 1950 as the dependent variable, the coefficient is positive and 1.5 times the size of its standard error. This suggests that foreign investment does, in fact, have an initial positive effect on economic growth.

One of the most interesting findings of this research is that the negative effects of foreign investment dependence do not appear to diminish over time. How are we to interpret this? I would argue that these persistent negative effects reflect two aspects of foreign investment dependence. First, it is a reflection of the stability of foreign investment over time. The infrastructure that develops in a country dominated by foreign capital is conducive to subsequent investment. The social and political structure that evolves, a small local elite whose interests are linked with those of the foreign investors, would ease the entry of future foreign investment. The economic infrastructure created to deal with issues of foreign property ownership, currency convertibility, and labor laws in a manner favorable to foreign interests would also make subsequent investment more likely.

There is empirical support for this argument, as indicated by the high correlation among the various measures of investment dependence used here with accumulated foreign stocks in 1967, as discussed earlier. A panel regression estimating the effects of LDEB49GDP on accumulated foreign stocks in 1967 (AFS67GDP), presented in Table 24.4, provides additional support. LDEB49GDP has a significant positive effect AFS67GDP, with an unstandardized coefficient of .37.

Further, this apparent continuous negative effect of foreign capital penetration on economic growth reflects cycles of indirect effects with different paths and varying lags. Differential productivity effects may exhibit a shorter lag time than the indirect consequences of negative externalities. And it is likely that these indirect effects, such as overurbanization, would take a significant time period to manifest their effects on economic growth.

It might be argued that these effects are spurious. There is a commonly held assumption that foreign capital is attracted to areas of relatively higher economic growth. It could be argued, therefore, that these findings actually represent the withdrawal of foreign capital and the subsequent decline in GDP growth resulting from this foreign capital flight.

Table 24.4   OLS Estimates of the Effects of Foreign Investment Dependence in 1949 on Foreign Investment Dependence in 1967

	Accumulated Foreign Stocks/GDP 1967		
	b	ß	*t*-value
LDEB49GDP	.37	.55	3.55**
LGDP1950	−.18	−.22	−1.38
LGDPpc1950	.33	.27	1.88
Constant	−5.76		−4.99**
Adjusted R^2	.47		

Note: –N=33.
**P < .01.

However, the data do not support this argument Bornschier and Chase-Dunn's (1985) PEN_1 measure of capital penetration was regressed on my earlier measures of GDP per capita, calculated as change scores over the time period in question. GDP growth 1940–65 did not have a significant effect on the amount of foreign investment penetration in 1967.

Conclusion

The results of this study confirm that peripheral countries with relatively high dependence on foreign capital exhibit slower economic growth than those less dependent peripheral countries. These findings have been replicated using different measures of foreign investment dependence, GDP data, countries, time periods, and statistical methods. This is a significant and persistent negative effect, lasting for decades. Further, a structure of dependency is created that perpetuates these effects. The consequences of these effects, as described in the literature, are pervasive: unemployment, overurbanization, income inequality, and social unrest, to name a few. This is what all the fuss has been about.

The next step in this research should be a more complete specification of this model, to explicate the mechanisms by which these dependency effects occur. Foreign investment dependence also needs to be examined from a world-systems perspective, a perspective that understands foreign investment dependence as a reflection of power relationships among countries that generates and maintains the core-periphery hierarchy in the world-economy. From this perspective, foreign investment dependence becomes a variable at the macro level of zones of the world-economy, rather than as a country-level variable.

References

Amin, Samir. 1974. *Accumulation on a World Scale: A Critique of the Theory of Under-Development,* 2 vols. New York: Monthly Review Press.

Arbuckle, James. 1996. "Full Information Estimation in the Presence of Incomplete Data." In *Advanced Structural Equation Modeling,* edited by George Marcoulides and Randall Schumacker. Mahwah, N.J.: Lawrence Erlbaum Associates.

Arrighi, Giovanni. 1994. *The Long Twentieth Century.* New York: Verso.

Bornschier, Volker. 1980. "Multinational Corporation and Economic Growth: A Cross-National Test of the Decapitalization Thesis." *Journal of Development Economics* 7:191–210.

Bornschier, Volker, and Thanh-Huyen Ballmer-Cao. 1979. "Income Inequality: A Cross-National Study of the Relationships between MNC Penetration, Dimensions of the Power Structure, and Income Distribution." *American Sociological Review* 44 (3):487–506.

Bornschier, Volker, and Christopher Chase-Dunn. 1985. *Transnational Corporations and Underdevelopment.* New York: Praeger.

Bornschier, Volker, and Peter Heintz, eds. 1979. *Compendium of Data for World Systems Analysis.* Zurich: University of Zurich, Sociological Institute.

Boswell, Terry, and William J. Dixon. 1990. "Dependency and Rebellion: A Cross-National Analysis." *American Sociological Review* 55:540–59.

Chase-Dunn, Christopher. 1975a. "The Effects of International Economic Dependence on Development and Inequality: A Cross-National Study." *American Sociological Review* 40:720–38.

———. 1975b. "International Economic Dependence in the World-System." Ph.D. dissertation. Stanford University, Department of Sociology.

Dixon, William J., and Terry Boswell. 1996. "Dependency, Disarticulation, and Denominator Effects: Another Look at Foreign Capital Penetration." *American Journal of Sociology* 102 (2):543–62.

Firebaugh, Glenn. 1992. "Growth Effects of Foreign and Domestic Investment." *American Journal of Sociology* 98 (1):105–30.

———. 1996. "Does Foreign Capital Harm Poor Nations? New Estimates Based on Dixon and Boswell's Measures of Capital Penetration." *American Journal of Sociology* 102 (2):563–75.

Frank, Andre Gunder. 1979. *Dependent Accumulation and Underdevelopment.* New York: Monthly Review Press.

Grimes, Peter. 1996. "Economic Cycles and International Mobility in the World-System: 1790–1990." Ph.D. dissertation. Johns Hopkins University, Department of Sociology.

IMF (International Monetary Fund). 1949. *Balance of Payments Yearbook.* Washington, D.C.: International Monetary Fund.

———. 1951. *Balance of Payments Yearbook.* Washington, D.C.: International Monetary Fund.

Kentor, Jeffrey. 1981. "Structural Determinants of Peripheral Urbanization: The Effects of International Dependence." *American Sociological Review* 46:201–11.

Kim, Jae-on, and James Curry. "The Treatment of Missing Data in Multivariate Analysis." *Sociological Methods and Research* 6:2.

Korzeniewicz, Roberto Patricio, and Timothy Patrick Moran. 1997. "World-Economic Trends in the Distribution of Income, 1965–1992." *American Journal of Sociology* 102:1000–1039.

Lewis, Cleona. 1948. *Debtor and Creditor Countries: 1938, 1944.* Washington, D.C.: Brookings Institution.

Little, Roderick, and Donald Rubin. 1989. "The Analysis of Social Science Data with Missing Values." *Sociological Methods and Research* 18:2–3.

London, Bruce. 1988. "Dependence, Distorted Development, and Fertility Trends in Non-Core Nations: A Structural Analysis of Cross-National Data." *American Sociological Review* 53:606–18.

Maddison, Angus. 1995. *Monitoring the World Economy, 1820–1992.* Paris: OECD.

Timberlake, Michael, and Jeffrey Kentor. 1983. "Economic Dependence, Over-urbanization, and Economic Growth: A Study of Less Developed Countries." *Sociological Quarterly* 24:489–507.

Wallerstein, Immanuel. 1974. *The Modern World System, Vol. 1, Capitalist Agriculture and the Origins of the European World-Economy in the Sixteenth Century.* New York: Academic Press.

———. 1979. *The Capitalist World Economy.* New York: Cambridge University Press.

———. 1980. *The Modern World System. Vol. 2, Mercantilism and the Consolidation of the European World-Economy, 1600–1750.* New York: Academic Press.

———. 1989. *The Modern World System. Vol. 3, The Second Era of Great Expansion of the Capitalist World-Economy, 1730–1840s.* New York: Academic Press.

CHAPTER 25

Income Inequality, Development, and Dependence: A Reconsideration

ARTHUR S. ALDERSON AND FRANÇOIS NIELSEN

Dependency theory not only predicts that foreign investment slows growth among poor countries, it also predicts that it produces greater levels of income inequality within those countries. These authors accept the Glenn Firebaugh critique of the impact of dependency on growth, and use it to examine its impact on income distribution. The study is based on eighty-eight countries for the period 1967–1994 and finds that inequality does increase as a result of increases in foreign investment. But they also find that as foreign investment grows to higher levels, income inequality declines, with a relationship that looks like an inverted-U. This is a novel finding, interpreted by the authors' results less from classic dependency effects and more from what they call "net direct investment position." By this logic, countries that have high levels of foreign investment per capita tend to conform to international standards that mitigate the inequality effect of lower levels of foreign investment. They conclude that income inequality is associated with the condition of "relative dependence" on external investment.

M OST THEORIES OF DEVELOPMENT SHARE THE VIEW THAT MODERN CAPI-
talism is inherently expansive. Through its own internal logic, capitalism is driven to incorporate ever larger areas of the globe. The paradigmatic debate in the field has been whether this process of incorporation has been progressive or regressive—that is, whether it promotes development or underdevelopment (Hoogvelt 1997:65). Over the

---

Reprinted with permission of the American Sociological Association and the authors from *American Sociological Review* (1999): 606–609, 617–628.

past several decades, a large literature has emerged in sociology that suggests that incorporation into the modern world system has had negative implications for everything in developing countries from economic growth (Bornschier and Chase-Dunn 1985) to the demographic transition (London 1988) to infant mortality and life expectancy (Wimberley 1990). In recent years, this dependency- and world-systems-oriented literature has fallen on hard times. As we see it, the challenge facing such studies has been part practical and part empirical.

On a practical level, as Bradshaw et al. (1993) note, there has been "a growing awareness that [dependency- and world-systems-oriented] perspectives are out of touch with recent developments in the world economy" (p. 634). For instance, as traditional sources of development finance have all but dried up in the wake of the debt crisis of the early 1980s, and as autarky has fallen out of fashion in response to the events of 1989, "openness" has found new favor in the eyes of policymakers across the developed world (Helleiner 1991). Paradoxically, this has occurred precisely as core countries generally have withdrawn from trade and investment relations with the periphery in the context of globalization (Alderson 1997). One might have expected these dramatic developments to have prompted a critical reassessment of dependency and world-system arguments. Unfortunately, our reading of the recent literature suggests these arguments have reached an impasse, yielding few new insights of relevance for students of development.

Empirically, confidence in the results of dependency- and world-system-oriented studies has been seriously undermined by Firebaugh's (1992, 1996) powerful critique of research on capital penetration. Firebaugh shows that the standard finding of a negative effect of long-term accumulations of foreign capital (the stock of foreign investment) on economic growth is actually consistent with a positive effect of the foreign investment rate on growth. While the importance of Firebaugh's critique has been widely acknowledged (e.g., Dixon and Boswell 1996; Kentor 1998), the debate has thus far been confined to the topic of economic growth. To our knowledge, no study has explored the possibility that a scenario of the sort suggested by Firebaugh might apply to other development outcomes that have been linked to foreign capital penetration. The present analysis redresses this critical omission in prior research.

The findings of the foreign capital penetration literature on inequality have been directly challenged by Tsai (1995), who suggests that the typical finding of a positive association between income inequality and foreign capital penetration may have emerged spuriously from a failure to control for regional differences. When such regional differences are

taken into account, foreign capital penetration does not contribute significantly to income inequality across broad swaths of the developing
world. We replicate Tsai's analysis to see if any observed effect of foreign investment emerges spuriously from the omission of region-specific effects.

We address these challenges as they relate to the dependency and
world-system-oriented literature on income inequality. Utilizing a much
larger data set than has previously been employed in such studies, we
estimate the effects of foreign capital penetration on income inequality,
. . . we investigate the implications of the Firebaugh critique, and we
replicate Tsai's regional analysis.

Trends in Income Inequality and Economic Development

The evolution of inequality in the course of development is a central
topic of sociology (Lenski 1966). In his pioneering investigation of historical trends in inequality in a handful of industrial societies (Great
Britain, Germany, and the United States), Kuznets (1955) discovered an
apparent inverted-U curvilinearity in the relationship of income
inequality with development. With some variation in timing, inequality
in these societies at first increased in the course of development in the
nineteenth and twentieth centuries, then leveled off and began to
decline as the society approached an advanced industrial stage. The
curvilinear relationship later was found to hold in cross-sectional studies: Inequality is relatively low in countries at the lowest development
levels, highest at intermediate levels, and lowest for developed industrial societies. Despite considerable scattering of observations around the
inverted-U shaped trend, the Kuznets curve has been generally well-
documented in cross-section for contemporary societies (Gagliani 1987;
Lecaillon et al. 1984; but see Papanek 1978). Many students of income
inequality, including those sympathetic to dependency and world-systems approaches, have discussed the Kuznets curve as an established
empirical regularity (Bornschier and Chase-Dunn 1985:117–30; Weede
and Tiefenbach 1981a).

A large literature focuses both on assessing the existence of the
inverted-U relationship postulated by Kuznets (1955) and on estimating
causal models relating income inequality to various social-structural
features of society suspected to affect the distribution of income, such
as educational expansion, political democracy, agricultural intensity,
and others (Ahluwalia 1976; Bollen and Jackman 1985a; Crenshaw
1992; Cutright 1967; Gagliani 1987; Jackman 1974, 1975; Lecaillon et

al. 1984; Muller 1985, 1988, 1989; Simpson 1990). In related work (Nielsen 1994; Nielsen and Alderson 1995, 1997), we proposed a model of the relationship of inequality with development that emphasizes the role of dualism, an explanation originally proposed by Kuznets (1955).
. . .

Much of the cross-national research on inequality adopts a dependency and world-systems approach in which the position of a country within the world system and the patterns of interactions among countries are emphasized as potential causes of internal inequality. . . . The variables emphasized in this approach are typically more "external" than those involved in developmental models, comprising such characteristics as the concentration of export partners and commodities, dependence on foreign trade. the structure of foreign trade (relative flows of raw materials and manufactured goods), and dependence on foreign capital.

While Kuznets's original intuition of the curvilinear relationship of inequality with development was based on longitudinal-historical evidence, the bulk of the subsequent research has been based on cross-sectional data. A typical research design approximates a true cross-section by collecting observations on income inequality and measures of the independent variables for a target year. However, the mechanisms postulated in most theories of the relationship of income inequality with development are strictly ahistorical, that is, they assume that the same structural configuration of a society (e.g., a certain composition of the labor force) will produce the same level of inequality ceteris paribus in that society in 1950 and in 1990 (Nielsen and Alderson 1995). It follows that estimation of models of income inequality can be based, in principle, on observations that are not simultaneous with respect to calendar time and that use the longitudinal variation that is available in the form of repeated measures of inequality over time for certain countries, in addition to variation between countries (Firebaugh 1980; Gagliani 1987:323; Jackman 1985). Our research takes advantage of both cross-sectional and longitudinal variation with a design that allows multiple observations, in different years, for the same country. The design is unbalanced—countries contribute different numbers of observations to the data set. This design provides a much larger number of cases than does a cross-section, and by allowing multiple observations at different dates it generates a data set with a panel structure that can be used to correct for potential sources of bias that cannot be addressed in cross-sections, such as effects of unmeasured time-invariant factors.

Inequality and Investment Dependence

In their review of theories of income inequality inspired by a world-system perspective, Weede and Tiefenbach (1981a) distinguish three broad traditions: (1) the school of thought initiated by Galtung (1971) focusing on the patterns of trade among countries; (2) the tradition associated with the work of Wallerstein (1974) and Rubinson (1976) emphasizing state power in relation to dependence on the world market; and (3) the foreign penetration school, exemplified by Bornschier and Ballmer-Cao (1979) and Bornschier and Chase-Dunn (1985). The first tradition focuses on such variables as the structure of foreign trade (specialization in export of raw materials and import of processed goods) and the concentration of export partners and of export commodities as factors in inequality. The second approach emphasizes the role of state strength (as measured by government revenue as a percentage of GDP) in protecting a society from inegalitarian world-system influences. The present analysis focuses on the third perspective (see Alderson and Nielsen [1995] for a companion treatment of the Galtung and Wallerstein-Rubinson traditions).

Investment Dependence and Inequality

The foreign capital penetration school emphasizes the role of the dependence of developing countries on foreign investment (Bornschier and Ballmer-Cao 1979; Bornschier and Chase-Dunn 1985; Bornschier, Chase-Dunn, and Rubinson 1978). Typically, results show that penetration by transnational corporations, measured as the stock of foreign direct investment, has a positive impact on income inequality in regression models (Bornschier and Chase-Dunn 1985:124). In their formulation of the dependency argument, Evans and Timberlake (1980) argue that dependence on foreign capital increases income inequality by distorting the occupational structure of Third World countries, "bloating" the tertiary sector and producing both a highly paid elite and large groups of marginalized workers. As Sullivan (1983) summarizes, "[I]t is the resultant marginalization of workers left out of the international sector, but displaced by its capital-intensive technology, and the embourgeoisement of those centrally associated with it that affects inequality levels" (p. 206). Bornschier and Chase-Dunn (1985:120–22) elaborate on this scenario by showing how penetration by transnational firms in three major sectors of the economy, namely (1) agricultural, mineral, and oil extraction; (2) manufacturing for the world market; and (3) manufacturing for the domestic market, leads in each case to increased inequality, albeit through different causal pathways. In this view, then, dependence on foreign investment is clearly expected to be associated with greater inequality.

The interpretation of the effects of foreign investment in the literature has been the object of a major critique by Firebaugh (1992). Researchers in the foreign capital penetration tradition typically estimate models of economic growth that include as independent variables both the short-term (yearly) flow and the long-term accumulation (or stock) of foreign investment. Results usually show a positive effect of flow on economic growth—interpreted as a short-term beneficial effect—and a negative effect of foreign investment stock—interpreted as a detrimental long-term effect of foreign investment on growth (Bornschier, Chase-Dunn, and Rubinson 1978). Firebaugh (1992) demonstrates, using the same cross-national data used by Bornschier and Chase-Dunn (1985), that the foreign investment rate (flow/stock) has a significant positive effect on economic growth, as predicted by standard economic theory (although this positive effect is not as large as the effect of the domestic investment rate). This result can be interpreted as indicating that foreign investment is beneficial to growth, although not as beneficial as domestic investment. Firebaugh then points out that the investment rate is calculated by dividing flow by stock, so that including both flow and stock as regressors amounts to estimating the effect of the denominator while keeping the numerator constant, and vice versa. Thus, a negative effect of foreign investment stock in such a model would indicate a positive effect of the foreign investment rate on growth because, keeping flow constant, the larger the stock the smaller the rate. Dependency and world-systems researchers thus mistakenly interpret the negative coefficient for stock as indicating a detrimental long-term effect of foreign investment on growth, when in fact it is the result of a denominator effect and is consistent with a positive effect of the foreign investment rate. Firebaugh further demonstrates this point by showing that, when both the flow and stock of domestic investment are introduced as regressors, the coefficient for the domestic investment stock is also negative. Of course, no researcher would claim that this negative coefficient indicates a detrimental long-term effect of domestic investment on economic growth (see Kentor 1998).

In a response to Firebaugh, Dixon and Boswell (1996) reassert the conceptual distinction between foreign investment and foreign capital penetration. Capital dependency research, they propose, does not argue that foreign investment per se has negative effects on economic growth, but rather that foreign control over an economy has negative effects. With this in mind, Dixon and Boswell (1996) distinguish between the differential productivity associated with foreign investment (the differential impact of foreign versus domestic investment on economic growth) and the negative externalities associated with foreign capital penetration such as disarticulation, "overurbanization," and inappropriate technology:

> Foreign investment is not as good as domestic investment at generating economic growth, a feature we termed *differential productivity.* Penetration . . . is harmful because it reduces growth in comparison to less penetrated economies because higher penetration implies a greater portion of invested capital from foreign sources and hence a greater portion hampered by differential productivity. More important, if somewhat more speculatively, we . . . hypothesized that foreign capital penetration also entails *negative externalities* that diminish growth beyond what is attributable to differential productivity. (p. 549, emphasis in original)

Dixon and Boswell simultaneously enter the foreign and domestic investment rates (flow/stock) and their measure of foreign capital penetration (stock of foreign investment/total stock or GDP) into regression equations to observe the effects of foreign capital penetration net of differential productivity and of the "denominator effects" identified by Firebaugh. Their results indicate that when investment rates are held constant, foreign capital penetration continues to have a significant negative effect on growth.

In his comment on Dixon and Boswell, Firebaugh (1996) observes that there are at least two (realistic) interpretations of their results. Given that their measure of foreign capital penetration is strictly the ratio of foreign stock to total stock, a negative coefficient for foreign penetration could mean either that (1) both domestic and foreign investment yield positive returns in terms of growth, with domestic stock yielding greater returns, or that (2) domestic stock yields positive returns while foreign stock yields negative returns. The foreign capital penetration literature clearly argues the latter—not merely that foreign investment is "not as good" as domestic investment (differential productivity), but that foreign investment has a negative impact on economic growth (negative externalities). In a reanalysis of the Dixon and Boswell findings, Firebaugh finds evidence for differential productivity but none for negative externalities. This result, he notes, is entirely consistent with the conclusion that the absolute effect of foreign investment is positive.

While Firebaugh's (1992, 1996) critique is directed at interpretations of the effects of foreign investment on economic growth, his analysis has cautionary implications for interpretations of the relationship between foreign investment and income inequality (among other development outcomes). Finding a positive effect of foreign investment stock on income inequality, as Bornschier and Chase-Dunn do (1985:124), may indicate a negative effect of the rate of foreign investment on inequality, because stock is the denominator of the rate. In light of Firebaugh's interpretation, findings such as those of Bornschier and Chase-Dunn must be viewed as indicating a beneficial role of foreign investment in reducing income inequality. We therefore estimate effects on inequality of the flow and rate of foreign investment, in addition to the stock. And in response to Dixon and Boswell (1996:560), we estimate the effects of the stock of foreign investment net of the foreign investment rate. Our interpretation of the results, however, is tempered by Firebaugh's (1996:573) observation that the results may be as open to multiple interpretations as are Dixon and Boswell's findings regarding the effects of foreign penetration on economic growth. Thus, we also attempt to determine whether foreign investment has a positive effect on inequality (as assumed in the literature) or whether foreign and domestic investment both have negative effects on inequality and foreign investment simply reduces inequality less (the possibility suggested by Firebaugh).

Tsai (1995) also reports results that challenge the original findings of the foreign capital penetration school. Applying ordinary least-squares regression (OLS) to an unbalanced panel containing a maximum of 60 observations on 33 less-developed countries, Tsai's initial results lend strong support to the dependency argument—he concludes that foreign capital penetration (measured as the stock of foreign direct investment/GDP) has a robust positive effect on inequality. However, as Tsai considers region-specific variables that are typically omitted from cross-national research on inequality, dramatically different conclusions are drawn.

Starting from the premise that countries in the same geographical region share a variety of (typically unmeasured) attributes that may affect income distribution, Tsai asks whether the distributional effects of foreign capital penetration might not be contingent on these regional differences. Tsai notes, for instance, that high levels of income inequality in Latin America, at least in earlier periods, were rooted in the concentration of land ownership. For reasons of data availability, however, many such potentially important region-specific variables are usually omitted from quantitative cross-national analyses of inequality. Might the omission of region-specific variables have created a spurious association between foreign capital penetration and inequality in prior studies? To answer this question, Tsai introduces indicator variables for Latin America and East/Southeast Asia (with a collection of African and Central and South Asian countries as the reference group) and interactions between these regional indicators and foreign capital penetration. The results indicate that when regional differences are taken into account, foreign capital penetration appears to have a significant effect on inequality only in East/Southeast Asian countries. For Latin American countries and countries in the reference group, foreign direct investment has no significant distributional effect, contradicting the "deep-rooted impression among the dependency theorists that [foreign direct investment] did most harm to the Latin American and African economies" (Tsai 1995:478).

Tsai's interpretation of these results rests on the notion of a "socially tolerable ceiling" for inequality. Tsai suggests that inequality in Latin America and Africa may have already reached such a ceiling by the time of the study. As a result, the marginal impact of foreign capital penetration, assuming it exists, would necessarily be small. East/Southeast Asian countries, in contrast, exhibit significantly lower levels of inequality than do other countries in the data set. Having more "room to move," the marginal effect of foreign direct investment would be most likely to be observed in this region.

In sum, then, while not ruling out the possibility that foreign capital penetration may have had important distributional implications in earlier periods of Latin American and African history, Tsai's analysis clearly questions the results of contemporary analyses that report a positive relationship between inequality and foreign capital penetration across broad cross-sections of countries. As Tsai (1995) concludes, "[T]he statistically significant positive correlation between [foreign capital penetration] and income inequality obtained in previous studies and our basic model is more likely to reflect the geographical difference in inequality than the pervasive distributional impact of [foreign investment]" (p. 479). We replicate Tsai's analysis to determine if any observed effect of foreign investment arises spuriously because of an association between inequality and unmeasured region-specific variables.

Analysis

The "Classical" Foreign Capital Penetration Model

We begin our analysis by loosely replicating the prototypical study of Bornschier and Chase-Dunn (1985:124, Table 12) to see if their finding of a positive effect of penetration on inequality is reproducible net of our internal-developmental model.

The regression results are presented in Table 25.1. Model 1 is the regression of income inequality on the baseline internal-developmental model, together with Gini based on income, year, and the Marxist-Leninist regime indicator (which is used in lieu of the "system-style" variable used by Bornschier and Chase-Dunn 1985). The Marxist-Leninist regime indicator has a strong negative effect on inequality, indicating that Communist countries have more equal income distributions. Net of other variables in Model 1, the Gini coefficient in state socialist countries is estimated to be 9.7 points lower than that in non-socialist countries. This pattern is compatible with a variety of technical and substantive explanations (Ahluwalia 1976; Atkinson and Micklewright 1992; Lydall 1979; Weede and Tiefenbach 1981a). The year of measurement of the dependent variable has a highly significant positive effect on inequality, consistent with the linear trend toward rising inequality. The coefficient of the Gini based-on-income indicator is positive and significant, suggesting that income-based Gini coefficients are roughly 6.9 points higher than expenditure-based Gini coefficients.

The four variables comprising the baseline model have significant effects on inequality in the expected directions (Nielsen and Alderson 1995). The negative effect of secondary school enrollment supports the venerable hypothesis, formulated by Mill (1848), that the spread of education reduces inequality. The positive effect of the natural rate of population increase is consistent with both interpretations of this effect—it is a result of the "swarming" of people in the poorer classes, or it acts as a proxy measure reflecting generalized dualism (Nielsen 1994:662). The two variables capturing effects of labor force shifts have significant effects consistent with expectations: The positive coefficient for sector dualism measures the contribution of between sectors inequality to overall inequality, and the negative coefficient for percent of the labor force in agriculture represents—controlling for sector dualism—the reduction in overall inequality due to lower inequality within the agricultural sector. The R^2 of Model 1 (.560) indicates that the baseline model accounts for a substantial proportion of the variance in inequality. We use this model as a benchmark to evaluate the effects of the foreign capital penetration variables.

Model 2 adds foreign investment stock/GDP as an independent variable. Its coefficient is positive and highly significant, confirming Bornschier and Chase-Dunn's finding of a positive association between foreign capital penetration and inequality net of the internal-developmental model (and with a much larger data set). Model 3 adds a term

Table 25.1 Unstandardized Coefficients from the Random-Effects GLS Regression of Income Inequality (Gini) on Selected Independent Variables: 88 Countries, 1967 to 1994

Independent Variable	Model 1	Model 2	Model 3	Model 4	Model 5	Model 6	Model 7	Model 8
Foreign investment stock/GDP (log)	—	3.677***	4.321***	3.373***	—	3.490***	—	2.941***
		(6.077)	(6.456)	(5.365)		(5.726)		(4.493)
(Foreign investment stock/GDP X core country)	—	—	-3.858*	—	—	—	—	—
			(-2.321)					
Core Country	—	—	-.351	—	—	—	—	—
			(-.134)					
Flow of foreign investment/GDP (log)	—	—	—	3.118	—	—	—	—
				(1.794)				
Foreign Investment Rate	—	—	—	—	.025**	.019*	.024**	.019**
					(2.998)	(2.267)	(2.916)	(2.370)
Domestic Investment Rate	—	—	—	—	—	—	-.026	-.008
							(-.853)	(-.247)
Secondary school enrollment	-.090***	-.093***	-.087***	-.089***	-.083***	-.087***	-.078***	-.084***
	(-4.037)	(-4.303)	(-4.003)	(-4.127)	(-3.730)	(-4.053)	(-3.553)	(-3.896)
Natural Rate of population increase	.180**	.163**	.134*	.170**	.206**	.185**	.203**	.187**
	(2.632)	(2.461)	(1.941)	(2.574)	(3.030)	(2.800)	(3.000)	(2.829)
Sector dualism	.194***	.170***	.153***	.175***	.192***	.171***	.201***	.177***
	(4.522)	(4.094)	(3.658)	(4.231)	(4.526)	(4.136)	(4.603)	(4.084)
Percent of labor force in agriculture	-070*	-.048	-.036	-.052	-.071*	-.051	-.062	-.046
	(-1.676)	(-1.191)	(-.886)	(-1.283)	(-1.715)	(-1.275)	(-1.468)	(-1.113)
Marxist-Leninist regime	-9.678***	-7.517***	-8.271***	-7.656**	-10.071***	-7.891**	-10.278***	-8.447**
	(-3.582)	(-2.827)	(-3.117)	(-2.914)	(-3.795)	(-3.017)	(-3.843)	(-3.206)
Year	.146***	.134***	.144***	.132***	.142***	.132***	.150***	.139***
	(5.785)	(5.497)	(5.117)	(5.408)	(5.674)	(5.432)	(5.949)	(5.602)
Gini based on income	6.898***	7.095***	7.520***	7.075***	6.964***	7.130***	7.250***	7.294***
	(8.069)	(8.592)	(9.046)	(8.594)	(8.217)	(8.678)	(8.676)	(8.906)
Constant	34.331***	31.027***	30.854***	27.115***	33.138***	30.451***	33.032***	30.498***
	(14.109)	(12.868)	(11.684)	(8.347)	(13.684)	(12.682)	(13.176)	(12.098)
R^2	.560	.577	.623	.576	.561	.579	.564	.582
Rho	.833	.837	.836	.833	.828	.831	.837	.835
Number of observations	488	488	488	488	488	488	480	480

Note: Numbers in parentheses are *t*-values.
* p < .05 ** p < .01 *** p < .001

for the interaction of foreign investment stock/GDP and core status. The coefficient for the term is negative and significant, implying that the overall positive effect of foreign capital penetration on inequality is cancelled out for core countries. This finding is similar to that obtained by Bornschier and Chase-Dunn (1985:124, Table 12).

Firebaugh 's Critique

Models 4 through 8 address issues raised by Firebaugh's (1992) critique of dependency models of economic growth and the more recent exchange between Dixon and Boswell (1996) and Firebaugh (1996). Firebaugh (1992) points out that the negative effect of the stock of foreign capital on economic growth often reported by researchers working in the investment-dependence perspective is compatible with the positive effect of the rate of investment (including foreign investment) on economic growth predicted by standard economic theory. The investment rate is calculated as investment flow divided by stock, and because the denominator of the rate is "stock," a larger stock entails a lower rate for a given flow of foreign investment. Thus, ceteris paribus, stock will have a negative effect on economic growth. Firebaugh's (1992) argument, together with his empirical evidence, calls into question the entire investment-dependence literature (Dixon and Boswell 1996).

Adapting the argument about economic growth to the context of income inequality, one might reason by analogy to Firebaugh (1992) that the positive effect on inequality of the stock of foreign investment might be a result of a negative effect of the rate of foreign investment. Because stock is the denominator of the rate, a larger stock would be associated with higher levels of inequality for a given flow of foreign investment. To assess this possibility, Model 4 includes both the stock and flow of foreign investment. If inequality is negatively related to the foreign investment rate, we would expect to find a negative effect of flow (the numerator of the rate), and a positive effect of stock (the denominator of the rate).

Model 4 shows that, while foreign investment stock/GDP retains its significant positive effect on inequality, the flow of foreign investment/GDP is neither significant nor negatively signed, as would be consistent with the Firebaugh scenario (Firebaugh 1992:120, Table 4). The results. therefore, do not support the conjecture of a negative effect of investment rate on inequality. Firebaugh (1992) implies that the investment rate (flow divided by stock) is the variable of central importance. Model 5 adapts this argument to the inequality context by entering the foreign investment rate directly into the equation, rather than entering stock and flow separately. The inequality scenario constructed by analogy to Firebaugh's (1992) critique of economic growth models predicts a negative effect of the foreign investment rate on inequality. Instead, the coefficient for the foreign investment rate is positive and significant. This result directly contradicts the idea that the reported positive effect of stock on inequality might simply be an artifact of a negative effect of the investment rate on inequality. Thus, the positive effect of stock is not the result of its role as the denominator of the rate.

In their response to Firebaugh, Dixon and Boswell (1996) reassert the conceptual distinction between foreign investment and foreign capital penetration. Analytically, this involves distinguishing between the effects of penetration and of (1) the differential productivity of foreign versus domestic investment and (2) the more general investment rate ("denominator effect") problem identified by Firebaugh (1996:551). Practically, they resolve this problem by entering foreign investment stock/GDP and the foreign investment rate into regression equations simultaneously. They claim this purges foreign investment stock/GDP of differential productivity and spurious denominator effects. Model 6 evaluates this claim. The significant positive effect of stock persists net of the foreign investment rate (Dixon and Boswell 1996:560, eq. 4). These results lend additional support to Dixon and Boswell's (1996) conclusion, based on an analysis of a cross-section of 39 countries, that "foreign capital penetration promotes income inequality independent of investment flows or rates or of hidden denominator effects" (p. 560).

Firebaugh (1996) observes that there are at least three possible interpretations of the results obtained by Dixon and Boswell (1996) and in the penetration literature generally. Given that their measure of foreign capital penetration (foreign investment stock/total stock or GDP) is, literally, the ratio of foreign stock to total stock, Firebaugh (1996) argues that the observation of a positive effect of foreign investment stock/GDP on inequality could mean that

> . . . both types of investment boost inequality, with foreign investment boosting it more; foreign investment boosts inequality whereas domestic investment reduces it; and both reduce inequality, with foreign investment reducing it less. In short, a positive sign for the PEN ratio is consistent with the statements that (a) foreign capital boosts inequality *and* (b) foreign capital reduces inequality. (p. 573, emphasis in original)

The implication of this observation is that the positive coefficient for foreign investment stock/GDP may simply reflect the fact that foreign investment has a positive effect on inequality relative to domestic investment (and thus that the absolute effect of foreign investment may be negative). Model 7 explores this possibility by directly entering both the foreign and domestic investment rates into the baseline model. The foreign investment rate has a significant positive effect on inequality while the effect of the domestic investment rate is negative and not significant. Thus, the results are most consistent with Firebaugh's second interpretation. We conclude that foreign capital appears to boost inequality as opposed to merely reducing inequality less than domestic investment does. Exploring further, Model 8 includes foreign investment stock/GDP along with the foreign and domestic investment rates. While the inclusion of the domestic investment rate measurably attenuates the positive effect of foreign investment stock/GDP found in Model 6, the investment rate variables exhibit the same pattern of effects observed in Model 7.

From the evidence examined thus far, it appears that foreign capital penetration has a positive effect on inequality. Controlling for the baseline internal-developmental model, foreign investment stock/GDP has a highly significant positive effect that is robust to our adaptations of Firebaugh's critique. Models 4, 5, and 6 indicate that the positive effect of foreign investment stock/GDP is not an artifact of a negative effect of the foreign investment rate on inequality. Model 6 shows that, when directly measured, the foreign investment rate has a positive effect on inequality. Models 7 and 8 indicate that the positive effect of foreign investment stock/GDP is not attributable to the fact that the variable is literally the ratio of foreign stock to domestic stock. When both the foreign and domestic investment rates are explicitly introduced into the model, the results rule out the possibility that both foreign and domestic investment reduce inequality and thus rule out the alternative explanation that the positive effect of foreign investment stock/GDP is simply an artifact of foreign investment reducing inequality less than does domestic investment.

Tsai's Regional Analysis

We turn next to Tsai's (1995) claim that, at least for some geographical regions, the observed association between inequality and foreign investment stock/GDP is spurious owing to the omission of region-specific variables. Tsai (1995) introduces indicators for Latin America and East/Southeast Asia and their interactions with foreign investment stock/GDP and finds (1) insignificant coefficients for foreign investment stock/GDP and for the interaction between the Latin America indicator and foreign investment stock/GDP, suggesting no significant pen-etration effects in Latin America or the reference group, and (2) a sig-nificant negative effect of the East/Southeast Asia indicator and a sig-nificant positive effect of its interaction with foreign investment stock/GDP. Model 9 in Table 25.2 presents the results of our replication of Tsai. Our findings deviate markedly from Tsai's (1995:478, Table 2). Foreign investment stock/GDP continues to have a significant positive effect on inequality net of the region variables and interactions, indicat-ing that the results presented in Model 2 do not emerge spuriously from specification error. Also, we find no evidence that East/Southeast Asian

Table 25.2   Unstandardized Coefficients from the Random-Effects GLS Regression of Income Inequality (Gini) on Selected Independent Variables: 88 Countries, 1967 to 1994

Independent Variable	Model 9		Model 10		Model 11	
	Coeff.	t-value	Coeff.	t-value	Coeff.	t-value
Foreign investment stock/GDP (log)	3.008***	(3.647)	3.415***	(5.773)	—	
Latin America X foreign investment stock/GDP	1.788	(1.331)	—		—	
East/Southeast Asia X foreign investment stock/GDP	−1.972	(−1.020)	—		—	
East/Southeast Asia	1.578	(.554)	—		—	
Latin America	6.546**	(3.081)	8.867***	(4.919)	—	
Asia	—		−2.215	(−1.210)	—	
Africa	—		3.020	(1.590)	—	
Foreign investment stock per capita[a]	—		—		6.135***	(3.946)
(Foreign investment stock per capita^2)	—		—		−.466**	(−2.372)
Secondary school enrollment	−.079***	(−3.740)	−.073***	(−3.412)	−.097***	(−4.422)
Natural rate of population increase	.062	(.917)	.063	(.940)	.206*	(3.107)
Sector dualism	.179***	(4.401)	.162***	(4.038)	.111**	(2.546)
Percent of labor force in agriculture	.004	(.089)	.005	(.115)	.019	(.440)
Marxist-Leninist regime	−7.311***	(−2.904)	−5.928**	(−2.418)	−5.412*	(−2.003)
Year	.132***	(5.401)	.114***	(4.493)	.103***	(3.816)
Gini based on income	6.762***	(8.331)	7.266***	(8.678)	6.868***	(8.303)
Constant	28.998***	(12.008)	28.038***	(11.540)	16.504***	(3.688)
R^2	.675		.697		.600	
Rho	.819		.811		.839	
Number of observations	488		488		488	

a. Deviated from median.
* $p < .05$ ** $p < .01$ *** $p < .001$

countries exhibit significantly lower inequality than other countries nor do we find evidence that foreign investment stock/GDP has a significantly different distributional impact in East/Southeast Asia. Finally, we find that Latin American countries exhibit greater inequality than other countries, but foreign investment stock/GDP does not appear to have any distinctive distributional impact on this region. In sum, our results fail to support Tsai's contention that the results reported in earlier penetration research merely reflect geographical differences in inequality.

Adhering to the spirit of Tsai's argument, Model 10 dispenses with the interactions and simply introduces indicator variables for Latin America, Asia (as opposed to East/Southeast Asia), and Africa. Again, relative to the reference group, we find significantly higher inequality in Latin America, but the key finding is that the results for foreign investment stock/GDP are again little changed over Model 2. Thus, net of the baseline model and of time-invariant, region-specific factors, the stock of foreign direct investment continues to have a strong positive effect on income inequality. What accounts, then, for the divergence between our results and those reported by Tsai? Further analysis suggests that Tsai's finding may be an artifact due to heterogeneity bias.

The Investment-Development Path

To further address the problems of interpretation that emerge from standardizing foreign stock by total stock (Firebaugh 1996), we also measured foreign capital penetration as foreign investment stock per capita. The bivariate relationship between inequality and foreign investment stock per capita is distinctly curvilinear, with low inequality at low levels of foreign investment stock per capita, rising inequality with greater investment, and declining income inequality at high levels. To capture this inverted-U relationship, Model 11 includes a polynomial function of foreign investment stock per capita. Net of the baseline internal-developmental model, both terms are significant and signed consistent with the relationship, . . . indicating that inequality first rises then declines with foreign investment stock per capita. Relative to Model 2, Model 11 also provides a marginally better fit ($R^2 = .600$). These results are strong evidence of an inverted-U relationship of income inequality with foreign investment stock per capita, a relationship that has not been reported in the literature.

The unexpected finding of an inverted-U relationship between income inequality and foreign investment stock per capita becomes interpretable when one recognizes that there is a strong positive rela-

tionship between inflows and outflows of foreign direct investment. . . .
Dunning (1981) found that the trend in net foreign direct investment
(outflow minus inflow) over the course of development is nonlinear,
taking the form of a J-curve that he termed the "investment-development path" . . . Countries at the lowest levels of development tend to
take part in little inward or outward foreign direct investment. As development proceeds, inflow typically mounts while outflow remains at or
near zero. Beyond some intermediate level of development, outflow
tends to take off and expand at a faster rate than inflow and, at the highest levels of development, typically surpasses inflow. This produces,
when inflow is subtracted from outflow, . . . a net foreign direct investment trend that grows increasingly negative (a growing excess of
inflow over outflow) from low to intermediate levels of development
and turns upward to eventually become positive at the highest levels of
development (an excess of outflow over inflow).

How might a society's net direct investment position be related to
its level of inequality? We suggest briefly that the observed effect of
foreign stock may simply be an artifact of autonomous developments
associated with the investment-development path. . . . Movement from
low to intermediate levels of foreign investment stock per capita may be
associated with rising inequality for many of the same reasons identified in the penetration literature (Bornschier and Chase-Dunn 1985;
Evans and Timberlake 1980; Sullivan 1983). Inasmuch as multinational
firms employ modern capital-intensive technologies and typically pay

In light of the investment-development path, note that while movement from low to intermediate levels of foreign investment stock per
capita (as stock is merely accumulated inflow, net of depreciation) is
consistent with growing dependence on foreign investment, movement
from intermediate to high levels of foreign stock in the course of development actually indicates declining relative dependence on foreign
investment. This suggests an intriguing possibility: What may have
been observed in the dependency and world-systems literature may be
less the effect of foreign capital penetration or, a la Firebaugh, of
investment rates and differential productivity, and more the effect of a
nation's net foreign investment position. This possibility has been con-
cealed by the construction and use of foreign penetration measures with
denominators like total stock or GDP—a procedure that has the effect
of "folding" the more highly developed countries in the sample (those
arrayed along a declining slope of inequality with foreign investment
stock per capita) into the space occupied by the least developed countries (those arrayed on an ascending slope of inequality with foreign
investment stock per capita).

at or above going rates in urban centers, a larger international sector should be associated with higher inequality in societies at low to intermediate levels of development—a phenomenon that is not entirely captured by our baseline internal-developmental model. The decline of inequality associated with movement from intermediate to high levels of foreign investment stock per capita has not been noted in the literature. We speculate that as indigenous firms bring their practices into line with international standards (and begin to engage in direct investment on their own), the distortion caused by the presence of multinationals fades. Moreover, given that the bulk of direct investment in more developed countries tends to be devoted to manufacturing, high levels of direct investment inflow might moderate inequality inasmuch as it boosts manufacturing employment, countering trends toward deindustrialization (Alderson 1996; Nielsen and Alderson 1997).

Conclusion

Our reconsideration of the role of foreign capital penetration in income inequality is based on a large cross-national data set in which we pooled multiple observations over time for 88 countries. The data set represents a nearly exhaustive compilation of the data available cross-nationally on income inequality and foreign capital penetration, spanning the period from 1967 to 1994. We used methods of pooling time-series of cross-sections based on the random-effects model that use the cross-sectional and longitudinal information contained in this unbalanced data set to correct for the presence of unmeasured heterogeneity among countries.

Firebaugh's (1992, 1996) critique of the literature on the role of investment dependence in economic growth is indeed devastating. However, we were unable to document, for income inequality, mechanisms equivalent to those he demonstrated for economic growth. Similarly, we were unable to confirm Tsai's (1995) finding that the foreign capital penetration effect arises spuriously from unmeasured regional effects. The finding of a significant association between the Gini coefficient of income inequality and the stock of foreign investment, one that is robust to our adaptations of Firebaugh's critique and Tsai's regional argument, clearly suggests an important role for foreign capital penetration in the generation of inequality.

Nevertheless, the relationship between income inequality and foreign investment is probably far more complex than has been assumed, as it appears to involve the balance of inflow and outflow across national boundaries, rather than inflow only (Alderson 1997). In sum, we conclude that it is *relative dependence* on foreign investment that is associated with greater inequality. Our alternative account proposes that investment dependence may be but one "stage" on the investment-development path and that, rather than "an expression of power relationships among *countries* that generates and maintains the core-periphery hierarchy in the world economy" (Kentor 1998:1043, emphasis added), it may reflect instead power relations among firms and the evolution of business organizations over the course of development (Dunning and Narula 1996). As foreign investment has found new favor in the eyes of policymakers across the developing world in recent years, these findings and conclusions deserve close attention and scrutiny.

It is important not to overstate the implications of our findings. World-system variables such as measures of investment dependence are "external" characteristics—pertaining to the interface of a society with the outside world—that are expected to affect inequality through their impact on the society's "internal" characteristics, such as the distribution of the labor force. This point is at least implicit in many theoretical discussions of world-system effects (Bornschier and Chase-Dunn 1985; Sullivan 1983). This implies that. paradoxically, a major strategy of future research on the role of the world system in internal inequality processes is to develop models incorporating better sets of internal controls. While research in this tradition has begun to focus on the interaction of internal and external phenomena (Bradshaw et al. 1993; Shen and Williamson 1997), a disproportionate emphasis upon external factors remains. We propose that the substance of such research would be better served by drawing out the causal links between external factors and internal outcomes in a more systematic fashion.

The fact that our baseline internal-developmental model fails to capture the internal processes producing the relationship between inequality and foreign capital penetration suggests that much work remains to be done in the way of identifying precisely these internal mechanisms. Identifying and measuring these processes—thereby reducing the effect of such "external" variables to insignificance— would not demonstrate the irrelevance of world-system variables, but would indicate that their role in generating income inequality has been fully specified. Future research developing models to explicate the effects of foreign penetration variables which would likely involve specification of the local factors determining a country's position on the investment-development path is an obvious example of this strategy.

Recently, the dependency- and world-systems-oriented literature has been subjected to a number of powerful criticisms. The wide-ranging reexamination that this has spurred is entirely appropriate. In recent years, researchers in this tradition have at times appeared to be fighting yesterday's battles, attempting, for instance, to convince the field of something that has been apparent to many (if not all) for some time now—that the larger political-economic context in which development proceeds (or does not proceed) matters. Having won the battle, advocates of the world-systems approach should take care not to lose the war (Wallerstein 1996). We have identified some avenues along which fruitful research might be done regarding income inequality and dependency. Our hope is that the results of the present analysis contribute to a renaissance of quantitative cross-national research on the world system.

References

Ahluwalia, Montek S. 1976. "Income Distribution and Development: Some Stylized Facts." *American Economic Review* 66:128–35.

Alderson, Arthur S. 1996. "Globalization and Deindustrialization: Direct Investment and the Decline of Manufacturing Employment in 17 OECD Nations." Paper presented at the annual meeting of the American Sociological Association, August, New York.

———. 1997. "Globalization, Deindustrialization, and the Great U-Turn: The Growth of Direct Investment in 18 OECD Nations, 1967–1990. Ph.D. dissertation. Department of Sociology.

Alderson, Arthur S., and François Nielsen. 1995. "Income Inequality, Development, and World System Position: Results from an Unbalanced Cross-National Panel." Presented at the Southern Sociological Society Meeting, April, Atlanta, Georgia.

Atkinson, Anthony B., and John Micklewright. 1992. *Economic Transformation in Eastern Europe and the Distribution of Income.* New York: Cambridge University Press.

Bollen, Kenneth A., and Robert W. Jackman. 1985a. "Political Democracy and the Size Distribution of Income." *American Sociological Review* 13:438–57.

Bornschier, Volker, and Thanh-Huyen Ballmer-Cao. 1978. "Multinational Corporations in the World Economy and National Development: An Empirical Study of Income per Capita Growth 1960–1975." *Bulletin of the Sociological Institute of the University of Zurich* 32:1–169.

———. 1979. "Income Inequality: A Cross-National Study of the Relationship Between MNC Penetration, Dimensions of the Power Structure and Income Distribution." *American Sociological Review* 44:487–506.

Bornschier, Volker, and Christopher Chase-Dunn. 1985. *Transnational Corporations and Underdevelopment.* New York: Praeger.

Bornschier, Volker, Christopher Chase-Dunn, and Richard Rubinson. 1978. "Cross-National Evidence of the Effects of Foreign Investment and Aid on Economic Growth and Inequality: A Survey of Findings and a Reanalysis." *American Journal of Sociology* 84:651–83.

Bradshaw, York W., Rita Noonan, Laura Gash, and Claudia Buchmann Sershen. 1993. "Borrowing Against the Future: Children and Third World Indebtedness." *Social Forces* 71:629–56.

Crenshaw, Edward. 1992. "Cross-National Determinants of Income Inequality: A Replication and Extension Using Ecological-Evolutionary Theory." *Social Forces* 71:339–63.

Cutright, Phillips. 1967. "Inequality: A Cross-National Analysis." *American Sociological Review* 32:562–78.

Dixon, William J., and Terry Boswell. 1996. "Dependency, Disarticulation, and Denominator Effects: Another Look at Foreign Capital Penetration." *American Journal of Sociology* 102:543–62.

Dunning, John H. 1981. *International Production and the Multinational Enterprise*. London, England: Allen and Unwin.

Dunning, John H., and Rajneesh Narula. 1996. *Foreign Direct Investment and Governments*. London, England: Routledge.

Evans, Peter B., and Michael Timberlake. 1980. "Dependence, Inequality, and the Growth of the Tertiary: A Comparative Analysis of Less Developed Countries." *American Sociological Review* 45:531–51.

Firebaugh, Glenn. 1980. "Cross-National versus Historical Regression Models: Conditions of Equivalence in Comparative Analysis." *Comparative Social Research* 3:333–44.

———. 1992. "Growth Effects of Foreign and Domestic Investment." *American Journal of Sociology* 98:105–30.

———. 1996. "Does Foreign Capital Harm Poor Nations? New Estimates Based on Dixon and Boswell's Measure of Capital Penetration." *American Journal of Sociology* 102:563–75.

Gagliani, Giorgio. 1987. "Income Inequality and Economic Development." *Annual Review of Sociology* 13:313–34.

Galtung, Johan. 1971. "A Structural Theory of Imperialism." *Journal of Peace Research* 8:811–17.

Helleiner, Gerald K. 1991. "Direct Foreign Investment and Manufacturing for Export in Developing Countries: A Review of the Issues." Pp. 12–33 in *Foreign Direct Investments*, edited by H. W. Singer, N. Hatti, and R. Tandon. New Delhi, India: Indus.

Hoogvelt, Ankie. 1997. *Globalization and the Postcolonial World*. Baltimore, MD: Johns Hopkins University Press.

Jackman, Robert W. 1974. "Political Democracy and Social Equality: A Comparative Analysis." *American Sociological Review* 39:29–45.

———. 1975. *Politics and Social Equality: A Comparative Analysis*. New York: Wiley.

———. 1985. "Cross-National Statistical Research and the Study of Comparative Politics." *American Journal of Political Science* 29:161–82.

Kentor, Jeffrey. 1998. "The Long-Term Effects of Foreign Investment Dependence on Economic Growth, 1940–1990." *American Journal of Sociology* 1024–46.

Kuznets, Simon. 1955. "Economic Growth and Income Inequality." *American Economic Review* 45:1–28.

Lecaillon, Jacques, Felix Paukert, Christian Morrisson, and Dimitri Germidis. 1984. *Income Distribution and Economic Development: An Analytical Survey*. Geneva, Switzerland: International Labour Office.

Lenski. Gerhard. 1966. *Power and Privilege: A Theory of Social Stratification.* Chapel Hill, NC: University of North Carolina Press.

Lydall, Harold. 1979. "Some Problems in Making International Comparisons of Inequality." Pp. 21–37 in *Income Inequality: Trends and International Comparisons*, edited by J. R. Moroney. Lexington, MA: Lexington Books.

Mill, John Stuart. 1848. *Principles of Political Economy.* London, England: John Parker.

Muller, Edward N. 1985. "Income Inequality, Regime Repressiveness, and Political Violence." *American Sociological Review* 50:47–61.

———. 1988. "Democracy, Economic Development, and Income Inequality." *American Sociological Review* 53:50–68.

———. 1989. "Democracy and Inequality." *American Sociological Review* 54:868–71.

Nielsen, François. 1994. "Income Inequality and Development: Dualism Revisited." *American Sociological Review* 59:654–77.

Nielsen, François, and Arthur S. Alderson. 1995. "Income Inequality, Development, and Dualism: Results from an Unbalanced Cross-National Panel." *American Sociological Review* 60:674–701.

———. 1997. "The Kuznets Curve and the Great U-Turn: Patterns of Income Inequality in United States Counties, 1970–1990." *American Sociological Review* 62:12–33.

Papanek, Gustav F. 1978. "Economic Growth, Income Distribution and the Political Process in Less Developed Countries." Pp. 259–73 in *Income Distribution and Economic Inequality*, edited by Z. Griliches, W. Krelle, H. Krupp, and D. Kyn. Frankfurt, Germany: Campus Verlag.

Rubinson, Richard. 1976. "The World-Economy and the Distribution of Income within States." *American Sociological Review* 41:638–59.

Shen, Ce, and John B. Williamson. 1997. "Child Mortality, Women's Status, Economic Dependency, and State Strength: A Cross-National Study of Less Developed Countries." *Social Forces* 76:667–94.

Simpson, Miles. 1990. "Political Rights and Income Inequality: A Cross-National Test." *American Sociological Review* 55:682–93.

Sullivan, Gerard. 1983. "Uneven Development and National Income Inequality in Third World Countries: A Cross-National Study of the Effects of External Economic Dependence." *Sociological Perspectives* 26:201–31.

Tsai, Pan-Long. 1995. "Foreign Direct Investment and Income Inequality: Further Evidence." *World Development* 23:469–83. United Nations Conference on Trade and Development (UNCTAD), 1995.

Wallerstein, Immanuel. 1974. *The Modern World-System: Capitalist Agriculture and the Origins of the European World-Economy in the Sixteenth Century.* New York: Academic.

———. 1996. "The Rise and Future Demise of World-System Analysis." Paper presented at the annual meeting of the American Sociological Association, August, New York.

Weede, Erich, and Horst Tiefenbach. 1981a. "Some Recent Explanations of Income Inequality: An Evaluation and Critique." *International Studies Quarterly* 25:255–82.

Wimberley, Dale W. 1990. "Investment Dependence and Alternative Explanations of Third World Mortality: A Cross-National Study." *American Sociological Review* 55:75–91.

PART 6

The State, Growth, and Inequality

CHAPTER 26

Big Bills Left on the Sidewalk: Why Some Nations Are Rich, and Others Poor

MANCUR OLSON JR.

During his lifetime Mancur Olson Jr. was one of the most influential champions of rational choice theory. Here he dismisses many of the proposed causes of the gap between rich and poor countries offered throughout this volume—access to productive knowledge, access to capital markets, population stresses, lack of natural resources, quality of human capital, culture, and so on—declaring that the cause is the quality of institutions and economic policies. Olson argues that all governments and policies are not made equally, countries do not produce as much as their natural endowments permit, but rather strong institutions that get the policy right is the decisive factor in a country's economic performance. According to Olson, convergence theorists are not right about convergence because most poor countries, despite having a higher propensity to grow than richer countries, have poorer economic policies and institutions than richer countries.

T HERE IS ONE METAPHOR THAT NOT ONLY ILLUMINATES THE IDEA BEHIND many complex and seemingly disparate articles, but also helps to explain why many nations have remained poor while others have become rich. This metaphor grows out of debates about the "efficient markets hypothesis" that all pertinent publicly available information is taken into account in existing stock market prices, so that an investor can do as well by investing in randomly chosen stocks as by drawing on expert judgment. It is embodied in the familiar old joke about the assistant professor who, when walking with a full professor, reaches down

Reprinted with permission of the American Economic Association from the *Journal of Economic Perspectives,* vol. 10, no. 2 (1996): 3–24.

for the $100 bill he sees on the sidewalk. But he is held back by his senior colleague, who points out that if the $100 bill were real, it would have been picked up already. This story epitomizes many articles showing that the optimization of the participants in the market typically eliminates opportunities for supranormal returns: big bills aren't often dropped on the sidewalk, and if they are, they are picked up very quickly.

Many developments in economics in the last quarter century rest on the idea that any gains that can be obtained are in fact picked up. Though primitive early versions of Keynesian macroeconomics promised huge gains from activist fiscal and monetary policies, macroeconomics in the last quarter century has more often than not argued that rational individual behavior eliminates the problems that activist policies were supposed to solve. If a disequilibrium wage is creating involuntary unemployment, that would mean that workers had time to sell that was worth less to them than to prospective employers, so a mutually advantageous employment contract eliminates the involuntary unemployment. The market ensures that involuntarily unemployed labor is not left pacing the sidewalks.

Similarly, profit-maximizing firms have an incentive to enter exceptionally profitable industries, which reduces the social losses from monopoly power. Accordingly, a body of empirical research finds that the losses from monopoly in U.S. industry are slight: Harberger triangles are small. In the same spirit, many economists find that the social losses from protectionism and other inefficient government policies are only a minuscule percentage of the GDP [gross domestic product].

The literature growing out of the Coase theorem similarly suggests that even when there are externalities, bargaining among those involved can generate socially efficient outcomes. As long as transactions costs are not too high, voluntary bargaining internalizes externalities, so there is a Pareto-efficient outcome whatever the initial distribution of legal rights among the parties. Again, this is the idea that bargainers leave no money on the table.

Some of the more recent literature on Coaseian bargains emphasizes that transactions costs use up real resources and that the value of these resources must be taken into account in defining the Pareto frontier. It follows that, if the bargaining costs of internalizing an externality exceed the resulting gains, things should be left alone. The fact that rational parties won't leave any money on the table automatically insures that laissez faire generates Pareto efficiency.

More recently, Gary Becker (1983, 1985) has emphasized that government programs with deadweight losses must be at a political disadvantage. Some economists have gone on to treat governments as institutions that reduce transactions costs, and they have applied the Coase theorem to politics. They argue, in essence, that rational actors in the polity have an incentive to bargain politically until all mutual gains have been realized, so that democratic government, though it affects the distribution of income, normally produces socially efficient results (Stigler, 1971, 1992; Wittman, 1989, 1995; Thompson and Faith, 1981; Breton, 1993). This is true even when the policy chosen runs counter to the prescriptions of economists: if some alternative political bargain would have left the rational parties in the polity better off, they would have chosen it! Thus, the elemental idea that mutually advantageous bargaining will obtain all gains that are worth obtaining—that there are no bills left on the sidewalk—leads to the conclusion that, whether we observe laissez faire or rampant interventionism, we are already in the most efficient of all possible worlds.

The idea that the economies we observe are socially efficient, at least to an approximation, is not only espoused by economists who follow their logic as far as it will go, but is also a staple assumption behind much of the best-known empirical work. In the familiar aggregate production function or growth accounting empirical studies, it is assumed that economies are on the frontiers of their aggregate production functions. Profit-maximizing firms use capital and other factors of production up to the point where the value of the marginal product equals the price of the input, and it is assumed that the marginal private product of each factor equals its marginal social product. The econometrician can then calculate how much of the increase in social output is attributable to the accumulation of capital and other factors of production and treat any increases in output beyond this—"the residual"—as due to the advance of knowledge. This procedure assumes that output is as great as it can be, given the available resources and the level of technological knowledge.

If the ideas evoked here are largely true, then the rational parties in the economy and the polity ensure that the economy cannot be that far from its potential, and the policy advice of economists cannot be especially valuable. Of course, even if economic advice increased the GDP by just 1 percent, that would pay our salaries several times over. Still, the implication of the foregoing ideas and empirical assumptions is that economics cannot save the world, but at best can only improve it a little. In the language of Keynes' comparison of professions, we are no more important for the future of society than dentists.

The Boundaries of Wealth and Poverty

How can we find empirical evidence to test the idea that the rationality of individuals makes societies achieve their productive potential? This question seems empirically intractable. Yet there is one type of place where evidence abounds: the borders of countries. National borders delineate areas of different economic policies and institutions, and so— to the extent that variations in performance across countries cannot be explained by the differences in their endowments—they tell us something about the extent to which societies have attained their potentials.

Income levels differ dramatically across countries. According to the best available measures, per capita incomes in the richest countries are more than 20 times as high as in the poorest. Whatever the causes of high incomes may be, they are certainly present in some countries and absent in others. Though rich and poor countries do not usually share common borders, sometimes there are great differences in per capita income on opposite sides of a meandering river, like the Rio Grande, or where opposing armies happened to come to a stalemate, as between North and South Korea, or where arbitrary lines were drawn to divide a country, as not long ago in Germany.

At the highest level of aggregation, there are only two possible types of explanations of the great differences in per capita income across countries that can be taken seriously.

The first possibility is that, as the aggregate production function methodology and the foregoing theories suggest, national borders mark differences in the scarcity of productive resources per capita: the poor countries are poor because they are short of resources. They might be short of land and natural resources, or of human capital, or of equipment that embodies the latest technology, or of other types of resources. On this theory, the Coase theorem holds as much in poor societies as in rich ones: the rationality of individuals brings each society reasonably close to its potential, different as these potentials are. There are no big bills on the footpaths of the poor societies, either.

The second possibility is that national boundaries mark the borders of public policies and institutions that are not only different, but in some cases better and in other cases worse. Those countries with the best policies and institutions achieve most of their potential, while other countries achieve only a tiny fraction of their potential income. The individuals and firms in these societies may display rationality, and often great ingenuity and perseverance, in eking out a living in extraordinarily difficult conditions, but this individual achievement does not generate anything remotely resembling a socially efficient outcome.

There are hundreds of billions or even trillions of dollars that could be—but are not—earned each year from the natural and human resources of these countries. On this theory, the poorer countries do not have a structure of incentives that brings forth the productive cooperation that would pick up the big bills, and the reason they don't have it is that such structures do not emerge automatically as a consequence of individual rationality. The structure of incentives depends not only on what economic policies are chosen in each period, but also on the long run or institutional arrangements: on the legal systems that enforce contracts and protect property rights and on political structures, constitutional provisions, and the extent of special-interest lobbies and cartels.

How important are each of the two foregoing possibilities in explaining economic performance? This question is extraordinarily important. The answer must not only help us judge the theories under discussion, but also tell us about the main sources of economic growth and development.

I will attempt to assess the two possibilities by aggregating the productive factors in the same way as in a conventional aggregate production function or growth-accounting study and then consider each of the aggregate factors in turn. That is, I consider separately the relative abundance or scarcity of "capital," of "land" (with land standing for all natural resources) and of "labor" (with labor including not only human capital in the form of skills and education, but also culture). I will also consider the level of technology separately, and I find some considerations and evidence that support the familiar assumption from growth-accounting studies and Solow-type growth theory that the same level of technological knowledge is given exogenously to all countries. With this conventional taxonomy and the assumption that societies are on frontiers of their aggregate neoclassical production functions, we can derive important findings with a few simple deductions from familiar facts.

The next section shows that there is strong support for the familiar assumption that the world's stock of knowledge is available at little or no cost to all the countries of the world. I next examine the degree to which the marginal productivity of labor changes with large migrations and evidence on population densities, and I show that diminishing returns to land and other natural resources cannot explain much of the huge international differences in income. After that, I borrow some calculations from Robert Lucas on the implications of the huge differences across countries in capital intensity—and relate them to facts on the direction and magnitude of capital flows—to show that it is quite impossible that the countries of the world are anywhere near the frontiers of aggregate neoclassical production functions. I then examine some strangely neglected natural experiments with migrants from poor to rich countries to estimate the size of the differences in endowments of human capital between the poor and rich countries, and I demonstrate that they are able to account for only a small part of the international differences in the marginal product of labor.

Since neither differences in endowments of any of the three classical aggregate factors of production nor differential access to technology explain much of the great variation in per capita incomes, we are left with the second of the two (admittedly highly aggregated) possibilities set out above: that much the most important explanation of the differences in income across countries is the difference in their economic policies and institutions. There will not be room here to set out many of the other types of evidence supporting this conclusion, nor to offer any detailed analysis of what particular institutions and policies best promote economic growth. Nonetheless, by referring to other studies—and by returning to something that the theories with which we began overlook—we shall obtain some sense of why variations in institutions and policies are surely the main determinants of international differences in per capita incomes. We shall also obtain a faint glimpse of the broadest features of the institutions and policies that nations need to achieve the highest possible income levels.

The Access to Productive Knowledge

Is the world's technological knowledge generally accessible at little or no cost to all countries? To the extent that productive knowledge takes the form of unpatentable laws of nature and advances in basic science, it is a non-excludable public good available to everyone without charge. Nonpurchasers can, however, be denied access to many discoveries (in countries where intellectual property rights are enforced) through patents or copyrights, or because the discoveries are embodied in machines or other marketable products. Perhaps most advances in basic science can be of use to a poor country only after they have been combined with or embodied in some product or process that must be purchased from firms in the rich countries. We must, therefore, ask whether most of the gains from using modern productive knowledge in a poor country are mainly captured by firms in the countries that discovered or developed this knowledge.

Since those third world countries that have been growing exceptionally rapidly must surely have been adopting modern technologies from the first world, I tried (with the help of Brendan Kennelly) to find out how much foreign technologies had cost some such countries. As it happens, there is a study with some striking data for South Korea for the years from 1973 to 1979 (Koo, 1982). In Korea during these years, royalties and all other payments for disembodied technology were minuscule—often less than one-thousandth of GDP. Even if we treat all profits on foreign direct investment as solely a payment for knowledge and add them to royalties, the total is still less than 1.5 percent of the *increase* in Korea's GDP over the period. Thus the foreign owners of productive knowledge obtained less than a fiftieth of the gains from Korea's rapid economic growth.

The South Korean case certainly supports the long-familiar assumption that the world's productive knowledge is, for the most part, available to poor countries, and even at a relatively modest cost. It would be very difficult to explain much of the differences in per capita incomes across countries in terms of differential access to the available stock of productive knowledge.

Overpopulation and Diminishing Returns to Labor

Countries with access to the same global stock of knowledge may nonetheless have different endowments, which in turn might explain most of the differences in per capita income across countries. Accordingly, many people have supposed that the poverty in the poor countries is due largely to overpopulation, that is, to a low ratio of land and other natural resources to population. Is this true?

There is some evidence that provides a surprisingly persuasive answer to this question. I came upon it when I learned through Bhagwati (1984) of Hamilton and Whalley's (1984) estimates about how much world income would change if more workers were shifted from low-income to high-income countries. The key is to examine how much migration from poorer to richer countries *changes* relative wages and the marginal productivities of labor.

For simplicity, suppose that the world is divided into only two regions: North and South, and stick with the conventional assumption that both are on the frontiers of their aggregate production functions. As we move left to right from the origin of Figure 26.1, we have an ever larger workforce in the North until, at the extreme right end of this axis, all of the world's labor force is there. Conversely, as we move right to left from the right-hand axis, we have an ever larger workforce in the South. The marginal product of labor or wage in the rich North is meas-

388   MANCUR OLSON JR.

Figure 26.1   Population Distribution and Relative Wages

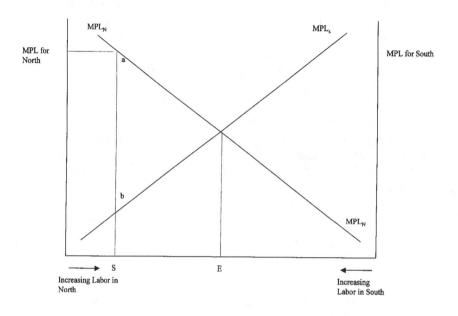

ured on the vertical axis at the left of Figure 26.1. The curve MPL_N gives the marginal product or wage of labor in the North, and, of course, because of diminishing returns, it slopes downward as we move to the right. The larger the labor force in the South, the lower the marginal product of labor in the South, so MPL_S, measured on the right-hand vertical axis, slopes down as we move to the left. Each point on the horizontal axis will specify a distribution of the world's population between the North and the South. A point like S represents the status quo. At S, there is relatively little labor and population in relation to resources in the North, and so the Northern marginal product and wage are high. The marginal product and wage in the overpopulated South will be low, and the marginal product of labor in the North exceeds that in the South by a substantial multiple.

This model tells us that when workers migrate from the low-wage South to the high-wage North, world income goes up by the difference between the wage the migrant worker receives in the rich country and what that worker earned in the poor country, or by amount ab. Clearly, the world as a whole is not on the frontier of its aggregate production, even if all of the countries in it are: some big bills have not been picked up on the routes that lead from poor to rich countries. Of course, the argument that has just been made is extremely simple, and international migration involves many other considerations. We can best come to understand these considerations—as well as other matters—by staying with this simple factor proportions story a while longer.

The Surprising Results of Large Migrations

This elementary model reminds us that, if it is diminishing returns to land and other natural resources that mainly explain international differences in per capita incomes, then large migrations from poorer to richer societies will, if other things (like the stocks of capital) remain equal, necessarily reduce income differentials. Such migration obviously raises the resource-to-population ratio in the country of emigration and reduces it in the country of immigration, and if carried far enough will continue until wages are equalized, as at point E in Figure 26.1.

Now consider Ireland, the country that has experienced much the highest proportion of outmigration in Europe, if not the world. In the census of 1821, Ireland had 5.4 million people, and Great Britain a population of 14.2 million. Though the Irish have experienced the same rates of natural population increase that have characterized other European peoples since 1821, in 1986, Ireland had only 3.5 million people. By this time, the population of Great Britain had reached 55.1 million. In 1821, the population density of Ireland was greater than that of Great Britain; by 1986, it was only about a fifth as great.

If the lack of "land" or overpopulation is decisive, Ireland ought to have enjoyed an exceptionally rapid growth of per capita income, at least in comparison with Great Britain, and the outmigration should eventually have ceased. Not so. Remarkably, the Irish level of per capita income is still only about five-eighths of the British level and less than half of the level in the United States, and the outmigration from Ireland is still continuing. As we shall see later, such large disparities in per capita income cannot normally be explained by differences in human capital. It is clear that in the United States, Britain and many other countries, immigrants from Ireland tend to earn as much as other peoples, and any differences in human capital could not explain the *increase* in wage that migrants receive when they go to a more productive country. Thus we can be sure that it is not the ratio of land to labor that has mainly determined per capita income in Ireland.

Now let us took at the huge European immigration to the United States between the closing of the U.S. frontier in about 1890 and the imposition of U.S. immigration restrictions in the early 1920s. If diminishing returns to labor were a substantial part of the story of economic growth, this vast migration should have caused a gradual reduction of the per capita income differential between the United States and Europe. In fact, the United States had a bigger lead in per capita income over several European countries in 1910 and 1920 than it had in the nineteenth century. Although many European countries did *not* narrow the gap in per capita incomes with the United States in the nineteenth century when they experienced a large outmigration to the United States, many of these same countries did nearly close that gap in the years after 1945, when they had relatively little emigration to the United States, and when their own incomes ought to have been lowered by a significant inflow of migrants and guest workers. Similarly, from the end of World War II until the construction of the Berlin wall, there was a considerable flow of population from East to West Germany, but this flow did not equalize income levels.

Consider also the irrepressible flow of documented and undocumented migration from Latin America to the United States. If diminishing returns to land and other natural resources were the main explanation of the difference in per capita incomes between Mexico and the United States, these differences should have diminished markedly at the times when this migration was greatest. They have not.

Several detailed empirical studies of relatively large immigration to isolated labor markets point to the same conclusion as the great migrations we have just considered. Card's (1990) study of the Mariel boatlift's effect on the wages of natives of Miami, Hunt's (1992) examination of the repatriation of Algerian French workers to Southern France, and Carrington and De Lima's (1996) account of the repatriates from Angola and Mozambique after Portugal lost its colonies all suggest that the substantial immigration did not depress the wages of natives.

Perhaps in some cases the curves in Figure 26.1 would cross when there was little population left in a poor country. Or maybe they would not cross at all: even that last person who turned the lights out as he left would obtain a higher wage after migrating.

Surprising Evidence on Density of Population

Let us now shift focus from changes in land/labor ratios due to migration to the cross-sectional evidence at given points in time on ratios of land to labor. Ideally, one should have a good index of the natural resource endowments of each country. Such an index should be adjusted to take account of changes in international prices, so that the value of a nation's resources index would change when the prices of the resources with which it was relatively well endowed went up or down. For lack of such an index, we must here simply examine density of population. Fortunately, the number of countries on which we have data on population and area is so large that population density alone tells us something.

Many of the most densely settled countries have high per capita incomes, and many poor countries are sparsely settled. Argentina, a country that fell from having one of the highest per capita incomes to third world status, has only 11 persons per square kilometer; Brazil, 16; Kenya, 25; and Zaire, 13. India, like most societies with a lot of irrigated agriculture, is more densely settled, with 233 people per square kilometer. But high-income West Germany, with 246 people per square kilometer, is more densely settled than India. Belgium and Japan have half again more population density than India, with 322 and 325 people per square kilometer, and Holland has still more density with 357. The population of Singapore is 4,185 per square kilometer; that of Hong Kong, over 5,000 persons per square kilometer (United Nations, 1986). These two densely settled little fragments of land also have per capita incomes 10 times as high as the poorest countries (and as of this writing they continue, like many other densely settled countries, to absorb migrants, at least when the migrants can sneak through the controls).

The foregoing cases could be exceptions, so we need to take all countries for which data are available into account and summarily describe the overall relationship between population density and per capita income. If we remember that the purpose is description and are careful to avoid drawing causal inferences, we can describe the available data with a univariate regression in which the natural log of real per capita income is the left-hand variable, and the natural log of population per square kilometer is the "explanatory" variable. Obviously, the per capita income of a country depends on many things, and any statistical test that does not take account of all important determinants is misspecified, and thus must be used only for descriptive and heuristic purposes. It is nonetheless interesting—and for most people surprising—to find that there is a positive and even a statistically significant relationship between these two variables: the greater the number of people per square kilometer the higher per capita income.

The law of diminishing returns is indisputably true: it would be absurd to suppose that a larger endowment of land makes a country poorer. This consideration by itself would, of course, call for a negative sign on population density. Thus, it is interesting to ask what might account for the "wrong" sign and to think of what statistical tests should ultimately be done. Clearly, there is a simultaneous two-way relationship between population density and per capita income: the level of per capita income affects population growth just as population, through diminishing returns to labor, affects per capita income.

The argument offered here suggests that perhaps countries with better economic policies and institutions come to have higher per capita incomes than countries with inferior policies and institutions, and that these higher incomes bring about a *higher population* growth through more immigration and lower death rates. In this way, the effect of better institutions and policies in raising per capita income swamps the tendency of diminishing returns to labor to reduce it. This hypothesis also may explain why many empirical studies have not been able to show a negative association between the rate of population growth and increases in per capita income.

One reason why the ratio of natural resources to population does not account for variations in per capita income is that most economic activity can now readily be separated from deposits of raw materials and arable land. Over time, transportation technologies have certainly improved, and products that have a high value in relation to their weight, such as most services and manufactured goods like computers and airplanes, may have become more important. The Silicon Valley is not important for the manufacture of computers because of deposits of silicon, and London and Zurich are not great banking centers because of fertile land. Even casual observation suggests that most modern manufacturing and service exports are not closely tied to natural resources. Western Europe does not now have a *high* ratio of natural resources to population, but it is very important in the export of manufactures and services. Japan has relatively little natural resources per capita, but it is a great exporter of manufactures. Certainly the striking successes in manufactures of Hong Kong and Singapore cannot be explained by their natural resources.

Diminishing Returns to Capital

We have seen that large migrations of labor do not change the marginal productivities of labor the way that they would if societies were at the frontiers of aggregate neoclassical production functions and that there is even evidence that labor is on average more *highly paid* where it is combined with less land. We shall now see that the allocation of capital across countries—and the patterns of investment and migration of capital across countries of *high and* low capital intensities—contradict the assumption that countries are on the frontiers of aggregate neoclassical production functions in an even more striking way.

This is immediately evident if we return to Figure 26.1 and relabel its coordinates and curves. If we replace the total world labor supply given along the horizontal axis of Figure 26.1 with the total world stock of capital and assume that the quantity of labor as well as natural resources in the North and South do not change, we can use Figure 26.1 to analyze diminishing returns to capital in the same way we used it to consider diminishing returns to labor.

As everyone knows, the countries with *high per* capita incomes have incomparably *higher capital* intensities of production than do those with low incomes. The countries of the third world use relatively little capital, and those of the first world are capital rich: most of the world's stock of capital is "crowded" into North America, western Europe and Japan.

If the countries of the world were on the frontiers of neoclassical production functions, the marginal product of capital would therefore be many times higher in the low-income than in the high-income countries. Robert Lucas (1990) has calculated, albeit in a somewhat different framework, the marginal product of capital that should be expected in the United States and in India. Lucas estimated that if an Indian worker and an American worker supplied the same quantity and quality of labor, the marginal product of capital in India should be 58 times as great as in the United States. Even when Lucas assumed that it took five Indian workers to supply as much labor as one U.S. worker, the predicted return to capital in India would still be a multiple of the return in the United States.

With portfolio managers and multinational corporations searching for more profitable investments for their capital, such gigantic differences in return should generate huge migrations of capital from the high-income to the low-income countries. Capital should be struggling at least as hard to get into the third world as labor is struggling to migrate into the high-wage countries. Indeed, since rational owners of capital allocate their investment funds across countries so that the risk-adjusted return at the margin is the same across countries, capital should be equally plentiful in all countries. (As we know from the Hecksher-Ohlin-Stolper-Samuelson discovery, if all countries operate on the same aggregate production functions, free trade alone is sometimes enough to equalize factor price ratios and thus factor intensities even in the absence of capital flows.)

Obviously, the dramatically uneven distribution of capital around the world contradicts the familiar assumption that all countries are on the frontiers of aggregate neoclassical production functions. A country could not be Pareto efficient and thus could not be on the frontier of its aggregate production unless it had equated the marginal product of capital in the country to the world price of capital. If it were not meeting this law-of-one-price condition, it would be passing up the gains that could come from borrowing capital abroad at the world rate of interest, investing it at home to obtain the higher marginal product of capital and pocketing the difference—it would be leaving large bills on the sidewalk. Accordingly, the strikingly unequal allocation of the world's stock of capital across nations proves that the poor countries cannot be anywhere near the frontiers of their aggregate production functions.

Sometimes the shortcomings of the economic policies and institutions of the low-income countries keep capital in these countries from earning rates of return appropriate to its scarcity, as we may infer from Harberger's (1978) findings and other evidence. Sometimes the shortcomings of the economic policies and institutions of poor countries make foreign investors and foreign firms unwelcome, or provoke the flight of locally owned capital, or make lending to these countries exceedingly risky. Whether the institutional and policy shortcomings of a country keep capital from having the productivity appropriate to its scarcity or discourage the investments and lending that would equalize the marginal product of capital across countries, they keep it from achieving its potential.

On top of all this, it is not rare for capital and labor to move *in the same direction:* both capital and labor are sometimes trying to move out of some countries and into some of the same countries. Of course, in a world where countries are on the frontiers of their aggregate production functions, capital and labor move in opposite directions.

Given the extraordinarily uneven allocation of capital across the countries of the world and the strong relationship between capital mobility and the economic policies and institutions of countries, the stock of capital cannot be taken to be exogenous in any reasonable theory of economic development.

Distinguishing Private Good and Public Good Human Capital

The adjustment of the amount of human capital per worker in Lucas's (1990) foregoing calculation for India and the United States raises a general issue: can the great differences in per capita income be mainly explained by differences in the third aggregate factor, labor, that is, by differences in the *human* capital per capita, broadly understood as including the cultural or other traits of different peoples as well as their skills? The average level of human capital in the form of occupational skills or education in a society can obviously influence the level of its per capita income.

Many people also argue that the high incomes in the rich countries are due in part to cultural or racial traits that make the individuals in these countries adept at responding to economic opportunities: they have the "Protestant ethic" or other cultural or national traits that are supposed to make them hard workers, frugal savers and imaginative entrepreneurs. Poor countries are alleged to be poor because they lack these traits. The cultural traits that perpetuate poverty are, it is argued, the results of centuries of social accumulation and cannot be changed quickly.

Unfortunately, the argument that culture is important for economic development, though plausible, is also vague: the word "culture," even though it is widely used in diverse disciplines, has not been defined precisely or in a way that permits comparison with other variables in an aggregate production function. We can obtain conceptions of culture that are adequate for the present purpose by breaking culture down into two distinct types of human capital.

Some types of human capital are obviously marketable: if a person has more skill, or a propensity to work harder, or a predilection to save more, or a more entrepreneurial personality, this will normally increase that individual's money income. Let us call these skills, propensities, or cultural traits that affect the quality or the quantity of productive inputs that an individual can sell in the marketplace "marketable human capital" or, synonymously, "personal culture." Max Weber's analysis of what he called the Protestant ethic was about marketable human capital or personal culture.

The second type of culture or human capital is evident when we think of knowledge that individuals may have about how they should vote: about what public policies will be successful. If enough voters acquire more knowledge about what the real consequences of different public policies will be, public policies will improve and thereby increase real incomes in the society. But this better knowledge of public policy is usually not marketable: in a society with given economic policies and institutions, the acquisition of such knowledge would not in general have any affect on an individual's wage or income. Knowledge about what public policy should be is a public good rather than a private or marketable good. Thus this second kind of human capital is "public good human capital" or "civic culture." Whereas marketable human capital or personal culture increases an individual's market income under given institutions and public policies, public good human capital or civic culture is not normally marketable and only affects incomes by influencing public policies and institutions.

With the aid of the distinction between marketable and public good human capital, we can gain important truths from some natural experiments.

Migration as an Experiment

As it happens, migration from poor to rich countries provides researchers with a marvelous (and so far strangely neglected) natural experiment. Typically, the number of individuals who immigrate to a country in any generation is too small to bring about any significant change in the electorate or public policies of the host country. But the migrant who arrives as an adult comes with the marketable human capital or personal culture of the country of origin; the Latin American who swims the Rio Grande is not thereby instantly baptized with the Protestant ethic. Though the migrant may in time acquire the culture of the host country, the whole idea behind the theories that emphasize the cultural or other characteristics of peoples is that it takes time to erase generations of socialization: if the cultural or other traits of a people could be changed overnight, they could not be significant barriers to development. Newly arrived immigrants therefore have approximately the same marketable human capital or personal culture they had before they migrated, but the institutions and public policies that determine the opportunities that they confront are those of the host country. In the case of the migration to the United States, at least, the data about newly arrived migrants from poor countries are sufficient to permit some immediate conclusions.

Christopher Clague (1991), drawing on the work of Borjas (1987), has found that individuals who had just arrived in the United States from poor countries, in spite of the difficulties they must have had in adjusting to a new environment with a different language and conditions, earned about 55 percent as much as native Americans of the same age, sex and years of schooling. New immigrants from countries where per capita incomes are only a tenth or a fifth as large as in the United States have a wage more than half as large as comparable American workers. Profit-maximizing firms would not have hired these migrants if they did not have a marginal product at least as large as their wage. The migrant's labor is, of course, combined with more capital in the rich than in the poor country, but it is not an accident that the owners of capital chose to invest it where they did: as the foregoing argument showed, the capital-labor ratio in a country is mainly determined by its institutions and policies.

Migrants might be more productive than their compatriots who did not migrate, so it might be supposed that the foregoing observations on immigrants are driven by selection bias. In fact, no tendency for the more productive people in poor countries to be more likely to emigrate could explain the huge increases in wages and marginal products of the migrants themselves. The migrant earns and produces much more in the rich country than in the poor country, so no tendency for migrants to be more productive than those who did not migrate could explain the increase in the migrant's marginal product when he or she moves from the poor to the rich country. In any event, developing countries often have much more unequal income distributions than developed nations, and the incentive to migrate from these countries is greatest in the least successful half of their income distributions. In fact, migrants to the United States are often drawn from the lower portion of the income distribution of underdeveloped countries (Borjas, 1990).

It is also instructive to examine the differences in productivity of migrants from poor countries with migrants from rich countries and then to see how much of the difference in per capita incomes in the countries of origin is likely to be due to the differences in the marketable human capital or personal culture of their respective peoples. Compare, for example, migrants to the United States from Haiti, one of the world's least successful economies, with migrants from West Germany, one of the most successful. According to the 1980 U.S. Census, self-employed immigrants from Haiti earned $18,900 per year, while those from West Germany earned $27,300; salaried immigrants from Haiti earned $10,900, those from West Germany, $21,900. Since the average Haitian immigrants earned only two-thirds or half as much as their West German counterparts in the same American environment, we may suspect that the Haitians had, on average, less marketable human capital than the West Germans.

So now let us perform the thought experiment of asking how much West Germans would have produced if they had the same institutions and economic policies as Haiti, or conversely how much Haitians would have produced had they had the same institutions and economic policies as West Germany. If we infer from the experience of migrants to the United States that West Germans have twice as much marketable capital as the Haitians, we can then suppose that Haiti with its present institutions and economic policies, but with West German levels of marketable human capital, would have about twice the per capita income that it has. But the actual level of Haitian per capita income is only about a tenth of the West German level, so Haiti would still, under our thought experiment, have less than one-fifth of the West German per capita income. Of course, if one imagines Haitian levels of marketable human capital operating with West German institutions and economic policies, one comes up with about half of the West German per capita income, which is again many times larger than Haiti's actual per capita income.

Obviously, one of the reasons for the great disparity implied by these thought experiments is the different amounts of tangible capital per worker in the two countries. Before taking this as given exogenously, however, the reader should consider investing his or her own money in each of these two countries. It is also possible that different selection biases for immigrants from different countries help account for the results of the foregoing thought experiments. Yet roughly the same results hold when one undertakes similar comparisons from migrants from Switzerland and Egypt, Japan and Guatemala, Norway and the Philippines, Sweden and Greece, the Netherlands and Panama, and so on. If, in comparing the incomes of migrants to the United States from poor and rich countries, one supposes that selection bias leads to an underestimate of the differences in marketable human capital between the poor and rich countries, and then makes a larger estimate of this effect than anyone is likely to think plausible, one still ends up with the result that the rich countries have vastly larger leads over poor countries in per capita incomes than can possibly be explained by differences in the marketable human capital of their populations. Such differences in personal culture can explain only a small part of the huge differences in per capita income between the rich and the poor countries.

History has performed some other experiments that lead to the same conclusion. During most of the postwar period, China, Germany and Korea have been divided by the accidents of history, so that different parts of nations with about the same culture and group traits have had different institutions and economic policies. The economic performances of Hong Kong and Taiwan, of West Germany and of South Korea have been incomparably better than the performances of mainland China, East Germany and North Korea. Such great differences in economic performance in areas of very similar cultural characteristics could surely not be explained by differences in the marketable human capital of the populations at issue.

It is important to remember that the foregoing experiments involving migration do not tell us anything about popular attitudes or prejudices in different countries regarding what public policy should be. That is, they do not tell us anything about the public good human capital or civic cultures of different peoples. As we know, the migrants from poor to rich countries are normally tiny minorities in the countries to which they migrate, so they do not usually change the public policies or institutions of the host countries. The natural experiments that we have just considered do not tell us what would happen if the civic cultures of the poor countries were to come to dominate the rich countries. For example, if traditional Latin American or Middle Eastern beliefs about how societies should be organized came to dominate North America or western Europe, institutions and economic policies—and then presumably also economic performance—would change.

The Overwhelming Importance of Institutions and Economic Policies

If what has been said so far is correct, then the large differences in per capita income across countries cannot be explained by differences in access to the world's stock of productive knowledge or to its capital markets, by differences in the ratio of population to land or natural resources, or by differences in the quality of marketable human capital or personal culture. Albeit at a high level of aggregation, this eliminates each of the factors of production as possible explanations of most of the international differences in per capita income. The only remaining plausible explanation is that the great differences in the wealth of nations are mainly due to differences in the quality of their institutions and economic policies.

The evidence from the national borders that delineate different institutions and economic policies not only contradicts the view that societies produce as much as their resource endowments permit, but also directly suggests that a country's institutions and economic policies are decisive for its economic performance. The very fact that the differences in per capita incomes across countries—the units with the different policies and institutions—are so large in relation to the differences in incomes across regions of the same country supports my argument. So does the fact that national borders sometimes sharply divide areas of quite different per capita incomes.

Old Growth Theory, New Growth Theory and the Facts

The argument offered here also fits the relationships between levels of per capita income and rates of growth better than does either the old growth theory or the new. As has often been pointed out, the absence of any general tendency for the poor countries with their opportunities for catch-up growth to grow faster than the rich countries argues against the old growth theory. The new or endogenous growth models feature externalities that increase with investment or with stocks of human or tangible capital and can readily explain why countries with high per capita incomes can grow as fast or faster than low-income countries.

But neither the old nor the new growth theories predict the relationship that is actually observed: *the fast-growing countries are never the countries with the highest per capita incomes but always a subset of the lower-income countries.* At the same time that low-income countries as a whole fail to grow any faster than high-income countries, a subset of the lower-income countries grows far faster than *any* high-income country does. The argument offered here suggests that poor countries on average have poorer economic policies and institutions than rich countries, and, therefore, in spite of their opportunity for rapid catch-up growth, they need not grow faster on average than the rich countries.

But any poorer countries that adopt relatively good economic policies and institutions enjoy rapid catch-up growth: since they are far short of their potential, their per capita incomes can increase not only because of the technological and other advances that simultaneously bring growth to the richest countries, but also by narrowing the huge gap between their actual and potential income (Barro, 1991). Countries with the highest per capita incomes do not have the same opportunity.

Thus the argument here leads us to expect what is actually observed: no necessary connection between low per capita incomes and more rapid rates of growth, but much the highest rates of growth in a subset of low-income countries—the ones that adopt better economic policies and institutions. During the 1970s, for example, South Korea grew seven times as fast as the United States. During the 1970s, the four countries that (apart from the oil-exporting countries) had the fastest rates of growth of per capita income grew on average 6.9 percentage points faster per year than the United States—more than five times as fast. In the 1980s, the four fastest growers grew 5.3 percentage points faster per year than the United States—four times as fast. They outgrew the highest income countries as a class by similarly large multiples. All of the four of the fastest-growing countries in each decade were low-income countries.

In general, the endogenous growth models do not have anything in their structures that predicts that the most rapid growth will occur in a subset of low-income countries, and the old growth theory is contradicted by the absence of general convergence.

Note also that, as the gap in per capita incomes between the relatively poor and relatively rich countries has increased over time, poor countries have also fallen further behind their potential. Therefore, the argument offered here predicts that the maximum rate of growth that is possible for a poor country—and the rate at which it can gain on the highest per capita income countries—is increasing over time. This is also what has been observed. In the 1870s, the four continental European countries with the fastest growth of per capita incomes grew only 0.3 of 1 percent per annum faster than the United Kingdom. The top four such countries in the 1880s also had the same 0.3 percent gain over the United Kingdom. As we have seen, the top four countries in the 1970s grew 6.9 percentage points faster than the United States, and the top four in the 1980s, 5.3 percentage points faster. Thus, the lead of the top four in the 1970s was 23 times as great as the lead of the top four in the 1870s, and the lead of the top four in the 1980s was more than 17 times as great as the top four a century before.

Thus neither the old nor the new growth theory leads us to expect either the observed overall relationship between the levels and rates of growth of per capita incomes or the way this relationship has changed as the absolute gap in per capita incomes has increased over time. The present theory, by contrast, suggests that there should be patterns like those we observe.

Picking Up the Big Bills

The best thing a society can do to increase its prosperity is to wise up. This means, in turn, that it is very important indeed that economists, inside government and out, get things right. When we are wrong, we do a lot of harm. When we are right—and have the clarity needed to prevail against the special interests and the quacks—we make an extraordinary contribution to the amelioration of poverty and the progress of humanity. The sums lost because the poor countries obtain only a fraction of—and because even the richest countries do not reach—their economic potentials are measured in the trillions of dollars.

None of the familiar ideologies is sufficient to provide the needed wisdom. The familiar assumption that the quality of a nation's economic institutions and policies is given by the smallness, or the largeness, of its public sector—or by the size of its transfers to low-income people—does not fit the facts very well (Levine and Remit, 1992; Rubinson, 1977; Olson, 1986).

But the hypothesis that economic performance is determined mostly by the structure *of* incentives—and that it is mainly national borders that mark the boundaries of different structures of incentives—has far more evidence in its favor. This lecture has set out only one of the types of this evidence; there is also direct evidence of the linkage between better economic policies and institutions and better economic performance. Though it is not feasible to set out this direct evidence here, it is available in other writings (Clague, Keefer, Knack and Olson, 1995; Olson, 1982, 1987a, 1987b, 1990).

We can perhaps obtain a glimpse of another kind of logic and evidence in support of the argument here—and a hint about what kinds of institutions and economic policies generate better economic performance—by returning to the theories with which we began. These theories suggested that the rationality of the participants in an economy or the parties to a bargain implied that there would be no money left on the table. We know from the surprisingly good performance of migrants from poor countries in rich countries, as well as from other evidence, that there is a great deal of rationality, mother wit and energy among the masses of the poor countries: individuals in these societies can pick up the bills on the sidewalk about as quickly as we can.

The problem is that the really big sums cannot be picked up through uncoordinated individual actions. They can only be obtained through the efficient cooperation of many millions of specialized workers and other inputs: in other words, they can only be attained if a vast array of gains from specialization and trade are realized. Though the low-income societies obtain most of the gains from self-enforcing trades, they do not realize many of the largest gains from specialization and trade. They do not have the institutions that enforce contracts impartially, and so they lose most of the gains from those transactions (like those in the capital market) that require impartial third-party enforcement. They do not have institutions that make property rights secure over the long run, so they lose most of the gains from capital-intensive production. Production and trade in these societies is further handicapped by misguided economic policies and by private and public predation. The intricate social cooperation that emerges when there is a sophisticated array of markets requires far better institutions and economic policies than most countries have. The effective correction of market failures is even more difficult.

The spontaneous individual optimization that drives the theories with which I began is important, but it is not enough by itself. If spontaneous Coase-style bargains, whether through laissez faire or political bargaining and government, eliminated socially wasteful predation and obtained the institutions that are needed for a thriving market economy, then there would not be so many grossly inefficient and poverty stricken societies. The argument presented here shows that the bargains needed to create efficient societies are not, in fact, made. Though that is another story, I can show that in many cases such bargains are even logically inconsistent with rational individual behavior. Some important trends in economic thinking, useful as they are, should not blind us to a sad and all-too-general reality: as the literature on collective action demonstrates (Olson, 1965; Hardin, 1982; Sandler, 1992; and many others), individual rationality is very far indeed from being sufficient for social rationality.

References

Barro, Robert J., "Economic Growth in a Cross Section of Countries," *Quarterly Journal of Economics,* May 1991, 106.2, 407–43.

Becker, Gary, "A Theory of Competition Among Pressure Groups for Political Influence," *Quarterly Journal of Economics,* August 1983, 98, 371–400.

Becker, Gary, "Public Policies, Pressure Groups, and Dead Weight Costs," *Journal of Public Economics,* December 1985, 28:3, 329–47.

Bhagwati, Jagdish, "Incentives and Disincentives: International Migration," *Weltwirtschaftliches Archiv,* 1984, 120, 678–701.

Borjas, George, "Self-Selection and the Earnings of Immigrants," *American Economic Review,* September 1987, 77, 531–53.

Borjas, George, *Friends or Strangers: The Impact of Immigrants on the U.S. Economy.* New York: Basic Books, 1990.

Breton, A., "Toward a Presumption of Efficiency in Politics," *Public Choice,* September 1993, 77:1, 53–65.

Card, David, "The Impact of the Mariel Boatlift on the Miami Labor Market," *Industrial and Labor Relations Review,* January 1990, 43:2, 245–57.

Carrington, William J., and Pedro J. F. De Lima, "The Impact of 1970s Repatriates from Africa on the Portuguese Labor Market," *Industrial and Labor Relations Review,* January 1996, 49:2, 330–47.

Clague, Christopher, "Relative Efficiency, Self-Containment and Comparative Costs of Less Developed Countries," *Economic Development and Cultural Change,* April 1991, 39:3, 507–30.

Clague, Christopher, P. Keefer, S. Knack, and Mancur Olson, "Contract-Intensive Money: Contract Enforcement, Property Rights, and Economic Performance." IRIS Working Paper No. 151, University of Maryland, 1995.

Great Britain Central Statistical Office, *Annual Abstract of Statistics.* London: H.M.S.O., 1988.

Hamilton, Bob, and John Whalley, "Efficiency and Distributional Implications of Global Restrictions on Labour Mobility Calculations and Policy Implications," *Journal of Development Economics,* January/February 1984, 14, 61–75.

Harberger, Arnold, "Perspectives on Capital and Technology in Less Developed

Countries." In Artis, M., and A. Nobay, eds., *Contemporary Economic Analysis.* London: Croom Helm, 1978, pp. 12–72.

Hardin, Russell, *Collective Action.* Baltimore: Johns Hopkins University Press, 1982.

Hunt, Jennifer, "The Impact of the 1962 Repatriates from Algeria on the French Labor Market," *Industrial and Labor Relations Review,* April 1992, 45.3, 556-72.

Ireland Central Statistics Office, *Statistical Abstract.* Dublin: Stationery Office, 1986.

Koo, Bohn-Young, "New Forms of Foreign Direct Investment in Korea." Korean Development Institute Working Paper No. 82-02, June 1982.

Krueger, Alan B., and Jörn-Steffen Pischke, "A Comparative Analysis of East and West German Labor Markets." In Freeman, Richard, and Lawrence Katz, eds., *Differences and Changes in Wage Structures.* Chicago: University of Chicago Press, 1995, pp. 405–45.

Landes, David, "Why Are We So Rich and They So Poor?," *American Economic Review,* May 1990, 80, 1–13.

Levine, Ross, and David Remit, "A Sensitivity Analysis of Cross-Country Growth Regressions," *American Economic Review,* September 1992, 82, 942–63.

Lucas, Robert, "'Why Doesn't Capital Flow from Rich to Poor Countries?," *American Economic Review,* May 1990, 80, 92–96.

Mitchell, Brian R., *Abstract of British Historical Statistics.* Cambridge, UK: Cambridge University Press, 1962.

Mitchell, Brian R., and H. G. Jones, *Second Abstract of British Historical Statistics.* Cambridge, UK: Cambridge University Press, 1971.

Mokyr, Joel, *My Ireland Starved: A Quantitative and Analytical History of the Irish 1800–1850.* London and Boston: Allen & Unwin, 1983.

Olson, Mancur, *The Logic of Collective Action.* Cambridge: Harvard University Press, 1965.

Olson, Mancur, *The Rise and Decline of Nations.* New Haven: Yale University Press, 1982.

Olson, Mancur, "Supply-Side Economics, Industrial Policy, and Rational Ignorance." In Barfield, Claude E., and William A. Schambra, eds., *The Politics of Industrial Policy.* Washington: American Enterprise Institute for Public Policy Research, 1986, pp. 245–69.

Olson, Mancur, "Diseconornies of Scale and Development," *The Cato Journal,* Spring/Summer 1987a, 7:1, 77–97.

Olson, Mancur, "Economic Nationalism and Economic Progress, the Harry Johnson Memorial Lecture," *The World Economy,* September 1987b, 10:3, 241–64.

Olson, Mancur, "The IRIS Idea," IRIS, University of Maryland, 1990.

Olson, Mancur, "Transactions Costs and the Coase Theorem: Is This Most Efficient of All Possible Worlds?" working paper, 1995.

Rubinson, Richard, "Dependency, Government Revenue, and Economic Growth, 1955–1970," *Studies in Comparative Institutional Development,* Summer 1977, 12:2, 3–28.

Sandler, Todd, *Collective Action.* Ann Arbor: University of Michigan Press, 1992.

Stigler, George J., "The Theory of Economic Regulation," *Bell Journal of Economics and Management Science,* Spring 1971, 2, 3–21.

Stigler, George J., "Law or Economics?," *The Journal of Law and Economics,* October 1992, 35:2, 455–68.

Thompson, Earl, and Roger Faith, "A Pure Theory of Strategic Behavior and Social Institutions," *American Economic Review,* June 1981, 71:3, 366–80.

United Nations, *Demographic Yearbook.* New York: United Nations, 1986.

Wittman, Donald, "Why Democracies Produce Efficient Results," *Journal of Political Economy*, December 1989, 97:6, 1395–424.

Wittman, Donald, *The Myth of Democratic Failure. Why Political Institutions are Efficient.* University of Chicago Press, 1995.

CHAPTER 27

Mauritius: A Case Study

ARVIND SUBRAMANIAN

Case study evidence of Mancur Olson's thesis from Chapter 26 is found here. In this chapter, Arvind Subramanian argues that Mauritius was able to achieve 5.9 percent economic growth between 1973 and 1999 due to the strength of its institutions and its economic policy. Robert Bates is well-known for highlighting the extreme corruption of marketing boards, but Subramanian argues that even though Mauritius has an export-processing zone, strong institutions allowed them to avoid the rent-seeking and corruption of other African countries. Like Olson, Subramanian points to institutions and policy as the keys to the economic success of Mauritius.

F EW SUB-SAHARAN AFRICAN COUNTRIES HAVE ACHIEVED HIGH STANDARDS of living. A notable exception has been Mauritius. Yet we had it on the highest possible authority—the economist and Nobel Prize winner James Meade, who prophesied in the early 1960s that Mauritius's development prospects were poor—that Mauritius was a strong candidate for failure, with its heavy economic dependence on one crop (sugar), vulnerability to terms of trade shocks, rapid population growth, and potential for ethnic tensions. History—or, rather, Mauritius—proved Meade's dire prognostication famously wrong.

Are Mauritius's achievements due to favorable initial conditions, good policies—especially openness to trade and foreign investment—sound domestic institutions, or other factors?

Reprinted with permission from *Finance and Development,* vol. 38, no. 4 (December 2001). Copyright © 2001 by the International Monetary Fund.

Achievements

Between 1973 and 1999, real GDP [gross domestic product] in Mauritius grew 5.9 percent a year, on average, compared with 2.4 percent for sub-Saharan Africa as a whole. Through the magic of compounding, the income of the average Mauritian more than tripled over a 40-year period, while that of the average African increased by only 32 percent.

Improvements in human development indicators have been equally impressive. Life expectancy at birth increased from 61 years in 1965 to 71 years in 1996; primary school enrollment increased from 93 to 107 per 100 children of school age between 1980 and 1996, while it decreased from 78 to 75 in the rest of Africa. (Enrollment rates may be higher than 100 percent because of repeaters, adults who are enrolled even though they are not in the age group being measured, and other discrepancies.) The income gap between the richest and the poorest Mauritians has narrowed considerably: the Gini coefficient (a measure of income inequality, with 0.0 representing total equality and 1.0 representing total inequality) declined from 0.5 in 1962 to 0.37 in 1986–87.

High growth rates have been achieved in a stable macroeconomic environment. Between 1973 and 2000, annual consumer price inflation averaged 7.8 percent in Mauritius, compared with more than 25 percent for sub-Saharan Africa as a whole. The unemployment rate declined from nearly 20 percent in 1983 to 3 percent in the late 1980s, although it has since edged up above 7 percent.

Social protection in Mauritius is similar to that seen in the industrial countries: a large and active presence for trade unions, which are able to engage in centralized wage bargaining, and generous social security benefits, particularly for the elderly and civil servants. Social protection is also afforded through price controls, especially on a number of socially sensitive items. In contrast with the member countries of the Organization for Economic Cooperation and Development, however, generous social programs in Mauritius have thus far not necessitated high taxes, reflecting both strong growth and favorable demographics, a large proportion of the population being of working age.

Initial Conditions

Did Mauritius grow fast because its inheritance was favorable? A retrospective answer can be provided based on the indicators that have been identified as important for long-term growth. On the one hand, a number of factors—especially the initial level of income, geography, and commodity dependence—have exerted a drag on long-term growth. For example, Mauritius is disadvantaged by being at least 25–30 percent more distant from world markets than the average African country. On the other hand, favorable demographic developments and very high initial levels of human capital have boosted growth. Formal analysis shows that on balance, however, the disadvantages outweigh the advantages: initial conditions have slowed growth by about 1 percentage point a year relative to the average African country and by nearly 2 percentage points relative to the fast-growing developing economies of East Asia.

Globalization Strategy

Perhaps the most interesting aspect of Mauritius's development has been its trade and development strategy. At one level, Mauritius can be seen as a case study proving that openness and an embrace of globalization are unambiguously beneficial. Since the mid-1980s, the volume of goods imported and exported by Mauritius has grown rapidly, at annual rates of 8.7 percent and 5.4 percent, respectively. Its openness ratio (the ratio of trade-in-goods to GDP) has increased from about 70 percent to 100 percent, while Africa's openness ratio has stagnated at around 45 percent. Particularly strong was the growth in manufacturing exports originating predominantly in Mauritius's export-processing zone.

There are three possible explanations for the impressive growth of trade: first, liberal trade policies; second, trade policies that, although interventionist, did not distort incentives in favor of the import-competing sector; third, openness to foreign direct investment.

The first explanation does not fit the facts. During the 1970s and 1980s, protection in Mauritius was high and dispersed throughout the economy. In 1980, the average tariff exceeded 100 percent, and it was still very high—65 percent—at the end of the 1980s. Moreover, until the 1980s, there were extensive quantitative restrictions in the form of import licensing, which covered nearly 60 percent of imports.

Clearly, by the usual measures, Mauritius had a highly restrictive import regime. But why did this not translate into an export tax and, hence, a tax on all trade? Not only was an effective institutional mechanism—the export-processing zone—in place but Mauritius's own domestic policies and the policies of its trading partners ensured very high returns to the export sector, effectively segmenting it from the rest of the economy and discouraging the diversion of domestic resources to the country's inefficient import-competing sector. First, all imported inputs entered the country duty free, ensuring that the export sector's competitiveness on world markets was not undermined by costly inputs. Second, a variety of tax incentives were provided to firms operating in the export-processing zone, which had the effect of subsidizing exports. Third, until the mid-to-late 1980s, labor market conditions in the export sector were different from those in the rest of the economy (in the import-competing sector, in particular): employers in the export-processing zone had greater flexibility to discharge workers, and the conditions of overtime work were more flexible. Most important, although the legal minimum wage was the same in the export-processing zone as in the rest of the economy, the minimum wage for women was lower than that for men. Because the export-processing zone employed a disproportionate number of women, their lower wages also implicitly subsidized exports, encouraging producers to concentrate on the export, rather than on the import-competing, sector.

However, these interventionist policies did not, on their own, fully offset the anti-export bias created by restrictive import policies. Preferential access provided by Mauritius's trading partners in the sugar, textile, and clothing sectors, which together accounted for about 90 percent of Mauritius's total exports, also implicitly subsidized the export sector and was responsible, to a large degree, for overcoming the anti-export bias of the import regime.

Since it gained its independence in 1968, Mauritius has been guaranteed a certain volume of sugar exports to the European Union (EU) at a price that was, on average, about 90 percent above the market price between 1977 and 2000. The resulting rents to Mauritius have amounted to a hefty 5.4 percent of GDP, on average, each year and as much as 13 percent in some years. From a macroeconomic perspective, these rents have played a crucial role in sustaining high levels of investment and explain why domestic, rather than foreign, savings have financed domestic investment during Mauritius's growth boom.

The preferential access given to textile and clothing exports from Mauritius has been equally important. The international regime known as the Multifiber Arrangement (MFA) was established by the United States and the European Union to limit imports of textiles and clothing by awarding country-specific quotas. As a result, imports were redistributed among the countries that produced these goods, to Mauritius's benefit.

The third explanation ascribes Mauritius's success to its openness to foreign direct investment, facilitated by the creation of the export-processing zone. The latter, a resounding success, has transformed the

Mauritian economy. Since 1982, output has grown by 19 percent a year, on average, employment by 24 percent, and exports by 11 percent. The export-processing zone accounts for 26 percent of GDP, 36 percent of employment, 19 percent of capital stock, and 66 percent of exports. Moreover, a growth-accounting analysis demonstrates the exceptional productivity of the zone. During 1983–99, total factor productivity growth in the export-processing zone averaged about 3.5 percent a year, compared with 1.4 percent in the economy as a whole. In the 1990s, productivity growth in the export-processing zone was remarkable, averaging 5.4 percent a year.

But these explanations, although plausible, do not really get at the underlying causes of Mauritius's trade and growth performance. Other developing countries had similar preferential trade opportunities and also created export-processing zones. But many of them failed where Mauritius succeeded. Clearly, there were deeper reasons for Mauritius's success.

Institutions

To a considerable extent, strong domestic institutions have contributed to Mauritius's success. Two examples illustrate the role played by domestic institutions. Mauritius successfully overcame its macroeconomic imbalances in the early 1980s. Macroeconomic adjustment was, in fact, implemented by three different governments of divergent ideological persuasions: this presupposed consultation and a recognition of the need to develop a national consensus in favor of adjustment. Further, a culture of transparency and participatory politics ensured that early warning signals and feedback mechanisms were in place, allowing emerging economic problems to be tackled at an early stage. Second, the export-processing zones established by other African countries may have provided the same incentives for investors but, unlike the zone in Mauritius, they have been plagued by rent seeking, abuses, and leakages deriving from weak administration.

Special Factors

Formal analysis of Mauritius's growth performance shows, however, that even after accounting for the positive role played by institutions, there is a sizable unexplained component. It is plausible that some factors specific to Mauritius may also have played an important role.

Foremost among these was the country's ethnic diversity and how it was managed.

First, some ethnic communities had important links with the rest of the world. The Chinese community, for example, attracted investment by Hong Kong entrepreneurs who sought overseas locations for their textile operations in an attempt to circumvent the textile quotas imposed on Hong Kong. Second, diversity, particularly the separation of economic and political power, helped ensure balance and prevented excessive taxation (by the politically powerful) of the sugar sector (owned by the economic elite), the country's cash cow. Third, diversity played an important role in the development of participatory institutions. Assuaging the misgivings of a large minority that had reservations about independence and were concerned about the possibility of domination by the majority made participatory politics in the post-independence era a necessity. These institutions ensured, in turn, the rule of law and respect for property rights that have made Mauritius attractive to investors. Perhaps, instilling confidence in the Mauritians in "their rights, their votes, the power of their opinions"—a major political achievement—was the key to Mauritius's economic success.

For further details, see Arvind Subramanian and Devesh Roy, 2001, "Who Can Explain the Mauritian Miracle: Meade, Romer, Sachs, or Rodrik?" IMF Working Paper 01/116 (Washington: International Monetary Fund), as well as their chapter in a forthcoming book, *Analytical Development Narratives,* ed. by Dani Rodrik, to be published by Princeton University Press. The challenges facing Mauritius in the period ahead are discussed in the IMF staff report for Mauritius's 2001 Article IV consultation (IMF Country Report No. 01/77).

CHAPTER 28

Why Aren't Countries Rich? Weak States and Bad Neighbourhoods

CHARLES KENNY

This chapter suggests that the emphasis on policy by Mancur Olson and Arvind Subramanian in the previous two chapters may be overdrawn. In this chapter, Charles Kenny argues that the common viewpoint that economic policy choices made by political leaders are the primary explanation for economic growth is wrong. Kenny poses the question, If all a country has to do is introduce the right policies in order to experience expanding wealth, why aren't they? His answer suggests that the policies a country follows are not always the ones the leaders want, but the ones that are possible. Kenny also proposes an interesting geographic hypothesis that asserts that one's neighborhood may be a determining factor in economic growth.

Introduction

IT IS A COMMON FEATURE OF THEORIES OF DEVELOPMENT ECONOMICS THAT the state is, for good or bad, central to the development process. The state is either the solution, the only way to combat structural weaknesses that hold back growth; or it is the problem, tying down the invisible hand; or it is the facilitator, vital for the efficient functioning of the free market. What is common to these ideas is that the ship of state is seen as a dreadnought, not a skiff. This paper will view the state as fragile— weakened by internal division of its people, unable to compensate for the vagaries of climate, and greatly affected by the condition of its

Reprinted with permission of Frank Cass Publishers from the *Journal of Development Studies* (1999): 26–29, 31–38, 43.

neighbours. Policies might be less effective than commonly thought. They might also be determined, to a large extent, by the environment in which the state is placed. Non-policy variables will appear as both an important determinant of policies and important determinants of growth in their own right.

This article will begin by studying some "stylized facts" regarding cross-country evidence on the growth process. Arguing that recent econometric results suggest that policy variables appear less than satisfactory as explanatory variables, it will turn to a range of non-policy variables. It discusses the idea that a nation-state—here proxied by common language and length of association—could be a prerequisite for growth in independent states. It will also look at two other "non-policy" factors (climate and neighbourhood wealth) which, together with the absence of nation-states, might be a major cause of the historical divergence in living standards. It then moves on to presenting statistical evidence supporting these propositions. The strongest statistical result from this analysis will be that no state is an island (although, it should be noted that in the regression sample this is literally true as well). Regional characteristics and the wealth of a country's neighbours will turn out to be strong correlates with country growth. The article concludes with a brief discussion of what these results might mean for the practice of development.

The Problem with Policy

It is perhaps worth reformulating the usual question, "what makes countries grow?" into the question, "why don't they?" The reason for adding a negative is that many present studies suggest that achieving a decent level of growth is reasonably straightforward [Dollar, 1993; Sachs and Warner, 1995]. Even more recent papers, such as Sachs and Warner [1997], while arguing that structural factors play a part, still conclude that there is a large role for the free choice of amelioratory policy reform. Some of the literature suggests that if a country introduces the right policies and formal political institutions, then convergence will follow. But if growth is merely a question of following a free choice to take the right policies, it seems surprising that everyone is not doing that.

Some recent studies have already suggested the difficulties in policy-centred explanations of growth performances based, for instance, on "large" or "small" states (as measured by government expenditure as a percentage of GNP [gross national product] or taxation) [Tanzi and Zee,

1997: 10; Easterly and Rebelo, 1993]. Levine and Renelt's study of common variables used in growth regressions also suggests that few of these variables are robust to being entered with different sets of other variables in regressions. This might be a sign of the high correlation between policy variables themselves and/or with causal country features that are the underlying reasons for differing growth rates [Levine and Renelt, 1992].

At the same time, studies of OECD [Organization for Economic Coordination and Development] countries suggest that developed country growth is well described as a process with constant mean and little persistence [Jones, 1995]. We can predict to within five per cent US GDP in 1987 looking at growth data from 1880 to 1929 alone. This suggests that there is a high level of persistence of growth at least within the OECD subsample of countries. Indeed, Pritchett [1997] notes that, between 1870 to 1989, two-thirds of the present high income industrialised countries had per annum GDP/capita growth rates within 0.2 per cent of the US rate. This relatively stable long-term growth rate further suggests that either policies have a limited role in explaining OECD growth rates, or that OECD countries have been following optimal policies, but such policies change over time and across countries—making cross-country, cross-period policy studies prone to error. Many US policies have changed dramatically over the period 1880–1987 (for instance, a massive increase on education, health and research expenditure), and policy differences between the US and countries such as Germany or Italy have been very large. It should be noted, however, that none of the OECD countries have consistently followed policies that were completely beyond the pale of economic rationality unlike some African countries. With that caveat, this work again suggests that there might be a role for more stable country characteristics to explain longer-term growth.

Another "stylized fact" about growth experiences also suggests that there is limited freedom for individual countries to grow at state-determined rates. Even a cursory glance at a map suggests that rich countries tend to be next to rich countries and poor next to poor. This relationship appears to work within countries, as well. In Mexico the industrialised North, next to the US border, is more wealthy than the central area dominated by Mexico City. In turn, the central region is far wealthier than the poverty-stricken South, including the Chiapas region, that has more in common with its Central American neighbours than with the rest of Mexico [Oppenheimer, 1996: 278]. This suggests one of two things. Either regional (as opposed to state) characteristics account for a large percentage of the differences between the wealth of countries or the wealth of a country's neighbours has a large impact on that country's wealth. In regression analyses, the importance of location has manifested itself in the persistence of region dummies. Easterly and Levine have also suggested neighbouring country's growth rates are a significant determinant of growth [1997b].

A third factor that has become increasingly clear in recent literature is the phenomenon of divergence. Pritchett [1997] argues that modern economic history suggests massive divergence across countries. Between 1820 and 1960, maximum average per annum growth rates of developing countries with GDP per capita of below $1,000 in 1960 is one per cent. Amongst present high income industrialised countries since 1870, growth has been close to 1.8 per cent/annum [Pritchett, 1997, 30–33]. Looking at long-term growth data from Maddison for 42 countries, the average per capita income of the poorest ten of those countries in 1900 was $637. The richest ten countries in 1900 had an average income of $3,696, approximately six times as much as the poorest. In 1992, the poorest ten countries had an average income of $1,831 compared to the richest ten's average of $18,765—approximately ten times as much as the poorest (calculated from Maddison [1995: 234]).

While Easterly, Kremer, Pritchett and Summers [1993] suggest that there is a limit to what country characteristics can explain in the short term, the fact of massive divergence suggests that over the long term there must be some correlation between growth in period one and growth in period two. The data suggest that, over the long term and on average, poor countries have grown significantly slower than rich ones. In the words of Lant Pritchett, there has been "divergence, big time." Poor continental regions have also grown slower than rich regions— where you are might be as important as what you do in explaining growth. At the same time, the low variation between growth in industrial countries and the low variation of growth over long periods of time within industrial countries is evidence that non-extreme policies cannot be that important (given policies have changed dramatically since 1870, and have varied across countries). There is a role for factors that are largely constant over very long periods, then; factors that can explain the long-term divergence in growth rates. These factors could affect growth rates directly (by increasing transactions costs, for instance) or indirectly, by inducing "extreme" polices of the kind not seen in the Twentieth-Century history of OECD countries. This is to see growth as a process of a violent random walk around a mean set by underlying institutional and structural factors.

What are some of the non-policy factors that might explain long-term growth? The recent explosion in work on institutions and economic growth might suggest some of the proximate causes. Work on the link between corruption, bureaucratic quality and civil liberties has produced some evidence of a link between such factors and economic performance [Alesina and Perotti, 1994]. King and Levine [1993] suggest that the development of the financial sector can have an important impact on economic growth, and show a robust connection between their measures of financial depth and GDP per capita growth. Levine's more recent work [1998] suggests a link with efficient legal and regulatory systems.

Clearly, the type of legal and regulatory system in a country is very much dependent on its history and location [Laporta, Lopez-de-Silanes, Schliefer, and Vishny, 1996]. This suggests that history and geography might have a role to play in explaining growth rates. In turn, this leads the discussion onto more permanent non-policy factors based on variables such as region, climate and culture, which might have an indirect impact through their effect on the nature of present institutions and policies as well as having a more proximate impact on growth.

For example, recent studies have already suggested that ethnic heterogeneity might play a role in development. Easterly and Levine's paper on "Africa's Growth Tragedy" [1997a] made use of the variable they labeled ETHNIC (and I report as ELF). This ethno-linguistic fractionalisation index is the chance that two randomly selected people from the same country will be of the same ethnic group. They show that ETHNIC is strongly correlated with measures of "minorities at risk," separatist movements and "ethnic tension." ETHNIC also makes the Africa dummy insignificant in their base regression. ETHNIC does not lead to political instability according to Easterly and Levine, but it is negatively correlated with school attainment, financial depth, infrastructure and the black market premium. Overall, they argue that ethno-linguistic effects probably account for one per cent of the growth difference between East Asia and Africa [Easterly and Levine, 1997a]. Hall and Jones [1996: 30] argue that countries where a large percentage of citizens speak one of eight international languages are significantly richer—twice as rich as similar countries where no international language is spoken.

Mauro used Business International's indices on corruption, bureaucratic red tape, political stability, terrorism and the legal system in 70 countries and found a link both between these measures themselves and with ETHNIC. ETHNIC has a $-.38$ correlation with the red tape index and a $-.41$ correlation with the political stability index. He also argues that GDP/capita, growth rate, and investment are correlated with bureaucratic competence [Mauro, 1995: 687].

These studies suggest that the absence of a nation-state as defined by language has a negative influence on the formal institutions of states and might encourage the types of extreme policies that damage long-term growth. Further studies by Sachs and Warner [1995, 1997] suggest that there is a (surprisingly negative) relationship between natural resources abundance and growth. Hall and Jones [1996: 30] show that countries in temperate regions are far richer than countries nearer to the equator. Wheeler [1984] and Hadjimichael et al. [1994] have both found drought a significant determinant of growth in Africa-only samples, and Sachs and Warner [1997] show that tropical countries tend to grow more slowly. Finally, Easterly and Levine also suggest that the growth rate of a country's neighbours can be a significant determinant of that country's growth [Easterly and Levine, 1997b].

I will examine three possible causes of growth connected with the ethnic, natural resource and neighbourhood wealth variables looked at in the above studies. First is a necessary but not sufficient cause of growth—the internal strength of the state. Strength, here, is defined as the ability to enforce reciprocity in state relations with its citizenry. I will argue that this strength is the result of a sense of nation that fosters legitimacy. Ethnic groups in Africa command far more loyalty than does the nationless state. The state therefore lacks legitimacy and is weakened. To capture the weak-state-low-legitimacy problem, I will use measures of ethnic division and state longevity taken from Easterly and Levine's work, along with a measure of the length of time since state leaders began the "political modernisation" process.

The second factor I will look at is an arbiter of agricultural productivity. Historically, agricultural revolutions have preceded or coincided with periods of very high growth. If some countries are prevented from achieving this high growth rate because of their climate—in this case low rainfall—this problem could trap them in a low growth trajectory. Third, I will look at the wealth of neighbouring countries. This factor appears to go a long way towards being a sufficient condition for growth. Beyond the role of neighbouring wealth in promoting catch-up, neighbourhood performance will capture regional characteristics that determine economic growth including ethnicity and climate, but also cultural and ideological groupings and resource availability.

Nation-States and Growth

One example of a relatively unchanging condition that appears to affect wealth is that countries with states capable of imposing controls on their interaction with citizens appear to be amongst the richer countries in the world. Even if one takes a minimalist position on the role of the state in development, it still has vital tasks to perform. Lal argues in *The Poverty of Development Economics* that the state has done too much, but admits that it sometimes has a role to correct the failings of "an inherently and inescapably imperfect economy" [Lal, 1983: 15]. To play this role requires an effective government, which in turn is predicated on a strong state.

The problem of the ethnically-induced internal weakness of the state as a whole perhaps helps to explains why it is so hard to find differences in the growth rates of democracies and non-democracies [Przeworski and Limongi, 1993: 6], or "large" and "small" states. These differences are secondary to those between strong and weak states. The formal constitutional nature of the government in Africa is relatively unimportant and irrelevant to the workings of the economy. The underlying, largely unchanging, cultural-institutional structure can weaken or redirect central efforts at control—be those efforts directed by the military or civilians. There is a further, linked, way in which ethnic division is likely to affect growth. It is in the way that a common culture is likely to increase trust—or at least understanding—between economic actors.

The variables that I will use to define "nations" are largely based on language. There is a long history of tying nations to their linguistic and/or religious cultural heritage. Dante tried to locate an Italian language to identify Italy in "On Vernacular Language" [Breuilly, 1985: 5–6]. Fichte, a founder of the modern philosophy of nationalism, argued that "Nothing seems more obviously opposed to the purposes of government than the unnatural enlargement of states . . . Those who speak the same language are joined to each other by a multitude of invisible bonds by nature herself . . . they belong together and are by nature one and inseparable whole . . ." [Fichte, 1962]. The variables STATEL and HOMELANG are both measures of the percentage of people who speak a country's official state language. HOMEL is the percentage of people in the country that speak the most popular language at home; it is also designed to capture the national homogeneity of states. A variation of this same concept is ELF, Easterly and Levine's ethno-linguistic fractionalisation index.

The examples of France and England suggest that, merely by being a state for long enough, a country can foster linguistic homogeneity and/or a sense of national identity. Belgium might be a reasonable example of a state that has limited linguistic homogeneity, but a reasonable sense of nationhood, born of 167 years as an independent country. This suggests that a measure of the amount of time a state has been an

independent administrative unit with its present borders might be a further useful measure for capturing the presence of a nation-state. The
variable YRIND60 comes from Easterly and Levine; it is the percentage of the number of years since 1776 that a country has been an independent state. This means that most African countries get a value of
zero because, despite the fact they were only formal colonies from the
end of the nineteenth century, they were not formal states within their
present borders before the European invasion. CONSOLIDATION is a
variation on this theme (used here as a robustness check). It is the
number of years up to 1990 since a country has begun the "consolidation of modernizing leadership" as defined by Black [1966], where this
consists of "the determination of leaders to modernize," a break from
agricultural institutional structures and the creation of a politically
organised society. As examples, this period began in 1776 for the US,
1861 for Russia, 1868 for Japan and 1964 for Malawi. CONSOL is the
same variable with years between independence and 1990 substituted
for countries where Black provides no data. All three variables
YRIND60, CONSOLIDATION and CONSOL are likely to act as proxies for an OECD dummy to some extent. Obviously, OECD countries
have been comparatively rich and independent for a long time—and
they colonised poorer countries. To that extent, these variables could
merely show once again that poor countries have remained poorer and
rich countries richer despite huge global increases in wealth. Perhaps
they suggest one reason why this might be so, however. Statebuilding
is a long process, which began earlier in the West than in most of the
rest of the world.

Other Initial Conditions: Rainfall and Regional Growth

One further factor that could be a large constraint to overall growth is a
limit to agricultural growth. It is clear that Britain's early industrial
growth was made possible by an increase in agricultural output that
allowed the country to escape the Malthusian trap. Morris and
Adelman's [1989] study of nineteenth-century development in 23 countries concluded that successful agricultural performance was necessary
(if not sufficient) for industrialisation to occur. More recently, the green
revolution in India has obviously been vital to that country's development. India's successes were made possible by high yielding varieties
of crops that required a certain quality of soil and consistency in water
availability not found in Africa, however [Lamb, 1982: 298]. It might
be that the climatic conditions in some countries prevent an agricultural

revolution that has been a necessary (if not sufficient) condition for long-term growth in other countries. For example, Africa's agricultural system is largely pastoral, with some rain-fed arable production. It is based on a system of production designed to minimise the catastrophe of drought rather than to maximise output [Lamb, 1982: 298]. This might be less receptive to productivity improvements than the irrigated, water-intensive rice production common in East Asia. Interseasonal differences in rainfall in Africa can alter smallholder cotton production yields by up to 400 kg/ha [kilograms/hectare], for example, while low rainfall can reduce the yield effect of fertiliser on cotton from 300 kg/ha to no effect at all [Carr, 1993: 2, 14]. Looking at rainfall levels might be suggestive in this regard, then.

The variable RAIN is a dummy which takes the value one if the lowest average monthly rainfall in a country's capital is below 10 mm for any month. Of course, this is not necessarily a good measure of the climatic conditions in the country's major agricultural areas. The weather in Beijing, Delhi, Moscow or Washington is not likely to be a good measure of weather across the entire agricultural areas of these countries. Too much rain can be as bad as too little, as recent floods in China attest, and further, variability can matter as much as quantity. RAIN, then, has to be seen as an exploratory variable. In future work, it might be worth looking at average rainfall during the growing season and/or the standard deviation of rainfall.

Neighbourhood wealth itself could be important in easing the benefits of catch-up. Attracting investment, exploiting trading opportunities, earning from migratory labour and learning about technological advances will be far easier for a poor country sharing a border with a rich neighbour than one surrounded by other poor countries. This might be seen as a "gravity theory" of catch-up, linked with Krugman's [1991] argument that there are strategic complimentarities in geographically concentrated capital accumulation and consistent with evidence of sigma convergence of per capita income across European Union countries, Japanese prefectures and US states [Barro and Sala-i-Martin, 1995]. The variables "NINT60" and "NINT90" are the unweighted average of available figures from within the 160-country dataset of land-bordering neighbours' GDP per capita, from the Summers and Heston dataset. This excludes islands and countries including South Korea that only border on countries for which there are no data. It also skews numbers for countries next to some other countries for which there is no data (China's NINT values exclude Russia, Pakistan's exclude Iran, for instance). GNINT is a measure of the unweighted average growth of neighbours over the period 1960–90.

Results

Using Easterly and Levine's 160-country sample as a basis, we can look at the significance of each of these factors. In turn: the average 1990 GNP per capita (Y90) from Summers and Heston for the 33 countries where under 60 per cent of the population spoke the most popular home language (and numbers are available) was $1,990; for the 79 countries where over 60 per cent spoke the most popular home language the average was $6,193. The average GNP per capita for those 41 countries whose land neighbours had an average GNP per capita of under $2,500 was $1,617. The average for those countries whose neighbours had an average GNP per capita of over $2,500 was $7,276. The average GNP per capita of those 52 countries which saw an average of under one centimetre of rain in their capital in any month was $2,475. For those 56 countries which always saw monthly average rainfall in the capital above one centimeter, the average GNP per capita was $7,320. For those 62 countries that had spent under 20 per cent of the time between 1776 and 1960 as independent states, the average income was $2,419. For those 52 countries that had spent more than 20 per cent of the time between the American War of Independence and 1960 as independent states, average GDP per capita in 1990 was $7,597. For the 14 countries that had linguistic diversity, poor neighbours, low rainfall and a short independent history, average per capita GDP was $969 in 1990. For the 26 countries blessed with linguistic homogeneity, wealthy neighbours, good rainfall and a short colonial history, average income was $9,849 in 1990.

If we look at regression studies of how well these factors predict wealth, when 1960 GNP/capita (Y60) is regressed against RAIN, HOMELANG and YRIND60, all are significant at below one per cent, enter with the expected sign and explain 43 per cent of the variation in wealth between countries (Table 28.1) (although average rainfall, unreported, but used as a robustness test for RAIN, was not significant).

Conclusion

The idea of all states as independent actors—"lithe leviathans"—is fundamental to much of the literature in development studies. Easterly, Kremer, Pritchett and Summers [1993] have shown that over the short term, it is external factors or "good luck" that cause changes in growth rates. Over the long term, this article argues that external factors remain vital, as do cultural and climatological factors which both determine

Table 28.1   Determinants of Income, 1960 (Dependent Variable is Y60, t-stats in italics)

	1	2	3	4	5	6
C	3159	3260	3378	218	379	593
	8.01	*7.97*	*8.56*	*1.09*	*0.88*	*1.23*
RAIN	−1562	−1539	−1522		−434	−475
	−4.59	*−4.5*	*−4.56*		*−1.52*	*−1.66*
HOMELANG	−17.6	−14.7	−19.8		−0.9	−3
	−3.57	*−2.51*	*−4.03*		*−0.21*	*−0.63*
YRIND60	1598	1434	1778		1128	1351
	3.45	*2.67*	*3.87*		*2.97*	*3.28*
NINT60				0.87	0.74	0.7
				12.97	*8.53*	*7.57*
AFRICA		−446				67
		−0.88				*0.87*
LATINCA			−1003			−558
			−2.39			*−1.56*
N	110	110	110	100	95	95
R-Squared	0.43	0.44	0.46	0.63	0.71	0.72

policy and have their own independent effect on growth. The constraints on state action are themselves a better prediction of growth than the actions that states take. These constraints take two forms. First, states can be weakened by internal division. This stops them acting (effectively not) to alter economic relations. A state capable of controlling economic relations is, I would argue, a precondition for growth. The second constraint is the external environment. With limited rainfall and poverty-stricken neighbours even an effective state will find growth at home very hard to nurture.

This is not to suggest that Africa will necessarily remain poor forever, but its growth is likely to be evolutionary, not revolutionary. Building a nation-state is obviously a long process, but it could be argued that Africa is moving towards that goal. Cheaper communications, the spread of education, the very presence of states (even if they are weak) will undoubtedly increase the sense of nation and national interest. Further, the nation-state's role as a necessary condition for growth might be reduced in the new global economy. If local factors are very important, reform also tends to be regional (everyone in Eastern Europe gave up on Communism, nearly everyone in Africa is moving towards the market). If there is a region-wide change, this could lead to region-wide mutually supporting growth. It might well be that technological change will render (or perhaps already has rendered) copious rainfall irrelevant to successful agriculture, or that other paths to growth avoiding agricultural revolution will be found. Overall, however, the article suggests that it is short-sighted to look at state policies alone to explain growth. Policies are only causal to a degree. Further, they are themselves the result of other factors—many of them regional. Policy prescriptions that do not recognise this fact might be difficult to implement successfully.

References

Alesina, A., and R. Perotti, 1994, "The Political Economy of Growth: A Critical Survey of the Recent Literature," *The World Bank Economic Review*, Vol. 8, No. 3.

Barro, Robert J., and Xavier Sala-i-Martin, 1995, *Economic Growth*, New York, NY: McGraw-Hill.

Black, C., 1966, *The Dynamics of Modernization*, New York: Harper & Row.

Breuilly, J., 1985, *Nationalism and the State*, Chicago, IL: University of Chicago.

Carr, S., 1993, "Improving Cash Crops in Africa: Factors Influencing the Productivity of Cotton, Coffee, and Tea Grown by Smallholders," World Bank Technical Paper 216.

Dollar, D., 1992, "Outward Oriented Developing Economies Really Do Grow More Rapidly," *Economic Development and Cultural Change*, Vol. 40.

Easterly, W., M. Kremer, L. Pritchett, and L. Summers, 1993, "Good Policy or Good Luck," *Journal of Monetary Economics*, No. 32.

Easterly, W., and R. Levine, 1997a, "Africa's Growth Tragedy: Policies and Ethnic Divisions," *The Quarterly Journal of Economics*, Vol. 112.

Easterly, W., and R. Levine, 1997b, "Troubles with the Neighbours: Africa's Problem, Africa's Opportunity," *Journal of African Economies*, Vol. 7, No. 1.

Easterly, W., and S. Rebelo, 1993, "Fiscal Policy and Economic Growth," *Journal of Monetary Economics*, Vol. 32.

Fichte, 1962, *Addresses to the German Nation*, New York: Harper.

Hadjimichael, M., D. Ghura, M. Muhleisen, R. Nord, and E. Ucer, 1994, "Effects of Macroeconomic Stability on Growth, Savings, and Investment in Sub-Saharan Africa," IMF Working Paper 94/98.

Hall, R., and Jones, 1996, "The Productivity of Nations," NBER Working Paper No. 5812.

Jones, C., 1995, "Time Series Tests of Endogenous Growth Models," *Quarterly Journal of Economics*, Vol. 110.

King, R., and R. Levine, 1993, "Finance and Growth: Schumpeter May Be Right," *Quarterly Journal of Economics*, Vol. 108, No. 3.

Krugman, Paul R., 1991, *Geography and Trade*, Leuven, Belgium: Leuven University Press.

Lal, D., 1983, *The Poverty of Development Economics*, London: Hobart.

Lamb, H., 1982, *Climate, History and the Modem World*, London: Methuen.

Laporta, R., F. Lopez-de-Silanes, A. Schliefer, and R. Vishny, 1996, "Law and Finance," NBER Working Paper No. 5661.

Levine, R., 1998, "The Legal Environment, Banks, and Long-run Economic Growth," *Journal of Money, Credit, and Banking*, Vol. 30, No. 3/2.

Levine, R., and D. Renelt, 1992, "A Sensitivity Analysis of Cross-country Growth Regressions," *American Economic Review*, Vol. 82.

Maddison, A., 1995, *Monitoring the World Economy 1820–1992*, Paris: OECD.

Mauro, P., 1995, "Corruption and Growth," *Quarterly Journal of Economics*, August.

Oppenheimer, A., 1996, *Bordering on Chaos*, Boston, MA: Little, Brown.

Pritchett, L., 1997, "Divergence Big Time," *Journal of Economic Perspectives*, Vol. ll, pp. 3–17.

Przeworski, A., and Limongi, 1993, "Political Regimes and Economic Growth," *Journal of Economic Perspectives*, Vol. 7, No. 3.

Sachs, J., and A. Warner, 1995, "Economic Convergence and Economic Policies," NBER Working Paper No. 5039.

Sachs, J., and A. Warner, 1995, "National Resource Abundance and Economic Growth," NBER Working Paper No. 5398.

Tanzi, V., and Zee, 1997, "Fiscal Policy and Long-run Growth," IMF Staff Papers, Vol. 44.

Wheeler, D., 1984, "Sources of Stagnation in Sub-Saharan Africa," *World Development*, Vol. 12, No. 1.

CHAPTER 29

Urban Bias and Inequality

MICHAEL LIPTON

Michael Lipton is the principal advocate of the thesis that the primary explanation for the internal gap between rich and poor is "urban bias." He argues that even though leaders of developing countries sympathize with the plight of the rural poor, they consistently concentrate scarce development resources in the urban sector. The result is that the urban sectors, which are already well-off in a comparative sense, get an increasing share of national income, which exacerbates the inequalities. In the book from which this chapter is drawn, Lipton tries to show that it is in the interests of the elites of developing countries to maintain this urban bias because they benefit directly from it. Critics of Lipton's thesis claim that historically there has been a rural bias in development and that much political power continues to reside in the hands of the rural elite. One might also ask if there is anything about the cultures found in developing nations that encourages policies favoring one sector over another; rural or urban biases (if they truly exist) might be a function of conditions estsablished by the international environment.

T HE MOST IMPORTANT CLASS CONFLICT IN THE POOR COUNTRIES OF THE world today is not between labor and capital. Nor is it between foreign and national interests. It is between the rural classes and the urban classes. The rural sector contains most of the poverty, and most of the low-cost sources of potential advance; but the urban sector contains most of the articulateness, organization, and power. So the urban classes

Reprinted with permission of Ashgate Publishing Limited from *Why Poor People Stay Poor: A Study of Urban Bias in World Development,* by Michael Lipton.

have been able to "win" most of the rounds of the struggle with the countryside; but in so doing they have made the development process needlessly slow and unfair. Scarce land, which might grow millets and beansprouts for hungry villagers, instead produces a trickle of costly calories from meat and milk, which few except the urban rich (who have ample protein anyway) can afford. Scarce investment, instead of going into water-pumps to grow rice, is wasted on urban motorways. Scarce human skills design and administer, not village wells and agricultural extension services, but world boxing championships in showpiece stadia. Resource allocations, within the city and the village as well as between them, reflect urban priorities rather than equity or efficiency. The damage has been increased by misguided ideological imports, liberal and Marxian, and by the town's success in buying off part of the rural elite, thus transferring most of the costs of the process to the rural poor.

But is this urban bias really damaging? After all, since 1945 output per person in the poor countries has doubled; and this unprecedented growth has brought genuine development. Production has been made more scientific: in agriculture, by the irrigation of large areas, and more recently by the increasing adoption of fertilizers and of high-yield varieties of wheat and rice; in industry, by the replacement of fatiguing and repetitive effort by rising levels of technology, specialization and skills. Consumption has also developed, in ways that at once use and underpin the development of production; poor countries now consume enormously expanded provisions of health and education, roads and electricity, radios and bicycles. Why, then, are so many of those involved in the development of the Third World—politicians and administrators, planners and scholars—miserable about the past and gloomy about the future? Why is the United Nations' "Development Decade" of the 1960s, in which poor countries as a whole exceeded the growth target,[1] generally written off as a failure? Why is aid, which demonstrably contributes to a development effort apparently so promising in global terms, in accelerating decline and threatened by a "crisis of will" in donor countries?[2]

The reason is that since 1945 growth and development, in most countries, have done so little to raise the living standards of the poorest people. It is scant comfort that today's mass-consumption economies, in Europe and North America, also featured near-stagnant mass welfare in the early phases of their economic modernization. Unlike today's poor countries, they carried in their early development the seeds of mass consumption later on. They were massively installling extra capacity to supply their people with simple goods: bread, cloth, and coal, not just luxury housing, poultry, and airports. Also the nineteenth-century "developing countries," including Russia, were developing not just market requirements but class structures that practically guaranteed subsequent "trickling down" of benefits. The workers even proved able to raise their share of political power and economic welfare. The very preconditions of such trends are absent in most of today's developing countries. The sincere egalitarian rhetoric of, say, Mrs. Indira Gandhi or Julius Nyerere was—allowing for differences of style and ideology— closely paralleled in Europe during early industrial development: in Britain, for example, by Henry Brougham and Lord Durham in the 1830s.[3] But the rural masses of India and Tanzania, unlike the urban masses of Melbourne's Britain, lack the power to organize the pressure that alone turns such rhetoric into distributive action against the pressure of the elite.

Some rather surprising people have taken alarm at the persistently unequal nature of recent development. Aid donors are substantially motivated by foreign-policy concerns for the stability of recipient governments; development banks, by the need to repay depositors and hence to ensure a good return on the projects they support. Both concerns coalesce in the World Bank, which raises and distributes some £3,000 million of aid each year. As a bank it has advocated—and financed—mostly "bankable" (that is, commercially profitable) projects. As a channel for aid donors, it has concentrated on poor countries that are relatively "open" to investment, trade and economic advice from those donors. Yet the effect of stagnant mass welfare in poor countries, on the well-intentioned and perceptive people who administer World Bank aid, has gradually overborne these traditional biases. Since 1971 the president of the World Bank, Robert McNamara, has in a series of speeches focused attention on the stagnant or worsening lives of the bottom 40 percent of people in poor countries.[4] Recently this has begun to affect the World Bank's projects, though its incomplete engagement with the problem of urban bias restricts the impact. For instance, an urban-biased government will prepare rural projects less well than urban projects, will manipulate prices to render rural projects less apparently profitable (and hence less "bankable"), and will tend to cut down its own effort if donors step up theirs. Nevertheless, the World Bank's new concern with the "bottom 40 percent" is significant.

These people—between one-quarter and one-fifth of the people of the world—are overwhelmingly rural: landless laborers, or farmers with no more than an acre or two, who must supplement their incomes by wage labor. Most of these countryfolk rely, as hitherto, on agriculture lacking irrigation or fertilizers or even iron tools. Hence they are so badly fed that they cannot work efficiently, and in many cases are unable to feed their infants well enough to prevent physical stunting and perhaps even brain damage. Apart from the rote-learning of religious texts, few of them receive any schooling. One of four dies before the age of ten. The rest live the same overworked, underfed, ignorant, and disease-ridden lives as thirty, or three hundred, or three thousand years ago. Often they borrow (at 40 percent or more yearly interest) from the same moneylender families as their ancestors, and surrender half their crops to the same families of landlords. Yet the last thirty years have been the age of unprecedented, accelerating growth and development! Naturally men of goodwill are puzzled and alarmed.

How can accelerated growth and development, in an era of rapidly improving communications and of "mass politics," produce so little for poor people? It is too simple to blame familiar scapegoats—foreign exploiters and domestic capitalists. Poor countries where they are relatively unimportant have experienced the paradox just as much as others. Nor, apparently, do the poorest families cause their own difficulties, whether by rapid population growth or by lack of drive. Poor families do tend to have more children than rich families, but principally because their higher death rates require it, if the aging parents are to be reasonably sure that a son will grow up, to support them if need be. And it is the structure of rewards and opportunities within poor countries that extracts, as if by force, the young man of ability and energy from his chronically stagnant rural background and lures him to serve, or even to join, the booming urban elite.

The disparity between urban and rural welfare is much greater in poor countries now than it was in rich countries during their early development. This huge welfare gap is demonstrably inefficient, as well as inequitable. It persists mainly because less than 20 percent of investment for development has gone to the agricultural sector (the situation has not changed much since 1965), although over 65 percent of the people of less-developed countries (LDCs), and over 80 percent of the really poor who live on $1 per week each or less, depend for a living on agriculture. The proportion of skilled people who support development—doctors, bankers, engineers—going to rural areas has been lower still; and the rural-urban imbalances have in general been even greater than those between agriculture and industry. Moreover, in most LDCs, governments have taken numerous measures with the unhappy side-effect of accentuating rural-urban disparities: their own allocation of public expenditure and taxation; measures raising the price of industrial production relative to farm production, thus encouraging private rural saving to flow into industrial investment because the value of industrial output has been artificially boosted; and educational facilities encouraging bright villagers to train in cities for urban jobs.

Such processes have been extremely inefficient. For instance, the impact on output of $1 of carefully selected investment is in most countries two to three times as high in agriculture as elsewhere, yet public policy and private market power have combined to push domestic savings and foreign aid into nonagricultural uses. The process has also been inequitable. Agriculture starts with about one-third the income per head as the rest of the economy, so that the people who depend on it should in equity receive special attention not special mulcting. Finally, the misallocation between sectors has created a needless and acute conflict between efficiency and equity. In agriculture the poor farmer with little land is usually efficient in his use of both land and capital, whereas power, construction, and industry often do best in big, capital-intensive units; and rural income and power, while far from equal, are less unequal than in the cities. So concentration on urban development and neglect of agriculture have pushed resources away from activities where they can help growth and benefit the poor, *and* toward activities where they do either of these, if at all, at the expense of the other.

Urban bias also increases inefficiency and inequity within the sectors. Poor farmers have little land and much underused family labor. Hence they tend to complement any extra developmental resources received—pumpsets, fertilizers, virgin land—with much more extra labor than do large farmers. Poor farmers thus tend to get most output from such extra resources (as well as needing the extra income most). But rich farmers (because they sell their extra output to the cities instead of eating it themselves, and because they are likely to use much of their extra income to support urban investment) are naturally favored by urban-biased policies; it is they, not the efficient small farmers, who get the cheap loans and the fertilizer subsidies. The patterns of allocation and distribution within the cities are damaged too. Farm inputs are produced inefficiently, instead of imported, and the farmer has to pay, even if the price is nominally "subsidized." The processing of farm outputs, notably grain milling, is shifted into big urban units and the profits are no longer reinvested in agriculture. And equalization between classes inside the cities becomes more risky, because the investment-starved farm sector might prove unable to deliver the food that a better-off urban mass would seek to buy.

Moreover, income in poor countries is usually more equally distributed within the rural sector than within the urban sector.[5] Since income creates the power to distribute extra income, therefore, a policy that concentrates on raising income in the urban sector will worsen inequalities in two ways: by transferring not only from poor to rich, but also from more equal to less equal. Concentration on urban enrichment is triply inequitable: because countryfolk start poorer; because such concentration allots rural resources largely to the rural rich (who sell food to the cities); and because the great inequality of power *within* the towns renders urban resources especially likely to go to the resident elites.

But am I not hammering at an open door? Certainly the persiflage of allocation has changed recently, under the impact of patently damaging deficiencies in rural output. Development plans are nowadays full of "top priority for agriculture."[6] This is reminiscent of the pseudo-egalitarian school where, at mealtimes, Class B children get priority, while Class A children get food.[7] We can see that the new agricultural priority is dubious from the abuse of the "green revolution" and of the oil crisis (despite its much greater impact on *industrial* costs) as pretexts for lack of emphasis on agriculture: "We don't need it," and "We can't afford it," respectively. And the 60 to 80 percent of people dependent on agriculture are still allocated barely 20 percent of public resources; even these small shares are seldom achieved; and they have, if anything, tended to diminish. So long as the elite's interests, background and sympathies remain predominantly urban, the countryside may get the "priority" but the city will get the resources. The farm sector will continue to be squeezed, both by transfers of resources from it by prices that are turned against it. Bogus justifications of urban bias will continue to earn the sincere, prestige-conferring, but misguided support of visiting "experts" from industrialized countries and international agencies. And development will be needlessly painful, inequitable and slow.

Notes

1. The UN target was a 5 percent yearly rate of "real" growth (that is, allowing for inflation) of total output. The actual rate was slightly higher.
2. Net aid from the donor countries comprising the Development Assistance Committee (DAC) of the Organization for Economic Cooperation and Development (OECD) comprises over 95 percent of all net aid to less-developing countries (LDCs). It fell steadily from 0.54 percent of donors' GNP in 1961 to 0.30 percent in 1973. The real value of aid per person in recipient countries fell by over 20 percent over the period. M. Lipton, "Aid Allocation When Aid is Inadequate," in T. Byres, ed., *Foreign Resources and Economic Development,* Cass, 1972, p. 158; OECD (DAC), *Development Cooperation* (1974 Review), p. 116.
3. L. Cooper, *Radical Jack,* Cresset, 1969, esp. pp. 183–97; C. New, *Life of Henry Brougham to 1830,* Clarendon, 1961, Preface.

4. See the mounting emphasis in his *Addresses to the Board of Governors,* all published by the International Bank for Reconstruction and Development, Washington; at Copenhagen in 1970, p. 20; at Washington in 1971, pp. 6–19, and 1972, pp. 8–15; and at Nairobi in 1973, pp. 10–14, 19.

5. M. Ahluwalia, "The Dimensions of the Problem," in H. Chenery et al., *Redistribution with Growth,* Oxford, 1974.

6. See K. Rafferty, *Financial Times,* 10 April 1974, p. 35, col. 5; M. Lipton, "Urban Bias and Rural Planning," in P. Streeten and M. Lipton, eds., *The Crisis of Indian Planning,* Oxford, 1968, p. 85.

7. F. Muir and D. Norden, "Comonon Entrance," in P. Sellers, *Songs for Swinging Sellers,* Parlophone PMC 111, 1958.

CHAPTER 30

Political Regimes and Economic Growth

ADAM PRZEWORSKI AND FERNANDO LIMONGI

In this chapter, Adam Przeworski and Fernando Limongi review the findings of eighteen articles that assess the relationship between regime type and economic growth. The authors show that the results have been inconclusive. According to Przeworski and Limongi, the confusion stems from the need for a more complex research design. Whereas the authors demonstrate that previous studies mistakenly attribute regime type as a cause of growth, they do not attempt to resolve the debate empirically. They state that ample evidence suggests that politics does affect growth, but they do not believe the debate over regime types captures the relevant differences between regimes that may be under investigation.

Arguments: How Democracy Might Affect Growth

ARGUMENTS THAT RELATE REGIMES TO GROWTH FOCUS ON PROPERTY RIGHTS, pressures for immediate consumption, and the autonomy of dictators. While everyone seems to agree that secure property rights foster growth, it is controversial whether democracies or dictatorships better secure these rights. The main mechanism by which democracy is thought to hinder growth is pressures for immediate consumption, which reduce investment. Only states that are institutionally insulated from such pressures can resist them, and democratic states are not. The

Reprinted with permission of the American Economics Association from *Journal of Economic Perspective,* vol. 7, no. 3 (summer 1993).

main argument against dictatorships is that authoritarian rulers have no interest in maximizing total output. . . .

The Statistical Evidence

In one way, the critics and defenders of democracy talk past each other. The critics argue that dictatorships are better at mobilizing savings; the defenders that democracies are better at allocating investment. Both arguments can be true but, as we shall see, the statistical evidence is inconclusive and the studies that produced it are all seriously flawed.

Table 30.1 summarizes the 18 studies we examined. These generated 21 findings, since some distinguished areas or periods. Among them, eight found in favor of democracy, eight in favor of authoritarianism, and five discovered no difference. What is even more puzzling is that among the 11 results published before 1988, eight found that authoritarian regimes grew faster, while none of the nine results published after 1987 supported this finding. And since this difference does not seem attributable to samples or periods, one can only wonder about the relation between statistics and ideology.[1]

For reasons discussed below, we hesitate to attach much significance to these results one way or another. Hence, we still do not know what the facts are.

Inferences Based on
Standard Regression Models Are Invalid

The reason social scientists have little robust statistical knowledge about the impact of regimes on growth is that the research design required to generate such knowledge is complex. This complexity is due to three sources: simultaneity, attrition, and selection.

Following the seminal work of Lipset (1960), there is an enormous body of theoretical and statistical literature to the effect that democracy is a product of economic development. This literature suffers from ambiguities of its own. While the belief is widespread that democracy requires as a "prerequisite" some level of economic development, there is much less agreement which aspects of development matter and why. Some think that a certain level of development is required for a stable democracy because affluence reduces the intensity of distributional conflicts; others because development generates the education or the communication networks required to support democratic institutions;

Table 30.1   Studies of Democracy, Autocracy, Bureaucracy, and Growth

Author	Sample	Time Frame	Finding
Przeworksi (1966)	57 countries	1949–1963	dictatorships at medium development level grew fastest
Adelman and Morris (1967)	74 underdeveloped countries (including communist bloc)	1950–1968	authoritarianism helped less and medium developed countries
Dick (1974)	59 underdeveloped countries	1959–1968	democracies develop slightly faster
Huntington and Dominguez (1975)	35 poor nations	the 1950s	authoritarian grew faster
Marsh (1979)	98 countries	1955–1970	authoritarian grew faster
Weede (1983)	124 countries	1960–1974	authoritarian grew faster
Kormendi and Meguire (1985)	47 countries	1950–1977	democracies grew faster
Kohli (1986)	10 underdeveloped countries	1960–1982	no difference in 1960s; authoritarian slightly better in 1970s
Landau (1986)	65 countries	1960–1980	authoritarian grew faster
Sloan and Tedin (1987)	20 Latin American countries	1960–1979	bureaucratic-authoritarian regimes do better than democracy; traditional dictatorships do worse
Marsh (1988)	47 countries	1965–1984	no difference between regimes
Pourgerami (1988)	92 countries	1965–1984	democracies grew faster
Scully (1988, 1992)	115 countries	1960–1980	democracies grew faster
Barro (1989)	72 countries	1960–1985	democracies grew faster
Grier and Tullock (1989)	59 countries	1961–1980	democracy better in Africa and Latin America; no regime difference in Asia
Remmer (1990)	11 Latin American countries	1982–1988 1982 and 1988	democracy faster, but result statistically insignificant
Pourgerami (1991)	106 less developed countries	1986	democracies grow slower
Helliwell (1992)	90 countries	1960–1985	democracy has a negative, but statistically insignificant effect on growth

still others because it swells the ranks of the middle class, facilitates the formation of a competent bureaucracy, and so on. Statistical results are somewhat mixed (Lipset 1960; Cutright 1963; Neubauer 1967; Smith 1969; Hannan and Carroll 1981; Bollen and Jackman 1985; Soares 1987; Arat 1988; Helliwell 1992). They suggest that the level of development, measured by a variety of indicators, is positively related to the incidence of democratic regimes in the population of world countries, but not necessarily within particular regions. Moreover, the exact form of the relationship and its relation to regime stability are left open to debate. Yet the prima facie evidence in support of this hypothesis is overwhelming: all developed countries in the world constitute stable democracies while stable democracies in the less developed countries remain exceptional.

Attrition is a more complicated issue. Following Lipset again, everyone seems to believe that durability of any regime depends on its economic performance. Economic crises are a threat to democracies as well as to dictatorships. The probability that a regime survives a crisis need not be the same, however, for democracies and dictatorships: one reason is that under democracy it is easier to change a government without changing the regime, another is that democracies derive legitimacy from more than their economic performance. We also have the argument by Olson (1963; also Huntington 1968) that rapid growth is destabilizing for democracies but not for dictatorships.

This evidence suffices to render suspect any study that does not treat regimes as endogenous. If democratic regimes are more likely to occur at a higher level of development or if democracies and dictatorships have a different chance of survival under various economic conditions, then regimes are endogenously selected. Since this is the heart of the statistical difficulties, we spell out the nature of this problem in some detail. (The following discussion draws on Przeworski and Limongi 1992.)

We want to know the impact of regimes on growth. Observing Brazil in 1988, we discover that it was a democracy which declined at the rate of 2.06 percent. Would it have grown had it been a dictatorship? The information we have, the observation of Brazil in 1988, does not answer this question. But unless we know what would have been the growth of Brazil in 1988 had it been a dictatorship, how can we tell if it would have grown faster or slower than under democracy?

Had we observed in 1988 a Brazil that was simultaneously a democracy and a dictatorship, we would have the answer. But this is not possible. There is still a way out: if the fact that Brazil was a democracy in 1988 had nothing to do with economic growth, we could look for some country that was exactly like Brazil in all respects other than its regime and, perhaps, its rate of growth, and we could match this country with Brazil. But if the selection of regimes shares some determinants with economic growth, an observation that matches Brazil in all respects other than the regime and the rate of growth will be hard to find. And then the comparative inferences will be biased: Whenever observations are not generated randomly, quasi-experimental approaches yield inconsistent and biased estimates of the effect of being in a particular state on outcomes. Indeed, this much is now standard statistical wisdom, as evidenced in the vast literature reviewed by Heckman (1990), Maddala (1983), and Greene (1990). Yet the implications of this failure are profound: we can no longer use the standard regression models to make valid inferences from the observed to the unobserved cases. Hence, we cannot compare.

The pitfalls involved in the studies summarized above can be demonstrated as follows. Averaging the rates of growth of ten South American countries between 1946 and 1988, one discovers that authoritarian regimes grew at the average rate of 2.15 percent per annum while democratic regimes grew at 1.31 percent. Hence, one is inclined to conclude that authoritarianism is better for growth than democracy. But suppose that in fact regimes have no effect on growth. However, regimes do differ in their probabilities of surviving various economic conditions: authoritarian regimes are less likely than democracies to survive when they perform badly. In addition, suppose that the probability of survival of both regimes depends on the number of other democracies in the region at each moment. These probabilities jointly describe how regimes are selected: the dependence of survival on growth constitutes endogenous selection, the diffusion effect represents exogenous selection.

In Przeworski and Limongi (1992), we used the observed regime-specific conditional survival probabilities to generate 5,000 (500 per country) 43-year histories obeying these assumptions, each beginning with the level and the regime observed in 1945. As one would expect, authoritarian regimes grew faster than democracies—indeed, we reproduced exactly the observed difference in growth rates—despite the fact that these data were generated under the assumption that regimes have no effect on growth. It is the difference in the way regimes are selected—the probabilities of survival conditional on growth—that generate the observed difference in growth rates. Hence, this difference is due entirely to selection bias.[2]

If one applies ordinary least squares to data generated in this way, with a dummy variable set to 1 for Authoritarianism and 0 for Democracy, the regime coefficient turns out to be positive and highly significant. Thus standard regression fails the same way as the comparison of means, even with controls. To correct for the effect of selection, we followed the procedure developed by Heckman (1978) and Lee (1978). Once we corrected the effects of selection, we generated the unbiased means for the two regimes and these, not surprisingly, reproduced the assumptions under which the data were generated: no difference in growth between the two regimes.

These methodological comments should end with a warning. Selection models turn out to be exceedingly sensitive: minor modifications of the equation that specifies how regimes survive can affect the signs in the equations that explain growth. Standard regression techniques yield biased (and inconsistent) inferences, but selection models are not robust (Greene 1990, 750; Stolzenberg and Relles 1990). While reverting to simulation provides at least the assurance that one does not attribute to regimes the effects they do not have, it may still fail to capture the effects they do exert.

Conclusions

The simple answer to the question with which we began is that we do not know whether democracy fosters or hinders economic growth.[3] All we can offer at this moment are some educated guesses.

First, it is worth noting that we know little about determinants of growth in general. The standard neoclassical theory of growth was intuitively unpersuasive and it implied that levels of development should converge: a prediction not born by the facts. The endogenous growth models are intuitively more appealing but empirically difficult to test since the "engine of growth" in these models consists, in Romer's (1992, 100) own words, of "ephemeral externalities." Statistical studies of growth notoriously explain little variance and are very sensitive to specification (Levine and Renelt 1991). And without a good economic model of growth, it is not surprising that the partial effect of politics is difficult to assess.

Secondly, there are lots of bits and pieces of evidence to the effect that politics in general does affect growth. At least everyone, governments and international lending institutions included, believes that policies affect growth and, in turn, scholars tend to think that politics affect policies. Reynolds (1983), having reviewed the historical experience of several countries, concluded that spurts of growth are often associated with major political transformations. Studies examining the impact of government spending on growth tend to find that the size of government is negatively related to growth, but the increase of government expenditures has a positive effect (Ram 1986; Lindauer and Velenchik 1992). Studies comparing the Far East with Latin America argue that there is something about the political institutions of the Asian countries which makes them propitious for growth. But while suggestive stories abound, there is little hard evidence.

Our own hunch is that politics does matter, but "regimes" do not capture the relevant differences. Postwar economic miracles include countries that had parliaments, parties, unions, and competitive elections, as well as countries run by military dictatorships. In turn, while Latin American democracies suffered economic disasters during the 1980s, the world is replete with authoritarian regimes that are dismal failures from the economic point of view.[4] Hence, it does not seem to be democracy or authoritarianism per se that makes the difference but something else.

What that something else might be is far from clear. "State autonomy" is one candidate, if we think that the state can be autonomous under democracy as well as under authoritarianism, as do Bardhan (1988, 1990) and Rodrik (1992). But this solution meets the horns of a dilemma: an autonomous state must be both effective at what it wants to do and insulated from pressures to do what it does not want to do. The heart of the neo-liberal research program is to find institutions that enable the state to do what it should but disable it from doing what it should not.

In our view, there are no such institutions to be found. In a Walrasian economy, the state has no positive role to play, so that the constitutional rule is simple: the less state, the better. But if the state has something to do, we would need institutions which enable the state to respond optimally to all contingent states of nature and yet prevent it from exercising discretion in the face of group pressures. Moreover, as Cui (1992) has argued, if markets are incomplete and information imperfect, the economy can function only if the state insures investors (limited liability), firms (bankruptcy), and depositors (two-tier banking system). But this kind of state involvement inevitably induces a soft-budget constraint. The state cannot simultaneously insure private agents and not pay the claims, even if they result from moral hazard.

Even if optimal rules do exist, pre-commitment is not a logically coherent solution. The reason is that just any commitment is not good enough: it must be a commitment to an optimal program. And advocates of commitment (like Shepsle 1989) do not consider the political process by which such commitments are established. After all, the same forces that push the state to suboptimal discretionary interventions also push the state to a suboptimal commitment. Assume that the government wants to follow an optimal program and it self-commits itself. At the present it does not want to respond to private pressures but it knows that in the future it would want to do so; hence, it disables its capacity to do it. The model underlying this argument is Elster's (1979) Ulysses.[5] But the analogy does not hold since Ulysses makes his decision *before* he hears the Sirens. Suppose that he has already heard them: why does he not respond to their song now and is afraid that he would respond later? If governments do bind themselves, it is already in response to the song of the Sirens and their pre-commitment will not be optimal.

Clearly, the impact of political regimes on growth is wide open for reflection and research.

Notes

1. Indeed, it is sufficient to read Scully (1992, xiii–xiv) to stop wondering: "The Anglo-American paradigm of free men and free markets unleashed human potential to an extent unparalled in history. . . . One needs evidence to persuade those who see promise in extensive government intervention in the economy. I have found such evidence, and the evidence is overwhelmingly in favor of the paradigm of classical liberalism." The evidence on the effect of democracy on growth consists of cross-sectional OLS regressions in which investment is controlled for, so that political effects measure efficiency but not the capacity to mobilize savings.

2. We could have gotten the same result in a different way. Suppose that (1) levels converge, that is, growth is a negative function of income, and (2) dictatorships occur at low levels while democracies are more frequent at high levels. Then we will observe fast growing dictatorships (at low levels) and slowly growing democracies (at high levels).

3. Note that we considered only indirect impacts of regimes on growth via investment and the size of the public sector, but we did not consider the impacts via income equality, technological change, human capital, or population growth.

4. As Sah (1991) has argued, authoritarian regimes exhibit a higher variance in economic performance than democracies: President Park of South Korea is now seen as a developmentalist leader, while President Mobutu of Zaire is seen as nothing but a thief (Evans 1989). But we have no theory that would tell us in advance which we are going to get. We do know, in turn, that until the early 1980s the democratic regimes which had encompassing, centralized unions combined with left-wing partisan control performed better on most economic variables than systems with either decentralized unions or right-wing partisan dominance.

5. Note that Elster (1989, 196) himself argues against the analogy of individual and collective commitment.

References

Adelman, Irma, and Cynthia Morris. 1967. *Society, Politics and Economic Development*. Baltimore: Johns Hopkins University Press.
Alesina, Alberto, and Dani Rodrik. 1991. "Distributive Politics and Economic Growth," National Bureau of Economic Research, Working Paper No. 3668.
Amsden, Alice H. 1989. *Asia's Next Giant: South Korea and Late Industrialization*. New York: Oxford University Press.

Arat, Zehra F. 1988. "Democracy and Economic Development: Modernization Theory Revisited," *Comparative Politics*, October, 21:1, 21–36.

Bardhan, Pranab. 1988. "Comment on Gustav Ranis' and John C. H. Fei's 'Development Economics: What Next?'" In Ranis, Gustav, and T. Paul Schultz, eds., *The State of Development Economics: Progress and Perspectives*. Oxford: Basil Blackwell, pp. 137–38.

Bardhan, Pranab. 1990. "Symposium on the State and Economic Development." *Journal of Economic Perspectives*, Summer, 4:3, 3–9.

Barro, Robert J. 1989. "A Cross-country Study of Growth, Saving, and Government," NBER Working Paper No. 2855.

Barro, Robert J. 1990. "Government Spending in a Simple Model of Endogenous Growth," *Journal of Political Economy*, October, 98:5, S103–S125.

Becker, Gary S. 1983. "A Theory of Competition Among Pressure Groups for Political Influence," *Quarterly Journal of Economics*, August, 98:3, 371–400.

Bollen, K. A., and R. W. Jackman. 1985. "Economic and Noneconomic Determinants of Political Democracy in the 1960s," *Research in Political Sociology*, 1, 27–48.

Collini, Stefan, Donald Winch, and John Burrow. 1983. *That Noble Science of Politics*. Cambridge: Cambridge University Press.

Crain, W. Mark. 1977. "On the Structure and Stability of Political Markets." *Journal of Political Economy*, August, 85:4, 829–42.

Cui, Zhiyuan. 1992. "Incomplete Markets and Constitutional Democracy," manuscript, University of Chicago.

Cutright, Philips. 1963. "National Political Development: Measurement and Analysis," *American Sociological Review*, 28, 253–64.

de Schweinitz, Karl Jr. 1959. "Industrialization, Labor Controls and Democracy," *Economic Development and Cultural Change*, July, 385–404.

de Schweinitz, Karl Jr. 1964. *Industrialization and Democracy*. New York: Free Press.

Dick, William G. 1974. "Authoritarian Versus Nonauthoritarian Approaches to Economic Development," *Journal of Political Economy*, July/August, 82:4, 817–27.

Dore, Ronald. 1978. "Scholars and Preachers." *IDS Bulletin*. Sussex, U.K.: International Development Studies, June.

Downs, Anthony. 1957. *An Economic Theory of Democracy*. New York: Harper and Row.

Elster, Jon. 1979. *Ulysses and the Sirens: Studies in Rationality and Irrationality*. Cambridge: Cambridge University Press.

Elster, Jon. 1989. *Solomanic Judgements. Studies in the Limitations of Rationality*. Cambridge: Cambridge University Press.

Elster, Jon, and Karl Ove Moene, eds. 1989. "Introduction." In *Alternatives to Capitalism*. Cambridge: Cambridge University Press, 1–38.

Evans, Peter B. 1989. "Predatory, Developmental, and Other Apparatuses: A Comparative Political Economy Perspective on the Third World State." *Sociological Forum*, December, 4:4, 561–87.

Fernandez, Raquel, and Dani Rodrick. 1991, "Resistance to Reform; Status Quo Bias in the Presence of Individual-Specific Uncertainty," *American Economic Review*, December, 81:5, 1146–55.

Findlay, Ronald. 1990. "The New Political Economy: Its Explanatory Power for the LDCS," *Economics and Politics*, July, 2:2, 193–221.

Galenson, Walter. 1959. "Introduction" to Galenson, W., ed. *Labor and Economic Development*. New York: Wiley.

Galenson, Walter, and Harvey Leibenstein. 1955. "Investment Criteria, Productivity and Economic Development," *Quarterly Journal of Economics*, August, 69, 343–70.

Gereffi, Gary, and Donald L. Wyman, eds. 1990. *Manufacturing Miracles: Paths of Industrialization in Africa and East Asia*. Princeton: Princeton University Press.

Greene, William H. 1990. *Econometric Analysis*. New York: Macmillan.

Grier, Kevin B., and Gordon Tullock. 1989. "An Empirical Analysis of Cross-national Economic Growth, 1951–80," *Journal of Monetary Economics*, September 1989, 24:2, 259–76.

Haggard, Stephan. 1990. *Pathways from Periphery: The Politics of Growth in the Newly Industrializing Countries*. Ithaca: Cornell University Press.

Hannan, M. T., and G. R. Carroll. 1981. "Dynamics of Formal Political Structure: An Event-History Analysis," *American Sociological Review*, February, 46:1, 19–35.

Heckman, James J. 1978. "Dummy Endogenous Variables in a Simultaneous Equation System," *Econometrica*, July, 46:4, 931–59.

Heckman, James J. 1990. "Selection Bias and Self-selection." In Eatwell, John, Murray Milgate, and Peter Newman, eds., *The New Palgrave Econometrics*. New York: W. W. Norton, 287–97.

Helliwell, John F. 1992. "Empirical Linkages Between Democracy and Economic Growth," NBER Working Paper #4066. Cambridge: National Bureau of Economic Research.

Huntington, Samuel P. 1968. *Political Order in Changing Societies*. New Haven: Yale University Press.

Huntington, Samuel P., and Jorge I. Dominguez. 1975. "Political Development." In Greenstein, F. I., and N. W. Polsby, eds. *Handbook of Political Science*, 3. Reading: Addison-Wesley, 1–114.

Kaldor, Nicolas. 1956. "Alternative Theories of Distribution," *Review of Economic Studies*, 23:2, 83–100.

Kohli, Atul. 1986. "Democracy and Development." In Lewis, John P., and Valeriana Kallab, eds. *Development Strategies Reconsidered*. New Brunswick: Transaction Books, 153–82.

Kormendi, Roger C., and Philip G. Meguire. 1983. "Macroeconomic Determinants of Growth: Cross-Country Evidence," *Journal of Monetary Economics*, September, 162: 141–63.

Landau, Daniel. 1986. "Government and Economic Growth in the Less Developed Countries: An Empirical Study for 1960–1980," *Economic Development and Cultural Change*, October, 35:1, 35–75.

Lee, L. F. 1978. "Unionism and Wage Rates: A Simultaneous Equations Model with Qualitative and Limited Dependent Variables," *International Economic Review*, June, 19:2, 415–33.

Levine, Ross, and David Renelt. 1991. "A Sensitivity Analysis of Cross-country Growth Regressions," World Bank Working Paper WPS 609.

Lindauer, David L., and Ann D. Velenchik. 1992. "Government Spending in

Developing Countries: Trends, Causes, and Consequences," *World Bank Research Observer,* January, 7:1. Washington, D.C.: The World Bank, 59–78.

Lipset, Seymour M. 1960. *Political Man.* Garden City: Doubleday, 1960.

Macaulay, Thomas B. 1900. *Complete Writings, 17.* Boston and New York: Houghton-Mifflin.

Maddala, G. S. 1983. *Limited-Dependent and Qualitative Variables in Econometrics.* Cambridge: Cambridge University Press.

Marsh, Robert M. 1979. "Does Democracy Hinder Economic Development in the Latecomer Developing Nations?" *Comparative Social Research,* 2:2, 215–48.

Marsh, Robert M. 1988. "Sociological Explanations of Economic Growth," *Studies in Comparative International Development,* Winter, 23:4, 41–76.

Marx, Karl. 1934. *The Eighteenth Brumaire of Louis Bonaparte.* Moscow: Progress Publishers.

Marx, Karl. 1952. *The Class Struggle in France, 1848 to 1850.* Moscow: Progress Publishers.

Marx, Karl. 1971. *Writings on the Paris Commune.* Edited by H. Draper. New York: International Publishers.

Neubauer, Deane E. 1967. "Some Conditions of Democracy," *American Political Science Review,* December, 61:4, 1002–9.

North, Douglass C. 1990. *Institutions, Institutional Change and Economic Performance.* Cambridge, U.K.: Cambridge University Press.

North, Douglass C., and Robert Paul Thomas. 1973. *The Rise of the Western World: A New Economic History.* Cambridge, U.K.: Cambridge University Press.

North, Douglass C., and Barry R. Weingast. 1989. "Constitutions and Commitment: The Evolution of Institutions Governing Public Choice in Seventeenth-Century England," *Journal of Economic History,* December, 49:4, 803–32.

O'Donnell, Guillermo. 1973. *Modernization and Bureaucratic-Authoritarianism.* Berkeley: UC Berkeley Press.

Olson, Mancur, Jr. 1963. "Rapid Growth as a Destabilizing Force," *Journal of Economic History,* December, 23, 529–52.

Olson, Mancur, Jr. 1991. "Autocracy, Democracy and Prosperity." In Zeckhauser, Richard J., ed., *Strategy and Choice.* Cambridge: MIT Press, 131–57.

Pasinetti, Luigi. 1961-62. "Rate of Profit and Income Distribution in Relation to the Race of Economic Growth," *Review of Economic Studies,* October, 29:81, 267–79.

Persson, Torsten, and Guido Tabellini. 19. "Is Inequality Harmful for Growth? Theory and Evidence." Working paper No. 91-155, Department of Economics, University of California, Berkeley, 1991.

Pourgerami, Abbas. 1988. "The Political Economy of Development: A Cross-national Causality Test of Development-Democracy-Growth Hypothesis," *Public Choice,* August, 58:2, 123–41.

Pourgerami, Abbas. 1991. "The Political Economy of Development: An Empirical Investigation of the Wealth Theory of Democracy," *Journal of Theoretical Politics,* April, 3:2, 189–211.

Przeworski, Adam. 1966. *Party Systems and Economic Development*. Ph.D. dissertation. Northwestern University.

Przeworski, Adam. 1990. *The State and the Economy Under Capitalism: Fundamentals of Pure and Applied Economics*, 40. Chur, Switzerland: Harwood Academic Publishers.

Przeworski, Adam, and Fernando Limongi. 1992. "Selection, Counterfactuals and Comparisons," manuscript, Department of Political Science, University of Chicago.

Przeworski, Adam, and Michael Wallerstein. 1988. "Structural Dependence of the State on Capital," *American Political Science Review*, March, 82:1, 11–29.

Ram, Rati. 1986. "Government Size and Economic Growth: A New Framework and Some Evidence from Cross-Section and Time-Series Data," *American Economic Review*, March, 76:1, 191–203.

Rao, Vaman. 1984. "Democracy and Economic Development," *Studies in Comparative International Development*, Winter 1984, 19:4, 67–81.

Remmer, Karen. 1990. "Democracy and Economic Crisis: The Latin American Experience," *World Politics*, April, 42:3, 315–35.

Reynolds, Lloyd G. 1983. "The Spread of Economic Growth to the Third World: 1850-1980," *Journal of Economic Literature*, September, 21:3, 941–80.

Rodrik, Dani. 1992. "Political Economy and Development Policy." *European Economic Review*, April, 36:2/3, 329–36.

Romer, Paul. 1992. "Increasing Returns and New Developments in the Theory of Growth." In Barnett, W. A., ed. *Equilibrium Theory and Applications*. New York: Cambridge University Press, 83–110.

Sah, Raaj K. 1991. "Fallibility in Human Organizations and Political Systems," *Journal of Economic Perspectives*, Spring 1991, 5:2, 67–88.

Schepsle, Kenneth. 1989. "Studying Institutions: Some Lessons from the Rational Choice Approach," *Journal of Theoretical Politics*, April, 1:2, 131–49.

Scully, Gerald W. 1988. "The Institutional Framework and Economic Development," *Journal of Political Economy*, June, 96:3, 652–62.

Scully, Gerald W. 1992. *Constitutional Environments and Economic Growth*. Princeton: Princeton University Press.

Sloan, John, and Kent L. Tedin. 1987. "The Consequences of Regimes Type for Public-Policy Outputs," *Comparative Political Studies*, April, 20:1, 98–124.

Smith, Arthur K. Jr. 1969. "Socio-economic Development and Political Democracy: A Causal Analysis," *Midwest Journal of Political Science*, 13: 95–125.

Soares, G. A. D. 1987. "Desenvolvimento Economico e Democracia na America Latina," *Dados*, 30:3, 253–74.

Stolzenberg, Ross M., and Daniel A. Relles. 1990. "Theory Testing in a World of Constrained Research Design," *Sociological Methods and Research*, May, 18:4, 395–415.

Wade, Robert. 1990. *Governing the Market: Economic Theory and the Role of Government in West Asian Industrialization*. Princeton: Princeton University Press, 1990.

Weede, Erich. 1983. "The Impact of Democracy on Economic Growth: Some Evidence from Cross-National Analysis," *Kyklos*, 36:1, 21–39.

Westphal, Larry E. 1990. "Industrial Policy in an Export-Propelled Economy: Lessons from South Korea's Experience," *Journal of Economic Perspectives*, Summer, 4:3, 41–60.

Wittman, Donald. 1989. "Why Democracies Produce Efficient Results," *Journal of Political Economy*, December, 97:6, 1395–1424.

World Bank. 1987. *World Development Report*. Washington, DC: The World Bank.

CHAPTER 31

Inequality as a Constraint on Growth in Latin America

NANCY BIRDSALL AND RICHARD SABOT

This chapter presents strong evidence that inequality and slow growth in the third world are not inevitable but are the direct outcome of choices made by governments. The chapter contrasts Latin America, where growth has been slow and inequality high, with East Asia, where growth has been extremely rapid and inequality very low. The empirical research on which the chapter is based demonstrates that large investments in education in East Asia help to explain a "virtuous circle" that leads to both higher growth and greater equality, whereas the low and stagnating investment in education in Latin America creates an opposite "vicious circle." Human capital investment is what sets East Asia apart from Latin America, a lesson many developing countries need to learn.

THE CONVENTIONAL WISDOM HAS BEEN THAT THERE IS A TRADEOFF between augmenting growth and reducing inequality, so that an unequal distribution of income is necessary for, or the likely consequence of, rapid economic growth. If this is so, however, why do we find in Latin America relatively low rates of economic growth and high inequality, and in East Asia low inequality and rapid growth? Figure 31.1 shows rates of GNP growth for the period 1965 to 1989 and levels of income inequality in the mid-1980s (measured by the ratio of the income shares of the top and bottom quintiles) for Latin American and East Asian countries. The difference between the two regions is striking: Latin American countries, concentrated in the southeast corner,

Reprinted from *Development Policy,* Inter-American Development Bank, vol. 3, no. 3 (September 1994): 1–5.

Figure 31.1   Income Inequality and Growth of GDP, 1965–1989

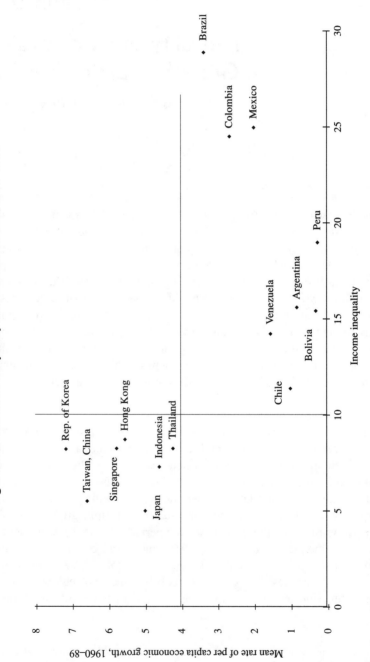

Source: World Bank, 1993. *The East Asian Miracle: Econmic Growth and Public Policy.*

experienced slow or negative growth with high inequality, while East Asian countries, concentrated in the northwest corner, achieved rapid growth with low inequality.

Differences in the political economy of the two regions may be part of the explanation. In the postwar period, governing elites in East Asia, their legitimacy threatened by domestic communist insurgents, sought to widen the base of their political support via policies such as land reform, public housing, investment in rural infrastructure, and, most common, widespread high-quality basic education. In Latin America governing elites appear to have believed they could thrive irrespective of what happened to those with the lowest incomes since tax, expenditure, and trade policies benefitted the poor relatively little. For example, East Asia's export oriented, labor-demanding development strategy contributed to rapid growth of output and, by increasing employment opportunities and wages, ensured that the benefits of that growth were widely shared. In contrast, Latin America's strategy tended to be biased against both agriculture and exports, resulting in relatively slow growth in the demand for labor. . . .

The association of slow growth and high inequality in Latin America could in part be due to the fact that high inequality itself may be a constraint on growth. Conversely, East Asia's low level of inequality may have been a significant stimulus to economic growth. If so, investment in education is a key to a sustained growth not only because it contributes directly through productivity effects, but also because it reduces income inequality.

Econometric Results

To assess the impact of the distribution of income on subsequent economic growth we regressed the growth rate of real per capita income of 74 developing countries over the period 1960–85 on determinants of growth such as per capita GDP and education enrollments at the start of the period and on a measure of income inequality, the ratio of the income shares of the top 40 percent and the bottom 20 percent. We found that inequality and growth are in fact inversely related: countries with higher inequality tend to have lower growth.

How big a constraint on growth is high inequality? It is substantial. The results suggest that ceteris paribus, after 25 years, GDP per capita would be 8.2 percent higher in a country with low inequality than in a country with inequality one standard deviation higher. How big was the constraint of high inequality in Latin America? The ratio of the income shares of the top 20 percent to the bottom 20 percent is 26 in Brazil and 8 in Korea. Simulations suggest that if, in 1960, Brazil had had Korea's lower level of inequality Brazil's predicted growth rate over the following 25 years would have been 0.66 percentage points higher each year. This implies that after 25 years GDP per capita in Brazil would have been 17.2 percent higher.

Poor Educational Performance, Slow Growth, and High Inequality in Latin America

Differences in educational performance help to explain why Latin America experienced relatively low rates of growth and high inequality while East Asia experienced high rates of growth and low inequality. Most countries in East Asia have significantly higher primary and secondary enrollment rates than predicted based on their per capita income; most Latin American countries have rates at or below those predicted. Moreover, where enrollment rates are low, as in Brazil and Guatemala, children of the poor are the least likely to be enrolled, perpetuating high income inequality.

Furthermore, in contrast to East Asia, where increases in quantity were associated with improvements in the quality of education, expansion of enrollments in many Latin American countries has resulted in the erosion of quality. In Brazil, the expansion of primary school coverage has been associated with declines in completion rates—probably a sign of failure to raise quality. By contrast, in East Asian countries, as quantity increased completion rates remained high. Declines in quality also tend to hurt the poor most, since they are least able to use private schools or change residence.

Education and Growth

Human capital theory says that education augments cognitive and other skills of individuals which, in turn, augment their productivity as workers. Our growth rate functions show that this accumulation of skills at the individual level translates into higher economic growth at the country level. Our statistical work also shows that increasing primary-school enrollments for girls, though they are less likely to become formal workers, is just as effective in stimulating growth as increasing primary enrollments for boys.

The reason: the economic payoff to educating girls is not confined to increases in the productivity of wage labor. It works through changes in behavior within households. For example, educated mothers have fewer children. Closing a virtuous circle, the fertility decline in East Asia that started in the mid-1960s resulted in a marked slowing of the growth of the school-age population in the 1970s. This made it easier to increase public expenditures on basic education per child, permitting rapid increases in the quantity of schooling as well as improvements in the quality of schools. . . .

Although fertility rates in Latin America have declined during the past two decades, they remain high relative to East Asian rates, particularly in the poorer countries. High fertility has placed added stress on already strained resources for education; per child spending on books, equipment, and teacher training in Latin America has declined. Declines in per-child spending in the region (from an estimated $164 per primary school child in 1980 to $118 in 1989) have probably contributed to declines in school quality and continued high repetition—the highest in the world—and high dropout rates. Between 1970 and 1990 expenditure on basic education per eligible child increased by 350 percent in Korea and 64 percent in Mexico. During the same period, the number of eligible children increased by 59 percent in Mexico, in Korea the number of eligible children actually declined by 27 percent. . . .

In addition, Latin America missed out on the positive feedback between rapid growth and household behavior with respect to human-capital accumulation. Investment in human capital by households is greater in East Asia than in Latin America in part because the demand for educated workers is greater, and consequently the returns to the household of investment in schooling are higher. In other words, stronger demand for educated workers elicits a greater supply. Furthermore, rapid economic growth in East Asia increased the numerator, while declining fertility reduced the denominator, of the ratio of public expenditures on basic education per school-age child. Neither in 1960 nor in 1989 was public expenditure on education as a percentage of GNP much higher in East Asia than in Latin America. However, it is obvious that the more rapid the growth of aggregate output, the more rapid the growth of the constant share of GDP that goes to education.

Education and Inequality

In Korea the proportion of high school and postsecondary graduates in the wage-labor force sharply increased between the mid-1970s and the mid-1980s, and the proportion of workers with elementary schooling or less declined to just 8 percent. As a consequence, the wage premium earned by educated workers in Korea declined. In Brazil the increment to the labor force of relatively well-educated workers was so small that it did not take much of an increase in the demand for educated workers to offset any wage compression effect of the increase in supply. As a result, the educational structure of wages barely changed in Brazil. What would the inequality of pay in Brazil have been had educational policy resulted in educational attainment comparable to that in Korea in the mid-1980s? Simulations indicate that Brazil would have had a log variance of wages in the mid-1980s some 17 percent lower than the actual. This 17 percent reduction represents over one-quarter of the gap between Brazil and Korea in the log variance of wages.

In Latin America there has also been a feedback effect, one that closed a vicious circle from high inequality to low enrollment rates. High income inequality limits household demand for education among the poor. Poor families may want to keep children in school, but they cannot afford to do so because they do not have money for school clothes or books or because they need children to work. Unable to borrow, poor households thus do not invest in their children's education even if they know that the benefits would be great. The pressing need to use income simply to subsist crowds out this high-return investment and reduces society's demand for education. High inequality makes this problem worse. For example, while the per capita income of Brazil (in 1983) slightly exceeded average income in Malaysia (in 1987) the bottom quintile received 4.6 percent of total income in Malaysia but only 2.4 percent of total income in Brazil. The per capita income of the poorest households in Brazil was thus only half the income of the poorest in Malaysia. Given an income elasticity of demand for basic education of 0.50 if the distribution of income were as equal in Brazil as in Malaysia, enrollments among poor Brazilian children would be more than 40 percent higher.

The Direct Effect of Inequality on Growth

Our results indicate that low inequality stimulates growth independent of its effects through education. However, using income transfers to reduce income inequality is unlikely to be good for growth: transfers often result in the diversion of scarce savings from investment to the subsidization of consumption; the targeted group is often not the one to benefit from transfers, reducing their effectiveness as a means of raising the standard of living, and hence the savings and investment rates, of the poor; transfers tend to distort incentives and reduce both allocative efficiency and X efficiency. But policies that increase the productivity and earning capacity of the poor may be quite a different matter.

Consider four ways in which low inequality can be a stimulus to growth:

- by inducing large increases in the savings and investments of the poor
- by contributing to political and macroeconomic stability—for example by reducing the tendency for fiscal prudence to be sacrificed to political expediency, by discouraging inappropriate exchange rate valuation, and by accelerating the adjustment to macroeconomic
- by increasing the "X-efficiency" of low-income workers, and
- by raising rural incomes, which limits intersectoral income gaps and the rent seeking associated with them, while increasing the domestic multiplier effects of a given increase in per capita income.

Conclusion

The contrasting experiences of Latin America and East Asia suggest that, contrary to conventional wisdom, inequalities in the distribution of both education and income may have a significant and negative impact on the rate of economic growth. The unequal distribution of education in Latin America, in terms of both quantity and quality, constrained economic growth in the region by forestalling opportunities to increase labor productivity and change household behavior. At the same time, the relatively small size of the educated labor force and high scarcity rents of the more educated contributed to high inequality in the distribution of income. Closing a vicious circle, slower growth and high income inequality, in turn, further limited the supply of, and demand for, education.

Education policy alone, however, does not explain the marked differences in equity and growth between Latin America and East Asia. Macroeconomic and sectoral policies in the former, which favored capital-intensive production and were biased against the agricultural sector, almost certainly exacerbated the inequality problem and have hindered growth as well. The East Asian development strategy promoted instead a dynamic agricultural sector and a labor-demanding, export-oriented growth path, thereby reducing inequality and stimulating growth. In

East Asia low inequality not only contributes to growth indirectly, for example, by increasing investment in education, but appears to have had a direct positive effect on the growth rate.

The experience of the two regions is sufficient to reject the conventional wisdom of a necessary link between high income inequality and rapid growth. While our analysis has not been sufficient to confirm the opposite, we hope others will now seriously consider the hypothesis that high inequality, and policies that ignore or even exacerbate inequality, constrain growth in the long run. The challenge in Latin America is to find ways to reduce inequality, not by transfers, but by eliminating consumption subsidies for the rich and increasing the productivity of the poor.

CHAPTER 32

The Myth of Asia's Miracle

PAUL KRUGMAN

The economic growth of the so-called "Asian Tigers" has been referred to as an economic miracle. Growth in that area of the world has been so spectacular that some authors point to the twenty-first century as being the "Asian century," and authors such as James Fallows argue that we ignore the lessons of the "Asian system" at our own peril. In this chapter, Paul Krugman cautions that development scholars may be reading too much into the Asian miracle and that we may be repeating a mistake of the past. Krugman argues that the Asian miracle is the result of an increase in investment and the education of workers in the Asian newly industrialized countries (NICs) and that the growth owes very little to increasing efficiency. This growth formula was not unlike that experienced in the Soviet Union. Whereas Krugman does not deny the improved economic conditions of the Asian NICs, he suggests that the "lessons" drawn from the Asian growth have been inaccurate.

C AN THERE REALLY BE ANY PARALLEL BETWEEN THE GROWTH OF WARSAW Pact nations in the 1950s and the spectacular Asian growth that now preoccupies policy intellectuals? At some levels, of course, the parallel is far-fetched: Singapore in the 1990s does not look much like the Soviet Union in the 1950s, and Singapore's Lee Kuan Yew bears little resemblance to the U.S.S.R.'s Nikita Khrushchev and less to Joseph Stalin. Yet the results of recent economic research into the sources of Pacific Rim growth give the few people who recall the great debate

Reprinted with permission from *Foreign Affairs,* vol. 73, no. 6. Copyright © 1994 by the Council on Foreign Relations, Inc.

over Soviet growth a strong sense of deja vu. Now, as then, the contrast between popular hype and realistic prospects, between conventional wisdom and hard numbers, remains so great that sensible economic analysis is not only widely ignored, but when it does get aired, it is usually dismissed as grossly implausible.

Popular enthusiasm about Asia's boom deserves to have some cold water thrown on it. Rapid Asian growth is less of a model for the West than many writers claim, and the future prospects for that growth are more limited than almost anyone now imagines. Any such assault on almost universally held beliefs must, of course, overcome a barrier of incredulity. This article began with a disguised account of the Soviet growth debate of 30 years ago to try to gain a hearing for the proposition that we may be revisiting an old error. We have been here before. The problem with this literary device, however, is that so few people now remember how impressive and terrifying the Soviet empire's economic performance once seemed. Before turning to Asian growth, then, it may be useful to review an important but largely forgotten piece of economic history.

"We Will Bury You"

Living in a world strewn with the wreckage of the Soviet empire, it is hard for most people to realize that there was a time when the Soviet economy, far from being a byword for the failure of socialism, was one of the wonders of the world—that when Khrushchev pounded his shoe on the U.N. podium and declared, "We will bury you," it was an economic rather than a military boast. It is therefore a shock to browse through, say, issues of *Foreign Affairs* from the mid-1950s through the early 1960s and discover that at least one article a year dealt with the implications of growing Soviet industrial might. . . .

Accounting for the Soviet Slowdown

When economists began to study the growth of the Soviet economy, they did so using the tools of growth accounting. Of course, Soviet data posed some problems. Not only was it hard to piece together usable estimates of output and input (Raymond Powell, a Yale professor, wrote that the job "in many ways resembled an archaeological dig"), but there were philosophical difficulties as well. In a socialist economy one could hardly measure capital input using market returns, so researchers were forced to impute returns based on those in market economies at similar levels of development. Still, when the efforts began, researchers were pretty sure about what they would find. Just as capitalist growth had been based on growth in both inputs and efficiency, with efficiency the main source of rising per capita income, they expected to find that rapid Soviet growth reflected both rapid input growth and rapid growth in efficiency.

But what they actually found was that Soviet growth was based on rapid growth in inputs—end of story. The rate of efficiency growth was not only unspectacular, it was well below the rates achieved in Western economies. Indeed, by some estimates, it was virtually nonexistent. . . .

Paper Tigers

At first, it is hard to see anything in common between the Asian success stories of recent years and the Soviet Union of three decades ago. Indeed, it is safe to say that the typical business traveler to, say, Singapore, ensconced in one of that city's gleaming hotels, never even thinks of any parallel to its roach-infested counterparts in Moscow. How can the slick exuberance of the Asian boom be compared with the Soviet Union's grim drive to industrialize?

And yet there are surprising similarities. The newly industrializing countries of Asia, like the Soviet Union of the 1950s, have achieved rapid growth in large part through an astonishing mobilization of resources. Once one accounts for the role of rapidly growing inputs in these countries' growth, one finds little left to explain. Asian growth, like that of the Soviet Union in its high-growth era, seems to be driven by extraordinary growth in inputs like labor and capital rather than by gains in efficiency.

Consider, in particular, the case of Singapore. Between 1966 and 1990, the Singaporean economy grew at a remarkable 8.5 percent per annum, three times as fast as the United States; per capita income grew at a 6.6 percent rate, roughly doubling every decade. This achievement seems to be a kind of economic miracle. But the miracle turns out to have been based on perspiration rather than inspiration: Singapore grew through a mobilization of resources that would have done Stalin proud. The employed share of the population surged from 27 to 51 percent. The educational standards of that work force were dramatically upgraded: while in 1966 more than half the workers had no formal education at all, by 1990 two-thirds had completed secondary education. Above all, the country had made an awesome investment in physical capital: investment as a share of output rose from 11 to more than 40 percent.

Even without going through the formal exercise of growth accounting, these numbers should make it obvious that Singapore's growth has been based largely on one-time changes in behavior that cannot be repeated. Over the past generation the percentage of people employed has almost doubled; it cannot double again. A half-educated work force has been replaced by one in which the bulk of workers has high school diplomas; it is unlikely that a generation from now most Singaporeans will have Ph.D.s. And an investment share of 40 percent is amazingly high by any standard; a share of 70 percent would be ridiculous. So one can immediately conclude that Singapore is unlikely to achieve future growth rates comparable to those of the past.

But it is only when one actually does the quantitative accounting that the astonishing result emerges: all of Singapore's growth can be explained by increases in measured inputs. There is no sign at all of increased efficiency. In this sense, the growth of Lee Kuan Yew's Singapore is an economic twin of the growth of Stalin's Soviet Union—growth achieved purely through mobilization of resources. Of course, Singapore today is far more prosperous than the U.S.S.R. ever was—even at its peak in the Brezhnev years—because Singapore is closer to, though still below, the efficiency of Western economies. The point, however, is that Singapore's economy has always been relatively efficient; it just used to be starved of capital and educated workers.

Singapore's case is admittedly the most extreme. Other rapidly growing East Asian economies have not increased their labor force participation as much, made such dramatic improvements in educational levels, or raised investment rates quite as far. Nonetheless, the basic conclusion is the same: there is startlingly little evidence of improvements in efficiency. Kim and Lau conclude of the four Asian "tigers" that "the hypothesis that there has been no technical progress during the postwar period cannot be rejected for the four East Asian newly industrialized countries." Young, more poetically, notes that once one allows for their rapid growth of inputs, the productivity performance of the "tigers" falls "from the heights of Olympus to the plains of Thessaly. . . ."

They Mystery That Wasn't

The extraordinary record of economic growth in the newly industrializing countries of East Asia has powerfully influenced the conventional wisdom about both economic policy and geopolitics. Many, perhaps most, writers on the global economy now take it for granted that the success of these economies demonstrates three propositions. First, there is a major diffusion of world technology in progress, and Western nations are losing their traditional advantage. Second, the world's economic center of gravity will inevitably shift to the Asian nations of the western Pacific. Third, in what is perhaps a minority view, Asian successes demonstrate the superiority of economies with fewer civil liberties and more planning than we in the West have been willing to accept.

All three conclusions are called into question by the simple observation that the remarkable record of East Asian growth has been matched by input growth so rapid that Asian economic growth, incredibly, ceases to be a mystery.

Consider first the assertion that the advanced countries are losing their technological advantage. A heavy majority of recent tracts on the world economy have taken it as self-evident that technology now increasingly flows across borders, and that newly industrializing nations are increasingly able to match the productivity of more established economies. Many writers warn that this diffusion of technology will place huge strains on Western society as capital flows to the Third World and imports from those nations undermine the West's industrial base.

There are severe conceptual problems with this scenario even if its initial premise is right. But in any case, while technology may have diffused within particular industries, the available evidence provides absolutely no justification for the view that overall world technological gaps are vanishing. On the contrary, Kim and Lau find "no apparent convergence between the technologies" of the newly industrialized nations and the established industrial powers; Young finds that the rates in the growth of efficiency in the East Asian "tigers" are no higher than those in many advanced nations.

The absence of any dramatic convergence in technology helps explain what would otherwise be a puzzle: in spite of a great deal of rhetoric about North-South capital movement, actual capital flows to developing countries in the 1990s have so far been very small—and they have primarily gone to Latin America, not East Asia. Indeed, several of the East Asian "tigers" have recently become significant exporters of capital. This behavior would be extremely odd if these economies, which still pay wages well below advanced-country levels, were rapidly achieving advanced-country productivity. It is, however, perfectly reasonable if growth in East Asia has been primarily input-driven, and if the capital piling up there is beginning to yield diminishing returns.

If growth in East Asia is indeed running into diminishing returns, however, the conventional wisdom about an Asian-centered world economy needs some rethinking. It would be a mistake to overstate this case: barring a catastrophic political upheaval, it is likely that growth in East Asia will continue to outpace growth in the West for the next decade and beyond. But it will not do so at the pace of recent years. From the perspective of the year 2010, current projections of Asian supremacy extrapolated from recent trends may well look almost as silly as 1960s-vintage forecasts of Soviet industrial supremacy did from the perspective of the Brezhnev years.

Finally, the realities of East Asian growth suggest that we may have to unlearn some popular lessons. It has become common to assert that East Asian economic success demonstrates the fallacy of our traditional laissez-faire approach to economic policy and that the growth of these economies shows the effectiveness of sophisticated industrial policies and selective protectionism. Authors such as James Fallows have asserted that the nations of that region have evolved a common "Asian system," whose lessons we ignore at our peril. The extremely diverse institutions and policies of the various newly industrialized Asian countries, let alone Japan, cannot really be called a common system. But in any case, if Asian success reflects the benefits of strategic trade and industrial policies, those benefits should surely be manifested in an unusual and impressive rate of growth in the efficiency of the economy. And there is no sign of such exceptional efficiency growth. . . .

PART 7

Conclusion

CHAPTER 33

Inequality in a Global Perspective: Directions for Further Research

MITCHELL A. SELIGSON

T HAT THERE IS A VAST GAP BETWEEN THE WORLD'S RICH AND ITS POOR IS beyond dispute. The causes and dynamics of the gap, however, are the subject of considerable debate, as the reader of this book will now know. Fortunately, debate over the gap differs considerably from the pattern normally encountered in the social sciences, debates that all too often do not lead to the development of a cumulative body of knowledge. Indeed, it can be said that research in this area represents one of the best illustrations of a cumulative social science continually deepening its understanding of a complex problem. In this concluding chapter I suggest some directions for future research so that continued rapid progress can be made in our understanding of the problem.

Evolution of Research on the Gaps

Once it became clear that the post–World War II hopes for rapid, universal development in the third world were not going to be fulfilled, social scientists set their minds to determining why that was the case. It was obvious, then as now, that unless development in the third world was to surge ahead, the gap between its economies and those of the increasingly prosperous developed countries would inevitably widen. The serious implications of this development for world peace are too great to be ignored.

Early thinking focused on the cultural distinctiveness of the third world. The observation that these cultures were indeed different from the industrial, capitalist development cultures found in the first world was enough to convince a generation of social scientists to view cultural barriers as the principal explanation for underdevelopment. Many of these explanations were intriguing, showed creative scholarship, and seemed to make a good deal of sense. As research proceeded, however, disenchantment with this perspective began to grow. The more that was known about the third world, the less cultural factors seemed to be able to explain its underdevelopment.

Many researchers found the explanation ethnocentric at best and insulting at worst. Studies also revealed many instances of a single "underdeveloped culture" producing vastly different developmental outcomes; wide variation was observed within supposedly monolithic cultures. In addition, people showed themselves to be highly capable of tailoring their cultures to conform to more "modern" ways of doing things. Cultures proved to be far more malleable and responsive than had been originally believed. Finally, despite putative cultural limitations, some third world nations made rapid strides in economic growth, and some middle-income countries, moreover, have in recent years been able to achieve higher growth rates than many industrialized countries.

Yet since the 1990s the debate on the impact of culture on development has resurfaced, and the empirical research reported in this volume in Chapter 19 shows that values might matter. This entire paradigm of thinking is reflected by Francis Fukuyama (1995a, 1995b), who has argued for the importance of trust in development. Also, Lawrence Harrison and Samuel P. Huntington (2002) have edited a book called *Culture Matters: How Values Shape Human Progress,* which collects a great deal of scholarship on this point. The debate has become more technical as a series of quantitative studies have attempted to reinvigorate the study of culture (Inglehart 1988, 1990), and other studies that have challenged this approach (Booth and Seligson 1984; Seligson and Booth 1993). One empirical study on the subject is included in this volume in Chapter 19, but that research, by Ronald Inglehart and his collaborators, has been strongly refuted by Robert Jackman and Ross Miller (1996b), and the entire approach has been criticized by the author of this chapter (Seligson 2002).

Whatever their power, cultural explanations no longer dominate the field, and as a result, other theories have emerged. Increasingly, thinking about development has become "globalized." The very nature of the gap problem probably forced such thinking to emerge. After all, in order to study the gap one must first specify the frame of reference in a comparative perspective. Studies can focus on the absolute or relative gap, but these terms have no meaning unless they are situated within a comparative framework; poor people are poor only with respect to rich people.

In this book extensive consideration has been given to the "inverted-

U curve" of development. In global terms, according to Simon Kuznets (Chapter 6) and other proponents of this thesis, developing nations are likely to experience a widening internal gap before they see the gap narrow in the later phases of industrialization. Dependency and world-system thinkers agree that the gaps are widening but do not believe that they will ultimately narrow as industrialization matures because both the widening internal and the widening external gaps between rich and poor are seen as a function of the world capitalist economic system.

The studies by Angus Maddison (Chapter 2) and by John Passé-Smith (Chapter 3) suggest strongly that the gaps are very wide and widening with each passing decade. Yet the controversy presented in Part 3, between those who argue that the economies of the world are on a path toward convergence and those who argue that the gaps are widening, shows that the issue has still not been resolved.

This disagreement has led some to examine more closely key cases of dependency and development. Chapter 21, by Heather-Jo Hammer and John W. Gartrell, shows that dependency is not confined to poor nations but seems to affect Canada as well, while Chapter 22 by Denis O'Hearn demonstrates its impact on Ireland. Yet the masterful analysis by Glenn Firebaugh (Chapter 23) shows that much of the slowed growth reportedly caused by dependency (Chapter 20) comes from a serious misreading of the data. Jeffrey Kentor (Chapter 24), however, disputes those conclusions and Arthur Alderson and François Nielsen (Chapter 25) find that dependency increases domestic income inequality. Like the culture paradigm before it, dependency and world-systems thinking no longer seem to offer the sole explanation for the gaps between rich and poor.

Considerable attention is focused on the role of the state, and some of the key thinking in that area is contained in the contributions in Part 6. Mancur Olson's (Chapter 26) careful comparison of cases such as North and South Korea—in which culture, history, and resources are largely held constant and what varies is the political system and the policies leaders make—presents a strong case that countries are not prisoners of their pasts or their environments but can make good or bad choices. Some states choose a capitalist route, but then engage in "rent-seeking" behavior that enables privileged groups to benefit from state policies, while producing an overall negative impact on the national level of economic development. Michael Lipton (Chapter 29) shows how rent seeking has a pernicious impact on development.

Rent-seeking states, therefore, seem bad for economic growth. At the same time, however, whether a state has a democratic or an authoritarian regime seems to make little difference in growth. For a long time it was thought that dictatorships do better than democracies, which allowed such highly regarded scholars as Samuel P. Huntington to suggest that in order to achieve development a state must pass through a protected period of strongman rule. Yet, as Adam Przeworski and Fernando Limongi show in Chapter 30, dictatorships seem no better at stimulating economic development than democracies. Indeed, in other work by this team, it has been shown that democracies do better on a per capita basis than dictatorships, and Erich Weede has found that democracies produce more stable growth than dictatorships. For a time it appeared the Asian newly industrialized countries (NICs) were demonstrating that interventionist, export-oriented states that promoted state capitalism were more successful at both growth and distribution. But the evidence presented by Paul Krugman (Chapter 32) shows that this is probably not the case. What does seem to be true, however, is that investment in human capital in the form of education and health really does spur growth and stem inequality (see Nancy Birdsall and Richard Sabot, Chapter 31).

Considerable data have been brought to bear on the various theories seeking to explain these dual gaps. It is in the analysis and interpretation of this data that we see the clearest example of cumulative social science in the making. This book presents some of the best examples of rigorous testing of theory with data. While it is too early to predict a definitive resolution of the debates, and it may be even too early to say which side seems to have the edge, it is possible to look ahead and suggest some directions for future research. A pessimistic interpretation of the present state of the debate is that each side is locked into its own respective positions and that future research will be stalemated. The vital importance of the problem of inequality, not only to the world's poor but also to those responsible for helping to secure peace, requires that such a stalemate be avoided. It is therefore appropriate to assess the directions in which fruitful further research might proceed.

The International Gap

By the early 1980s, in terms of gross national product per capita (GNP/pc), a small group of oil-exporting nations enjoyed incomes higher than the average income found among industrial market economies. In 1981, Saudi Arabia had a GNP/pc of $12,600; Kuwait, $20,900; and the United Arab Emirates, $24,660; while the mean income of the industrial market economies was $11,120. None of the industrialized countries came even close to exceeding the income of Kuwait and the

United Arab Emirates; Switzerland had $17,430, the highest GNP/pc of the industrial countries. The United States, traditionally the world's GNP/pc leader, was far behind at $12,820. Oil-rich Libya was moving up rapidly, with its GNP/pc reaching $8,450, only slightly behind that of the United Kingdom ($9,110).

Yet we now know that much of the dramatic increase in the GNP of the oil states was a short-term phenomenon owing to the sharp price rises of petroleum in the 1970s. By 2001, the World Bank (2003: 234–235) was reporting that Saudi Arabia had income per capita of only $7,230, compared to the United States with $34,870. Kuwait, still recovering from the Gulf War, had declined to a GNP of $18,030.

The rapid growth and equally rapid decline of the oil states, however, is the exception to the rule. As John Passé-Smith has shown in Chapter 3, there is very little movement over the long term, from rich to poor and vice-versa. While South Korea, Taiwan, and Malaysia have been growing rapidly, they have incomes that are only a fraction of those found in the industrialized countries. Consider China, which has had very strong growth for over ten years; the per capita income there was only $890 in 2001. In GNP/pc terms, it seems clear, there is a near-universal widening gap between rich and poor.

This conclusion, however, is based on a single indicator, GNP/pc, recently renamed gross national income (GNI) by the World Bank. The use of a single indicator for any social phenomenon has long fallen into disrepute in the social sciences. Why then base conclusions about such an important subject entirely on per capita income data? The response from those who use it in their research as a sole indicator of income is that it is by far the most widely accepted indicator. The principal problem emerges not because of the unreliability of data collected on each nation but because of validity problems associated with converting local currency values into dollars using exchange rates, the standard currency normally employed by those who compare such data.

In order to convert the multitude of currencies used around the world into a single standard, it has long been common practice to use the exchange rate of the foreign currency in U.S. dollars. The exchange rate appeared for a long time to be the only reasonable way to compare the value of different currencies. In fact, however, it is now known that such comparisons introduce considerable distortion in the data. The exchange rate comparisons do not accurately measure differences in the relative domestic purchasing power of currencies. The net result is that the exchange-rate GNP measures can greatly exaggerate the gap between rich and poor countries. This exaggeration occurs in part because international exchange rates are susceptible to fluctuations from equilibrium value. In addition, according to the "law of one price," the cost of goods and services that are traded (among countries) tend to equalize. For a developing country in which most of the production does not enter the world trade market, the exchange rate–converted GNP figures will be an underestimate of true income.

In order to correct for this bias, the United Nations has undertaken the International Comparisons Project, which has provided some revealing findings. Using purchasing power parity (PPP) rather than exchange rates, Passé-Smith (Chapter 5) finds that the gap is less expansive than it is when measured with exchange rate–converted GNP, but it is still considerable. For some countries the change was large; for example, Sri Lanka exhibits a gap nearly four times as large when the traditional measure is used as when the new, purchasing power index is computed. Colombia and Mexico also reveal considerable differences, although these differences are not as great as in Sri Lanka. Because of these shifts, the appendix of this book provides PPP figures as well as GNI figures.

It would seem appropriate to suggest that future research on the international gap employ the purchasing power index rather than the exchange rate–based comparison in order to obtain a truer picture of income comparisons (as Firebaugh does in Chapter 23). When measured with purchasing power–converted GNPs, the gap remains, although it is slightly smaller overall. Hence, despite the dramatic narrowing of the international gap in the case of Sri Lanka, as noted above, even using the purchasing power index that country's income per capita in 2001 was only 10.2 percent of that of the United States. Kenya, in which the GNP/pc is more than quadrupled with the new index, still confronts income levels that are only 2.9 percent of those of the United States (World Bank 2003: 234–235). The revised measure, therefore, does not eliminate the gap between rich and poor. It does, however, provide what appears to be a more appropriate standard of comparison. The mere fact that the gap narrows through the use of the new index does not necessarily imply that there is an overall trend toward a narrowing of the international gap. Fortunately, the World Bank now annually reports these purchasing power parity measures in its annual *World Development Report.*

Another way of looking at the gap question is to shift the focus away from per capita income measures and to look at human needs and human development instead. Using these criteria, one obtains a rather different perspective on the international gap question. According to studies conducted by the World Bank, major strides have been made in the reduction of absolute poverty since the close of World War II (1980:

32–45). These studies have found that the proportion of people around the world living in absolute poverty has declined. In addition, there has been a worldwide increase in literacy levels such that over the past 30 years literacy in low-income countries has increased from 30 percent to 63 percent of the population. Even more dramatic improvements have been experienced in the area of health. Infant mortality rates have dropped considerably and life expectancy has been extended. For example, citizens of low-income countries in 1950 had a life expectancy of only 35.2 years, whereas by 2001 that had risen to 59 years (World Bank 1980: 34; 2003: 235). The World Bank stated that "the gaps in education and health have narrowed—by 15 percentage points in adult literacy and five years in life expectancy" between the industrial countries and the middle-income countries (1980: 35).

Research more consciously directed at these indicators of basic human needs may provide a clearer picture of the impact of the gap than that presented by income figures alone. But before one leaps to the conclusion that the human needs approach can demonstrate that the gap is narrowing, some additional context needs to be added to the discussion. While it is true that the *proportion* of people who are experiencing improved education, health, and life expectancy has increased, the absolute number of poor people in the world has increased dramatically because of high birth rates in the developing world. Hence, the World Bank estimated that despite the increases in the levels of literacy, the number of illiterate people had grown by some 100 million since 1950 (1980: 35). And by 1995, in the low-income countries of the world alone, the number of illiterate adults had grown to 1.1 billion compared to 800 million in 1980 (World Bank 1980: 110; 1995: 214). Moreover, there is increasing evidence that the quality of education in much of the developing world outside of East Asia lags far behind that found in the industrialized countries. The quality gap is especially acute in secondary and higher education, where technical advances are so very rapid and the cost of obtaining modern training equipment ever more expensive. It is increasingly difficult for developing countries to train their young people adequately for the skills they need to compete in the high-technology world.

The education gap has two particularly pernicious implications. First, the increasing frustration that the brightest youngsters face in developing countries as a result of antiquated equipment and poorly prepared teachers results in an increasing tendency for them to migrate to the industrialized nations. Hence, the problem of the "brain drain" is a growing one, which promises to continue to adversely affect the ability of poor nations to develop, as they steadily lose that sector of their population with the greatest intellectual potential. Second, the high-technology nature of contemporary society seems to be creating a higher and more impenetrable barrier between rich and poor countries. The efficiency of modern manufacturing techniques along with increasing requirements for exceptional precision make it more and more difficult for developing nations to compete with the industrialized nations. The price advantage that developing nations have as a result of their considerably lower labor costs remains an advantage only for those items that require relatively low technical inputs. Hence, the proliferation of in-bond industries (i.e., "maquiladoras") in the Far East and Latin America, where consumer goods are assembled for re-export, only highlights the technology gap, as nearly all of the machinery and a good deal of the managerial skill used in those factories are imported from the industrialized nations. Even without tariff barriers, the third world faces a growing gap in technology, which is serving to reinforce the income gap.

In sum, the use of improved income measures and basic needs data provides important avenues of research for those who wish to study the international income gap. A look at some of these data gives reason for optimism that conditions in poor countries are improving. At the same time, however, there is little reason to believe that the international income gap is narrowing. In fact, it would appear that each passing day finds the world inhabited by a larger *number* of people who live in absolute poverty, even though the *proportion* of the world's population in absolute poverty may be declining. This gap, then, seems to remain the single most serious problem confronting the family of nations, and one that cries out for the attention of policymakers.

The Internal Gap

However problematical the reliability, validity, and availability of data on the international gap, they present an even more formidable barrier to the study of the internal gap. The empirical testing of dependency/world-system explanations for the internal gap has produced widely varying results. Any reader of the major social science journals today would be rightly confused by the varied findings reported in the ever more frequently appearing articles on this subject. In reviewing this growing body of research, Edward N. Muller (1993) has pointed out a number of the weaknesses of those articles, and he goes a long way toward correcting many of them. Nonetheless, there are at least four chronic problems that beset macrolevel empirical tests of internal gap theories and that may ultimately lead down a blind alley of inconclusive findings even after the "best" methodology has been applied.

The first difficulty plaguing these macroanalytic investigations concerns sample skewing. Inequality data are difficult to obtain because many nations do not collect them (or at least do not publicly acknowledge that they do), a problem noted in several of the chapters included in this volume. In spite of the availability problem, researchers have proceeded with the data that are available, following the time-honored tradition in the social sciences of making do with what one finds rather than postponing research indefinitely. While such a procedure is often justifiable in many research situations, one wonders if it is justifiable in this one. The principal reason for sounding this cautionary note is that it is probably not the case that the countries reporting income distribution data are a random sample of all nations. Rather, one suspects that there are at least two factors that tend to skew the sample. First, the poorest, least developed nations often do not have the resources (financial and technical) to conduct such studies, and indeed there may not even arise the need for such data to be collected in some of these nations. Second, nations in which the income distributions are very badly skewed are probably reluctant to authorize the collection of such data, and even if the data are collected, governments may not make them publicly available. Hence, the data we do have may reflect a sample that has fewer cases of the poorest nations and fewer cases of highly unequal distribution than one might expect if the sample were random.

The second major problem with macroanalytic investigations is a direct outgrowth of the first. I call this problem the Mauritania effect, that is, the dramatic differences in regression results that are produced from the inclusion or exclusion of as few as one or two countries. In one investigation, for example, the inclusion of Mauritania, with a population of only 2.8 million people, had a major impact on the results of a key regression equation. The findings tend not to be robust when minor variations in sample design occur; one's confidence in the results, therefore, is shaken. "It seems impossible to predict with any confidence what would happen if inequality data on all or about twice as many countries were to become available" (Weede and Tiefenbach, 1981).

The third problem concerns the general lack of cross-time data. However limited the sample of countries may be for the present period, even less reliable information exists on developing countries for the pre–World War II period. This is a particularly serious problem because both dependency/world-system analysis and the traditional developmental approach propose longitudinal hypotheses, whereas data limitations generally impose cross-sectional designs. While such cross-sectional designs can sometimes be a useful surrogate for longitudinal studies, the problem of skewed samples reduces the value of these studies.

One serious manifestation of the lack of longitudinal data emerges in studies that include Latin American cases. As a region, Latin America is more developed than most of the third world and, not surprisingly, has somewhat more income distribution data available. Latin American nations have also been found to exhibit comparatively high levels of both dependency and income inequality. One might leap to the conclusion, as some have, that this proves that inequality is a function of dependency. However, there is another equally appealing thesis, which suggests that inequality in Latin America is part of a corporatist bureaucratic/authoritarian political culture considered to be characteristic of the region. It is uncertain, therefore, if Latin America's comparatively high level of inequality is a function of its intermediate level of development (as Kuznets, Chapter 6, would suggest), or its dependency (as the dependency/world-system proponents would suggest, Chapters 20–25), or its political culture (Chapters 16–19). To determine which hypothesis is correct would require longitudinal data to explore the dynamics of dependency, development, and inequality.

A final difficulty with the macroanalytic research is that there is no meeting of the minds as to suitable standards of verifiability. For example, there is a wide gulf separating many dependency/world-system theorists on the one hand, and those researchers who seek to test their hypotheses with quantitative data on the other. F. H. Cardoso and E. Faletto (1979), whose book on dependency theory is among the most influential works on the subject (see Packenham 1982: 131–132), argue that empirical tests of dependency theory have largely missed the target. Cardoso (1977: 23, n. 12) explains that this is so because the tests have been "ahistorical." In addition, although not rejecting empirical verification as useful, he questions the validity of many of these studies, even those sustaining the dependency approach. Finally, in the preface to the English edition of their book, Cardoso and Faletto argue that "statistical information and demonstrations are useful and necessary. But the crucial questions for demonstration are of a different nature" (1979: xiii). The thrust of the demonstrations proposed are ones heavily grounded in historical detail and therefore highlight all the more the problem of the lack of longitudinal income distribution data.

In the coming years, it is likely that many more macroanalytic empirical investigations will be published and will continue to add to our understanding. However, it is difficult to imagine how the four major problems enumerated above will be overcome entirely. Given the difficulties apparently inherent (to a greater or lesser degree) in the macroanalytic studies conducted to date, more attention needs to be paid to methodologies that will examine from a microanalytic perspective the question of the origin of domestic inequality. In concluding an extensive review of the dependency/world-system literature, Gabriel Palma argues for microstudies of "specific situations in concrete terms" (1981: 413). V. Bornschier, C. Chase-Dunn, and Richard Rubinson conclude by arguing for microsociological studies that would "clarify the specific mechanisms by which these processes operate" (1978)

Problems of data availability need not cause the abandonment of future studies of the internal gap. Rather, a series of microanalytic studies would seem like a promising alternative. Such investigations would make it possible to trace the ways inequality is stimulated in developing countries. The emphasis needs to be placed on drawing explicit links, if they exist, between income distribution and factors such as culture, dependency, rent-seeking, and urban bias. Indeed, even if the data problems were not as serious as they in fact are, and if macroanalytic empirical research were to demonstrate unequivocally the existence of a connection between, for example, culture and domestic inequality, one would still need to understand *how* one affects the other, something that cannot be known from the macrostudies. Without knowing how the process works, it is not possible to recommend policy "cures."

Some research has already been published that opens the door to this type of analysis. Studies of transnational corporations in Colombia (Chudnowsky 1974) and Brazil (Evans 1979; Newfarmer 1980) reveal much about the internal dynamics of dependency. Another microstudy, however, has demonstrated that imperialist penetration in one African state, Yorubaland, at the end of the nineteenth century, produced a "vibrant and creative" reaction on the part of Yoruba traders in response to new opportunities in the international market (Laitin 1982: 702).

These microanalytic studies, helpful though they are in beginning to penetrate the "black box," reflect weaknesses that would need to be overcome by those seeking to test the various explanations of income inequality proposed in this volume. First, these detailed case studies, while providing a wealth of rich, descriptive material, betray all of the limitations of generalizability inherent in the case study method. It is to be hoped, of course, that the accumulation of these various cases ultimately will lead to a synthesis, but given the widely divergent methods, time periods, and data bases employed in these studies, it is unclear at this juncture if such optimism is warranted. What is clear is that if a cumulative social science is to continue to emerge in this field, future research will need to be not only microanalytic but self-consciously comparative as well. Only by applying the comparative method at the outset of a study of the internal causes of inequality will the data generated allow immediate comparisons and subsequent theory testing.

In sum, an appropriate study ought to be (1) microanalytic, (2) comparative, and (3) capable of testing the relative merits of competing paradigms. That certainly is a tall order for any researcher, but one way to achieve this goal and still plan a project of manageable proportions is to focus on key institutions through which dependency mechanisms are thought to operate. In an effort to accomplish this task, one study analyzed exchange rate policies as the "linch-pin" that helps "uncover the mechanisms through which these various [dependency] effects occur" (Moon 1982: 716). A major advance of this study over previous work is its explicit linking of dependency effects to particular policies of third world governments. Hence, the analysis goes far beyond most dependency literature, which typically makes frequent reference to the so-called internal colonialist *comprador* elite without revealing precisely how such elites affect income distribution. Such studies, which examine the impact of other such crucial "linch-pins" through which dependency is thought to operate, are to be encouraged.

Two efforts, therefore, need to be made if one is to hope for the advancement of the debate beyond its present state. First, historians need to assist those working in this field to develop measures of income distribution for prior epochs. Creative use of historical records (e.g., tax roles, property registers, census data, etc.) might permit the reconstruction of such information. This, in turn, would provide the longitudinal data so sadly lacking at this time. John H. Coatsworth (1993) has already done precisely this for Latin America, and the payoffs of his approach are evident, as he seems to have been able to refute dependency theory and make a case for the role of institutions on development and underdevelopment. William Glade (1996) has recently extended this argument. Second, once the historical data have been gathered, social scientists need to direct their attention to the various linch-pins of the causes of growth and inequality and study them in a comparative context. Perhaps with these two efforts under way, significant advances are possible in a relatively short period of time.

Conclusion

The research offered here was not written in a vacuum. Investigators study problems such as the gap between rich and poor because they are concerned; and the great majority of them hope that their findings ultimately will be translated into public policy. Even though definitive findings are still far from our grasp, as has been made clear by the debate presented in this volume, many world leaders already have sought to implement policies to correct the problem.

As the gaps between rich and poor grow wider throughout the world, the debate grows more heated. Discussions in international forums are characterized by increasing intolerance. It is hoped that this collection of studies along with the suggestions made in this concluding chapter will help, in some small way, to moderate tempers and guide thinking and research toward more productive answers to this important question.

References

Biel, R. 2000. *The New Imperialism: Crisis and Contradictions in North-South Relations.* London: Zed Books.

Booth, J. A., and M. A. Seligson. 1984. "The Political Culture of Authoritarianism in Mexico: A Reexamination." *Latin American Research Review,* no. 1: 106–124.

Bornschier, V., C. Chase-Dunn, and R. Rubinson. 1978. "Cross-National Evidence of the Effects of Foreign Investment and Aid on Economic Growth and Inequality: A Survey of Findings and a Reanalysis." *American Journal of Sociology* 84 (November).

Cardoso, F. H. 1977. "The Consumption of Dependency Theory in the United States." *Latin American Research Review* 12, no. 3: 7–24.

Cardoso, F. H., and E. Faletto. 1979. *Dependency and Development in Latin America.* Berkeley: University of California Press.

Chudnowsky, D. 1974. *Empresas multinacionales y ganancias monopolicias en una economía latinoamericana.* Buenos Aires: Siglo XXI Editores.

Coatsworth, J. H. 1993. "Notes on the Comparative Economic History of Latin America and the United States." In W. L. Bernecker and H. W. Tobler, eds., *Development and Underdevelopment in America: Contrasts of Economic Growth in North and Latin America in Historical Perspective.* Berlin and New York: Walter de Gruyter.

Collier, D., ed. 1979. *The New Authoritarianism in Latin America.* Princeton: Princeton University Press.

Evans, P. 1979. *Dependent Development: The Alliance of Multinational, State, and Local Capital in Brazil.* Princeton: Princeton University Press.

Fukuyama, F. 1995a. "Social Capital and the Global Economy." *Foreign Affairs* 74 (September/October): 89–103.

————. 1995b. *Trust: The Social Virtues and the Creation of Prosperity.* New York: The Free Press.

Glade, W. 1996. "Institutions and Inequality in Latin America: Text and Subtext." *Journal of Interamerican Studies and World Affairs* 38 (Summer/Fall): 159–179.

Harrison, L. E., and S. P. Huntington. 2002. *Culture Matters: How Values Shape Human Progress.* New York: Basic Books.

Hoogvelt, A. 2001. *Globalization and the Postcolonial World.* 2d ed. Baltimore: Johns Hopkins University Press.

Inglehart, R. 1988. "The Renaissance of Political Culture." *American Political Science Review* 82 (December): 1203–1230.

————. 1990. *Culture Shift in Advanced Industrial Societies.* Princeton: Princeton University Press.

Jackman, R. W. 1982. "Dependency on Foreign Investment and Economic Growth in the Third World." *World Politics* 34 (January): 175–197.

Jackman, R. W., and R. A. Miller. 1996a. "The Poverty of Political Culture." *American Journal of Political Science* 40, no. 3: 697–717.

————. 1996b. "A Renaissance of Political Culture?" *American Journal of Political Science* 40, no. 3: 632–659.

Kravis, I., et al. 1975. *A System of International Comparisons of Gross Product and Purchasing Power.* Baltimore: Johns Hopkins University Press.

————. 1982. *World Product and Income: International Comparisons of Real GDP.* Baltimore: Johns Hopkins University Press.

Laitin, D. D. 1982. "Capitalism and Hegemony: Yorubaland and the International Economy." *International Organization* 36 (Autumn): 687–714.

Moon, B. E. 1982. "Exchange Rate System, Policy Distortions, and the Maintenance of Trade Dependence." *International Organization* 36 (Autumn): 715–740.

Muller, E. N. 1993. "Financial Dependence in the Capitalist World Economy and the Distribution of Income Within States." In M. A. Seligson and J. T Passé-Smith, *Development and Underdevelopment: The Political Economy of Inequality.* Boulder: Lynne Rienner.

Newfarmer, R. 1980. *Transnational Conglomerates and the Economics of Dependent Development: A Case Study of the International Electrical Oligopoly and Brazil's Electrical Industry.* Greenwich, Conn.: JAI Press.

O'Donnell, G. 1973. *Modernization and Bureaucratic Authoritarianism: Studies in South American Politics.* Politics of Modernization Series, no. 9. Berkeley: Institute of International Studies of the University of California.

Packenham, R. A. 1982. "Plus ça change . . . : The English Edition of Cardoso and Faletto's *Dependencia y Desarrollo en América Latina.*" *Latin American Research Review* 17, no. 1: 131–151.

Palma, G. 1981. "Dependency: A Formal Theory of Underdevelopment or a Methodology for the Analysis of Concrete Situations?" In P. Streetin and R. Jolly, eds., *Recent Issues in World Development.* New York: Pergamon.

Ray, J. L., and T. Webster. 1978. "Dependency and Economic Growth in Latin America." *International Studies Quarterly* 22 (September): 409–434.

Seligson, M. A. 2002. "The Renaissance of Political Culture or the Renaissance of Ecological Fallacy?" *Comparative Politics* 34: 273–292.

Seligson, M. A., and J.A. Booth. 1993. "Political Culture and Regime Type: Evidence from Nicaragua and Costa Rica." *Journal of Politics* 55 (August): 777–792.

Weede, E., and H. Tiefenbach. 1981. "Some Recent Explanations of Income Inequality." *International Studies Quarterly* 25 (June): 255–282.

World Bank. 1980. *World Development Report 1980.* New York: Oxford University Press.

———. 1982. *World Development Report 1982.* New York: Oxford University Press.

———. 1983. *World Development Report 1983.* New York: Oxford University Press.

———. 1995. *World Development Report 1995.* New York: Oxford University Press.

———. 2003. *World Development Report 2003.* New York: Oxford University Press.

Basic Indicators of the Gaps Between Rich and Poor for 207 Countries

Appendix   Basic Indicators of the Gaps Between Rich and Poor for 207 Countries

	Gross National Income (GNI), 2001	PPP Gross National Income (GNI)	Gross Domestic Product per capita Growth, 2000–2001	Life Expectancy at Birth (years), 2000	Adult Illiteracy Rate (% of people age 15 and above), 2000	Survey Year for Income Inequality	Percentage Share of Income and Consumption (highest 10%)
Afghanistan	e	—	—	43	—	—	—
Albania	1,230	3,880	5.50	74	15	—	—
Algeria	1,630	5,150c	0.30	71	33	1995i,j	26.8
American Samoa	d	—	—	—	—	—	—
Andorra	e1	—	—	80	—	—	—
Angola	500	1,550c	0.30	47	—	—	—
Antigua and Barbuda	9,070	9,870	-0.40	75	—	—	—
Argentina	6,960	11,690	-4.80	74	3	—	—
Armenia	560	2,880	9.40	74	2	1996i,j	35.2
Aruba	e1	—	—	—	—	—	—
Australia	19,770	25,780	1.30	79	—	1994k,l	25.4
Austria	23,940	27,080	0.90	78	—	1995k,l	22.5
Azerbaijan	650	3,020	8.20	72	—	1995k,l	27.8
Bahrain	9,370	14,410	—	73	12	—	—
Bangladesh	370	1,680	3.30	61	59	1995–96i,j	28.6
Barbados	9,250	15,020	—	75	—	—	—
Belarus	1,190	8,030	4.40	68	0d	1998i,j	20
Belgium	23,340	28,210	0.80	78	—	1996k,l	23
Belize	2,910	5,350	0.20	74	7	—	—
Benin	360	1,030	3.10	53	63	—	—
Bermuda	e1	—	—	—	—	—	—
Bhutan	640	1,530c	4.00	62	—	—	—
Bolivia	940	2,380	-1.20	63	14	1999i,j	32
Bosnia and Herzegovina	1,240	—	3.80	73	—	—	—

(continues)

Appendix continued

	Gross National Income (GNI), 2001	PPP Gross National Income (GNI)	Gross Domestic Product per capita Growth, 2000–2001	Life Expectancy at Birth (years), 2000	Adult Illiteracy Rate (% of people age 15 and above), 2000	Survey Year for Income Inequality	Percentage Share of Income and Consumption (highest 10%)
Botswana	3,630	8,810	4.80	39	23	—	—
Brazil	3,060	7,450	0.20	68	15	1998k,l	48
Brunei	e,l	—	—	76	8	—	—
Bulgaria	1,560	5,950	5.10	72	2	1997k,l	22.8
Burkina Faso	210	1,020c	3.20	44	76	1998i,j	46.8
Burundi	100	590c	1.30	42	52	1998i,j	32.9
Cambodia	270	1,520	3.20	54	32	1997i,j	33.8
Cameroon	570	1,670	3.10	50	24	1996i,j	36.6
Canada	21,340	27,870c	0.60	79	—	1994k,l	23.8
Cape Verde	1,310	4,870c	0.40	69	26	—	—
Cayman Islands	e,l	—	—	—	—	—	—
Central Africa Republic	270	1,180c	0.00	43	53	1993i,j	47.7
Chad	200	930	5.80	48	57	—	—
Channel Islands	e,l	—	—	79	—	—	—
Chile	4,350	9,420	1.70	76	4	1998k,l	45.6
China	890	4,260	6.50	70	16	1998k,l	30.4
Colombia	1,910	5,980	-0.20	72	8	1996k,l	46.1
Comoros	380	1,610c	-0.50	61	44	—	—
Congo, Dem. Rep. of	e	—	—	46	39	—	—
Congo, Rep.	700	580	0.10	51	19	—	—
Costa Rica	3,950	8,080	-1.00	77	4	1997k,l	34.6
Côte d'Ivoire	630	1,470	-3.30	46	53	1995i,j	28.8
Croatia	4,550	8,440	4.10	73	2	1998k,l	23.3
Cuba	h	—	—	76	3	—	—
Cyprus	12,370	20,780c	—	78	3	—	—
Czech Republic	5,270	14,550	3.60	75	—	1996k,l	22.4

(continues)

Denmark	31,090	27,950	0.70	76	—	1992[k,l]	20.5
Djibouti	890	2,120	-0.30	46	35	—	—
Dominica	3,060	5,040	-5.00	76	—	—	—
Dominican Republic	2,230	5,870	1.10	67	16	1998[k,l]	37.9
Ecuador	1,240	3,070	3.30	70	8	1995[i,j]	33.8
Egypt	1,530	3,790	1.40	67	45	1995[i,j]	25
El Salvador	2,050	4,500	0.00	70	21	1998[k,l]	39.5
Equatorial Guinea	700	5,640	-1.30	51	17	—	—
Eritrea	190	970	2.50	52	44	—	—
Estonia	3,810	10,020	5.30	71	0	1998[k,l]	29.8
Ethiopia	100	710	5.40	42	61	1995[i,j]	33.7
Faeroe Islands	e[1]	—	—	—	—	—	—
Fiji	2,130	5,140	1.10	69	7	—	—
Finland	23,940	25,180	0.50	77	—	1991[k,l]	21.6
France	22,690[f]	25,280	1.60	79	—	1995[k,l]	25.1
French Polynesia	17,290	23,340[c]	—	73	—	—	—
Gabon	3,160	5,460	0.00	53	—	—	—
Gambia	330	1,730[c]	2.70	53	63	—	—
Georgia	620	2,860	4.60	73	—	1996[k,l]	27.9
Germany	23,700	25,530	0.50	77	—	1994[k,l]	23.7
Ghana	290	1,980[c]	1.90	57	28	1999[i,j]	30.1
Greece	11,780	17,860	3.90	78	3	1993[k,l]	25.3
Greenland	e[1]	—	—	—	—	—	—
Grenada	3,720	6,720	-5.70	72	—	—	—
Guam	e[1]	—	—	78	—	—	—
Guatemala	1,670	3,850	-0.60	65	31	1998[k,l]	46
Guinea	400	1,980	0.70	46	—	1994[i,j]	32
Guinea-Bissau	160	710[c]	-2.00	45	62	—	—
Guyana	840	3,750[c]	0.80	63	2	—	—
Haiti	480	1,450[c]	-3.50	53	50	—	—
Honduras	900	2,450	0.10	66	25	1998[k,l]	42.7
Hong Kong, China	25,920	26,050	-0.10	80	6	1996[k,l]	43.5
Hungary	4,800	12,570	4.00	71	1	1998[i,j]	20.5

(*continues*)

	Gross National Income (GNI), 2001	PPP Gross National Income (GNI)	Gross Domestic Product per capita Growth, 2000–2001	Life Expectancy at Birth (years), 2000	Adult Illiteracy Rate (% of people age 15 and above), 2000	Survey Year for Income Inequality	Percentage Share of Income and Consumption (highest 10%)
Iceland	28,880	29,830	1.90	80	—	—	33.5
India	460	2,450	2.70	63	43	1997i·j	26.7
Indonesia	680	2,940	1.80	66	13	1999i·j	—
Iran	1,750	6,230	3.00	69	24	—	—
Iraq	h	—	—	61	44	—	—
Ireland	23,060	27,460	5.60	76	—	1987k·l	27.4
Isle of Man	d	—	—	—	—	—	—
Israel	16,710	19,330	—	78	5	1997k·l	28.3
Italy	19,470	24,340	1.80	79	2	1995k·l	21.8
Jamaica	2,720	3,650	0.40	75	13	2000i·j	30.3
Japan	35,990	27,430	-0.60	81	—	1993k·l	21.7
Jordan	1,750	4,080	1.20	72	10	1997i·j	29.8
Kazakhstan	1,360	6,370	13.50	65	—	1996i·j	26.3
Kenya	340	1,020	-1.00	47	18	1997i·j	36.1
Kiribati	830	—	-0.80	62	—	—	—
Korea, Dem. Rep.	e	—	—	61	—	—	—
Korea, Rep. of	9,400	18,110	2.30	73	2	1993i·j	24.3
Kuwait	18,030	18,690	—	77	18	—	—
Kyrgyz Republic	280	2,710	4.20	67	—	1999i·j	27.2
Lao PDR	310	1,610c	2.90	54	51	1997i·j	30.6
Latvia	3,260	7,870	9.00	70	0d	1998k·l	25.9
Lebanon	4,010	4,640	0.00	70	14	—	—
Lesotho	550	2,670c	1.70	44	17	1986–87i·j	43.4
Liberia	e	—	—	47	46	—	—
Libya	d	—	—	71	20	—	—
Liechtenstein	e1	—	—	—	—	—	—

(continues)

Country							
Lithuania	3,270	7,610	4.30	73	0[d]	1996[i,j]	25.6
Luxembourg	41,770	48,080	3.80	77	—	—	—
Macao, China	14,580[l]	18,190[c]	—	79	6	—	—
Macedonia	1,690	4,860	-4.70	73	—	1999[i,j]	28.6
Madagascar	260	870	3.70	55	34	—	—
Malawi	170	620	0.70	39	40	—	—
Malaysia	3,640	8,340	-1.80	73	13	1997[k,l]	38.4
Maldives	2,040	4,520[c]	4.50	68	3	—	—
Mali	210	810	-0.90	42	59	1994[i,j]	40.4
Malta	9,120	16,530[c]	—	78	8	—	—
Marshall Islands	2,190	—	-0.70	65	—	—	—
Mauritania	350	1,680	1.40	52	60	1995[i,j]	28.4
Mauritius	3,830	10,410	6.10	72	15	—	—
Mayotte	d	d	—	—	—	—	—
Mexico	5,540	8,770	-1.80	73	9	1998[k,l]	41.7
Micronesia, Fed. Sts.	2,150	2,420	-0.90	68	—	—	—
Moldova	380	—	6.30	68	1	1997[k,l]	30.7
Monaco	e l	e l	—	—	—	—	—
Mongolia	400	1,800	0.40	67	1	1995[i,j]	24.5
Morocco	1,180	3,690	4.80	67	51	1998–99[i,j]	30.9
Mozambique	210	1,000[c]	6.70	42	56	1996–97[i,j]	31.7
Myanmar	e	e	—	56	15	—	—
Namibia	1,960	6,700[c]	2.60	47	18	1995–96[i,j]	29.8
Nepal	250	1,540	3.40	59	58	1994[k,l]	25.1
Netherlands	24,040	26,440	0.40	78	—	—	—
Netherlands Antilles	e l	e l	—	76	3	—	—
New Caledonia	15,060	21,820	—	73	—	—	—
New Zealand	12,380	19,130	1.30	78	—	—	—
Nicaragua	e	e	—	69	33	1998[i,j]	48.8
Niger	170	770[c]	1.70	46	84	1995[i,j]	35.4
Nigeria	290	830	1.60	47	36	1996–97[i,j]	40.8
Northern Mariana Islands	e l	e l	—	—	—	—	—
Norway	35,530	30,440	0.80	79	—	1995[k,l]	21.8

(continues)

Appendix continued

	Gross National Income (GNI), 2001	PPP Gross National Income (GNI)	Gross Domestic Product per capita Growth, 2000–2001	Life Expectancy at Birth (years), 2000	Adult Illiteracy Rate (% of people age 15 and above), 2000	Survey Year for Income Inequality	Percentage Share of Income and Consumption (highest 10%)
Oman	d	—	—	74	28	—	—
Pakistan	420	1,920	0.90	63	57	1996–97i·j	27.6
Palau	6,730	—	-1.00	70	—	—	—
Panama	3,290	5,720c	-1.30	75	8	1997i·j	35.7
Papua New Guinea	580	2,150c	-5.80	59	36	1996i·j	40.5
Paraguay	1,300	4,400c	-3.00	70	7	1998k·l	43.8
Peru	2,000	4,680	-1.40	69	10	1996k·l	35.4
Philippines	1,050	4,360	1.50	69	5	1997i·j	36.6
Poland	4,240	9,280	1.20	73	0d	1998i·j	24.7
Portugal	10,670	17,270	-0.30	76	8	1994–95k·l	28.4
Puerto Rico	d	—	—	76	6	—	—
Qatar	e1	—	—	75	19	—	—
Romania	1,710	6,980	5.50	70	2	1998i·j	25
Russian Federation	1,750	8,660	5.50	65	0d	1998i·j	38.7
Rwanda	220	1,000	4.30	40	33	1983–85i·j	24.2
Samoa	1,520	5,450c	9.30	69	20	—	—
San Marino	e1	—	—	80	—	—	—
São Tomé and Príncipe	280	—	0.80	65	—	—	—
Saudi Arabia	7,230	11,390	—	73	24	—	—
Senegal	480	1,560	3.20	52	63	1995i·j	33.5
Seychelles	7,050	—	—	72	—	—	—
Sierra Leone	140	480	3.10	39	—	1989i·j	43.6
Singapore	24,740	24,910	—	78	8	—	—
Slovak Republic	3,700	11,610	3.20	73	—	1992k·l	18.2
Slovenia	9,780	18,160	2.90	75	0d	1998k·l	23
Solomon Islands	580	1,680c	-11.50	69	—	—	—

(continues)

Somalia	[e]	—	—	48	—	—	—
South Africa	2,900	9,510[c]	1.20	48	15	1993–94[i,j]	45.9
Spain	14,860	20,150	2.70	78	2	1990[k,l]	25.2
Sri Lanka	830	3,560	1.00	73	8	1995[i,j]	28
St. Kitts and Nevis	6,880	11,730	1.60	71	—	—	—
St. Lucia	3,970	5,200	-4.80	71	—	—	—
St. Vincent and the Grenadines	2,690	5,250[c]	-1.30	73	—	—	—
Sudan	330	1,610	4.00	56	42	—	—
Suriname	1,690	3,310[c]	1.20	70	—	—	—
Swaziland	1,300	4,690[c]	-0.60	46	20	—	20.1
Sweden	25,400	24,670	1.00	80	—	1992[k,l]	25.2
Switzerland	36,970	31,320	0.90	80	—	1992[k,l]	—
Syria	1,000	3,440	1.00	70	26	—	—
Tajikistan	170	1,150	4.10	69	1	1998[i,j]	25.2
Tanzania	270[g]	540[g]	2.30	44	25	1993[i,j]	30.1
Thailand	1,970	6,550	0.90	69	5	1998[i,j]	32.4
The Bahamas	*14,960*	*16,400*	*-0.10*	*69*	*5*	—	—
Togo	270	1,420	2.50	49	43	—	—
Tonga	1,530	—	—	71	—	—	—
Trinidad and Tobago	5,540	9,080	4.30	73	6	1995[k,l]	31.8
Tunisia	2,070	6,450	4.20	72	29	1994[i,j]	32.3
Turkey	2,540	6,640	-7.80	70	15	1998[i,j]	31.7
Turkmenistan	950	4,580	18.40	66	—	—	29.8
Uganda	280	1,250[c]	2.00	42	33	1996[i,j]	23.2
Ukraine	720	4,150	10.00	68	0[d]	1999[i,j]	—
United Arab Emirates	[e,l]	—	—	75	24	—	—
United Kingdom	24,230	24,460	1.90	77	—	1995[k,l]	27.7
United States	34,870	34,870	0.30	77	—	1997[k,l]	30.5
Uruguay	5,670	8,710	-3.70	74	2	1989[k,l]	32.7
Uzbekistan	550	2,470	2.60	70	1	1998[i,j]	32.8
Vanuatu	1,050	2,710	-6.10	68	—	—	—
Venezuela	4,760	5,890	0.70	73	7	1998[k,l]	36.5
Vietnam	410	2,130	4.70	69	7	1998[i,j]	29.9

(continues)

Appendix   continued

	Gross National Income (GNI), 2001	PPP Gross National Income (GNI)	Gross Domestic Product per capita Growth, 2000–2001	Life Expectancy at Birth (years), 2000	Adult Illiteracy Rate (% of people age 15 and above), 2000	Survey Year for Income Inequality	Percentage Share of Income and Consumption (highest 10%)
Virgin Islands, U.S.	e1	—	—	78	—	—	—
West Bank and Gaza	1,350	—	-15.50	72	—	—	—
Yemen, Rep. of	460	770	-1.00	56	54	1998i·j	25.9
Yugoslavia	h	—	4.90	72	—	—	—
Zambia	320	790	3.20	38	22	1998i·j	41
Zimbabwe	480	2,340	-9.80	40	11	1995i·j	40.4

Source: World Bank *World Development Report, 2003* (Washington, DC: World Bank, 2003), tables 1, 2, 1a, pp. 234–237, 242.

Notes: Figures in italics are for years other than those specified.

a. Preliminary World Bank estimates calculated using the World Bank Atlas method.

b. Purchasing power parity; see the Technical Notes in the *World Development Report, 2003*.

c. The estimate is based on regression; other are extrapolated from the latest International Comparison Programme benchmark estimates.

d. Estimated to be upper middle income ($2,976 to $9,205).

e. Estimated to be low income ($745 or less).

e1. Estimated to be high income ($9,206 or more).

f. GNI and GNI per capita estimates include the French Overseas departments of French Guiana, Guadeloupe, Martinique, and Reunion.

g. Data refer to mainland Tanzania only.

h. Estimated to be lower middle income ($745 to $2,975).

i. Refers to expenditure shares by percentiles of population.

j. Ranked by per capita expenditure.

k. Refers to income shares by percentiles of population.

l. Ranked by per capita income.

INDEX

ABOUT THE BOOK

Presenting both classic pieces and the most up-to-date arguments in the debates about issues of economic growth and inequality, *Development and Underdevelopment* is a guide to understanding the causes and dynamics of the persistent income gap between rich and poor countries, as well as the rich and poor within the poor countries. The editors' short introductions to each reading, highlighting the significance of the selections, remain a key feature of this new edition.

Mitchell A. Seligson is Daniel H. Wallace Professor of Political Science at the University of Pittsburgh. **John T Passé-Smith** is associate professor of political science at the University of Central Arkansas.